SHIPWRECKS
in the
AMERICAS

Diver surfacing with an intact coral-encrusted sword from a Spanish shipwreck.

SHIPWRECKS
in the
AMERICAS

BY *ROBERT F. MARX*

DOVER PUBLICATIONS, INC., NEW YORK

For Ileana and Ruth

Copyright © 1971, 1975, 1987 by Robert F. Marx.
All rights reserved under Pan American and International Copyright Conventions.

Published in Canada by General Publishing Company, Ltd., 30 Lesmill Road, Don Mills, Toronto, Ontario.

Published in the United Kingdom by Constable and Company, Ltd.

This Dover edition, first published in 1987, is a revised republication of the edition originally published (as *Shipwrecks in the Americas*) by Bonanza Books, an imprint of Crown Publishers, Inc., New York, in 1983. This Bonanza edition was itself an unabridged republication of the work first published by The World Publishing Company, New York, in 1971 (and later reissued, with a new preface, by David McKay Company, New York, in 1975) under the title *Shipwrecks of the Western Hemisphere, 1492–1825*. The present edition features a new selection of pictures in a totally new layout, with corresponding captions; a list of illustrations is included for the first time. The "Preface to the New Edition" is here called "Preface to the 1975 Edition."

Manufactured in the United States of America
Dover Publications, Inc., 31 East 2nd Street, Mineola, N.Y. 11501

Library of Congress Cataloging-in-Publication Data

Marx, Robert F., 1933–
    Shipwrecks in the Americas / by Robert F. Marx.
        p.   cm.
    "Revised republication"—T.p. verso.
    Bibliography: p.
    Includes index.
    ISBN 0-486-25514-X (pbk.)
    1. Shipwrecks—America—Directories. 2. Treasure-trove—America—Directories. 3. Underwater archaeology—America—Directories. 4. Excavations (Archaeology)—America—Directories. 5. America—Antiquities—Directories. I. Title.
VK1250.M36   1987
909'.09812—dc19   87-23756
                                                   CIP

Contents

List of Illustrations

LEFT: The author holding an amphora from a UNESCO-sponsored excavation of a sixth-century B.C. Phoenician wreck found in Tyre, Lebanon. BELOW: The author's 72-foot salvage vessel with a prop-wash on the stern.

Preface to the 1975 Edition

Ten years ago those engaged in quest of sunken treasure were considered romantic crackpots foolishly chasing a pot of gold at the end of the rainbow. Today treasure hunting is "big business," and the latest in scientific knowledge and equipment is often brought into play. There are a number of nationally known companies that spend as much as $15,000 a day in the search for sunken treasure although, ironically, most of the major discoveries of the past few years have been made by amateur Scuba divers propelled by bubble-bright visions of gleaming doubloons and chests crammed with jewels.

Interest in underwater archaeology has also grown by leaps and bounds, but its future hinges on encouraging the motivated amateur diver to acquire the basic skills necessary for obtaining useful archaeological information. The funds available for training professionals are limited and so it is the amateur diver, for whom underwater archaeology is an avocation, who must fill the void.

I believe most divers would rather make a contribution, even a small one, to archaeology than just destroy shipwreck sites in a hurried, indiscriminate quest for gold and other treasures. How much more exciting to research the name, history, and exact fate of the wreck they are working. A few professional underwater archaeologists have worked closely with amateurs on such excavations and have been pleased with the results of the collaboration—but closer cooperation on a larger scale is still needed.

The British were the first to take the logical step of coordinating the activities of amateur wreck divers and professional underwater archaeologists who for so long had been in conflict with each other. The Committee for Nautical Archaeology was formed for this purpose and, in almost every instance in which an old wreck has been located, the divers have reported their finds to the Committee, which in turn has provided assistance, both technical and financial, for the excavation of the site. The Committee recently formed a school at Plymouth for the express purpose of teaching divers short courses in the accepted techniques they should employ on underwater sites. Unfortunately there is no comparable body in any other country.

Within three weeks of the first printing of this book in 1971 all 7,500 copies were sold, and then the book went out of print because the company that published it went out of the trade book business. While I have heard stories, perhaps apocryphal, of would-be treasure hunters offering as much as $100 for a copy, I can vouch for the countless letters I have received asking how copies could be obtained. Consequently it was imperative that the book, which many divers refer to as "the bible for treasure divers" be reissued. Rarely a month has passed since this book first came out that I haven't received letters from divers telling me of finds they have made using the information contained in these pages. My sincere hope is that everyone who uses it will have the same results.

R.F.M.

Introduction

When I first became interested in old shipwrecks many years ago, there were several books on the subject that were extremely exciting to read—galleons intact with chests of treasure in their holds and skeletons at the wheel—as well as numerous "Authentic Treasure Charts" denoting the locations of many wrecks "containing millions in treasure." Like many of my other friends in this business, we had to learn the hard way.

After spending three exciting years in Mexican waters locating and excavating several old wrecks that yielded a vast number of important artifacts and some treasure, I was anxious to locate other wrecks. Why spend weeks and months snorkeling over coral reefs and the sea floor searching for wrecks when all I had to do was to use the information I had already accumulated from the various books and treasure charts? I selected one hundred different wrecks scattered all over the Caribbean and then set off to track them down.

Fifteen months later, after exploring from the Gulf of Honduras to the San Blas islands off Panama and from Trinidad to the Bahamas— diving on almost every island, reef, and rock in between—I had located only two of the one hundred wrecks, and both had nothing of interest on them. This was not surprising, as I was to learn later during my years of original research in the European depositories. Out of the one hundred "authentic wrecks," seventy-four never existed at all but were merely the creation of some of the imaginative authors of the books I had used as my sources. Of those that existed, eighteen had in fact sunk with treasure on board, but on the high seas, where there was little chance of recovery, and not in the shallow waters close to land, where these same authors had conveniently placed them; four others had sunk in shallow waters, but hundreds of miles from the locations I had obtained from my sources; the remaining four existed—two of which I had located—but they had carried nothing of interest when they sank.

Professional wreck-hunters have long since realized that most of the information contained in such books is fictional, so they label the wrecks "Ghost Wrecks" and have a good laugh whenever they hear of newly organized expeditions setting out after them. I know of several groups of "professionals," however, who have spent over $100,000 searching for a Spanish wreck that sank in 1656 with a vast amount of treasure on board. In a book—considered the most reliable on the subject—the author placed the wreck in the Florida Keys. My research in the Spanish archives has since proved that the shipwreck occurred in the Bahamas.

Even the assistance of so-called experts on maritime history cannot always be relied upon. A good example is Kip Wagner, who is looked upon as the most successful treasure-hunter in the world. In his early days, before he realized that the only place to get authentic information was in the Spanish archives, he sought assistance from an expert of the Smithsonian Institution and was told that the 1715 treasure fleet was lost in the Florida Keys. If Kip had followed this expert's advice, he probably would never have discovered the fantastic treasure that he and his team eventually recovered more than 200 miles from the place the expert claimed it was.

There are people who erroneously believe that only a limited amount of research is necessary to locate an old shipwreck, because with to- day's fantastic underwater electronic location equipment, any wreck can be located if only the general location of its site is known. Re- cently, a well-known mineral company decided to enter the field of treasure-hunting. Equipped with a deep submersible vehicle and the latest in electronic detection gear, it proudly announced that it would make the biggest treasure recovery in history. Upon hearing of their plans, I contacted the director of the operation and offered to supply them with authentic original documentation. The shipwreck was lost off the coast of Colombia during a naval engagement between the Spaniards and the English. The ship, which was the flagship of a Spanish treasure fleet, carried over 22 million pesos in treasure and was blown up in about 600 feet of water. My assistance was refused, as they claimed that with only the general location of the disaster they could easily locate the wreck site. Three months later, with over a quarter of a million dollars wasted, they were begging for my research, but I had since decided to go after that wreck myself one day and did not help them. Their submarine has since been put back to use in searching for marine deposits, the original purpose for which it was designed.

Yet there have been quite a few important underwater-treasure recoveries made by persons who never did a bit of research—and fortunately did not use "Ghost Wrecks" information. One good example is Teddy Tucker of Bermuda, one of the world's most successful treasure-hunters. Teddy started off by searching the reefs surrounding Bermuda, using a glass-bottom bucket. When he sighted something that did not appear to be made by nature, he would dive and check it out. This led to the various big discoveries he has made over the years. But for the few who have been successful, there have been hundreds who have failed miserably. Most professionals agree that it is best to have the odds in your favor, which means doing proper research before you set out after a wreck.

There are two schools of thought on the business of wreck research. One is to first find a wreck—in the manner that Tucker did—and then do the research to determine everything you can about the wreck—such as its identity, what it carried, etc.; the other is to first decide on an area you want to work in and research those wrecks that are the most promising, or do research to determine what areas have the most promising wrecks. The latter method has proven the most successful to myself and many others in the business.

This book is written in order to assist the treasure-hunter who has already located a wreck to identify it, and to convince a wreck-hunter that a certain area would be the best to search or that a certain wreck might be the most lucrative to go after.

From my research I have amassed a file comprising data on more than 28,500 shipwrecks around the world, dating from the time of the Greeks to modern days. To write about these wrecks would amount to a work of many volumes, so I had to be very selective and concentrate on the most significant shipwrecks lost in the Western Hemisphere dating from the time of Columbus until about 1825. In a future book I plan to tackle all the important wrecks postdating 1825.

Actually, if a diver locates a wreck postdating 1825, it is fairly simple to establish its identity and uncover all the important information. The reason for this is that newspapers of the period contained notices of ship disasters, and once the treasure-hunter can pinpoint the date of disaster by dating the artifacts recovered on the wreck within ten or twenty years, he simply has to consult old newspapers of the place in which he located the wreck. He may also learn its identity by reading history books on the area in question or from a local historian or museum curator.

It is even simpler to obtain information on ships that were lost off the coast of the United States after 1825, as records of these losses can easily be obtained from various governmental agencies. The best source is in the Treasury section of the National Archives in Washington, D.C. Other good sources are the archives of the United States Coast Guard, the United States Naval Hydrographic Office, and United States Maritime Commission, all located in Washington, D.C. Over the years the Public Information Division of the United States Coast Guard has published lists of ship losses, which can be obtained free of charge. Two currently in print are: *Principal Marine Disasters 1831–1932*, which lists over six hundred shipwrecks; and *United States Merchant Ship Losses, December 7, 1941–August 14, 1945*.

Of the many books currently available containing information on shipwrecks postdating 1825, I can recommend only the following as completely reliable: *A Guide to Sunken Ships in American Waters*, by Lieutenant Commander Adrian L. Lonsdale and H. R. Kaplan, which contains information on over 1,100 shipwrecks off the coast of the United States as well as in the Great Lakes and major rivers; a forty-two-volume work entitled *Records of the Navies of the Civil War*, published by the U.S. Government Printing Office, which contains data on almost every military and merchant ship lost during the Civil War; and *Graveyard of the Atlantic*, by David Stick, which lists over eight hundred shipwrecks off the coast of North Carolina.

If I were to write a multivolume work listing every shipwreck I have collected information on, it would still be far from a complete list of every ship lost in the Western Hemisphere over the centuries. First, hundreds of ships have been lost without a trace, and many of these were no doubt lost in waters of the Western Hemisphere. A Portuguese fleet consisting of twenty-one ships carrying 23,740 ounces of gold in different forms and 439,980 crusadoes of silver sailed from Pernumbuco, Brazil, in 1746, heading for Lisbon. About a week out of port it was struck by a storm and had to run before it, heading toward the Caribbean. The fleet was still intact when it passed within sight of Barbados, but shortly afterward the storm developed into a full hurricane and the ships were widely dispersed. Thirteen disappeared without a trace.

Documents carrying news concerning various shipwrecks back to Europe or elsewhere were in many cases lost because the ships themselves were lost. Many documents concerning shipwrecks are in various European depositories, but until they are cataloged—which might take many years—they are not accessible to researchers. The major reason that information on many shipwrecks will never be discovered, however, is that thousands upon thousands of historical documents have been destroyed by man and nature.

All of the documents predating 1670 that were kept in Old Panama City were destroyed by fire when Henry Morgan and his men burned the city to the ground. Documents postdating 1670 have been destroyed by the humid climate of the Panama area. Complete archives in Cartagena and Bogotá, Colombia, were destroyed during the War of Independence; likewise, a great number of documents were destroyed in Veracruz and Mexico City during the Mexican War of Independence. When Cuba revolted against Spain near the end of the last century, the colonial archives were fortunate to survive. After the war the Cubans turned over the whole archives to the Spaniards, who took them back to Seville. Seventy years later these thousands of bundles of historical documents still remain as stacked and unopened as they were when they arrived, collecting dust and being chewed up by rats in an old building in Seville. The main archive in Lima, Peru, was destroyed twice by earthquakes in the eighteenth century. Even in Spain, vast numbers of documents have been destroyed—such as in 1551, when the House of Trade building burned to the ground, and as recently as 1962, when thousands of documents were destroyed during a flood.

Spanish colonial history is not alone in suffering the destruction of documents. Most of the other major European nations have shared similar fates. Portugal suffered by far the worst when in 1763 its main depository of historical documents—the Casa da India—sank into a Lisbon river during a terrible earthquake. Even during World War II there were great losses of historical documents due to fires caused by bombing in London, Paris, Rotterdam, and Amsterdam.

The greatest collection of Spanish colonial records is stored in the Archives of the Indies in Seville, which was the original House of Trade building. The original state archives of Spain was the Simancas Archives, located near Valladolid. It became so overcrowded with documents that in 1784 the King ordered all documents dealing with the New World shipped to Seville, thus creating the Archives of the Indies. However, in recent years it has been discovered that about six hundred to seven hundred bundles (called *legajos*) of documents dealing exclusively with the New World still remain in the Simancas Archives. And I have discovered that vast numbers of documents on the *flotas* and shipwrecks are in erroneously titled *legajos* in Simancas. While doing research on sixteenth-century Portuguese voyages to India, I found four large *legajos* entitled "Papers of Portugal—Sixteenth Century," but to my amazement I found that they contained nothing on Portugal or these voyages. Instead, there were thousands of pages dealing with the day-by-day salvage operations on the 1715 shipwrecks on the coast of Florida.

There is also documentation on Spanish maritime history in other depositories in Spain, such as the Museo Naval, Museo Nacional, Biblioteca Nacional, Archivo Histórico Nacional, and Academia Real de la Historia, all of which are in Madrid. But compared with the Archives of the Indies in Seville, their documentation is not much.

If a team of one hundred researchers spent their whole lives searching through the more than 250,000 large *legajos* in the Archives of the Indies, I doubt that they could locate all the important documents concerning Spanish maritime history in the New World. The majority of the *legajos* are not cataloged, and about 20 percent of those shipped from Simancas in 1784 have never been opened.

Very few documents concerning Dutch maritime history in the New World have survived the ravages of man and nature, and there is virtually nothing known on Dutch shipwrecks in the New World other than what can be found in Spanish or British depositories. Although many documents on French maritime history in the New World have been lost, eventually we will be able to learn more about the ships they lost in the New World. But this cannot be effected until their archives are better cataloged.

For a researcher, England is the easiest place to work, as the depositories are generally well-cataloged and the staffs very helpful. The main depositories for research on shipwrecks in the waters of the New World are The British Museum, Public Records Office, Admiralty Archives, the National Maritime Museum, and the Archives of Lloyd's of London, all of which are in or very near London.

In making the best use of the information concerning shipwrecks in this book, the following factors should be taken into consideration. All of the information on Spanish shipwrecks was obtained from original documents. In some cases a wreck or wrecks were mentioned in only a few words while in others there were thousands of pages concerning the loss of a fleet, or even an individual wreck. Where vital information is lacking on a wreck, it is because it could not be found in the original documents.

Where I have stated the amount of treasure reported to be carried on a ship, two things must be remembered. First a wreck might have been salvaged over the years, and no record exist to indicate how much might have been salvaged. Secondly, smuggling of treasure back on Spanish ships was done on such a large scale that sometimes a ship might carry as much as four or five times the amount registered on a ship's manifest. A good example of this occurred in 1743, when some English warships captured a Spanish galleon named *San Antonio*. Her manifest indicated that she was carrying slightly over 800,000 pesos, but the English discovered over 4 million pesos in treasure on her.

In some cases I have given the modern place-name where a shipwreck occurred, but only when I was positive that the place-name in the documents corresponded to place-names today. In many cases I have used the original place-name as given in the document, because the place cannot be identified today, or because the place-name was used at different places at different periods. Cayo de Viboras is a good example: in some sixteenth-century documents all of the Florida Keys are called Cayos de los Vivoras; on some seventeenth-century charts it is shown near Plantation Key; and on eighteenth-century charts it is shown between Vaca and Matacumbe Keys.

There are various reasons for the precise locations of shipwrecks being vague in original documents. In the early days—which would apply mainly to Spanish shipwrecks—there were very few place-names on charts of the coast of Florida used by the Spanish navigators. On most sixteenth-century charts only two places are named: Martires (spelled many different ways), which was the Florida Keys; and

Cabo del Canaveral, or Cape Canaveral. By the middle of the seventeenth century a few more place-names had been added: Las Tortugas, The Dry Tortugas, Vivoras, Matacumbe, Rio de Ais, and La Florida, which was the name for St. Augustine. By the beginning of the eighteenth century, many other places were named, rendering charts more accurate.

Another important reason that the Spanish documents were vague on locations of shipwrecks is that when writing to Spain telling of a disaster, it mattered little to the officials in Seville exactly where the shipwreck had occurred. What mattered mainly was what was lost and what could be or was recovered.

Some of the information in this book concerning English, French, Dutch, and American shipwrecks is brief and their location vague. Charts with too few landmarks for reference is not the excuse, since most of these shipwrecks occurred after good charts had come into existence. The main reason is that those who wrote about the occurrence did not consider it important to mention the precise wreck location. If a ship could be salvaged, it was usually done long before news of the disaster ever reached Europe or America, so it was not essential that the precise location of a wreck be made known to either the admiralty, in the case of naval vessels, or to the public or insurance firms, in the case of merchant vessels.

Due to the Great Fire of London in 1666, there are virtually no extant documents on British shipwrecks in the New World prior to this date; but then again, there was not much British shipping to the New World prior to this date. Between 1666 and 1740, there is a limited amount of original documentation on British shipwrecks in New World waters, but I found very little concerning shipwrecks in the Western Hemisphere. Since 1740 the best sources of information on British shipwrecks have been *Lloyd's List* and *Gentleman's Magazine*, both of which were first published in that year.

Lloyd's List was basically a newspaper giving the movements of British shipping around the world, as well as brief accounts of ship losses and the movements of other foreign shipping, such as the Spanish *flotas* or the returning French fleet from the Caribbean. In many cases the names of foreign ships, persons, and place-names were misspelled in the *List*, and I have corrected only those I am positive were misspelled.

Although *Lloyd's List* has been in continual existence to the present day, the volumes for various years are missing and no copies are known to exist. The years of the missing volumes are: 1742, 1743, 1745, 1746, 1754, 1756, 1759, 1776, and 1778. The *Lists* from October 15, 1770, through the end of that year are also missing. While doing research in the Archives of Lloyd's of London (I preferred it over various libraries because on many of the printed *Lists* notes had been added by contemporary members of the staff), I learned that there is never any mention of merchantmen or other ships carrying cannon, although we know that most of them did indeed carry cannon. It should also be noted that when the *List* mentions "a cargo being saved," this does not necessarily mean that it was saved before the ship sank or broke up, as in those days the word "saved" was also used to mean "salvaged."

All of the ships built and used by the American colonies until the War of Independence were under British registry, and most of the documentation on these ships' losses I found in British Archives. After the United States became independent and our ships were of American registry, the vast majority were insured by Lloyd's of London and the *List* carried notices of the majority of American ship losses. A limited number was also found in early American newspapers, which I consulted in the Library of Congress.

I have also taken the liberty of converting all the dates of ships' losses and other events mentioned in this book to our modern calendar. In 1582, Pope Gregory XIII ordered that ten days of that year be omitted to bring the calendar and sun into correspondence again, creating the Gregorian calendar, which we use today. All of the Protestant nations stuck to the old calendar, however, not changing over to the new for many years; England not until 1752. Until England made this change, her new year began on March 25; so a date of February 11, 1733, to the English was February 21, 1734, to all the other European nations.

Finding no reliable means to convert the value of the monetary units used in the old days to our present-day monetary system, I have used the values of treasures and cargoes in the terms in which they are described in the old documents.

TOP: Two divers holding gold coins next to an iron cannon from an English wreck dating 1780. BOTTOM: Archaeologist tagging timbers on the wooden remains of an early seventeenth-century Dutch merchant ship.

PART ONE

LEFT: Television Search and Salvage System (TVSSS) for recovering items from wrecks lying as deep as 5,000 feet. BELOW: Small, grappling-type anchor being raised by a "lift bag."

CHAPTER ONE

The Ships

BETWEEN 1492 AND 1830 the Spaniards mined a total of 4,035,156,000 pesos of gold and silver in the mines of the New World, which was registered in the Royal Mints. Of this amount, 493 million pesos, or slightly over one-tenth, consisted of gold and the remainder of silver. About 40 percent of the above total was mined in Mexico, while almost all of the remainder came from Peru, with a small amount also from Colombia and Chile.

During this period, in an average year, about 17,500,000 pesos of gold and silver were shipped back to Spain, while small amounts remained in the Spanish colonies for local use. There are no means by which to determine the amount of unregistered gold and silver mined during this period, but it is estimated that it amounted to between 1 and 2 billion pesos. Some of this unregistered treasure was smuggled back to Spain, but the majority was used in purchasing contraband goods from other European nations, goods which reached Europe aboard foreign ships.

Until the discovery of the New World by Columbus, all of the European nations were in a very stagnant condition due to the severe lack of precious metals, which were the main ingredients in meeting an expanding mercantile trade. One of the principal motives that led to the discovery of the New World was the belief that by sailing westward from Europe or Africa, Marco Polo's Golden Land of Zipango (Japan) might be reached and result in bringing back great quantities of gold and silver to satisfy the needs of the European nations. As it turned out, however, treasure was not obtained from Zipango but from the mines of Peru and Mexico.

The importance of the treasure from the New World to Spain can readily be understood from the following dispatch sent by the Venetian ambassador in Spain to the doge in September 1567:

At the time of writing my last dispatch to you, I informed you that there was great anxiety all over Spain, over the delay of the arrival of the treasure fleet from the Indies and, when the Genoese bankers informed the King that unless the fleet reached port shortly, that they would be unable to negotiate any further loans for him, Philip II fell into such a state of shock that he had to be confined to bed by his physicians. The King then ordered about 10,000 Ducats, which was about all the treasure left in his royal coffers, to be sent all over his realm and distributed to various churches and monasteries for the saying of masses for the safe arrival of the treasure fleet. I am happy to inform you that news has just arrived from Seville that the fleet has made port safely and there is now great rejoicing not only here in the Royal Court, but all over the land as well.

From the thousands of documents that have survived in various European archives, I discovered that the above account was by no means exceptional; in fact, it was almost a yearly occurrence over a period of three centuries. The importance of the Indies treasure was such that any delay in its arrival damaged Spanish credit disastrously and caused great concern in all the major financial centers of Europe. Although generally between a quarter and a third of the returning Indies treasure was consigned to the Crown, it never seemed to be enough and the Crown was constantly in debt to international bankers; sometimes the Crown's share of the Indies treasure was pledged to these bankers for as much as four or five years in advance.

Treasure from the New World was of equal importance to all the other European nations as well, as it provided nearly 95 percent of the precious metals on which their monetary systems were based. There is a popular misconception that only Spain benefited, when in fact she benefited less than England, France, Holland, and Italy. The reason is that throughout the sixteenth, seventeenth, and eighteenth centuries, when heavily laden and usually cranky ships carried immense amounts of treasure, there was virtually no industry of any kind in Spain, which was totally dependent on other nations for manufactured goods, both for export to the New World and domestic consumption. Therefore nearly all her treasure was used to pay for these goods.

From the very beginning the city of Seville held a monopoly on New World trade until superseded by the seaport of Cadiz early in the eighteenth century. During the first five decades following the discovery of the New World, Seville was really the best choice as the main terminus for ships sailing to and from the New World, as it was the main commercial and financial port of Spain. Although it was located 60 miles up the Guadalquivir River, it offered no handicap, as in those days ships were quite small and could easily navigate. Around the middle of the century, however, when the first organized fleet came into existence and ships began to double in size, Seville could not accommodate large numbers of ships and it became extremely hazardous for the bigger ships to navigate. As a result, even though the main control of the Indies trade remained in the hands of merchants and royal officials in Seville, the seaports of Sanlucar and Cadiz had to replace Seville as the main ports.

Both of these ports also had various drawbacks. Sanlucar, which is situated at the mouth of the Guadalquivir River, had a very dangerous sandbar over which ships had to cross when leaving port. During the three-century period when treasure ships were plying the seas between Spain and the New World, more than two hundred ships were lost on this sandbar. Cadiz, although much larger than Sanlucar, was vulnerable to attacks by enemy fleets and a dangerous wind called a levanter. As a result of these obstacles, over five hundred additional ships of the Indies navigation were lost during that period.

In 1503, when Columbus was in the New World on his fourth voyage of discovery, the Indies trade was put on an organized basis with the founding of the House of Trade in Seville, at the orders of Queen Joanna. Its purpose was to promote and regulate trade and navigation with the New World, make certain that all royal orders were carried out, collect the taxes and duties on both outward-bound and returning cargoes, and to supervise the preparations and dispatching of all the ships sailing for the New World. At first the officials of the House of Trade made their headquarters in the Cathedral of Seville, much to the great discontent of the local populace. But finally, in 1572, construction was begun on a new building; and when it was completed a few years later it served as the home for the House of Trade officials until the Indies trade monopoly was transferred to Cadiz. Today this building is the Archives of the Indies, in which millions of pages of priceless documents dealing with the ships in the Indies navigation and other aspects of New World history are kept.

In 1519, the year that Cortez sailed from Cuba to begin his infamous conquest of Mexico, Charles I, finding that the business of administering the affairs of the New World was taking up too much of his time, created a new administrative body, the Council of the Indies. The Council was part of his royal court, and its main function was to keep the King advised on matters concerning his New World possessions, to appoint both royal officials to govern in the New World and commanders of the treasure fleets, to organize the conquest of new lands in the New World, and to act as a middleman between the House of Trade and the King.

In 1543, still another administrative body was created to aid in trade and navigation. It was called the Merchant Guild, and its officials were selected from among the richest and most influential merchants engaged in commerce with the New World. Its three main functions were: the supervision of marine insurance, which was necessary to equalize losses due to shipwrecks and ships captured by enemies or pirates; a clearing house for all manufactured goods arriving from European nations for transshipment to the New World; and the maintenance of civil jurisdiction for its members, all of whom were merchants and businessmen engaged in trade with the New World.

One of the earliest laws concerning the Indies navigation was that ships must be of Spanish construction and ownership. Over the entire period of the Indies navigation, about half of the ships that sailed for the New World were of foreign construction, for rarely was there a sufficient quantity of Spanish-built ships available. However, the Spanish-ownership law was more strictly enforced.

During the first half of the sixteenth century, ships were astonishingly small—most of them less than 100 tons and many as small as 30 to 40 tons, which was the size of the Niña, the smallest vessel used by Columbus on his first voyage of discovery. To obtain a better idea of the smallness of these early ships, one has only to look at their size: a ship of fifty tons would only be from 35 to 40 feet long and from 12 to 15 feet in the beam; while a ship of 100 tons was from 50 to 55 feet in length and 16 to 18 feet in the beam. These ships were in a class called caravels but were often referred to in documents as *naos,* which merely means a ship. Caravels were first built early in the fifteenth century by the Portuguese for voyages of exploration, and by making slight modifications in their sails and rigging, the Spaniards found them well-adapted for transatlantic voyages. Although they were quite fast and much more seaworthy than any of the later classes of ships used by the Spaniards for the Indies navigation, their relatively small size was soon found to be a handicap, as it restricted the amount of cargo that could be carried and afforded very limited quarters for crew and passengers.

In the early 1540s, when the New World's demand for imports from Europe and Spain's demand for exports from the New World increased greatly, it was necessary to replace the caravel with a much larger vessel. At that time the standard vessel in Europe for carrying large cargoes was called a carrack and ranged in size from 100 to 800 tons. It was a large, round, bulky tub, and although capable of carrying large cargoes its shape made it such a slow sailer that after several years of trial and error on the transatlantic voyages to the New World it was found impractical and never used again.

The Spaniards next tried using galleys, which were larger and faster than caravels, but they too were found impractical. Although larger than caravels, they could carry less cargo, as a great portion of the space in their hold had to be utilized for carrying the large quantity of water and victuals necessary for the large number of slaves needed to propel them. Also, built very low in the water, they were extremely hazardous in any kind of storm.

By the early 1550s, when large quantities of treasure began reaching Spain from the New World, the Spaniards were hard-pressed to find a suitable vessel. Not only must the vessel be larger in size but more defendable, since hostilities had broken out between France and Spain and many of the smaller caravels began falling prey to French privateers. The solution was found by Don Alvaro de Bazan, Spain's foremost naval leader in the sixteenth century. By combining the bulkiness of the carracks with the swift-sailing lines of the galleys and the sail patterns and rigging used on caravels, he invented the galleon, which became the standard class of ship used throughout the remainder of the Indies navigation. Its average size was from 300 to 600 tons, but late in the sixteenth century many were as large as 1,200 tons. They were constructed with two or three spacious decks, large fore-and-stern castles, and carried from three to four masts. Though slower than caravels or galleys, when not overloaded and with their bottoms properly cleaned they could average about four knots on a transatlantic crossing, which was more than twice as fast as the carracks. Their disadvantage was the massive size of the fore-and-stern castles, which made the ships topheavy and placed them in great peril of capsizing in storms. Not until early in the eighteenth century was this danger properly understood and these castles reduced in size.

Although the galleon became the standard vessel used in the Indies navigation, this vessel was only called a galleon when it carried a large number of cannon. When it was used as a merchant ship and carried only a small amount of cannon, it was called a *nao*. Thus on one voyage to the New World, a ship might be called a *nao* and on the next a galleon.

Besides the galleons and *naos,* other classes of smaller vessels, ranging in size from 40 to 100 tons, were also used in the Indies navigation. Although they were of many different types of construction and rig—such as caravels, pinks, flyboats, sloops, and pinnaces—the Spaniards referred to them all as *pataches.* They served various purposes, such as reconnaissance vessels in convoys, advice boats between Spain and the New World, and to carry small cargoes to such small outposts as St. Augustine, Florida, which, as a settlement of minor importance, did not warrant the sending of a larger ship.

Although the main terminus for the Indies navigation was centered in southern Spain, very little suitable timber was available in this area, thus most of the Spanish-built ships were built in the provinces of northern Spain; after the turn of the seventeenth century a large number were also built in Cuba and other New World ports. Most of the masts, spars, and other heavy rigging came from as far away as Russia and Poland; cordage and sails were imported from Scandinavia and Holland; and until the end of the sixteenth century, when factories producing a good grade of iron were founded in Biscay Province in northern Spain, most of the metal fittings, anchors, and iron cannon were imported from various countries of northern Europe.

From the beginning even the small caravels were obliged to carry several pieces of artillery, the number depending on its size and the purpose it served. For example, a galleon of 400 tons that was being used as a merchant *nao* would be required to carry only ten or twelve cannon, whereas the same vessel serving as a flagship of a convoy and entrusted with bringing back a large amount of treasure would be required to carry as many as fifty cannon of various caliber. Iron cannon, unless new, was used merely to fire salutes or as a signal between ships, as it heated too quickly after firing and would crack or burst apart, often rendering more damage to those firing than those fired upon. When the galleons superseded the earlier class of Indies vessels, it became standard pratice for them to carry only brass cannon, except in times when it was scarce. The largest brass cannon used on the galleons in the sixteenth and seventeenth centuries was called a demi-culverin, which weighed about 2 tons and fired an iron ball weighing from 7 to 12 pounds at a maximum distance of 1,000 paces at point-blank range and more than twice that distance when fired in a trajectory. In those early days, ships usually sailed in small convoys, not only for the sake of mutual protection against corsairs and foul weather but to pool navigational knowledge, for there was a great scarcity of navigators.

During the first three decades of the sixteenth century, before sizable conquests had been made in Mexico and Peru, virtually all the shipping between Spain and the New World was directed to Hispaniola. The number of ships sailing each year depended on the availability of ships, number of corsairs cruising in wait for the returning ships near the Azores and off Portugal and Spain, and the amount of exports and number of settlers going to the New World in that particular year. For example: In 1508, sixty-six ships sailed to the New World; in 1520 the number reached 108; in 1529, when the number of French privateers operating off the Azores was great, only sixty sailed, and of the forty-two that attempted to return to Spain, eleven were captured by French privateers.

Corsairs and privateers were a menace from the very beginning. Columbus was the first to have dealings with them. On his very first voyage of discovery in 1492, when approaching the Canaries, he sighted two French corsair vessels, but because his ships were better-armed the corsairs gave him a wide berth. Returning from his third voyage, only foul weather saved his flagship from falling prey to a fleet of French corsairs off Cape St. Vincent, located at the southern tip of Portugal. Although the corsairs were lucky enough to capture a few returning Indies ships each year from 1505 onward, they never got any of major importance until 1521, when two caravels loaded with treasure for the King were captured.

This resulted in the formation of a special fleet, which was maintained by a special tax—called *avería*—placed on all cargoes to and from the New World. The purpose of this fleet, which was named the Armada of the Ocean Sea, was to escort convoys of ships from Spain as far as the Canaries and then take up station off the Azores, where it would search out and destroy corsair vessels and meet homeward-bound convoys and escort them to Spain. This fleet of warships became of such major importance to Spain that it became the Royal Fleet of Spain and existed throughout the duration of the Indies navigation.

In 1537, when war with France broke out once again, the first fleet that could be called a "treasure fleet" sailed to the Indies. This fleet consisted of six warships and twenty merchant ships. It sailed directly to Nombre de Dios on the Isthmus of Panama to collect the treasures sent up from Peru, then to Cartagena to receive gold and emeralds sent down from the interior and pearls sent from the Island of Margarita, located off the coast of Venezuela. Then it sailed to Havana, where it met with ships arriving from Veracruz with treasures and products from Mexico. After taking on water and provisions at Havana, it sailed up through the Bahama Channel and headed for the Azores, where it united with the Armada of the Ocean Sea and they sailed jointly for Spain. This system of treasure fleets was kept in effect until about 1552, when galleons first came into use and a new convoy system was established.

This new convoy system consisted of sending two separate convoys of ships each year to the New World and although the other European nations referred to these convoys as treasure fleets, the Spaniards called them *flotas,* which means just plain fleet. Each of these *flotas* consisted of four heavily armed galleons of at least 300 tons and two 80-ton *pataches,* plus from ten to ninety merchant *naos.* One *flota* generally sailed in March and the other in September. After passing the Canaries they would generally make their first landfall at either Guadeloupe or Martinique in the Caribbean. There the ships would split up: those sailing for Mexico would sail with those heading for Puerto Rico, Hispaniola, Cuba, Jamaica, and Honduras; and the four galleons and two *pataches* would sail with those heading for Venezuela, Colombia (which was then called the Nuevo Reino de Granada), and the Isthmus of Panama. The galleons would make their usual stops at Nombre de Dios and Cartagena and then go to Havana to await the arrival of the ships from all the other Spanish settlements in the New World before starting back to Spain. In theory, only the four galleons were permitted to carry treasure on the voyage to Spain, but this regulation was very often broken by merchants, who preferred to carry their treasure on the ships they were sailing on.

The organization of this *flota* system had one big disadvantage. After the ships split up upon making their Caribbean landfall, many of those sailing with the ships bound for Mexico were left without the protection of the four galleons and two *pataches* and fell prey to corsairs and privateers. As a result of this deficiency, a much better *flota* system was put into effect in 1564 and retained for nearly a century.

There were still two *flotas* sailing to the New World each year, one called the Tierra Firme Flota and the other the New Spain Flota. Each consisted of two heavily armed galleons and two *pataches*, plus the merchant *naos* sailing under their protection. The larger galleon, which was the flagship, was called the *Capitana* and the smaller the *Almiranta*. The New Spain Flota would generally sail from Spain in April; however, due to the incurable dilatoriness of the Spaniards it was difficult to get either of the *flotas* dispatched on time. The voyage from Spain to Veracruz generally took from two to three months, depending on the weather and condition of the ships. The ships sailing for the Greater Antilles islands and Honduras would sail with this *flota*. By this time such a large number of ships had been lost in the Gulf of Mexico, due to ships or fleets sailing from Veracruz between October and February—which is the time of the year when dangerous "northers" blow in the Gulf—that it became the practice for the *flotas* to winter in Veracruz. Then they would sail the following year in February or March, either to wait in Havana and sail jointly with the Tierra Firme Flota or to continue on alone for Spain.

The Tierra Firme Flota usually sailed in August, taking under its protection all the ships destined for ports along the Spanish Main. After it received the treasure from Peru in Nombre de Dios, it would go to Cartagena and winter there, like the New Spain Flota was doing in Veracruz. Then in January it would sail for Havana and either meet with the New Spain Flota or continue on back to Spain alone. Political conditions in Europe during this period sometimes made it necessary to increase the number of galleons in the Tierra Firme Flota to six or eight, in which case it was called the Armada of Tierra Firme, or simply the Galleons. During such times the New Spain Flota either sailed back to Spain with the Galleons or left the Mexican treasure in Havana to be picked up by the Galleons.

In 1591, due to a dangerous threat by the English to capture homeward-bound treasure-laden galleons, the Indies navigation was re-organized and continued in use until about 1650. The new system entailed the dispatching of three fleets each year to the Indies. The Tierra Firme Flota and the New Spain Flota were still maintained, except for the fact that the former would sail earlier in the year and instead of wintering in Cartagena would return to Spain the same year, usually in convoy with the new fleet, which was called the Armada of Tierra Firme, the Silver Fleet, or simply the Galleons. This new fleet consisted of eight to twelve galleons and two or more *pataches,* and, like the *Capitana* and *Almiranta* in the *flotas,* it was not permitted to carry cargo to or from the New World, except for treasure. The average size of these galleons was about 600 tons, but the *Capitanas* and *Almirantas* were sometimes as large as 1,000 tons. Besides being heavily armed with brass cannon, they each carried a company of two hundred marines. With the reorganization of the Indies navigation, the Tierra Firme Flota usually sailed first in March and the Galleons either sailed at the same time or a month or so later. The New Spain Flota would now sail in May or June, hopefully to reach Veracruz before the "northers" started blowing in October. After the Galleons picked up the treasure in Nombre de Dios, or later Porto Bello, it would go to Cartagena and then sail alone or with the Tierra Firme Flota to Havana, where it would either meet with the previous year's New Spain Flota or pick up the treasure this *flota* had left in Havana. Then it would sail for Spain. Only on a few occasions between 1591 and 1650 did the New Spain Flota carry treasure back to Spain unescorted by the Galleons, and this only when the treasure was urgently needed in Spain to avoid royal bankruptcy.

Throughout the three centuries of the Indies navigation, besides the ships sailing in convoys, single ships—called *sueltos*—were also permitted to sail to the New World. The number sailing each year was from a few to as many as fifty, depending on the political climate in Europe. Most of the *sueltos* were small ships and their destinations out-of-the-way places that the larger merchant *naos* didn't visit. Although they were easy prey to enemy or corsair ships, the Crown benefited from their sailing, as they afforded a year-round communication system with the New World colonies. To protect these *sueltos,* as well as the smaller and not too well-protected settlements, Spain maintained a squadron of from four to eight galleons—called the Windward Armada—in the Caribbean.

After the conquest of Peru had been completed in the early 1540s, a squadron of from two to four ships—the Armada of the South Seas—was created for the purpose of carrying treasure from Peru to Panama City, from where it was transferred to either Nombre de Dios or Porto Bello, and to carry the European products and passengers brought over from Spain down to Peru. The home port of this armada was Callao, a seaport located 6 miles from Lima.

The most dangerous navigation undertaken by the Spaniards during these three centuries was the one between Manila in the Philippines and Acapulco, Mexico. From 1565 onward and nearly annually until 1815, ships called Manila Galleons made the perilous voyage between Manila and Acapulco. Until 1593, when a law was passed keeping the number of these sailing down to two a year in each direction, three or four sailed. They were the largest ships used by the Spaniards: In the sixteenth century they averaged about 700 tons; in the seventeenth century the average was 1,500 tons; and in the eighteenth they were between 1,700 and 2,000 tons.

The voyage from Acapulco to Manila was usually pleasant, with only an occasional storm unsettling the routine sailing of from eight to ten weeks. On the other hand, the voyage from Manila to Acapulco was known as the most difficult navigation in the world and dozens of ships were lost over the years. Because the winds in latitude of the Philippines are from the east, the Manila Galleons had to beat their way as far north as Japan before reaching the belt of westerly winds, which would carry them across the Pacific until they made a landfall on the coast of California and worked their way down to Acapulco. This voyage took from four to eight months, depending on luck. Counting the crews, from 300 to 600 persons would sail on these galleons, and an average of from 100 to 150 persons would perish on each voyage from epidemics, scurvy, thirst, starvation, or the cold. On one of two Manila Galleons sailing jointly in 1657, all 450 persons died from a smallpox epidemic and about half of the 400 on the other.

Notwithstanding the great risks involved in this navigation to ships, property, and life, the financial gain made by those involved in this trade and to the Royal Crown seemed well worth the hardships. The cargoes carried from Acapulco to Manila were basically the same as those carried on the *flotas* between Spain and the Indies ports, except for the fact that silver specie and bullion were also carried on these galleons, coming from the mines of Peru and Mexico to pay for the cargoes sent from Manila. The Crown restricted the amount to be sent to Manila at 500,000 pesos a year, but like most other laws, this one was always disobeyed and an average of 3 to 5 million pesos was sent to Manila each year. In 1597 the fantastic amount of 12 million pesos reached Manila.

The cargoes carried from Manila to Acapulco were of a more interesting and diversified nature. The main item was Chinese and Japanese silks of various styles and descriptions. There were also crepes, velvets, taffeta, damasks in cloth materials; fans, rugs, combs, exquisite jewelry (rings, bracelets, pendants, earrings, etc.); devotional pieces, such as crucifixes, reliquaries, and rosaries; jewel-studded sword hilts, ornaments made of pearls, objects made of ivory and sandalwood, copper cuspidors, gold bells, beautiful porcelainware, and a variety of different drugs and spices.

After the Manila Galleons reached Acapulco, merchants arrived from as far away as Peru and a fair was held in which the bulk of the goods was sold. Peruvian merchants would carry their goods down to Panama City and sail later in the year on the ships of the Armada of the South Seas. Mexican merchants had their goods carried over the mountains by mules. The agents who represented the merchants of Seville also used mules and traveled all the way to Veracruz to board the New Spain Flota back to Spain.

All of the officers and royal officials serving on all the ships in the Indies navigation, with the exception of navigators—who were often either Portuguese or Italian—were Spanish citizens by birth. On the other hand, the crews on these ships were made up of men and boys of every European country. Although this was prevalent throughout the history of the Indies navigation—with Spaniards sometimes making up less than 20 percent of the crew—it was contrary to royal regulations, but due to the shortage of seafaring Spaniards, the officials of the House of Trade turned a blind eye. At times on a single merchant *nao* there were as many as twelve different European nations represented among the men in the crew, all of whom spoke different languages, resulting in a great deal of confusion and constant fighting between the seamen.

The maximum number of passengers permitted on each ship was computed to be thirty for each 100 tons of shipping. The ship's owner or captain was responsible for providing each passenger with 1½ pounds of biscuit, 2 pints of drinking water, and 1 pint of water for bathing purposes. All other victuals and liquids needed by the passengers had to be provided by themselves.

The seamen and marines on both the galleons and merchant *naos* had the same diet, and it varied very little through the course of the three centuries. Their daily rations consisted of 2 pounds of biscuit, 1 quart of wine, and 1 quart of water each day; four days a week they received 8 ounces of dried fish and 2 ounces of peas or beans; on the other three days they received 8 ounces of salt pork and 1½ ounces of rice. Once a week they also received a small amount of olive oil, vinegar, and cheese. They supplemented this rather monotonous diet by catching fresh fish during the course of the voyage.

Officers and royal officials had to supply their own victuals and, depending upon how wealthy they were, determined their bill of fare during the voyage. The lists of their personal victuals included every known species of live domestic beast and fowl, smoked hams, bacon, sausages, salted cows' tongue, various types of pickled or dried fish, olives, olive oil, biscuit, bread, chocolates, noodles, rice, beans, spices, starch, lentils, and as many as twenty different varieties of wines and stronger liquors.

The preparations for dispatching a *flota* were always a long-drawn-out frustrating affair to those involved in the undertaking, as they required from three to five months, depending on the availability of supplies, ships, men, and the money to buy what was needed. The merchant *naos* were the responsibility of their owners, but the House of Trade officials were in charge of preparing the *Capitanas* and *Almirantas* and *pataches* of the *flotas,* as well as all the ships in the Galleons. These officials not only had to prepare the galleons and *pataches* for sailing but constantly inspect the merchant *naos* to ensure that they were suitable to make the voyage, that they carried sufficient armaments and munitions, that all the cargoes carried were properly registered and all the taxes and duties had been paid on them, that only licensed passengers were aboard the ships, and many other things. The officials were sometimes aided in these inspections by officers and officials of the *flotas,* who knew that if a merchant *nao* was overloaded or unfit to make the voyage, it would slow down the progress of the convoy, since it had to sail at the speed of the slowest ship.

The early colonists in the New World had to depend on Spain for almost every essential item needed for their subsistence. The cargoes of those early ships consisted basically of foodstuffs, tools, agricultural and mining implements, domestic animals, seeds, and weapons. Even the ballast of these early ships consisted of bricks or dressed stones, which were used for building in the new settlements. After the discovery of the rich mines in the New World and the foundation of the *flota* system around the middle of the sixteenth century, the nature of the cargo began to change. By this time the colonists were able to supply themselves with their own foodstuffs, and because of the wealth they were obtaining from the mines they demanded vast quantities of manufactured goods, not just hardware, weapons, and household items, but luxury items: books, paper, musical instruments, religious objects, leather goods, etc.

The departure of a fleet from Spain was a ceremonious occasion and brought crowds of spectators from far and wide to witness the event. The sailing date was always preceded by several days of fiestas and religious ceremonies. Once at sea, after the excitement of the departure had died down, the normal routine of each ship would be set and kept throughout the voyage: The men would be placed in different watches, assigned sleeping areas and messmates, and read the rules that would have to be obeyed during the voyage.

Spaniards were never noted for cleanliness, especially on ships, and most of the epidemics that broke out aboard their ships came as a result of this problem. An Englishman writing in the early seventeenth century said: "Their ships are kept foul and beastly, like hog-sties and sheets-cots in comparison of ours; and no marvel, for there is no course taken to correct that abuse by appointing men purposely for that office as we do in our ships."

In comparison with a crossing from Manila to Acapulco, an Atlantic crossing from Spain to the New World was like child's play. Even so it was still a long and trying experience. Quarters were painfully restricted for all but the senior officers and rich passengers, and the quantity and quality of the victuals left much to be desired. To break the monotony of the voyage they improvised mimic bullfights, held cockfights, celebrated as many religious holidays as possible, and did a great deal of fishing. But the main pastime for most of the crew and passengers was gambling, which, although forbidden by royal decree, met with little opposition from the officers and officials in charge of the ships. Prognosticating the weather was a continuous source of interest. Old salts could fairly accurately predict the weather by various means. For example: A heavily clouded sky at night meant rain would soon fall; when extra-large rays were seen emitting from a rising or setting sun, it meant bad weather was near at hand; the brighter the moon at night, the better the weather the following day; deep red clouds on the horizon at dawn or dusk meant the approach of a tempest; a halo around the moon threatened rain, etc. Some old salts predicted bad weather when they suffered from rheumatism, and this has been proven to be true, as the high humidity that precedes most storms at sea also causes discomfort to persons with rheumatism. The one sign that was dreaded most was finding the sea exceptionally calm for several days, with the water extraordinarily clear and many more fish than usual seen near or on its surface, followed by huge ocean swells when there was no wind about. This was a positive sign of a hurricane approaching.

From beginning to end, the voyage to and from the New World was a hazardous undertaking. Shipwrecks were the greatest danger. During the three centuries slightly more than 5 percent of the ships in the Indies navigation were shipwrecked, mostly due to bad weather but also to incompetent navigators. A small percentage were lost due to capsizing because of overloading and to fires on board. There were also other small losses due to ships being destroyed or captured by enemy or corsair ships.

Throughout the Indies navigation, once the ships sailing for the New World passed over the dangerous sandbar at Sanlucar, very few were lost until after they reached the Caribbean. The winds in this ocean crossing were nearly all in their favor, there was little danger of bad storms in the latitudes these ships sailed in, and, of course, there was little danger of running up on a reef in the deep ocean waters.

The return voyage was always considered the most dangerous, and for many reasons. In addition to sometimes being twice as long as the voyage over, the ships were in a bad way due to worms eating at the wooden hulls and heavy growths of barnacles and moss growing below the waterline, slowing the speed of the ships considerably. The passage homeward passed many dangerous areas, such as the hostile reefs and shoals on both sides of the Bahama Channel. Another problem was that the crews were less in number due to desertion and deaths in the New World.

Among the most interesting aspects were the methods, or lack of methods, used in navigation. Many have written scornfully of Spanish navigational practices, and among these critics were many Spaniards. Shortly after the foundation of the House of Trade in Seville, a school of navigation was also founded there for the express purpose of providing good navigators. The science of navigation came into being during the early fifteenth century under the auspices of such Portuguese as Prince Henry the Navigator. By the time Columbus sailed for the New World, navigation appeared to have reached its zenith and very few improvements were made until the nineteenth century. Basically, the navigator depended on dead-reckoning navigation, as there were no means by which to establish longitude until the nineteenth century. The compass was used to keep a course, instruments such as astrolabes and quadrants were available to obtain a ship's latitude at midday, various methods were in use to estimate a ship's speed, and a great deal of guesswork, such as in deciding a ship's drift in ocean currents or the magnetic variation of the compass, made up part of the navigator's skills. Charts were generally so inaccurate that many navigators preferred to rely on their own knowledge and experience.

Rarely could two navigators in the same convoy agree on the position of the ships or even the proper compass headings to take, which resulted in many ships being wrecked. In a New Spain Flota sailing in 1582, the captain-general summoned all the navigators to his ship to determine the position they were in after five weeks at sea. The estimates ranged from two weeks to only one day from sighting Guadeloupe. The majority placed the convoy ten days from the island while only one predicted they were quite close and would reach the island within twenty-four hours. He was laughed at, but that very night he was proven right when the three leading ships ran upon reefs on the eastern side of the island.

Once the *flota* system was established, the routes sailed to and from the New World were followed with little variation except during times of war, when they had to be altered to avoid capture or destruction at the hands of enemy fleets. Upon leaving Spain, all the fleets would pass within sight of the Canary Islands and then make their landfall at either Guadeloupe or Martinique, where they would spend a day or two refreshing themselves. The New Spain Flota would then set a course for St. Croix, Virgin Islands, and pass within sight of the southern coast of this island. While dropping off various ships along its way, it would continue along the south side of both Hispaniola and Cuba and, after sighting Cape San Antonio, on the western tip of Cuba, would head for Cape Catoche on the Yucatan peninsula and stay in sight of land until it finally reached Veracruz. The voyage from Veracruz to Havana generally took from four to five weeks, as the *flotas* had to take an indirect route due to contrary winds. After leaving Veracruz they headed north until they sighted land in the vicinity of Pensacola, at which point they would turn and follow the whole length of Florida's west coast, where the winds were usually favorable. Not until reaching the vicinity of the Dry Tortugas in the Florida Keys could they steer a direct course for Havana.

Both the Tierra Firme Flota and the Galleons followed the same routes. After leaving Guadeloupe or Martinique, they steered for a point on the Spanish Main called Cabo de la Vela, or Cape of the Sail, so called because from a distance this cape resembled a large sail. Once in sight of this cape, they stayed within sight of the coast until reaching Cartagena. To sail from Cartagena to Nombre de Dios, or Porto Bello—which superseded Nombre de Dios near the end of the sixteenth century—the fleets sailed in a direct line due to the prevailing winds but would first have to sail northwest for several days before changing course to southwest. The voyage back to Cartagena was more direct and generally made within sight of land all the way.

In sailing between Cartagena and Havana, the Spaniards used an unorthodox method, which they also did in sailing between Havana and Spain. Instead of attempting to steer a course to pass between the dangerous reefs of Serrana and Serranilla on the west and Pedro Shoals on the east, they would steer directly for either one of these dangerous reefs, believing that it was more important to know they had reached a dangerous area by sighting it rather than trying to sail between the dangerous areas on both sides of their course and not knowing where their position was or that of the dangerous reefs. Naturally, on various occasions these reefs ripped the bottoms out of ships that happened to reach them on dark nights. After sighting whichever of these dangerous reefs the fleet had been steering for, they would then change course, heading for Grand Cayman Island. Upon sighting it they would again alter course at a point on the southwestern coast of Cuba. Once in sight of the Cuban coast, they would hug it until reaching Havana.

After departing from Havana on the voyage for Spain, they once again executed the unorthodox practice of heading directly for the Florida Keys, an area that has claimed more Spanish shipwrecks than any other in the New World. With the Bahama Channel being no narrower than 50 miles at any point, it seems incomprehensible that they would not try to steer up its middle rather than so close to such a dangerous area. However, in that day and age the method of navigation dictated sighting as many known points of land as possible to establish a ship's true position, and not even the loss of a great number of ships on the Florida Keys was enough to change this practice. Once the Keys were sighted, a more northerly course was taken, and generally the ships stayed within sight of the Florida coast until sighting Cape Canaveral, when they would change course, heading for Bermuda. While Bermuda also claimed many Spanish ships on its reefs, navigators felt it was absolutely necessary to sight Bermuda in order to know their true position before turning on an easterly and heading toward the Azores.

The route used on the return voyages to Spain remained constant throughout the Indies navigation. However, around 1650, when most of the islands of the Lesser Antilles began to be settled by the English and other European nations, both fleets sailing to Mexico and the Spanish Main had to change their routes. The New Spain Flota would make its first Caribbean landfall in the vicinity of the Virgin Islands and then pass along the northern coast of Puerto Rico and sail south down the channel separating Puerto Rico from Hispaniola. Once in sight of the southern coast of Hispaniola, the rest of the route was the same as before. The fleets sailing for the Spanish Main would make their first landfall at Trinidad and Tobago and pass between both these islands on the body of water that retains the name of Galleon Passage. They would then head directly for Cabo de la Vela and proceed along the routes used previously. The main ports visited were Nombre de Dios, Porto Bello, Cartagena, Havana, and Veracruz.

At first the Caribbean terminus for receiving the Peruvian treasures was at Nombre de Dios, the narrowest point on the Isthmus. However, because of the unhealthiness of this port, which was surrounded by marshy swamps, in 1584 the Crown ordered the town moved to Porto Bello, which stood a few miles to the southeast and was a much safer port for shipping. The actual move was delayed for some time because a new trail had to be cut out of the jungle to connect Porto Bello to Venta Cruz, which was the midway point along the trail between Porto Bello and Panama City. However, the move was greatly hastened by Drake's destruction of Nombre de Dios in 1596, when Porto Bello finally superseded it. Porto Bello was never a settlement of any large size. Except at the time of the visit of the fleets, the town was more or less a ghost town containing a small garrison of Spanish soldiers who manned the forts and several hundred Negroes and mulattoes.

The main Peruvian port was Callao, which was located 6 miles from Lima. It consisted of a natural harbor defended by a strong fort and was the home base of the Armada of the South Seas. This armada was formed after the rich ore discoveries at Potosi and usually consisted of from two to four galleons that was responsible for carrying the Peruvian treasures up to Panama City and returning with cargoes brought from Spain. The Potosi mines were located high up in the mountains, so it took about two weeks to have the treasures carried overland on llamas down to the nearest port, which was Arica. From Arica to Callao the treasure was carried on small *pataches,* and this usually took about eight days. The voyage of the Armada of the South Seas from Callao to Panama City took an average of three weeks, but the return voyage was twice and sometimes three times as long, as the ships had to buck contrary currents and winds.

Usually, a few weeks before the Galleons were to depart from Spain, an advice boat was sent ahead to Nombre de Dios (or Porto Bello) with news of the approach of the Galleons. Both by sea and land, this news was rushed down to Lima so measures could be taken to assure that the Peruvian treasures would be in Panama City about the time the Galleons arrived at the Isthmus. Once the Galleons reached the Isthmus, word was rushed overland to Panama City for the transportation of the treasure to Nombre de Dios or Porto Bello. This was executed in one of two ways: either the treasure was transported entirely overland on mules, or partly by mules and partly on water. A short distance south of Porto Bello is the mouth of the Chagres River, which has its head at Venta Cruz, the halfway point across the Isthmus. Provided the water was high enough on the river, treasure would be taken off the mules at Venta Cruz and placed aboard flat-bottomed barges and carried down the river. At the mouth of the river, where there was a strong fort, the treasure would then be transferred to either galleys or other small vessels and taken up to Porto Bello. Upon arrival of the treasure in Porto Bello, the bars of silver were stacked like heaps of stones in the streets or the main square without causing any fear or suspicion of loss, since the owner of each bar had his marks stamped on it. The gold, all coinage, and the King's treasure were kept in the large Customs Warehouse.

Each year a fair was held in Nombre de Dios or Porto Bello and the town was called upon to accommodate an enormous crowd of traders, soldiers, sailors, etc. Shelter and food were only obtainable at outrageous prices. Merchants paid as much as a thousand pesos for a moderate shop or store to house their goods. Porto Bello wasn't much healthier than Nombre de Dios had been, and each year large numbers would die from dysentery and malaria. The fair generally lasted a month, but occasionally epidemics or the urgent need for the treasure in Spain would cut its duration as short as a week. Once the fair ended and the ships sailed for Cartagena, the port would once again become a ghost town.

Cartagena served as the port for Santa Fe de Bogotá, which was the capital of New Granada (today called Colombia). Here the pearls from the various fisheries along the Spanish Main were placed aboard the galleons, as well as the gold and emeralds sent down from Bogotá. Before the fleets left for Havana, they would obtain fresh victuals and water and make any needed repairs to the ships.

Veracruz was the most dangerous port used by the *flotas,* exposed as it was to hurricanes in the summer and violent "northers" during most of the fall and winter months. It was an open roadstead, and entry to the port was dangerous due to many sandbars and reefs at its mouth. From the beginning, the large ships anchored at or were tied up in the lee of a small island named San Juan de Ulua, located 15 miles down the coast from Veracruz, and the goods destined for Mexico City and elsewhere had to be carried on small boats from there to Veracruz. In 1600 the town of Veracruz was completely transferred down the coast directly opposite San Juan de Ulua. This town, like all others visited by the fleets, was never of major importance, being nothing more than a shanty town that served as a base for the *flotas* that wintered there. The only buildings of any note were the forts, a customs house, and several churches. A fair was held there, as in Porto Bello, and when it was over, goods were carried overland on mules to Mexico City and other places, including far-away Guatemala City.

Havana was the only Indies port at which nearly every ship returning from the Indies to Spain stopped. The town itself was the most impressive of any visited by the fleets, and it was here that the fleets would unite for the homeward voyage. The surrounding countryside provided plenty of victuals for the homeward-bound ships as well as wood for all necessary ships' repairs.

Without the discovery of the rich mines of precious metals in the New World, there would not have been any treasure fleets and the whole course of American history would have taken a different turn. The first treasure to reach Spain was brought by Columbus. It was followed by much larger amounts from Hispaniola during the next two decades, amounts obtained by the use of Indian slave labor. When this source soon became exhausted, others emerged with the conquests of Peru and Mexico. By 1530 some enterprising Spaniards, and a large number of Germans sent by the Emperor, began serious mining by digging out deposits of ore, mainly silver ore, from rich surface deposits, and each year larger and larger amounts were shipped back to Spain.

The breakthrough came in the year 1545 in Peru with the discovery of the prodigious mountain of Potosí (today located in Bolivia), which contained the greatest concentration of silver found anywhere in the world. This mine was discovered by an Inca Indian named Hualpa. While stalking a deer up the steep slopes of this mountain, he grabbed hold of a shrub to pull himself up. The shrub gave way and in the cavity in the ground he discovered a mass of pure silver. A short time later the Spaniards began working this mine on a large scale. Just three years later two other rich silver mines were discovered in Mexico —Zacatecas and Guanajuato—and a silver rush overtook both of these areas.

The Spanish Crown never exploited the mines on their own account—with the exception of the Huancavelica mercury mine in Peru—but received its revenue from the collection of the King's Royal Fifth on all the precious metals mined. Although some Spaniards, and even Indians, worked small claims by hand, the typical silver miner was a capitalist, as a great deal of investment was needed to mine, refine, and transport the gold and silver to the seaports.

Another boost in the amount of precious metals reaching Spain came in 1555 with the discovery by an unknown German alchemist of refining precious metals with the use of mercury or quicksilver. Within a year this process—which was called the mercury amalgamation process—was being used in the New World with good results. The Spanish Crown, realizing that supplying the miner with a steady supply of mercury could be a lucrative source of income, shrewdly placed a Crown monopoly on mercury. The mercury mine of Huancavelica, which had been discovered prior to 1555, was seized by the Crown and its owners miserably compensated. This mine served all the needs for South-American mines until the nineteenth century, except during rare periods when the mercury production of the mine was halted due to cave-ins or flooding. No mercury mines were ever discovered in Mexico, and all the mercury used there had to be shipped from Peru and Spain. The mercury brought from Spain came from two sources: a mercury mine named Almaden in southern Spain, which had been producing mercury since the days of the Romans, was exploited, but when it couldn't produce sufficient quantities to meet the demands of the Mexican mines, large quantities were imported yearly from Hungary, which was the nearest source of mercury. Mercury was so important that any interruption in its delivery resulted in great financial problems to the Crown, since it meant a decrease in the amount of precious metals refined and subsequently lesser amounts of revenue paid to the Crown.

Before the discovery and exploitation of the silver mines, the main wealth in precious metals was obtained from gold, which was mainly obtained from the conquests of new lands and in panning rivers and streams. Gold was always being discovered but was generally found too expensive to mine in comparison with silver, which produced better benefits. Between 1550 and 1700 so little gold was mined that of the total value of precious metals it accounted for less than 1 percent, and most of this was obtained as a by-product in the mining and refining of silver.

Silver production expanded continuously throughout the second half of the sixteenth century and reached its peak during the last decade. Then production began declining slowly between 1600 and 1630, but after 1630 the decline was precipitous. The main reason for this decline was that as the deposits near the surface were exhausted, the miners had to dig deeper and deeper and this greatly increased production costs. Also the deeper they mined, they found lower and lower grades of ore. For example: at the Potosí mine in 1560 a pound of silver ore was yielding two ounces of pure silver, but by 1630 it took over one ton of ore to yield an equal amount of pure silver. Besides necessitating a much greater labor force in mining these poorer grades of ore, much greater amounts of mercury were also needed in the refining of the ores, and the supply of the mercury was never enough to meet demands. By the middle of the seventeenth century, over half the mines that had been in operation in 1600 had to close down, either because they could not make a profit, due to a lack of labor, or because of technical difficulties, such as not being able to drain deep shafts, prevent cave-ins, and supply adequate ventilation to the miners.

Around the end of the seventeenth century the production of both gold and silver took a turn for the better, mainly as a result of great technical advances being made in mining techniques—such as being able to drain and provide ventilation down the deep shafts. By 1700, and during every year of the eighteenth century, more precious metals were being mined in America than during even the peak years during the last decade of the sixteenth century. Many of the gold mines that had been discovered as much as two centuries earlier and which hadn't been mined were soon put into production, and throughout the eighteenth century the value of mined gold was about 10 percent that of the total value of precious metals.

The refining of both gold and silver was left in the hands of individual miners, but the Crown provided assayers to test all the precious metals for their fineness and also collected the King's Royal Fifth and other, smaller taxes. There were royal mints in most of the major cities of the New World, such as Lima, Mexico City, Guatemala City, Bogotá, and even at Potosí. Most of the King's Royal Fifth was kept in bars or smaller wedges of silver. Some of it was used in the Indies to pay the salaries of royal officials and soldiers. After private individuals had paid their Royal Fifth, they were free to keep the gold or silver in bars or wedges, or have it minted into coins. Most of the coins minted in the Indies remained there for use—except for the large amounts that changed hands at the fairs in Porto Bello or Veracruz—and were carried back on ships by merchants who had sold their wares at the fairs. Gold coins were called escudos, or doubloons (as they were called from about 1700 onward). Silver coins were called reals, and both gold and silver were minted in denominations of 8, 4, 2, 1 and halves. The value of gold coins as compared with silver in the sixteenth and seventeenth centuries was sixteen to one; but during the eighteenth century, when gold production was greatly increased, this value dropped to eight to one.

There were all sorts of frauds committed by the persons entrusted with the refining, assaying, and minting of gold and silver. On many occasions, silver bars were detected having their centers made of lead or copper, and occasionally with baser metals. In minting coins, baser metals were also added, and even platinum—which was valueless in those days—was used as a substitute for silver. Another fraud was minting coins less in weight than they should have been.

Before any treasure was embarked on the galleons, manifests, or registers, were made in triplicate of every bar, wedge, or chest of coins. The bars and wedges had various marks on them: where it was mined and assayed, the Royal Fifth paid on it, the owners' mark, the mark of the assayer, the fineness of the metal, its weight, and the value of each piece. The average weight of a silver bar was 70 pounds, a wedge was between 10 and 20 pounds, and gold bullion weighed from several ounces up to 30 pounds.

Smuggling of unregistered cargoes, both to and from the Indies, was the most frustrating problem that the Spanish Crown was confronted with throughout the period of the Indies navigation. In 1510 an ordinance was issued ordering that any unregistered treasure brought back from the Indies was subjected to confiscation and the smuggler fined four times the value of the treasure. All sorts of precautions were exercised by the officials of the Crown, but they were never totally effective. Before a fleet entered Sanlucar, all other ships were forced to move to Cadiz so that no treasure could be sneaked aboard them from the returning Indies ships. Patrol boats were stationed up and down the coasts between Cape St. Vincent and Gibraltar to make sure no boats approached or left the returning Indies ships. Along the beaches, special patrols utilizing wild dogs were used. From 1576 onward, informers were paid one-third of the value of any unregistered treasure recovered. Every ship returning from the Indies was also closely inspected by royal officials of the House of Trade. Notwithstanding these precautions, about 20 percent of the gold and silver mined in the New World was still smuggled into Spain or other European nations in return for payment of contraband goods that had been sold in the Indies by foreigners.

Gold, being more valuable than silver, was naturally the choice item to smuggle into Spain, but great amounts of silver, both in specie and bullion, also were smuggled, and the smugglers never seemed to tire of devising new methods to avoid detection. On one occasion a royal official became suspicious over a painted ship's anchor. Upon scraping it he discovered it was made of solid gold. The most common method used, however, was smuggling the gold and silver in bales, boxes, or chests of unimportant commodities like sugar, molasses, tobacco, etc., as it was almost impossible for the royal officials to open every single container on board ship.

In some cases the amounts of unregistered treasure on board ships was greater than the registered. A good example was in 1555, when a ship returning from New Spain wrecked on the southern coast of Spain between Cadiz and Gibraltar. Divers were employed to salvage the wreck and over 500,000 pesos in treasure was recovered, of which less than 150,000 pesos was registered. This resulted in all the officers aboard that ship being sent to serve as galley slaves for ten years.

A gradual decline began in the overall *flota* system around 1600, and by 1650 the whole *flota* system almost ceased to exist at all. The reasons for this are many, with the most important being: the decline in silver production in the Indies; a great increase in contraband goods being sold in the Indies by foreigners; insufficient shipping and crews for use in the Indies navigation; poor leadership by inept rulers; bankruptcy of the Crown on several occasions; and the depredations executed on the shipping and American colonies by Spain's enemies.

As the American colonists' demand for merchandise from Spain decreased yearly—due to the ever-increasing amounts of contraband brought over by foreigners and sold at more attractive prices—the number of ships in the *flotas* kept decreasing. So great was the amount of contraband goods reaching Porto Bello that 1648 was the last year that a Tierra Firme Flota ever sailed to the Indies. Thereafter the small amount of goods carried there was embarked aboard the Galleons. A few years later, with so little merchandise to carry, and the mining industry in such a poor state, the Crown seriously considered the cessation of the whole *flota* system.

From 1650 onward the New Spain Flota and the Galleons, which previously had sailed yearly, began sailing only at irregular intervals of every four or five years, and the number of ships in these fleets was negligible. To give an example of how bad the decline was at this time one has only to compare it with the past: Between 1570 and 1599 there was an average of 110 ships sailing yearly to the Indies; between 1600 and 1610 they dropped to 55; between 1640 and 1650 to 25; and between 1670 and 1690 to only 17. Things were so bad that in 1661 the Spaniards had to use a Dutch fleet of twenty ships under the command of Admiral Ruiter to protect their returning treasure ships, as the English were after them. The Dutch were willing, since most of the returning treasures were consigned to Dutch merchants in payment for goods they had shipped over earlier in the year.

Even after 1700, when the production of gold and silver in the American mines greatly increased, the overall *flota* system showed very little improvement, the main reason being that the Spanish-American colonists preferred buying most of their European merchandise from the English, Dutch, and French, all of whom had already established settlements throughout the West Indies. During the War of Spanish Succession, which lasted from 1700 to 1713, the French virtually took over complete control of the *flota* system, and most of the ships used were French and carried predominantly French crews as well.

Between 1715 and 1736, small *flotas* continued to sail to Veracruz every two or three years, but during this same period of twenty-one

years only five convoys of treasure galleons sailed to Porto Bello and
Cartagena. In 1736, due to the threat of war with England, the Spanish
Crown suspended the sailing of the New Spain Flota and the Galleons.
In 1740 the Crown went a step further and ended the sailings of the
Galleons permanently. Thereafter a new system was devised to bring
back the Peruvian treasures. Large, solitary galleons, or occasionally
two sailing together, would sail directly from Cadiz to Callao and
back again. Great improvements in the design and rigging of the
galleons made the perilous voyage around Cape Horn a lot safer.
Some foreign ships, mainly French, had been making this long voyage
from 1700 onward.

Due to the long war with England, the resumption of the sailings
of the New Spain Flota didn't come into effect until 1754, and during
the long period when no *flotas* sailed to Veracruz, single registered
sueltos made the voyage yearly. Between 1754 and 1778, the year when
the last New Spain Flota returned to Spain, only six *flotas* sailed to
Veracruz, and all of them had to be escorted by large squadrons of
warships, which made the expense too great in maintaining their
future sailings. In 1778, when the Spanish Crown finally declared free
trade all over her American colonies, the *flota* system came to an
end. Spanish ships still sailed to the New World with European products and returned with treasure, but no longer in convoys—usually
two or three ships sailed jointly, and sometimes only one.

Throughout the sixteenth century the waters of the New World were
more or less a "Spanish Lake" and virtually all the ships sailing in
these waters were Spanish-built, had Spanish crews, and carried
cargoes and treasures between Spain and the Spanish-American colonies. Ships of other European nations made occasional voyages to the
New World, however, generally to the detriment of the Spaniards.
The Portuguese were the one exception. Soon after the founding of the
early Spanish settlements, the Portuguese were granted exclusive permission by the Spanish Crown to carry limited numbers of African
Negroes to be sold in the New World ports as slaves. They were in
especially great demand in areas where the indigenous population
were decimated, either by the wholesale massacres affected by the
Spaniards or various diseases the Spaniards had brought with them
from the Old World. During the period 1525 to 1550 an average of
six to eight Portuguese slave ships visited various ports in the New
World, sometimes making additional profits by selling contraband
European products to the Spanish colonists at much cheaper prices

than they could obtain from the Seville monopolists. With the great increase in the mining of precious metals after the middle of the sixteenth century, the number of these Portuguese slave ships increased to as many as forty to fifty annually. This continued until 1640, when Portugal revolted against the Spanish Crown and eventually won total independence. The Dutch, and later the English, took over the lucrative trade of supplying the Spanish colonies with a steady supply of African slaves.

The first interlopers in the waters of the New World were the French pirates and privateers, who appeared during the third decade of the sixteenth century. Throughout the century the French made sporadic voyages to the New World, generally for the sake of attacking Spanish settlements and shipping. They also made several abortive attempts to establish settlements on the coast of Florida. The English, on the other hand, began their first voyage with the intent of making peaceful trade with the Spanish colonists—such as those made by John Hawkins and others—but the Spaniards had such complete mastery over their colonies that these voyages were rarely profitable. It took the English many years, but they finally realized that the only way to make any profit in the New World was to take what they wanted by force. During the last three decades, Francis Drake and a host of other famous English privateers sailed to the West Indies and to other Spanish New World colonies for the express purpose of waging war on the Spaniards and accumulating great amounts of plunder. But many of these voyages were profitless, as the Spaniards were not always easy to overcome.

The Dutch showed no interest in the New World until the last two decades of the sixteenth century, and this came about not because of greed or plunder or to make a profit out of contraband trade with the Spaniards but because of their great need for salt. The main industry of the Netherlands in the sixteenth century was fishing, and vast amounts of salt were necessary to process their catches. Until 1580, when Portugal was annexed to Spain, they obtained almost all of their salt from the Portuguese, who had great salt pans on their southern coast. When Spain took over the government of Portugal, however, she discouraged further trade with the Dutch (with whom Spain had been at war for over twenty years), which threatened their economy with disaster. The Dutch soon discovered that there were vast deposits of salt available in the New World, specifically in several of the Bahama Islands, St. Martins Island, and at Punta de Araya on the coast of Venezuela. As early as 1582 there were as many as 150 Dutch ships making voyages to the Caribbean for salt. By 1600 this number increased to over 200 ships annually (actually more ships than were sailing from Spain to the New World at this time), and in the year 1616 a total of 279 Dutch ships made the voyage over and back, most of them obtaining the salt from Punta de Araya, where they had constructed permanent warehouses to store any surplus of salt that might accumulate. They continued extracting vast amounts of salt from the Caribbean until near the close of the seventeenth century, when large salt mines were discovered in Germany and elsewhere in Europe.

Early in the seventeenth century, Sir Walter Raleigh founded several small English settlements near the Orinoco River on the northeastern section of the South-American coast. The Dutch and the French soon followed with their own settlements in the same general area, but none of these settlements amounted to much until later in the century, when the settlements were put on a firmer footing (some are still held today). Most of the ships returning from these settlements to Europe sailed directly home and did not come up through the Bahama Channel except when a captain decided to chance the occasion of meeting some small Spanish ship he might capture.

The second quarter of the seventeenth century opened a new era in the maritime history of the New World, and within a few decades the "Spanish Lake" myth was broken. The English, French, and Dutch were no longer content to be thought of by the Spaniards as interlopers and soon established themselves as permanent settlers.

The English first settled the Island of St. Christopher (St. Kitts) in 1624, and the following year a large group of French settlers joined them. To avoid friction between the colonists, the island was divided in two. In 1627 the first English colonists reached Barbados, and in 1628 other Englishmen settled on Nevis Island and Providencia (called Santa Catalina by the Spaniards), located in the western Caribbean off the coast of Nicaragua.

The Spaniards were by no means happy about this situation. On September 7, 1629, a Spanish fleet of over thirty large ships under the command of Admiral Fadrique de Toledo dropped anchor at Nevis Island and captured and destroyed several English ships anchored there. Then Spanish soldiers were sent ashore to ravage the few buildings the new settlers had just built. The fleet then moved to St. Kitts, which is only a few miles to the north of Nevis, and although the English and French put up some resistance the Spaniards quickly

Spanish galleon in a battle.

TOP: Seventeenth-century Dutch ships. BOTTOM: Spanish galleon wrecking on a beach.

captured it. Admiral Toledo provided several ships and ordered the settlers to return to their respective countries (for which he was severely criticized by the King of Spain). Although most of the French colonists returned to France, most of the English soon returned to St. Kitts and began all over again. Some of the English ships sailing between England and Virginia or New England preferred taking the southern route in crossing the Atlantic, and on many of these voyages additional colonists were brought to St. Kitts and other newly founded English settlements.

The Dutch, not wanting to be outdone by their French and English neighbors, were quick to grab the islands they wanted and to found their own settlements. In 1628 they settled on Tobago Island, but it was a bad choice, as Trinidad, the next island to the south, was settled by the Spaniards. The Spaniards, making use of the cannibalistic Carib Indians, soon forced the Dutch to flee from Tobago in 1630. However, the directors of the Dutch West Indies Company, who were entrusted with the founding of these settlements, sent another group of colonists to Tobago in 1633, but in 1637 the Spaniards mounted a surprise attack and put every one of the settlers to the sword.

The Dutch had better luck on other Caribbean islands. By the time of the Treaty of Westphalia in 1648, when the war between the Dutch and Spaniards finally came to an end after almost a hundred years of bloody warfare, the Dutch had permanent settlements on Aruba, Bonaire, Curaçao, Saba, St. Martin, and St. Eustatius; and the Spaniards were forced to recognize the existence of these Dutch colonies in the New World.

In 1635 the French formed the Compagnie des Iles d'Amerique to compete with the Dutch and English. By 1648 they had settlements on Martinique, Guadeloupe, St. Bartholomew, St. Croix, St. Lucia, and Grenada. By this time the English had gobbled up most of the remaining islands in the Lesser Antilles and later were to win, through the spoils of war, some of those in French hands; yet they were still unsatisfied.

No foreign nation had attempted to take an inhabited Spanish possession by force until in 1655 Cromwell sent a massive military force to the Caribbean. After failing to capture either Puerto Rico or Santo Domingo, he finally took the Island of Jamaica, more or less as a consolation prize. Spain was too weak to recapture this island, so in a peace treaty with England in 1670 she ceded Jamaica to England.

Jamaica soon became England's most profitable overseas possession; first through privateering, then by illegal commerce with the Spanish colonies, and eventually through agriculture—mainly through the cultivation of sugar and its by-products. The French soon followed the English capture of Jamaica with one of their own on the eastern half of Hispaniola, which was finally ceded to them by Spain in 1697.

Thus throughout the seventeenth century—and especially during the second half—there was a great number of ships of the different major European powers sailing Caribbean waters and returning through the Bahama Channel. The majority of these ships sailed singly or in small groups and carried back cotton, tobacco, indigo, spices, lumber, and rum, as well as gold, silver, and whatever else they obtained from the Spaniards through plunder or illegal trade. Toward the end of the century the English first organized merchant fleets—generally convoyed by warships—to and from the Mother Country. The usual practice was for the convoy to split up when reaching the Caribbean while the merchant ships sailed to various islands to unload cargoes and load homeward-bound cargoes. Then all of the ships would sail to Kingston in Jamaica and sail back to England in a large convoy, passing through the Bahama Channel. As early as 1697 one of these fleets numbered 116 merchantmen and 6 warships. In 1758, a fleet leaving Jamaica numbered 150 ships, and this was only one of two fleets that sailed from there that year. As early as 1723 there were three fleets sailing from England to the Caribbean: one to Barbados and two to Jamaica, totaling over 425 ships for that year. Not all of them sailed to England; many went to various ports in the American colonies. The American colonies, as well, were sending substantial numbers of merchant ships to the Caribbean, supplying the English islands with items they could not get from the Mother Country or those they could supply at cheaper prices, such as a wide variety of food-stuffs and various types of lumber. As years passed and the population grew, maritime traffic also increased. By 1750, in Kingston alone, more than eight hundred ships from other Caribbean islands, Europe, Africa, North America, and the Spanish colonies entered port.

The Dutch colonies were small in comparison with the English, and they did not make use of convoys. The French, although their colonies were not as large as those of the English, soon used a convoy system of their own, but the majority of their homeward-bound traffic did not pass through the Bahama Channel. French ships from the Lesser Antilles would unite in one of their several Hispaniola ports and then sail through what was known as the "Windward Passage"—passing to the east of Great and Little Inagua and Mayaguana islands and to the west of Caicos Island out into the Atlantic Ocean. The largest French merchant fleet to leave Hispaniola sailed in 1782 and totaled 190 ships.

Not all the shipping of these nations was of mercantilistic nature. Warships were used to escort the merchant fleets and to wage war on their neighbors, which seemed to be a continuous occurrence throughout both the seventeenth and eighteenth centuries. The warships were also utilized when these nations were at war with the Spaniards in attempts to capture returning Spanish *flotas*. Although at least fifty different serious attempts were made by the English, French, and Dutch between 1550 and 1750 to capture an entire *flota*, it was only accomplished once. In 1628 a Dutch West Indies Company fleet under the command of Peit Heyn, captured all twenty-four ships of the New Spain Flota commanded by Captain-General Juan de Benevides y Bazan and won a booty of over 14 million pesos.

Smaller vessels also sailed the waters of the Caribbean and passed through the Bahama Channel. There were packet boats that brought news from and took news back to the Mother Country; and there were fishing vessels of various kinds: coastal, or interisland, traders, salvage boats, and numerous pirate and privateering vessels (about which so much has been written).

As the New World colonies of the European nations grew rapidly in population, shipping between Europe and the Western Hemisphere became greater. In 1785 there was a total of 1,347 European ships that sailed to the Western Hemisphere and to Europe. And with a greater number of ships plying the seas, the number of losses increased.

Early Salvors, Treasure-Hunters, and Marine Archaeology

MAN HAS GONE down to the depths of the sea since the earliest of times. From archaeological evidence we know that free divers were used in Mesopotamia as early as 4500 B.C. to recover the murex shells, from which an important dye was obtained. Divers were also used by the Egyptians around 3200 B.C. to recover mother-of-pearl shells; and Greek divers were bringing up sponges as early as 2500 B.C.

The earliest account of the use of divers to recover sunken treasure is mentioned in the writings of Herodotus, a Greek historian around the middle of the fifth century B.C. About fifty years earlier a Greek diver named Scyllias and his daughter Cyane had been employed by Xeres, the King of Persia, to recover an immense treasure from several Persian galleys that had been sunk during a battle with a Greek fleet. They managed to recover the treasure, but Xeres cheated them out of the reward he had promised them. There are hundreds of other accounts of divers recovering great treasures from sunken ships all over the seas of the Old World. Diving was an old profession long before the discovery of the New World.

We know that diving was done by the Indians of Peru as early as the third century A.D. Long before the white man reached the Western Hemisphere, it was practiced by many aborigines, mainly as a means of obtaining food. North-American Indians used diving as a basic hunting technique: by swimming under water and breathing through reeds they were able to approach unwary fowl and game and capture them with nets, spears, or their bare hands. Diving for pearls did not become a major occupation until the coming of the white man, but it was done on a small scale in the Caribbean by the Lucayan, Carib, and Arawak tribes. In 1498, during Columbus' third voyage of exploration, his small fleet anchored at the Island of Cubagua, near the coast of Venezuela, to obtain a supply of fresh water and fruits. While some of his men were ashore they noticed a Carib Indian woman wearing a pearl necklace. They made inquiries, then informed Columbus that the natives possessed great quantities of exquisite and valuable pearls that were to be found in the waters all around the island. Columbus sent Indian divers in search of the pearl oysters, and the results confirmed the story of his men. Returning to Spain, Columbus reported this to the King, who ordered that a pearl fishery be established on Cubagua at once.

Other large pearl beds were discovered during the next few years in the same area, including the area around Margarita Island, which eventually became the center of the pearl industry, a position it has maintained. The Caribbean pearl fisheries furnished Spain with a source of wealth surpassed only by the gold and silver from the mines of Peru and Mexico.

Soon after the opening of the pearl fisheries around Cubagua and Margarita, the local supply of divers was expended: Many died from diseases carried by the Spaniards, others from overwork at the hands of the greedy employers, who often forced them to dive as many as sixteen hours a day. The next source of divers tapped by the Spaniards was the Lucayan Indians of the Bahamas, who were then considered the best divers in the New World. The Spanish historian Oviedo, writing in 1535, gave an account of his visit to the pearl fishery at Margarita in which he marveled at the fantastic abilities of the Lucayan divers and stated that they were able to descend to depths of 100 feet and remain submerged as long as fifteen minutes (no doubt an exaggeration). He added that, unlike the Carib Indians, who had less stamina, they could dive from sunrise to sunset, seven days a week, without appearing to tire. As the divers of the Old World had done for thousands of years, they descended by grasping stone weights in their arms and jumping overboard, completely naked except for a net bag around their necks in which to deposit the oysters they found on the sea floor. So great was the demand for the Lucayan Indians that in a few years all their people were enslaved and the Bahamas were bereft of their former inhabitants, the first natives Columbus and his men had seen on their epic voyage of discovery.

Like the Carib Indians before them, the Lucayans were soon expended. Thus by the middle of the sixteenth century the Spaniards were again hard-pressed for divers. They solved the problem by importing Negro slaves from Africa, most of whom had never dived and in many cases had never seen the sea until their enforced voyage. Amazingly, they adapted at once and became good divers. Women slaves were preferred to men, probably because the extra layers of body fat in their tissues prevented chilling and enabled them to spend longer hours in the water than the men could endure.

The Spaniards, who knew when they were on to a good thing, soon found another use for their talents just as important as pearl-diving, or even more so: salvage work on shipwrecks. In major colonial ports like Havana, Veracruz, Cartagena, and Panama, teams of Negro divers were kept aboard salvage vessels that were ready to depart on short notice to attempt the recovery of sunken treasure and other valuable cargoes. During the sixteenth century, and on to the end of the eighteenth, more than 100 million pesos in just treasure alone was recovered by these Negro divers. Ironically, when the other European nations began colonizing the New World, these same divers were instrumental in depleting the Spanish exchequer: Their new employers made use of them in salvaging Spanish wrecks, but this time the profits went into English, French, and Dutch treasuries.

The English were next to enter the salvage field, which they called "wracking," soon after they settled in Bermuda at the beginning of the seventeenth century and worked their wracking vessels all over the Caribbean. During the second half of the century, Port Royal, in Jamaica, became the center of the wrackers, and it was there that the American William Phips came to recruit divers to help salvage a Spanish galleon, laden with a great treasure, that had sunk in 1641 on

Silver Shoals, off the northern coast of Hispaniola. Using Negro divers, he recovered the greatest amount of treasure from any single wreck until the twentieth century.

The Spaniards learned quite early that the Indians of Florida were also very good divers but failed to utilize their diving abilities, for they were considered too dangerous to work with. There are documents dated as early as 1544 stating that Indians on the coast of Florida were diving for and recovering vast amounts of treasure from shipwrecks. Although no known pearl deposits exist today in Florida waters, there are several sixteenth-century accounts stating that these Indians dived for pearl oysters along the east coast of Florida. The famous Dutch historian John Huigehen Van Linschoten wrote in 1598: "Gold and silver wherewith the Indians trafficke, they had it out of ships which fall on ground (wreck) upon the Cape of Florida, because most of the ships lost here are lost on this said cape. . . ."

Although the diving bell was first invented early in the sixteenth century, neither the Indian nor the Negro made much use of it, preferring instead to stay below for as long as they could hold their breath. On some occasions white men actually did the diving on wrecks, and they almost always made use of diving bells.

Since something like 99 percent of the ships that have been lost over the centuries in the New World went down in very shallow waters— generally by wrecking on shallow reefs or shoals—almost all of these wrecks were in depths that the early salvors could reach. This would more or less indicate that very little treasure or other items of historical value should remain on shipwrecks, but such is not the case. When ships broke up on reefs or on a coastline—especially during hurricanes —their cargoes were often scattered over wide areas and covered by shifting sands. A good example was the loss of the 1715 fleets on the eastern coast of Florida. Although the Spaniards carried out extensive salvage operations on these wrecks, they were only able to recover about half the treasure. An exception occurred with the loss of the 1733 fleet in the Florida Keys when more treasure was recovered than had been registered.

There were also many cases where ships were lost and there were no survivors—either all the people drowned or were killed by the Indians. Without knowing the locations of these wrecks, naturally the Spaniards did not salvage them. Some of these virgin wreck sites have been discovered by nineteenth- and twentieth-century salvors and fishermen.

Key West, which was founded primarily as a base for salvors, at the beginning of the nineteenth century was actually a latecomer in the game. Nassau, founded a century earlier, had superseded Port Royal as the main base of Caribbean wreck salvors. With salvage vessels working out of both ports from the early years of the nineteenth century onward, there were very few shipwrecks that were not salvaged even before they broke up and their cargoes scattered or hidden beneath shifting sands or coral growth.

During the first half of the twentieth century very few attempts were made to recover sunken treasures or salvage old shipwrecks. Many fictional articles and several books were gobbled up by a gullible public, however, telling of brave divers finding intact Spanish galleons with skeletons still at the wheel and holds crammed with chests of treasure. But usually a giant octopus or schools of voracious sharks prevented the actual recovery of the treasure. In fact, it was one of these fascinating and romantic stories that got me interested in old shipwrecks at an early age. The author spun a good yarn about having gone to Jamaica in the thirties and diving on the sunken city of Port Royal. He had the water ten times deeper than it actually is and told of walking the streets of the sunken city in helmet diving gear, locating a standing cathedral full of golden church relics that were guarded by a 12-foot crab, taverns in which skeletons sat at tables with tankards in their bony hands, and chests of gold and precious stones ready for the taking everywhere. What a surprise I was in for when I eventually got to dive on the sunken city!

The only major recovery of sunken treasure of this century until more recent years—more of an archaeological value than an intrinsic one—occurred not in the sea but in fresh water. For centuries a legend persisted about the Mayans sacrificing virgin maidens covered with ornaments of gold and jade in a sacred well, called a *cenote*, at the ruins of Chichén Itzá in Yucatán, Mexico. In 1904 a young American, Edward Thompson, who was the American consul to Mérida, Yucatán, decided to see if there was any truth to this legend. The depth of the murky waters of the *cenote* was between 60 and 70 feet, with a great amount of mud on its bottom. Thompson first learned to dive with a helmet, then enlisted the services of a professional Greek diver to assist him. They had no luck at first, but Thompson was persistent. Eventually they found gold jewelry and ornaments, as well as a vast amount of archaeological treasure. Realizing that the bulk of the treasure was beneath the mud on the bottom of the *cenote*, Thompson rigged a drag-bucket at the top of the *cenote* and recovered a great deal more. However, with his primitive equipment he did not thoroughly salvage all of the treasure. Recently, several well-equipped expeditions have recovered a great amount of other priceless artifacts and treasure. The value of what Thompson recovered was about $100,000.

In 1906 a fisherman from Grand Cayman Island was working in the area of Pedro Shoals, which is located about 130 miles south of Kingston, Jamaica. While rowing over a shallow reef he sighted something bright. Without any diving equipment at all, he dove and brought up a Spanish gold bar. On subsequent dives he brought up six other gold bars and several handfuls of gold Spanish coins. Not realizing the value of his find, he sold all of the treasure for its gold value. When news of his find spread, several expeditions arrived but found nothing. Unknown to them at that time was the fact that the rest of the treasure and cargo of this shipwreck was probably buried under coral growth or sand. In recent years over a dozen expeditions have set out to find this particular wreck, but none have been successful, as the exact location where the fisherman found his treasure has been lost.

There have been tales about Greek helmet divers who worked out of Tarpon Springs, Florida, diving for sponges in Florida and Bahamian waters and recovering various sunken treasures, but I have been unable to verify any of these tales.

During the summers of 1934 and 1935, the Mariner's Museum of Newport News, Virginia, conducted salvage operations on two British warships that were sunk in the York River during the Siege of Yorktown in 1781. The locations of both wrecks were found by oystermen who accidentally snagged their nets on them. Helmeted divers were employed to use water-jets and removed the mud over the wrecks, which were in 40 feet of water. A great number of interesting artifacts were recovered: cannon, cannonballs, swords, axes, tools of various types, many pieces of rigging, a brass ship's bell, sounding leads, glass bottles of many descriptions, and other personal items belonging to the crews of these ships. Fortunately, great efforts were undertaken to preserve these artifacts and most of them can today be seen in the Mariner's Museum.

In December 1938, several Negro fishermen sighted a large number of coral-encrusted cannons on a reef off Key Largo. They reported this to Charles Brookfield, who had long dreamed of locating sunken treasure. Brookfield hired a young diver and the cannons were relocated.

Besides cannons, they brought up many cannonballs, lead musketballs, bits of rope, anchors, a silver porringer, and several silver and brass coins. Their most interesting recovery was small fragments of pages from a prayer book that was found beneath a cannon. Through the British Admiralty, whom they contacted after identifying the cannon as British from the markings on them, they learned the identity of the shipwreck: It was H.M.S. *Winchester*, of 933 tons and sixty guns, which was lost on September 24, 1695.

During World War II, when there was a great demand for scrap iron, salvage boats stripped thousands of old cannons and anchors of old shipwrecks all along the East Coast of the United States and the Caribbean and sold them for their scrap-iron value. Probably unknown to these salvors at that time, they destroyed the chances of future marine archaeologists and wreck-divers of locating many of these old shipwrecks, as cannon and anchors are the main signposts that indicate the presence of an old wreck.

In the chapters of this book that list shipwrecks of the Western Hemisphere, I have covered the most significant recoveries since the introduction of scuba-diving equipment as well as other pertinent information that will help the wreck-diver.

The first people to show an interest in marine archaeology were a group of English archaeologists and antiquarians who, in 1775, sponsored an expedition to recover historical artifacts from the Tiber River, near Rome. Greek divers, using a diving bell, worked for three years with very little success, for they had no means of removing the accumulation of river mud that covered the Greek and Roman artifacts they were hoping to recover. After that there was very little interest in recovering relics until early in the twentieth century, when objects brought up from the Mediterranean by Greek and Turkish sponge-divers aroused the interest of archaeologists working on land sites nearby. The archaeologists hired divers to recover more artifacts, which turned out to have a historical importance as great as anything dug up on land sites.

Today, almost all marine archaeological work is confined to the Mediterranean. In the late 1930s, even before scuba equipment was available, the famous underwater explorer Dimitri Rebikoff began exploring, surveying, and excavating dozens of ancient shipwrecks and sunken cities off the coast of France, Italy, and Greece. He was followed by Jacques Cousteau and his team of divers, who worked several ancient shipwrecks off France and Tunisia.

In recent years a great amount of marine archaeological work has been undertaken in Greek and Turkish waters, largely because of the enthusiasm of an American, Peter Throckmorton, who in 1959 discovered thirty-five ancient shipwrecks. His most important find is a shipwreck dating from 1200 B.C. called the "Bronze Age Wreck," which lies in 120 feet of water off Cape Gelidonya, Turkey. Soon after making his discovery, Throckmorton became associated with the Department of Archaeology of the University of Pennsylvania, and under the direction of Dr. George Bass, major excavations have taken place on several of these shipwrecks during the past six summers. During the past summer no less than twenty major marine archaeological expeditions took place all over the Mediterranean: in Spain, France, Italy, Greece, Yugoslavia, Turkey, Israel, Tunisia, Malta, and Crete. The sad fact is that most of the Americans who are qualified to conduct a proper marine archaeological excavation prefer working on the more ancient sites in the Mediterranean, resulting in a scarcity of archaeologists to aid the amateurs working at sites in the Western Hemisphere.

The most difficult, expensive, and time-consuming marine archaeological project ever undertaken in Europe was the raising of the Swedish sixty-four-gun warship *Vasa*, which sank in Stockholm Harbor in 1628 shortly after being launched from the ways. Early salvage efforts failed, as the deepest parts of the wreck lay in 100 feet of water, a depth too great for the diving bells then in use. From the higher parts of the wreck within reach of the diving bells, however, a few cannon were recovered. The wreck lay at the bottom of the harbor for more than three hundred years, and because there are no sea teredo, or shipworms, in the harbor, the ship remained totally intact.

In 1956 a Swedish petroleum engineer, Anders Franzen, became interested in the *Vasa* and, by using a core sampler, located the wreck. Swedish naval divers were sent down to investigate the wreck and, when discovering that it was intact, plans were made to raise the ship. With the aid of the Swedish government and funds from private sources, a team of helmeted divers under Franzen's supervision went to work. It was no easy task, as the *Vasa* was huge, having a displacement of 1,400 tons; also, the wreck was deeply buried in the mud. First the divers had to remove all of the loose objects aboard. Next, with the use of a water-jet, they had to blast tunnels under the wreck (a perilous task, for the ship could easily have slipped farther into the mud and crushed them) so that steel lifting cables could be inserted under the wreck. The construction of the tunnels alone took three years. While it was going on, other divers were busy removing the masts, spars, and rigging. Two more years were spent sealing off all the gun ports and other openings in the ship, as well as tying down all the cannons to prevent them from moving and possibly damaging the hull. Finally, cables were strung through the tunnels and attached to pontoons on the surface. On April 24, 1961, five years after the work began, the *Vasa* broke the surface. It was placed in a specially constructed drydock, where it is still undergoing preservation. To date, over $6 million has been spent in the salvaging and preservation of this ship.

The first marine archaeological excavation in the Western Hemisphere was undertaken by Edward Thompson at Chichén Itzá (mentioned earlier in this chapter). Under the dynamic leadership of Pablo Bush Romero, the founder and president of CEDAM (the Marine Archaeological Society of Mexico), two other excavations took place in the Sacred Well in 1960–61 and 1967–68. Over the past ten years, CEDAM has also conducted other serious excavations on shipwrecks in Mexican waters.

During the past fifteen years the Smithsonian Institution has sponsored a series of excavations in Bermudan waters, working mainly on sites discovered by Teddy Tucker and his associates.

The most important marine archaeological excavation undertaken in the Western Hemisphere was my own work on the sunken city of Port Royal, which was conducted over a period of three complete years in which more artifacts were recovered than had been gathered from all the old shipwrecks salvaged in the Western Hemisphere in the last twenty years. In the chapter dealing with Jamaica, and later in this chapter, I will go into more detail on Port Royal.

Marine archaeology, a science still in its infancy, poses problems that do not arise in the excavation of a land site. Ideally, archaeological excavation should be taken stratigraphically, or layer by layer, with the exact depth of each find recorded. Stratigraphical digging on land often leads to very precise determination of the age of the object uncovered and reconstruction of the society it belonged to. On most marine sites, because the sea floor is constantly subjected to the disturbances of currents, storms, and the like—to say nothing of the disturbances caused by man—such results are the exception rather than the rule.

One case in which land archaeological methods were applied under water with outstanding results occurred a few years ago, when Dr. George Bass undertook the excavation of the three-thousand-year-old

"Bronze Age Wreck" in Turkish waters discovered by Peter Throck-morton. Bass had every advantage. The wreck lay in crystal-clear water at a depth of 150 feet, too deep for salvors of the past to reach. No storm had broken it to pieces over the centuries, nor had currents disturbed the artifacts aboard. Besides having sufficient funds with which to finance his work, Dr. Bass had a full archaeological team of divers, draftsmen, artists, a photographer, a historian, a classicist, and several preservation experts. With their help, he was able to map the site properly on a grid chart, dig stratigraphically, and record the position and depth of the timbers remaining on the ship as well as every artifact recovered. Later, he was able to reconstruct the wreck completely, ascertaining how the ship was built, what it carried, and how each item was stored aboard the ship. His work on this site was an archaeologist's dream, the equivalent of the Roman city of Pompeii, which was covered over by volcanic ash in A.D. 79 and remained a fantastic time capsule of history until archaeologists began excavating it over fifty years ago.

Certainly the chances of obtaining such sensational results are rare in the Western Hemisphere, where almost every marine archaeological site is located in shallow waters and has been subjected to countless disturbances from nature and man. The exception would be the discovery of an old shipwreck that sank in at least a depth of 100 feet. But unfortunately only a small number of old wrecks are known to have sunk in such depths, and even so, unless the wreck was known to be carrying treasure there is little likelihood that anyone would attempt to excavate it, because of the great expense involved in working a wreck at such a depth. If the scholarly world would shift their efforts from the Mediterranean, however, it would be possible to duplicate Bass's work.

The sunken city of Port Royal is the only site in the Western Hemisphere in which any attempt has been made to thoroughly and completely excavate under the accepted archaeological standards of the "old school" archaeologists. It was excavated using methods similar to those used by land archaeologists and Bass, which meant gridding the site off, making a thorough survey, recording the position and stratigraphy of all the artifacts and buildings uncovered, making drawings and photographing everything recovered, carrying out proper preservation work, and—most important—publishing the scientific results of the overall excavation. However, as in Bass's case, I had many advantages that other archaeologists and divers will not have on other sites in this hemisphere. The city sank quickly and was soon covered over by harbor sediment, which more or less kept all the artifacts and buildings *in situ*. Because the site is in a protected harbor, it has not been greatly disturbed by storms or currents, unlike most shipwreck sites, which lie exposed in shallow-water areas. However, a certain amount of disturbance was caused over the centuries by ships dragging their anchors through the site, and this resulted in artifacts being moved from their original positions. Also, the site suffered a great deal from contamination, items lost aboard shipwrecks, and trash thrown into the area over the years by local inhabitants.

Since most sites in this hemisphere do not fit into the category of most Mediterranean sites or Port Royal, just how much archaeological information can they yield to science? Archaeologists and historians would like to learn the following about most old shipwrecks: How and out of what material were the ships constructed? What type of rigging, anchors, and armament did they carry? What were their cargoes and where were they stored aboard the ships? Some of these questions can be answered from the average shallow-water wreck, but others—like where the cargoes were stored—can only be answered from deep-water shipwrecks.

More than 99 percent of all shipwreck losses in the Western Hemisphere have occurred due to a ship wrecking in shallow water. Either immediately upon wrecking, or soon after (even when ships wrecked in good weather), the ship has broken up. The superstructure was the first to go. Being buoyant, it was generally washed up on a beach or into a more shallow area, spilling cannon and other items along the way after it broke away from the main hull. And what remained of the main hull was generally lost. On reefs the wood would either be eaten by teredo or broken up and carried away by wave action or currents, causing most of the items stored in the hull to be widely scattered over the reef or caught in sand pockets. When a ship wrecked on a sandy or muddy bottom, generally the lower section of the hull— keel, keelson, and lower ribs—would be buried while the higher sections were either eaten by worms or washed away, and again the original position of the items carried would be widely scattered. This results in the fact that there is virtually no way to determine the original position of cannon, anchors, equipment, or cargo. Nor can very much be learned about type and methods of construction of the actual ships, except for the lowest sections, which might be buried beneath sand or mud. The marine archaeological data that can be collected are: what these ships carried aboard them, even if we cannot determine where and how it was carried. When a ship is properly identified and dated, the items recovered from it are of immense value to science because they can be used to corroborate dates of items found on land archaeological sites. Yet this is not always foolproof, because a wreck can be contaminated in several ways: Salvors may throw things on a shipwreck many years after it was wrecked, or items from a later shipwreck might be carried into the area.

The big problem with regard to marine archaeology, as already mentioned, is that there are too few qualified people working in the field and the average wreck-diver has no one to go to for assistance in recording the archaeological data he has obtained from a site. The exception is in Mexico and Florida, where the governments provide archaeological assistance to divers working wreck sites.

My advice to anyone working a shipwreck or other marine archaeological site is to gather all the archaeological data possible: This includes a description and drawings of the site, photographs of everything uncovered (both *in situ* underwater and when brought to the surface), and any other pertinent information. Then turn it all over to some scholarly authority who might put the information to scientific use.

CHAPTER THREE

Locating Shipwrecks

APPROXIMATELY 98 PERCENT of all ships lost in the Western Hemisphere prior to 1825 were lost in shallow waters at depths of 30 feet or less, which makes them much easier to locate and salvage. In the Mediterranean, however, the reverse is true, as at least 95 percent of the shipwrecks lie in depths of over 100 feet. The major causes for ships being wrecked in shallow waters were storms driving them onto reefs, shoals, or coastlines; and faulty navigation, which is easy to understand when we see the primitive navigational equipment and inaccurate charts they used. Of the 2 percent lost in deep waters, the major causes were ships breaking up or capsizing in storms, fires at sea, ships sunk in battle, and ships either scuttled to prevent capture or scuttled by their captors after being stripped of their valuables.

About 95 percent of the ships lost in shallow waters are located on sandy bottoms, with the remaining 5 percent almost equally divided between those covered by mud and silt in harbors such as Havana and Veracruz and at rivermouths and those covered by coral growth on reefs.

First we should consider what happens to ships that wreck in shallow water. When a ship struck on shallow reefs, sometimes it was so badly broken up that no trace of its wooden hull remains, as the wood either floated away or was completely devoured by the teredo. Teddy Tucker has worked several such sites in Bermuda; and the *Matanceros* site, which I worked on the coast of Yucatán, is another good example, as we found only a few pieces of ship timbers buried under sand. Other ships wrecked on shallow reefs sometimes had all or part of their hulls carried to sandy bottoms or small sand pockets by wave action or currents, so that their timbers were covered over by sand before the worms could totally destroy them. Coral growth varies a great deal in different areas of tropic and subtropic waters, the determining factors being water temperature, salinity of the water, and wave action. In areas where coral growth is slow, most of the items on the ship are carried away to areas at varying distances, depending on the weight and shape, and very little—in some cases nothing at all—can be found on the reef where the ship was wrecked. Along the Caribbean coastline of Yucatán, for instance, the coral growth is rapid, so the major portion of the ship's cargo would be buried under coral growth before it could be washed ashore or off the area of the wreck site. Another good example of rapid coral growth is on Silver Shoals, on the eastern edge of the Bahama archipelago. When the divers of Sir William Phips located a richly laden treasure galleon in 1682—only forty-one years after it had been wrecked— they reported that the wreck was completely buried in coral and that in some places the coral growth was 5 feet thick, which prevented them from entirely salvaging the wreck.

Ships lost in mud or silt are generally the best preserved, as the weight of the ship forces the lower hull of the vessel down into the sediment very quickly, preventing attacks on the wood by the teredo. In the harbor of Cartagena, Colombia, I dived on two large Spanish warships that had been scuttled by the Spaniards in 1740 to prevent their capture by the English. Several months before my arrival, both wrecks had been uncovered during dredging operations to deepen the harbor. I found them to have most of their hulls in a remarkable state of preservation. Other examples are the two ships run aground in 1504 by Columbus in St. Anne's Bay, on the northern coast of Jamaica. Due to bad leaks on both ships, they were full of water and a great part of their lower hulls were pushed down into the soft silt of the bay, preserving them to this day. The main disadvantage of excavating a wreck lying on a mud or silt bottom is that during the actual excavation, underwater visibility is generally reduced to nil because of the stirring up of the sediment.

Ships wrecked on sandy bottoms are preserved to varying degrees, depending on two major factors: how quickly the weight of the wreck pushes the hull down into the sand, and when ocean or tide currents cause sand to rapidly build up over a wreck. In some areas there are only a few inches of sand covering a limestone or coquina bottom, in which case very little of a ship's hull will be preserved. Sometimes wrecks were covered over so quickly that even contemporary salvors were prevented from salvaging them, despite the fact that they knew their precise locations. The *Atocha*, which was lost in 1622 in the Florida Keys, is a prime example. Since it sank on the edge of the Gulf Stream, where the currents run between one and three knots, the sand built up so rapidly over the wreck that within two months Spanish divers reported that only the masts remained above the sea floor and there was an average of two fathoms of sand over the main deck of the wreck. There is also a great deal of documental evidence that this occurred to other wrecks.

When ships are wrecked during hurricanes, generally their hulls and cargoes are scattered over wide areas, sometimes covering several square miles, but there are exceptions. During the disaster of the 1715 fleet, ten of the ships were completely broken up. Very little of the hulls exists today and cargoes are scattered over large areas. Yet the eleventh ship of this fleet was wrecked close to shore and its hull remained intact for a long period, thus enabling the Spaniards to salvage her complete cargo.

During the hurricane of 1733 in which twenty-one Spanish ships were wrecked off the Florida Keys, the majority of the ships remained almost totally intact until the Spaniards salvaged them. Then they burnt those parts of the wrecks that remained above the waterline.

Recently I spent several months excavating the *San José*, which was one of the 1733 fleet. From our excavation I discovered the following facts. The ship apparently struck on an offshore reef with an average depth of 10 feet, or it may have been thrown completely clear over the reef due to the high seas during the hurricane. About a quarter-mile closer to shore from the reef the ship struck on a sandy bottom approximately 20 feet deep, losing its rudder, five cannons—which were possibly carried on the stern—and a substantial amount of cargo that spilled out of the ship in this general area. The main hull of the ship was carried about 250 feet farther, sinking in 30 feet of water, probably due to losing her stern section, which would result in her rapidly filling with water. Most of the cannon she carried was discovered either right on top of the ballast on the lower deck or relatively close to the main section of the lower hull. Most of the starboard section of the hull was lying between 10 and 20 feet from the lower section of the wreck, which consisted of the lower deck over the ship's keel. Covering the lower deck, we discovered about 200 tons of ballast rock, with a trail of ballast rock leading to the area where the ship had lost its rudder and part of its stern.

From these discoveries we can assume that the *San José* was one of the ships that remained intact after wrecking, otherwise we wouldn't have discovered most, or all, of her cannon so close to the main section of the wreck. This would also indicate that most of the cargo she carried would have remained inside the hull of the wreck, or fairly close to it.

In cases such as the ships of the 1715 fleet, we know—both from contemporary documents and actual salvaging of the wrecks—that when they broke up during the hurricane the lower sections of the hulls, containing the ballast and most of the bulky cargoes, sank farther offshore than the upper decks and superstructures. This is verified by the fact that most of the cannon, carried on the upper decks of the ships, was discovered closer to shore than the main ballast piles; and by the fact that most of the gold jewelry was discovered close to shore. The most valuable items—such as gold and silver—were always carried in the captain's, or some other ranking officer's, cabin in the superstructure of the old ships, generally in the stern castle. This was done so that the chests of valuable treasure could be kept under close surveillance. When a vast amount of silver, either in specie or bullion, was carried, it was always stored in the main hold over the ballast.

There are also instances in which ships were wrecked during good weather and their cargoes lost over large areas. Sometimes when a ship struck on a reef, sustaining holes in the hull, the captain would keep the sails up and try to run the ship as close to shore as possible to lessen the loss of lives and facilitate salvage operations. This would result in the ship spilling a great deal of her ballast and cargo between the area where she had hit and eventually sank. I worked on a good illustration of this type of disaster near Providencia off the coast of Nicaragua. A Portuguese ship, being chased by several Spanish warships in 1641, struck on a shallow reef fairly close to shore. To elude the pursuers the captain kept the ship sailing, staying right over the dangerous reef, either hoping that the pursuers would also wreck on it or that they would cease their pursuit to avoid the danger. The ship traveled over 2 miles before it finally sank. In searching for the wreck, by snorkeling I discovered the area where the ship had first struck the reef, so I followed the trail of ballast stones until reaching the main section of the wreck. Mixed in with the trail of ballast rock were a large number of artifacts that had fallen out through the hole in the ship's hull.

The three main signposts in locating an old shipwreck are the cannon, anchors, and ballast; however, finding any of the three does not always indicate that you have found a shipwreck.

When a ship was in danger of capsizing during a storm, on many occasions some or all of a ship's cannon were thrown overboard. When a ship ran aground on a reef or shallow area, cannon were thrown overboard to lighten the ship and sometimes the ships were refloated. At times even large amounts of a ship's ballast and cargoes of the least value were thrown overboard to lighten and refloat a stranded ship. I have also dived off several areas close to old forts on different Caribbean islands and discovered large numbers of cannon that were not from shipwrecks but from the forts. They could have gotten into the sea for a number of reasons: during hurricanes and earthquakes they might have fallen into the sea when sections of the forts collapsed; or they may have been thrown in because they were too old and dangerous to use, or to prevent their capture by an enemy, or thrown in by the enemy after the capture of a fort.

Old cannon were sometimes used as ballast on ships and occasionally jettisoned when not needed. An instance of this is found off the eastern end of the Bon Aire Island. Diving there some years ago I located over 200 cannon in a relatively small area, but what amazed me the most was the fact that they ranged over a period of 250 years. By consulting with a local historian soon afterward, the mystery was cleared up. This had been the area where ships coming from Holland anchored to take on cargoes of salt from the island; these cannon had been used as ballast on various ships and jettisoned when they took on heavy cargoes of salt.

Generally, finding anchors that are not near cannon or a ballast pile simply signifies that a ship lost an anchor. However, there are exceptions to this rule. When a storm drove a ship toward a dangerous reef or coastline, anchors were naturally thrown out to prevent the ship from wrecking. In these situations one or more anchors would have been lost seaward from the shipwreck and can provide a clue to the location of a wreck. Since most—in some cases all—of a ship's anchors were carried high on the bow and stern of the ship, and we know that in many cases these sections of a shipwreck were carried closer toward shore than the main section of a shipwreck, anchors can also be found shoreward from a wreck site, providing a clue in the locating of the main wreck site. In either event, whether the anchor is seaward or shoreward from a wreck, knowing the wind and sea direction as well as the current directions prevalent to the area are extremely useful in determining the approximate position of the wreck site.

As mentioned earlier, finding a ballast pile does not always indicate a shipwreck, especially when they are discovered near or in ports or harbors. Many ships occasionally sailed without cargoes, and this necessitated carrying large amounts of ballast to stabilize sailing ships. Before or after entering a port where a heavy cargo was to be loaded aboard a ship, most and sometimes all of the ballast was thrown overboard. If the ship remained in the same position when this operation was underway, the ballast pile would resemble one similar to that of a shipwreck site. If the ship was swinging on its anchor, then the ballast would be scattered such as on a wreck site where the wreck had been badly broken up and the ballast strewn over a large area.

The ancient mariners were not overly cautious about sanitation on their ships, particularly the Spaniards, who were known to have the dirtiest ships afloat. Since many seamen—as well as the poorer passengers—lived below deck a great amount of fish, animal, and fowl bones, broken pieces of ceramic, glassware, etc., were thrown into the hold with the ballast. This resulted in items that a modern-day salvor might associate with artifacts from a shipwreck being mixed in with ballast rock. Thus these items would also be thrown overboard with the ballast rock and can mislead a salvor into believing that the ballast pile is indeed associated with a shipwreck.

Most old ships carried round ballast rocks ranging in size from several ounces to 200 pounds. The larger rocks are usually placed over the lowest deck, then the smaller rocks fill in the spaces between the larger ones. On some of the early French and English ships, a substantial amount of ballast rock was cemented together with mortar for use as permanent ballast. I have not discovered whether ships of other nationalities followed this practice.

Since most ships took on their ballast in ports or harbors, and most of them had rivers or streams emptying into them, the round "pebble" or "river rock" ballast was the most commonly used. However, there were many instances where this type of rock was not available, so they were forced to use other types of rock. Their preference was naturally round rocks, as they did not have sharp edges that could pierce through the wooden hulls in rough weather.

A late-sixteenth-century wreck, either of Spanish or French origin, salvaged by Teddy Tucker in Bermuda contained flint rock for ballast. Documents dated 1570 tell of a Spanish merchantman sailing from Cuba to Spain with copper ore for ballast; of another Spanish ship sailing in 1638 from Venezuela to Spain with saltpeter for ballast; and still another sailing in 1760 from Cadiz to Venezuela with gypsum rock for ballast.

As early as 1614 there are mentions of Spanish ships carrying bars of iron from Spain to America as ballast, but this was done only when iron was being carried for sale or use in the New World colonies. From 1700 onward, English warships used pigs of iron as ballast, practice that took hold with French warships from 1707.

For several reasons, a wreck site may not have any ballast on it at all. When ships carried vast cargoes they avoided being dangerously overweighted by not taking on ballast. Or again, when ballast rocks were scarce, sand was used. Also, on small vessels the limited space below decks necessitated an alternate means of carrying ballast. Therefore, as the casks and barrels containing water, beer, wine, vinegar, etc., were consumed, they were filled with sea water. This method had the advantage of lightening a ship quickly during a storm. The casks and barrels could either be emptied into the bilges and the salt water pumped overboard, or they could be jettisoned quickly, unlike ships carrying ballast in the form of rocks or pig iron.

Before going into the various methods in locating shipwrecks, several facts should be considered. Over the centuries, shorelines have receded in some places and have extended farther into the sea in others. Those that have built out mainly affect the modern-day salvors, since many shipwrecks have undoubtedly been covered over by land. A good example is the city of Port Royal, which sank in 1692. Today approximately 60 percent of the original city is covered by land. Near Port Royal but on the other side of the harbor, the shoreline has been built out by sediment brought down by rivers. Recently three eighteenth-century shipwrecks have been found buried on the land. And this has occurred in many other known areas.

Many small islands or cays that existed years ago have disappeared, others have built up—some are actually manmade. On modern charts there is an area called Mysterious Bank, which has a shallow depth of only four fathoms on some parts of it and is located west of Grand Cayman Island. Throughout the sixteenth century various navigators mentioned passing a small island in this area, but sometime around 1600 it disappeared beneath the sea. Many old charts also show several small islands or cays north of Memory Rock, on the Little Bahama Bank, but they no longer exist.

The mouths of rivers and streams have in some cases moved considerable distances due to the body of water changing its course. Several inlets on Florida's east coast have closed up and others opened, some by nature and others by man.

Special caution should be exercised with old charts, as many are very inaccurate. When making use of old charts in an attempt to locate an old shipwreck, I make it a general practice to do the following. First I consult as many charts that were published around the time of the disaster as possible, as place-names change considerably over the centuries. Memory Rock, for example, had six different names on Spanish charts over a three-hundred-year period and still other names on charts of different nations. We can assume that old navigators were using the most up-to-date charts, so the place-names on them would be the ones they used to describe the location of a shipwreck.

Positions of latitude taken on a rocking ship were not always accurate, but it was generally the practice to establish the latitude of a shipwreck by taking the position from the nearest piece of firm ground. I have found that on the whole these positions are accurate to within a few miles, even from the earliest days of navigation in the New World.

The distance, or measurement, of a mile and league was not universal in the old days. From the end of the fifteenth and well into the nineteenth century, the Spanish and Portuguese divided a degree of latitude into 70 miles of 5,000 feet each, or into 17½ leagues of 4 miles each. The English and French divided it as we know it today: 60 nautical miles, or 20 leagues of 3 miles each. The Dutch divided it into 60 nautical miles, and 15 leagues of 4 miles each.

All nations used the fathom as the unit to describe depths of water, but its true depth, or length, was not uniform. It depended on the size of the seaman who made the measurement, especially during the sixteenth and seventeenth centuries. A sounding lead on a line was lowered and the depth established by the seaman pulling in the line. If he had short arms the fathom could be as little as 5½ feet; if he had long arms it could be as long as 6½ feet—the measurement was obtained by measuring the distance between the fingers of his extended arms.

In areas where there is considerable difference in tide levels, care must be exercised in using depths given in old documents, since there is never any mention of what state the tide was in when the depth was measured. I have also found that when a document states that "a ship was lost in so many fathoms" it does not always indicate the true water depth in the area but the depth from the surface to the main deck of a shipwreck.

Depending on circumstances—such as how accurate a position one might have of a ship location, its size, the depth and area in which it was lost, the cause of the disaster, and other factors—various methods should be used by the modern-day salvor. I shall try to cover them all in this chapter.

Assuming that a modern-day salvor has decided to locate one or more particular shipwrecks in the same area, I suggest that he undertake it more or less in this manner. The first prerequisite is to obtain permission from the government in whose water the wreck is located. Then it is a good practice to establish contact with local historians or archaeologists in the area near the wreck site, as they can be very helpful to you in many ways, such as providing you with pertinent historical data on the wreck you are trying to locate.

Depending on the nationality of the wreck, write to the major archives, libraries, and naval museums of the country and request any historical information they can give you. In the case of, say, a Spanish shipwreck, it would be advisable to write to the Naval Museum in Madrid and the Archives of the Indies in Seville. Do this well in advance, for it sometimes takes many months for them to locate the material you are requesting. Further information can often be obtained by writing to the nearest port captain or harbor master in the area you plan to explore, as fishermen who might drag up some artifacts from a shipwreck usually report these facts to the port authorities.

You should read every history book on the area, especially those written shortly after the period in which your wreck was lost. These are not easy to find, but major American libraries will probably have them; they can also be obtained through the interlibrary system. Personally, before heading for any new area to search for shipwreck, I usually spend a few days or a week at the Library of Congress in Washington, D.C., and read any books that may be helpful. The Library of Congress also has the most complete collection of old charts and maps of the Western Hemisphere, and I have photocopies made of those I might be able to use.

Several times old charts alone have resulted in my discovering shipwrecks, and on a few occasions even modern charts produced the same result when they contained place-names that aroused my suspicion. I located the *Matanceros* wreck off the coast of Yucatán by becoming suspicious of why modern charts called it "Punta Matanceros"—"Slaughter Point." This, I assumed, could have been a place where many persons were slaughtered by Indians after staggering ashore from a shipwreck.

Modern charts are useful in many other ways. Studying them before actually going to the area of the shipwreck, one can determine from water depths, positions of reefs and other shallow areas, direction of the prevailing currents and winds, the possible or most promising areas to search. Sailing directions and coastal pilot books also provide a vast amount of information essential in the success of the search.

Weather is one of the major factors that cause so many expeditions to fail. As much meteorological data as possible should be obtained concerning the area you plan to explore. Then you must select the best time of the year for the venture. The summer months are generally the best throughout the Western Hemisphere, but there are a number of exceptions. Off Padre Island, Texas, the winter months are best, as the seas are calm and the water visibility clear. Remember that south of the equator the seasons are the opposite of those north of the equator, so the best months down there are our winter months.

The science of weather-forecasting is still in its infancy as far as I am concerned, for I have experienced the opposite weather pattern from that predicted before I started out on various expeditions. In 1963 I took a major expedition down to Serranilla Bank during the month of June, supposedly the best of the year. The result was that during the thirty days we were in the area the wind never dropped below twenty knots and we could not even attempt to search for the wrecks we were after. The following year I decided to spend August and September on Serrana Bank, actually living on a small cay and working out of a small skiff. Meteorological experts assured me that no hurricane had ever visited that area during those months. But one struck anyway, and if a passing vessel had not stopped by to pick me up and get me to safety, I would have perished, as the hurricane washed most of that cay away.

Hurricanes can be helpful or harmful to salvors. Some of them may completely uncover a shipwreck, making the locating and salvaging of it much easier. On the other hand, hurricanes have also deposited as much as 15 feet of sand over known wreck sites. The huge seas associated with hurricanes generally help establish shipwreck locations in two ways: Artifacts that may be buried offshore on a wreck are often thrown up on adjacent beaches; also, when beaches become badly eroded by the wave action, artifacts, treasure, and sometimes even parts of the ship may be revealed. Upon arriving in a new area, it is always advisable to inquire about items the local inhabitants might find on the beach. Remember that the main reason the 1715 fleet shipwrecks were discovered is that Kip Wagner found coins and other items from these shipwrecks that had been washed up on the beaches between Sebastian and Fort Pierce inlets on the eastern coast of Florida.

After arriving in the area you plan to work, make contact with the authorities who have granted you permission to work in their territorial waters. This applies not only when one is in a foreign country, but in one's own as well. A few days spent in the local archives and libraries will also prove useful. If the wreck you are after occurred after the area was first settled, chances are more than likely that some newspaper was in existence at the time and carried some information about it. The local archives might also have some documents concerning the loss of the ship, provided documents have survived over the years.

In my experience I have found local fishermen to be one of the best sources of information on shipwreck locations. On my first night ashore I usually visit several bars frequented mainly by fishermen. While they may not be very talkative to a stranger during the working day, they generally loosen their tongues when you are buying the drinks. If you just ask them if they know the locations of any wrecks, they will probably lead you to a modern-day shipwreck. It is much better to ask them if they have ever seen any "old guns" or a pile of "river stones." They usually know the surrounding areas as well as the palm of their hand. In many of the Caribbean islands they dive on known ballast piles to recover the rocks to use as ballast on their own fishing boats.

If the wreck you are after is completely buried under the sea floor, then they may not be able to assist you.

Local divers are also good contacts. Throughout the Caribbean and Bahamas there are thousands of divers who spearfish, grab lobsters, or dive for conch. If your wreck is in a harbor or port there are commercial divers who know the surrounding bottom and can lead you to different wrecks—one of which may be the one you are seeking. I also consult the captains or operators of dredging barges, since they can tell you where they may have accidentally dredged up items from shipwrecks.

After checking out all the locations supplied by your contacts, if the water visibility is clear you should make an aerial survey of the suspected area. The preferred tool for an aerial survey is a balloon, which proved very successful for Teddy Tucker in Bermuda. Also useful are either a seaplane, a Bensen Gyrocopter or helicopter, and a light single-engine plane. The balloon and the Bensen Gyrocopter can be made compact enough to enable the explorer to ship it to the area he plans to search. Remember that helium is virtually impossible to obtain outside the United States, however, so a hot-air balloon may be a better bet. The reason I prefer the balloon is that it has to be towed by a surface vessel, and it is always easier to obtain a good position with electronic equipment from a surface vessel than from an aircraft. Furthermore, as soon as something is sighted from a balloon it can be hauled in and divers sent to investigate the suspected area. If a balloon is not available, then I suggest using either a seaplane, a Gyrocopter, or a helicopter with floats, as this enables the explorer to land right over the suspected area and inspect it, provided sea conditions are good. Prior to obtaining his balloon, Teddy Tucker used a small, light seaplane around Bermuda, locating over fifty wrecks by this method. Dimitri Rebikoff is currently using a Sea-B seaplane for this same purpose, and aboard it he not only carries sufficient diving equipment but a small portable air-compressor for refilling his scuba tanks.

When an aircraft cannot land on suspicious areas, then I suggest that a surface vessel be used in conjunction with the search. By radio communications the surface vessel can be directed to suspect areas and divers sent down to investigate, or a vessel can assist in placing buoys over the area for future investigation. Without the aid of a surface vessel it is often difficult to establish the precise position of a shipwreck even when you sight it from the air, especially if the location is not close to some noteworthy landmark. If you are operating alone in the air, there are several different methods that can be used. A loran or lorac set is your best tool. Flying several timed compass headings from the wreck site to known positions is another method; still another is the use of a radio directional finder, but it is not as accurate as the other methods. From the Gyrocopter or helicopter, buoys can be dropped on top of the wreck, but it is more difficult to do this from a circling plane. Recently, several small sonar transmitters have become available. Dropped over a wreck site, some produce a continuous sonar signal for as long as two thousand hours, and with the use of a boat and sonar-receiving equipment the position can be located.

To obtain the best results from an aerial survey the sea should be flat calm and the altitude between 100 and 500 feet. Polaroid glasses are a must, as is a good chart of the area in order to mark the approximate position of anything you might sight. Not only can items such as ballast piles, cannon, and anchors be sighted, I have also located wrecks that were completely buried under sand. On wreck sites that have a great deal of metal—such as large cannon—the iron oxide from the large metal masses generally makes the sand a darker color over a site. Another good indication is when you sight a small, solitary coral reef, or several small patches of coral reefs, in areas where there are no others. In most instances these small reefs started building up when some part of a shipwreck was exposed above the sand and continued to grow after the wreck was buried.

Photography can also be very helpful in locating shipwrecks. Using infrared film in a 35-mm still camera, I located three shipwrecks on a reef along the northern coast of Jamaica that I had not seen from a light plane. Regular color film with the use of a Polaroid filter occasionally produces good results. The main difficulty with aerial photography lies in establishing the precise area of the photographed wreck.

Provided a wreck is not buried under sand, sediment, or coral growth, there are many simple methods that can be used in searching for it. I shall begin with the simplest and cheapest methods and progress up to the more elaborate and costly.

If the water is reasonably clear, and you have good eyes and have had considerable experience, you can use the "Teddy Tucker Method," which is to stand either on the bow or a higher spot on a boat and search for large objects like ballast piles, cannon, etc. However, as when doing an aerial survey, the sea must be flat calm—as it is in

Bermuda for months at a time. Once, using this method under ideal conditions, I located fourteen old wrecks on the Little Bahama Bank in less than three hours. Polaroid glasses are very useful when using this method.

When I first started—and I still use this method whenever it is feasible—I preferred searching for wrecks either by snorkeling on the surface or by being dragged behind a small boat holding on to a line. This simple method has resulted in my locating over two hundred old wrecks. Its two disadvantages are that it is more time-consuming than most other methods—such as a magnetometer—and that it is dangerous in areas with heavy concentrations of sharks. Whenever sharks have forced me to abandon these two methods I have usually resorted to a glass-bottom boat.

Other divers prefer using different types of sea sleds or towing vans, but I prefer the freedom of snorkeling or the towline behind a boat, as I find that these methods afford me greater freedom of movement.

Various types of sea scooters and the Rebikoff Pegasus can also be used. Their big disadvantage is that the maximum length of time they can operate is two hours, after which they usually require from eight to twenty-four hours for recharging. To overcome this major problem, Rebikoff Underwater Products recently came out on the market with another type of Pegasus, which I have found much more adaptable to searching for shipwrecks in shallow water. It is powered by a surface engine that is floated on a small pontoon and connected by an umbilical power line to the underwater vehicle, which drags it behind on the surface. In recent tests we mounted a magnetometer on this new-type Pegasus and it worked quite well.

Wet submarines offer no advantage over any of the above methods other than giving the diver some protection in the event of a shark or barracuda attack. And while I highly recommend dry submarines for locating deep shipwrecks, I have found them practically useless on shallow-water searches. Not only are they quite expensive to operate and maintain but they require constant maintenance; also, due to their weight they generally require large surface support vessels and are difficult to launch or retrieve in rough seas.

In 1963 I rented the original Perry Cubmarine for a month, and from the start it was a headache. Before sailing for our wreck location in the Caribbean we decided to test it at Fort Lauderdale. During the test it ventured too close to the salt-water-intake system of the city's electric-power plant and was sucked against the huge pipe's protective screen. The two men inside were trapped for eight hours before we finally located it and had the plant intake pump stopped for a few minutes. On the few occasions we got to use it, we constantly suffered from electric shocks due to minor water leaks reaching the batteries, which were located under both seats. Navigating it in shallow water, we repeatedly collided with coral reefs.

To locate shipwrecks that are completely buried or lying in areas with poor underwater visibility, other, more sophisticated methods must be used. Sometimes these methods should also be used in clear water, for they reduce considerably the time involved in locating the wreck. Also, some of them will locate the shipwreck whether it is visible or buried. In areas of poor visibility, especially in bays and harbors, until recent years the old method of locating a shipwreck—provided that some part of it protruded above the sea floor—was to drag a cable between two vessels or to drag a line with grappling hooks from a single vessel. The big disadvantage of this method was that it could be used with a degree of success only when the sea floor was flat and reefs and rocks were not prevalent. Otherwise the drag line was constantly snagging on underwater obstructions.

Although I suggest that every vessel carry a good fathometer so that it knows the depth it is in, this instrument is practically useless in locating shipwrecks in shallow and even deep water. To get a reading on the fathometer, a considerable part of the wreck must remain above the sea floor and the surface search vessel has to go directly over it.

Sidescan sonar—which was originally developed during the last war to detect submerged submarines—is useful in locating wrecks, but only if some part remains above the sea floor. In 1954 this method proved very successful in helping to pinpoint the location of the U.S.S. *Monitor,* the Civil War ironclad that was lost off Cape Hatteras, North Carolina, in 1862. It also proved very useful in 1967 in locating a Roman wreck in 300 feet of water off Yassi Ada, Turkey. In 1962 a beautiful bronze sculpture was recovered by a Turkish sponge-dragger but only the general area of the find was known. An expedition sponsored by the University of Pennsylvania Museum used the sidescan sonar, developed by Dr. Harold Edgerton of the Massachusetts Institute of Technology, to locate the wreck; then they verified and photographed it with the use of their submarine, *Asherah.*

Dr. Harold Edgerton also invented another type of sub-bottom sonar, called the "pinger" and "boomer," which locates and records the shape and position of objects buried beneath the sea floor. Both units have been used with great success on many marine archaeological sites all over the globe. During January and February of 1968, I was fortunate to have Dr. Edgerton run his sub-bottom sonar surveys at both Port Royal and St. Anns Bay, the site of the two Columbus shipwrecks he located in only several hours.

Most of his efforts were devoted to mapping the sunken city of Port Royal. A series of shore points, all about 10 meters apart, were first located, numbered, and then plotted on an existing map of the area. Offshore buoys had to be placed, also 10 meters apart; then the survey ship, with its sonar equipment, made runs between the shore markers and buoys at a constant speed. Since the site extends almost a mile in length, this sonar survey took about three weeks; however, the results were excellent. From the hundreds of feet of sonar recording paper, and with the aid of several draftsmen, we produced four large charts that covered the whole site and showed the precise position of a tremendous number of walls of the old buildings, as well as of several shipwrecks. Another important feature of this survey was that it defined the total extent of the whole site.

Magnetometers were also developed during World War II as a means to detect submerged submarines. Basically, a magnetometer detects gradients in the earth's magnetic field produced by local concentrations of ferro-magnetic materials such as cannon, anchors, or any other ferrous metal objects on a shipwreck. The larger the object is and the longer it has remained in the same position, the better the chances are of locating the wreck. There are four types of magnetometers, each working on a different principle: the rubidium, proton, caesium, and differential flux-gate. The usual method of operating a magnetometer is to tow it behind a boat at speeds of from 2 to 10 knots, depending on the sensitivity of the particular instrument and the size of the object one is searching for. On several occasions shipwrecks have been located by using a magnetometer from a helicopter, in which the sensing probe of the magnetometer was dragged through the air.

During the fifties a few attempts were made to utilize magnetometers to locate shipwrecks, but none of them met with much success. One was developed by Fay Fields of Treasure Salvors Company and proved successful. According to its developer, his magnetometers have located more than a hundred ancient shipwrecks just off the coast of Florida.

Until a few years ago a good magnetometer cost well over $15,000, with some as high as $30,000. Today some are selling for as low as

$500, but, of course, they are not as sensitive as the costlier ones. Recently a magnetometer came out on the market that is as sensitive, if not more so, than the $30,000 models and sells for $3,500. It is a Differential Flux Gate magnetometer and has several important features that many of the other magnetometers lack: It operates at full efficiency regardless of geographic location; it eliminates problems resulting from orientation in the earth's magnetic field, and it is unaffected by ignition interference and atmospheric conditions. The control unit is watertight and tested to a depth of 200 feet. It has negative buoyancy and, with an optional sensing probe, can be operated by a diver in an underwater environment. Indications of magnetic anomalies are provided both visually and aurally. The visual indication is a 4-inch meter, calibrated in field strength (Gamma), with an 0 to 10 scale, subdivided into two-tenths divisions. Eight field-strength scales are provided, 0 to 3 Gamma, the most sensitive, and decreasing by a factor of our per-switch position, *i.e.*, scale 8 is 0 to 3 Gamma, scale 7 is 0 to 12 Gamma, etc. Aural indication is provided by earphones.

Power is provided by the power case and consists of rechargeable nickel cadmium cells. Total drain is approximately 4.5 watts. The power case will provide twenty-hour operation between charges. A charger operating from 115 v. A.C., with overcharge protection and undervoltage protection, is part of the power case.

This magnetometer senses gradients in the earth's magnetic field produced by local concentrations of ferro-magnetic material. It employs two sensors, elements that are mounted in a rigid submersible container, and measures the difference between the two sensor outputs. These sensors are balanced, so that orientation in the earth's magnetic field is not critical. The instrument is also insensitive to ignition interference and atmospherics. This device can detect magnetic-field strength at the two sensors less than 0.5 Gamma, independent of the external-field strength as long as this field does not exceed three times the maximum value of the earth's field. This makes the unit's operation independent of geographic location. The instrument consists of three basic units: sensing probe, control unit and power case. The sensing probe is designed to be towed and a 100-foot cable is supplied. The towable sensing probe is extremely stable and can be adjusted to run at predetermined depths to 200 feet. A given underwater altitude can be maintained over a range of several hundred engine RPM's. Buoyancy is slightly negative. Altitude is maintained during turns.

The usual method in using the magnetometer is to get up a search pattern using buoys, although this has always proved quite time-consuming. Recently a new system has been developed by MacDowell Associates and is now on the market. Called the Plot Position Locator System, magnetometer surveys can be made without the use of a single buoy, as this instrument guides the survey vessel on its prescribed grid course.

This same firm has also developed and is currently marketing another useful instrument, the Underwater Beacon Transponder. Buoys left on a shipwreck have a nasty habit of disappearing. Some are accidentally cut by passing boats, others break loose in heavy seas, and still others are lost for a number of different reasons. Even with the most elaborate electronics equipment, a considerable amount of time is required to relocate the position of a shipwreck, provided that it was plotted accurately in the first place. The beacon transponder eliminates this problem as well as the possibility of pirate divers sighting your buoys on a wreck site and diving on it when you are not there. This problem is especially troublesome in the Florida Keys, where there are a great number of divers who make a good living poaching on wrecks belonging to others. The Beacon, with its operational life of up to several years, depending on the size of the battery power source, can be attached to some part of the wreck. The salvage vessel, returning to the general area by regular navigational means, can then activate the beacon transponder from the salvage vessel and home in on it to the wreck site.

Locating shipwrecks in deep waters, which is attracting more and more interest these days with the development of mixed-gas saturation diving, can be accomplished by one or a combination of several methods.

Unless a shipwreck location is narrowed down to a relatively small area, the use of neither submersible vehicles nor underwater television is of much use, as their range is too small to cover a substantial area of the sea floor. Both sidescan and sub-bottom sonar and magnetometers are by far the best methods. A combination of using all of these methods together, either from the surface or from a submersible vehicle, would certainly produce good results.

For the very best results, I would recommend the POODLE, which was invented by Dimitri Rebikoff and has already proved very useful in locating a large number of ancient shipwrecks in the Mediterranean. It consists of an unmanned submersible vehicle, very similar in shape and size to the Pegasus, which is controlled from the surface by remote control by means of a tether cable. It carries both sidescan and sub-bottom sonar, a magnetometer, a wide-angle distortion-correction television camera, different types of motion- and still-picture cameras, lights when required, and its own self-contained navigation system. Plans are now in action to equip it with hydraulic grab-arms so that it can bring up small objects from the sea floor.

With the current interest in oceanography in the United States and elsewhere, I feel certain that progressively better equipment will eventually be developed and adapted for use in locating shipwrecks in both shallow and deep waters.

RIGHT: Proton precession magnetometer at work. BELOW: Using a Pegasus scooter to search visually for a wreck.

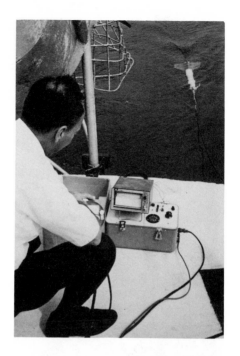

LEFT: Setting up an electronic instrument to find a wreck. BELOW: Diver finding a gold coin by use of an underwater metal detector.

CHAPTER FOUR

Surveying, Mapping, and Excavating a Site

SURVEYING:

One of the major mistakes made by modern-day salvors is their failure to make a proper survey of a wreck site after it has been located and before beginning the excavation of the wreck. This has repeatedly resulted in many expeditions failing and the loss of great expenditures of capital.

A prime example took place quite recently. A group from Miami, armed with historical documents giving the location of a rich galleon wreck in the Bahamas, first used a magnetometer dragged from a helicopter. In less than a week they located a wreck in the general area given in the documents as the location of the sunken galleon. Instead of first making a survey of the site to determine if the wreck was the one they were after, they foolishly outfitted a large vessel for salvaging the site, then quickly realized their mistake. The wreck turned out to be a late-nineteenth-century vessel with nothing of value on it and these salvors lost over twenty thousand dollars. This group should have learned their lesson after this venture, but they repeated it. After returning to Miami with their salvage vessel, they resumed their magnetometer search from the helicopter and located what they once again believed to be their galleon wreck. But once again they failed to make a survey of the suspected area and brought their large salvage vessel back to the Bahamas. This time they discovered a modern missile cone instead of their wreck. In both cases they could have undertaken a survey—costing a small amount of capital and time—on the suspected areas by renting a small vessel and taking a minimum of diving and excavating equipment.

And there are other reasons why a wreck site should be surveyed before bringing in a salvage vessel. Establishing the overall extent of the site is important because it will indicate how long the excavation will take and if it is economically feasible to salvage the wreck. A wreck contained in a small area—say, about the size of a football field—is certainly more economical to excavate than one spread over an area of several square miles. Another reason for surveying is to determine the best type of excavation equipment required. Failure to do this resulted in the failure of an expedition in the Bahamas. In this case the salvors located a wreck site visually from the air, sighting a large number of cannon on a sandy bottom. Believing that the wreck was buried in sand, they outfitted their salvage vessel with airlifts and a prop-wash. Arriving at the wreck site, they quickly discovered that the sand was only several inches deep and that the wreck was buried in thick coral growth. They lacked the proper equipment, such as pneumatic hammers or powerful water-jets to salvage the wreck.

In areas such as Florida, where salvors must obtain a pinpoint lease on a wreck site, it is imperative that the total extent of the site is known, since the salvor may not get a lease covering the total area. When this occurs—and it has on several occasions—others are able to obtain leases adjacent to those obtained by the original discoverers of the shipwrecks.

The initial step of any survey should be to locate all visual traces of the wreck by diving and placing buoys over the objects located. In doing this, I make it a practice to have someone follow me in a small skiff. After I place a buoy over each object, I surface and identify the object and the person in the skiff records and plots it on a chart. Mapping and identifying the objects as they are located eliminates the danger of not relocating them if the buoys placed over them are lost.

The next step is to locate all concentrations of metal, which is necessary when no trace of a wreck is visible above the sea floor. A good magnetometer will locate the metallic objects and, from the size of the anomalies recorded, a good magnetometer operator can determine the size of the metallic concentration. This information should also be plotted on a chart.

Sub-bottom-penetrating sonar can be used to locate large metallic objects as well as ballast piles and wood. Hand-held magnetometers and metal detectors should be used for locating the smaller metal objects on the site, but this can be very time-consuming if the wreck is scattered over a large area. When time and capital permit, however, I recommend it.

Bill Mahan proved the value of a metal detector on a wreck during the summer of 1968. Wanting to test a new detector which he had recently invented, he decided to use it on the wreck of the H.M.S. *Looe,* which had been worked over by hundreds of different divers. Everyone assured him that there was nothing left on the wreck. Although all of the sandy areas had been excavated with airlifts, many artifacts were buried in coral growth, which Mahan easily located with his detector. On his first day he discovered a silver plate, a silver spigot, a pewter plate, two pewter spoons, a pewter tankard, a brass scale weight, four copper coins, lead musket balls, many iron cannonballs, and several other items made of iron.

The next step in surveying a wreck site will depend on the nature of the sea floor. Things buried in coral growth are the most difficult to survey, as test holes must be made all over the area until the overall extent of the site is determined, and this can be a lengthy undertaking. If the coral growth is soft, either a strong water-jet or coring device can be used. In hard coral growth—such as we experienced on the *Matanceros* wreck off the coast of Yucatán—small pneumatic hammers should be used; if they are not available, small sledge hammers and chisels can be used. On most reefs where wrecks are located, there are generally many small pockets of sand not more than a few inches deep. I have found that a scuba tank with several feet of hose attached used as an air-jet is quite effective for blowing away the sand. Fanning the sand away by hand can also be attempted, but it is more time-consuming.

Various other methods can be used in surveying a site located in mud or silt after magnetometer and sub-bottom sonar surveys have been done (or when these sophisticated instruments are not available). The fastest, but not always the most effective, method would be to make test holes on the site using an airlift, hydrolift, or small prop-wash. In some areas these excavation tools can be used when there is only a few feet of sediment over the site, as small test holes can be made quickly. If the sediment is hard and compact, small test holes can be made with these tools to reach quite deep in the sediment. When the sediment is soft and silty, however, much larger test holes have to be made, as the sediment continually caves in. At Port Royal I found areas where the sediment was so soft that in order to make a test hole with an airlift to a depth of 20 feet, the diameter of the hole had to be over 60 feet. To overcome the problem I followed this method. I used five sections of concrete water pipe, which were 4 feet in diameter and 5 feet long. After driving the first section as far down into the sediment as possible, I began excavating with a small airlift, and as I went deeper the pipe also sank. When it sank below the level of the sea floor I attached the next length of pipe and continued this method until I reached the desired depth. This method had one big disadvantage: It was almost impossible to retrieve the concrete water pipes without excavating a large hole around them, which in my case did not really matter, since I had access to an unlimited amount of these water pipes.

I recently learned a simpler method to obtain the same results from Art McKee, who developed it by making test holes on wreck sites located in deep sand. Instead of using water pipes, he uses a long metal tube and an airlift. The diameter of the tube should be a few inches wider than the airlift-tube diameter. His method is quicker and safer than mine, for the diameter of his test hole is smaller, requiring less time but obtaining the same results; the metal tube is easier to handle than the larger water pipes; and instead of the diver operating the airlift in the water pipe—as I did at Port Royal—he remains on the sea floor operating the airlift as it and the metal tube sink deeper into the sediment. He does not face the risk of the water pipe's collapsing and trapping him under tons of sediment. To determine the stratigraphical depth beneath the sea floor in which items are located by the airlift, the diver simply measures the length of the metal tube remaining above the sea floor and subtracts it from the total length of the tube. Recovering the metal tube from the sediment can be accomplished with the aid of lifting bags or lifting equipment from a boat, such as an anchor winch.

At Port Royal, to locate large objects that were buried under up to 10 feet of mud I used a quarter-inch-thick and 12-foot-long iron rod with a wooden handle and found it to be quite effective. By using this method I located hundreds of brick walls of the old buildings as well as large artifacts, even two shipwrecks. With a little experience I was able to determine the nature of the object I had struck—such as brick, ballast stones, wood, iron—by the sound of the metal rod striking and the hardness of the object.

After we had located the two Columbus ships with Dr. Edgerton's sonar equipment, I first attempted to determine the overall extent of both wrecks by using the metal-rod-probe method. The sonar indicated that both wrecks were under from 10 to 12 feet of sediment. In some areas on both wrecks I was able to reach these stratigraphical levels and discovered the presence of wood and ballast rock. However, in others my probe would not penetrate more than several feet, due to concentrations of very hard mud. Instead I used another tool, which I have named the Judd air probe.

Dr. George Bass had assisted me in obtaining a coring device from Columbia University for bringing up test samples of the wreck to prove their identity; Columbia also sent a qualified person, Bob Judd, to help me operate it. When Judd saw the problems I was having with my metal-rod probe, he invented his air probe right on the spot. It consisted of a 20-foot section of galvanized iron water pipe of 1-inch diameter. The air hose of an aquanaut diving unit was attached to the top of the pipe, sending down a continuous stream of compressed air that cut through the concentrations of hard mud. It not only penetrated into the sediment quickly but was also easy to pull back out because of the compressed air blowing out of the bottom of the pipe.

Coring tubes are not only useful in mud or silt but can be used on sandy bottoms and even in soft coral growth. Those generally used by marine geologists are driven into the sea floor by explosives or other equipment operated from a surface vessel. Those used by divers can be much simpler, like the one I used on the two Columbus shipwrecks. It consisted of 4-foot sections of 4-inch-diameter iron tubing. One diver held the tube vertically while another drove it into the sediment by hitting the top of the tube with a heavy sledge hammer. As each section sank into the sediment another was attached, and the operation continued until we reached a depth of 20 feet beneath the sea floor. Before the coring tube was pulled up by means of a lifting bag, a rubber plug was inserted into the top of the coring tube to maintain suction in the tube, otherwise the sediment and artifactual sample in the tube would fall out as the tube was pulled up through the sediment. Either aboard a vessel or ashore, the sample in the tube was recovered by simply removing the plug and holding the tube almost horizontally and shaking it lightly. We were not only able to recover sufficient amounts of artifacts—such as wood, glass, flint, iron nails and tacks, small ballast rock, animal bones, ceramic sherds, beans—but to determine their exact stratigraphical depth as well. This method also eliminated the danger of disturbing the archaeological nature of the site.

If a coring tube is used in coral growth, the bottom of the tube will require a sharp edge for cutting through the coral and will often have to be sharpened during the operation. The length of each section of the coring tube should not exceed 4 feet, as this length enables the diver who is pounding the tube into the sediment to stand on the sea floor, giving him more power in swinging the sledge hammer than if he had to swing it while swimming underwater.

Surveying a wreck site on a sandy bottom is easier to accomplish than those in coral growth or on mud or silt bottoms. Test holes can be made with small airlifts, hydrolifts, or small prop-washes on small boats. I have operated both small airlifts and hydrolifts without the use of even a small boat when the sites were located relatively close to shore. The air compressor for an airlift and the water pump for the hydrolifts were mounted on a platform floated on an inner tube of a truck. A small prop-wash, which would be effective only on a shallow-water site no deeper than 10 or 12 feet, can even be mounted over the propeller of an outboard engine. The advantage of the airlift and hydrolift in making test holes is that they can be used in any reasonable depth of water; however, an airlift will not work in less than 10 feet of water.

Test holes can also be made in areas of shallow sand over a wreck by using an air-jet or water-jet, both of which can be operated from a small float or boat. In shallow water the air-hose from an aquanaut diving unit can be used effectively. Since the unit has two hoses, one can provide the diver with air to breathe and the other to make test holes. I do not recommend the use of the air- or water-jets in muddy areas, as they quickly reduce your underwater visibility to nothing.

Several salvage groups are now using a good system of surveying a wreck site. With a prop-wash mounted on a large vessel, they dig long test trenches by continually excavating with the prop-wash and "walking" the vessel on a straight course over a large area. This is done by first determining the length of time needed to excavate to the desired depth in the sand and by playing out the stern anchor lines and taking in on the two bow anchors respectively. While the vessel is "walking" and excavating the trench, divers follow behind the vessel at a safe distance and search in the trench. The advantage of this system lies in covering a larger area much faster than by using any of the other equipment mentioned in making test holes. Its disadvantage is that it requires a large vessel, which increases the cost of the survey.

MAPPING:

Another common mistake made by modern-day salvors is their failure to map a wreck site. They consider it too time-consuming and believe that the information obtained is useful only to archaeologists. But they are wrong. By mapping and recording all the information gathered during the surveying of a wreck site, the salvor not only determines the overall extent of his site but a great deal of other information. The pattern in which the wreck lies can enable the salvor to determine the cause of the loss of the vessel, which is useful in trying to establish whether it was salvaged by contemporary salvors. For example: A wreck that has remained intact for a long period is more likely to have been salvaged than one that is scattered over a large area. A wreck lying on the surface of the sea floor or not buried very deep was most likely salvaged soon after being lost and again over the centuries by other salvors, whereas a wreck buried deep was most probably covered over before anyone could have salvaged it. Another use in mapping a wreck is to establish its size, which is useful in identifying a wreck if its size, tonnage, or the number of cannon it carried is known. This can be done by measuring the length of the keel of a wreck—when it exists—estimating the amount of ballast the ship carried, or discovering the number and size of cannon.

Mapping or plotting the locations of major artifacts discovered during the actual excavation also aids the salvor in many ways. From the nature of the different items recovered, the salvor can determine which end of the wreck is the bow and stern. For example: The largest anchors were generally carried on the bow of the ship, so— provided the ship was wrecked more or less intact—anchors found on one end of a ballast pile or section of a wreck generally indicate that this was the bow of the ship. But this is not always a safe assumption, as anchors were also carried on the stern, and sometimes several were stored in the hold as spares; and if a ship threw several over off her bow before wrecking, she might wreck with some on her stern, confusing the issue. Most salvors make an attempt to distinguish the bow and stern of a wreck as quickly as possible, knowing that most of the important treasure carried on old ships was carried in the stern castle, so they naturally want to excavate that section of a wreck first.

In many cases the most likely areas of finding treasure on a wreck, provided it was not badly scattered, can also be determined through mapping the position of the artifacts recovered. Since the officers and rich passengers lived in the stern castle, where the most valuable treasure was kept, this is the most likely area in which good silver or pewterware, fine chinaware, or other items are discovered. However, the salvor should take many facts into consideration before making general assumptions. If all the items show no sign of use, such as knife-scratch marks on a pewter or silver plate, then these items could have been carried as cargo elsewhere on the ship.

There are various methods by which the mapping of a wreck can be accomplished, and the method the salvor selects will depend on many different conditions. In areas where underwater visibility is very limited, special methods must be applied. In areas where the wreck site is located a large distance from shore, still other methods must be used.

The grid system is most commonly used by land archaeologists but has also been used on several underwater excavations. When underwater visibility is good, the sea floor more or less level, the wreck contained in a relatively small area, and a prop-wash not used (the prop-wash will blow the grid lines away), then the grid system can be used. Grid lines can be laid out in a predetermined pattern, generally running on a north-south and east-west axis and spaced from 10 to 20 feet apart, making squares of equal size. Each square is marked with a number under water and plotted on a chart. As each square is excavated, the locations of the major artifacts are plotted on the chart as well as that of other data, such as amounts of ballast rock, ship's timber, and other items that cannot be raised (like a heavy cannon).

In most cases, the grid system is neither practical nor economically feasible. On wrecks that are scattered over large areas, with parts lying in the shore breakers, this system cannot be used.

Mendel Peterson, of the Smithsonian Institution, developed a fairly simple method of mapping wrecks contained in a relatively small area that is both less time-consuming and less expensive than the grid system. It consists of an azimuth circle marked with the degrees of the compass, which is mounted on a brass rod and driven into the bottom near the center of the wreck site and becomes the datum point. Using an underwater compass, the azimuth circle is lined up with magnetic north. A chain is connected to the center of the circle and distances are marked on the whole length of the chain. When the chain is stretched to a cannon—or whatever is to be mapped— the diver notes the compass bearing on the azimuth circle to the object and the distance from the datum point. This information is then plotted on a chart. This system has an advantage over the grid when the bottom is not uniformly level. The device is compact and can be built for only a few dollars.

If the wreck site is close to shore, the best method is to erect shore markers and plot their positions on a chart. Compass bearings taken on these shore markers will indicate the position of the items that must be plotted on the chart. Taking compass bearings from a rocking boat is not easy, nor accurate. After first surveying the wreck site, buoys should be placed on all important items. Their locations can be obtained by taking their compass bearings from the shore. During the salvage operation someone could also take the compass bearings whenever required. Some form of communications would have to be used between the person ashore and the salvage vessel.

At Port Royal I used the method of shore markers, which were erected by the Jamaican Survey Department and plotted on special grid charters for my use. When major finds were made, one of my team on shore established the precise position of the find by taking compass bearings from three or more shore markers to the top of the airlift tube, which protruded vertically above the water right over the position of the recovery. Since stratigraphical information was useful on this particular site, the stratigraphical depth of the recovered item was simultaneously established by determining the length of the airlift tube remaining above the surface of the water. Taking the water depth and state of the tide into consideration, the exact stratigraphical depth could be determined.

Mapping a wreck site that is scattered over a large area and not close to shore is the most difficult. First, using good electronic equipment and a sextant, a datum point must be established. A buoy placed on the datum point would provide one compass-bearing source, but at least two others would be required—preferably forming a triangle—and the other buoys would have to be placed in precisely known locations, possibly by measuring the distance and bearing from the datum point. I used this method recently on the excavation of the *San José* (wrecked in 1733 in the Florida Keys). Fortunately, we were in sight of land, so we obtained the precise position of the actual hull of the shipwreck and its ballast pile. A datum point was established on the seaward end of the wreck and buoys positioned over other areas of the overall wreck site. The State of Florida official aboard the salvage boat used these buoys to take compass bearings and map our excavation. On several occasions when one or more of these buoys disappeared during bad weather, it was easy to locate their original position by establishing their compass bearing and distance from the datum point and placing new ones out.

The most accurate way to map a site is with a Brunton transit or other sophisticated land-surveying equipment, but this method is too complicated and expensive for the average salvor. It was utilized on the two Columbus shipwrecks in St. Anns Bay because of their great historical importance.

Underwater photography can be used in mapping a wreck site, provided there is good visibility and the wreck site is contained in a small area. Generally, the wreck is first marked with the grid system, a grid frame is used to hold the camera, and photographs are taken of each square grid. The photographs are then made into a large mosaic showing the whole area of the wreck. Marine archaeologists have photographs taken of each square at many different stratigraphical levels and, provided the wreck sank relatively intact in deep water and has not been disturbed by man or nature over the years, obtain a great deal of information concerning the ship's construction, how and where the cargo was carried, and other pertinent data. On shallow-water wreck sites, however, the same information cannot be obtained.

I recommend that salvors make a photographic mosaic of wreck sites when large sections of the actual ship may exist, as it will enable

TOP: The azimuth circle is used for plotting the position of items found on a wreck (Smithsonian Institution). BOTTOM: Diver using a transit underwater in mapping a shipwreck.

LEFT: Diver, using a Desco breathing rig, seated on timbers of a sixteenth-century wreck. BELOW: Divers digging out treasure from a coral reef.

them to establish the type, size, and sometimes the nationality and identity of the ship. This must be done after the wreck has been uncovered and all of the ballast stones removed from it. The best method for making a good mosaic of a wreck site, and one that is not too expensive, is to use the Pegasus or some similar underwater vehicle with a pulse camera mounted on it. The focal width of the camera lens and the clarity of the water will determine the elevation above the wreck from which the photographs will be taken and the total number of photographs required to make a complete mosaic. In making a complete mosaic of the *San José* site, which encompassed a 200-by-100-foot area, only fourteen individual photographs were required. This was due to the good underwater visibility in the area and the depth of the wreck, which averaged 30 feet, and by using the wide-angle corrected Rebikoff lens on the camera from a height of 25 feet over the wreck.

Hand-held cameras can also be used to make a photographic mosaic of a wreck site, but the diver must remain at a constant eleva-tion over the wreck and swim on a straight course, otherwise the mosaic will not be accurate and it will be difficult to match the photographs when putting the mosaic together. The Pegasus eliminates this problem, as it has a complete navigational system and can be flown at a constant depth and on a straight course.

EXCAVATION:

Before mentioning the different tools and methods of exca-vating a wreck site, I shall discuss the equipment used by the divers. Most divers prefer using a surface-supplied source of air, which eliminates having to surface and change scuba tanks every hour or so. Back in the 1930s, when Art McKee started exploring shipwrecks, the standard diving rig was the bulky shallow-water diving helmet, which required the diver to keep his head upright so that large amounts of water would not enter. After World War II this rig was superseded by the Desco diving mask, which consisted of a full-face mask connected to the surface air compressor by means of a rubber hose, like the shallow-water helmets. The Hookah diving rigs came into use around 1955, consisting of the breathing air reaching the diver through a regular scuba regulator connected by an air hose to the surface air compressor.

In 1965 the Outboard Marine Corporation introduced a new SAS

(Surface Air Supply) diving rig that I found far superior to those I had used in the past. The exact same unit—except for different exterior colors—is distributed by Johnson Motors as the Air Buoy and by Evinrude Motors as the Aquanaut. The retail price for the unit is $279.00. The unit, which weighs only 40 pounds, consists of an engine-pump assembly that is encircled and floated on the surface by an inflatable tube. The 2-HP, 2-cycle engine delivers 2.5 CFM of clean air to each diver at a depth of 25 feet, which is the length of the two hoses provided with each unit. This is actually twice the amount of air required at this depth. I found that by attaching additional lengths of hose I could safely and comfortably use my Aquanaut as deep as 50 feet. Depending on the carburetor adjustment, the unit will run from forty-five to sixty minutes on each filling, taking a quart of regular gasoline with an oil mixture of 24:1. The cost of operation is only ten to fifteen cents an hour, much cheaper than the cost of compressed-air refills for scuba.

It has several unique features that I particularly like. The air delivered by the unit is the cleanest I have ever breathed under water, the hoses do not kink or sink to the bottom and get tangled on obstructions, and the full-face mask fits every face, whether child or adult. Another great advantage of the unit is the relatively little maintenance it requires—and I'm speaking from long experience, as my divers and I logged over thirteen thousand hours with these units during the three-year excavation of Port Royal. About every thirty or forty hours the sparkplugs had to be cleaned, and about every hundred hours we would have to take off the exhaust and scrape out the carbon deposits. Other than a few times when some idiot failed to put gas in the fuel tank, the unit did not stop dead, cutting off our air supply.

The only disadvantage it has is the small capacity of its fuel tank. Rather than come topside every hour to refuel, however, we ran each unit continuously for eight to ten hours daily, and about every forty minutes someone topside would refuel the units without stopping them. The only inconvenience was when someone goofed and spilled some gas on the unit, which resulted in gas fumes being pumped down to the divers, causing some discomfort for a few minutes. The compact size and light weight of this unit is another of its great advantages over the other sources of breathing air for a wreck-diver. It is especially useful when going to a remote area to search or undertake a survey on a wreck site and can even eliminate the need of a boat if the wreck is located close to shore.

None of the surface-air-supply diving rigs should be used when excavating with a prop-wash, due to the danger of the air hose being caught in the vessel's turning propeller, which could result in the hose being cut or, even worse, being wrapped around the propeller and pulling the diver into it. Instead, scuba-diving equipment should be used. It should also be used for deep-water shipwrecks.

Even in the warm waters of the Caribbean, rubber suits are needed, as a diver will get chilled after several hours in the water. They also offer protection from coral cuts and scratches, burns from fire coral, stings from jellyfish, and bites from small fish. During the actual excavation of a wreck, large amounts of sea worms and other marine life are uncovered. This provides a feast for many small fish, and during their eating sprees it is not uncommon for them to take bites out of a diver. Trigger fish are especially aggressive, and I carry several scars from their bites. The most common area bitten by these small fish are the fingers—which resemble sea worms to the hungry fish—so gloves are essential on most excavations. The only protection against sea urchins is to destroy them, which is usually the first course of action taken each day. The same applies to moray eels. The deeper you excavate into a wreck, the more areas you uncover that make good homes for the eels.

The danger of attacks by sharks or barracudas is always a possibility, but I have found that the noise during a salvage operation tends to scare them away. Spearfishing should never be done around a wreck site, nor should garbage be thrown in the water, as it can attract sharks and barracudas.

All divers engaged in excavating a wreck should be instructed as to the physical appearance of what different items will look like after long years under the sea. A silver coin, for example, may be mistaken for a dark sea shell. Most iron objects that become heavily encrusted with coral growth are very difficult to distinguish from ordinary pieces of coral. Divers should also be instructed in how to handle fragile artifacts. Small, fragile items should be placed in a jar or plastic bag and brought to the surface; bigger items can be placed in plastic buckets or larger containers.

The usual method of sending up nonfragile items is in metal buckets or baskets made of wire mesh. Heavy objects can be raised by pulling them aboard the salvage vessel by lines or lifting bags. Some salvage vessels are rigged with heavy-lifting equipment to raise cannon, anchors, and other items. There are also lifting bags on the market with a lifting capacity as great as a ton. The use of 55-gallon fuel drums is the most common method of raising large items to the surface. The drums are sunk and attached by steel cables or lines to the item, then filled with compressed air, which raises them to the surface. Using this method, I have seen salvors recover large cannon and anchors while operating from a small boat. After the drums and items attached to them are lifted to the surface, the salvors tow them to shore, where they can be raised out of the water by different methods.

A small cloth or plastic bag, commonly called a "goodie bag," should be carried by every diver and used to store all small items (coins, musket balls, etc.) until he surfaces. Many valuable items have been lost by divers trying to hold them inside their gloves or rubber suits. Use of the goodie bag may also prevent a diver from "accidentally" forgetting about a gold coin he may have found and placed inside his rubber suit for safekeeping.

Surveying the wreck site will assist the salvor in deciding on the best method of operation and excavation tools required. Other factors should also be considered—such as surface and tidal currents—when excavating areas where sand, mud or silt is being removed from a wreck. The currents should be used to carry the sediments away from the wreck site, or at least into areas that have already been excavated. A common mistake of salvors is to begin their excavation in the middle of the site. This usually results in the excavated sediment being deposited in areas not yet excavated, so in many cases the same sediment has to be moved many times. Thus selecting the proper area to begin your excavation is very important.

The most difficult wreck site to excavate is that which is embedded in coral growth, like the *Matanceros* wreck in Yucatán. On this wreck our main excavation tools were sledge hammers and chisels to chop into the coral and extract artifacts. We usually attempted to chop or cut out pieces of coral about the size of a basketball, or larger. These pieces were raised aboard the salvage vessel and later broken apart to extract the artifacts they contained. In many instances we had no idea of the contents of a chunk until it was broken apart. From one clump of coral weighing about 20 pounds, we extracted over two hundred individual artifacts. In most areas, parts of artifacts could be seen embedded in the surface growth, so we dug into these areas, sometimes as deep as 5 feet, until there were no more artifacts to be recovered. In areas where no artifacts were seen in the surface of the coral, we dug as deep as 3 feet before locating any artifacts.

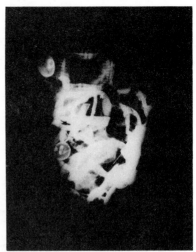

TOP LEFT: Coral-encrusted conglomerate containing many artifacts (Empire Photosound). TOP RIGHT: X-ray of the same object showing buckles, pins, needles, buttons, earrings, and cuff links (Empire Photosound). BOTTOM: Diver using an airlift to remove sand from a wreck site (Gerhard Kapitan).

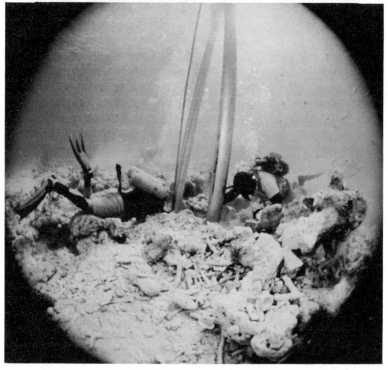

TOP: Large prop-wash used to blow sediment off a shipwreck. BOTTOM: Airlift at work on a coral reef.

Large artifacts (pewter plates, wine bottles, etc.) were carefully excavated from the coral on the bottom, as it was too difficult to dig out a large enough section of the coral growth that contained the artifact.

During my third year of excavation on this wreck, I obtained three pneumatic hammers, which proved quite effective in chopping through the coral growth and recovering items. The largest was used only in excavating cannons and anchors. The medium, which was only 12 inches in length and had a cutting chisel 6 inches long and 2 inches wide, was used on excavating the basketball-size chunks of coral containing the smallest artifacts. For excavating fragile items like glass wine bottles or small items like a brass medallion or crucifix, the smallest pneumatic hammer, with a chisel only 4 inches long and three-fourths of an inch wide, was used.

The overall area of the *Matanceros* wreck site is smaller in extent than a football field, and although over the years thousands of man-hours have been spent by hundreds of divers chopping into the coral growth on this wreck, it is far from being completely excavated. This wreck was the most difficult to excavate that I have ever seen or heard about. Other wrecks located in coral growth have proved easier to excavate because, in most cases, a large portion of the wreck was actually buried in sand pockets on a reef and most of the parts buried under coral growth were in much softer coral than that at the *Matanceros* site and high-pressure water-jets could be used to blast the coral apart.

Explosives have been used to excavate wrecks embedded in coral growth, but this is not a recommended method, as it destroys most of the fragile objects and brings on sharks, attracted by the noise and the fish killed by the explosion. Once sharks establish an area as a feeding zone, they tend to remain in it for long periods, and this certainly increases the chances of an attack on the divers.

When excavating on muddy or silty bottoms, the only recommended excavation tool is an airlift. It consists of a metal tube into which a continuous stream of compressed air is ejected through one or more holes, depending on the size or diameter of the tube, which also determines the pressure and volume of air required. A 3-inch-diameter airlift requires between 20 and 50 cubic feet of air per minute at a pressure of about 50 PSI. One of 6-inch diameter requires 50 to 200 cubic feet of air per minute and about 100 PSI of pressure. The effective working depth of an airlift depends on the air pressure being provided, which must be greater than the surrounding water pressure. For example, the maximum effective depth for an airlift using only 50 PSI of air pressure is 40 feet, whereas one using 100 PSI of air pressure can work in depths up to 100 feet.

The principle of the airlift is that when air is forced into its bottom it rises rapidly, creating suction and sucking up bottom sediment and small artifacts. There should be a control valve on all airlift tubes so the diver can control the amount of air entering the tube. When removing overburden, the airlift is run at full power to remove as much sediment as possible, but when areas containing artifacts are reached, the speed of the suction is reduced to permit the diver to grab the artifacts before they are sucked up by the tube or damaged by striking against the bottom of the tube. When small objects—such as coins, buttons, musket balls, etc.—are sucked up by the tube, the spill from the top of the tube should be directed onto a floating screen, or onto a boat or barge containing a screen.

Under no circumstances do I recommend anyone using an airlift with a diameter larger than 6 inches, as they are difficult for divers to control and result in a great number of artifacts being destroyed or lost. This occurred during the 1959 six-week excavation of the sunken city of Port Royal when a 12-inch-diameter airlift was used.

During my excavation of Port Royal I used a 4-inch-diameter airlift with good results. On the bottom of the tube I had two wires attached, crossing the tube in opposite directions, which permitted only the smallest artifacts to go up the metal tube. These landed on a screen placed on a barge, and two men stood guard to recover them the moment they landed on the screen. Using only 50 PSI of air pressure resulted in removing the sediment at a slower rate than if I had used a higher pressure, but it prevented artifacts from being sucked with great force against the bottom of the tube and being damaged.

The advantage of using the airlift on muddy or silty bottoms is that spill from the top of the airlift can be directed and carried away by the current, preventing underwater visibility from becoming too bad. At Port Royal there was rarely any underwater visibility—and then for only a few inches—so the only advantage in using the currents to carry away the sediment pump-up was to prevent it from sinking back down on unexcavated areas. Until the development of the prop-wash, the airlift was also the main excavation tool used on wrecks in sandy areas, and it is still used on many wrecks today, especially on those lying in waters below the effective working depths of the prop-wash.

The prop-wash—which is also called the "blaster" or "mailbox" by some divers—was invented early in the century for the purpose of blowing away sediment covering oyster beds in Chesapeake Bay. In 1962, salvors working on the 1715 wrecks off the coast of Florida accidentally discovered its use as an effective excavation tool. Confronted with having to dive in waters of very little underwater visibility, they devised a type of prop-wash for the purpose of pushing clear water from the surface down to the bottom, which is always dirtier and darker. To their great surprise, they discovered that it was a much better excavation tool than the airlifts and hydrolifts they had been using.

The prop-wash is simple and inexpensive to construct and easy to operate. It consists of an elbow-shaped metal tube several inches larger in diameter than the vessel's propeller diameter and is attached to the transom of the salvage vessel so that the wash of the propeller is forced into the tube and deflected downward to the sea bottom. Generally, the upper end of the tube is attached from 1 to 3 feet behind the propeller and a wire-mesh cage covers the propeller area to prevent divers from being cut. On twin-screw vessels, two prop-washes can be used side-by-side. The length of the prop-wash will depend on the diameter of the tube. On a small prop-wash, such as those used on outboard engines, they are generally about 3 feet in length. On larger vessels, such as those having propellers as large as 4 feet in diameter, the length of the tube is usually 6 to 8 feet long, and half of this length is used in the section of the tube running out horizontally from the propeller to the elbow part of the tube.

Four anchors must be put out to hold the salvage vessel in place when the prop-wash is being used. The vessel's engine is then started and the propeller turned at different speeds, depending on the depth of water and amount of sediment that must be blasted away. The wash of the prop deflected downward creates a whirlpool action that forces water to the bottom at a terrific velocity and blasts away the sediment at a rapid rate. It is so powerful that it also cuts through coquina, a type of limestone coral growth, almost as fast as through sand.

Its effective depth depends on two factors: the size of the prop-wash tube and the highest velocity at which the vessel's propeller can be run. A small prop-wash on an outboard engine is effective only up to 15 feet. Those on a vessel with a propeller of 2 to 3 feet in diameter can be used up to 35 feet, and on one with a 4-foot-diameter propeller it can be used up to 50 feet. In 20 feet of water a prop-wash of 2 to 3 feet in diameter can excavate a hole 20 feet in diameter to a depth of 15 feet into the sediment in only a few minutes. A larger prop-wash can excavate a hole in 50 feet of water to a diameter of 50 feet and 20 feet deep into the sediment in the same period of time.

The secret in using a prop-wash is being able to properly control its speed: running it at high speeds to remove overburden on a wreck and knowing when to slow it down when the level of the wreck or artifacts is reached to prevent the artifacts from being blown away. I have learned that in order to remove 12 feet of sand over a wreck, I must run the engine so that the propeller makes 1,200 revolutions per minute for a period of exactly three minutes. Then I reduce the speed to 400 RPM and send divers down to operate under this slow speed picking up artifacts as they are uncovered. At this speed the prop-wash will remove approximately an inch of sand per minute, which is slow enough to enable the divers to catch all the artifacts before they are blown away. If the prop-wash is not properly controlled, many artifacts will be destroyed or blasted away into other areas. Running a prop-wash at full speed I have seen a 6-pound cannonball blasted over 50 feet from its original position. Some prop-washes are so powerful that they can be used to remove ballast stones off a wreck, but I do not recommend this, as there generally are many valuable artifacts mixed in with most ballast piles and these are also blasted away.

When a good area—say, one where many pieces of jewelry or gold coins, or priceless porcelain chinaware—is uncovered by the propeller, it is advisable to stop the prop-wash and use a method of excavation in which the diver on the bottom has more control. I have had several experiences where a prop-wash uncovered a layer containing a large number of coins and other items and, even while it was running at its slow speed, still I was unable to grab all the items before they were blasted away by the prop-wash. Stopping the prop-wash and continuing the excavation, either by fanning by hand or using a small airlift or hydrolift, is advisable.

The one disadvantage in using the prop-wash is that as it excavates a hole, sediment is thrown or blasted over unexcavated areas, and this overburden must always be removed from the virgin areas. But due to the speed in which the prop-wash can excavate, this is really a minor problem.

The hydrolift, which is also known as a transfer tube and gold dredge, is mainly used in surveying a wreck or when excavating in a hot area, like that mentioned above. It works on the same principle as the airlift, except that water pressure is used instead of air pressure to create the suction in the tube. The tube used is rarely more than 6 feet long and instead of discharging its spill on the surface it discharges it behind the diver. The spill should either be directed to fall on a screen so the small artifacts can be found or a diver should be stationed at the exhaust end of the tube to search for artifacts as they are blasted out of the tube.

Water-jets, which consist of nothing more than a hose pushing water out at a high pressure, and air-jets, which operate on the same principle, are mainly useful as tools to blow away sediment under a ship's timbers or in ballast piles, where an airlift or prop-wash might not be used as effectively.

The depth into sediment or coral growth that one must excavate can only be determined by trial and error. I have worked on some wrecks in which everything found was under the first 2 feet of sediment, and on others in which 25 feet of overburden had to be removed before everything was discovered in the next 5 feet.

The ballast piles of every wreck should be thoroughly investigated, as many valuable artifacts will be found mixed in with the ballast rock. Moving ballast rock is the most time-consuming and hardest on any wreck excavation. The best method is to excavate all the adjacent areas to a ballast pile and then move the ballast rock into these areas. Sending the ballast rock to the surface vessel in baskets can require months of time and is not really necessary, provided the same ballast rock can be moved on the bottom to an area already excavated. A close friend of mine is currently developing a system of moving the ballast rock on a wreck site to other areas by means of a conveyer belt.

Nothing is more frustrating than to excavate a hole and then discover a beer can that one of your crew has flung overboard. This can be avoided by keeping proper records. Systematically excavating and mapping a wreck is the best method, but unfortunately many modern-day salvors fail to do this. They use intuition and ESP to decide where to excavate, which results in their jumping from one spot to another and in many cases missing the best finds. When a wreck is worked systematically the salvors can easily keep track of the areas excavated each day. At the end of the day, all of the artifacts should be laid out on the deck of the salvage vessel. Then a Polaroid photograph can be taken of the artifacts and the location in which they were recovered can be recorded. This will prove most useful in mapping the wreck site.

CHAPTER FIVE

Identification and Dating of Shipwrecks and Their Cargoes

THE IDENTIFICATION and dating of shipwrecks and equipment and cargoes they carried is often very difficult and time-consuming. When assistance from experts is available, the salvor should make use of their expertise. Even with a library numbering over a thousand books and scientific reports on this subject, I realized a long time ago that I could not become an expert on identifying and dating the thousands of different items that might be found on a shipwreck. Very often my books and reports do enable me to establish a positive identification and date of an item, particularly when a great deal of material has been published on it. Still, to avoid any possibility of error, I consult experts specializing in various articles for verification. On items on which little or nothing has been published, I rely solely on the assistance of experts. Some items cannot be properly identified, as either nothing has been published about them or there are no experts in those items. Some examples of such things are: ship's pumps, fastenings, construction, rigging, lead shipping seals, sewing thimbles.

Because the average salvor may not have a large reference library or access to a public library containing the book he needs to identify and date a shipwreck, and because weeks or even months might be required to obtain an answer from an expert, I will attempt to assist the salvor in establishing the possible identification and date of some of the items found on shipwrecks. In some instances I can only recommend obtaining assistance from the experts.

There are many problems associated with properly identifying and dating a shipwreck and its items. The more articles the salvor has to work with, the better his chances are of establishing a positive identification and date. Artifact contamination postdating a shipwreck is always possible: Items from other wrecks lost in the same area might get mixed in with an earlier shipwreck; articles thrown off a passing ship or a ship salvaging a shipwreck may also contaminate a site.

During a recent salvage operation in the Florida Keys the first item recovered was an anchor dating from the second half of the nineteenth century. If the salvors had relied on dating their shipwreck from just this one item they would have made a grave mistake. The anchor had apparently been lost after snagging on a seventeenth-century wreck, thus contaminating the shipwreck site.

On the other hand, many shipwrecks will have items predating the period of the shipwreck. From reading old documents I have found many instances where items carried on ships were much older than the ships and men sailing them. A Spanish sea captain wrote to the King in 1728 that he would defend his ship against any enemy attacks with the same sword that one of his ancestors had used during the famous Battle of Lepanto in 1571. Another captain reported in 1682 that since he was unable to obtain the required number of cannon for his ship making a voyage to Mexico, he had hired divers to recover several from a shipwreck in Cadiz Bay dating from the middle of the sixteenth century. He knew they could not be fired and admitted that he carried them to make his ship appear heavily armed to enemy ships he might encounter. An English ship was lost without a trace in 1794 somewhere in the Caribbean during a hurricane; its principal cargo consisted of treasure recovered from a Spanish galleon that had sunk on the coast of Panama around 1560.

I have had firsthand experience with this problem. While I was living in Seville the director of the local archaeological museum requested that I make a survey on a shipwreck recently located by fishermen near Málaga. He reported that the fishermen had sighted a large marble statue on the shipwreck. The statue was of Roman origin, but the rest of the ship's cargo as well as the ship itself dated from the latter part of the nineteenth century. Through research we discovered that the ship had been sailing from Sicily to Spain with a general cargo. Either the statue was being brought to Spain to be sold or was being used as ballast.

Establishing the nationality of a shipwreck from the items discovered on it is often impossible for a number of reasons. As I mentioned in an earlier chapter, the majority of the cargoes brought from Spain to the New World were manufactured in many different countries. This also applies to ships of other nationalities. Even during times of war, when the rulers prohibited trade between their subjects and the enemy, trade continued as usual, sometimes by using merchants of neutral nationals as middlemen. A good example of this fact was discovered on the *Matanceros* shipwreck. Although Spain and England were at war at this time, over 50 percent of the cargo carried on the ship was of British origin. To further complicate the identification of this wreck, the major portion of the remainder of the ship's cargo came from countries other than Spain, such as France, Germany, England, Holland, and Brazil.

At the close of our first season of excavation on the shipwreck, we sought the assistance of an expert from the Smithsonian Institution in identifying and dating the wreck. According to this expert, he assured us that the wreck was definitely an English merchantman. My partners and I disagreed with him, mainly because the ship carried a vast number of Catholic religious articles, which we felt certain no English ship would carry. Consequently, through our research efforts we were able to positively identify the shipwreck as a Spanish merchantman. After obtaining copies of the original ship's cargo manifest from the Archives of the Indies in Seville, we were able to compare the majority of the items we recovered from this wreck with those listed on the cargo manifest.

There are many cases in which ships of other European nations also carried cargoes manufactured in various other countries. In 1620 a Dutch merchantman was captured after entering a small port in Cuba to carry on illegal trade with the local residents. The bulk of its cargo consisted of merchandise from England, France, and Italy.

Many ships of different nations sailing from Europe to the New World made it a practice to stop at one of the Canary Islands to take on fresh water and victuals before making the long ocean crossing. Often they also purchased Spanish wine and other spirits, so it would not be unusual to find large numbers of Spanish olive jars, in which these liquids were carried, on non-Spanish ships. Other items manufactured in Spain—such as swords made in Toledo—and held in great esteem by men of different nationalities might also have been obtained in the Canaries.

Ships of all nations sailing from the Western Hemisphere back to Europe would also have carried goods manufactured in various countries. Items such as navigational equipment might have been carried throughout the life of the ship, whereas other trade items might have been obtained by carrying on trade in the ports they visited or items the ships originally brought over to sell but failed to do so. These items could also have been obtained by capturing them from ships of other nations.

Discovering Spanish specie or bullion on a shipwreck does not identify it as a Spanish ship. For instance, Spanish coinage was used as the chief currency by all the European nations possessing settlements in the New World, and even in the United States it was used as legal tender until the beginning of the nineteenth century. The reason for this was the vast amount of silver and gold mined and minted by the Spaniards and the scarcity of these precious metals in all the other European nations. However, through trade—both legal and illegal—as well as plunder, most of the precious metals mined in Spanish America eventually reached other European countries. In many of these nations, rather than melt the precious metals down to make new coins, Spanish coinage was used on a large scale. On various occasions the English Crown did have vast amounts of Spanish coinage melted and recoined into English coinage, but very few of these coins ever reached the New World. To encourage the English subjects to purchase only that merchandise manufactured in Mother England, merchant ships sailing to the New World were forbidden to carry English currency. Thus the thousands of English merchantmen that came to obtain New World products were able only to secure cargoes in exchange for English-manufactured merchandise.

Large amounts of Spanish coinage were also used throughout the rest of the world. Each year huge sums were shipped from Mexico to the Philippines to purchase goods to be shipped to Acapulco from the Orient. Large amounts of this specie eventually reached other nations. A Dutch ship, the *Golden Dragon*, wrecked in 1656 on the west side of Australia, was recently salvaged. Among the items recovered were 7,500 silver coins dated 1654–55 from the Mexico City and Potosí mints.

The nationality and date of some shipwrecks can be established by the size of the vessel and the objects found on them, but again, caution must be exercised, as there are many exceptions that can confuse the salvor.

During the period covered in this book, most likely the smallest vessels were those used by early explorers like Columbus; advice or mail boats; reconnaissance boats; salvage vessels; and coastal, or inter-island, trading vessels.

The small caravels and pinnaces used by early explorers should be fairly easy to identify by the artillery they carried, as they differed a great deal in size and construction from all types of later-period ships. Due to the risk involved in sailing in uncharted waters, the officers and crew avoided bringing such valuable items as silverware or glassware. Instead they would eat and drink from wooden or ceramic objects. An exception occurred when one of these ships carried colonists or government officials to a newly settled area, in which case they would bring all their earthly possessions with them. Such a ship usually carried agricultural, mining, masonry, and carpentry tools. These items should enable the salvor to differentiate between a vessel on an exploratory or colonizing voyage. If any treasure is found on the shipwreck, it will most likely be gold or silver of an unrefined and un-minted nature, or items manufactured by the Indians.

Advice and mail boats, and even reconnaissance boats, for that matter, appear very similar in appearance under water. Unlike the early exploratory or colonizing vessels, these carried more armament and could be dated from the armament. They were not armed to fight large vessels but only to repel ships their own size and smaller ones that might overtake them. Their lightness and construction enabled them to outrun the larger vessels. To maintain fast speeds, these vessels had to be light, so they rarely carried any cargo at all. On occasion, Spanish advice boats returning to Spain did carry small amounts of treasure to drop off at places along the way to pay officials or garrisons; and sometimes they carried it to the hard-pressed Spanish kings to tide them over until the treasure fleets reached Spain at later dates.

Small pirate and privateering vessels would also fit into this description and would be difficult to distinguish from the other vessels.

Salvage vessels also carried a substantial amount of armament to protect the items they might salvage. Finding diving bells, or any of the many instruments used in early salvage operations, might aid the modern-day salvor in identifying the type of ship he has located. If the early salvors were successful, then a diversified cargo of treasure and artifacts might also be found on the wreck.

Due to a constant shortage of artillery throughout the Western Hemisphere during the entire period covered in this book, very few small trading vessels carried it. If they did, the pieces were rarely ever larger than swivel guns and generally used for repelling boarders but of little use in combat with other vessels. Lack of armament and slow speeds, due to the weight of their cargoes, made them very vulnerable to attack by all other shipping, so consequently they sailed only when it was safe. And even when they did sail, they usually carried cargoes of little value because of the risk of capture involved. Small Spanish vessels were forbidden by the Crown from carrying any treasure; however, this rule was not strictly enforced, since documents tell of many of them being lost with treasure aboard. Occasionally these small trading vessels were used to carry large amounts of treasure, but then they were guarded by armed galleys or other warships. The gold and emeralds that were sent annually from Bogotá to Cartagena for transshipment to Spain were brought down the Magdalena River in these small vessels and sailed along the coast to Cartagena. When the Chagres River was used to transport the treasure by rafts from the Pacific to the Caribbean side of the Isthmus, the small trading ships carried the treasure from the mouth of the river to Nombre de Dios or Porto Bello. Virtually all the nonprecious cargoes —such as lumber and agricultural products—carried on these small traders would have disappeared long ago on a shipwreck with few traces of a wreck remaining today, especially if the ship carried no armament or ballast.

Many of the larger merchant ships also suffered the same fate over the years, as the cargoes they carried back to Europe consisted of similar perishable products, such as tobacco, cocoa, sugar, rum, cotton, drugs, indigo, cochineal, and lumber. Finding a shipwreck that fits this description could falsely convince a salvor that he had located a ship that had been sailing without cargo when lost, since only shipboard items—cannon, anchors, weapons, and cooking and eating utensils— would be found.

Due to the nature of their cargoes, which in most cases consisted of objects of various metals, glass, and ceramic ware (things that would not disappear from a shipwreck over the years), by far the easiest to identify are the merchantmen arriving from Europe. Remember that many of the items carried on these merchantmen to be sold in the New World were also used on all types of ships. Thus a large number of different individual articles must be recovered before a salvor can determine that he has found a merchantman. It would be normal to find several dozen, or even several hundred, shoe buckles on a number of different types of shipwrecks, but finding thousands of them, as we did on the *Matanceros* wreck, enabled us to realize that it was a merchantman.

A Spanish treasure galleon is easily identifiable from the large amounts of treasure it carried as well as the number and size of its cannon, which was also greater in number and size than the average merchantman's. The size of the ship furnishes another clue, as the largest ships were generally used to carry the treasures back to Spain. During the second half of the sixteenth century the average size of a Spanish merchantman was about 450 tons and for the galleons around 800 tons. During the seventeenth century the merchantmen averaged 600 tons and the galleons between 800 and 1,000 tons. During the eighteenth century the merchantmen barely increased in size, but most of the treasure-carrying galleons used were between 1,500 and 2,000 tons. Galleons were required to carry anywhere from 100 to 250 marines, and discovering a large number of weapons in association with great amounts of treasure will help identify a shipwreck as a galleon.

All treasure-laden ships were not necessarily Spanish galleons, as ships of other nations also carried Spanish treasure back to Europe from the New World. In 1755, a period when no Spanish ships were available to carry treasure to Spain, as Spain and England were at war, a French ship named *Notre Dame de Deliverance* disappeared without a trace somewhere between Havana and Cadiz. Her cargo consisted of 1,170 pounds of gold bullion carried in seventeen chests, 15,399 gold doubloons, 153 gold snuff boxes weighing 6 ounces each, a gold-hilted sword, a gold watch, 1,072,000 pieces of eight, 764 ounces of virgin silver, 31 pounds of silver ore, a large number of items made of silver, six pairs of diamond earrings, a diamond ring, several chests of precious stones, plus general cargo consisting of Chinese fans, cocoa, drugs, and indigo.

Discovering a large ship with many cannon and weapons but little or no treasure will most likely identify the ship as a warship. Generally, warships of all nations were forbidden to carry cargo of any description, and the scarcity of artifacts normally found on merchantmen will aid in identifying a wreck as a warship. In most cases it is impossible to distinguish between a Spanish treasure galleon arriving from Europe to a New World port and a warship, as neither would be carrying cargo and both would carry large numbers of cannon and hand weapons. Occasionally mercury was shipped from Spain to the New World on the treasure galleons, so discovery of this on a wreck site would normally identify it as a treasure galleon arriving from Spain.

British warships are easily identifiable because of the broad-arrow mark on many objects found on shipwrecks of this type. I have seen the broad arrow on cannon, weapons, copper sheathing, cutlery, bottles, and many other articles. The origin of the mark is obscure, but it was in regular use by the second half of the sixteenth century to denote all Crown property and continued until the end of the nineteenth century. Finding a few items with the broad arrow on a shipwreck will certainly indicate that the items once belonged to the British admiralty, but not necessarily that the shipwreck is British. Items marked with the broad arrow were found not only on several of the 1715 Spanish shipwrecks but also on wrecks that proved to be non-British.

Slave ships sailing to or from the New World are usually identifiable by the equipment found on them. One located recently near Panama contained hundreds of leg and arm bracelets attached to chains, used on the poor human cargoes these ships carried. Due to the fact that almost every inch of a slave ship was used to carry the slaves and water and victuals to maintain them, most ships of this type carried only a few cannon. Other than the slaves, the only cargo these ships carried was ivory and gold dust, also obtained on the African coast. After selling their cargoes on this side of the Atlantic, they returned to Europe with gold or silver specie or bullion received as payment for their human cargoes.

Before discussing the identification and dating of items discovered on shipwrecks by their physical appearance, I shall mention the various scientific methods that can be utilized in establishing the place of origin or the date, or both, of the various materials discovered on a wreck.

The most well-known method of dating an old object is Radiocarbon 14, or C-14, although this is only feasible on organic material—

such as wood, bone, charcoal, peat, shell, plants. This method was conceived by the noted nuclear physicist W. F. Libby, who discovered that all organic material absorbs carbon-14 from the earth's atmosphere until it dies, and that this absorption ceases and disintegrates at a known rate over periods of time. By measuring the amount of C-14 remaining in organic material, scientists can determine the length of time that has elapsed since the object died or was destroyed by man, such as when a tree is cut down. Only small samples of the materials are required for this method of dating an object, but the object should be kept wet (if discovered in the sea) until the tests are made on it. Many universities have facilities for C-14 dating and there are also a number of commercial laboratories that do it; the average price is about $150 and requires from two to six weeks to be accomplished.

The main disadvantage in using this method to date shipwrecks located in the Western Hemisphere lies in the uncertainty of the date obtained. Recently I submitted a wood sample from a shipwreck and received a date of 420 years, plus or minus 150 years. This meant that the wood sample could date from 1400 to 1700, which was no help at all. When C-14 dating is used on items that are many thousands of years old, the plus or minus factor is of little significance; but on items only several hundreds of years old, it is important. Furthermore, in many cases the date obtained by this method will have no relationship to the date of the shipwreck. The ship may have been many decades old—some were used for as long as fifty years—when it sank and the ambiguous date obtained by this method would relate to the date when the tree was cut. There are many instances when a ship was constructed from timbers from older ships, which in turn could have been constructed from the timbers of an even older ship. Other articles —such as bone or charcoal found on a shipwreck—are preferable to date, since they date within a few years of the loss of the ship.

Establishing the place of origin of wood can be accurately settled by dendrologists; in many cases they not only can identify the country from which the wood came but even narrow it down to a small section of the country. This information is extremely useful in establishing the country in which the ship was constructed. This was one of the factors that contributed to the positive identification of the two shipwrecks of Columbus discovered in St. Anns Bay, Jamaica.

Another method is the science of botany. During our preliminary survey of the site we found several black beans that botanists identified as a species grown only in Spain. On another occasion a botanist identified several tobacco leaves I had found on a shipwreck as coming from Venezuela, thus aiding me in identifying the shipwreck. Most plants or seeds discovered on shipwrecks can also be identified as to their species and place of origin.

Zoologists are helpful in identifying bones of animals, birds, and fish. Identifying large numbers of human bones on a shipwreck would indicate either that many of the persons were killed during a sea battle or as a result of a hurricane that caused the ship's loss. Investigating a shipwreck site near Jamaica, I noticed that there were a great many fish bones mixed in with the ballast. At the time I assumed that they were either from fish that had died over the years on the wreck or were the remains of meals eaten by the ship's crew. The latter assumption was correct. I took a selection of the fish bones to a marine zoologist, who identified them as belonging to a species of herring caught in the North Sea. This information, combined with my discovery of many Dutch items on the wreck, identified it as being a Dutch merchantman.

Information obtained from geologists, who can establish the place of origin of most ballast rock found on a shipwreck, can be used to identify the ship's nationality. There are certainly exceptions to the rule, but generally a ship will be carrying ballast rock from its home port or other ports belonging to the same country either in the Old or New World.

Scientists specializing in metalography can determine, through microscopic study and other means, the exact origin of the minerals and metal alloys used in different metal items. This will not necessarily identify the particular nationality of a wreck but will give the precise origin of the metallic objects carried on it. Where metal fastenings were used in the construction of a ship's hull, this information is especially useful, as these fittings were probably manufactured near the source of the minerals of which they are composed; this would identify the locality where the ship was constructed.

The Corning Glass Museum of Corning, New York, has conducted extensive research in methods of identifying and dating glassware. Throughout history, different methods and minerals have been used in making glassware, and through scientific analysis they are able to identify the place of manufacture of most glassware. Several years ago, Dr. Robert Brill (of the museum) developed a method of precisely dating glass recovered from the sea. By counting the number of layers of the weathering crust on the glass fragment, he established the length of time it has been under the sea. I have submitted many different samples of glassware from dated shipwrecks, and his findings are always accurate to within a year or two of the known date of the wreck.

Ceramic and other objects made from clay, such as building bricks, can be rather accurately dated by a new process called thermoluminescence, which was developed at the Oxford Research Laboratory in England only a few years ago. This process is based on the fact that radioactivity from certain isotopes in clay are trapped there until a ceramic object is fired in a kiln. The firing releases the electrons in a "thermoluminescence glow." When the object cools, the electrons are again trapped but continue to increase with the process of decay, and the number of electrons released increases with the length of time. By measuring the number remaining in the object, its date can be established with from 5- to 10-percent accuracy.

From consulting hundreds of documents concerning the size and tonnage of ships of different types and nationalities, I have devised the following table to assist the salvor in establishing the size and draft of old ships. The salvor may know from documental sources that his ship was of 500 tons and, provided he locates the correct shipwreck, the length of the keel should be about 92 feet. This information can be used in reverse. Locating a shipwreck, the salvor might discover that the keel length was 120 feet; this would indicate that his ship was 1,400–1,500 tons, which would aid him greatly in identifying the ship. The figures in the table are given in feet.

Establishing the nationality of a ship at the time it was lost from a visual inspection of the remains of a shipwreck is very difficult for many reasons. Some were captured by all the European nations and used in their own navies and merchant fleets; others were bought or hired from different nations. In 1593, due to a scarcity of Spanish shipping, the King ordered the seizure of all foreign ships in Spanish ports so that a fleet could sail to the New World. Of the sixty-two ships in this fleet, only fourteen were Spanish-built. The others came from twelve European nations, including Greece and Sweden.

In shallow waters, too little remains on shipwrecks to aid in establishing the place where the ship was constructed. And even if it were established, it would not indicate the nationality of the ship at the time it was lost. One of the 1715 ships was originally built in England, serving as a warship for many years until it was captured by the French and converted into a merchantman; she was eventually sold to the Spaniards, who converted her to a treasure galleon.

The spikes, nails, tacks, and other metal fastenings are no help in

Tonnage	Length of Keel	Width of Beam	Draft
100	52	19	7½
200	66	24	9½
300	76	27⅓	10½
400	84	30	12
500	92	33	13
600	98	35	14
700	102	36¾	14⅝
800	104	37½	15
900	107½	38½	15¼
1,000	109	39⅕	15⅓
1,100	110	40	15½
1,400–1,500	120	44	16
1,600	132	48	16
2,000	152	60	18

identifying the nationality or date of the ship, as their shapes and sizes changed very little over the centuries. Brass tacks discovered recently on a Roman shipwreck dating from the third century A.D. were identical to those found on an eighteenth-century French warship. Treenails (wooden pegs), used to fasten the planking to the frame of the ship, are no help either in dating a ship, since they remained the same in shape over the centuries. If they were turned on a lathe rather than shaped by hand, it indicates only that the wreck is dated after 1825. Nor will the types of wood used in a ship's construction provide the salvor with any valuable clues, as the types of wood used by the various nations depended on what was most readily available. The earliest mention of a ship built in Europe using teakwood was in 1821. A ship built with mahogany planking might indicate that it was built near Honduras, which was the major source of mahogany in the old days.

Preventing the borings of the teredo and accumulation on the hulls was a constant problem. One method used by most of the European nations was to careen their ships and burn the ships' bottoms, then apply a number of different compounds basically consisting of a tar and pitch base. The Spaniards generally used a mixture of tar and lime. Some Spanish ships in the eighteenth century used a layer of wooden sheathing and placed a compound of tar and animal hair between the sheathing and hull. The English used many different compounds on their ships' bottoms, too numerous to mention here. In 1745 it consisted of one hundred parts of pitch, thirty parts of brimstone, and thirty-five parts of brick or marble dust; all mixed together.

The earliest mention of Spanish ships being sheathed with lead was in 1508. This practice was continued until 1567 when the King ordered it to cease, claiming that its added weight caused his ships to sail too slowly. In 1605, lead sheathing was again applied to Spanish ships sailing to the New World, but only to those going to Mexico. The reason for this was to protect their hulls from the teredo during the long months that these ships wintered in Veracruz. Those going to other Spanish settlements were still forbidden to use lead sheathing. The only other nation that used lead sheathing was England, and only on a small scale, mainly as an experiment on their warships in the Caribbean during different periods.

There was a brief mention in 1735 that twenty English warships were sheathed, but the type of material used was not mentioned. In 1766, several English warships were sheathed with copper, and by 1780 this was done on all their ships, both naval and merchantmen. The first French ships to use copper sheathing sailed in 1775, but this practice did not catch on with the Spaniards or Portuguese until the first decade of the nineteenth century.

The majority of the masts, yards, spars, and rigging used on ships of all nations came from the Baltic region; their shapes differed so little over the years that they are neither useful in identifying the nationality nor the age of a ship. However, the size of these items could be used to establish the size of the ship.

Anchors are very difficult to date because their shapes changed very little over the centuries; nor can their place of origin be established by the shape of the anchor. From the time of the Vikings until about 1825, all anchors were hand-forged from several pieces of iron. After this period many were cast in one piece. The stocks were made of wood until the middle of the nineteenth century, when they were replaced by iron bars. The first mention of chains being used on an anchor occurred in 1817 and referred to those on an English warship.

The number and size of anchors carried depended on the size and type of ship. Anchors were constantly being lost, so many extra ones were carried. Until 1579 there was no regulation as to the number of anchors a ship must carry, but that year the King issued an order stating that ships over 100 tons going to Tierra Firme must carry five anchors and those going to Mexico must carry seven. The first mention of their sizes occurred in 1620, when a galleon of 500 tons carried seven anchors on a voyage to Veracruz: one of a ton weight, two of 1,800 pounds, two of 1,600 pounds, one of 450 pounds, and one of 350 pounds. In 1709 an order was issued that the total weight of anchors on all Spanish warships must be equal to 5 percent of the total weight of the ship.

From 1634 onward, French merchantmen were required to carry a minimum of four large anchors and warships at least six. One large French warship lost in the Caribbean near the end of the seventeenth century was carrying ten anchors at the time, while another, lost during the same hurricane, had only two available, resulting in her loss when both of their cables parted and she wrecked on a reef.

In 1688, English warships were required to carry the following number of anchors: a ship of 2,000 tons, known as a first-rater, carried nine anchors weighing a total of 17 tons; a second-rater of 1,500 tons carried nine weighing a total of 12½ tons; a third-rater of 1,000 tons carried six weighing a total of 8½ tons; a fourth-rater of 700 tons carried six weighing a total of 5½ tons; and a fifth-rater of 500 tons carried five weighing a total of 4½ tons.

Cannon are very useful in establishing the size, type, and approximate date of the ship, but not always the nationality, because cannon manufactured in many different countries might be found on a single ship. During the second half of the sixteenth century the majority of the cannon carried on Spanish ships were made in England and Holland, and during the seventeenth and eighteenth centuries a large percentage were of foreign manufacture. A Spanish merchant ship sailing to Veracruz in 1616 had three English, one Italian, three Dutch, two Portuguese, five French, and three Spanish cannon as her armament. In 1623 the *flotas* and treasure galleons were unable to sail for the New World because of a grave shortage of cannon due to the fact that all the ships that had gone to the New World the previous year had not returned to Spain. To arm the ships, thirty were bought from Portugal, two hundred from Denmark and three hundred from England. Many of the ships of other European nations also carried cannon of foreign manufacture, most of which were obtained by capturing ships of other nations.

Most bronze and iron cannon were struck with dates at the time they were founded and many also carried the coat of arms of the monarch of the country of manufacture. The majority of the English cannon were struck with a crowned rose and the initials *GR*—"George Rex" or "King George." On bronze cannon these marks always survive, but on the many iron cannon discovered the markings have disappeared due to oxidation of the exterior of the pieces. When no markings bearing the date the cannon was founded are visible, they can still be dated by their shapes and other distinctive characteristics. All the European nations have artillery museums, and their experts can generally date the pieces to within fifty years. In the United States the Smithsonian Institution and the National Park Service also have experts that can aid a salvor in identifying and dating cannon. Various books have been published on cannon of different nations, but the majority are written in foreign languages and are difficult to obtain in the United States.

During the voyages made by Columbus, his ships were armed with two different types of cannon; Lombards and Versos, also called swivel guns. The Lombards were made of forged-iron strakes running the length of the barrel and held together by iron bands spaced every 4 to 6 inches. The piece was opened at both ends and a breech block loaded with powder was wedged against the back end of the piece after a ball was inserted. The cannon was mounted on a wooden cradle and carried on the main deck of the ship. These pieces varied from 6 to 12 feet in length, weighed from 500 to 2,000 pounds, and fired a ball of stone between 4 and 10 inches in diameter. The weight of the stone depended on the type of rock used in making the ball. A distinctive feature of this type of cannon was the absence of trunnions on the cannon, unlike any other cannon used at later dates.

The Versos were either cast in bronze or made of iron in the same manner as the Lombards. Around the end of the sixteenth century they began casting them in iron as well. They were mounted on a pivoting frame and attached to the bulwarks of the ships. They varied in length from 4 to 10 feet, weighed between 150 and 1,800 pounds, and fired a stone or iron ball between 1½ and 3 inches in diameter. These small-caliber guns were mainly used to attack the personnel on the decks and castles of an enemy ship rather than a ship's hull, which was capable of resisting the shock of such small projectiles. This type of cannon was carried on ships of all types and nations as late as the end of the eighteenth century. It was also used as a signal gun and by officers at times of mutinies.

As early as 1504 some of the larger Spanish ships sailing to the New World were carrying bigger cannon, which were mounted on two-wheeled wooden gun carriages. A merchant *nao* sailing to Santo Domingo this same year carried: one bronze Demiculverin, 11 feet in length, weighing 2 tons, and firing a 12-pound ball; four Iron Cannon Serpentines, 8 feet in length, weighing 2½ tons, and firing a 40-pound ball; one bronze Saker, 7 feet in length, weighing 1,200 pounds, and firing a 6-pound ball; and three Versos of unknown size and weight but firing a 4-pound ball.

In 1552 a royal order was issued that all Spanish ships sailing to the New World had to carry the following amounts of armament. Merchant ships between 100 and 170 tons were required to carry: one bronze Saker, one bronze Falconet, six iron Lombards; and twelve iron Versos. A ship of 170 to 220 tons must carry: one bronze Demiculverin, one bronze Saker, one bronze Falconet, eight iron Lombards, and eighteen iron Versos. Ships of 220 to 320 tons must carry one iron Demiculverin, two bronze Sakers, one bronze Falconet, ten iron Lombards, and twenty-four iron Versos. Treasure galleons of between 400 and 600 tons were required to carry all bronze cannon, which consisted of thirty to fifty Culverin cannon, four to six Demiculverins, two to four Sakers, four Falconets, and an unknown number of Versos.

The Demiculverins fired balls weighing from 7 to 12 pounds, were twenty-five to forty times their bore diameter in length, and weighed between 3,000 and 4,000 pounds. The Sakers fired balls weighing from 5 to 10 pounds, were from 5 to 8 feet in length, and weighed between 1,700 and 2,400 pounds. The Falconets fired a 3- or 4-pound ball, were thirty to thirty-six times their bore diameter in length, and weighed between 1,500 and 2,500 pounds. At this time the Lombards were made with trunnions and were about the same size and weight as the earlier types. The same applies to the Versos. The Culverin cannon were the main armament for fighting against enemy ships. They were made in many different sizes and fired balls weighing between 20 and 40 pounds. Their lengths were thirty to thirty-two times their bore diameter and their weight from 2 to 3 tons.

Around 1570, when the scarcity of copper prevented the manufacture of a sufficient number of bronze Culverins and other types of cannon on the Spanish ships, many began carrying larger numbers of iron cannon. The largest was called just plain Cannon: it fired a 40-pound ball, was seventeen times its bore diameter in length, and weighed 6,200 pounds. There were also Demi-Cannons, which fired

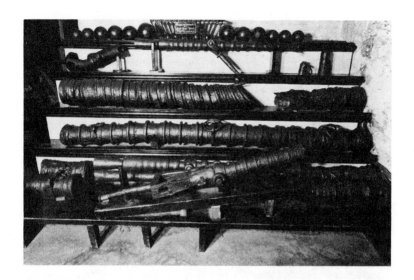

TOP: Early sixteenth-century Spanish shipboard artillery (Tower of London).
BOTTOM: Seventeenth-century saker, mainly used on merchantmen.

LEFT: Inspecting an iron cannon after removing the coral growth on it. BELOW: Divers preparing a cannon for raising.

balls weighing between 12 and 20 pounds, were between twelve and twenty times their bore diameters in length, and weighed between 2,300 and 3,600 pounds.

Small vessels frequently used several other types of cannon: the Pasavolante, which fired a ball weighing between 2 and 15 pounds; the Moyana, which fired a ball weighing from 6 to 10 pounds; and the Esmeril, of which very little is known.

The principal cannon carried on English ships during the sixteenth century are given below with their average weights and measurements.

During the sixteenth and seventeenth centuries a type of cannon named Pedrero was occasionally carried on Spanish ships, but very little is known about this cannon. At times, documents mentioned some firing balls of only a few pounds, being small in size and weight; and at other times they were mentioned as weighing as much as 2 tons and firing 40-pound balls. The balls they fired were always made of stone.

With the exception of the Lombards, which went out of use near the end of the sixteenth century, all the other cannon described above remained in use until the beginning of the nineteenth century, when Carronades replaced most of the larger cannon on Spanish ships.

In 1599 the Spaniards apparently had a sufficient supply of bronze cannon, as all twelve galleons in the Tierra Firme Armada carried only bronze cannon along with the *Capitanas* and *Almirantas* of both *flotas*. In 1605 a royal order stated that all treasure galleons and the *Capitanas* and *Almirantas* of the *flotas* must carry only bronze cannon

Name	Weight in Pounds	Length in Feet	Caliber in Inches	Weight of Shot in Pounds
Robinet	200	5	1¼	1
Falconet	500	4	2	2
Falcon	800	6	2½	2½
Minion	1,100	6½	3½	4½
Saker	1,500	7	3½	5
Demiculverin	3,000	10	4½	9
Bastard Culverin	3,000	8½	4½	11
Culverin	4,000	11	5½	18
Demi-Cannon	5,000	9	6½	30
Cannon	7,000	12	8	60

and that all merchantmen must carry a minimum of two bronze pieces. By 1644, however, only the two main flagships of the Tierra Firme Armada carried only bronze cannon, while the other galleons carried but a few. All of the merchantmen sailing that year carried only iron cannon. In a fleet made up of eleven ships sailing to the New World in 1680, of the 467 cannon carried only sixteen were bronze. And in 1715 all the cannon on the twelve ships returning to Spain were iron; and again on the twenty-one ships returning to Spain in 1733, with the exception of several small-caliber pieces.

The principal cannon carried on English ships during the seventeenth century are given below with their average weights and measurements.

Of the above-mentioned English-made cannon, the Robinet, Falconet, Falcon, Minion, Saker, Demiculverin, and Culverin were generally made of bronze. The different types and sizes of Cannon were generally made of iron.

A new type of cannon was introduced on English ships in 1779 called the Carronade, easily recognizable from those of earlier years because of its large bore diameter and short length of only 3 to 6 feet. They fired balls weighing 9, 12, 24, 32, 42, and 68 pounds. Those made up to 1800 had low trunnions, and after 1800 the trunnions were centered. After 1825, however, many of them had no trunnions but were mounted with lugs on the gun carriages. From 1800 onward the Carronade replaced most of the large-caliber cannon on

Name	Weight in Pounds	Length in Feet	Caliber in Inches	Weight of Shot in Pounds
Robinet	120	3	1¼	¾
Falconet	210	4	2	1¼
Falcon	700	6	2¾	2¼
Minion	1,500	8	3	4
Saker	2,500	9½	3½	5¼
Demiculverin	3,600	10	4½	9
Culverin	4,000	11	5	15
Demi-Cannon	6,000	12	6	27
Cannon	7,000	10	7	47
Cannon Royal	8,000	8	8	63

ships of all nations.

The principal cannon carried on English ships during the eighteenth century, until the introduction of the Carronades, are given below with their average weights and measurements.

The number and types of cannon carried on English merchantmen depended on the size of the ship and their availability, as cannon were also scarce in England. This also applied to English warships until about the middle of the seventeenth century, when the admiralty issued an order specifying the number and types of cannon that must be carried on their ships.

In 1762 a first-rater of 100 cannon carried thirty 42-pounders, twenty-eight 24-pounders, thirty 12-pounders, ten 8-pounders, and two 6-pounders. A second-rater of 90 cannon carried twenty-six 32-pounders, twenty-six 18-pounders, twenty-six 12-pounders, ten 8-pounders, and two 6-pounders. A third-rater of 74 cannon carried twenty-eight 32-pounders, thirty 24-pounders, fourteen 9-pounders, and two 6-pounders. A fourth-rater of 50 cannon carried twenty-two 24-pounders, twenty-two 12-pounders, and six 6-pounders. A fifth-rater of 36 cannon carried twenty-six 12-pounders and ten 6-pounders. A sixth-rater of 28 cannon carried twenty-four 9-pounders and four 6-pounders.

French cannon were very similar in size, shape, and weight to the English cannon, but were generally lavishly marked with decorations, especially those cast in bronze. The number and types carried

Name	Weight in Pounds	Length in Feet	Caliber in Inches	Weight of Shot in Pounds
Robinet	150	$3\frac{1}{2}$	$1\frac{3}{4}$	$\frac{1}{2}$
Falconet	700	$4\frac{1}{2}$	3	3
Falcon	800	6	$3\frac{1}{4}$	4
Minion	2,000	$7\frac{1}{2}$	$3\frac{3}{4}$	6
Demiculverin	2,600	8	$4\frac{1}{2}$	9
Culverin	3,200	9	$4\frac{3}{4}$	12
18-Pound Cannon	3,900	9	$5\frac{1}{3}$	18
24-Pound Cannon	4,600	9	$5\frac{4}{5}$	24
32-Pound Cannon	5,500	$9\frac{1}{2}$	$6\frac{1}{2}$	32
42-Pound Cannon	6,500	10	7	42

on their merchantmen and warships varied greatly until 1643, when the King issued an order concerning the armament on all French ships. Merchantmen sailing to the New World were required to carry the following number and sizes: a ship between 200 and 300 tons must carry six Demiculverins of 2,400-pound weight, twelve Sakers of 1,600-pound weight, two Minions of 1,000-pound weight, one Falconet of 300-pound weight, and one Robinet of 200-pound weight. The ships of larger sizes had to carry the smaller number and sizes of cannon, with the exception of the number and weight of the Demiculverins, which increased with the size of the ship. A 300-ton vessel carried nine Demiculverins of 3,000-pound weight, a 500-ton ship carried sixteen Demiculverins of 3,200-pound weight, and a 700-ton ship carried twenty-two Demiculverins of the same weight.

All first- and second-raters were required to carry only bronze cannon, with all the smaller French warships being required to carry one-quarter of their cannons made of bronze and the remainder of iron.

Dutch cannon were also very similar to the English and French; they used bronze cannon almost exclusively on all of their ships, including the majority of their large merchantmen. Portuguese cannon differed vastly in shape from any of the others manufactured in Europe, and many of those carried on Portuguese ships were actually manufactured in India or in other Portuguese Far East possessions.

The basic cannon projectile was the round shot, generally made of iron, but sometimes of stone or lead. The size of the shot used for each cannon was one-quarter inch smaller in diameter than the caliber of the piece. Because there was no difference in the appearance of the round shot made by all the countries, the only information that can be obtained from them establishes the caliber of the cannon carried on the shipwreck in the event that the cannon were previously salvaged.

The table on page 105 gives the average weight of iron round shot in relation to its size.

Bar shot and chain shot were primarily used during sea battles to destroy the sails and rigging of enemy vessels. The first mention of bar shot was by the Dutch in 1819. Some were made by attaching an iron bar measuring 6 and 12 inches in length between two round shot; others were made with two halves of a round shot, and some with round disks. Chain shot was introduced by the Dutch in 1666, as a chain replaced the iron bar of the bar shot.

Diameter in Inches	Weight in Pounds and Ounces		Diameter in Inches	Weight in Pounds and Ounces	
2	1	2	5¼	20	1
2¼	1	9	5½	23	2
2½	2	2	5¾	26	6
2¾	2	14	6	30	
3	3	12	6¼	34	
3¼	4	12	6½	38	
3½	6	1	6¾	42	
3¾	7	5	7	48	
4	8	15	7¼	53	
4¼	10	10	7½	58	
4½	12	10	7¾	64	
4¾	14	14	8	71	
5	17	5	8¼	78	

Two types of antipersonnel shot were also used: grape shot and canister shot, sometimes called case shot. The earliest mention of grape shot was in 1556 aboard English ships. It consisted of twenty to fifty small cast-iron balls of 1 to 2 inches in diameter held in place between two or more wood or metal disks connected to a central rod. The balls were lashed to the frame with cords or leather and the cylindrical projectile was covered with canvas and coated with wax, paint, or pitch. The diameter of the projectile depended on the caliber of the cannon; its height was between 6 and 12 inches. Canister shot, introduced by the French in 1745, consisted of a thin cylindrical metal can containing various-shaped objects, such as glass fragments, nails, tacks, musket balls, and small pebbles.

Carcass shot was an incendiary projectile, consisting of a hollow cast-iron ball filled with combustible materials. When fired, flames streamed out through small holes in the side of the ball. The period when this projectile first came into use is unknown, except that it was during the second half of the seventeenth century.

Carronade shot also consisted of a hollow cast-iron ball but did not contain any combustible material or have holes in it.

Weapons of many different types were carried on the ships, and it is relatively simple to identify them and establish their date and place of manufacture, as there are many books available on this subject. On ships of all nationalities, even passengers were required to carry at least one hand-held weapon. Crossbows were used until the end of the sixteenth century, but generally only small numbers of these weapons were carried aboard ships, as harquebuses and muskets were considered better weapons.

Matchlock harquebuses, which were introduced in the fourteenth century, were generally 5 or 6 feet long, weighed as much as 60 pounds, and fired an iron or lead ball ranging from half an inch to an inch in diameter. The firing mechanism consisted of an S-shaped lever pivoted to the stock near its center and forked at its upper end to hold the match. By pressing the lower end of the lever the match was forced down into the flashpan and ignited the primer. The disadvantage in using this weapon was the necessity of keeping the match lit or having the means to light it when needed. In 1517 a German invented the wheel lock, which replaced the matchlock, consisting of two main parts. A steel-tooth wheel was wound up by a key to tighten a spring; by pulling the trigger, the wheel, which contained a lump of pyrite or a flint, struck the firing pan and ignited the primer. Another improvement was introduced on the firing mechanism around the end of the sixteenth century, when the flintlock superseded the wheel lock. In the flintlock, a piece of flint held in the jaws of the cock was released by pulling the trigger of the weapon, which struck against a piece of steel, sending a shower of sparks into the priming powder pan. The flintlock remained in continuous use on all firearms until about 1820, when it was replaced by the percussion lock. Although it was invented near the end of the sixteenth century, some nations did not make use of it for many years. In France it was not used on a large scale until 1670.

Muskets, introduced in 1521, were the largest guns fired by a single man. Some were as long as 10 feet and weighed over 100 pounds and, because of its size and heavy recoil, had to be supported by a rest. The average size of the ball was about 1 inch in diameter. They gradually decreased in size and by 1690 the average musket was about 5 feet in length. From about 1700 onward the name "musket" was used to identify any type of firearm shot from the shoulder.

Carbines were introduced by the English during the second half of the sixteenth century. Similar in appearance to a musket, they were much smaller and fired a lead ball less than an ounce in weight.

Pistols were first used in England in 1521, and in most other European countries soon afterward. Actually, they were a smaller version of the harquebus; lighter and easier to handle, primarily invented for use by men on horseback who could use only one hand. By the middle of the sixteenth century they were standard equipment for all officers aboard ships.

The firing mechanisms on the muskets, carbines, and pistols changed at the same time as those of the harquebuses.

Full suits of armor were not used aboard ships during the period covered in this book. However, armored breast plates and helmets were used until the end of the sixteenth century. Other primitive weapons still in use were boarding axes, pikes, lances, and shields.

Swords, daggers, rapiers, and poniards were worn by all officers and wealthy passengers on ships, and many of these weapons have been discovered on shipwrecks. Cutlasses were used by the seamen and marines during battles from about the middle of the sixteenth century onward.

Bayonets were introduced by the Spaniards in 1580, but not adopted by the French until 1647 and the English until 1690.

Hand grenades were used on ships as early as 1467 and remained in use until the middle of the nineteenth century. They were made in many forms, but were usually round, made of different metals, glass, or ceramic, and were filled with gunpowder. A small hole held a fuse, which was lit before the grenade was thrown.

Establishing the place and date of manufacture of most navigation instruments can be done only by experts, as very few reference books on the subject are available to the average underwater explorer. The navigation instruments used at the time of Columbus consisted of astrolabes and quadrants to establish the ship's latitude; nocturnals to establish the approximate time of night; the compass and dividers to mark off distances on charts. About the middle of the sixteenth century, the cross-staff, or Jacob-staff, came into general use. The sextant was invented simultaneously in 1732 by John Hadley in England and Thomas Godfrey in Philadelphia, but it did not come into general use until about 1750.

Several brass astrolabes and a large number of dividers have been recovered from shipwrecks, but none of the other navigation instruments mentioned above have been discovered on shipwrecks, with the exception of several sextants dating in the nineteenth century. Quadrants and the cross-staves were made of wood and probably have not been found either because they floated away or were devoured by the worms. Nocturnals were made of brass, so it is strange that none have been discovered. The same applies to compasses, as the compass housings were usually made of lead or other nonmagnetic metals.

Glass bottles are very good for establishing the date of a shipwreck, as their shape changed quite often and they can be dated to within ten years of their date of manufacture.

Glass was first discovered by the Phoenicians and the Egyptians, who made many beautiful glass objects. At the time of Columbus' discovery of America, Venice was the only place in Europe manufacturing glassware, specializing in drinking glasses and decanters. Glass factories were founded in Antwerp in 1550 and in London in 1557. Another was founded in Jamestown, Virginia, in 1608, but it went out of business in 1624. One was started in Salem, Massachusetts, in 1632, making bottles to transport rum and cider to the West Indies and England. The next glassworks to open was in Brussels in 1662, and soon after others were founded in Spain, France, Holland, and Germany.

Glass bottles that contained any type of liquor are generally called "wine bottles." The first ones manufactured were those in Salem, Massachusetts, in 1632. The exact date they were being manufactured elsewhere is not known, but it is believed that they were being made in England around 1650. Other European nations were not manufacturing wine bottles until well after 1700. At least 95 percent of all wine bottles discovered on seventeenth- and eighteenth-century shipwrecks will be of English manufacture, as the English produced them on a large scale and exported them all over Europe. Wine bottles manufactured in Holland are very similar in appearance to those of the English, but those made in other European countries have their own distinct characteristics, so nationality can be established.

Some bottles bear the dates of manufacture and others bear identification seals of the persons for whom they were made, such as the owner of a tavern. Bottles were sealed with cork until near the end of the seventeenth century, when brass wire was used to hold the corks in place. Late in the eighteenth century, copper wire came into general use to hold them in place.

All bottles were blown by hand until the second decade of the nineteenth century, when they began to be manufactured in molds. Thus any bottle discovered with mold marks or with the maker's or owner's name molded on it must date later than 1810.

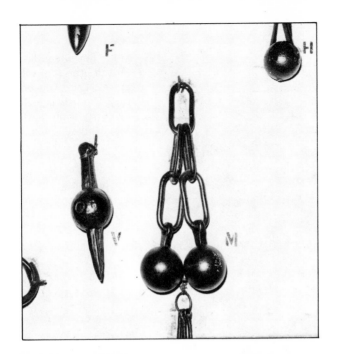

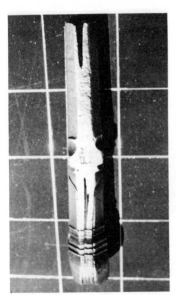

TOP: Different types of cannon shot found on shipwrecks (Tower of London).
BELOW LEFT: Seventeenth-century Spanish brass dividers for navigation.
BELOW RIGHT: Sea astrolabe, probably Spanish (National Maritime Museum).

LEFT: Seventeenth-century Dutch glass gin bottle. BELOW: Late eighteenth-century English rum bottles. OPPOSITE: Evolving shapes of wine bottles.

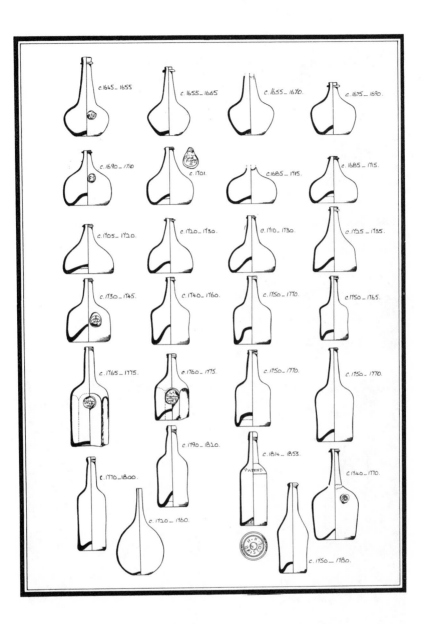

c. 1645 — 1655.

c. 1655 — 1665.

c. 1655 — 1670.

c. 1675 — 1690.

c. 1690 — 1710.

c. 1701.

c. 1685 — 1715.

c. 1685 — 1715.

c. 1705 — 1720.

c. 1720 — 1730.

c. 1710 — 1730.

c. 1725 — 1735.

c. 1730 — 1745.

c. 1740 — 1760.

c. 1750 — 1770.

c. 1750 — 1765.

c. 1765 — 1775.

c. 1760 — 1775.

c. 1750 — 1770.

c. 1750 — 1770.

c. 1770 — 1800.

c. 1790 — 1810.

c. 1814 — 1853.

PATENT

c. 1740 — 1770.

c. 1720 — 1760.

c. 1450 — 1780.

LEFT: Man's face on bowl of clay smoking pipe. BELOW: Maker's initials on two clay smoking pipes. OPPOSITE: Evolving shapes of clay smoking pipes.

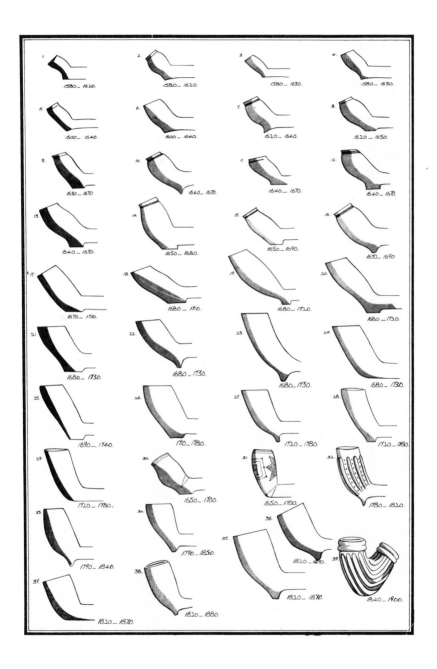

LEFT: Spanish olive jar, ca. 1571. OPPOSITE: Evolving shapes of Spanish olive jars. BELOW: Bellarmine stoneware bottles and jugs. Top row: 1650–1700, 1650–1700, 1700–1750 (Fulham), 1650–1700. Middle row: 1620–1640, 1580–1600, 1600–1620, 1650–1700. Bottom row: 1570–1600, 1570–1600, 1600–1620.

spanish Olive Jars.

C.1500 - 1580.

C.1580 - 1780

C 1780 - 1850

LEFT: Maker's touch plate on the back of a pewter plate: "Alex. Cleaves." BELOW: Hallmarks on the back of a silver plate.

There are various books available to identify and date drinking glasses, but I suggest sending photographs and measurements of any glasses discovered on a shipwreck to the Corning Glass Museum. Glass plate for windows and mirrors was first made in England in 1673.

White clay smoking pipes are also very valuable for establishing the date, but not for establishing the possible nationality of a shipwreck, as almost all of them were manufactured either in England or Holland and were exported all over Europe. Most clay pipes can be dated to within ten years of their date of manufacture, with the exception of a few that were manufactured in Virginia and Jamaica. Unlike many other items discovered on shipwrecks, the lifespan of a clay pipe was short, so those located on a wreck will date very close to the time when the ship was lost. The short lifespan was due to the fact that pipes were quite fragile and broke easily. They were very inexpensive to purchase and as expendable as cigarettes are today.

The use of tobacco was unknown in Europe until after the discovery of the New World. Columbus and his men saw Indians on various Caribbean islands smoking cigars, and later explorers in North America saw Indians smoking tobacco from clay pipes. Although the Spaniards started cultivating and exporting tobacco to Spain from her New World colonies about the end of the sixteenth century, the use of tobacco in Spain was prohibited by the Church until the beginning of the nineteenth century. Most of the tobacco imported into Spain was sold to England and Holland.

On his voyage to the West Indies in 1565, John Hawkins gathered a large amount of tobacco and introduced it to England upon his return. The first mention of the manufacture of clay pipes in England occurred in 1573, and by the end of the sixteenth century the use of tobacco and clay pipes was widespread both in England and Holland. By 1619 there were so many manufacturers of clay pipes in England that they incorporated into a guild, with the Dutch doing the same in 1660. Clay pipes were first made in Denmark in 1655 and in Switzerland in 1697, but very little is known concerning the dates when they were first manufactured in the other European nations. It is believed—but not certain—that small numbers were being manufactured in Virginia and Jamaica in the late seventeenth century, but it wasn't until about the beginning of the nineteenth century that the United States first manufactured clay pipes on a massive scale.

There are many distinctive features about clay pipes that aid in dating them. When smoking first came into vogue in England and Holland the cost of tobacco was very expensive, as all of the tobacco used was purchased from the Spaniards, so consequently the size of the pipe bowls was small. After the English began cultivating tobacco in the New World and exporting it to England, the cost became progressively less and the size of the pipe bowls progressively increased; and with the increase the shapes of the bowls changed. Thus pipe bowls can be dated to within ten or twenty years by their shapes. Prior to my excavation of the sunken city of Port Royal it was believed that clay pipes could be dated by the diameters of the bore of their stem. The theory was based on the assumption that as the pipe bowls grew larger the diameter of the bore became smaller. At Port Royal I discovered a total of 7,133 pipes with intact bowls and over 5,000 with semi-intact bowls. From a very thorough examination of these clay pipes, ranging in dates from 1650 to 1850, I found that this theory was baseless and should never be used in trying to establish a date on a pipe.

A large majority of the pipes manufactured in England were marked with either the initials or full name of the manufacturer. Records exist in England listing 3,400 pipe-makers from 1600 onward. Several good reference books on the subject are available to enable a salvor to identify the maker, place of manufacture, and date range of any particular pipe. These marks can be found on the bowls, heels, spurs, or stems of the pipes.

Decorated pipes were made as early as 1600, with the earliest having patterns of the fleur-de-lis or rosettes etched on them. Later types contained oak leaves, a bowl or bunch of grapes, flowers, anchors, and many other designs. From the end of the eighteenth century to the middle of the nineteenth century, decorations on pipes became much more elaborate, with some being adorned with busts of the British monarchs and fancy coats-of-arms.

Practically nothing is known about the markings on the pipes made in other European nations until well into the nineteenth century. The same applies to the red clay pipes believed to have been made in Virginia or Jamaica.

The discovery of large numbers of pipes on a shipwreck usually identifies it as being English or Dutch, but small numbers have been discovered on a few Spanish shipwrecks. The use of snuff came into general use around 1700, so the discovery of snuffboxes on a wreck would date it after 1700. Tobacco stoppers, generally made of brass or pewter, are first mentioned as being used in 1640, and many contain distinctive markings that can be used to establish a date or place of manufacture.

Items made of gold, silver, or pewter are usually easy to identify and date. At Port Royal, for example, I found tankards, spoons, knives, etc., and with only a few exceptions I was able not only to identify the place and date of manufacture but in many cases the names of the actual owners of the items. Some of the items contained the full name of the owner, but the majority were only stamped with the owner's initials. From historical records in the Jamaican archives I was able to match these initials with the names of their owners, enabling me to determine the identity of the owners of the buildings I was excavating. I have also been able to do this with items recovered from various shipwrecks by matching the names or initials on items recovered with passenger or crew lists of the ship.

There has been a great deal published on these items to enable a salvor to establish a precise date and place of manufacture. The majority contain hallmarks and touchmarks that can be identified, and those that do not can be identified by their shape or form.

The English had a virtual monopoly on the manufacture of these items; more than 95 percent of those found on shipwrecks are of English manufacture, with the exception of jewelry. A small quantity of silver items—mainly spoons, forks, plates, and cups of Spanish and French manufacture—have been found on various shipwrecks, and all contained sufficient markings to identify and date them. However, even on most Spanish wrecks, the vast majority of items of this type were made by the English. On the *Matanceros* shipwreck, over a hundred pewterware and silverware articles were found, all—with the exception of one fork of Spanish make—of English manufacture.

All items made of gold, silver, or pewter discovered on shipwrecks of all dates were used throughout the period covered in this book, with the exception of snuffboxes and forks. Large serving forks were in use as early as 1300, but the use of small forks to transfer food from the plate to the mouth is not mentioned until the latter part of the sixteenth century, when they came into general use for the upper class. Their use did not catch on with the lower class until the end of the seventeenth century. The cutlery used by the lower classes until late in the eighteenth century was usually made of iron or brass.

Only the very rich could afford articles of gold or silver, so only small quantities of such items will be found on shipwrecks. Items made of pewter were used by the vast majority of the upper and middle classes. Pewterware was first used by the Romans and has remained in continual use until the present time.

There are different types of markings on all pewterware, and they can all be identified. The touchmark on all pieces identifies the manufacturer. After being admitted to the Pewterers Guild each pewter-maker was given permission to strike a mark of his own choice—from 1 to 2 inches in height—on all pieces he made to identify their maker. The touchmarks of over six thousand English pewter-makers are recorded and have been published in various reference books. The majority consist of some type of design—flower, animal, crown—with the maker's name or initials around it. On many, even the place of manufacture is mentioned. The crowned Tudor rose mark signifies that the item was manufactured in London; the letter X with a crown above it denotes items made of extraordinary quality. In addition, many items were stamped with their place and date of manufacture.

Many articles of pewterware contained hallmarks similar to those used on gold or silverware. These marks were not authorized for use by the Pewterers Guild, however, and were illegally struck by the pewter-makers. They were struck in the shapes of shields or cartouches, averaged about three-eighths of an inch in height, and were aligned in a straight row, unlike the marks mentioned above. The first hallmark denoted the place of manufacture. The crowned leopard's head was the mark of the London manufacturers; the anchor for those in Birmingham; and a plain crown for those in Sheffield. The second mark consisted of a letter of the alphabet and denoted the year of manufacture. Every twenty-seven years they would start the alphabet all over again. The third hallmark denotes that the piece was made of good quality. In England the lion was used; and elsewhere in the British Isles other devices, such as the thistle in Edinburgh. The fourth hallmark denoted the identity of the maker and usually consisted of his initials.

Gold and silverware used the same kinds of hallmarks described above in addition to other distinctive marks that can easily be identified. American-made silverware of the seventeenth and eighteenth centuries contained only the maker's mark; thus these pieces can only be dated as being made sometime during the lifespan of the known craftsman.

Silver plating on copper items was first done in 1743, but not on a large scale until 1833, when electroplating was invented.

Large amounts of porcelain have been found on many different ship-wrecks and most pieces can be identified and dated fairly accurately. The distinguishing feature of porcelain is that it is translucent, as opposed to pottery, which is opaque. All porcelain found on a six-teenth-century shipwreck, and the majority found on shipwrecks of the seventeenth century, is of Chinese or Japanese manufacture. All these pieces bear marks of the province in which they were made, in addition to the name of the reigning ruler of the country at that time.

The first exact date or place of manufacture of porcelain in Europe is not known, but it is believed to have been in Florence around the close of the sixteenth century and was done on a small scale and not for export. The English first began producing small amounts of porcelain about 1745, the Dutch a few years later. Most of these pieces bear manufacturers' marks, making it possible to establish the date and place of manufacture. Most of the other European nations and the United States did not begin manufacturing porcelain until the nineteenth century. Identification of unmarked porcelain should only be attempted by experts, but approximate dates and places of manufacture can be obtained by amateurs using various references.

The most common type of pottery discovered on shipwrecks is utilityware, which consists of a coarse hard paste, usually red but sometimes gray or brown. Only small amounts of utilityware were glazed, generally green. This was the pottery used by the lower classes, so it was rarely decorated or had any other distinctive feature that would facilitate identifying its place or date of manu-facture. Approximate dates can be fixed by the shapes of various vessels of this type, provided the vessel is found intact or enough pieces are found to establish its original shape.

On all Spanish ships, and on many of other nations, a type of vessel resembling the amphoras used by the Greeks and Romans was used to carry liquids and other things. These vessels, known as Spanish "olive jars," were manufactured in Seville and the surrounding countryside and exported all over Europe and the New World. An approximate date can be obtained from the shape of the vessel and by the maker's mark found on some of them. They were made of utilityware, usually of a gray exterior, and ranged in size from 2 to 6 gallons in capacity.

Another type of large vessel that can be dated fairly accurately was the bellarmine jug. These were manufactured in Germany of a type of ceramic called stoneware. The clay used had flint in its composition, fired at much greater temperatures than utilityware, and coated with a salt-glaze that give it a distinctive whitish-gray interior and brownish exterior. Most of the necks of the jugs were decorated with a human face and some have armorial medallions on the bodies. These jugs range in size from 1-pint to 5-gallon capacity.

Another commonly used type of pottery is known as delftware. It was called that by the English, Dutch, and most other northern European countries, but in France and Italy it was called faience and in Spain and its New World possessions majolica. Widely manufactured in every country and used mainly by the upper and middle classes, it was generally made of the same clay as utilityware but was coated with a glaze of tin oxide, which appeared white in color after firing. The surface of the glaze was then decorated in a wide range of colors and designs.

Most of the pieces manufactured in Europe, and some of the later pieces made in the New World, have distinctive makers' marks on them, which can be used to establish the date and place of origin. Experts should be consulted to date all unmarked pieces.

Coins can generally be used to date a shipwreck within a few years of its loss, especially when large numbers of coins bearing the same dates or dates that span a short period of time are discovered. However, coins have been found that were more than a hundred years older than the shipwreck itself. Remember that a shipwreck must date from the same year, or later, than the latest dated coin found on it. Due to the fact that probably 99 percent of all coinage carried on any shipwreck dating prior to 1825 in the waters of the Western Hemisphere will be of Spanish-American colonial mintage, I shall describe only these coins and the means by which they can be dated.

Very little is known about the earliest coins minted in the New World. Several documents mention that private persons minted their own issues of gold and silver coins in Mexico City as early as 1528, but nothing is known concerning their descriptions or how long this practice continued. In 1535 a mint was established in Santo Domingo, where copper maravedi coins were first minted. Practically nothing is known about this coin, except that it was also minted at Mexico City and Panama City, among other places, and was used until the beginning of the nineteenth century. Very few were stamped with distinctive markings such as dates, mint marks, or assayers' initials. Some, dating from the second half of the sixteenth century and minted in Santo Domingo, had an anchor on one side and a fort on the other. Others, minted there in 1636, had a fort on one side and two ships on the other. Occasionally, maravedi coins minted in Spain and bearing dates and other marks have been discovered on shipwrecks. The known denominations of these coins were 8, 4, and 2 maravedis, but they may have been minted in other denominations as well. Their actual buying value was small and they were basically used as small change in the New World. A silver one-real coin was worth 34 maravedis and an eight-real coin, or piece of eight, was worth 272 maravedis.

Silver coins were first officially minted at Mexico City in 1536, at Lima in 1568, at Potosí in 1572, at Bogotá in 1622, at Guatemala City in 1733, and at Santiago (Chile) in 1751. It is believed that they were also minted at Cartagena and Panama City for short periods at various times during the seventeenth century. The basic silver coin was the eight-real piece, which weighed an ounce. The other real denominations were the 4, 2, 1, ½ and ¼ coins, which were smaller in size and weight.

Gold coins were first officially minted at Cartagena in 1615, at Bogotá in 1635, at Mexico City in 1679, and at Lima and Potosí about 1697. They were also minted for a six-month period during the year 1698 and again after 1750 at Cuzco, Peru. The gold coins are of the same size and weight as the silver and are in denominations of 8, 4, 2, 1, and ½ escudos.

Although the screw press was used to mint round milled coins in England as early as 1610, it was not used in Spanish America until 1732, when the first round milled coins were made at the Mexico City mint. The Lima mint did not produce round milled coins until 1752, and the other mints at even later dates.

Prior to 1732 almost all gold and silver coins minted in the New World were not round in shape but of many irregular patterns. There were some exceptions: The silver coins minted in Mexico City during the first twenty or thirty years of operation were almost perfectly round, and over the years all the mints made small numbers of perfectly round gold and silver coins. The round gold coins are known as royals and are quite rare. It is believed that each mint made several royals each year and sent them to the King to show that they were capable of producing good coinage.

The irregular-shaped gold and silver coins were called cobs, a name probably derived from *cabo de barra*, which means "end of a bar." The method for making these coins was as follows: The molten metal was poured out on a flat surface in long, thin strips. When the metal cooled, pieces of the approximate size and weight of the desired coin were cut from the strip, then trimmed to their proper weight. The planchet was then placed between two dies and struck with a heavy hammer. Since one or both sides of the coin were not perfectly flat, the dies only marked the highest surfaces of these sides. This resulted in the majority of the cob coinage not having full die marks. Also, because such large quantities of coins were minted each year, care was not always exercised in marking them, so many only bear die marks on various sections of their surfaces. The coins made at the Mexico City mint during the seventeenth and eighteenth centuries are poor in quality, show faulty die marks, and are the most difficult to date. Of the coins recovered from the 1715 shipwrecks—with at least 95 percent from the Mexico City mint—only 15 percent of the gold coins and less than 1 percent of the silver coins show dates. Other mints appeared to have exercised better workmanship, as larger amounts of both their gold and silver coins are found with fuller die marks in addition to bearing dates. At Port Royal I recovered about 2,500 silver coins from the Potosí and Lima mints dated from 1658 to 1690, and 98 percent of these coins had dates on them.

There are numerous books that can be used to date Spanish-American colonial coins; also, in most large cities there are numismatists who can be consulted. When dates are not visible on the coins, there are other means by which they can be dated fairly accurately. The majority of the coins had the shield or coat-of-arms of the monarch on the obverse side, so the coin can be dated to the period in which the king reigned. From 1772 to 1825, the end of Spanish rule in America, both the gold and silver coins carried the portrait of the Spanish King. All coins were also marked with the initials of the assayer and cover the period in which a particular assayer was in charge of a mint. On small numbers of coins the reigning monarch's name or initials were also marked.

The place in which a coin was minted can be determined from the mint marks on each coin. The letter *L* for Lima, *P* for Potosí, *M* for Mexico City, *C* for Cartagena, *G* for Guatemala, *S* for Santiago, and *NR* for Bogotá. When the mint marks are not visible on the coin, the place where it was minted can be identified by its die markings. Almost all of the Mexico City coins had a Jerusalem cross—a square cross with balls on all four ends—on the reverse side, as did some of the Bogotá- and Cartagena-minted coins. The Lima- and Potosí-minted coins had a plain cross with the arms of Castile and León on their reverse sides. If only a small amount of the die is visible, the place in which it was minted can generally be established.

TOP LEFT: Spanish gold coin of 1732. TOP RIGHT: Dutch coin, early seventeenth century. BOTTOM: Gold and silver coins from a 1715 shipwreck.

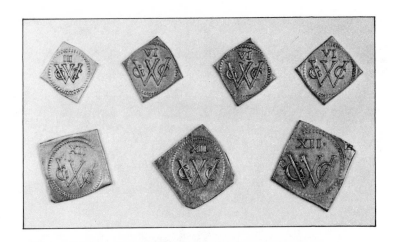

TOP: Dutch gold coins found by the author on a wreck in Brazil. BOTTOM: Large iron chests such as this were used to transport the most valued treasure aboard the galleons.

Platinum was probably discovered at an early date in the New World, but the first mention of its use in coinage was in 1757, when it was illegally used in both gold and silver coins in Lima. When this fact was discovered the assayer of the mint was beheaded and its further use strictly forbidden, but it might have been used both before and after this date. It was not considered a precious metal until late in the nineteenth century.

CHAPTER SIX

Preservation of Artifacts

SOME ITEMS that are lost on a shipwreck, such as gold and porcelain, do not in any way suffer from their long underwater immersion and are recovered in a perfect state of preservation. On the other hand, the majority of the items deteriorate in varying degrees, and the purpose of this chapter is to acquaint the salvor with the proper methods of protection after bringing them to the surface, to restore them to their original state when possible, and to preserve them for posterity.

Most organic items, like wood, come under immediate attack from the teredo, fungi, and different bacteria. The more these items are exposed to salt water, the more they suffer and the quicker some of them disappear. Many of the same objects, when buried deep under sediment, will suffer less, or not at all, and on occasion can be discovered in an excellent state of preservation.

Of the various types of metals lost on a shipwreck, iron and silver suffer the most, due to the effects of electrolysis under water. Different types of metal and salt water act as a gigantic galvanic battery. With the salt water forming the electrolyte, metals of two or more different molecular weights become opposite poles and a current of electrons is created between them. The galvanic current following between the different metals will attack them with the highest electrode potential and convert them to one of its compounds. Silver converts to silver sulfide and iron to iron oxide. The metals with the lowest electrode potential are preserved by cathodic protection. The effects of electrolysis on different metals occur when the metals are buried under sediment or are exposed to sea water on the surface of the sea floor.

Items recovered from the sea can be divided into three distinct classes: those recovered in their original condition—like gold—that require no treatment at all, or only a brief immersion in fresh water to remove the salts on their exterior surfaces; those that have suffered marked physical and chemical changes and can be preserved by different methods; and those that have suffered to such a degree that they cannot be restored to their original state. In this case, what remains of the original object can be saved by completely embedding it in plastic. In some cases nothing will remain of the original object other than a hollow form inside a coral-encrusted conglomerate, which can be recorded through X-ray photography or by making a replica of it by using the hollow form as a mold.

Any shipwreck-recovered item that requires preservation should not be exposed to the air for any length of time and must be kept wet, preferably in salt water. But due to the heavy weight of water, it is not always possible to transport it. An item can be wrapped in Saran Wrap or placed in an airtight plastic bag or container. Large items are best transported from the salvage vessel to a preservation laboratory in wooden barrels or boxes containing moist sawdust.

SILICEOUS AND RELATED MATERIALS:

Hard gem stones—sapphires, rubies, emeralds, and agate—do not suffer from immersion in sea water and are recovered in their natural state. Softer gem stones, such as beryl, are sometimes found scratched, due to the abrasive action of sand and other materials moving against them under water, and these scratches should be removed only by lapidary treatment.

Glass is affected in varying degrees, depending on its composition.

Optical glass generally survives in a good state of preservation but is occasionally found pitted on its exterior.

White-lead glass objects, such as plate glass, wine glasses, tumblers, and pharmaceutical vials or medicine bottles, are generally found free of calcareous deposits—though most will be covered with a thin coating of lead oxide and sometimes iron oxide—when discovered in close association with iron objects. To clean and preserve these items the following method should be used: Place the item in a 10-percent solution of nitric acid for the time required to remove the lead oxide. If iron oxide is present, then use a 5-percent solution of sulfuric acid to remove the oxide, then follow through with several thorough washings in distilled water. If, after drying, the item shows signs of flaking on its exterior, it should be coated with several layers of clear plastic spray, such as Krylon.

As a rule, most bottles postdating 1750 require very little preservation, as they are recovered in a good state of preservation. Sediment inside the bottle can be removed with a high-pressure hose or various types of tools, such as a wire or an icepick. The removal of exterior calcareous growth can be done by tapping gently on the bottle with a rubber mallet or by immersion in a bath consisting of 0.2 solution of sulfuric acid for from several hours to as long as a week, depending on the amount of growth on it. It must then be thoroughly washed in several baths of fresh water, or distilled water when available, until the glass is free of alkalis. The litmus-paper test is the best means to determine if the glass is free of alkalis. Upon drying, the surface of some bottles may tend to look dull, or develop a very thin layer of pearly iridescence in spots. No further treatment is necessary, although the iridescence, if especially fragile, may tend to flake off.

The preservation of badly decomposed glass, which is the state of most bottles predating 1750, is a difficult treatment. If the glass is not impregnated in some way, it is very likely that the exterior weathering crust will crumble away when it dries out. This may be a matter of minutes or of some months, depending on the item itself. This was one of the major preservation problems encountered during the Port Royal excavation. In consultation with Dr. Robert Brill of the Corning Glass Museum, I attempted to discover why the wine bottles were recovered in a worse state of preservation than others of the same manufacture and period that were found elsewhere. The weathering crust on those at Port Royal was thicker than on other bottles of the same period, and this made them more difficult to preserve. We theorize that the heavy concentration of bauxite in the harbor sediment was the major cause, as it may have created electrolysis with the lead components in the glass, thus causing the greater amount of deterioration.

Most bottles predating 1750 can be cleaned and preserved in the following manner. The 0.2-percent solution of sulfuric acid will remove the calcareous growth and stains. Depending on the fragility of the bottle, a high-pressure hose or probe can be used to remove the sediment inside the bottle. Then it must be thoroughly rinsed in distilled water until free of all alkalis. Then, without letting the bottle dry completely, it must be bathed in alcohol—either wood, denatured ethyl, or rubbing alcohol—which will tend to remove the remaining water without causing the decomposition crust to crumble away. Then it must be air-dried for a short period, and then impregnated with several coatings of clear spray lacquers.

Through experimentation I discovered that this method did not preserve the more badly decomposed bottles, such as those recovered at Port Royal. After several months the glass began flaking under the lacquer coatings, and in many cases the bottles completely disintegrated. To prevent this, we follow the same procedure as described above, except that instead of coating the bottles with lacquer we immersed them for a week or two in a solution consisting of 50 percent distilled water and 50 percent vinyl acetate, which is the same material used in making the glue used in bookbinding (it is marketed as Padding Cement). After removing the bottle we wiped off the excess solution with a slightly damp cloth, then air-dried it in a cool area. After it was completely dried, we coated it with several layers of lacquer.

For mending or piecing together broken glass or bottles, any number of convenient epoxy cements can be used—and a small amount of cement works better than a large. The most important step in cementing glass is the cleaning of the surfaces to be joined. Caution must be exercised in cementing the glass correctly the first time, because once the cement sets, the bonds are permanent and cannot be loosened.

Different types of ceramics are affected in varying degrees due to immersion in salt water. Porcelain survives the best, although its painted exterior may have eroded away. Due to its nonporous surface it is rarely found with any calcareous marine growth adhering to it. When there is growth on it, however, it can be removed by tapping it lightly with a rubber tool or by bathing it in a 10-percent solution of nitric acid. Iron- or lead-oxide stains can be removed by a bath in a 5-percent solution of sulfuric acid. When calcareous deposits and oxides stains are on porcelain, the sulfuric-acid bath will remove both. Thorough washing in fresh water will remove all traces of alkalis from the acids.

Glazed pottery, being covered with a waterproof vitreous layer, survives much better than unglazed pottery. If, however, the glazed layer is incomplete or imperfect, soluble salts may get into the body of the ware and crystallize, forming efflorescence, and cause the glaze to flake off. If the glazed layer on the piece is intact, the methods used on porcelain to remove calcareous deposits and oxide stains can be used. If the glaze is not intact, or is flaking—which occurs on a great deal of the delftware items recovered—no acid of any kind should be used to remove the deposits or stains. The pieces should be thoroughly bathed in fresh water to remove the sea salts, then air-dried and coated with several layers of clear plastic or lacquer spray.

No acid of any type should be used on unglazed porous pottery, such as utilityware or olive-jar pottery. Removal of calcareous deposits must be done with small tools, then the pieces should be bathed for several days in several baths of fresh water to remove the sea salts. To assure that these pieces are free of water they must be dehydrated in several baths of alcohol and then coated with plastic spray. This treatment should be used only on ceramic objects that show signs of crumbling. Approximately 95 percent of ceramic pieces will require no treatment other than the freshwater baths to remove sea salts.

Nature handles the removal of calcareous deposits on clay smoking pipes. After their recovery they should be air-dried. When this is completed the pipe actually decreases slightly in size and this causes the calcareous deposits to fall off on their own. The removal of various stains on the pipes is best accomplished by washing with a mild detergent and soft brush.

Repairing or piecing together all types of ceramics is relatively simple. The joints must be first cleaned of any foreign bodies and then cemented together with Durofix or Elmer's Glue. While the glue is drying the pieces should be held in place by tape or placed in a sandbox.

ORGANIC MATERIALS:

All organic material recovered from salt water must be bathed in fresh water from two to four weeks, depending on its size, to remove all sea salts before preservation treatment can be attempted. If possible, the bath should consist of running fresh water, which will carry away the sea salts as they are leached from the items. Large items, like wooden ship's timbers, can be placed in a freshwater stream or river, provided the water is not contaminated by industrial waste. If a running-water bath cannot be provided, the bathwater should be changed at least daily.

Such organic materials as sisal or hemp fibers, beans and pods, tortoise shell, hair, textiles, leather, horn, bone, or paper will generally totally disintegrate upon drying if the proper preservation treatment is not exercised. Sometimes organic materials—such as wood or bone —are completely preserved by being saturated by iron oxide while lying close to iron objects under water, as they tend to become mineralized and hard in texture.

To preserve organic animal materials they must first be thoroughly dehydrated in successive baths of alcohol to remove all water. The first bath should consist of 40 percent alcohol and 60 percent water, the second of 60 percent alcohol and 40 percent water, and the third of 100 percent alcohol. The length of each bath depends on the size of the object—say, an hour for a small fragment of leather and several hours for a bone object weighing several pounds. Then the object must be placed in two successive baths of xylene, the first for a week and the second for four weeks. In the second bath, paraffin chips should be added until a saturated solution of paraffin is obtained. After the object is removed from the second bath and allowed to solidify by air-drying, a small amount of paraffin crystals may remain on the exterior of the object. They can be removed by heating the object in an oven until the excess crystals melt off or by brushing the object with a fine-bristle brush.

Very fragile organic animal materials—which might suffer by preserving them by the above method—such as small objects of ivory or horn, can best be preserved by embedding them in clear plastic blocks after they have been dehydrated.

Organic vegetable materials—such as wood, sisal and hemp fibers, textiles, paper, and beans and pods—can also be preserved by the method described above for the organic animal materials, but there are several other methods that can be used. The alum and glycerine process has been used with good results, especially on wood, because the alum crystallizes and replaces the water in the wood, preventing it from shrinking or losing its original shape. After all foreign matter has been removed from the object, it is immersed in a boiling bath solution containing equal parts, by weight, of alum, glycerine, and water. As soon as the object is placed in the bath it is taken away from its heat source and allowed to cool slowly. The object should remain in the bath from one to two days, depending on its size. After the object has hardened and air-dried, it should be coated with a solution of 50 percent turpentine and 50 percent linseed oil. The polyethylene glycol process has also proven to be quite successful. The great advantage in using this process is the elimination of dehydrating the object before it is immersed in its chemical bath. The preservatives are sold commercially under the trade names of Polywax and Carbowax. Polyethylene glycol is a polymer formed by the condensation of ethylene glycol into a waxlike water-soluble preservative. The length of time that the object must remain in the chemical bath varies from four hours to several weeks, depending on the type of Polywax or Carbowax used and the size of the object.

INORGANIC MATERIALS:

Approximately 95 percent of all metal objects discovered on a shipwreck consist of iron, which provides some of the most difficult problems for preservation, due to its highly corrosive nature. In many cases cast-iron objects corrode into a crystalline form and are so totally destroyed that only powdered oxide remains. Wrought-iron objects are not as corrosive, probably because they contain a greater nickel content. The same applies to steel, which has a high nickel content. The amount of metal remaining in the object can best be determined by its weight or by application of a magnet. If the object has no magnetic attraction, it is evident that it is completely oxided. When laboratory facilities are available, this can also be determined by the use of X-ray photography or a fluoroscope.

The first step in the treatment of ferrous metals—iron or steel—is the removal of the exterior calcareous encrustations, and this can only be attempted when a substantial amount of the orginal metal remains

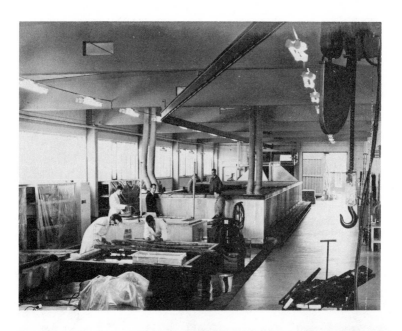

TOP: Wood and textile preservation hall of the *Vasa* recovery project, Stockholm (Maritime Museum and the Warship Wasa). BOTTOM: Sixteenth-century Spanish cannon being preserved.

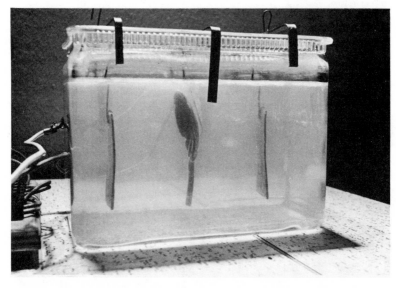

TOP: Two coins, one as it came from the sea, the other after cleaning in an electrolytic reduction bath. BOTTOM: Spoon in an electrolytic reduction bath.

in the object. These deposits can best be removed on large objects (a cannon) by tapping gently with a hammer or other hand tool. Small, delicate objects can be cleaned in ultrasonic electrical baths or chemically. Ultrasonic baths range in price from one hundred dollars upward and are easy to operate. The chemical process consists of a bath in a solution of 10 percent nitric acid and 90 percent water, with several washes in fresh water to remove the alkalis. Then the object must be treated by electrochemical reduction. It is placed in a bath consisting of 10 percent sodium hydroxide and 90 percent water and soaked for a period of four to eight weeks. The object is then removed and a new bath of the same solution is made, following which the entire object is covered with zinc chips or surrounded by zinc plates. Soon after the zinc is added to the bath the solution will begin to bubble, and this will continue throughout the two to four weeks the object is kept in the bath. Upon removal the object will be covered with a white coating, which can be removed by placing the object in another bath consisting of 5 percent sulfuric acid and 95 percent fresh water.

The next step is placing the object in a running-water bath for at least a week, then in a bath of distilled water for another week. The bath should be tested to make sure that it is free of both alkalis and chlorides. If it is not free of these elements, then more baths in distilled water are required until there are no traces. The object is then dried, preferably in an oven at a high temperature. After drying it can be coated by melted paraffin wax or a clear synthetic plastic or lacquer to seal its exterior and prevent further corrosion.

When little or none remains of the original ferrous metals, they can be treated by one of the following two methods. The object can be embedded in a plastic resin, such as Selectron 5,000. The object must first be thoroughly dehydrated, either by heat or the alcohol process, otherwise it will continue to disintegrate inside the plastic blocks. This can be a lengthy process if the object is large, as only very thin layers of the plastic can be placed in the mold containing the object.

An exact replica of the object can be made of plaster of Paris or other materials. By X-raying the object, its size and location in the encrusted conglomerate can be determined, then the conglomerate must be cut in half by a diamond saw. The two halves will be hollow inside where the original object was and will serve as the mold into which the plaster of Paris is placed to make the replica. Another method is to drill a hole into the conglomerate and force the plaster-of-Paris compound into the cavity of the conglomerate. After hardening, the exterior encrustation can be removed by grinding or hand tools.

Nonferrous metals are always recovered in a far better state of preservation than the ferrous and are usually easier to clean and preserve. Some of the metals are recovered in such condition that they require no treatment other than cleaning with fine steel wool and water.

Gold is almost always recovered as bright and shiny as the day it was minted and requires no preservation treatment. Occasionally it will be found tarnished, due to close underwater association with other metals, and this can best be removed by soaking it in a bath of 10 percent nitric acid and 90 percent water. The same bath should be used to remove any calcareous deposits on gold.

Silver is affected in varying degrees under water, depending on conditions. A silver coin lying on the sea floor and not protected by electrolysis from other metals—even other silver coins—may be converted to silver sulfide, and nothing can be done to preserve it, other than casting it in plastic. When this occurs to a silver coin, or other small silver object, it will weigh as little as one-fifth of its original weight and may be two or three times its original thickness. Caution must be exercised in handling silver in this fragile condition, as it will easily disintegrate into powder forms.

When silver has been protected by electrolysis it will survive intact, sometimes with only a superficial amount of corrosion, which can be removed by different methods. This can be accomplished by the electrochemical bath, as used for preserving the ferrous metals.

Another method is the electrolytic reduction process. The semi-corroded silver object is made the negative electrode (cathode) and is placed between two plates of sheet iron (acting as the positive electrode, or anode) in a glass or plastic container filled with water and a 5-percent amount of caustic soda, which acts as the electrolyte. Electrical current, generally from a 6- or 12-volt battery, is also required. The object is connected by copper wire to the negative pole of the battery, and the iron anodes are connected to the positive pole through an ammeter and adjustable resistance unit. When current passes into the bath, hydrogen is evolved at the cathode, with the result that the corrosion is gradually reduced. As the reduction progresses, chlorides are transferred from the cathode to the iron anode. The length of the process depends on the amount of corrosion on the object. The object should be removed and inspected periodically until all corrosion has been removed. When this has been completed, there will be a smaller layer of insoluble oxides and metallic powder on the object.

These can be removed by brushing under running water. Then the silver object should be rubbed with a paste of water and baking soda.

On some occasions—such as when large amounts of silver coins or items are found together—the majority will be in a very good state of preservation and require only cleaning by the paste method to remove the black silver-sulfide patina on them.

Pewter is generally found in a good state of preservation. Of the pewter recovered from the sunken city of Port Royal, about 20 percent required very little treatment. Rubbing it with a soft cloth in water and a mild detergent removed a thin black film from its surface and its luster was restored by the paste treatment. The remaining 80 percent was recovered with only a small amount of external corrosion and occasionally with small amounts of calcareous deposits. Both were removed by immersion in a bath consisting of a solution of 20 percent hydrochloric acid and 80 percent fresh water followed by thorough washings in running fresh water, generally for a period of several hours. Then the surface was rubbed gently with fine steel wool to remove the black patina and again placed in a bath of running water for several hours. The same paste treatment is used to restore its original luster.

On some sites, pewter is occasionally found badly corroded, and in some cases the only means of preservation is embedding it in plastic. Badly corroded pewter can be cleaned and preserved as follows. A lye bath is prepared by dissolving a pint of lye in 2 gallons of fresh boiling water. When the object is placed in the bath it is taken off its heat source and allowed to cool. Generally, a period of ten to thirty minutes is required to remove the corrosion. Caution must be observed to prevent the lye solution from contact with your skin or eyes. Then the same procedure is carried out as on the pewter objects cleaned by the hydrochloric-acid process. If the object is bent out of its original shape, the best time to restore it—usually done with a rubber mallet—is when it is taken out of the lye bath, as the metal will be warm and easily shaped.

Lead objects suffer very little in the sea other than obtaining a thin coating of lead oxide on their surfaces, which is easily removed in a bath of 10 percent acetic acid and 90 percent fresh water followed by a running-water bath for several hours. Due to the softness of this metal, many pieces are bent and lose their original shape on shipwrecks.

Copper, brass, and bronze objects are also little affected by salt-water immersion. Calcareous deposits on large objects can be removed by tapping with a rubber mallet and on smaller objects by immersion in a bath consisting of 10 percent nitric acid and 90 percent fresh water followed by a washing for a short time in running water. The acid bath is used to remove the green patina found on these objects, but this can also be accomplished with the use of steel wool.

Objects made entirely of magnesium, tin, aluminum, zinc, or nickel will not be discovered on a shipwreck predating 1825, so their preservation will not be discussed here.

At the time of writing this chapter, a chemical firm, Zurcon, Inc., of Zieglersville, Pennsylvania, announced publicly that it had developed a process to clean and preserve every type of item, both organic and inorganic, which are discovered on shipwrecks. The inventor of this revolutionary process, Norman B. Larson, plans to keep it a secret for as long as possible, as his firm intends large-scale preservation for profit. I have seen many different types of objects—from iron cannon to small bits of wood—which were treated by his process, and all of them appear to be in a much better state of preservation than that obtainable by any of the other methods described in this chapter. My hope is that he reveals his process publicly, which will make most, maybe all, of the known processes obsolete and will result in the better preservation of all objects recovered from shipwrecks.

PART TWO

Artifacts from a Spanish merchant ship lost in 1741.

CHAPTER ONE

Canada

BAD WEATHER, rough seas, and ice-cold water most of the year make Canada one of the least attractive areas in the Western Hemisphere for underwater explorations and salvage work. For these reasons, very little has been accomplished on old shipwrecks in Canadian waters. In fact, most of the Canadian divers who are interested in old shipwrecks head south to Bermuda or the Bahamas for their serious diving.

During the summer months of the past six years, amateur divers under the supervision of archaeologists from the Toronto Museum and the National Historical Park Service have been employed to locate and salvage several small vessels that were sunk in lakes and rivers during the French and Indian Wars.

The only major salvage operation in Canadian waters occurred during the summers of 1965 and 1966, when three amateur divers located the eighteenth-century French warship *Le Chameau*, off Nova Scotia. They found the site by dragging a grappling hook in the general vicinity in which the ship was known to have been lost, and when something was snagged a diver was sent down to inspect the object. Actually, the shipwreck was first located in 1914, when a helmet diver surveying a modern shipwreck spotted a large number of gold and silver coins on the sea floor. He hoped to recover the treasure as soon as his work on the modern shipwreck was accomplished, but he drowned a few days later and the secret of its location was lost with him. The three divers—Alex Storm, David MacEachern, and Harvey MacLeod—worked under very difficult conditions. The water temperature was never higher than 45 degrees, and due to high tides there were always currents of several knots around their site. During the two summers, however, they discovered over two thousand French louis d'or (gold coins) and eleven thousand French livres (silver coins), as well as a silver pocketwatch, silver and pewter cutlery, weapons of different types, a vast number of cannonballs, cannon, ceramics, and many other artifacts.

When they had begun their work on this wreck there were no laws concerning the recovery of sunken treasure, but soon after they brought up their first finds the Canadian government ordered them to turn all of it over to its officials while the matter was investigated, which prevented them from selling anything to raise more capital to carry on their work. A court battle ensued over the legal ownership of the treasure and artifacts until 1968 when the courts finally decided that the Canadian government should retain only 10 percent of the find and return the rest to the salvors. The cargo manifest of the ship stated that she was carrying over 300,000 livres, so the trio still has a great deal of work left to complete the job. The Canadian government has since passed a law stating that no work on any ancient shipwreck can be undertaken without permission from the National Historical Park Service and that a competent archaeologist must supervise all of the salvage operations.

One of the greatest concentrations of shipwrecks in Canadian waters is on Sable Island, located 150 miles off the coast of Nova Scotia. Due to its strategic location so far from the mainland and because several different ocean currents flow toward the island, over five hundred ships have been wrecked on this island from the earliest time up to the present. Although more than 90 percent of these wrecks are dated after 1825, many of them carried various amounts of treasure as well as interesting cargoes. However, working conditions in these waters are extremely difficult and shifting sands have tended to cover most of the shipwrecks very soon after they wrecked.

List of Shipwrecks in Canadian Waters

1. **Year, sometime before 1583.** English warship *Delight*, in the fleet of Admiral Sir Humphrey Gilbert, sank on a shoal near Sable Island, off Nova Scotia.

2. **Year 1710.** In late August, a fleet of New Englanders set out to capture Port Royal, a port in eastern Canada, but one of the troop-transport ships from Rhode Island, the sloop *Caesar*, Captain Jeremiah Tay (or Taye), ran ashore on Digby Cut in the Bay of Fundy and twenty-six men aboard her were lost.

3. **Year 1725.** The French frigate of war *Le Chameau* sailed from Louisburg, a French stronghold on the eastern tip of Cape Breton Island, Nova Scotia, heading for Quebec carrying a valuable treasure of gold and silver as well as a large number of passengers. As the ship was rounding Cape Lorenbec, Nova Scotia, a squall struck and the ship capsized and sank with almost a complete loss of her crew and passengers. Many of the bodies washed ashore, but nothing of the wreck was ever found until recent times.

4. **Year 1748.** During a very violent gust of wind on February 26 nearly every French merchant and warship in the harbor of Louisburg, Cape Breton Island, Nova Scotia, was sunk.

5. **Year 1752.** During a hurricane that struck Louisburg Harbor on October 1, over fifty merchant and warships were driven ashore or sunk.

6. **Year 1752.** English merchantman *Elizabeth*, Captain Carter, coming from Poole, England, was lost in the harbor of Fogo, in Newfoundland.

7. **Year 1753.** During a very bad storm on October 7, over forty large ships were wrecked at Cape Breton Island, Nova Scotia.

8. **Year 1755.** English warship H.M.S. *Mars*, 64 guns, Captain John Amherst, was wrecked at Halifax, Nova Scotia, during June.

9. *Year 1755.* English merchantman *Jersey,* Captain Giffred, coming from Jersey Island, off the coast of France, was wrecked on the coast of Newfoundland.

10. *Year 1757.* During a hurricane on September 24, two English warships were sunk in Louisburg Harbor: H.M.S. *Tilbury,* 60 guns, Captain Henry Barnsley, and H.M.S. *Ferret,* 10 guns, Captain Arthur Upton.

11. *Year 1757.* English merchantman *Buchanan,* Captain Lawrence, sailing from Gibraltar to Maryland, was captured by a French privateer and on her passage to Louisburg was wrecked on Sable Island, Nova Scotia, on April 22.

12. *Year 1758.* The following ships were scuttled by the French in Louisburg Harbor on June 28 because they did not have enough men to man them for an impending attack by the English: *Apollon,* 50 guns; *Fidéle,* 26 guns; *Chérre* and *Biche,* each of 16 guns. While still awaiting the English attack, three of the major French warships were burnt by accident in the same harbor: *Entreprenant,* 74 guns, *Capricieux* and *Célébre,* each of 64 guns. During the English attack, which took place a few weeks later, an English frigate, H.M.S. *Tilbury,* which was the payship for Admiral Edward Boscawen's fleet, was wrecked on a reef near Louisburg.

13. *Year 1759.* Four ships were wrecked in the St. Lawrence River: the English warship H.M.S. *Terrible,* 74 guns; and three French warships: *Le Sinecterre* and *Le Soleil Royal,* each of 24 guns, and *Duc de Fronfac,* 20 guns.

14. *Year 1760.* English merchantman *Cupid,* Captain Trimett, sailing from Newfoundland to the Leeward Islands, was lost returning to St. John's Harbor, Newfoundland, because of bad weather.

15. *Year 1760.* Two English warships were wrecked in the St. Lawrence River: H.M.S. *Lowestoft,* 28 guns, Captain Joseph Deane, on May 17; and H.M.S. *Eurus,* 20 guns, Captain John Elphinstone.

16. *Year 1760.* During an attack by an English fleet commanded by Captain Byron, twenty-five French ships were sunk in Chaleur Bay, in the Gulf of St. Lawrence, on July 8. Twenty-two of the ships were small vessels carrying provisions and stores; the other

three were warships: *Marchault,* 32 guns, *Bienfaisant,* 22 guns, and *Marquis Marloze,* 18 guns.

17. **Year 1761.** Four ships were lost on the St. Lawrence River: the English ship *Success,* Captain Friend, wrecked on the river approaching Quebec, coming from London; English merchantman *General Gage,* Captain Power, wrecked in the river after leaving Quebec for London; English ship *Isaac and William,* Captain Gregory, lost on the Orleans Shoals in the river after leaving Quebec for London, but her cargo was saved; and the French warship *Leopard,* 60 guns, was burnt at Quebec because it arrived with the plague on board.

18. **Year 1762.** English merchantman *Charming Nancy,* Captain Hume, coming from London, sank at Quebec but most of her cargo was recovered.

19. **Year 1762.** English ship *Charming Nancy,* Captain Haynes, sailing from London to Halifax, Nova Scotia, was lost entering this port and nothing was saved from her.

20. **Year 1763.** Two English merchantmen were wrecked in the St. Lawrence River: *Providence,* Captain Pinkham, sailing from Quebec to Ireland and London, the crew and some of her cargo were saved; and the *Good Intent,* Captain Wood, sailing from London to Quebec, most of her cargo was saved.

21. **Year 1763.** English ship *Bonetta,* Captain Feampton, sailing to Poole, England, was lost near St. Mary's in Newfoundland with a total loss of crew and cargo.

22. **Year 1764.** Three English merchantmen were lost in the Gulf of St. Lawrence: *Lord Elbank,* Captain Warrell, sailing from New York to Quebec, was lost near Gaspe, New Brunswick, but part of her cargo was saved; *Margaret & Harriot,* Captain Cordova, sailing from Plymouth, England, to Quebec, was lost on rocks near the island of Anticosti, one member of the crew drowned and the rest were forced to spend six months in great misery on that deserted island; and the *Greyhound,* Captain Shaw, sailing from Liverpool to Quebec, was lost out of sight of land but her crew was saved.

23. **Year 1765.** English troop-transport *Loyal Pitt,* Captain Davis, sailing from London to Quebec, was lost in strong gale of wind on

the St. Lawrence River between the islands of Caudre and Travers on August 6.

24. *Year 1765.* A small American schooner, while acting as a tender for the frigate H.M.S. *Maidstone,* foundered on the south shoal of George's Bank, off Nova Scotia, all twelve of her crew perished.

25. *Year 1766.* American or English ship *Minehead,* Captain Gwyn, sailing from Bristol, England, to Boston, was a total wreck on Sable Island, off Nova Scotia, fifteen of the crew drowned.

26. *Year 1768.* English ship *Mary & Susannah,* Captain Muire, sailing from London to Quebec, was a total loss in the St. Lawrence River.

27. *Year 1771.* Ship of unknown registry, *Rose,* Captain King, sailing from Quebec to Cork, Ireland, was lost on the St. Lawrence River.

28. *Year 1771.* Three English merchantmen were lost at Nova Scotia: *Nassau,* Captain Smith, sailing from London to Boston, was a total wreck near Canso but her crew was saved; *Swansey,* Captain David, sailing from Rhode Island to Newfoundland, was lost on Sable Island; and the sloop *Grandy* (or *Granby*), Captain Hay, was wrecked off the Lighthouse Rocks in Halifax Harbor and all sixteen men aboard her were lost. She carried military stores and 3,000 pounds sterling in coins for the Halifax Navy Yards.

29. *Year 1773.* English merchantman *Sophia,* Captain Hastington, sailing from Philadelphia to Quebec, was lost on Sable Island, Nova Scotia.

30. *Year 1773.* English ship *Matilda,* Captain Blyth, sailing from Philadelphia to Quebec, was lost on October 18 in the St. Lawrence River after being on rocks for five days.

31. *Year 1775.* English merchantman *Sally,* Captain Brame, sailing from London to Quebec, was lost off Newfoundland.

32. *Year 1775.* English warship, H.M.S. *Savage,* 8 guns, Captain Hugh Bromelge, was lost near Louisburg, Cape Breton Island, Nova Scotia.

33. *Year 1776.* Two English ships were lost near Halifax, Nova Scotia: *Dolphin,* Captain Thomas, sailing from Newfoundland to

Halifax, was lost near that port; *Euphrates,* Captain Gordon, a transport coming from London, was lost entering the port of Halifax.

34. *Year 1776.* An English transport ship, *Favorite,* Captain Bishipprick, was lost in the Gulf of St. Lawrence.

35. *Year 1776.* Two English ships were lost on the St. Lawrence River: *Bosphorus,* a victualer; and *St. George,* Captain Gill, was wrecked on Red Island in the river but the crew was saved.

36. *Year 1777.* Three ships were lost off Nova Scotia: English ship *Mary & Frances,* Captain Sutton, sailing from Cork, Ireland, to Quebec, was lost in the Bay of Canso; the English ship *Aurora* was lost on Sable Island, and when survivors got ashore from this wreck they found seven Negro women who had been wrecked there sixteen years earlier on a French ship.

37. *Year 1777.* English merchantman *Lock,* Captain Gowland, coming from London, sank in the St. Lawrence River.

38. *Year 1777.* Two English warships foundered off Newfoundland: H.M.S. *Pegasus,* 16 guns, Captain J. Hamilton Gore; and H.M.S. *Vestal,* 20 guns, Captain James Shirley.

39. *Year 1778.* English warship H.M.S. *Dispatch,* 14 guns, Captain J. Botham, capsized in the Gulf of St. Lawrence.

40. *Year 1778.* Three English warships were lost off Newfoundland: the armed transport *Grampus,* 32 guns, Captain John Frodsham, foundered; H.M.S. *Cupid,* 16 guns, Captain William Carlyon, foundered; and H.M.S. *Spy,* 12 guns, Captain Thomas Lenox Frederick, was wrecked near the island.

41. *Year 1779.* English armed-transport *Tortoise,* 32 guns, Captain Jahleel Brenton, foundered off Newfoundland.

42. *Year 1779.* Two ships were lost near Nova Scotia: a ship of unknown registry, *Fame Murphy,* was wrecked on Sable Island; and the English armed-transport *North,* 20 guns, Captain George Selby, was wrecked near the coast of Nova Scotia.

43. *Year 1780.* English ship *Margaretta Christina* foundered on a voyage between Halifax, Nova Scotia, and Newfoundland but the crew was saved.

44. *Year 1780.* English merchantman *Jane,* Captain Wilson, sailing from London to Halifax, was lost on Sable Island, Nova Scotia, but the crew was saved.

45. *Year 1780.* Three English ships were lost at Quebec: the *Sharp,* the *Valiant,* and the *Lizard.*

46. *Year 1780.* English warship H.M.S. *Viper,* 16 guns, Captain John Augustua, was wrecked in the Gulf of St. Lawrence on October 11.

47. *Year 1780.* Three English merchantmen were lost at Newfoundland: *William,* Captain Washman, coming from Lisbon, was wrecked on the coast and all of its crew perished; *Peggy,* also known by the alias *Wolf,* coming from Liverpool, was wrecked on St. Peter's Island; and the *Adventure,* sailing from St. Eustatius Island to Newfoundland, was forced onshore by an American privateer near the Port of St. John's, vessel and cargo a total loss.

48. *Year 1781.* English ship *Ann,* Captain M'Clue, sailing from Quebec to Barbados, was wrecked on the Isle of Orleans, in the Gulf of St. Lawrence.

49. *Year 1781.* English ship *Potowmack,* Captain Mitchell, sailing from London to Quebec, was captured by an American privateer and later wrecked on Sable Island, Nova Scotia.

50. *Year 1781.* Three English ships sank in the St. Lawrence River: *General Haldemand,* Captain Love, one man drowned; *Harvey,* Captain Harvey [*sic*], her crew was saved; and the *London,* Captain M'Cullough, her crew was saved.

51. *Year 1781.* Two English ships wrecked at Newfoundland: warship H.M.S. *Dutchess of Cumberland,* 16 guns, Captain Edward March; and merchantman *Venus,* Captain Millet, sailing from Jamaica to Quebec, wrecked at Cape Ray, with a total loss of men and cargo.

52. *Year 1782.* Two English ships were lost going up the St. Lawrence River. One was not identified, except as a transport, and the other was the *Christie,* Captain Bodfield.

53. *Year 1782.* Two English warships were lost at Newfoundland: H.M.S. *Placentia,* 14 guns, Captain Charles Anderson, wrecked near the island; and H.M.S. *Hector,* 74 guns, Captain John Bourchier, sank on the Grand Banks of Newfoundland.

54. Year 1782. Two English merchantmen were lost at Nova Scotia: *Endeavour*, Captain Simpson, coming from Exeter, England, to Quebec, was wrecked 25 leagues eastward of Halifax, in December, and part of its cargo was saved; *Tom*, Captain Smart, sailing from Antigua to Halifax, was lost at the entrance of the port but all of its cargo was saved.

55. Year 1783. Three English merchantmen were lost on the St. Lawrence River: *Hope*, Captain Cameron, sailing from Tortola to Quebec, was lost 2 leagues below Tadefase but part of its cargo was saved; *Betsey*, Captain Anderson, sailing from Quebec to Barbados, was totally wrecked by a violent gust of wind on Hare Island on October 24 and one of the crew drowned; and the *Noble*, Captain Taylor, sailing from Halifax to Quebec, was lost near Quebec but all of its cargo was saved.

56. Year 1783. Three English ships lost at Nova Scotia: *Peter*, Captain Bruce, sailing from St. Lucia Island to Halifax, was lost near that port; a transport ship, *Lion*, Captain Davis, was lost near Cape Sable; and a merchantman, *Sampon*, Captain Wood Whitehove, sailing to Quebec, was totally wrecked on Cape Breton Island and three of the crew drowned.

57. Year 1785. English merchantman *Coleman*, Captain Pickmore, was wrecked on Newfoundland but the crew was saved.

58. Year 1785. English packet boat *Hermoine*, sailing from Halifax to Port Roseway, was wrecked on Cape Sable, Nova Scotia.

59. Year 1785. English merchantman, *Warrior*, Captain M'Donough, sailing from St. John's Island to Cadiz, was wrecked at Merrygomish in the Gulf of St. Lawrence on December 28, her total cargo was lost but the crew was saved.

60. Year 1786. Ship of unknown registry, *Telemachus*, Captain Sargeant, sailing from Georgia to Amsterdam, was lost with most of her cargo on Sable Island, Nova Scotia.

61. Year 1786. English ship *Renuse*, Captain Bully, was lost at Newfoundland.

62. Year 1788. English merchantman *Favorite*, Captain Robertson, sailing from London to Quebec, was lost on the lower part of the St. Lawrence River.

63. *Year 1788.* English merchantman *Elizabeth and Mary*, Captain Lethbrige, was lost at Newfoundland.

64. *Year 1788.* Three English merchantmen lost at Nova Scotia: *White*, Captain Gill, sailing from Cowes, England, to Quebec was lost at Seaton off the Cape Breton Island; *William*, Captain Losh, sailing from London to Quebec, was lost near Cape Breton on April 28; and *Betsey*, Captain Young, sailing from Scotland to Halifax, was lost on the coast but the crew was saved.

65. *Year 1790.* Ship of unknown registry, *St. Joseph*, Captain Barnveth, was lost onshore at Newfoundland shortly after sailing from there.

66. *Year 1790.* English ship *Lynx*, Captain Murphy, sailing from Newfoundland to Cape Breton, was lost on July 9 near the Laun Islands, in the Gulf of St. Lawrence.

67. *Year 1791.* English merchantman *Fanny*, Captain Bugs, arriving from Grenada Island, was burnt at St. Andrews, New Brunswick.

68. *Year 1791.* Four English merchantmen lost around Newfoundland: *Hope*, Captain Anderson, coming from London, wrecked on the coast; *Monkey*, Captain Palmer, was a total loss on the Banks of Newfoundland but the crew was saved; unidentified ship sailing from Liverpool to Quebec was lost off Cape Ray; and *Fame*, Captain Meggetson, sailing from London to Quebec, was wrecked on St. Pierre Island, near Newfoundland, but the crew and part of her cargo were saved.

69. *Year 1792.* Two ships of unknown registry were lost on Sable Island, Nova Scotia: one was not identified; the other was the *Rambler*, Captain Kaquet, sailing from Philadelphia to Boston.

70. *Year 1793.* Three English merchantmen were wrecked on the coast of Newfoundland: *Diana*, Captain Greaves, coming from Dartmouth, England, but the crew was saved; *Hornett*, Captain Priddes, coming from St. Ubes, England; and *Manacles*, Captain Jones.

71. *Year 1794.* Two English merchantmen were lost on the coast of Labrador: *Charlotte*, Captain Godfrey, coming from Dartmouth, England; and *Polly*, Captain Graves.

72. *Year 1794.* English warship, H.M.S. *Placentia,* Captain Alexander Shippard, was lost near Newfoundland.

73. *Year 1794.* Two English ships were lost on the St. Lawrence River: *Augusta,* Captain Cole, sailing from Quebec to the West Indies, was burnt by accident in the river on October 24; and the schooner *Charlotte,* sailing from Quebec to Halifax.

74. *Year 1795.* Two English merchantmen lost at Nova Scotia: *York,* Captain Norton, sailing from Liverpool to Boston, was wrecked at Cape Negro; and *Orb,* Captain Brigs, sailing from Liverpool to Halifax, was wrecked on Sable Island on January 6.

75. *Year 1795.* Two unidentified English merchantmen were lost on the Grand Banks of Newfoundland but both crews were saved.

76. *Year 1796.* English warship H.M.S. *Active,* 32 guns, Captain Edward Leverson Gower, was wrecked in the St. Lawrence River on July 5.

77. *Year 1797.* Two English ships were lost at Nova Scotia: merchantman *Stag,* leaving Halifax Harbor for Jamaica, overset when leaving the harbor and was lost; warship H.M.S. *Tribune,* 32 guns, Captain Scory Barker, was wrecked near Halifax on November 16.

78. *Year 1798.* English warship H.M.S. *Rover,* 16 guns, Captain George Irwin, was wrecked on June 23 in the Gulf of St. Lawrence.

79. *Year 1798.* English merchantman *Susannah,* Captain Doucett, sailing from Quebec to Halifax, was lost in the St. Lawrence River.

80. *Year 1798.* English merchantman *Britannia,* Captain Adney, was lost at New Brunswick but the crew was saved.

81. *Year 1798.* During a gale in Halifax Harbor on September 25, many ships were sunk. Among them were two American ships: the *Liberty* and *Penelope;* a Danish ship; the English warship H.M.S. *Lynx;* and the brig *Betsey,* of unknown registry. Total loss of shipping was over 100,000 pounds sterling.

82. *Year 1799.* English merchantman *Lucy,* sailing from Quebec to Greenock, England, was lost on September 11 on the coast of Labrador but part of her cargo was saved.

83. *Year 1800.* English merchantman *Enterprize*, Captain Cummings, sailing from London to Quebec, was lost in November on Anticosti Island in the Gulf of St. Lawrence.

84. *Year 1800.* English ship *Francis*, sailing from London to Halifax, was totally lost on Sable Island, Nova Scotia, and all of the crew perished.

85. *Year 1800.* English merchantman *Turk*, Captain Thomas, sailing from Bristol, England, to Newfoundland, was lost on the Banks of Newfoundland.

86. *Year 1801.* English merchantman *Sovereign*, Captain Ramshaw, sailing from London to Quebec, was lost in May at Cape Breton, Nova Scotia.

87. *Year 1801.* Two English merchantmen were lost in the St. Lawrence River: *Industry*, Captain Young, sailing from Quebec to Leith, Scotland; and *Dalrymple*, Captain Marsh, sailing from Barbados to Quebec, but part of its cargo was saved.

88. *Year 1802.* Two English warships foundered off Newfoundland: H.M.S. *Scout*, 18 guns, Captain Henry Duncan, and H.M.S. *Fly*, 14 guns, Captain Thomas Duvall, both with a total loss of crews.

89. *Year 1802.* Three English merchantmen were lost at Nova Scotia: *Union*, Captain Hooper, sailing from Spain for Boston, wrecked on July 10 on Sable Island, but the crew was saved; the *Mars*, Captain Clemente, sailing to India, and the *Eagle*, sailing to the West Indies, were lost at Cape Sable but their crews were saved.

90. *Year 1802.* Ship of unknown registry, *Terpsichore*, Captain Burge, sailing from Quebec to Bristol, England, was lost on Flatt Island in the Gulf of St. Lawrence but its crew was saved.

91. *Year 1802.* During the winter months ten ships were lost on the St. Lawrence River but only one was identified: *Mary*, Captain Montburne, sailing from Newfoundland to Quebec.

92. *Year 1803.* Twelve unidentified vessels were lost on the St. Lawrence River.

93. *Year 1805.* English merchantman *Atlanta*, Captain Gammell, sailing from Grenada Island to Halifax, was wrecked at Torbay, Newfoundland, on January 29 but part of its cargo was saved.

94. *Year 1806.* Two ships of unknown registry were lost in the St. Lawrence River: the brig *Minerva,* heading to Quebec, on March 19; and the *Liberty,* Captain Clark, sailing from Quebec to Plymouth, England.

95. *Year 1807.* English storeship H.M.S. *William,* 12 guns, Captain John Foxton, was wrecked in the Gut of Canso, Nova Scotia, on November 11.

96. *Year 1807.* English schooner *Doncet,* coming from Halifax, was totally lost in the St. Lawrence River but the crew was saved.

97. *Year 1808.* Three English ships were lost on the St. Lawrence River: warship H.M.S. *Banterer,* 22 guns, Captain Alexander Shippard, on December 4; merchantman *Speedwell,* Captain Lawson, sailing from Madeira Island to Quebec, but most of its cargo was saved; and the merchantman *Hamilton,* Captain Gilchrist, sailing from Clyde, Scotland, to Quebec, but most of the cargo was saved.

98. *Year 1810.* English warship H.M.S. *Plumper,* 12 guns, Captain W. Frissel, foundered in the St. Lawrence River in November.

99. *Year 1812.* English warship H.M.S. *Avenger,* 16 guns, Captain Urry Johnson, was wrecked off St. John's, Newfoundland, on October 8.

100. *Year 1812.* Three English warships were lost at Nova Scotia: H.M.S. *Chubb,* 4 guns, Captain Samuel Nisbett, capsized off Halifax on August 14 with all hands lost; H.M.S. *Emulous,* 18 guns, Captain Williams Howe Mulcaster, and H.M.S. *Barbadoes,* 28 guns, Captain Thomas Huskisson, were wrecked on Sable Island on August 3 and September 28, the latter ship was carrying over $500,000 in gold and silver specie and bullion.

101. *Year 1813.* English warship H.M.S. *Atalante,* 18 guns, Captain Frederick Hickey, was wrecked off Halifax, Nova Scotia, on November 10.

102. *Year 1813.* English warship H.M.S. *Bold,* 12 guns, Captain John Skekel, was wrecked on Prince Edward Island, in the Gulf of St. Lawrence, on September 27.

103. *Year 1813.* English warship H.M.S. *Tweed,* 18 guns, Captain

William Mather, was wrecked in Shoal Bay, Newfoundland, on November 5.

104. *Year 1814.* Three English warships were lost near Halifax, Nova Scotia: H.M.S. *Fantóme,* 18 guns, Captain Thomas Sykes, wrecked on November 24; H.M.S. *Cuttle,* 4 guns, foundered; and H.M.S. *Herring,* 4 guns, Captain John Murray, foundered —date of losses of last two ships not known.

105. *Year 1814.* English troopship, H.M.S. *Leopard,* 50 guns, Captain Edward Lowther Crofton, was wrecked on Anticosti Island, in the Gulf of St. Lawrence, on June 28.

106. *Year 1815.* English troopship, H.M.S. *Penelope,* 36 guns, Captain James Galloway, was wrecked off Newfoundland on May 1.

107. *Year 1822.* English warship, H.M.S. *Drake,* 10 guns, Captain Charles Adolphus Baker, was wrecked with the loss of many lives off Newfoundland on June 20.

108. *Year 1822.* French ship *L'Americaine,* carrying over a million dollars in gold and silver bullion and specie, was lost in 72 feet of water off Wallace Lake, on Sable Island, Nova Scotia.

CHAPTER TWO

The United States

UNTIL RECENTLY, only Florida had laws concerning the salvaging of ancient shipwrecks. However, several other states —Texas, Georgia, South and North Carolina, and Virginia—have just passed new laws on this matter, and I suspect that other states will do the same in the near future. Before attempting to carry out salvage work in any body of water in the United States, it is wise to determine if permission is required from the state or federal government. This move may prevent the seizure of any part of whatever is recovered.

Due to underwater-visibility conditions, the best time of the year varies throughout the states. It is advisable for prospective salvors to make their own investigations. Some areas have rather unusual seasons in which diving conditions are the best: for example, off the Gulf Coast of Texas the best time for diving and salvage operations is winter, when the water is the clearest.

I have excluded a total of 1,167 shipwrecks, as their locations were too vague in the documents. For example: Over three hundred shipwrecks were listed only as being lost on "the New England Coast"; others were lost on "the Carolinas," on "the American Coast," or on "the North-American Continent."

I have listed only a few shipwrecks on the Pacific coast, as there was virtually no shipping at all in this area prior to 1825. Several other books list treasure-laden Manila galleons as being lost off the coast of California on Santa Catalina Island, Cortez Bank, and elsewhere, and many divers have searched in vain for these shipwrecks. According to the research I have undertaken to corroborate their existence, the reason for their failure is that the galleons never existed.

Because of the large number of shipwrecks in Florida waters, I have made a separate chapter to cover this state.

List of Shipwrecks in Waters of the United States

EAST COAST:

MAINE:

1. **Year 1743.** English warship H.M.S. *Astrea,* Captain Robert Swanton, was accidentally burnt at the mouth of the Piscataqua River and several of the crew perished.

2. **Year 1758.** English merchantman *Phoenix,* Captain Barter, sailing from England to Boston, wrecked in Casco Bay but some of her cargo was saved.

3. **Year 1779.** Four American warships were burnt on August 14 at Portland to prevent their capture by the British: *Warren,* 32 guns, Captain Dudley Saltonstall; *Diligent,* 14 guns, Captain Brown; *Hazard,* 16 guns, Captain John Foster Williams; and the *Tyrannicide,* 14 guns, Captain Cathcart. Some of the cannon were recovered several years later.

4. **Year 1807.** American merchant schooner *Charles,* Captain Adams, was wrecked on a reef of rocks to the westward of the Portland Lighthouse and only six of her crew of twenty-two were saved.

NEW HAMPSHIRE:

5. *Year 1760.* English merchantman *Friends Adventure,* Captain Hamilton, sailing for Jamaica, was lost when leaving Portsmouth Harbor.

6. *Year 1774.* American merchantman *Scripio,* Captain Moore, sailing for the West Indies, was wrecked on a rock at Fernands Point in Piscataqua Harbor.

7. *Year 1780.* Three unidentified American merchantmen returning from Jamaica with rum and sugar products were totally lost on Appledore Island, on the Isle of Shoals, and many persons from the crews were lost.

8. *Year 1817.* American merchantman *Commerce,* Captain Roberts, sailing from Jamaica to New York, was totally lost on May 14 on Portsmouth Beach but the crew and some of her cargo of rum were saved.

MASSACHUSETTS:

9. *Year 1624.* Small English vessel, *Sparrow Hawk,* carrying settlers and supplies to the newly founded Virginia Colony, was wrecked on the beach near the site of the present town of Orleans on Cape Cod. She was recently excavated and many recovered items were placed in a museum.

10. *Year 1678.* An unidentified French merchantman coming from Canada with a cargo of hides was totally lost on Nantucket Shoals.

11. *Year 1709.* English warship H.M.S. *Solebay,* 32 guns, was totally lost on December 25 at Boston Neck and all of her crew perished.

12. *Year 1714.* English sloop of war H.M.S. *Hazard,* bringing munitions from England, was wrecked in Green Bay, about 30 miles from Boston, all of her crew perished.

13. *Year 1717.* Pirate ship *Whidah,* Captain Black Sam Bellamy, wrecked on a shoal near Wellfleet on Cape Cod, only one of her crew of 102 survived. She was reported to be carrying a considerable treasure at this time.

14. *Year 1731.* Two English merchantmen lost: the *John & Mary*, Captain Quirk, near Boston; and the *Anne*, Captain Goodridge, coming from Barbados, on Martha's Vineyard.

15. *Year 1744.* English warship H.M.S. *Astrea*, 20 guns, Captain John Barker, was accidentally burnt in Boston Harbor but no lives were lost.

16. *Year 1749.* During a hurricane on October 8, seven unidentified ships were wrecked on Martha's Vineyard and many lives were lost.

17. *Year 1757.* American merchantman *Clinton*, Captain Hughes, coming from Jamaica and South Carolina, was wrecked on August 12 on No-man's Land, a small island near Martha's Vineyard, but some of her cargo was saved.

18. *Year 1760.* English merchantman *Claremont*, Captain Newton, sailing to Jamaica, was wrecked on Cape Cod, several of her crew perished.

19. *Year 1762.* English merchantman *Mary*, Captain Nain, sailing from Halifax to Gibraltar with a cargo of hides and furs, was lost near Boston.

20. *Year 1766.* English merchantman *Pembroke*, Captain Taylor, arriving from England with a valuable cargo, was wrecked on Lynn Beach, near Boston, but some of her cargo was saved.

21. *Year 1767.* Scottish merchantman *Betsey*, Captain MacFarlan, sailing for London, was wrecked after leaving Boston near Race Point, on Cape Cod, but most of her cargo was saved.

22. *Year 1768.* American merchantman *Hawke*, Captain Norton, carrying a cargo of salt from the Bahamas, was wrecked on Shagg Rock, near Boston, but all of her crew was saved.

23. *Year 1773.* English troop-transport *Britannia*, Captain Walker, after arriving from London, was accidentally burnt in Boston Harbor but there was no loss of life.

24. *Year 1774.* During a gale in December, two unidentified merchantmen arriving from the Leeward Islands and a schooner from Virginia were totally lost in Buzzards Bay.

25. *Year 1778.* English frigate of war H.M.S. *Somerset,* 70 guns, Captain George Curry, carrying a large cargo of war materials, was wrecked near Provincetown, on Cape Cod.

26. *Year 1782.* English warship H.M.S. *Blonde,* 32 guns, Captain Edward Thornborough, was wrecked on a rock on Nantucket Shoals and several of her crew perished.

27. *Year 1783.* During a gale on October 9, three unidentified ships sank in Boston Harbor.

28. *Year 1784.* Three ships were lost: Spanish merchantman *Julius Caesar,* coming from Cadiz, on Cape Cod; American merchantman *Peace & Plenty,* Captain Calahan, on Cape Cod; and a ship of unknown registry, *Fanciculetta,* arriving from Tobago Island, on Nantucket Shoals.

29. *Year 1785.* American packet boat *Ross,* sailing from Newfoundland to New York, sank after entering Boston Bay.

30. *Year 1786.* Unidentified French brig sailing from the Caribbean to France, was lost on July 31 on Nantucket Shoals but all of her crew was saved.

31. *Year 1789.* English merchantman *Mary & Ann,* Captain Evers, arriving from London, wrecked on Plumb Island, four persons of her crew were lost.

32. *Year 1791.* English merchantman *Hopewell,* Captain Harrison, arriving from London, was wrecked near Boston.

33. *Year 1792.* Three merchantmen were lost: English ship *Rodney,* Captain Wytock, sailing from Boston to the Caribbean, on Cape Cod; American ship *Marretta,* Captain Barnes, on Cape Cod; and American ship *Columbia,* Captain Chauncey, arriving from Liverpool, off Plymouth, only two of her crew survived.

34. *Year 1793.* Danish merchantman *Gertrude Maria,* Captain Klein, arriving from Copenhagen, was lost near Boston, some of her cargo was saved.

35. *Year 1794.* American merchantman *Fanny,* Captain Stevens, arriving from Virginia, was totally lost on Martha's Vineyard.

36. *Year 1795.* Three merchantmen were lost: English ship *Clarissa,* Captain Scott, arriving from London, on Nantucket Isle, crew and cargo were saved; ship of unknown registry, *Margaret,* Captain Mackay, arriving from Amsterdam, near Cape Ann; and American ship *Industry,* Captain Barnes, sailing from Portsmouth to Boston, totally lost near Cape Ann, with total loss of lives.

37. *Year 1796.* English ship *Julianna,* Captain Ingraham, arriving from South Carolina, was lost at Nantucket Isle.

38. *Year 1797.* English merchantman *Three Sisters,* Captain Delano, arriving from Liverpool, was wrecked on Cape Cod but all of her crew was saved.

39. *Year 1798.* Three merchantmen were lost: American ship *Charming Betsey,* Captain Foffey, arriving from Martinique, wrecked on Martha's Vineyard; English ship *Delight,* Captain Wilson, sailing from Virginia to London, lost on Cape Cod; and English ship *Commerce,* sailing from Havana to Bristol, lost on Nantucket Shoals.

40. *Unidentified year prior to 1799.* On a Spanish chart of New England published this year, it mentions that two Spanish warships—the *Magnifico* and *Cibila*—were sunk in Boston Harbor at a previous date.

41. *Year 1800.* English merchantman *Delight,* Captain Williams, arriving from Gibraltar, was wrecked on a shoal off Martha's Vineyard.

42. *Year 1802.* Four merchantmen were lost on Cape Cod: American ship *Astrea,* sailing from Boston to the West Indies; English ship *Minerva,* Captain Phelim, arriving from Madeira Island, on January 11; two ships of unknown registry—*Brutus,* Captain Brown, and *Ulysses,* Captain Cock—both sailing from Salem to Europe.

43. *Year 1804.* Three merchantmen were lost: American ship *Semiramis,* Captain Smith, arriving from South Carolina, on Nantucket Shoals, only small part of her cargo was saved; Spanish ship *Protecto,* sailing from Boston to Lima, Peru, on Cape Cod; and French ship *Alert,* arriving from France, near Boston on December 24.

44. *Year 1811.* Five merchantmen were lost: American ship *Four Brothers,* arriving from Russia, all of her cargo was saved; English

ship *Neutrality*, Captain Forster, arriving from Liverpool; ship of unknown registry, *Florenza*, Captain King, arriving from London, crew and some of her cargo saved; French ship *Abeona*, Captain Blunt, sailing from Boston to Portsmouth, her crew saved; and Irish ship *Alknomack*, carrying immigrants from Ireland to New York, her crew and all passengers were saved. The first four were lost on Cape Cod and the fifth on Martha's Vineyard.

45. Year 1812. American merchantman *Alfred*, sailing from Russia to Boston, was lost on January 3 near Cape Ann, her crew was saved.

46. Year 1813. American ship *Princess*, sailing from London to New York, was totally lost on April 27 on Cape Cod, salvors failed to recover several chests of silver specie from this wreck.

47. Year 1814. Swedish merchantman *Nordkoping*, Captain Nordstrom, sailing from Cuba to Boston, was lost on Nantucket Shoals in July.

48. Year 1815. English merchantman *Matchless*, after arriving from London, sank at anchor in Boston Harbor during a gale on September 23.

49. Year 1817. Three vessels were lost: American packet boat *Dispatch*, Captain Lovett, arriving from the Virgin Islands, wrecked near Boston; American merchantman *Fox*, Captain Williams, arriving from Guadeloupe Island, wrecked January 18 on Martha's Vineyard; and the English merchantman *Robert Todd*, Captain Campbell, arriving from Liverpool and the Bahamas, totally lost on Nantucket Shoals on October 21.

50. Year 1818. Two American merchantmen were lost on Cape Cod: *Mary Ann*, Captain Robinson, arriving from Baltimore, part of her cargo saved; and the *Warren*, Captain Knowles, arriving from Brazil, during the month of November.

51. Year 1821. American merchantman *Paragon*, Captain Hardon, arriving from Havana, totally lost on February 16 near Cape Ann.

52. Year 1822. American merchantman *Favorite*, Captain Webster, sailing from Honduras to Boston, wrecked on May 7 near Edgarton but her crew was saved.

53. *Year 1824.* American merchantman *Federal George,* Captain Davis, sailing from Philadelphia to Boston, was totally lost on January 20 near the Scititate Lighthouse off Boston Harbor, her crew and part of her cargo saved.

RHODE ISLAND:

54. *Year 1738.* German ship *Princess Augusta,* Captain Brook, carrying 350 German immigrants from Amsterdam to New York, was wrecked on the northern tip of Sandy Point, Block Island. Previous to the disaster, 250 immigrants and some of the crew died from contaminated water. The ship was reported to be carrying a considerable amount of personal treasures belonging to the immigrants.

55. *Year 1765.* Irish merchantman *Golden Grove,* Captain Chitty, sailing from Cork to Halifax with a cargo of dried meats and butter, was wrecked on Block Island, crew and some of her cargo saved.

56. *Year 1772.* Two English ships were lost near Newport Harbor: warship H.M.S. *Gaspee,* on June 10; and merchantman *London,* Captain Folger, sailing for London.

57. *Year 1777.* Two English warships wrecked near Point Judith: H.M.S. *Triton,* Captain Woolcomb; and H.M.S. *Syren,* 20 guns, Captain Toblas Furneaux, on November 10.

58. *Year 1778.* Seven English warships were burnt and sunk in Narragansett Bay during the War of Independence: H.M.S. *Kingfisher,* 16 guns; H.M.S. *Juno,* 32 guns, Captain Hugh Dalrymple; H.M.S. *Lark,* 32 guns, Captain Richard Smith; H.M.S. *Orpheus,* 32 guns, Captain Charles Hudson; H.M.S. *Flora,* 32 guns, Captain John Brisbane; H.M.S. *Cerberus,* 28 guns, Captain John Symons; and H.M.S. *Falcon,* 16 guns, Captain Harry Harmood.

59. *Year 1779.* American ship *Minerva,* Captain Cranston, sailing to New York, was wrecked near Westerly.

60. *Year 1805.* Ship of unknown registry, *Anna and Hope,* coming from France, was totally lost on Block Island.

61. *Year 1806.* English schooner of war H.M.S. *Redbridge,* 12 guns, Captain Edward Burt, wrecked on November 4 near Providence.

62. *Year 1807.* English ship *Brutus*, Captain Tobey, arriving from Liverpool, was wrecked on Block Island.

63. *Year 1813.* American merchantman *Ann*, Captain McDonald, wrecked near Barrington, her crew and cargo were saved.

64. *Year 1815.* During a hurricane on September 23 at Providence, four large ships, nine brigs, seven schooners, and fifteen sloops were wrecked or sunk.

65. *Year 1818.* American ship *Governor Hopkins*, arriving from Savannah, Georgia, wrecked during a storm in December on Brenton's Reef but most of her cargo was saved.

66. *Year 1819.* Two American merchantmen were lost: the *Montgomery*, arriving from Honduras, near Sakonnet Point; and the *American*, Captain Lincoln, sailing from the West Indies to Boston, on May 25 off Block Island.

CONNECTICUT:

67. *Year 1770.* During a hurricane on October 19, two unidentified large merchantmen were wrecked at New London.

68. *Year 1812.* American merchantman *Osprey*, Captain Cook, sailing from Pernambuco to New York, wrecked during a gale in February near New London.

69. *Year 1816.* Spanish merchantman *Anion*, sailing from Italy to New York, sank during October near New London because of a bad leak.

70. *Year 1817.* Two American merchantmen were lost: the *George*, Captain Speeding, sailing to Grenada, October 16, near New London, her crew and cargo saved; and the *Mary*, Captain Hanly, sailing for Liverpool, March 25, while crossing the bar at Darien.

NEW YORK:

71. *Year 1657.* Dutch ship *Prins Maurits*, carrying immigrants to Nieuw Amsterdam (New York City), was lost on Fire Island, but Indians rescued all of the crew and passengers.

72. *Year 1710.* German ship *Herbert*, bringing immigrants from the Palatinate, wrecked on July 7 on the east end of Long Island, no lives were lost but only a small part of her cargo was saved.

73. *Year 1719.* Spanish privateer of 12 guns and 133 men was blown up during a battle with a New York privateer off the east end of Long Island, ninety-one of the Spaniards perished.

74. *Year 1760.* Scottish merchantman *Adventure*, Captain Auld, sailing from New York for Dublin, was lost in lower New York Bay.

75. *Year 1761.* American ship *City of Werry*, Captain Patterson, arriving from Boston, was sunk in the Narrows of New York Bay but her crew was saved.

76. *Year 1763.* American coastal schooner *Marey*, Captain Samuel Vetch, wrecked at Montauk Point, Long Island, carrying a cargo of contraband goods from French Canada.

77. *Year 1769.* Scottish merchantman *Elizabeth*, Captain Consy, arriving from Dublin, was totally lost on the south side of Long Island.

78. *Year 1773.* Scottish merchantman *Hope*, Captain Stewart, sailing from New York City to Dublin, was wrecked on Staten Island but her crew was saved.

79. *Year 1776.* American troop-transport *Generous Friends*, sank near Coney Island but no lives were lost.

80. *Year 1777.* Four ships were lost: English warship H.M.S. *Liverpool*, 28 guns, Captain Henry Bellow, wrecked on the south side of Long Island; Irish merchantman *Diamond*, Captain Lanning, arriving from Cork, struck on some rocks at the entrance to the East River and sank near a wharf close to Manhattan; American warship *Congress*, 28 guns, burnt on the Hudson River to prevent her capture by the British; American warship *Montgomery*, 24 guns, captured and blown up on the Hudson River by the British.

81. *Year 1778.* Three ships were lost: English warship H.M.S. *Mercury*, 24 guns, Captain James Montagu, wrecked near New York City; American naval vessel *Rose*, Captain Anderson, wrecked during a gale in December on Staten Island; and American merchantman *Jenny*, sailing for London, wrecked during a gale on Staten Island.

82. *Year 1779.* Three ships were lost: American merchantman *Colpoys*, arriving from St. Kitts, totally lost on Long Island but

only one man drowned; English troop-transport *James & William*, arriving from Rhode Island, totally lost at Hell Gate on the East River of New York City but all of her crew was saved; and the English warship H.M.S. *Hussar*, 28 guns, Captain Charles Maurice Pole, sank at Hell Gate, quite close to the *James & William*. Although there have been several articles in recent years stating that the *Hussar* was carrying a large amount of treasure, I have not discovered any documentary evidence to support this claim.

83. *Year 1780.* Four ships were lost: English troop-transport *Betsey*, Captain Obrien, was wrecked on some rocks in lower New York Bay and many lives were lost; English ship *Mercury*, Captain Monkhouse, sailing to Portugal, lost on March 2 during a gale on Long Island; American ship *Watt*, Captain Coulthard, sailing to Jamaica, was totally lost on Long Island and twenty-six men perished; and American privateer *Patience*, Captain Chase, wrecked on Long Island.

84. *Year 1781.* Two English warships were wrecked on Long Island: H.M.S. *Swallow*, 16 guns, Captain Thomas Wells; and H.M.S. *Culloden*, 74 guns, Captain George Balfour, on January 23.

85. *Year 1783.* Three ships were lost: English troop-transport *St. James*, wrecked on Staten Island; English supply ship *Elizabeth*, Captain Griffith, wrecked on Long Island; and American merchantman *Huzzar*, Captain Wilson, arriving from Jamaica, wrecked on Long Island but part of her cargo was saved.

86. *Year 1784.* Unidentified French packet boat was wrecked on Long Island on January 15 and several of her crew perished.

87. *Year 1785.* Two ships were lost: Spanish merchantman *Nuestra Señora del Rosario*, Captain Moratus, arriving from the Canaries, was wrecked near New York City but part of her cargo was saved; and the Swedish ship *Alstromer* was wrecked on Governor's Island during a gale on September 29.

88. *Year 1786.* Ship of unknown registry, *Mary Ann*, Captain Stewart, coming from the Far East, wrecked on Long Island in August.

89. *Year 1788.* English merchantman *Betsey & Amy*, Captain Watts, arriving from Liverpool, wrecked on Long Island.

90. *Year 1789.* American merchantman *Sally*, Captain Mathews, arriving from Grenada, wrecked on Coney Island.

91. *Year 1792.* Two ships of unknown registry were wrecked on Long Island: the *Eliza*, Captain Hughes, arriving from Jamaica, and *George*, Captain Gregorio, arriving from Madeira Island.

92. *Year 1795.* American merchantman *Neptune*, Captain Wallace, arriving from Dominica Island, wrecked on the south side of Long Island but some of her cargo was saved.

93. *Year 1796.* During a gale at New York City on January 11, eight unidentified ships sank at anchor or at the wharves, one of them was an English packet boat.

94. *Year 1797.* Spanish merchantman *Enrique*, Captain Cuzana, arriving from Cadiz, wrecked on Long Island but crew and some of her cargo saved.

95. *Year 1798.* American merchantman *Jenny*, Captain Dickson, sailing to Jamaica, wrecked in lower New York Bay.

96. *Year 1800.* Two ships were lost: German ship *Ocean*, sailing from Bremen to Philadelphia, wrecked on the south side of Long Island, only the captain perished; and the American merchantman *Experiment*, arriving from Havana, sank shortly before reaching Manhattan.

97. *Year 1801.* Three ships were lost: English merchantman *Thomas*, sailing for Londonderry, totally lost on the East River; American ship *Traveller*, Captain Russell, sailing from the West Indies to Boston, wrecked on Long Island; and a ship of unknown registry, *Ann*, sailing from New York City to Liverpool, wrecked on Long Island, near Brookhaven.

98. *Year 1802.* Two ships were lost: Dutch ship *Mary*, Captain Seimen, arriving from Amsterdam, lost in lower New York Bay; and a ship of unknown registry, *Catherine Ray*, Captain Benthall, arriving from Lisbon, wrecked on February 21 on Long Island, crew and part of her cargo saved.

99. *Year 1804.* Ship of unknown registry, *Nelly*, Captain Nueller, arriving from Newfoundland, wrecked on Long Island.

100. *Year 1805.* American merchantman *Cato*, Captain Updell, arriving from New York, wrecked on January 16 on Long Island.

101. Year 1806. Scottish merchantman *Edward*, Captain Babcock, arriving from Dublin, was totally lost on Long Island but all of her crew was saved.

102. Year 1807. Three merchantmen of unknown registry were lost: the *Nereus*, Captain Stowe, arriving from St. Vincent's, wrecked on Long Island; the *Selby*, Captain Pratt, arriving from Jamaica, wrecked on March 25 near Manhattan; and the *Mississippi*, Captain Stedmore, arriving from London, wrecked in lower New York Bay, crew and some of her cargo saved.

103. Year 1808. Two American merchantmen were lost: the *Flora*, Captain Adams, arriving from New Orleans with a cargo of cotton, burnt on the East River; and the *Little George*, arriving from Newfoundland, wrecked on January 29 near Long Island.

104. Year 1809. American merchantman *True American*, Captain Newson, arriving from Haiti, wrecked on February 20 near The Narrows in upper New York Bay.

105. Year 1810. American merchantman *Cincinnati*, bound for Lisbon, wrecked on Governor's Island during a gale on November 10.

106. Year 1811. During a violent storm on December 23 and 24, between fifty and sixty large unidentified ships were wrecked on the south side of Long Island. Two other ships were lost on Long Island earlier in the year: the English merchantman *Olive Branch*, Captain Newman, arriving from Liverpool, crew and passengers were saved; and the English warship H.M.S. *Thistle*, 10 guns, Captain George McPherson, on March 6, six of her crew of fifty perished.

107. Year 1812. American ship *Lucy & Elizabeth*, Captain Bray, arriving from Lisbon, lost in lower New York Bay but all of her crew was saved.

108. Year 1815. Four English ships were lost: warship H.M.S. *Sylph*, 18 guns, Captain George Dickens, wrecked on Southampton Bar, Long Island, 115 of her crew of 121 perished; and three merchantmen—*Nelson*, Captain Scoffin, arriving from London, sank in lower New York Bay; *Vidette*, Captain Hammond, arriving from Guadeloupe, wrecked October 28 on Long Island, three persons drowned; and the *Friendship*, sailing from Halifax to Jamaica, wrecked during a gale on September 23 on Staten Island but most of her cargo was saved.

109. *Year 1818.* English merchantman *Albion,* Captain Cox, wrecked on Coney Island in February, her crew and cargo saved.

110. *Year 1821.* During a hurricane on September 4, New York City suffered severe damages. A large ferryboat sank at Whitehall Dock, a sloop sank at Coenties Slip, ten large ships sank at the Quarantine, twelve other large ships sank at Public Store Dock #12, four ships wrecked at Fountain Ferry, five ships wrecked at the Kilm, and a large number were wrecked along the south side of Long Island. Earlier in the year, two American merchantmen were wrecked on Long Island: the *Savannah,* Captain Holdridge, arriving from Savannah, but most of her cargo was saved; and the *Albert,* Captain Salter, sailing from Portsmouth, New Hampshire, to Philadelphia.

111. *Year 1822.* Four American merchantmen wrecked on Long Island: the *Savannah,* Captain Cole, arriving from Liverpool, during October, with a total loss of lives; the *Elizabeth,* Captain Williams, arriving from Amsterdam, on May 22, all of her crew and part of her cargo saved; the *Ruth,* Captain Hughson, sailing from South America to Canada, near Mount Desart on April 2; and the *Augusta,* Captain Peterson, during a gale on October 27, at Shrewsbury Beach.

112. *Year 1823.* Spanish schooner *Ligera,* Captain Rock, arriving from Havana, wrecked at Montauk Point, Long Island, and only a small part of the specie she carried was recovered.

113. *Year 1824.* Three merchantmen wrecked on Long Island: the American ship *Pocahontas,* Captain Grover, arriving from Jamaica, on April 11, one person drowned; English ship *Edward Douglas,* Captain Carlew, sailing to Haiti, on September 14, no lives lost; and the English ship *Nestor,* Captain Pease, arriving from Liverpool, on November 28.

114. *Year 1825.* During a hurricane on June 3 or 4, the Colombian warship *Venezuela* wrecked in New York Harbor and the American schooner *Hornet* foundered off Long Island.

NEW JERSEY:

115. *Year 1704.* A privateer vessel, *Castle del Rey,* 18 guns, 130 tons, Captain Otto Van Tyle, was struck by a gale after sailing from

Manhattan and wrecked on a shoal near Sandy Hook. Of her crew of 145, only thirteen survived, as the ship quickly went to pieces.

116. *Year 1768.* English merchantman *Sally,* Captain Rankin, sailing from England to Philadelphia, wrecked off Little Egg Harbor.

117. *Year 1777.* Irish merchantman *Norbury,* Captain Wood, sailing from Cork to New York, wrecked at Sandy Hook, crew and most of her cargo saved.

118. *Year 1778.* English warship H.M.S. *Zebra,* 16 guns, Captain Henry Collins, wrecked during October at Egg Island Harbor.

119. *Year 1779.* Three American merchantmen were lost: *Mary,* Captain Peppard, arriving from St. Kitts, sank near Sandy Hook during a gale; an unidentified ship, arriving from Antigua with a cargo of rum, was also lost at the same time near the above-mentioned ship; and the *Betsey,* Captain Parke, sailing from Providence, Rhode Island, to New York was wrecked at Great Egg Harbor.

120. *Year 1783.* Nine merchantmen were lost: *Jupiter,* Captain Rumage, sailing from Jamaica to New York, totally lost off Cape May, two men perished. During a gale on September 19, four others were lost at Cape May: *New York,* Captain Fortey, sailing from Glasgow to New York, but her crew was saved; *Two Friends,* Captain Bevan, sailing to Philadelphia; *Betsey,* Captain Brown, sailing to Philadelphia; and the *Mercury,* Captain Herpin, sailing from Dunkirk to Philadelphia. During another gale, on October 8, two unidentified ships sank at Cape May and two others near Great Egg Harbor.

121. *Year 1784.* American merchantman *Charming Nancy,* Captain Penkham, sailing from Philadelphia to the West Indies, wrecked during a gale at Cape May Roads but some of her cargo was saved.

122. *Year 1789.* American merchantman *Nymph,* Captain Palmer, sailing from Oporto to New York, wrecked during November near Barnegat.

123. *Year 1791.* Two ships were lost: English merchantman *Betsey,* Captain Douglas, sailing from London to New York, wrecked at Barnegat; and a ship of unknown registry, *Boston & Liverpool,*

Captain Laud, sailing from Liverpool to Philadelphia, wrecked near Barnegat.

124. *Year 1792.* Two merchantmen of unknown registry were lost: *Fanny,* Captain Johnson, sailing from the Virgin Islands to Philadelphia, wrecked at Cape May; and the *Wilhelmina,* Captain Steele, sailing from New London to Dublin, wrecked north of Cape May but her crew was saved.

125. *Year 1793.* Three merchantmen were lost: English ship *Manchester,* Captain Clay, sailing from Liverpool to Philadelphia, wrecked on Egg Island Shoals; American ship *Swallow,* Captain Wright, sailing from Antigua to New York, wrecked near Sandy Hook; and the American ship *Edward,* Captain Goodrich, arriving from Turk's Island, Bahamas, lost on Barnegat Shoals.

126. *Year 1794.* Italian ship *St. Francesco de Paula Costellina,* Captain Genovese, sailing from France to New York, lost on Little Egg Harbor Bar.

127. *Year 1802.* Spanish warship *Juno,* 34 guns, sailing from Mexico to Spain, was driven off course by strong winds and due to many bad leaks sank on October 29 near Cape May, carrying all of her 425 persons and over 300,000 pesos in silver to the bottom.

128. *Year 1803.* American ship *Virginia,* Captain Darby, sailing from London to New York, lost south of Sandy Hook, several of her crew and passengers perished.

129. *Year 1804.* Two American merchantmen were lost: *William,* Captain Ashton, arriving from the Canary Islands, sank near Sandy Hook; a gale caused an unidentified ship to wreck on Absecon Beach (present-day Atlantic City) on October 9.

130. *Year 1805.* English brig *Recovery,* sailing from England to New York, wrecked at Sandy Hook.

131. *Year 1806.* Two American merchantmen were lost: the *Columbia,* Captain Lewis, sailing from Lisbon to New York, totally lost near Little Egg Harbor on January 4; during a hurricane on August 24, the *Rose in Bloom* sank off the central New Jersey coast.

132. *Year 1807.* Ship of unknown registry, *Walters,* Captain Homer, sailing from Amsterdam to New York, wrecked on January 16, near Sandy Hook but all of her crew was saved.

133. *Year 1808.* Three merchantmen were lost: English ship *Ida*, sailing from Lisbon to Philadelphia, lost near Cape May on February 16; Italian ship *Thetis*, Captain Granbury, wrecked on Cape May on February 16; and American ship *Cato*, Captain Darrell, arriving from the Bahamas, lost November 11 at Sandy Hook.

134. *Year 1809.* American merchantman *Harnett*, Captain Gardner, arriving from Jamaica, lost on February 20 near Sandy Hook.

135. *Year 1810.* Ship of unknown registry, *Sally*, Captain Moffet, sailing from England to New York, totally lost on September 22 near Barnegat.

136. *Year 1811.* Three merchantmen were lost: American ship *Success*, Captain Forbes, sailing from the Virgin Islands to New York, wrecked on January 16 near Sandy Hook; English ship *Amelia*, sailing from England to New York, wrecked February 16 at Sandy Hook; and a ship of unknown registry, *Belle Air*, Captain Allen, sailing from Norway and Cork to Philadelphia, wrecked near Egg Harbor but her crew was saved.

137. *Year 1815.* American ship *Clarendon*, Captain Gainess, sailing from Bermuda to New York, wrecked at Sandy Hook on April 7, crew and passengers saved.

138. *Year 1816.* English merchantman *Robert Walne*, sailing from London to New York, wrecked on Sandy Hook on August 22, a small part of her cargo was saved.

139. *Year 1817.* Ship of unknown registry, *Hannah*, Captain Askwith, sailing to New York, wrecked on April 19 off Tom's River, crew and cargo saved.

140. *Year 1819.* English merchantman *Andrew*, Captain Hathaway, sailing from Liverpool to Philadelphia, wrecked at Barnegat, her crew was saved.

141. *Year 1820.* English merchantman *Caledonia*, Captain Struthers, sailing from Liverpool to New York, wrecked on December 28 about 10 miles south of Sandy Hook, three persons were drowned.

142. *Year 1821.* English ship *Syren*, sailing from the Caribbean to Boston, wrecked around February at Great Egg Harbor. During a hurricane on September 3, a large number of unidentified ships sank in the vicinity of Cape May.

143. *Year 1822.* Three merchantmen were lost: English ship *Enterprize*, sailing from Maine to Philadelphia, lost in May near Little Egg Harbor, her crew was saved; Scottish ship *Hind*, sailing from Dundee to New York, wrecked at Sandy Hook on January 28; and a ship of unknown registry, *Citizen*, Captain Loring, sailing from Manila to New York, wrecked on April 9 on Brigantine Shoals, near Egg Harbor, but then drifted off and sank in 5 fathoms of water, her crew was saved.

144. *Year 1823* American ship *Union*, Captain Cotter, sailing from Londonderry and Bermuda to New York, wrecked at Sandy Hook but her crew was saved.

145. *Year 1824.* Two merchantmen of unknown registry were lost: the *Rebecca*, Captain Stairs, sailing from the West Indies to Halifax, wrecked on December 2 at Sandy Point; and the *Hunter*, sailing from France to Philadelphia, wrecked at Cape May, crew and cargo saved.

146. *Year 1825.* American merchantman *Trumbell*, Captain Hitchcock, sailing from Trinidad to New York, wrecked at Sandy Hook.

DELAWARE COAST, BAY, AND RIVER:

147. *Year 1741.* English merchantman *Mercury*, Captain Hogg, sailing from Philadelphia to London, lost near the Delaware River.

148. *Year 1757.* Three English merchantmen lost: *Sally*, Captain Saze, sailing from Philadelphia to Antigua, lost at Brandy Wine on the Delaware River; *Pusey*, Captain Good, arriving from Jamaica, wrecked on Reedy Island in the Delaware River; and the *Cornelia*, Captain Smith, sailing from Philadelphia to Gibraltar, sank between capes Henlopen and May, three of her crew perished.

149. *Year 1760.* Scottish merchantman *Molly*, Captain Stewart, sank in the Delaware River.

150. *Year 1763.* Two English merchantmen lost: the *Vaughan*, Captain Foster, sailing from Bristol to Philadelphia, wrecked in Delaware Bay; and the *Pitt Packet*, Captain Montgomery, sailing from Belfast to Philadelphia with a large number of passengers, foundered in Delaware Bay with a total loss of life.

151. *Year 1766.* American merchantman *Charlestown,* Captain Simpson, sailing from Hamburg to Philadelphia, wrecked on January 25 on the Branclawine Bank in Delaware Bay.

152. *Year 1768.* Ship of unknown registry, *Kildare,* Captain Nicholson, sailing from Barbados to Philadelphia, lost at the mouth of the Delaware River.

153. *Year 1771.* English merchantman *Commerce,* Captain Addis, sailing from England to New York, wrecked at Cape Henlopen, very little of her cargo was saved.

154. *Year 1774.* English merchantman *Severn,* Captain Hathorn, sailing from Bristol to Philadelphia, wrecked in Delaware Bay but all of her crew was saved.

155. *Year 1775.* English merchantman *Endeavor,* Captain Caldwell, sailing from Philadelphia to Londonderry, caught fire and sank off Reedy Island in the Delaware River but most of her cargo was saved.

156. *Year 1777.* Seven American warships were lost during a battle with the British in Delaware Bay: *Washington,* 32 guns; *Effingham,* 28 guns; *Sachem,* 10 guns; *Independence,* 10 guns; *Dolphin,* 10 guns; *Wasp,* 8 guns; and the *Mosquito,* 4 guns. Another American warship, the *Andrea Doria,* 14 guns, was burnt to prevent her capture, also in Delaware Bay.

157. *Year 1783.* During a severe gale in the fall, nine large unidentified ships were wrecked at Cape Henlopen and many lives were lost.

158. *Year 1874.* Ship of unknown registry, *Peace,* Captain Star, sailing from London to Virginia, wrecked on Hog Island, in Delaware Bay, some of her cargo was saved.

159. *Year 1785.* Scottish immigrant ship *Faithful Stewart,* Captain M'Causland, sailing from Londonderry to Philadelphia, sank near Cape Henlopen, over two hundred persons perished.

160. *Year 1788.* Spanish merchantman *Santa Rosalea,* Captain Pardenus, sailing from Baltimore to Havana, wrecked near Cape Henlopen but some of her cargo was saved.

161. *Year 1789.* English ship *Pomona*, Captain Hopkins, coming from Quebec, sank in Delaware Bay on October 30.

162. *Year 1790.* English merchantman *John*, Captain Staples, arriving from England, wrecked December 5 on the Delaware River, near Philadelphia but some of her cargo was saved.

163. *Year 1793.* American merchantman *Industry*, Captain Carson, sailing from France to Philadelphia, sank in Delaware Bay, near Cape May.

164. *Year 1794.* Two merchantmen were lost in Delaware Bay: a Spanish ship, *San Joseph*, sailing from Philadelphia to Cuba, lost due to ice crushing her hull; the American ship *Peggy*, sailing from Philadelphia to Savannah.

165. *Year 1795.* Ship of unknown registry, *Lively*, Captain Lawrence, sailing from Amsterdam to New York, sank near Lewes, only her crew was saved.

166. *Year 1796.* Three American merchantmen were lost: *Henry & Charles*, sailing from Philadelphia to Hamburg, wrecked near Cape Henlopen; *Favorite*, sailing from Cadiz to Philadelphia, sank in Delaware Bay; and the *Minerva*, sailing from Lisbon to Philadelphia, wrecked near the mouth of the Delaware River, seven of her crew perished.

167. *Year 1797:* American ship *John*, Captain Folger, sailing from Hamburg to Philadelphia with over three hundred immigrants, wrecked near Cape Henlopen.

168. *Year 1798.* English warship H.M.S. *De Braak*, 16 guns, Captain James Drew, capsized and sank near Lewes, thirty-five of her crew perished. At the time of the disaster she carried 70 tons of copper ingots and a large amount of gold and silver bullion and specie. Over the years there have been many attempts to locate this shipwreck and recover her treasure but all have failed.

169. *Year 1799.* American merchantman *New Jersey*, Captain Clay, sailing from Puerto Rico to Philadelphia, wrecked on the west side of Delaware Bay.

170. *Year 1800.* Three merchantmen were lost: English ship *George*, preparing to sail for England, sank at Philadelphia; American

ship *Susannah,* Captain Medlin, sailing from Hamburg to Philadelphia, wrecked in Delaware Bay; and an unidentified ship sank near the mouth of the Delaware River.

171. *Year 1801.* Two American merchantmen sank in Delaware Bay: *Adriana,* sailing from Philadelphia to Dublin, due to heavy ice, and the *Constellation,* sailing for New York.

172. *Year 1804.* During a hurricane on October 9, a large newly arrived unidentified ship sank at Philadelphia.

173. *Year 1805.* Two merchantmen of unknown registry sank in Delaware Bay: *China,* Captain M'Pherson, sailing from Batavia to Philadelphia, part of her cargo was saved; and the *Fanny,* Captain Wing, sailing from France to Philadelphia.

174. *Year 1811.* American ship *Matilda,* sailing from the Canary Islands to Baltimore, wrecked on the north side of Delaware Bay, crew and part of cargo saved.

175. *Year 1824.* American merchantman *Adeline,* Captain Israel, sailing from North Carolina to Philadelphia, wrecked December 9 at Cape Henlopen.

MARYLAND:

176. *Year 1753.* English merchantman *Swan,* Captain Clarkson, sailing from Baltimore to London with three hundred hogsheads of tobacco, burnt shortly after leaving Baltimore.

177. *Year 1766.* English merchantman *Hawke,* Captain Price, sailing for Cadiz, sank in the upper reaches of Chesapeake Bay but all of her crew was saved.

178. *Year 1769.* Scottish merchantman *Earl of Chatham,* Captain Wolsey, sailing from Dublin to Maryland, was lost near Cambridge but some of her cargo was salvaged.

179. *Year 1770.* English merchantman *Boyne,* Captain Howard, arriving from St. Kitts, wrecked in Chesapeake Bay near Baltimore.

180. *Year 1775.* English ship *Totness,* Captain Waring, was set afire by Indians and totally destroyed near St. Mary's City but no lives were lost.

181. Year 1781. Early in the year a storm severely damaged the British fleet, and the H.M.S. *Culloden*, 74 guns, was lost, except for her masts, which were later salvaged. Later in the year the British scuttled three of their warships in the northern part of Chesapeake Bay: H.M.S. *Guadeloupe*, 28 guns, Captain Hugh Robinson; H.M.S. *Charon*, 44 guns, Captain Thomas Symonds; and the fire ship, H.M.S. *Vulcan*, 8 guns, Captain George Palmer.

182. Year 1806. English merchantman *Ruthy*, after arriving from Liverpool, wrecked at the mouth of the Baltimore River, crew and some cargo saved.

183. Year 1808. Ship of unknown registry, *Mary*, Captain Hunt, was lost during a gale on September 12 at Baltimore.

184. Year 1817. Canadian brig *Hannah*, arriving from St. Johns, New Brunswick, wrecked at the mouth of the Potomac River at the end of May.

VIRGINIA:

185. Year 1689. English warship H.M.S. *Deptford*, 10 guns, Captain Thomas Berry, wrecked on August 26 near Cedar Island but no lives were lost.

186. Year 1706. During a hurricane a fleet of fourteen unidentified merchantmen were lost on the northern coast of Cape Charles after setting sail for England.

187. Year 1724. During a hurricane on August 12, several ships were wrecked on the James River but most of their cargoes were saved.

188. Year 1739. In January, an unidentified ship carrying over three hundred immigrants from Germany to the James River wrecked off Cape Henry, there were only ten survivors.

189. Year 1741. English merchantman *Sea Nymph*, Captain Ecles, sailing for England, was lost on Hog Island, many of her crew perished.

190. Year 1746. Two Scottish merchantmen, *Prince George*, Captain Coulter, and the *Glasgow*, Captain Montgomery, were captured near Cape Charles by a French warship. After the crews and cargoes were transferred to the French ship, both merchantmen were burnt.

191. *Year 1749.* English merchantman *Tamphough,* Captain Brag, arriving from England, wrecked on Cobb Island but her crew was saved.

192. *Year 1750.* A hurricane on August 18 struck the New Spain Flota of Captain General Juan Manuel de Bonilla off Cape Hatteras, North Carolina, and four ships were lost in this vicinity. Three other Spanish ships were lost on the coast of Virginia: *Nuestra Señora de los Godos,* near Cape Charles, *La Galga,* 15 leagues north of Cape Charles, and an unidentified brigantine, 6 leagues north of this cape. The *Capitana Nuestra Señora de Guadalupe* and the galleon *Zumaca* reached Norfolk; however, both ships and twelve unidentified English merchantmen were lost during another hurricane several weeks later.

193. *Year 1751.* English merchantman *King's Fisher,* Captain Bibby, sailing from New England to South Carolina with a cargo of prisoners, was captured by these prisoners, who murdered the captain and crew, then wrecked the ship at Wallop's Island.

194. *Year 1753.* Two merchantmen were lost: Irish ship *Flower of Cork,* Captain Chip, arriving from Cork, was wrecked on the coast 5 leagues south of Cape Henry but the crew was saved; American ship *Lucy,* sailing from Maryland to Lisbon with a cargo of wheat, wrecked on the Middle Ground, between capes Henry and Charles.

195. *Year 1754.* English ship *Pearl* caught fire and blew up in the vicinity of Cape Charles.

196. *Year 1757.* Five English merchantmen were lost: *Duke,* Captain Maitland, sailing for London, foundered four days after setting sail; *Lydia,* Captain Teague, foundered near Cape Henry; *Duke of Cumberland,* Captain Ball, sailing from the Canaries to Virginia, was lost 9 leagues south of Cape Henry and twenty-five of her crew perished; at the same time a brig and a snow were lost in the area, all of the snow's crew perished.

197. *Year 1760.* Two English merchantmen were wrecked 25 miles south of Cape Henry: *Neptune,* Captain Burdon, and the *Thomas & Richard,* Captain Wilkinson, both arriving from London.

198. *Year 1761.* English merchantman *Russel,* Captain Calder, sailing for Barbados, lost when passing Cape Henry, crew and part of cargo saved.

199. *Year 1762.* English merchantman *Sally*, Captain Pritchard, sailing from Philadelphia to Lisbon, and two unidentified ships were lost off Cape Charles but both crews were saved.

200. *Year 1764.* Two merchantmen were lost: English ship *Brothers*, Captain Morrison, sailing for London, was wrecked near Cape Henry but her crew was saved; American schooner *Friendship*, Captain Clark, sailing from Barbados to Philadelphia, was wrecked on November 25 a little southward of Cape Henry, two of her crew perished.

201. *Year 1766.* English merchantman *Rogers*, Captain Wignell, arriving from Liverpool, wrecked on the Middle Ground, between capes Henry and Charles, but the crew was saved.

202. *Year 1768.* English merchantman *Charles*, Captain Waterman, arriving from London, was totally lost on Cobb Island, several of her crew perished.

203. *Year 1769.* During a hurricane on September 7 and 8, four large English merchantmen were wrecked on the York River and two on the James River. In November, the English merchantman *Randolph*, Captain Andrews, arriving from Bristol, wrecked off Cape Henry but all of her crew was saved.

204. *Year 1770.* English merchantman *Gorel*, Captain Rymey, arriving from Liverpool, was lost 3 leagues north of Cape Charles but most of her cargo was saved.

205. *Year 1771.* American merchantman *Kitty*, Captain Shaw, sailing for England, sank off Cape Charles during a gale.

206. *Year 1772.* Dutch merchantman *Jane Pierre*, Captain Veffer, sailing from the Caribbean to Amsterdam, foundered on December 24 near Cape Henry, her crew was saved.

207. *Year 1775.* Three English merchantmen were lost: *Hibernia*, Captain Morrison, arriving from Londonderry, wrecked during a violent storm on September 2 about 10 leagues south of Cape Henry; *Five Oak*, Captain Peaton, arriving from the Leeward Islands, totally wrecked on Hog Island, only two of the crew

saved; and the *Minerva,* Captain Ewing, arriving from Londonderry, wrecked on September 4 at Cape Charles.

208. Year 1776. English merchantman *Molly,* Captain Collins, preparing to sail for Liverpool, was burnt at Norfolk.

209. Year 1781. During the British siege of Yorktown during the month of October, at least six British warships and other smaller support vessels were sunk.

210. Year 1784. Ship of unknown registry, *Cox,* Captain Mason, sailing from Barbados to Philadelphia, was wrecked on Assateague Island but her crew was saved.

211. Year 1785. During September and October, many severe storms struck the vicinity of Virginia and several large ships were sunk or destroyed along the coasts and in the rivers. During one tremendous gale at Portsmouth, several large ships were carried a long way into the woods. Earlier in the year the English ship *Grange,* arriving from England, was wrecked at Cape Charles but all of her cargo was saved.

212. Year 1786. American packet boat *Maryland,* Captain Brown, arriving from London, was wrecked on Cape Henry, her crew was saved.

213. Year 1787. English merchantman *Nonsuch,* Captain Wallace, arriving from London, was lost on the Middle Ground between capes Charles and Henry, her crew was saved.

214. Year 1788. During a bad gale at Norfolk on July 23, many unidentified ships were destroyed and sunk.

215. Year 1790. Six merchantmen were lost: Scottish ship *William,* Captain Church, sailing for Dublin, wrecked on Cape Charles, her cargo was saved; American ship *Jane & Dianna,* Captain Handwith, sailing from Norfolk to Spain, lost near Cape Henry; English ship *Kitty & Alice,* arriving from Jamaica, lost near Cape Henry; Scottish ship *Lovely Ann,* arriving from Glasgow, wrecked near Cape Charles; French ship *Fanny,* arriving from the Channel Islands, wrecked near Cape Charles; and the American ship *Flora,* Captain Finlay, sailing from London to Philadelphia, wrecked about 25 miles north of Cape Charles.

216. Year 1791. Three English merchantmen were lost: *Rainbow*, Captain Coward, sailing from Newfoundland to Philadelphia, near Cape Henry, her crew was saved; *Nanty*, Captain Foster, sailing to London, lost in Hampton Roads; and the *Swan*, Captain Dale, sailing for London, lost on Hog Island.

217. Year 1795. During a gale on August 2, a large unidentified ship sank off Cape Charles with a total loss of lives.

218. Year 1797. Two English ships were lost: merchantman *Martin*, sailing for London, lost at Hampton Roads; and the warship H.M.S. *Hunter*, 18 guns, Captain Tudor Tucker, wrecked December 27 on Hog Island, seventy-five of her crew of eighty perished.

219. Year 1798. Two merchantmen of unknown registries were lost: *Antony Mangin*, Captain Stafford, sailing from Hamburg to Baltimore, lost near Cape Charles; and the *Inclination*, Captain Coster, sailing from Bremen to Baltimore, wrecked on Hog Island.

220. Year 1800. English merchantman *June*, Captain Rexburg, sailing from Liverpool to Baltimore, was totally lost on Hog Island, only a few of the crew survived.

221. Year 1801. American merchantman *Suffolk*, Captain Doggett, sailing from New York to Norfolk, was totally lost on the Middle Ground between capes Henry and Charles, crew and passengers saved.

222. Year 1804. Ship of unknown registry, *Samuel Smith*, Captain Stiles, arriving from the Far East with a valuable cargo, wrecked south of Cape Henry, many of her crew perished.

223. Year 1805. American merchantman *Adventure*, Captain Smith, arriving from Jamaica, wrecked September 7 on Cape Henry but her crew and some of her cargo were saved.

224. Year 1806. Two ships wrecked near Cape Henry: English merchantman *Sheperdess*, Captain Wells, arriving from London, crew and passengers saved; and the French warship *Impetueux*, 74 guns, forced ashore by two British frigates and destroyed.

225. Year 1807. American merchantman *Betsey*, Captain Tredwell, fully laden and ready to sail for Liverpool, was accidentally burnt at anchor at Norfolk and sank.

226. Year 1808. English merchantman *William Murdock*, Captain Brooks, sailing in ballast from Rotterdam to the Potomac River, wrecked on Cape Charles in January but no lives were lost.

227. Year 1809. American merchantman *Robert*, Captain Stocking, sailing from Jamaica to Philadelphia, wrecked on August 31 at Cape Henry but her crew was saved.

228. Year 1810. American merchantman *Lucy*, Captain Pickman, sailing from Madeira Island to Baltimore, wrecked on Cape Henry but crew and some wine cargo were saved.

229. Year 1811. Two ships were lost: French privateer *Revanche du Cerf* was captured by an American naval vessel and taken into Norfolk, where it was stripped and burnt on April 16; and an American ship, *Heroine*, Captain Maxwell, sailing from Lisbon to Norfolk, wrecked April 14 on Hog Island but no lives were lost.

230. Year 1813. French ship *Tamerlane*, after being captured, was totally lost on Cape Henry, only a small part of the large amount of silver and gold specie was saved.

231. Year 1818. American merchantman *Clotilda*, Captain Brotherdon, sailing from New Orleans to Philadelphia, wrecked on Cape Henry on March 5 and eleven men drowned.

232. Year 1821. During a hurricane that struck Norfolk on September 3, two American war frigates—*Congress* and *Guerriere*—plus a large number of brigs, schooners, and smaller vessels were sunk or wrecked.

233. Year 1822. Four merchantmen were lost: one, unidentified, wrecked near the boundary line of Virginia and North Carolina, no lives were lost; Spanish ship *La Plata*, sailing from Havana to Baltimore, was totally lost on October 22 near Cape Charles, no lives were lost; Dutch ship *Janus*, Captain Windt, arriving from Bremen, totally wrecked on Cape Henry, no lives were lost; and a ship of unknown registry, *Seaflower*, Captain Bascombe, arriving in ballast from St. Vincent, lost near Cape Henry, crew and sails saved.

234. Year 1824. Two merchantmen were lost: English ship *Liverpool*, Captain Nash, arriving from Jamaica, lost March 10 to the southward of Cape Henry, crew and part of cargo saved; and American ship *Mary & Ann,* Captain Barlow, sailing from Havana to Philadelphia, wrecked November 19 on Hog Island Shoals.

NORTH CAROLINA:

235. *Year 1526.* A small unidentified Spanish brigantine, which was sent from Cuba on a voyage of exploration along the eastern coast of the United States, was wrecked during the month of June at Cape Fear. The survivors made a smaller vessel from the wreckage and managed to reach Santo Domingo with great hardship.

236. *Year 1585.* English ship *Tiger,* on a voyage of exploration, wrecked on June 29 at Ocracoke Inlet but no lives were lost.

237. *Year 1665.* An unidentified English fly-boat was wrecked at Cape Fear but no lives were lost.

238. *Year 1666.* An unidentified English sloop wrecked at Cape Lookout but all cargo was salvaged by the survivors.

239. *Year 1710.* English warship H.M.S. *Garland* was wrecked November 29 on a small sandbar a little southward of Currituck Inlet and fifteen of her crew perished. The wreck sanded over before anything could be salvaged.

240. *Year 1728.* During a hurricane, an unidentified English ship was wrecked 6 miles seaward from Ocracoke Inlet and there were only a few survivors.

241. *Year 1739.* English merchantman *Adriatick,* Captain Hanney, sailing from London to Virginia, wrecked at Cape Hatteras with a large loss of lives.

242. *Year 1741.* Two English merchantmen were lost off Cape Hatteras: *Hoylin,* Captain Cunningham, arriving from Bristol, no lives were lost, and the *Woolford,* Captain Kenlock, sailing from Jamaica to London.

243. *Year 1743.* American coastal trader *George,* Captain Raitt, sailing from Boston to North Carolina, wrecked near Oregon Inlet but no lives were lost.

244. *Year 1744.* Two English merchantmen sailing for London were lost on Diamond Shoals: *Katherine & Elizabeth,* Captain Webster, and the *Neptune,* Captain Knowler.

245. *Year 1749.* During a hurricane on October 7 and 8, eleven English merchantmen were totally lost: at Ocracoke Inlet, seven sank inside the bar and two were wrecked 5 miles north of the inlet; at Cape Fear the *Dolphin,* Captain Cleavers, sank; and the *John & Jane,* Captain Close, foundered 9 leagues seaward of the Cape Fear bar.

246. *Year 1750.* During a hurricane on August 18, four ships of the New Spain Flota of Captain General Juan Manuel de Bonilla were lost: the galleon *Nuestra Señora de la Soledad,* wrecked 10 leagues north of Ocracoke Inlet; the merchant *nao El Salvador* wrecked 15 leagues north of Ocracoke Inlet; an unidentified *nao* wrecked at Topsail Inlet and another at Drum Inlet. The Spaniards and the English recovered the majority of the treasure. During the hurricane an unidentified English merchantman was lost off Cape Hatteras with a total loss of lives.

247. *Year 1751.* English merchantman *Greyhound,* Captain Cook, sailing from Boston to North Carolina, wrecked during bad weather near Salmon Creek, in the Chowan River, but no lives were lost.

248. *Year 1752.* Three merchantmen were lost: two unidentified schooners arriving from Virginia wrecked on the Ocracoke Bar; and an unidentified English brigantine, Captain Murray, sailing for London, wrecked near Cape Fear.

249. *Year 1757.* Three ships were lost at Cape Hatteras: American merchantman *Union,* Captain Hammond, coming from Rhode Island, lost in January; English packet boat *Virginia Packet,* Captain Ball, sailing from Bristol to Virginia; and an unidentified American schooner, Captain Hayman, sailing to the Leeward Islands.

250. *Year 1758.* Three English merchantmen were lost at Cape Hatteras: *Friendship,* Captain Briscal, arriving from England, no lives were lost; *Peggy,* Captain Abercrombie, sailing from Philadelphia to South Carolina; and the *Princess Amelia,* Captain Freizwell, sailing from Halifax to South Carolina.

251. *Year 1759.* English merchantman *Tyrrel,* wrecked July 3 off Bacon Island Roads, all of the crew were saved.

252. *Year 1760.* Six ships were lost: English merchantman *Nancy,* Captain M'Carroll, sailing from Philadelphia to Cape Fear, wrecked near Cape Hatteras; ship of unknown registry, *Four Lantons*, Captain Tasker, arriving from Jamaica, lost entering Edenton; English merchantman *Anne*, Captain Thresher, arriving from Cadiz, lost on the Cape Fear bar; English slave ship *Racehorse*, Captain Barker, carrying slaves from Africa to South Carolina, wrecked June 22 on Frying Pan Shoals and many lives were lost; English ship *Kingston*, Captain Goodman, sailing from Havana to Philadelphia, foundered off Cape Fear but the crew was rescued by a passing ship; and the Scottish merchantman *Charming Betsey*, Captain Watts, sailing from Lisbon to Virginia, foundered off Cape Hatteras, nine of the crew perished.

253. *Year 1763.* Two English merchantmen were lost: *Royal Charlotte*, Captain Severy, sailing from Montserrat to Georgia, wrecked at Long Bay; and the *Union*, Captain Blackburn, sailing from Barbados to North Carolina, was lost crossing the Cape Fear bar but her crew was saved.

254. *Year 1764.* Scottish merchantman *Shannon*, Captain Williamson, sailing from Virginia to Glasgow, wrecked at Currituck Inlet, crew and part of cargo saved.

255. *Year 1765.* English merchantman *Revenge*, Captain Whittingham, sailing from Curaçao to Norfolk, wrecked in June, two miles north of Currituck Inlet, only the crew was saved.

256. *Year 1767.* English slave ship *Good Intent*, Captain Copeland, arriving from Africa with over three hundred slaves, lost off Cape Hatteras.

257. *Year 1768.* Two merchantmen were lost: English ship *Beggars Bennison*, Captain Boyd, on Cape Lookout Shoals; and Scottish ship *Enterprize*, Captain Reid, totally lost during a gale on February 3, on Linger Shoals, inside the Cape Fear bar.

258. *Year 1770.* English merchantman *Charming Polly*, Captain Shoemaker, arriving from London, was totally lost off Cape Hatteras.

259. *Year 1771.* Two English merchantmen were lost: *Betsey*, Captain Roberts, arriving from London, at Old Topsail Inlet, no lives were lost; and the *Lively*, Captain Read, arriving from Grenada, off Cape Hatteras.

260. *Year 1772.* During a hurricane at the beginning of September, fourteen or fifteen unidentified large merchantmen were totally lost near the Ocracoke Inlet bar; and earlier in the year the English merchantman *Betsey*, Captain Leadbeater, was lost crossing this bar.

261. Year 1774. Two English merchantmen were lost: *Charming Betsey*, Captain Waugh, sailing from Baltimore to London, wrecked on Ocracoke Island, only a small part of her cargo was saved; and the *Sally*, Captain Keith, sailing from Maryland to Gibraltar, was lost on Cape Hatteras.

262. Year 1775. During a hurricane that struck the North Carolina coast on September 2, a large number of ships were lost, but only the English merchantman *Hector*, Captain Quince, arriving from London, lost on Frying Pan Shoals, was identified. Four other English merchantmen were lost during the year: *Royal Exchange*, Captain Daverson, bound for London, at Cape Lookout, all of her crew was saved; *Clementina*, Captain Weir, arriving from London, at Cape Hatteras; *Elizabeth & Mary*, arriving from England, lost entering Cape Fear Inlet; and the *Austin*, Captain Sarrat, sailing from Tobago to Liverpool, lost off Cape Hatteras.

263. Year 1776. Ship of unknown registry, *Aurora*, a brigantine, wrecked September 19 on Portsmouth Island.

264. Year 1777. English troop-transport *Aurora*, Captain Bishop, was lost on November 11 off Cape Hatteras, very few survivors.

265. Year 1783. American merchantman *Peggy*, Captain McNeil, sailing from the Virgin Islands to New York, was lost off Cape Hatteras, only a small part of her cargo was saved.

266. Year 1784. Ship of unknown registry, *Betsey*, Captain Flynn, sailing to Antigua, was totally lost near Cape Fear.

267. Year 1786. English ship *Britannia*, Captain Dunlop, arriving from England, wrecked south of the Cape Fear River but no lives were lost.

268. Year 1788. During a hurricane on July 23 and 24, seventeen ships were wrecked at Ocracoke Inlet but only a few lives were lost.

269. Year 1789. English merchantman *Molly*, Captain Baker, sailing from Dunkirk to Virginia, was wrecked at Cape Hatteras.

270. *Year 1790.* American ship *Pusey Hall,* Captain Simpson, sailing from Jamaica to Virginia, wrecked at Cape Lookout.

271. *Year 1791.* English merchantman *St. James Planter,* Captain Paxton, sailing from Jamaica to London, was lost near Cape Lookout but part of her cargo was saved.

272. *Year 1792.* Two merchantmen were lost: English ship *Pitt,* Captain Cook, arriving from Antigua, lost on the Ocracoke Inlet bar; and the American ship *Experiment,* Captain McDonald, sailing to New York, lost off Cape Hatteras.

273. *Year 1793.* Two American merchantmen were lost: the *Polly,* wrecked near Beaufort, no lives were lost; and the *Nancy,* Captain Beacon, sailing from Jamaica to Virginia, wrecked on a shoal off Currituck, no lives were lost.

274. *Year 1795.* During a bad gale on August 2, six unidentified ships were wrecked on the Ocracoke Inlet bar; during the same storm a fleet of eighteen Spanish ships, sailing from Havana to Spain, was struck off Cape Hatteras, an undisclosed number of these ships were lost.

275. *Year 1797.* American sloop *Betsey,* lost on September 6 at Currituck Inlet.

276. *Year 1798.* American merchantman *Industry,* Captain Woodend, sailing from St. Vincent to Virginia, was lost on Cape Hatteras.

277. *Year 1799.* German immigrant ship *Christian,* Captain Deetjen, sailing from Bremen to Baltimore, was lost near Cape Lookout, no lives lost and part of cargo saved.

278. *Year 1802.* Two English merchantmen were lost on Cape Hatteras: *Expectation,* Captain Baker, sailing from Antigua to North Carolina, and the *Brunshill,* Captain Bacon, sailing from England to Virginia, her crew was saved.

279. *Year 1804.* Four ships were lost: American packet boat *Wilmington Packet,* wrecked on September 8 at Bald Point, after first striking on Frying Pan Shoals; English ship *Lydia,* Captain Hatton, sailing from Wilmington to England, lost on Cape Hatteras; American merchantman *Molly,* Captain Mill, arriving from Jamaica, wrecked near Cape Hatteras; and a Spanish merchantman, *Santa Rosa,* Captain Fernandez, sailing from Havana to Bilbao with a great amount of treasure aboard, was lost near Wilmington about the middle of November.

280. *Year 1805.* Portuguese merchantman *Fortura,* Captain Rhode, sailing from Brazil to Baltimore, lost on Cape Hatteras but part of her cargo was saved.

281. *Year 1810.* Four merchantmen were lost: English ship *Rhine,* Captain Turnly, arriving from the Bahamas, lost crossing the Wilmington bar in September, no lives were lost; French ship *Maria,* sailing from Martinique to New York, lost on Cape Hatteras; English ship *Olympus,* arriving from England, was totally lost near Wilmington at the end of November; and the American ship *Lively Lass,* sailing from New Orleans to Liverpool, drifted onshore at Ocracoke Island at the end of September without any persons aboard.

282. *Year 1811.* English merchantman *Young Factor,* sailing for London, was lost crossing the Wilmington bar but no lives were lost.

283. *Year 1813.* Two ships were lost: American pilot boat *Patriot,* lost during January at Nags Head, and the Spanish brig *San Antonio,* Captain Fabre, was totally lost on February 18 near Wilmington but all of her crew were saved.

284. *Year 1814.* American gunboat *#140* wrecked on September 23 on Ocracoke Island.

285. *Year 1815.* During a hurricane early in September, more than twenty ships were wrecked or sunk at Ocracoke Inlet and on Ocracoke Island. During the year, three other ships were lost: American brig *Atlanta* on November 8 on Diamond Shoals but the crew was saved; English merchantman *Sero,* Captain Robinson, coming from Cuba, wrecked on September 25 off Cape Hatteras; and the American merchantman *Superior,* Captain Spence, sailing from Martinique to Philadelphia, lost October 3 near Cape Hatteras, crew and part of cargo saved.

286. *Year 1816.* Five merchantmen were lost: American ship *Eliza,* Captain Steele, sailing from Jamaica to Philadelphia, lost on Ocracoke Island, crew and part of cargo saved; American ship

Bolina, Captain Lee, sailing from New York to Charleston, wrecked on Boddy Island on September 26, crew and part of cargo saved; American ship *Little Dick,* sailing from Jamaica to Wilmington, lost crossing the Wilmington bar; English ship *Nancy,* Captain Scott, sailing from the Virgin Islands to Edenton, wrecked on January 23 near Newburn but the crew was saved; and a ship of unknown registry, *Mary,* sailing from Norfolk to Trinidad, wrecked on April 15 on Currituck Beach, most of her cargo was saved.

287. *Year 1817.* Five merchantmen were lost: American ship *Voucher,* Captain Howland, sailing from New York to Charleston, wrecked November 19 at Chicamacomico, all of crew, passengers, and cargo saved; ship of unknown registry, *Emperor of Russia,* sailing from Amsterdam to Boston, lost March 18 near Currituck Inlet, crew and part of cargo saved; American ship *John Adams,* sailing from Charleston to Norfolk, lost May 19 on Cape Hatteras, crew and some cargo saved; ship of unknown registry, *Rosetta,* Captain Sissen, arriving from New York, lost March 4 crossing the Ocracoke Inlet bar, crew and all cargo saved; and the American ship *Mary & Francis,* Captain Marsh, sailing from Madeira to Baltimore, wrecked during March near Cape Hatteras but most of her cargo was saved.

288. *Year 1818.* Five merchantmen were lost: during a storm on October 3, two unidentified American ships were wrecked near Cape Hatteras and the English ship *Fly* sank on Frying Pan Shoals. The American ship *William Carlton* wrecked May 15 at Kill Devil Hills and the English brig *Georgia,* Captain Colesworth, coming from New York, was wrecked July 15 at Currituck Inlet, crew and most of wood cargo saved.

289. *Year 1819.* Two American ships were lost: the schooner *Phoenix,* Captain Coffin, sailing to Philadelphia, wrecked May 13 on Cape Hatteras, and the sloop *Revenge* during January at Currituck Inlet.

290. *Year 1820.* Three American ships were lost: the sloop *Henry* during January on Ocracoke Island; the merchantman *Islington,* Captain Wilson, on March 16 at Cape Hatteras, and the ship *Horatio,* Captain Martin, during April on Diamond Shoals.

291. Year 1821. Four merchantmen were lost: an unidentified English ship of about 125 tons, with a cargo of rum, wrecked at Cape Hatteras in September, with a total loss of lives; American ship *Charles K. Mallory*, Captain Driver, arriving from St. Thomas, wrecked September 10 on Cape Hatteras, with a total loss of lives; English ship *Martha*, sailing from Bermuda to New London, wrecked at Currituck Sands; and American schooner *Sophia*, Captain Massey, sailing from Philadelphia to Norfolk, wrecked 10 miles north of Currituck Inlet, only one survivor.

292. Year 1822. Three ships were lost: a ship of unknown registry, *Nereus*, Captain Bosse, sailing from Bremen to Virginia, totally lost January 1 on Cape Hatteras; English merchantman *Statira*, sailing from Havana to London, lost on Frying Pan Shoals, no lives were lost; and the American schooner *Enterprize*, wrecked October 27 at New Inlet.

293. Year 1823. American ship *Peter Francisco*, Captain Reerson, sailing from New York to Mobile, wrecked October 7 on Bodies Island, crew, passengers, and all cargo saved.

294. Year 1824. Two ships were lost on the Ocracoke Inlet bar: the American schooner *Susan*, sailing from Demarara to Philadelphia, on June 1; and the French merchantman *Caroline du Nord*, Captain Grace, on January 19, no lives were lost.

295. Year 1825. During a hurricane on June 4, more than twenty-five unidentified ships were wrecked north of Ocracoke Inlet on the Outer Banks. During the year, seven other American ships were lost: *Washington*, coming from Jamaica, on January 24, at Ocracoke Island; *Nancy*, Captain Hatch, February 21, on the Ocracoke Inlet bar; merchantman *Horam*, Captain Eldridge, sailing from Boston to Jamaica, April 6, on the Ocracoke Inlet bar; schooner *Emulous*, January 22, at Kitty Hawk; schooner *Diomede*, January 23, at Kitty Hawk; schooner *Harvest*, Captain Murphy, November 18, at Bodie Island; and the schooner *Victory*, December, at Kitty Hawk.

SOUTH CAROLINA:

296. Year 1520. Unidentified Spanish *nao*, Captain Lucas Vázquez de Ayllon, wrecked near Cape Romain, no lives were lost.

297. *Year 1700.* Scottish merchantman *Rising Sun,* lost during a hurricane on September 3 on the Charleston bar.

298. *Year 1713.* During a hurricane in September, a large number of ships were sunk and wrecked in Charleston harbor.

299. *Year 1728.* During a hurricane on September 14, a great part of the town of Charleston was destroyed and eight ships were sunk in the harbor and fifteen badly damaged.

300. *Year 1750.* English merchantman *Caesar,* Captain Sparks, sailing from the Bay of Honduras for England, was forced to enter Charleston for repairs but was lost crossing the bar of this port.

301. *Year 1751.* Scottish merchantman *Martha,* Captain Shea, arriving from the Canary Islands, was wrecked on Cape Romain, all of her crew was saved.

302. *Year 1752.* During a hurricane on September 15, more than twenty large English merchantmen and three warships were totally lost in Charleston harbor. On September 30, another hurricane struck and twelve more newly arrived English merchantmen were also sunk. In April the English merchantman *Bennet,* Captain Wadham, preparing to sail for London, was accidentally burnt in Charleston harbor.

303. *Year 1757.* Slave ship of unknown registry, *Anamaboo,* Captain Ferguson, sailing from Africa to Rhode Island with a cargo of slaves, was totally lost near St. Helena Sound, only a few of the crew survived.

304. *Year 1758.* English merchantman *Marcella,* Captain Way, arriving from Lisbon, wrecked February 18 on a sandbank about 3 leagues from Charleston, totally salvaged and no lives were lost.

305. *Year 1759.* English merchantman *Judith,* Captain Martin, sailing from North Carolina to England, wrecked on Cape Romain.

306. *Year 1761.* Five ships were lost in Rebellion Road at Charleston during a hurricane on May 4: the English merchantman *Polly & Betsey,* Captain Muer; English merchantman *Success,* Captain Clark; English merchantman *Daniel,* Captain Lake; English ship *Britannia,* Captain Wilson; and an unidentified Bermudian schooner.

307. *Year 1766.* English merchantman *Speedwell,* Captain Redman, arriving from London, lost crossing the Charleston bar.

308. *Year 1767.* Two merchantmen were lost: Portuguese ship *St. Anthony,* Captain Arnold, sailing from Charleston to Oporto, foundered soon after leaving port, no lives were lost; and the English ship *Mary,* Captain Loveday, arriving from London, wrecked a bit south of Charleston but the crew, rigging, and sails were all saved.

309. *Year 1768.* English merchantman *York,* Captain Randell, sailing from Jamaica to London, forced into Charleston for repairs but lost in November while crossing the bar of this port, all cargo lost but crew saved.

310. *Year 1770.* English merchantman *Sergeant Glynn,* Captain Mogridge, arriving from London, totally lost near Port Royal Sound but no lives were lost.

311. *Year 1775.* English merchantman *Nancy,* Captain Cummingham, sailing from London to North Carolina, wrecked several leagues north of Charleston.

312. *Year 1776.* English warship H.M.S. *Acteon,* 28 guns, Captain Christopher Atkins, burnt in Charleston harbor by her crew on June 29.

313. *Year 1777.* English warship H.M.S. *Cruiser,* 8 guns, Captain Francis Parry, was burnt off Charleston by her crew to prevent its capture by the Americans.

314. *Year 1780.* During a battle off Charleston, a British fleet commanded by Vice-Admiral Arbuthnot, destroyed and sank three American naval vessels: *Bricole,* 44 guns; *General Moultrie,* 20 guns; and the *Notre Dame,* 16 guns. The British privateer *Vigilant,* 20 guns, Captain Thomas Goldesbrough, was burnt at Beaufort.

315. *Year 1781.* Six ships were lost: English warships *Thetis* and *London* sank at the Charleston docks during a hurricane on August 9; English merchantman *Despatch,* arriving from Jamaica, was driven ashore near Charleston by several American privateers and totally lost; English troop-transport *Leeds Industry,* Captain Hobkirk, sank in Charleston harbor; ship of unknown registry,

Jamaica, Captain McLeon, arriving from New York, capsized and sank in Charleston harbor; and the English merchantman *Port Morant,* sailing from Jamaica to London, wrecked on October 10 on a sandbank called Martin's Industry, to the eastward of Port Royal, but no lives were lost.

316. *Year 1784.* Three English merchantmen were lost on the Charleston bar: *America,* Captain Jameson, arriving from Scotland; *Swift,* Captain Craig, arriving from St. Augustine; and the *Suffolk,* Captain Warton, sailing for London, part of her cargo was saved.

317. *Year 1785.* English merchantman *Dispatch,* Captain Shields, fully loaded and ready to sail for London, totally lost at Georgetown harbor.

318. *Year 1787.* Two merchantmen were lost: English ship *Hope,* Captain Worsley, sailing to Hamburg, lost on the Charleston bar; and the Scottish ship *Three Friends,* Captain McElcheran, arriving from Tobago, wrecked near Charleston but some of her cargo was saved.

319. *Year 1791.* American ship *Governor Bickney,* Captain Hall, sailing to Hispaniola, wrecked on the Charleston bar.

320. *Year 1792.* During a severe gale on October 30, several large unidentified merchantmen were lost in Charleston harbor.

321. *Year 1796.* Two English merchantmen were lost: *Powhaton,* Captain Shaw, sailing from Liverpool to Jamaica, on the Charleston bar, most of her cargo was saved; and the *Grampus,* arriving from Liverpool, wrecked southward from Charleston.

322. *Year 1797.* Two merchantmen were lost: English ship *Three Friends,* Captain Bradford, sailing to London, lost on the Charleston bar; and the American ship *Polly,* Captain Higgins, arriving from Havana, wrecked near Charleston.

323. *Year 1799.* Ship of unknown registry, *Seaflower,* Captain Williams, arriving from Jamaica, was lost on the Georgetown bar, some of her cargo was saved.

324. *Year 1800.* English merchantman *Argus,* Captain Johnson, sailing for Liverpool, was lost on the Charleston bar but most of her cargo was saved.

325. *Year 1801.* English ship *Patrick,* Captain Salmon, arriving from Honduras, was lost on the Charleston bar.

326. *Year 1802.* American ship *Monticello,* Captain Newell, coming from the Leeward Islands, wrecked on Morris Island but some of her cargo was saved.

327. *Year 1804.* During a hurricane on September 11, five ships were sunk and eleven severely damaged in Charleston harbor.

328. *Year 1805.* Two English merchantmen were lost in Charleston harbor: *Northumberland,* Captain Gibb, arriving from Jamaica, October 14, the crew was saved, and the *Jack Park,* sailing for Liverpool, while crossing the bar.

329. *Year 1806.* Two English slave ships were wrecked when attempting to enter Charleston harbor: *John,* Captain Cummings, and the *Swan,* Captain Smith, no lives were lost on either ship.

330. *Year 1810.* Two English merchantmen were lost near Charleston: *Sarah,* Captain Milner, sailing from Havana to Jamaica, on May 7 on Morris Island, and the *Cracklow,* arriving from London, several miles south of the harbor.

331. *Year 1811.* English ship *Benson,* Captain Wilmot, sailing from Honduras to London, wrecked on March 23 near Charleston.

332. *Year 1813.* During a hurricane at Charleston on August 27 and 28, a large number of ships were sunk in the river and harbor and others wrecked on the shore. On November 24 a sloop of unknown registry, *General Hodgkinson,* arriving from Curaçao, wrecked off Charleston.

333. *Year 1814.* English warship H.M.S. *Peacock,* 18 guns, Captain Richard Coote, during August, foundered off Charleston, total loss of lives.

334. *Year 1815.* Two merchantmen were lost: English ship *Spring,* Captain Smith, sailing from Liverpool to Wilmington, was totally lost on Cape Romain Shoals during August but no lives were lost; and the American ship *Hercules,* Captain Duncan, arriving from Jamaica and the Bahamas, was totally lost off Charleston.

335. *Year 1816.* American ship *Harriet,* Captain Folson, sailing from Havana to Wilmington, wrecked on August 6 on Sullivan's Island.

336. Year 1818. English merchantman *Margaret,* sailing for Liverpool, wrecked August 9 on the Charleston bar, crew and cargo saved.

337. Year 1820. English ship *Dee,* Captain Dixon, arriving from Liverpool, was totally lost on December 24 to the southward of the Charleston Lighthouse, crew, four chests of specie, and mail saved.

338. Year 1821. Ship of unknown registry, *Minerva,* Captain Neilson, arriving from France, wrecked January 3 on Edisto Island, her crew was saved.

339. Year 1822. American ship *Calcutta,* Captain Winslow, arriving from Amsterdam, wrecked on April 10 about 4 miles north of the lighthouse on Folly Island.

340. Year 1824. English merchantman *Plantagenet,* Captain Key, arriving from Liverpool, totally lost February 20 on the Charleston bar, only her crew was saved.

GEORGIA:

341. Year 1763. English merchantman *Friends Endeavour,* Captain Wake, sailing for London, was lost crossing over Sunbury bar, only her crew was saved.

342. Year 1769. English merchantman *Prudence,* Captain Smith, arriving from Cadiz, totally lost on Cumberland Island.

343. Year 1779. English warship H.M.S. *Rose,* 20 guns, Captain John Brown, was deliberately sunk in September to block the bar at the entrance of Savannah.

344. Year 1780. Two ships were lost: English warship H.M.S. *Defiance,* 64 guns, Captain Maximillian Jacobs, wrecked February 18 on the Savannah bar; and the English merchantman *Jamaica,* Captain Redman, arriving from Jamaica, was lost on the Savannah River.

345. Year 1781. English warship H.M.S. *Hope,* 16 guns, Captain William Thomas, wrecked off Savannah.

346. Year 1785. English merchantman *Polly,* Captain Newell, preparing to sail for London, accidentally burnt in Savannah Harbor.

347. Year 1787. Scottish merchantman *Dutchess of Argyle,* Captain Miller, sailing from Jamaica to Philadelphia, wrecked on Cumberland Island but no lives were lost.

348. *Year 1791.* English merchantman *Eliza,* Captain Shelburn, arriving from Barbados, totally lost on the Savannah bar.

349. *Year 1792.* Ship of unknown registry, *Conception,* Captain Towers, arriving from Philadelphia, wrecked on St. Simon Island.

350. *Year 1794.* English packet boat, *Grenada,* after being captured by a French privateer was brought into Savannah Harbor and burnt.

351. *Year 1799.* American brig *Minerva,* Captain Bunker, lost during April near St. Andrews Sound.

352. *Year 1803.* Scottish merchantman *Whydah,* Captain Balfour, arriving from Clyde, lost January 6 near Savannah, crew and part of cargo saved.

353. *Year 1804.* During a hurricane on September 11, a large number of unidentified ships were sunk in Savannah Harbor.

354. *Year 1806.* American merchantman *Mary,* Captain Firth, sailing to Barbados, was lost going down the Savannah River, crew and cargo saved.

355. *Year 1808.* Ship of unknown registry, *Triton,* Captain Cox, sailing from Amsterdam to Baltimore, was totally lost near Savannah.

356. *Year 1810.* Ship of unknown registry, *Pezzarro,* Captain Fosh, sailing for Liverpool, was wrecked at Savannah, crew and cargo saved.

357. *Year 1811.* Two American merchantmen were totally lost on the Savannah bar: *Active,* arriving from Lisbon, at the end of November, and the *Edward,* Captain Lewis, laden with timber for England.

358. *Year 1815.* Three English merchantmen were lost: *Mars,* Captain Taylor, arriving from London, on December 2, near Savannah, no lives were lost; *Achilles,* on the Martha's Industry Shoals; and the *Speculator,* Captain Hardy, on December 10, near Savannah, seven of her crew perished.

359. *Year 1816.* Two English merchantmen were lost near Savannah: *Velina,* Captain Wickham, arriving from England, on March 3, crew and part of cargo saved, and the *Braddock,* Captain Johnson, arriving from Liverpool, on November 21.

360. *Year 1817.* Three merchantmen were wrecked near Savannah: American ship *Goleah,* Captain Payne, arriving from France, in March; the American ship *Jupiter,* arriving from Havana; and the English ship *Rose in Bloom,* Captain Lake, sailing from New Orleans to Amsterdam, on May 6, crew and small part of cargo saved.

361. *Year 1821.* English ship *Jason,* Captain Thomson, arriving from England, wrecked on the South Breakers of the St. Simon Island bar but no lives were lost.

362. *Year 1824.* English merchantman *Albion,* Captain Stephenson, sailing from Honduras to London, wrecked on St. Catherine's Island, only six survivors.

THE GULF COAST:

ALABAMA:

363. *Year 1814.* English warship H.M.S. *Hermes,* 20 guns, Captain William Henry Percy, was sunk while attacking the batteries in Mobile Bay on September 15.

364. *Year 1821.* American merchantman *Mississippi,* lost on June 20 at the entrance to Mobile Bay.

365. *Year 1822.* American merchantman *Margaret Ann,* Captain Bodfish, arriving from New York, wrecked on September 25 at Mobile Point, crew and some cargo saved.

MISSISSIPPI:

366. *Year 1643.* Two unidentified Spanish caravels, sent on an exploration voyage from Veracruz, were wrecked on the south side of Ship Island, several lost from both crews. The island was named after these two shipwrecks.

367. *Year 1818.* American merchantman *Hibernia,* Captain Latham, sailing from Madeira to New Orleans, wrecked on Petit Bois Island but no lives were lost.

368. *Year 1819.* American warship, the schooner *Firebrand,* 12 guns, 150 tons, crew of seventy-five men, Captain Cunningham, wrecked on a shoal off the west end of Cat Island during a hurricane in July.

LOUISIANA:

369. *Sometime before 1550.* A Spanish fleet commanded by Captain Narvay, on a voyage of exploration, lost one of its ships at the entrance to the Mississippi River.

370. *Year 1722.* During a hurricane on September 12 and 13, a large number of unidentified ships were sunk at and near New Orleans.

371. *Year 1772.* Spanish merchant brigantine *Nuestra Señora del Amparo*, alias *El Principe de Orange*, Captain Pedro Dias Baladonque, sailing from New Orleans for Veracruz, was struck by a hurricane on September 2 and wrecked at the entrance of the Mississippi River, where she quickly went to pieces, only six survivors.

372. *Year 1779.* A Spanish fleet of warships commanded by Governor Bernardo de Galvez, while preparing to attack the English fort at Baton Rouge, was struck by a hurricane on August 18, all ships, except one, were sunk. The number of ships lost was not stated, only the name of one of them: the *America La Reseda*.

373. *Year 1780.* During a hurricane that struck New Orleans on August 24, dozens of ships were sunk on the Mississippi River and the lakes surrounding New Orleans, and the town was leveled.

374. *Year 1782.* French merchantman *Deux Freres*, sailing from New Orleans to London, was lost south of the port on the Mississippi River.

375. *Year 1785.* French merchantman *Savanne*, Captain Basques, arriving from Jamaica, was totally lost on a sandbar on the Mississippi River below New Orleans, some of her cargo was saved.

376. *Year 1793.* Four merchantmen were wrecked on the Mississippi River, south of New Orleans, during a storm in August, two of them were American ships from Philadelphia, captains Towers and McClanahon.

377. *Year 1812.* During a hurricane on August 19 a large number of ships were lost at New Orleans and on Lake Ponchartrain.

378. *Year 1817.* American merchantman *Rolla*, arriving from Lisbon, wrecked on May 30 on the New Orleans bar.

379. Year 1821. During a severe gale on March 6, three ships were lost at New Orleans: an unidentified ship from Cuba; American merchantman *Blanch,* having arrived from Charleston, no lives were lost; and a French brig coming from France with a valuable cargo and $30,000 in specie aboard, many persons perished on this ship. Two other ships were lost: the French merchantman *Navigator,* Captain Chaureaux, arriving from France, lost in March on Chandelier Island; and the English merchantman *Hannah,* Captain Rose, arriving from Liverpool, on August 19, about 60 miles south of New Orleans on the Mississippi River.

TEXAS:

380. Year 1553. About five days after the New Spain Flota sailed from Veracruz for Havana and Spain, it was struck by a hurricane and the twenty or more ships in this fleet were widely scattered over the Gulf of Mexico. Three of the ships managed to reach Spain and one Veracruz, but none of the others were ever heard from. Three of these ships, all carrying substantial amounts of treasure, were wrecked on Padre Island: *San Estevan,* 220 tons, Captain Francisco del Mecerno; *Sancta Maria de Yciar,* 220 tons, Captain Alonso Ozosi; and an unidentified *nao.* On two of the ships, it is not known whether there were any survivors, but on the other, most of the crew and passengers reached shore only to be massacred by Indians. Only two persons survived and eventually reached civilization. In recent years, one of these wrecks has been located and a substantial amount of treasure and artifacts have been recovered.

381. Year 1766. During a hurricane on September 4, all five ships of a Spanish fleet carrying treasure from Veracruz to Spain were wrecked on Galveston Island, two were identified: *El Nuevo Constante,* and *La Caraqueña* (alias the *Guipuzcuana*). The majority of the treasure and persons on these ships were saved.

382. Year 1811. Spanish warship *San Pedro,* sailing from Veracruz to Spain, carrying more than 500,000 pesos in gold and silver specie, was wrecked on Padre Island. Salvors recovered most of the treasure shortly afterward.

383. Year 1818. During a hurricane on September 12, four ships of the pirate Jean Lafitte were wrecked on the northern tip of

Galveston Island, but it is not known if they were carrying anything of value.

WEST COAST:

CALIFORNIA:

384. *Year 1540.* In 1539, at the orders of the conquistador Hernán Cortez, three small caravels under the command of Captain Francisco de Ulloa explored the coast of California. Before reaching Californian waters, one of the ships was scuttled and another sent back to Mexico. The remaining ship, the 35-ton *Trinidad,* continued on alone and during the summer of 1540 was in the vicinity of San Diego. Due to sickness, all of the men were placed ashore, and during a storm the small vessel disappeared (apparently the anchor cable parted and the vessel drifted off to places unknown). In recent years there has been a great deal of publicity concerning persons claiming to have located this wreck as well as claims that a substantial amount of treasure has been recovered from it. No proof has turned up, however, to substantiate the claim of its discovery, and there is little chance that it carried any treasure at all, except for the few personal effects of its crew.

385. *Year 1599.* A large Manila galleon, the *San Agustin,* Captain Sebastian Camenon, was wrecked in the vicinity of San Francisco on its voyage from the Philippines to Acapulco and the majority of the persons aboard her perished. Although several books on sunken treasures state that she carried an immense treasure in gold and silver, this statement is false. Her main cargo was silks, spices, and porcelains, with only a small amount of gold and silver ornaments and jewelry.

386. *Year 1600.* The *Capitana* of a small squadron commanded by General Juan de Velasco, which was sent from Peru in search of Dutch warships reported cruising in the area of Panama, lost its rudder during a storm near Panama and drifted for weeks until it finally wrecked somewhere on the southern coast of California. But the only clue of her possible location is that it was somewhere north of San Diego.

387. *Year 1823.* A large French merchantman, *Nereide,* Captain

Betaille, sailing from the Far East for South America, was lost somewhere on the coast of California and only ten of the crew of more than three hundred men managed to reach civilization.

OREGON:

388. *Sometime after 1679.* The remains of an unidentified Spanish ship were discovered around the turn of the century near the mouth of the Nehalem River. Along the beach, wooden fragments from the wreck—ceramic sherds and large amounts of beeswax—have been recovered. One of the large pieces of beeswax had the date 1679 on it, others had markings that indicated that they were of Spanish origin. It is possible that this may be one of the many Manila galleons that disappeared during their long voyages.

THE GREAT LAKES:

389. *Year 1679.* Small French frigate *Griffon*, Captain Robert La Salle, sank during September carrying a small amount of gold specie aboard on Birch Island Reef, on Lake Huron.

390. *Year 1721.* French frigate *Le Jean Florin* sank on July 2 about 10 to 15 miles northeast of Erie, Pennsylvania, on Lake Erie, and was reported to be carrying some treasure at the time.

391. *Year 1764.* French ship *Le Blanc Henri* wrecked on June 17 on Wolf Island Spit, near Kingston, Ontario, carrying some treasure aboard.

392. *Year 1783.* English sloop *Ontario* sank on November 23 about 3 miles off Oswego, on Lake Ontario, 190 persons perished and a great amount of treasure was lost.

393. *Year 1803.* American sloop *Lady Washington* vanished November 11 on Lake Ontario carrying a general cargo including a large amount of chinaware.

CHAPTER THREE

Florida

FLORIDA is the world's main center for underwater treasure-hunting. More work has been done on shipwrecks in Florida waters than throughout the rest of the Western Hemisphere. There are several reasons for this. The Florida Keys and the east coast of Florida were lined with off-lying reefs and shoals and there were no safe places to enter during bad weather. Almost all ships returning from the New World to the Old, from the time of Columbus until the introduction of steamships, had to sail up the dangerous Bahama Channel. But even in good weather the prevailing winds and Gulf current pushed all shipping toward the coast of Florida. Large numbers of "wreckers" were established in the Bahamas from the early eighteenth century and at Key West from the second decade of the nineteenth century, and it was only natural that they would work on shipwrecks near them rather than travel elsewhere. Like California, Florida was one of the first places were skin-diving and scuba-diving caught on in the United States; and many divers, bored with spearfishing or underwater photography, switched to old shipwrecks. Many out-of-state divers also became interested in old wrecks, but lacking the capital to roam the Caribbean (as they would have preferred), they began combing the reefs off Florida in quest of treasure and artifacts.

Even before skin-diving caught on there were a handful of professional treasure-hunters—Art McKee, Bill Thompson, Ed Ciesinski, and others—doing most of their exploring and salvaging in the Florida Keys. As early as 1950 they had located and worked on most of the ships of the fleet of 1733—including the H.M.S. *Winchester* and the H.M.S. *Loo*—and had recovered a vast number of artifacts but very little treasure. Their diving and salvage equipment was primitive by today's standards—shallow-water helmets were used for diving, and most of their excavation was done by hand or with small water-jets.

With the introduction of scuba gear a new breed of treasure-hunter followed in their wake, and they had better equipment, such as air lifts for excavating, metal detectors for locating metallic deposits, and greater freedom on the bottom with their more advanced diving gear. For the most part, they worked on the same wrecks as their predecessors, making even better discoveries. On the whole, however, most of these divers only worked at it on a part-time basis, mostly working weekends or during summer vacations.

During the past five years things have changed drastically in regard to working shipwrecks in Florida waters. More than a dozen commercial companies have been formed for salvaging wrecks, and they are employing the best locating and excavation equipment available, with large numbers of professional divers working on a full-time basis the year-around. The Real Eight Company, which is the largest and most successful, started as a small but determined group of amateur divers and was led by Kip Wagner, a building contractor. Kip had been beachcombing for years—using a World War II metal detector —when he located a large number of silver and gold coins along the beach between Sebastian Inlet and Fort Pierce. Since none of the coins were dated later than 1714, he assumed—and correctly—that they had all come from the same fleet. Further research into historical documents convinced him that these coins were coming ashore from various shipwrecks of the 1715 fleet (lost during a hurricane). Not himself a diver, he contacted different divers, who were either in the military or worked at Cape Canaveral, and together they searched offshore for the source of the coins. Soon after locating several of the shipwrecks they began excavating with a hydrolift, but because they held full-time jobs at the Cape they could work only on a part-time basis and when the weather permitted. In 1963 they signed a contract with Treasure Salvors, a group of professional divers from California who had just recently become treasure-hunters, having enjoyed very little success until this time. The Real Eight divers had already recovered over 100,000 silver coins and a few gold ones as well. During the summer of 1964 the Treasure Salvors hit it big—recovering over $1 million in gold specie and bullion as well as jewelry and other priceless artifacts. Ever since this find, the two groups have worked together and made big discoveries each year. Due to weather conditions, however, their diving season is limited from May (or June) until the first hurricane hits, which is generally in late August or early September. Nineteen sixty-nine was the first year in which they were able to work as late as October 10 before the bad weather set in. Although they have located ten of the eleven ships lost in the 1715 fleet, it will take at least another ten years to completely salvage all of these wrecks. So far they have recovered over $6 million worth of treasure.

Real Eight is now a public corporation and most of the original divers have left the military and their jobs on the space program to work full-time for the company. When weather prohibits salvage work on the 1715 wrecks, its divers are kept busy salvaging others in the Bahamas, Colombia, and several other places. Treasure Salvors also works elsewhere when not on the 1715 wrecks.

As far as working on shipwrecks in Florida waters, the Florida Keys are considered the best area because of good underwater visibility; also, weather conditions permit year-around salvage work. Off most of the East Coast and the coasts in the Gulf of Mexico, the diving season is limited to the summer months.

The State of Florida has very strict laws for locating and recovering treasure or artifacts from a shipwreck. The Florida Board of Archives and History, in Tallahassee, is in charge of all diving operations on shipwrecks. The state employs a marine archaeologist, who is instrumental in aiding salvors in dating and identifying their finds, as well as approximately a dozen conservation officers, who supervise the day-by-day operations on the salvage boats. Until June of 1969 the state declared jurisdiction only on shipwrecks within 3 miles of the shore, but—after lengthy controversy—it has been extended to 10 miles.

Anyone interested in searching for shipwrecks must first apply for an exploration permit from the Board. After a shipwreck has been located (provided that someone else does not already have a lease on the site), the potential salvors must apply for a pinpoint lease on the site. This is not always easy to obtain, as the Board works on a very limited budget and is able to employ only about a dozen men to work on salvage boards. In 1966 more than a hundred individuals and groups applied for leases, but only about ten were issued. This naturally infuriated many people, so a large number of those refused leases joined forces and sued the state, but they lost the case. One state official, when notifying a diver that he was not able to get a lease that year, had four of his teeth knocked out by the infuriated diver.

The state receives 25 percent of everything recovered, but also has the right to buy part or all of the salvors' remaining share. After the division has been made between the state and the salvors, the salvors can dispose of their share in any way they wish.

Two controversies have raged in recent years between the State of Florida and two different groups of salvors: a young boy was spearfishing between Vero Beach and Fort Pierce and accidentally located a large number of American gold coins on a ship carrying a U.S. Army payroll lost in this area in 1857. At the time of this discovery neither the boy nor his father, who helped him recover the coins, had a search or salvage permit. However, they reported their find and the state asked for and received its normal 25 percent. The salvors reported recovering 582 gold coins. Sometime later the state, which employs a team of criminal investigators, brought the salvors to court, claiming that they had actually recovered 3,264 gold coins, valued at $271,000. Even now, after three years in the courts, the case is still pending, as the state has failed to prove that the salvors cheated on their find.

Another group, led by Tom Gurr, discovered the Spanish merchant ship *San José*, of the 1733 fleet, outside the 3-mile limit in 1968. During the summer of 1968 it recovered a large number of interesting artifacts valued at over $50,000. Then, after the new law was passed extending the state's limits of offshore rights to 10 miles, Gurr was forced to stop his salvage operation. He threatened to sue the state, but the state finally gave him a lease on this wreck and, in gratitude, Gurr turned over half of what he had recovered during 1968, even though the wreck was not within the boundaries of the state at the time.

Besides the wrecks I have listed in this chapter, there are over a hundred others lost between 1540 and 1825 that are listed in original documents only as lost in the Bahama Channel, Strait of Florida, or

Diver at work on a wreck in the Florida Keys.

TOP: Clump of silver spoons recovered from a Revolutionary War wreck off Florida. BOTTOM: Complete silver serving set from the *San José*, which sank in 1733 in the Florida Keys.

Gulf of Florida. Some of these shipwrecks were no doubt lost on the high seas.

List of Shipwrecks in Florida Waters

1. **Year 1521.** Spanish merchant *nao San Anton,* 100 tons, Captain Gonzalo Rodríguez, was lost in the Florida Keys after leaving Cuba enroute to Spain.

2. **Year 1525.** A caravel that was part of the expedition of Don Lucas Vasquez de Ayllon, which sailed from Spain in 1524, was lost near Cape St. Helen and natives massacred all of its two hundred survivors.

3. **Year 1545.** A vessel was wrecked upon the coast of Florida and some of its crew of two hundred were slain by natives and the remainder reduced to slavery.

4. **Year 1550.** *Nao* (type of vessel), *Visitación,* 200 tons, Captain Pedro de la Torre, sailing alone from Veracruz for Spain, was wrecked in the Florida Keys.

5. **Year 1551.** *Nao San Nicolas,* 200 tons, Captain Juan Christoval, was wrecked near Fort Pierce and Indians recovered a great deal of what it carried. The ship was coming from Nombre de Dios and Cartagena on its way to Spain, and there was no mention of whether it stopped in Havana or of its cargo.

6. **Year 1554.** *Nao Santa Maria del Camino,* 350 tons, Captain Diego Diaz, owned by Sr. Bolaños, part of the Armada de Tierra Firme of Captain-General Bartolome Carreño, was lost on the coast of Florida, everything it carried was salvaged by the Spaniards.

7. **Year 1554.** The ship of Farfan (probably its owner) sank near Fort Pierce, richly laden with gold and silver, and Indians of the King of Ais recovered a great deal from the wreck.

8. **Year 1555.** Several ships of the Flota de Tierra Firme, commanded by Cosme Rodríguez Farfan, were separated from the convoy in the Bahama Channel after a storm hit and never heard of again.

9. **Year 1556.** Indians of the King of Ais were reported to have recovered, near Cape Canaveral, over a million pesos in bars of gold

and silver and many precious pieces of jewelry made by the Indians of Mexico from ship or ships of the Nueva España Flota, of which it is said the son of Pedro de Menéndez was the general. The document containing this information is dated 1570, and although the Indians made this recovery in 1556, the ship or ships might have wrecked at an earlier date. The wording of the document makes it impossible to determine if only one ship, several, or the whole fleet sank, but it was probably only one or several ships, otherwise there would have been a great deal more mention in other contemporary documents.

10. *Year 1556.* Three *naos* under the command of Captain Gonzalo de Carbajal, sailing from Puerto Rico to Spain, were lost on the coast of Florida. Only two were identified: *Sancta Salbador,* 120 tons, Captain Guillen de Lugo; and the other, with the identical name and weight, Captain Martín de Artaleco.

11. *Year 1559.* A fleet of thirteen vessels sailed from Veracruz under the command of Don Tristán de Luna y Arellano, Governor of Florida, on June 11, where they planned to found a new colony. On August 14 the fleet anchored in the Bay of Santa Maria and on the night of September 19 it was struck by a tempest from the north, which lasted twenty-four hours and shattered five ships, a galleon, and a bark to pieces with great loss of life. It swept a caravel with its cargo into a grove of trees more than the distance of a harquebus shot from the shore.

12. *Year 1564.* A Spanish historian briefly mentions the loss of three ships of Don Juan Menéndez on the Florida coast near Fort Pierce.

13. *Year 1565.* Two ships of the Frenchman Ribaut were wrecked during a storm along the shore between Matanzas and Mosquito Inlet. Some of both crews drowned in attempting to reach shore, and Indians captured and killed most of the others.

14. *Year 1567.* On the coast of Florida, one of the *naos* of Pedro Menéndez de Aviles was lost.

15. *Year 1567.* While Spaniards were exploring the area of Tampa Bay in 1567 they discovered a Portuguese trader from the port of Algarve, Portugal. He was the only survivor from a ship that had wrecked there and had been a prisoner of the Indian chief

Tocobaya. All others from the wreck had been killed by the Indians.

16. *Sometime before 1570.* The ship *Viscayo,* on which Don Anton Granado was a passenger, wrecked, richly laden, near Fort Pierce Inlet and the Indians of the King of Ais salvaged a great deal of her treasure.

17. *Unidentified year sometime before 1570.* A Spanish privateer, *El Mulato,* wrecked, richly laden, near Fort Pierce, where the Indians recovered a great deal of her treasure.

18. *Year 1571 or 1572.* Two ships that were going from Mexico to Santo Domingo to receive a cargo of sugar and hides were lost due to a storm off Cape Canaveral, and as the crews were journeying to the fort of St. Augustine, which was a distance of 30 leagues, the Indians massacred most of them.

19. *Year 1572.* Adelantado Pedro Menéndez de Aviles left St. Augustine in two small tenders and a bark heading for Havana. While sailing down the coast of Florida the vessels were separated by a storm. The bark reached Havana safely but the tender, in which Aviles and some Jesuits were sailing, was wrecked near Cape Canaveral. All thirty persons on board reached shore, however, and constructed a small fort from the wreckage. Sometime later they walked safely back to St. Augustine. The other tender wrecked onshore in the province of Ais, where the crew was killed and their vessel burnt.

20. *Year 1576.* The Armada de Tierra Firme, commanded by Captain-General Cristobal de Eraso, left Havana for Spain. A few days later this armada was struck by a tempest in the Bahama Channel and one of the *naos* was separated from the other ships. It arrived in a sinking condition at Puerto Escondido, which is near Puerto de las Palmas, on the coast of Florida, but soon after entering port the ship sank. Salvage operations were soon under way and all of its gold and silver was recovered.

21. *Year 1577.* Don Gutierres de Miranda wrote the King from Havana on February 13, 1578:

> While I was coming in a boat from St. Augustine to this town, off the Florida Keys three Indians came in a canoe out to me, from

which I understood by signs, that two vessels had been wrecked, which had been sent from this town in the month of August last past. As I knew not their language, I brought one of them to this town, where they understand it, and he said that the loss of the ships was a fact and that the Indians had killed all the people except two, whom two caciques are holding captive.

22. *Year 1579.* Don Antonio Martínez Carvajal wrote to the King from Havana on November 3, 1579, stating that "we set out for St. Augustine and by reason of a tempest, one of the two frigates we had was lost . . . the General and the rest of the people were saved from the wreck of said frigate, whence he went by land to the fort of St. Augustine." This wreck occurred somewhere on the east coast of Florida.

23. *Year 1587.* A hurricane hit the *flota* of General Francisco de Noboa and during the storm the *nao* of maestre Hernán García Marín sank off the coast of Florida with a great quantity of gold, silver, and pearls, but almost all was saved and carried to the *Capitana* in a launch before the ship sank.

24. *Year 1589.* The Dutch historian Linchoten tells us that in 1589 all but one out of one hundred large ships in the Tierra Firme Flota were wrecked in the Florida Channel, and that of 220 ships sailing that year for Spain and Portugal from various possessions of the Spanish Crown (Portugal was under Spanish rule at this time), only fourteen or fifteen arrived safely. No doubt Linchoten is grossly incorrect. The Spanish historian Duro states that 1589 was not a particularly bad year (but he goes on to say that fourteen ships were lost at San Juan de Ulua, in Veracruz, in 1590 due to a "norther"). From the abundance of documents for this year there is no doubt that Linchoten was wrong, as only four Spanish ships were lost and only one Portuguese ship, returning from Goa, in India. This is just one instance of false information concerning losses to Spanish shipping.

25. *Year 1589.* For protection against an English squadron that was known to be waiting for the return of Spanish ships from the West Indies, at the King's orders the Armada and Flota de Tierra Firme and the Flota de Nueva España met in Havana, forming a convoy of about one hundred ships, and sailed from Havana on September 9. Soon after entering the Bahama Channel the convoy was struck by a hurricane. The *Almiranta* of the Flota de Nueva España developed a bad leak and fired cannon for assistance, but before aid could reach her she sank with a great treasure at the mouth of the Bahama Channel in very deep water. While running up the Bahama Channel before the hurricane, three merchant *naos* also sank in 30 fathoms of water in about 30 degrees of latitude. Only the names of two were given in the documents: *Santa Catalina,* 350 tons, Captain Domingo Ianez Ome, owned by Fernando Ome, coming from Mexico, and the *Jesús María,* 400 tons, Captain Francisco Salvago, owned by Domingo Sauli, also coming from Mexico. There is no mention of what their cargoes consisted of, but it is certain that the *Almiranta,* at least, was carrying treasure.

26. Year 1591. A Spanish fleet of seventy-five ships left Havana after spending the winter there, leaving all of their treasure in Havana at the King's orders. The treasure reached Spain safely, by-passing an English blockade aboard small but fast *zabras.* After the convoy, consisting of ships from Mexico and South America, left Havana on July 27, it suffered many storms and no less than twenty-nine were lost, many off the coast of Florida. This information was obtained from English sources, and as the Spanish sources for this year are vague on the matter, it cannot be disputed. Only one Spanish document, dated March 26, 1592, briefly states that "due to the fact that so many ships were lost returning from the Indies during the past year, there are very few ships available to be sent to the Indies for this year." Since the lost ships were not carrying treasure—at least not registered treasure or any belonging to the King—this is probably the reason there is so little mention of them in the Spanish documents.

27. Year 1592. A frigate coming from Havana to St. Augustine sank on the coast near Cape Canaveral and all the men made it ashore; however, all but one were killed by the Indians before aid could reach them—and that one was being tortured when soldiers from St. Augustine arrived to save him.

28. Year 1600. Unnamed 200-ton *nao* (originally built in France), of Captain Diego Rodríguez, coming from Mexico in the Flota de Nueva España, sank on the coast of Florida.

29. Year 1618. An unnamed *patache*, sent as an advice boat from Veracruz, was wrecked in March on its twenty-eighth day of sailing at "la Boca de Matasissos," on the coast of Florida. Some of the survivors reached St. Augustine safely but others were killed by the Indians. Some mail and cargo washed ashore and was recovered by the Indians.

30. Year 1618. On October 10 the governor of St. Augustine received news from Indians that a very large ship had sunk near the Fort Pierce Inlet. He sent men to aid the survivors—only fifty-three—who arrived and identified the ship as the *Almiranta* of Honduras. Indigo and cochineal—the ship's main cargoes—and hides were washed all over the coast. At the same time, a smaller, unidentified *nao* had also sunk nearby, so the governor sent a frigate to locate both wrecks. There was no other document telling the identity of the latter shipwreck, or if either ship was located by the Spaniards.

31. Year 1619. On March 24 an unidentified ship coming from Campeche sank in the Florida Keys with a cargo of hides and indigo. All of the crew escaped to shore and reached St. Augustine.

32. Year 1621. An unidentified small *patache*, serving as an advice boat on a voyage from Veracruz to Spain, was capsized by a large wave about 3 leagues off the Dry Tortugas and sank. The number of persons aboard was not given, but thirty drowned and the rest reached one of the cays of the Dry Tortuga group. They were soon rescued, along with the mailbags they had saved from the ship, by a passing Spanish ship, which they had signaled by use of fires made on the cay.

33. Year 1622. On the morning of September 4 a large convoy consisting of the Armada de Tierra Firme and the Tierra Firme Flota, commanded by the Marqués de Cadereita, sailed for Spain from Havana harbor against the better judgment of the main pilots of the convoy, who warned that there were imminent signs of a hurricane. On September 6 (some accounts give the date as the seventh) the convoy was struck by a fierce hurricane, which scattered the ships over a wide area. Nine were lost in the Florida Keys and several others were probably lost on the high seas, as they were never accounted for. The surviving ships got back to

Havana in battered condition. Of those that reached Havana, all had lost their masts and many had been forced to jettison cannon and parts of their cargoes. This disaster was considered the worst to have occurred to the *flotas* in over fifty years. Of the nine ships that were wrecked in the Florida Keys, three were treasure-laden galleons, five were merchant *naos,* and one a *patache* that served as a reconnaissance boat for the convoy. Only the locations of the three galleons and the *patache* are given in the documents, and only four of the nine are identified.

The galleon *Nuestra Señora de Atocha,* 600 tons, built two years earlier in Havana, Captain Jacome de Veider, owned by the Administrators of the Averia (a branch of the House of Trade in Seville that regulated and collected a special tax on all returning treasure and products from the New World for the maintenance of a fleet of warships that generally met all returning fleets off the Azores and escorted them on their final leg of the voyage to Spain), was lost in 10 fathoms of water off Matacumbe Key with a cargo valued at over 1 million pesos, mostly consisting of silver bullion and specie and a small amount of tobacco belonging to the King. The wreck location was lost soon after the disaster, due to the buoy placed over the wreck being lost in bad weather, and before it could be relocated it was covered over by sand and never salvaged.

The galleon *La Margarita,* 600 tons, Captain Pedro Guerrero de Espinosa, carrying over half a million pesos in silver bullion and specie and a small amount of tobacco belonging to private merchants, sank near the *Atocha,* in 5 fathoms of water, off Matacumbe Key. The majority of the treasure on this shipwreck was recovered by divers, but before all could be recovered it also sanded over and the remainder of the treasure was lost. While salvage work was being done on this galleon, the salvors reported locating a ballast pile from an older shipwreck nearby, from which they recovered several silver bars.

The galleon *Nuestra Señora del Rosario,* 600 tons, Captain Francisco Rodríguez Rico, owned by Admiral Gaspar de Vargas, was wrecked at the Dry Tortugas with about half a million pesos of silver bullion and specie aboard. Salvors recovered all of the treasure and twenty cannon from the wreck. The *patache* was wrecked very close to this galleon and everything of value aboard it was recovered.

Of the five merchant *naos*, only the identity of one is known: *Jesús y Nuestra Señora del Rosario*, 117 tons, originally built in Portugal, Captain Manuel Diaz, owned by Juan de la Torre. Neither her location nor that of the other four were precisely given, only that they were lost in the Florida Keys, in the vicinity of the other shipwrecks.

34. **Year 1622.** *Nao Santa Ana María*, 180 tons, Captain Goncalo [*sic*] de la Rocha, sailing alone from Santo Domingo and Havana for Spain, was sunk in a storm on the high seas off the coast of Florida.

35. **Year 1623.** In early spring two galleons were sent to the Florida Keys to protect the salvors at work on *La Margarita* from attack by Dutch privateers who were reported cruising in that area. The *Capitana* of this small squadron was wrecked on the Florida Keys, 4 leagues to windward of the shipwreck of the *Nuestra Señora de Atocha*, but none of the crew was lost. Ten days later these survivors reached Havana aboard rafts made from their shipwreck. The galleons carried fourteen bronze cannon.

36. **Year 1623.** The Tierra Firme Flota, commanded by Captain-General Antonio de Oquendo, sailed from Havana on April 26. Upon reaching the mouth of the Bahama Channel it was struck by a storm that created waves so huge that the ships were tossed about like corks. The treasure-laden galleon *Espíritu Santa el Mayor*, 480 tons, Captain Antonio de Soto, opened up and sank so quickly that only fifty of the three hundred persons aboard her could be saved by other ships, and all of her treasure—amounting to more than 1 million pesos, was totally lost. The *Almiranta* of the *flota*, the galleon *Santisima Trinidad*, 600 tons, Captain Ysidro de Cepeda, also sank, but not as quickly, as there was time for several *pataches* to recover all of her treasure—which amounted to 1 million pesos—and all the people aboard her. Contemporary accounts differed as to the loss of both ships. Several state that they wrecked on the coast of Florida in the vicinity of Ais and others that they sank on the high seas.

37. **Year 1624.** An unidentified frigate sank on the coast of Florida sometime before July 30, and eight of the twelve iron cannon it carried, as well as several anchors, were recovered from it.

38. **Year 1626.** A small frigate sent from Havana with the salaries and supplies for the officials and soldiers at St. Augustine ran aground

on the bar at the entrance to St. Augustine and was a total loss. Only a few pipes of wine that washed ashore were recovered from this wreck.

39. Year 1627. When news of the above loss reached the viceroy of Mexico, he ordered a frigate sent from Veracruz with supplies and money to pay the garrison at St. Augustine, which was threatening to mutiny if not paid promptly. The governor of Florida, Don Luis de Rojas, wrote the King on February 15, stating that the frigate that had been sent from Veracruz had also wrecked on the same bar as the one in 1626 and was a total loss. The crew of the frigate, along with 12,000 pesos in eight-real silver coins, were saved. Of the 200 barrels of flour it carried, only eleven were salvaged. The ship had also carried four bronze and four iron cannon, but only two of the iron cannon could be salvaged as mud covered the wreck over quickly.

40. Year 1630. Two galleons of the Armada de Tierra Firme were sent under the command of the Maestre de Campo Antonio de Oteyca to carry supplies to St. Augustine from Havana but both were wrecked at the head of the Florida Keys. All of the men on both wrecks were saved and the fifty-six bronze and iron cannon on both wrecks were recovered and taken to Havana.

41. Year 1632. As a large convoy was making its way up the Bahama Channel, sailing from Havana to Spain, two ships were wrecked on the coast of Florida during the night of April 2 because they became separated from the convoy and currents forced them too close to the coast of Florida. One was the *Almiranta de Honduras* and the other was an unidentified frigate coming from Maracaibo, Venezuela, with a cargo consisting mainly of cocoa. The location of the two wrecks was probably in the vicinity of present-day Miami, as an advice boat passing that area a few days later reported sighting two ships wrecked shortly after passing the head of the Florida Keys.

42. Year 1633. On November 15, the governor of Florida wrote to the King, stating:

> On the 10th of November, my soldiers captured three Englishmen from London. Their ship was carrying supplies and aid to the English settlement at Alxacan [probably somewhere in Virginia or New England], but it sank on our coast. Forty of them reached shore

safely, but the Indians had killed all but the three my soldiers captured. I will send them back to Spain for questioning on the first available vessel. The location of their shipwreck was 70 leagues south of our town [St. Augustine].

43. *Year 1634.* On December 20 the governor of Florida wrote to Captain-General Antonio de Oquendo, who was wintering in Havana with his Armada de Tierra Firme, stating:

> I received news that a ship of the Flota de Nueva España, commanded by Captain-General Lope de Hoces, had wrecked on my coast. We found some Indians that told us that some other Indians had salvaged some treasure off this wreck. We stationed some soldiers opposite the site of the wreck and sent others after the Indians who had recovered the treasure, but they were never located. I went with several canoes and some divers to the said wreck and in one day's time we recovered the 100,000 pesos in bullion and specie which the ship had been carrying as registered cargo and we took this treasure to my fort at St. Augustine.

44. *Year 1641.* A convoy consisting of the Nueva España Flota, commanded by Captain-General Juan de Campos, and the Armada de Barlovento (a squadron used for protecting returning *flotas* during time of war), was struck by a hurricane on September 27 in the latitude of 30 degrees north and five ships of the Flota were wrecked on the coast of Florida. Four of the five ships were merchant *naos*, and there were no survivors. Another was the *patache* of the Flota, which was located by another *patache* from Havana some days later. They found the wrecked *patache* about 5 leagues from the shore with some survivors still aboard. Others had tried to swim ashore, including a priest, but they were all eaten by sharks. Other ships in this same convoy were in such bad condition that they sank on the high seas. Another, the *Almiranta* of the Flota, lost all her masts and developed such a bad leak that she eventually drifted and was wrecked on a reef in the Bahamas called Abreojos, located north of Hispaniola. Today this reef is called Silver Shoals as a result of the more than 2 million pesos in silver that was lost on this shipwreck, of which the majority was recovered about forty years later by Sir William Phips.

45. *Sometime before 1677.* On May 4, 1677, the governor of Cuba sent Don Martín de Melgar with a frigate to savalge cannon from a Dutch ship that had wrecked at Key West.

46. *Sometime before 1685.* The governor of Cuba sent two brigantines under the command of captains Martín de Riva and Pedro de Iriarte to St. Bernards Bay, on the coast of Florida, to salvage what they could from several French ships that had been wrecked there. Divers recovered only four cannon and some other objects of little value.

47. *Year 1688.* Brief mention that an unidentified Spanish merchant *nao* was lost in the Florida Keys.

48. *Year 1689.* Frigate *Nuestra Señora de Concepción y San Josefe* was lost at Key Largo.

49. *Year 1695.* British man-of-war *Winchester,* 50 guns, Captain John Soule, sailing from Jamaica to England, was wrecked near Cape Florida on some reefs.

50. *Year 1696.* British merchantman *Burroughs* (or *Smith*), from the port of Bristol, sailing from Port Royal, Jamaica, in a convoy of twelve or thirteen ships was wrecked on September 23 north of Jupiter Inlet.

51. *Year 1696.* British barkentine *Reformation,* Captain Joseph Kirle, sailing from Port Royal, Jamaica, in a convoy of twelve or thirteen merchant ships, sank on September 23 a bit north of Jupiter Inlet, close to shore. Her exact location was 27 degrees and 8 minutes of north latitude. She carried twenty-five passengers and crew, and her cargo consisted of sugar, rum, beef, molasses, and some Spanish money.

52. *Year 1696.* British merchant bark *Nantwitch,* Captain John Smith, part of the same convoy as the above two ships, was wrecked south of Fort Pierce Inlet, about one-third of the distance between Fort Pierce and St. Lucie inlets.

53. *Year 1698.* Brief mention that two ships of unknown nationality were forced ashore on the coast of Florida about 40 leagues from the Island of New Providence, in the Bahamas, by a notorious pirate named Kelly.

54. Year 1705 or 1706. The governor of Florida wrote the King on January 31, 1706, stating that one of the two ships—named *Santo Cristo de Maracaibo*—sent by the viceroy of Mexico to bring supplies to St. Augustine sank 8 leagues southwest of St. Augustine during a storm.

55. Year 1711. Merchant *nao Nuestra Señora del Rosario y San Cristobal,* sailing alone from Havana to Spain, was lost on the coast of Florida in 30 degrees and 20 minutes of north latitude.

56. Year 1715. At sunrise on July 24 a convoy consisting of twelve ships set sail from Havana Harbor for the long voyage back to Spain. The convoy was composed of the five ships of the New Spain Flota, commanded by Captain-General Don Juan Esteban de Ubilla, six ships of the Squadron of Tierra Firme, commanded by Captain-General Don Antonio de Echeverz y Zubiza, and a French ship named *Grifon,* commanded by Captain Antonio Daire. The *Grifon* was not part of Ubilla's *flota* or Echeverz's Squadron but just happened to be in Havana at the time and received permission to sail back to Europe in the convoy.

Echeverz's Squadron had sailed from Spain and gone directly to Cartagena, Colombia, carrying assorted merchandise for sale at Cartagena, Porto Bello, and Havana. Upon arriving in Cartagena, Echeverz sent word to the viceroy of Peru to send up the treasure of Peru and Chile to Panama City, where it was then generally transported overland on mules to Porto Bello, where a fair was held. Then the treasure was placed aboard the ships of the Squadron of Tierra Firme and carried back to Spain. Echeverz also notified both the viceroy of New Granada, in Bogotá, to send treasure and the governor of the Island of Margarita to send pearls. Due to the fact that the last Squadron of Tierra Firme had been destroyed near Cartagena in 1708 by an English fleet under the command of Admiral Wager, the viceroy of Peru did not send the treasure to Panama City as requested by Echeverz but had it transported overland to Buenos Aires, then by ship to Spain. For some unknown reason, neither the viceroy of New Granada nor the governor of Margarita Island heeded the request. So instead of a large amount of treasure from South America, Echeverz received so little that it was hardly worth his effort. The only treasure he received was from the governor of Cartagena and his royal officials, and some belonging to private persons. The royal treasure consisted of 46,095 pesos, 6 reals, and 10 maravedis in gold doubloons (escudos), 300 castellanos, 7 tomines, 6 grains of gold dust, and 646 castellanos in two small gold bars. All of it was carried on Echeverz's *Capitana*. Also put aboard his *Capitana* were 19 gold bars valued at 26,063 pesos, 2,650 pesos in gold doubloons, 1,485 pesos in silver specie, three gold chains valued at 747 pesos, 47 serons of cocoa, and 1½ tons of brazilwood (a dyewood). Aboard his *Almiranta* he put eight gold bars valued at 8,978 pesos, 3,150 pesos in gold doubloons, 175 pesos in silver specie, two chests of ceramic jugs, one chest of gifts, 2½ tons of brazilwood, 28 serons of cocoa, one chest of vanilla, two chests of tortoise shells, and 650 cured half-hides. Aboard the *Nuestra Señora de Concepción* he put 3,000 pesos in gold doubloons, four gold bars valued at 5,703 pesos, 15 serons of cocoa, one chest of vanilla, 15¾ tons of brazilwood, 1,440 cured half-hides, and some tobacco. The ship *El Ciervo* only carried 96 tons of brazilwood. On his other two ships we know of no cargo or treasure being loaded aboard in Cartagena or Porto Bello, but like all the other ships in this squadron it is believed that they received a large cargo of tobacco in Havana. There is a possibility that there were actually seven ships in Echeverz's squadron, making a total of thirteen sailing together from Havana, but the documents are confusing.

Ubilla's *flota* consisted of eight ships when it sailed from Spain to Veracruz, but four were lost during a bad storm while in that port, and when he sailed from Veracruz for Havana he had only four ships. In Havana he added a small frigate to his *flota*. Ubilla's *Capitana* carried the following treasure and cargo: 611,409 pesos in silver specie for the King, 169,111 pesos in silver specie for the wages of the members of the Council of the Indies in Madrid, 2,559,917 pesos in silver specie belonging to private persons. All of this treasure was contained in 1,300 chests. It also carried a small amount of silver bars; twenty-three chests of silverware; one small chest containing an undisclosed number of gold doubloons, gold bars, and pearls; a small chest containing jewelry for the Queen; and another small chest of gold jewelry belonging to a nobleman. The cargo consisted of Chinese porcelain, indigo, cochineal, drugs, hides, brazilwood, gifts, copper disks, and ceramic drinking vessels. In Havana it received 36,000 pesos worth of silver specie, gold disks, and several other bars that had been salvaged off a ship that sank in 1711. The *Almiranta* also received a similar amount in Havana. It carried 990 chests of silver specie, of which 611,408 pesos belonged to the King and 2,076,004 pesos belonged to private persons. Other treasure consisted of fifty-three chests of silverware. Her general cargo was the same as that of the *Capitana*, but in addition she carried sarsaparilla, cocoa, and three Chinese folding screens. According to documents, she carried no gold treasure in any form, so the gold coins which Real Eight members found on this shipwreck must have been contraband.

The *Refuerzo* (also called the *Urca de Lima*) carried no royal treasure but did carry eighty-one chests and some loose sacks of silver specie valued at 252,171 pesos belonging to private persons. In addition it carried thirteen chests of worked silver and, like the *Capitana* and *Almiranta*, a general cargo. It also carried snuff and balsam.

The *Patache*, which was a much smaller vessel than the above three of Ubilla's *flota*, carried no royal treasure but did carry 44,000 pesos of silver specie in twelve chests and some loose sacks of leather. Since Real Eight members have found a sufficient number of gold coins on this shipwreck in recent years, these coins were undoubtedly contraband. This ship also carried a general cargo. In addition it carried a type of incense.

Documents do not indicate whether the small frigate Ubilla bought in Havana carried any cargo or treasure, but it is unlikely that it carried any treasure.

The total value of registered treasure carried on the four ships of Ubilla's *flota*—excluding the silverware, jewelry, and a small number of gold coins—was 6,388,020 pesos. The total amount of treasure carried on three of the ships of Echeverz's squadron was 98,046 pesos in silver and gold specie, plus the 955 castellanos in gold dust and bars. The total carried in the overall convoy was 6,466,066 pesos and 955 castellanos. According to the records there were virtually no gold coins carried on any of the ships, which means that those being recovered by Real Eight members were contraband. This is substantiated by the fact that most of the gold disks being recovered by Real Eight are not marked the way registered gold bars had to be at that period.

After the convoy left Havana it made its way up the Bahama Channel. During the night of July 30 it was struck by a fierce hurricane that wrecked all the ships upon the coast of Florida, with the exception of the *Grifon,* which miraculously escaped. Over a thousand persons lost their lives, including Ubilla and his principal officers. About 1,500 persons reached shore by floating aboard pieces of wreckage, or swimming, and some of them perished from exposure, thirst, and hunger before aid reached them from Havana and St. Augustine.

Salvage efforts on the wrecks began immediately, and by the end of December the officials in charge of operations reported that they had already recovered all of the King's treasure and the major part of the treasure belonging to private persons, totaling 5,200,000 pesos. The following spring they recovered an additional small amount of treasure, so that by July, when the Spaniards ended all further salvage efforts, they had recovered a reported total of 5,241,166 pesos in silver specie and bars, excluding the gold specie and bars, silverware, and general cargoes. We also know that after the Spaniards ended their salvage operations, for several years Englishmen from Jamaica and the Bahamas also salvaged unknown amounts off these wrecks. When the Spaniards ended their salvage operations, there supposedly remained a total of 1,244,900 pesos of registered treasure, but the amount will never be known, as the survivors and salvors robbed unknown amounts. Furthermore, we have no means to determine how much unregistered treasure remains to be recovered. Gold, in terms of weight worth sixteen times the value of silver, was the most common item smuggled back to Spain, and since there were virtually no gold coins registered aboard the ships, it is possible that a substantial amount was being smuggled in this convoy. But we have no way of proving this until Real Eight has completely worked all of the wrecks of this convoy.

57. *Year 1731.* Unidentified merchant *nao* was lost on the coast of Florida on a voyage between Havana and Spain, near the mouth of the St. John's River.

58. *Year 1733.* A merchant *nao* sailing alone back to Spain was lost at Rico Seco, on the coast of Florida.

59. *Year 1733.* On July 13 the Nueva España Flota, commanded by Don Rodrigo de Torres, set sail for Spain; documents give either twenty-one or twenty-two as the total number of ships in this

fleet. The names of the ships are also confusing, as some ships had two: a religious name and an alias. However, the majority of the documents reveal that the following ships were in the fleet when it sailed from Havana.

1. The *Capitana El Rubi*, 60 cannon, Captain Baltazar de la Torre y Alfaro, owned by the King (her tonnage not given in any document), carried 104 castellanos in worked gold, 3,200 pesos in gold specie, 5,080,285 pesos in silver specie and bullion, and 6,099 marcos in worked silver, all the property of private citizens.

2. The *Almiranta Nuestra Señora de Balvaneda* (alias *El Gallo*), 60 cannon, Captain Bernardo de Maturana, owned by the King (her tonnage not given in any documents), carried 196 castellanos in worked gold, 3,200 pesos in gold specie, 4,895,216 pesos in silver specie and bullion, 2,579 marcos in worked silver, and 285 marcos of "plata pasta," all the property of private citizens.

Note that in addition the *Capitana* and *Almiranta* carried 1,519,527 pesos in silver specie and bullion, 4,110 "granos" in gold, an unspecified amount of worked gold and silver, and copper ingots, all of which was the property of the King. The precise percentage of what each of the two ships carried of this amount is not given in the documents, only that it was equally divided aboard both ships. Documents also state that unspecified amounts of gold and silver specie and bullion were carried on both ships as the property of the Church of Spain.

3. Galleon *Nuestra Señora de Balvaneda* (alias *El Infante*), Captain Domingo de Sanz, owned by the King (neither the number of cannon nor tonnage given in the documents), carried 562,509 pesos in silver specie and bullion and 643 marcos in worked silver, plus large amounts of indigo, vanilla, and ceramic jars, jugs, and plates.

4. Pink *Nuestra Señora del Populo* (alias *El Pinque*), Captain Francisco Ibernon, owned by the King. Documents do not reveal the number of cannon, tonnage, or what cargo this small vessel carried.

5. Merchant *nao San José de las Animas* (sometimes listed as *San José y las Animas*), Captain Cristobal Fernández Franco, owned by José del Duque y Muñoz, English-built ship, 326½ tons (number of cannon not given for any of the privately owned merchant ships), carried 30,435 pesos in silver specie and bullion,

plus sugar, chocolate, indigo, cochineal, dyewoods, cocoa, hides, ceramicware, tobacco, vanilla and various types of drugs.

6. Merchant *nao Nuestra Señora del Rosario* (*San Francisco Javier y San Antonio de Padua*), the captain and owner was Don Luis Lozana, French-built of 205½ tons, carried 12,000 pesos in silver specie and bullion and a cargo of products similar to that of the above ship.

7. Merchant *nao Nuestra Señora de Belem y San Antonio de Padua*, her captain and owner was Don Luis de Herrera, English-built, 242¼ tons, carried 12,000 pesos in silver specie and bullion, 359 marcos in worked silver, and a cargo similar to those of the above two ships.

8. Merchant *nao Nuestra Señora del Rosario, San Antonio y San Vicente Ferrer*, Captain Juan José de Arizon, owner Jacinto de Arizon, carried 24,000 pesos in silver specie and bullion and a general cargo as the above ships; in addition, an item listed as *tinta*, which could either be coffee or some type of dye.

9. Merchant *nao Nuestra Señora del Carmen, San Antonio de Padua y las Animas*, captain and owner Don Antonio de Chaves, Genovese-built of 220⁹⁄₁₀ tons, carried no treasure, only a cargo similar to that of the above ships.

10. Merchant *nao Nuestra Señora de Belem y San Juan Bautista*, Captain Diego de la Corte y Andrade, owner Francisco Lebrum, foreign-built, 212⅝ tons. This ship carried no treasure, only the usual cargo, and was probably better known by an alias, which is not revealed in the documents.

11. Merchant *nao Nuestra Señora de los Dolores y Santa Isabel* (alias *El Nuevo Londres*), Captain Antonio de Loaysa, owner Nicolas Fernández del Castillo, English-built, 296 tons, carried the usual cargo plus an unspecified small amount of silver specie.

12. Merchant *nao Nuestra Señora del Rosario y Santo Domingo*, Captain Tomás de Astiguieta, owners were the captain and Doña María Teresa de Astiguieta (probably his wife), Spanish-built, 522½ tons, carried 31,281 pesos in silver specie and bullion, 495 marcos in worked silver, and the usual cargo.

13. Merchant *nao Nuestra Señora de los Reyes, San Fernando, y San Francisco de Paula*, Captain José Cabeza, owner Francisco de Soto y Posada, Genovese-built, 328 tons, carried 16,000 pesos in silver (not disclosed if in specie or bullion, or both), 226 marcos of worked silver, and the usual cargo.

14. Merchant *nao San Pedro*, Captain Gaspar López Gonzales,

owner Gaspar de Larea Berdugo, Dutch-built, 287¼ tons, carried 16,000 pesos in silver specie and bullion and the usual cargo plus several boxes of Chinese porcelain.

15. Merchant *nao San Felipe,* Captain José del Villar y Andrade, owner the Marqués de Cañada, English-built of 485⅘ tons, carried 34,000 pesos in silver specie and bullion, 326 marcos of worked silver, and the usual cargo.

16. Merchant *nao Nuestra Señora de las Angustias y San Rafael,* Captain Francisco Sánchez de Madrid, owner José Sánchez de Madrid, English-built, 328½ tons, carried 27,000 pesos in silver specie and bullion, 605 marcos of worked silver, the usual cargo plus an unspecified amount of Chinese porcelain.

17. Merchant *nao El Gran Poder de Dios y Santa Ana,* alias the *Aná Agustina,* the captain and owner was Francisco Sánchez de Madrid (note: same name as that of above captain), built in Hamburg, Germany, of 181¾ tons, carried 14,000 pesos in silver specie and bullion, 139 marcos in worked silver, and the usual general cargo.

18. Merchant *nao San Ignacio,* captain not identified, owner Francisco de Alzaibar, English-built, 292⅘ tons, carried 12,000 pesos in silver specie and bullion, 696 marcos of worked silver in six boxes, the usual cargo plus some boxes containing gifts from China.

19. Merchant *nao San Francisco de Asis,* captain and owner was Cristobal de Urquijo, English-bulit, 264⅔ tons, no mention in any document of what its cargo was, but it can be assumed that it was the usual.

20. Merchant *nao San Fernando,* no data.

21. Frigate *Floridana,* no data.

22. A vessel only identified as a *balandra* (or schooner), which might be the reason for the different accounts stating that there were twenty-one or twenty-two ships in the fleet when it sailed from Havana. This type of vessel was quite small, and in some accounts it might not have been included as a ship of the fleet.

After setting sail from Havana on July 13, the following day they sighted the Florida Keys. Around nine that evening the wind blew very strongly from the north. By sunup the following morning the wind had swung around to the south at hurricane force and prevented the ships from trying to reach the safety of Havana. By nightfall of this same day, all or most of the ships had been wrecked on the Florida Keys, scattered in different areas between Key Biscayne and Vaca Key. Many documents, as well as charts showing the locations of the wrecks, differ as to the names of the shipwrecks, their locations, and the total number of ships that were lost. Following are the probable locations of the lost ships.

1. *Capitana El Rubi*, listed as being wrecked at Cayo Tabamos in most documents and at Cayo Largo (Key Largo) in a few others.

2. *Almiranta El Gallo*, listed as being wrecked at Cayo de Vivoras in all the documents and charts.

3. Galleon *El Infante*, listed as being wrecked at Cayo Tabamos in all documents and charts.

4. Pink *El Pinque*, listed as being wrecked at the Cabeza de los Martires (head of the Florida Keys) and Key Biscayne in different documents and charts.

5. *San José de las Animas*, listed as being wrecked at Cayo Tabamos. On one chart showing the locations of the shipwrecks of this fleet, a shipwreck denoted as *Africa* is shown in the same location that other charts show the *San José de las Animas*, which was probably her alias.

6. *Nuestra Señora del Rosario, San Francisco Javier y San Antonio de Padua*, listed in some documents as being wrecked at Cayo de Vivoras and in others as having survived the hurricane and safely returned to Havana.

7. *Nuestra Señora de Belem y San Antonio de Padua*, listed in documents as being wrecked at Cayo de Matacumbe el Viejo (Upper Matacumbe Key), but on the charts it is not shown by this name. However, the charts do list a shipwreck by the name of *Herrera*, which is probably the same ship, as the captain and owner of this ship was named Herrera.

8. *Nuestra Señora del Rosario, San Antonio y San Vicente Ferrer*, is not listed in any document or shown on the charts. However, on two charts a shipwreck named *Arizon*—the name of the captain and owner of this ship—is shown, and on another chart in the same location a shipwreck named *Terri* is shown as being lost at Cayo de Vivoras. Several documents also mention a ship named *Terri* (or *Terry*) as being lost at Cayo de Vivoras, and it is probably the same ship as above.

9. *Nuestra Señora del Carmen, San Antonio de Padua y las*

Animas, is listed in both documents and charts as being wrecked at Cayo de Matacumbe el Viejo, or Matacumbe Grande, both names used for Upper Matacumbe. In the documents, this ship was sometimes called simply *Chaves,* the name of captain and owner, and on all of the charts it was also denoted by the name *Chaves.*

10. *Nuestra Señora de Belem y San Juan Bautista* is mentioned in documents as being wrecked at Cayo de Matacumbe el Viejo (Upper Matacumbe) and not shown on any charts by this name. However, the charts do show a ship named *Tres Puentes* as being lost at Upper Matacumbe, and this was probably the ship's alias.

11. *Nuestra Señora de los Dolores y Santa Isabel* is not mentioned as being lost in the documents, nor shown on any of the charts, but she might have been mentioned by an alias.

12. *Nuestra Señora del Rosario y Santo Domingo* made it safely back to Havana.

13. *Nuestra Señora de los Reyes, San Fernando y San Francisco de Paula,* was wrecked at Cayo de Vivoras.

14. *San Pedro* is listed as being wrecked at Cayo de Matacumbe el Mozo (Lower Matacumbe), and at Cayuelo de Matanzas.

15. *San Felipe* is not mentioned in any documents as being lost, nor returning to Havana, nor shown on any of the wreck charts.

16. *Nuestra Señora de las Angustias y San Rafael* was wrecked at Cayo de Vivoras.

17. *El Gran Poder de Dios y Santa Ana* is listed by this name and by *Sánchez de Madrid,* the name of the captain and owner, as being wrecked at Cayo de Bacas del Leste (Vacas Key).

18. *San Ignacio,* listed as being wrecked at Cayo de Bocas and Cayo de Vacas. One document calls this ship *San Ignacio de Urquijo,* which was the name of the captain of the *San Francisco de Asis.* As the documents do not reveal the name of the captain of the *San Ignacio,* it is possible that this was his name as well.

19. *San Francisco de Asis* was wrecked at Cayo de Vivoras.

20. *San Fernando* is not mentioned in the documents or shown on any charts as being lost, but it was probably mentioned by its alias, if it had one.

21. *Floridana* is listed in some documents as having escaped and in some others as being wrecked at Cayo de Vivoras.

22. The unidentified *balandra* is probably the Key Biscayne

shipwreck mentioned in documents and shown on the charts as *El Aviso* (an advice boat).

To add to the confusion, documents and charts mention the following ships as being wrecked at different places. They might be aliases for some of the ships that were wrecked or for those whose fate was not mentioned in documents. Or they might be ships that were not even part of the fleet but were sailing separately.

1. *El Sueco,* wrecked at Cayo de Bacas del Leste.

2. *Sánchez,* which is probably the *El Poder de Dios y Santa Ana,* wrecked at Cayo de Bacas del Leste.

3. *Murguia,* wrecked at Cayo de Matacumbe el Mozo.

4. *Ledieque,* wrecked at Cayo de Tavanos (probably the same place that is listed as Cayo Tabamos).

5. *Valandrita,* wrecked at Matacumbe el Grande.

The Spaniards carried out thorough salvage operations on all of these wrecks, and several, which were not identified by name, were refloated. Fifteen, which could not be refloated, were burnt to their waterlines after salvage operations were completed. Within three months after the disaster occurred, the King was informed by royal officials in Havana that not only had all of the registered treasure been recovered but a substantial amount of unregistered treasure as well. Most of the other cargo was also recovered but a great amount of it had been destroyed by the salt water, especially the sugar, indigo, and cochineal. What little the Spaniards failed to recover has been searched for in the past few decades, but very little of real value has been discovered other than various items of historical and archaeological value. Small amounts of silver coins have been found by modern-day salvors, but nothing of the magnitude such as has been recovered from the wrecks of the 1715 fleet.

60. *Year 1734.* Brief mention of a ship of Don Gerónimo Barroso (he could have been the captain or owner, or both) that was lost near Rio Seco on the coast of Florida.

61. *Year 1741.* Brief mention of an unidentified Spanish frigate being lost at Cayo de Lobos on the coast of Florida.

62. *Year 1741.* In March the H.M.S. *Wolf,* a 14-gun sloop, captain's name not given, was wrecked on the east coast of Florida. These

British war-sloops generally carried eight regular iron cannon and twelve swivel guns, also called *patereroes,* which were counted as half a gun.

63. *Year 1741.* British merchantman *Naffaw,* Captain Bradshaw, sailing from Jamaica for Bristol, England, lost on the Florida Keys, the crew was saved by a vessel bound for Virginia.

64. *Year 1742.* British man-of-war H.M.S. *Tyger* was lost in the Florida Keys, where the crew built a small fort from the timbers of the wreck. The Spanish admiral Torres sent several small vessels to make prisoners of the survivors but they were not successful, as the Englishmen beat them off.

65. *Year 1742.* Spanish galleon *Fuerte,* 60 cannon, lost near the H.M.S. *Tyger.* When Admiral Torres learned that his forces had been repelled by the crew of the *Tyger,* he sent this larger ship with a great number of Spanish soldiers aboard, but they wrecked themselves.

66. *Year 1744.* British man-of-war (called a frigate in some accounts) H.M.S. *Looe* (sometimes called *Loo*), 44 guns, Captain Uting, was lost in the Florida Keys along with a Spanish ship she had captured shortly before but all the men on both ships were saved. The site of the wreck was called *la Pareda* by the Spaniards, but shortly later the area was referred to as Looe Reef, as it is still called today. The date of the accident was February 5, 1744.

67. *Year 1748.* British merchantman *Dolphin,* Captain Smith, sailing from Carolina to Antigua, and several other vessels were lost on the coast of Florida.

68. *Year 1748.* British ship *Dolphin,* Captain Bagat, bound for North Carolina, was captured by the Spaniards but soon afterward wrecked near Cape Florida.

69. *Year 1748.* American merchant vessel *Howlet,* on a trading voyage from Boston to the Gulf of Mexico, was driven ashore by strong winds near Cape Florida, where the crew was captured by Indians and—except for a black slave who later escaped—put to death.

70. *Year 1748.* British warship H.M.S. *Fowey,* 20 guns, Captain Francis William Drake, was wrecked in the Florida Keys (area

now known as Fowey Rocks), along with a Spanish merchantman named *Judith* (or *Judan*), which was carrying $57,000 (pesos) and a large cargo of cocoa. The crews of both ships and the cargo of the Spanish prize were all saved and transferred to a sloop and carried to Carolina.

71. **Year 1750.** British merchantman *Betsey*, Captain Slater, sailing from Jamaica to Bristol, was lost in the Gulf of Florida but the crew was taken up by a passing vessel.

72. **Year 1752.** The following ships were lost in the Gulf of Florida during a hurricane on October 22: British merchantman *Alexander*, Captain Mudis, sailing from Jamaica to London; British merchantman *Lancaster*, Captain Lowry, sailing from Jamaica to Lancaster; British merchantman *Dolphin*, Captain Pedrick, sailing from Jamaica to Liverpool; British merchantman *Queen Anne*, Captain Rymer, sailing from Jamaica to Bristol; British merchantman *May*, Captain Crawford, sailing from Jamaica to Glasgow; American merchantman *Rhode Island*, Captain Ball, sailing from Jamaica to New York; American merchantman *Statea*, Captain Jones, sailing from Honduras to Rhode Island; an unidentified Spanish man-of-war; an unidentified Spanish schooner; and three other ships of unknown identity.

73. **Year 1763.** British merchantman *Albinia*, sailing from Jamaica to London, was wrecked on the coast of Florida but the crew was saved.

74. **Year 1763.** British merchantman *Alexander*, Captain Johnson, sailing from Jamaica to London, was lost in the Florida Keys.

75. **Year 1764.** British ship *Industry*, Captain Lawrence, in the government service installed in Charleston, South Carolina, from New York bound for east and west Florida, having on board a number of craftsmen and other settlers and their families, was lost on the St. Augustine bar but the crew and all passengers were saved.

76. **Year 1765.** British ship *Grenville Packet*, Captain Curlett, with mail from Falmouth, in her route from Pensacola ran ashore on February 27 upon the Dry Tortugas and was lost but the crew was saved.

77. **Year 1766.** Unidentified Spanish ship from the Bay of Campeche, enroute to Pensacola, was wrecked off Isle of Rosey, within a few leagues of Pensacola, the ship was a total loss but her cargo was saved.

78. **Year 1766.** British or American ship *Nelly*, Captain Smith, sailing from Philadelphia to St. Augustine, was lost on the St. Augustine bar, crew and part of cargo saved.

79. **Year 1766.** British ship *General Conway*, Captain Bail, from Jamaica, was lost in the Florida Keys but the crew was saved.

80. **Year 1766.** Unidentified French ship, commanded by Monsieur Pierre Viaud, was wrecked on the coast of Florida between Pensacola and Mobile.

81. **Year 1766.** On October 22 and 23, a violent hurricane caused considerable damage to shipping in the harbor of Pensacola. This same hurricane also caused five large and richly laden Spanish galleons, sailing from Veracruz for Spain, to be wrecked in the Bay of St. Bernard, which is WSW from Pensacola.

82. **Year 1768.** Unidentified shipwreck shown on a chart as "A Wreck in 1768," located between Mount Tucker and Cape Kennedy.

83. **Year 1768.** Spanish ship *Jazo e Santa Ana* (alias *La Nimsa del Puerto*), captain's name unknown, sailing from Havana to Cadiz, was lost in the Florida Straits.

84. **Year 1768.** A vessel of Captain Codington, coming from Montego Bay, Jamaica, to Rhode Island with rums, in coming through the Florida Straits was set on fire by lightning and entirely consumed, all lives were lost.

85. **Year 1768.** Spanish ship *San Antonio*, Captain Font, from Havana, was lost on January 22 on a reef near Key West, the crew and passengers, after surviving for twenty-two days on this reef, were rescued by a turtling sloop and carried back to Havana.

86. **Year 1768.** British packet boat *Anna Theresa*, Captain Dyer, sailing from Pensacola to Falmouth, was wrecked on the Florida Keys. On the morning of July 30 the British ship *Prince George*, Captain Collier, was sailing past the Florida Keys and saw this wreck aground on a reef and afire. Seeing three sloops anchored near

the wreck, he sent a boat to investigate and was told that the crew of the ship had been carried to New Providence, the Bahamas. He was also told that a few days earlier a Spanish ship and a brig from Boston—whose captain's name was Bostley —had been lost in the same area.

87. *Year 1769.* British ship *Prince George,* sailing from London to St. Augustine, was lost going into St. Augustine.

88. *Year 1769.* British merchant snow *Ledbury,* Captain John Lorain, sailing from Jamaica to Bristol, was driven on shore about fifteen leagues northward of Cape Florida, in a violent gale of wind on September 29, crew and part of cargo saved.

89. *Year 1769.* Unidentified shipwreck location shown on Bernard Romans' map of Florida as "Wreck 1769," at Mount Tucker, north of Cape Canaveral.

90. *Year 1770.* News reached London from Jamaica that a large Spanish ship, sailing from Caracas, Venezuela, for Cadiz, was wrecked in the Florida Keys during a violent gale of wind, ship and cargo totally lost.

91. *Year 1771.* British ship *Eagle,* arrived in Bristol from Jamaica, where it had left on July 26. The captain reported seeing five large ships and one brig wrecked in the Florida Keys and on the coast of Florida. One of the ships had lost her main and mizzen masts, and he noted that the current set very strong toward the Florida coast.

92. *Year 1771.* British ship *Hope,* Captain Clutsam, who, while passing through the Florida Straits, reported that he saw a Spanish man-of-war; sometime later it caught on fire and blew up.

93. *Year 1771.* Captain Bratt, who arrived in London in early October, reported seeing seven large ships wrecked on the shores of Florida.

94. *Year 1771.* Spanish merchant *nao El Nauva Victoriosa,* Captain Josef Varan, which had sailed from Cadiz on November 3, 1770, in a *flota* going to Veracruz, sank sometime in 1771 at the entrance of the Bahama Channel, on the head of the Florida Keys, in the vicinity of Key Largo, with only her crew being saved.

95. *Year 1772.* British merchantman *Maria Beckford,* Captain Boyd, was wrecked at Cape Florida and was a total loss.

96. *Year 1772.* British ship *Fortune,* Captain Richardson, sailing from Jamaica to London, was lost on November 18 near the coast of Florida, only two men were drowned.

97. *Year 1773.* A ship of unknown nationality, *Sally,* Captain Mathews, sailing from Lisbon to South Carolina, was lost on February 22 in a snowstorm near St. Augustine and all of the crew except the mate perished.

98. *Year 1773.* British merchantman *East Florida Merchant,* Captain Losthouse, sailing from London to St. Augustine, was lost on the St. Augustine bar and two-thirds of its cargo was saved.

99. *Year 1773.* British ship *Dove,* captain's name unknown, was lost on October 18 on the coast of Florida, enroute from Africa to St. Augustine, eighty out of one hundred slaves, plus the captain and two of the crew, were lost.

100. *Year 1774.* Captain Addis of the ship *Green River,* sailing from Jamaica to London, reported that on April 23 he saw a ship wrecked at Cape Florida without main or mizzen masts, and believed it was the *Mill,* Captain Hays, which was sailing in ballast from Jamaica to Boston.

101. *Year 1774.* British ship *Rhee Galley,* Captain Hunter, sailing from Honduras to Bristol, was lost in the Florida Keys.

102. *Year 1774.* Captain Magness of the ship *Ann & Elizabeth,* arrived in London from Jamaica and reported that on August 8 he saw a large brig onshore to the northward of Cape Florida being stripped by several wreckers.

103. *Year 1774.* British merchantman *Montague,* Captain Pickels, sailing from Jamaica to Liverpool, was lost at Cape Florida, but the crew and about thirty hogsheads of sugar were saved and carried to New Providence Island in the Bahamas.

104. *Year 1774.* British ship *Diana,* Captain Buckley, sailing from Jamaica to Rhode Island, was lost on Cape Florida, the crew was saved, but the cargo and ship were a total loss.

105. *Sometime before 1775.* A historian wrote: ". . . a little cay lying before Matacumbe is a dreadful monument of this [the cannibal-

ism of the Colossas Indians], it is called Matanca [*i.e.*, "slaughter"], from the number near four hundred wretched Frenchmen, who being cast away, fell into the hands of these monsters. . . ."

106. **Year 1776.** British ship *Belieze* [*sic*], Captain Gillis, sailing from Honduras to London, was lost on October 12 on the east coast of Florida.

107. **Year 1777.** A ship of unknown nationality, *Minerva*, Captain Callahan, was lost on the east coast of Florida.

108. **Year 1777.** On May 16 the Spanish ship *Begoña* entered Cadiz, coming from Veracruz it had sighted an English vessel of Captain Williams just ready to sink off the coast of Florida. The Spaniards rescued the crew from this ship and took them to Cadiz.

109. **Year 1777.** British ship *Claudina*, Captain Valliant, sailing from London to Pensacola, was totally lost on the coast of Florida.

110. **Year 1778.** British warship H.M.S. *Otter*, 10 guns, Captain John Wright, was wrecked off the east coast of Florida.

111. **Year 1778.** During a hurricane on October 9, fourteen large and many small ships were sunk at Pensacola, among which were the *Sarah & Elizabeth*, Captain Tovet, laden with lumber for Jamaica, and the *Mary*, Captain Blackwell, both of British registry.

112. **Year 1778.** British ship *Mary*, Captain Hoincastle, sailing from Jamaica to London, was lost in December off Cape Florida in attempting to escape from two American privateers.

113. **Year 1781.** Spanish frigate *Francesa*, Captain Andromaca, carrying a large cargo of war materials, ran aground on April 19 on a shoal in Pensacola Bay. The exact location of this shipwreck is shown on a chart in the Naval Museum of Madrid.

114. **Year 1781.** British warship H.M.S. *Mentor*, 20 guns, Captain Robert Deans, was burnt at Pensacola.

115. **Year 1782.** Brief mention that an English ship sank on the Florida Keys sometime during the year.

116. **Year 1782.** British ship *Fanny*, Captain Farquar, sailing from Jamaica to Liverpool, on March 7 ran aground to the northward of Cape Florida and broke up quickly, people and some cargo rescued by a privateer from Nassau.

117. **Year 1783.** British ship *Mary*, Captain Stafford, sailing from St. Augustine to London, was lost on the St. Augustine bar on April 19.

118. **Year 1783.** British merchantman *Tony*, Captain Welsh, sailing from Charlestown to St. Augustine and London, was lost on the St. Augustine bar.

119. **Year 1785.** Captain Earl of the ship *Joseph*, sailing from Honduras to England, on August 31 reported seeing a large ship wrecked on the Florida Keys. Two small vessels were near her on the inside of the reef.

120. **Year 1787.** A vessel sailing from Jamaica to London picked up the crew of a British ship wrecked on the east coast of Florida.

121. **Year 1787.** British ship *Noble Bounty*, Captain Herbert, sailing from Jamaica to London, was wrecked on the Cape Florida Reef but her crew was saved by the *Friendship*, Captain Black.

122. **Year 1788.** British ship *Betsey*, Captain Grant, sailing from Nassau to Florida, was lost on the Mosquito bar on the coast of Florida.

123. **Year 1788.** British merchantman *Evenly*, Captain Hebden, sailing from Honduras to London, was wrecked on the Florida Keys.

124. **Year 1788.** British merchantman *Mary & Jane*, Captain Pennymont, sailing from Jamaica for Liverpool, was lost on the Florida shore but the crew was saved.

125. **Year 1789.** British merchantman *Hazard*, Captain New, sailing from Honduras to London, was totally lost near Cape Florida but the crew was saved.

126. **Year 1789.** British ship *Fly*, Captain Walker, sailing from Jamaica to Africa, was lost on the Florida Keys.

127. **Year 1790.** A ship of unknown nationality, *Santa Marie*, Captain Wicks, sailing from St. Augustine to Havana, was lost on the St. Augustine bar.

128. **Year 1790.** British merchantman *Elizabeth*, Captain Sims, came from Jamaica to Bristol after having run aground on the coast of Florida, where it was refloated by throwing part of its cargo overboard. On August 12, Captain Sims, then in 25 degrees and

4 minutes of latitude, saw four ships on the Florida reef. On the nineteenth he saw two other ships at Cape Florida wrecked on the reef: the *Apollo*, Captain Cragg, and the *Edmund & George*, Captain Rainy—both had been bound for London. Two other ships had been on shore in Florida but got off by throwing parts of their cargoes overboard.

129. *Year 1790.* British merchantman *Hope*, Captain Chappel, sailing from Jamaica to Charlestown, was lost on the coast of Florida.

130. *Year 1791.* British merchant brig *Lively*, Captain Morse, sailing from Jamaica for Bristol, was lost in the Florida Keys but most of her cargo was saved.

131. *Year 1792.* Captain Graham of the ship *Mary*, on June 5 reported seeing a large ship wrecking on the Florida Keys. It was a total loss, and although he was within a mile of her he could not establish her identity.

132. *Year 1792.* Captain M'Donald of the ship *Trelawney Planter* on August 14 reported sighting a ship ashore on Carysford Reef with several wreckers about her.

133. *Year 1792.* American merchantman *Lovely Ann*, Captain Green, sailing from Jamaica to New York, was lost in the Florida Keys.

134. *Year 1793.* British warship H.M.S. *Carysford*, a frigate of 28 guns, Captain Francis Laforey, was lost on Carysford Reef in the Florida Keys.

135. *Year 1793.* British merchantman *General Clark*, Captain Lilburn, sailing from Jamaica to Savannah, was totally lost on a reef of the Florida Keys but the crew was saved.

136. *Year 1794.* British merchantman *Catherine Green*, Captain Rose, sailing from Jamaica for London, was wrecked on August 8 on a reef in the Florida Keys but most of her cargo was saved.

137. *Year 1795.* American merchantman *Noah's Ark*, captain's name unknown, sailing from New Orleans to Philadelphia, was lost in the Florida Keys.

138. *Year 1796.* A brig of unknown nationality, *Hope*, Captain West, sailing from Havana to a port in America, was lost near Cape Florida.

139. *Year 1796.* British naval transport *Maria*, Captain Giltchrist, sailing from Jamaica, was lost on Ludberry Reef in the Florida Keys.

140. *Year 1796.* British merchantman *Speedwell*, Captain Brownlow, sailing from Honduras to Charlestown, was lost on August 28 on Carysford Reef, crew and ship's materials saved.

141. *Year 1796.* A ship of unknown nationality, *Jolly Tar*, captain's name unknown, sailing from Jamaica to Norfolk, was wrecked on the coast of Florida, crew and cargo saved.

142. *Year 1797.* A number of American vessels were cast away on the east coast of Florida during a hurricane on October 15 or 16. Some were also lost in the Bahamas.

143. *Year 1798.* British ship *Flora*, Captain Scott, sailing from Charlestown to Havana, was lost on the Florida Keys.

144. *Year 1799.* British sloop-of-war *Amaranthe*, Captain John Blake, 14 guns, was wrecked on the coast of Florida on October 25 and twenty-two of the crew of eighty-six were lost.

145. *Year 1800.* A ship of unknown nationality, *Hector*, captain's name unknown, sailing from Havana to Nassau, was lost on a reef in the Florida Keys.

146. *Year 1801.* American ship *Eagle*, Captain Dennet, sailing from Havana to Philadelphia, was wrecked on December 15 on the Florida side of the Maranzie Reef in the Florida Keys, crew and cargo saved.

147. *Year 1802.* British ship *Neptune*, Captain Cushley, sailing from New Orleans to Nassau, was lost on the coast of Florida, crew and most of cargo saved.

148. *Year 1802.* A ship of unknown nationality, *Neptune*, Captain Cosbury, sailing from New Orleans to Greencock, out fourteen days from New Orleans, was lost on the coast of Florida, crew and small part of cargo saved.

149. *Year 1802.* American schooner *Phoebus*, Captain Dominique, sailing from Norfolk, was lost on the St. Augustine bar.

150. *Year 1803.* A Spanish ship and a Spanish snow, both from Cadiz, were wrecked and totally lost in January on the Mocus Reef on the Florida Shore.

151. *Year 1803.* British merchantman *Maria,* captain's name unknown, sailing from Honduras to Charlestown, was wrecked on the Florida coast, crew, materials, and cargo saved.

152. *Year 1803.* British merchantman *Britannia,* Captain Wright, sailing from Jamaica to London, was lost on the Florida Keys but part of her cargo was saved by wreckers and carried to Nassau.

153. *Year 1804.* American merchantman *Calliope,* Captain Nash, sailing from Jamaica to Virginia, was lost on the reefs of the Florida Keys.

154. *Year 1804.* During a fierce northeast gale on September 6 or 7, eight ships were sunk in St. Augustine Harbor.

155. *Year 1805.* British warship H.M.S. *Fly,* Captain Powoll Bast Pellew, was wrecked in May on the Carysford Reef and all 121 men of the crew were saved. Gilly states that the wreck occurred on March 3.

156. *Year 1805.* British merchantman *Rattler,* Captain Balmond, sailing from Honduras to London, was totally lost on Carysford Reef and only a small part of her cargo was saved.

157. *Year 1805.* A ship of unknown nationality, *Providence,* Captain Gibson, sailing from New Orleans to Bordeaux, wrecked on September 17 in the Florida Keys.

158. *Year 1805.* A ship of unknown nationality, *Andromache,* Captain Hickles, sailing from Jamaica to New York, was wrecked on December 6 in the Florida Keys. The principal part of her cargo was salvaged and carried to Nassau.

159. *Year 1806.* British schooner H.M.S. *Zenobia,* 10 guns, captain's name unknown, was wrecked on the coast of Florida and the crew was lost.

160. *Year 1806.* A ship of unknown nationality, *Maria,* Captain Rundle, sailing from Jamaica to Halifax, was wrecked on the Dry Tortugas.

161. *Year 1807.* A ship of unknown nationality, *Seaflower,* Captain Pitch, sailing from Jamaica and Havana to New York, was lost on the east coast of Florida.

162. *Year 1807.* British merchantman *Flora,* Captain Adams, sailing from New Orleans to Liverpool, was wrecked on the coast of Florida.

163. *Year 1808.* American merchantman *Ohio,* Captain Hall, sailing from Jamaica to New York, was wrecked on January 15 near Cape Florida but the crew and a great part of the cargo were saved.

164. *Year 1810.* During a hurricane at the end of October, five American ships were wrecked on the Florida shore and went to pieces but the greatest part of their cargoes were recovered.

165. *Year 1810.* British merchantman *Susan,* Captain Beard, sailing from Amelia Island to Clyde, was lost at Amelia Island, crew and cargo saved.

166. *Year 1810.* American merchantman *Fame,* Captain Bennett, sailing from New Orleans to Liverpool, was lost on the coast of Florida but the crew was saved.

167. *Year 1810.* Two British merchantmen, *Hanover,* Captain Baxter, and *George,* Captain Decone, sailing from Liverpool to Amelia Island, were lost about October 20 on Amelia Island.

168. *Year 1810.* Four merchantmen of unknown nationality were lost about October 25 on the Florida shore: *Caroline,* Captain Curtis, sailing from New Orleans to Liverpool; *Union,* captain's name unknown, sailing from Havana to London; *African,* Captain Garcia, sailing from Havana to New York; and the *Triton,* Captain Hand, sailing from Havana to Richmond.

169. *Year 1810.* American schooner, name of ship unknown, Captain Fowler, sailing from St. Mary's to Savannah, laden with salt and cotton, was wrecked at St. Augustine.

170. *Year 1811.* British merchantman *Cabinet,* Captain Montgomery, sailing from New Orleans to Liverpool, was lost October 26 on a reef of the Florida Keys, crew and most of cargo saved.

171. *Year 1811.* British merchantman *Minerva,* Captain M'Nelly, sailing from Londonderry to Amelia Island, was lost on March 2 on Amelia Island but crew was saved.

172. *Year 1811.* Ship identified only by its name, *North Star,* was wrecked at Amelia Island.

173. *Year 1811.* A ship of unknown nationality, *Horatio,* Captain Turner, was totally wrecked at Amelia Island.

174. *Year 1811.* British merchantman *Lady Provost,* Captain Clary, struck on a bar at Amelia Island and was lost on May 9.

175. *Year 1811.* Two British merchantmen were lost at Amelia Island: *Windsor,* Captain Low, sailing from Liverpool to Savannah and Amelia Island, wrecked on Amelia Bar; and the *Maria,* Captain Forster, sailing from London to Amelia Island, was blown up at Amelia Island.

176. *Year 1811.* On October 17 the Spanish ship *Araucana,* Captain Benito de la Rigada (with an official rank of *Teniente de fragata*), sailed from Havana with mail for Spain, but due to a hurricane on October 26 it was totally wrecked on Elliot Key. The crew came ashore on this key and was picked up by a vessel and carried to Nassau and then Havana.

177. *Year 1811.* In October the *Eagle,* sailing from Liverpool, and the *Maria,* of and to London, with five of six other vessels, names unknown, were lost on Amelia Island bar.

178. *Year 1811.* A ship of unknown nationality, *Fair Weather,* captain's name unknown, sailing from Amelia Island to England, was lost on Amelia Island bar.

179. *Year 1811.* British merchantman *Mary,* Captain Forbes, was totally lost at Amelia Island in October.

180. *Year 1811.* British ship *Earl Bathurst,* Captain Heron, sailing from Liverpool, was wrecked at Pensacola.

181. *Year 1812.* American merchantman *Orion,* Captain Brown, sailing from Aux Cayes to Philadelphia, was lost on February 20 on a reef in the Florida Keys.

182. *Year 1812.* British ship *Betsey,* Captain Telley, sailing from St. Vincent, was totally lost at Amelia Island.

183. *Year 1812.* British merchantman *Highlander,* Captain Cuthbert, sailing from Jamaica to London, was lost on July 15 on Carysford Reef, the crew was picked up by the ship *Hopewell.*

184. *Year 1812.* American ship *Juno,* Captain Pratt, sailing from New Orleans to Boston, was lost on June 16 on the Carysford Reef.

185. *Year 1813.* Spanish merchantman *Flor de Guadiana,* captain's name unknown, with between 800 and 900 bags of cotton aboard, was driven on shore at Amelia Island and broke up during a violent storm on September 17.

186. *Year 1814.* Spanish merchantman *Americano,* Captain Abrew, sailing from Havana to Lisbon, was wrecked on July 26 on a reef in the Florida Keys.

187. *Year 1814.* Ship identified only by its name, *Santa Rosa,* coming from Liverpool, was lost on Amelia Island bar.

188. *Year 1814.* Ship identified only by its name, *Oscar,* bound for Liverpool, was burnt at Amelia Island.

189. *Year 1814.* Spanish ship *Intrépido,* commanded by Alferez de Navio Marqués del Moral, was wrecked on a beach of Pensacola during a storm.

190. *Year 1814.* A ship of unknown nationality, *Nicholas Adolph,* Captain Hoas, was lost on November 10 on the Amelia Island bar, part of her cargo was saved.

191. *Year 1815.* Spanish ship *Empecinada,* 6 guns, commanded by Captain Juan Villacencio, left Havana on December 19, 1814, with four other Spanish ships. On January 8, 1815, due to bad weather, it was wrecked at Amelia Island bar while trying to enter this port, where it immediately went to pieces, crew and cargo saved.

192. *Year 1815.* Spanish ship *Volador,* 10 cannon, commanded by Captain Joaquin Veal, entered the port of Pensacola on March 25 carrying a large cargo of goods and rifles. That night a strong wind caused the ship to run aground and it soon went to pieces. Two of the crew and all its cargo were lost.

193. *Year 1815.* Ship identified only by its name, *Santa Anna,* coming from Bermuda, was lost on March 7 off Amelia Island.

194. *Year 1815.* A ship of unknown nationality, *Watt,* Captain M'Gee, sailing from Jamaica to New York, was lost on a reef in the Florida Keys.

195. *Year 1815.* Spanish ship *Jerusalem,* captain's name unknown, sailing from Havana to Africa, was lost on November 13 on a reef of the Florida Keys, crew and cargo saved.

196. Year 1815. An unidentified ship was reported to be wrecked on Carysford Reef on December 6.

197. Year 1816. The following vessels were wrecked in the Gulf of Florida during the violent gales between June 5 and 8: *Atlas,* Captain Thompson, of and heading for Glasgow, coming from Jamaica, on a reef in the Florida Keys; *Martha Brae,* Captain Farish, from Jamaica to Whitehaven, near Cape Florida, with loss (total) of cargo and two men; *Cossack,* from Havana to Hamburg, in the Florida Keys, crew and part of cargo saved; *General Pike,* Captain Emery, from Charlestown to Matanzas, Cuba, at Sound Point, part of its cargo saved; and the *Zanga,* Captain Russell, of Nassau, at Sound Point, all of its cargo saved.

198. Year 1816. The following ships of unknown nationality were wrecked near St. Augustine in early June: ship *Huron,* Captain Snow, sailing from Charlestown to St. Mary's; the schooners *Due Bill* and *Water Witch,* of Savannah; and several unidentified vessels.

199. Year 1816. British ship *Three Sisters,* captain's name unknown, of and heading for Nassau, from New York, was lost on the Carysford Reef.

200. Year 1816. American ship *Three Sisters,* Captain Arnington, of New York, bound for New Orleans, was wrecked on August 30 on Carysford Reef, the crew was saved.

201. Year 1816. Two ships of unknown nationality were wrecked "at Florida": *Rebecca,* captain's name unknown, sailing from Cadiz and Havana to Savannah; and *Catherine Osmond,* Captain Vicaiz, sailing from Havana to Salem. Parts of their cargoes were saved and carried to Nassau.

202. Year 1816. American merchantman *Frolic,* Captain Kennedy, sailing from Havana to Charelstown, was wrecked on Anastasia Island, crew and cargo saved.

203. Year 1816. A ship of unknown nationality, *Sir John Sherbroke,* Captain Cowan, sailing from Jamaica to New York with a general cargo and $60,000 in specie, struck a reef off the Dry Tortugas and the ship went to pieces. The crew was saved and made off with the specie.

204. *Year 1816.* British merchantman *Magdalen,* Captain Sawyer, sailing from New Orleans to Liverpool, was wrecked on a reef in the Florida Keys, its cargo was saved.

205. *Year 1816.* British merchantman *Neptune,* Captain Conolly [*sic*], sailing from Amelia Island to Jamaica, wrecked on the Amelia Island bar and went to pieces.

206. *Year 1816.* Ship identified only by its name, *Amiable Antoinetta,* sailing from Charlestown, wrecked on December 26 near St. Augustine, crew and cargo saved.

207. *Year 1817.* The ship *Hambro,* Captain Patterson, sailing from St. Ubes to Savannah was wrecked about March 12 at a distance of 12 miles to the south of St. Augustine, the crew was saved but the cargo was a total loss.

208. *Year 1817.* Ship identified only by its name, *Anna Maria,* sailing from New Orleans to Philadelphia, wrecked on Bason Bank off east Florida on March 23, the crew was saved, also the few dry goods she had on board.

209. *Year 1817.* Ship identified only by its name, *Julian,* sailing from St. Ubes to Savannah, was lost on March 15 at Anastasia Island, crew, passengers, and part of cargo saved.

210. *Year 1817.* The ship *Brandt,* coming from New Orleans arrived in New York on June 3 and reported seeing a ship and a brig aground on Carysford Reef with eight wreckers around them.

211. *Year 1817.* A ship of unknown nationality, *Europa,* Captain Rich, sailing from St. Jago de Cuba for America, wrecked on a reef in the Florida Keys in May.

212. *Year 1817.* American merchantman *Despatch,* Captain Field, sailing from Havana for Charlestown, wrecked on June 15 on Carysford Reef, crew and cargo saved.

213. *Year 1817.* Portuguese ship *Marquis de Pombal,* captain's name unknown, sailing from Pernambuco to Oporto, was captured by the *Patriola,* an insurgent privateer, but was run aground on May 5 on a reef in the Florida Keys, her cargo was saved and carried to Nassau.

214. *Year 1817.* British merchantman *Sisters,* Captain Swiney, sailing from Jamaica to London, was lost on August 3 on Grand Cayman

Island but her crew was picked up by the ship *Unity,* Captain Lambourn, sailing from Jamaica to London. The *Unity* was then lost on August 13 on Carysford Reef and the crews of both ships were saved by another passing ship.

215. Year *1817*. American brig *Merrimack,* captain's name unknown, sailing from Havana to New York, was wrecked in the Florida Keys and her cargo completely lost but her crew was saved and taken to Nassau by the wreckers.

216. Year *1817*. A ship of unknown nationality, *Venus,* Captain Pinder, sailing from Jamaica to New York, was lost on the east Florida coast, crew and part of cargo saved.

217. Year *1818*. American merchantman *Betsey,* Captain Grafton, sailing from Havana to Rhode Island, was lost on a reef in the Florida Keys, part of her cargo was saved and carried to Nassau.

218. Year *1818*. A large plain ship with yellow sides and black-painted parts was seen wrecked on the Carysford Reef about August 15.

219. Year *1818*. British merchantman *Solway,* Captain Bennett, sailing from Jamaica to Withsharon, wrecked August 10 on a reef of the Florida Keys. Eighteen different wrecking vessels were reported to have recovered the greatest part of her cargo.

220. Year *1818*. British merchantman *Quebec,* Captain Fiott, sailing from Jamaica to London, was totally lost on a reef in the Florida Keys on August 7, only her crew was saved.

221. Year *1818*. A ship of unknown nationality, *Eliza,* Captain Murphey, sailing from Jamaica to Philadelphia, was lost on Carysford Reef, crew and six boxes of dollars saved.

222. Year *1818*. British merchantman *Acasta,* Captain Parkin, sailing from Jamaica to Liverpool, was wrecked sometime before December 5 on the Dry Tortugas, crew and most of cargo saved.

223. Year *1819*. Ship identified only by its name, *Bonee Adelle,* coming from Havana, was wrecked on the coast of east Florida on February 5, only the crew was saved.

224. Year *1819*. A brig with a white bottom and a white streak was seen wrecked on a reef along the Florida Keys on February 24.

225. Year *1819*. French ship *Modeste,* Captain D'Barron, was wrecked at Key Largo on May 21.

226. Year 1819. American ship *General Jackson*, Captain Taylor, sailing from New Orleans for Rotterdam, was wrecked on Cape Florida but most of her cargo was saved.

227. Year 1819. British merchantman *Sandwich*, Captain Fraser, sailing from Havana to Guernsey, was wrecked in the Florida Keys and only a small part of her cargo was saved.

228. Year 1819. A ship of unknown nationality, *Anie of Scarbro* [*sic*], Captain Stanley, enroute to England, was lost June 29 on a reef in the Florida Keys, only five of the crew were saved.

229. Year 1819. On August 12 a large vessel was seen aground on Carysford Reef with three small vessels—presumably anchored nearby.

230. Year 1819. Two American ships were driven over a reef in the Florida Keys and lost: the brig *Barilla*, Captain Jones, sailing from New Orleans to Philadelphia, and the schooner *Lively*, Captain Avery, sailing from New Orleans to Baltimore. The cargoes of both vessels were saved.

231. Year 1821. American ship *Hope for Peace*, Captain Baker, sailing from New Orleans for Charlestown, was dismasted and overset in the Gulf Stream on January 25. The ship then drifted and wrecked on the coast of Florida on January 30 but the crew was saved.

232. Year 1821. A ship of unknown nationality, *Supply*, Captain Fisher, sailing from Jamaica to Havana, heading for the Cape Verde Islands, was totally lost on the coast of Florida at a latitude of 26 degrees and 20 minutes during a heavy gale on January 26 but the crew was saved.

233. Year 1821. At the end of February a ship was seen wrecked and totally dismasted on Carysford Reef.

234. Year 1821. British merchantman *Pearl*, Captain Johnson, sailing from Havana to Gibraltar, was lost near Cape Florida on March 8, only the captain and four of the crew survived.

235. Year 1821. French ship *Royal Desire*, Captain Feuardant, sailing from Havana to Le Havre, was lost early in June near the Florida Coast but the crew was rescued.

236. Year 1821. During a hurricane September 15 several ships were lost in Pensacola Bay.

237. *Year 1821.* A ship of unknown nationality, *Cosmopolite*, Captain Selliman, sailing from Charlestown to New Orleans, was wrecked during a gale on September 14 in the Florida Keys.

238. *Year 1821.* American sloop *General Jackson*, captain's name unknown, was wrecked on the coast of Florida but the crew was saved and carried to Havana, arriving there on October 5.

239. *Year 1822.* English brig *Nelson*, captain's name unknown, was wrecked on the Florida shore on January 31 but the crew was saved and taken to Jamaica.

240. *Year 1822.* British merchantman *Frances & Lucy*, Captain Barnaby, sailing from Jamaica to Halifax, was lost on a reef in the Florida Keys on January 14.

241. *Year 1822.* On April 25, a full-rigged brig was reported wrecked on Carysford Reef. Two other brigs were also aground on Ledbury Reef—one appeared to be over the reef—and there were six or seven wreckers around the two wrecks.

242. *Year 1822.* British merchantman *Ann of London*, Captain Campbell, sailing from Havana to Buenos Aires, was lost around the end of April on the east Florida Keys, only part of her cargo was saved.

243. *Year 1822.* A French brig laden with indigo, logwood, and mahogany, coming from Honduras, was wrecked on the east Florida Keys around the end of April.

244. *Year 1822.* On May 19 a ship with plain yellow sides was reported wrecked on Carysford Reef.

245. *Year 1822.* During a hurricane on July 7 the sloop *Lady Washington* ran aground on Ship Island near Pensacola.

246. *Year 1822.* British merchantman *Neptune*, Captain Duncan, sailing from Jamaica to Dublin, was wrecked on the east Florida shore and broke up quickly.

247. *Year 1822.* On June 27 a large vessel was seen wrecked on a reef in the Florida Keys with six large wreckers around her.

248. *Year 1822.* British ship *Waterloo*, Captain Kelcher, sailing from Jamaica to Cork, was wrecked during October on the east Florida shore but all of its cargo was saved and carried to Nassau.

249. *Year 1823.* American sloop *Leopard,* captain's name unknown, sailing from St. Augustine to Havana, was lost in the Florida Keys but the crew was saved and taken to Havana.

250. *Year 1823.* American merchantman *Franklin,* Captain Taper, sailing from Philadelphia for Pensacola, was wrecked in the Florida Keys, crew and principal part of cargo saved and taken to Nassau.

251. *Year 1823.* Ship identified only by its name, *Andromache,* sailing from Jamaica to New York, was wrecked November 18 on a reef in the Florida Keys.

252. *Year 1823.* Spanish ship *Intrépido,* commanded by Captain José Usel de Guimbarda, was lost in the Bay of Pensacola.

253. *Year 1824.* British merchantman *George III,* Captain Danning, sailing from Honduras to Dublin, was lost February 24 on Carysford Reef, only her crew was saved.

254. *Year 1824.* On March 14 a brig, painted black with a white streak, was seen wrecked on a reef in the Florida Keys.

255. *Year 1824.* The sloop *Theodore* reported that a British brig, sailing from Honduras to England, was wrecked on a reef in the Florida Keys. The *Theodore* was driven away from the wreck by American wreckers.

256. *Year 1824.* On March 26, in latitude of 25 degrees, near Caesar Creek, a long black vessel with painted ports was seen wrecked on a reef with her masts cut down.

257. *Year 1824.* A ship of unknown nationality, *Swift,* Captain Miller, coming from Havana, was wrecked at night on Long Island: 900 boxes of sugar and all the indigo and cochineal she had on board were saved by wreckers and landed at Key West.

258. *Year 1824.* On August 5 a large bright-sided American brig, deeply laden, was seen wrecked on the southwestern end of Carysford Reef with several wreckers alongside.

259. *Year 1824.* On August 29 a large brig was seen wrecked on the Florida coast near Palmerstone Inlet with several small vessels around her.

260. *Year 1824.* British brig *Sarah,* Captain Rowe, laden with logwood and mahogany, was wrecked 8 miles from St. Johnson's bar, east Florida.

261. *Year 1824.* Ship identified only by its name, *Ceres,* coming from New Orleans, was wrecked on the Dry Tortugas but the crew was saved and carried to Havana.

262. *Year 1825.* French merchantman *Pointe-a-Petre,* captain's name unknown, sailing from New Orleans to Bordeaux, was lost on a reef in the Florida Keys on February 7, crew and part of cargo saved.

263. *Year 1825.* Ship identified only by its name, *Johan Carl* (or *Carl John*), sailing from Havana to the Mediterranean, was lost in the Florida Keys, and out of a thousand boxes of sugar aboard only seventy-four were saved.

CHAPTER FOUR

Mexico

ON MANY OCCASIONS I have been asked in which area of the Western Hemisphere I prefer to work on old shipwrecks. My answer has always been Mexico because of the vast number of virgin shipwrecks lying in its waters. Unlike the Bahamas or Florida, where salvors have been picking the shipwrecks clean over the centuries (except for ships that were lost close to Veracruz), most of the old shipwrecks were not salvaged, or only partially so. The reason is that many ships were lost in desolate areas on the Yucatán Peninsula, or on small keys or reefs in the Gulf of Mexico, and even if survivors had been able to reach civilization, they could not accurately report the locations of their shipwrecks. Even today most of the coastline of the Yucatán Peninsula is barren, and outstanding landmarks are few and far between.

Besides the shipwreck locations I have listed in this chapter, there

are no doubt many others on which no documentation has survived—
if indeed there was ever anything written about them. This would
include many small trading vessels that plied between Mexico and
Cuba and other ports of the Caribbean as well as privateering and
pirate vessels of different nationalities.

The reason there is little mention of ships being lost on the Pacific
side of Mexico is that in the old days there was virtually no shipping
in those waters. There were the annual departures and arrivals of the
Manila Galleons, but none were known to have been lost in Mexican
waters. Trade between Mexico, Panama, and Peru was prohibited,
except on rare occasions, to prevent the carrying of contraband by
them.

It must be remembered that prior to 1600 the town of Veracruz was
located 15 miles west of the present port of Veracruz, so any ships
listed as being lost at or near Veracruz prior to 1600 were located at
the site of the old town. Ships mentioned as being lost at San Juan
de Ulúa are today located in the present harbor of Veracruz, as the
former name is no longer in use. In the past fifty years a great deal of
dredging has been done in Veracruz Harbor and vast amounts of
treasure and artifacts have been brought up by accident, but there is
still a great deal to be recovered by modern-day salvors.

When a ship was reported as being "lost on the Coast of Campeche,"
this did not necessarily mean near the present port of Campeche, as
the whole Yucatán Peninsula was known as the Coast of Campeche
as late as 1800. Some of the place-names I have used in this chapter
are no longer used on modern charts or maps but can be found on old
nautical charts.

From my own experience I know that most of the eastern section of
the Yucatán Peninsula can be worked the year around, but in the Gulf
of Mexico the best season is summer, when the strong north winds do
not blow. Except around rivermouths, or in large commercial ports,
the underwater visibility is generally as good as that found in the
Bahamas.

The Mexican Government is very strict about foreigners working on
shipwreck sites in their territorial waters, and in recent years several
treasure-hunting parties have been arrested for diving illegally in
Mexican waters. Permission can be obtained only through CEDAM
or CEDAM International.

In 1959, CEDAM (Club of Explorations and Aquatic Sports of
Mexico) was founded by Pablo Bush Romero, a noted sportsman and

businessman. It was the first marine archaeological society created in the Western Hemisphere. Its function was not just to undertake serious salvage work but to protect all ancient shipwrecks from being plundered by foreigners. Each year since its founding, members of CEDAM have participated in large-scale expeditions in Mexican waters and have recovered a great deal of interesting artifacts from various sites.

From its inception, Americans were admitted as members. In 1966, CEDAM International was founded, which consists of hundreds of Americans interested in salvaging shipwrecks in Mexican waters. Combined, there are over a thousand members in both groups, which work jointly on Mexican shipwreck sites each summer.

List of Shipwrecks in Mexico

1. **Year 1511.** When Hernando Cortez stopped at Cozumel Island in 1519 he found a Spaniard named Jerónimo de Aguilar, a native of Ecija, Spain. In 1511 they and fifteen other men and two women left Darien for the Island of Santo Domingo but their ship was blown off course and wrecked on Alacranes Reef in the Gulf of Mexico. In the ship's boat they reached Yucatán, where most of their companions were sacrificed by the Indians.

2. **Year 1519.** After Cortez had begun his conquest of Mexico, he had nine of the ten vessels with which he had arrived at San Juan de Ulúa either burnt or sunk. Various accounts differ as to how the ships were destroyed; however, all accounts agree that all of the ships were stripped of everything of value, such as rigging, cordage, etc., before they were destroyed. None of the accounts indicate the type of ships they were, except that some were large and others small. During the summer of 1958 a group of divers led by Pablo Bush Romero attempted to locate these shipwrecks but failed, as the land has built out farther into the sea and the area in which these ships were lost is believed to be under land.

3. **Year 1519.** A *nao* of Captain Diego Camargo sank in the Tampico River and all of the men aboard her were lost.

4. **Year 1524.** The lawyer Alonso Zuazo, who was then the governor of Santiago de Cuba, sailed from there in January of 1524 to visit Cortez in Mexico. On January 20 his ship was wrecked on Los

Triángulos and quickly went to pieces. Only forty-three persons were saved, and Zuazo lost his books and a great deal of gold, silver, and jewels. The wreck occurred near a small cay, 10 paces wide and 100–150 paces long. There was another small cay located about 3 leagues away, from which they obtained water. From the wreckage of the ship they built a small boat and eventually reached Veracruz. Other accounts of this event place the wreck on Los Alacranes, but from the description of the area it was most likely on Los Triángulos.

5. *Year 1526. Las Nicolasa* sank at Isla Cancun near Isla Mujeres. This was a ship sailing from Cuba to Veracruz with supplies for the conquistadors. Members of CEDAM recovered several lombard cannon from this wreck in 1959, and a few years earlier several fishermen from Isla Mujeres recovered a bronze cannon in excellent condition.

6. *Year 1527.* The conquistador Francisco de Montejo, when he began his conquest of Yucatán in 1527, had two of his ships—a brigantine and a caravel—burnt at Punta Soliman on the coast of Quintana Roo, which is located between the ruins of Tulum and Xehla. I located the site of these wrecks in 1957 and recovered a small anchor, iron cooking caldron, miscellaneous iron fittings, various ceramic shards, and some ballast stones.

7. *Year 1527.* Two *naos* of the armada of General Alvaro de Saavedra, which were sent by Cortez from the west coast of Mexico to search for the ships of Loaysa, were believed to have been lost on the Straits of Gaspar, near the coast of Mexico, but the exact location of this strait is not known. The names of the ships were the *Santiago* and *Espíritu Santo.*

8. *Year 1532.* An unidentified brigantine, built in Mexico at the orders of the Marquis del Valle for the purpose of making new discoveries in the South Seas (Pacific Ocean), was lost on the coast of Mexico near Aldeanueva.

9. *Year 1539.* Loss of the ship carrying the explorer Francisco de Ulloa, who after exploring the Gulf of California headed north and was never again heard from.

10. *Year 1545.* An unidentified merchant *nao* coming from Spain was lost "on the reefs of Veracruz" and all of its cargo worth over 100,000 pesos, was totally lost but the people were saved.

11. *Year 1545.* An unidentified ship of the Flota de Nueva España was wrecked because of a "norther" on Isla de Terminos and the survivors reached Campeche in a canoe.

12. *Year 1553.* Merchant *nao La Magdalena,* 150 tons, Captain Juan Rodríguez, sailing from Veracruz to Spain, was lost on the coast of Mexico but all the gold she was carrying was recovered and taken to Spain in another ship.

13. *Year 1555.* *Nao Espíritu Santo,* 220 tons, Captain Damyan Martin, preparing to sail for Spain, was sunk in the port of San Juan de Ulúa but all the gold and silver she carried was salvaged.

14. *Year 1555.* On January 21 the *nao Santa María la Blanca,* 220 tons, Captain Francisco de Santana, owned by Diego Felipe, was lost. One document states that she was lost in the port of San Juan de Ulúa and another that she was lost on some reefs as she was leaving port. All of her cargo, which consisted of 850,000 pesos de oro, 28,000 marcos of silver (recovered from three *naos* that had been wrecked on the coast of Florida in 1554), and a large amount of cochineal, were salvaged but eighty-five people were drowned.

15. *Sometime before 1557.* In 1557 the bishop of Yucatán, Diego de Landa, wrote that about fifteen years earlier a bark was lost with many people and a great amount of dry goods near the Bay of Ascension, on the coast of Quintana Roo. The ship foundered and all the people, except a man named Majuelas and four others, were lost. They clung to a fragment of the ship's mast and floated for three or four days trying to reach one of the small islands in this bay. Only Majuelas survived. He built a small raft and reached the mainland.

16. *Year 1558.* On February 6 nineteen merchant *naos* under the command of General Pedro de Ruelas sailed from Sanlúcar de Barrameda for the Indies. After making their Caribbean landfall, Ruelas took eleven of the ships and sailed for Cartagena. The other eight, under the command of Admiral Antonio de Aguayo, sailed for Mexico. When they were in sight of Roca Partida, which was about 50 leagues from Veracruz, they were struck by a storm that lasted three days. The *urca* of Maestre Pedro de Mata was lost near Rio Alvarado and sixty persons aboard her were

drowned. Another *nao, La Inglesa,* was lost nearby and only the people aboard her were saved. The remaining six ships entered San Juan de Ulúa on May 23.

17. *Year 1565.* An unidentified *nao* coming from Cabo Verde (probably with a cargo of Negro slaves) was wrecked on the coast of Coatzacoalcos during a "norther" and her captain, Juan Gallego, and some of her crew were saved. Some of the general merchandise she carried was also later salvaged.

18. *Year 1566.* The *nao El Santo Crucifijo de Burgos,* 400 tons, Captain Sebastián de Porras, one of the merchant ships in the Flota de Nueva España of Captain-General Juan Velasco de Barrio, was wrecked on the coast of Coatzacoalcos while enroute to Veracruz.

19. *Year 1566.* After the aforementioned Flota had anchored and was in the process of discharging its cargo in the port of San Juan de Ulúa, a "norther" struck the port on October 4 and caused a great deal of damage to the ships, sinking an unidentified ship of Captain Armijo.

20. *Year 1567.* The Flota de Nueva España, commanded by Captain-General Cristobal de Eraso and numbering over twenty merchant *naos,* sailed from Sanlúcar on July 7 and entered the port of San Juan de Ulúa during the first week of October. On the night of October 16 a strong "norther" struck the port and three of his *naos* were sunk but the people and most of their cargoes were saved.

21. *Year 1568.* The Flota de Nueva España, commanded by Captain-General Francisco de Luxan and Admiral Juan de Ubillo, sailed from Sanlúcar near the end of July and reached San Juan de Ulúa on September 21, where they found eight ships under the command of the Englishman John Hawkins already anchored in port. Most sources vary as to the number of ships Hawkins had— five to eight. Although a truce was effected by the opposing forces, a battle broke out and the *Almiranta* of the Flota, the *Santa Clara,* 500 tons, Captain Alonso Arfran, was blown up and sank carrying 184 quintales (100 pounds) of mercury. During the battle five or six of the English ships were also burnt or sunk (Spanish sources say six and English five), and the names of five

are known: *Jesus, Swallow, Grace of God, William & John,* and *Angel.* Although Hawkins' flagship the *Jesus* was lost, he escaped aboard the *Minion;* another ship, the *Judith,* under command of Francis Drake, also escaped and reached England.

22. **Year 1571.** Four merchant *naos* of the Flota de Nueva España, commanded by Captain-General Cristobal de Eraso, sailing from Sanlúcar to Veracruz, were wrecked on the coast of Tabasco in October or November. The ships were: the *urca San Juan,* 300 tons, Captain Luis Gutiérrez; *nao La María,* 550 tons, Captain Alonso Rodríguez de Norruega; *nao Santo Catalina,* 400 tons, Captain Andrés de Paz; and the *nao La Magdalena,* 886 tons (a very large ship for this period), Captain Gonzalo Monte. Extensive salvage operations were carried out on all these wrecks and most of the mercury, wine, and other types of merchandise were recovered.

23. **Year 1574.** The Flota de Nueva España, commanded by Captain-General Antonio Manríquez, sailed from Spain with twenty-seven ships on June 29 and, after reaching the Gulf of Mexico, was struck by a bad storm that scattered the ships widely. The *nao Sanct' Ana,* 300 tons, Captain Pedro de Paredes, and two unidentified *naos* owned by Antonio Sánchez de Armas and a man identified only by the surname of Carrejas, were sunk. An unidentified *urca* was also wrecked on the coast of Coatzacoalcos and five men were drowned but all of its cargo was saved.

24. **Year 1582.** The Flota de Nueva España, commanded by Captain-General Alonso de Quiñones and consisting of thirty-nine ships, sailed from Sanlúcar on June 20 and reached Veracruz on September 18 or 19. The *Almiranta Nuestra Señora de la Rosa,* 650 tons, Captain Alonso Conquero, and an unidentified small *nao* were sunk inside the port. The *Almiranta* was carrying 450 quintales of mercury, all of which was recovered.

25. **Year 1584.** The Flota de Nueva España, commanded by Captain-General Diego de Alcega and consisting of forty-seven ships, sailed from Sanlúcar on July 11. On September 10 four *naos* of this Flota were wrecked on Las Cabezas, which is located 10 leagues from Veracruz. One of these *naos* was carrying mercury, but there is no mention if the mercury, or any of the cargoes of the other ships, was salvaged.

26. Year 1586. The Flota de Nueva España, commanded by Captain-General Francisco de Nova Feijo and consisting of fifty-five ships, sailed from Sanlúcar on July 18. While passing in sight of Cabo Catoche, two *naos* were wrecked: *Santa María de Begonia,* 140 tons, Captain Cristobal Sánchez Melgareza, and the *Santiago El Mayor,* 200 tons, Captain Vasco Martín. The *nao La Trinidad,* 125 tons, Captain Gaspar de Cubas, was also lost on the coast of Tabasco.

27. Year 1588. The Flota de Nueva España, commanded by Captain-General Martín Pérez de Olozabal and consisting of fifty-two ships, sailed from Sanlúcar on July 5 and had an uneventful voyage until reaching the Gulf of Mexico, where on September 23 it was struck by a storm that separated many of the ships from the main convoy. Although the storm lasted for several days, none of the ships were lost. All the ships were then reunited to the main convoy and entered Veracruz in September. The *Almiranta Ascension,* 500 tons, Captain Juan de Lambarri (the last ship in the convoy to enter the port), was struck by a freak wind and sank on a reef at the entrance of the port. Salvage operations were quickly started and most of her mercury was recovered.

28. Year 1590. The Flota de Nueva España, commanded by Captain-General Antonio Navarro de Prado and consisting of sixty-three ships, sailed from Sanlúcar on August 1. Early in November the *flota* was struck by a fierce "norther" while in the Gulf of Mexico and sixteen ships were lost along the Mexican coast. The surviving ships entered Veracruz on November 8. Only four of the lost ships were identified: *nao La Trinidad,* 280 tons, Captain Bernardo de Paz, lost trying to enter Veracruz during the storm; a Portuguese *nao, La Piedad,* 180 tons, Captain Cristobal Sánchez Melgarejo, lost on the bar of Veracruz with only eighteen persons saved but most of its cargo; *nao Nuestra Señora del Socorro,* 220 tons, Captain Pedro Diaz Franco, lost in the Canal Gallega in Veracruz; and the Portuguese *nao Nuestra Señora de la Concepción,* 130 tons, Captain Miguel Rodríguez, which was lost near Veracruz. More than a thousand men and over 2 million pesos in cargo were lost on the sixteen ships.

29. Year 1597. The Flota de Nueva España, commanded by Captain-General Pedro Menéndez Márquez and consisting of sixty-eight ships, sailed from Cadiz on June 22 and entered San Juan de

Ulúa on August 30. Two ships were wrecked at the entrance of this port: *nao San Buenaventura,* 700 tons, Captain Pedro de Venastequi, and *nao La Pandora,* 600 tons, Captain Julio López de Cubeleus. The accident occurred when the fluke of an anchor on the bow of *La Pandora* caught the rigging of the *San Buenaventura,* which was sailing too close to it, causing them to collide and sink.

30. *Year 1597.* A hurricane struck the port of San Juan de Ulúa on September 22 and two ships were sunk: *nao San Buenaventura,* 250 tons, Captain Pedro de Bestiqui, and *nao La María,* 140 tons, Captain Manuel de Gaya. (Note the similarity between the names of the two captains of two ships named *San Buenaventura* of the same *flota.*)

31. *Year 1600.* The Flota de Nueva España, commanded by Captain-General Pedro D'Escobar Melgarejo, sailed from Cadiz on May 15 with sixty ships in the convoy. A hurricane struck the *flota* on September 12, when it was about 20 leagues from the coast of Villa Rica, and six ships were lost. Three of them sank soon after the storm began: *nao San Antonio de Padua,* 300 tons, Captain Juan de Morales; *nao Santa Catalina de Siena,* 280 tons, Captain Andrés Ximénez, and an unidentified *nao,* 700 tons, Captain Mathea Letieta, which was carrying a great deal of mercury. Two other ships, unidentified, disappeared and were presumed to have sunk. One was 350 tons and its captain Rafael Ferrifino. During the same storm a small *patache* of 50 tons, Captain Ganucho, was also wrecked on the coast of Tabasco and sixty men were drowned. After the hurricane abated, the ships that survived rejoined the main convoy and continued on to Veracruz, which they sighted on September 26, but a "norther" began blowing, so the ships were forced to anchor offshore for the night. Some of the ships anchored in the lee of Isla de Sacrificios and many were forced to cast their cannon, anchors, and part of their cargoes overboard to prevent them from capsizing. The *nao* of Captain Juan Minquez cast overboard 500 ceramic jugs of wine and 160 jugs of olive oil off this island. Before the "norther" died out, eight more ships were lost: frigate *La Caridad,* 300 tons, Captain Francisco Morales, owned by Augusting de Paz, was wrecked near Isla Verde and thirty men were drowned; *nao Santa María del Juncal,* 100 tons, captain's identity unknown, was wrecked

near Isla de Gavias and later divers were able to recover part of her cargo; *nao San Pedro,* 300 tons, Captain Diego de Bodes, was wrecked on the coast near the Medellin River and some of her cargo washed ashore; *nao La Catalina,* 100 tons, Captain Duarte de Quiros, was wrecked on the coast about 5 leagues from Coatzacoalcos and only her men and forty or fifty new muskets were recovered; a Scottish-built felibote, *Nuestra Señora del Rosario,* 170 tons, Captain Hernán García, was wrecked on the coast at Las Aguas Locas and many pipes of wine from her were washed ashore and recovered; English-built frigate *San Benito,* 135 tons, Captain Lazaro de Arpide, struck the coast near the Alvarado River and some pipes of wine were salvaged. French-built ship *Santa Buenaventura,* 125 tons, Captain Juan Francisco Grimaldi, sank near the Tuscla River, off the Sierras de San Miguel, and sixty persons were drowned. Some pipes of wine from her washed ashore and were recovered; *nao La Esperanza,* 400 tons, Captain Tomás Gallardo, struck on the coast near Mimcapa and thirteen men were drowned. All 110 boxes of mercury she carried were lost.

Some brief contemporary accounts state that all fourteen ships were lost when trying to enter Veracruz, but other accounts, which are written in greater detail, state the true facts. The total loss of life was reported to be about one thousand persons, and the value of the ships and their cargoes, lost or jettisoned, was valued at over 10 million pesos. French and English contemporary accounts date this occurrence as 1601, perhaps because news of it reached these two countries at a late date.

32. *Year 1604.* Shortly after the Flota de Nueva España, commanded by Captain-General Juan Gutiérrez de Garibay, reached Veracruz on September 5, the *nao Santa María de Begonia,* 700 tons, Captain Sanctorin de Bengochea, carrying 239 quintales of mercury as well as a general cargo of merchandise, was lost inside the harbor.

33. *Year 1605.* The Armada de Barlovento, consisting of five ships commanded by Admiral Fajardo, surprised seventeen Dutch ships near Manzanillo (engaged in trading contraband merchandise with unscrupulous Spanish colonists of Mexico) and gave battle. Two of the Dutch ships were sunk during the battle and the others escaped.

34. **Year 1610.** Soon after the Flota de Nueva España, commanded by Captain-General Pedro de Armendáriz, reached Veracruz, on September 10 a hurricane struck and many frigates were lost on the coast near the port.

35. **Year 1610.** An unidentified ship, carrying over a million pesos in gold and silver and coming from Peru to Mexico, was wrecked by strong winds about a league from shore on the coast of Zacatula, fifty-three persons were drowned and thirty-two saved. Many pieces of the wreck, as well as some boxes, drifted ashore the same day. Divers were used and some of the treasure was recovered.

36. **Year 1610.** Brief mention that an unidentified richly ladened ship carrying gold and silver was sunk in front of Acapulco and nothing was recovered from her.

37. **Year 1611.** After the Flota de Nueva España, commanded by Captain-General Antonio de Oquendo, was anchored in San Juan de Ulúa and all of the cargoes had been taken ashore, on December 4 the *Almiranta San Pablo*, 600 tons, commanded by an unidentified admiral, sank during a storm.

38. **Year 1614.** A special armada, composed of twenty-one warships of various sizes, was sent to the Indies under the command of Admiral Juan Bermúdez de Castro to search for pirates and contraband traders. Several ships of this armada were lost on the coast of Campeche.

39. **Year 1614.** The Flota de Nueva España, commanded by Captain-General Juan de la Cueva y Mendoza and consisting of forty-one ships, sailed from Cadiz on July 7. Seven unidentified merchant *naos* of this *flota*, which carried over a million and a half pesos in merchandise and 876 quintales of mercury, were wrecked during the night on the coast of Yucatán between Cabo Catoche and Isla Mujeres. Salvage boats were sent from Havana but very little was recovered, as they broke up quickly and their cargoes were buried deep under sand.

40. **Year 1615.** The Flota de Nueva España, commanded by Captain-General Martín de Vallecilla and consisting of forty-one ships, sailed from Cadiz on July 6. On August 30, when the *flota* was located 20 leagues from Islas Tranquilo and Arena, in 22 fathoms

of water, it was struck by a storm from the southeast and the *nao San Miguel,* 500 tons, Captain Gaspar Conquero—which was carrying a cargo of 700 pipes of wine, 3,000 ceramic jugs of wine, 150 boxes of mercury, and 75 bales of general merchandise—split in two and quickly sank. Nothing was saved, not even the crew or passengers. On September 4 the *flota* reached Veracruz and the *nao Espíritu Santo,* 100 tons, Captain Juan Ortuño de Olano, ran aground. Attempts to pull her off the shoals were successful, but then she sank in deeper water. While she was sinking, over a thousand men were put aboard her and, working quickly, threw most of the cargo into boats alongside.

41. Year 1616. The Flota de Nueva España, commanded by Captain-General Juan de la Cueva y Mendoza and consisting of thirty-nine ships, sailed from Cadiz on July 7. It was struck by a storm while only 6 leagues from the entrance of the port of Veracruz and the *nao Nuestra Señora de la Candelaria,* 200 tons, Captain Antonio de Obregón, sank, crew and part of cargo saved.

42. Year 1617. The Flota de Nueva España, commanded by Captain-General Juan de Salas y Valdes and consisting of thirty-one ships, sailed from Cadiz on July 16 and reached Veracruz on September 17. While entering port the *nao* of Captain Domingo de la Guardia sank, but was totally salvaged.

43. Year 1618. The Flota de Nueva España, commanded by Captain-General Carlos de Ibarra and consisting of twenty-three ships, sailed from Cadiz on July 6 and reached Veracruz on September 16. While in the Gulf of Mexico the *flota* was struck by a storm and one unidentified *nao* sank but her cargo was saved.

44. Year 1621. As the Flota de Nueva España, commanded by Captain Juan de Benavides y Bazan, was leaving the port of Veracruz, the *nao Nuestra Señora del Rosario,* 370 tons, caught fire and sank but her silver was saved and transferred to the *Capitana* and *Almiranta.*

45. Year 1623. The *navío, Nuestra Señora de la Piedad,* Captain Pascual Farina (probably Portuguese), coming from Angola with a cargo of 282 Negro slaves, was wrecked at Isla Mujeres. Two frigates were sent from Veracruz for the survivors—the crew and 170 of the slaves.

46. **Year 1623.** A Captain Sancho de Urdanivia was sent with war materials from Spain to Punta de Araya, Venezuela, but on his return to Spain his ship was wrecked on Cozumel Island.

47. **Year 1623.** *Navío La Candelaria,* 250 tons, Captain Juan de Paternina, sailing from Santo Domingo to Spain, was wrecked on Cozumel Island.

48. **Year 1623.** The Armada de Tierra Firme, commanded by Captain-General Antonio de Oquendo, was forced to spend the winter in Havana when many of its ships were damaged in a storm while sailing up the Bahama Channel. Because of a shortage of victuals in Havana, a *patache* was sent to Mexico for supplies but was lost at Cabo de Contón. Its men and artillery were saved.

49. **Possibly before 1628.** On December 3, 1628, the governor of Cuba wrote to the King from Havana: "Because of bad weather they have not been able to search for the *Almiranta* which was lost at Matacumbe Cay [in the Florida Keys], but at my own expense I sent a frigate, two longboats and two canoes to salvage a galleon that I received notice had been lost in the Bahía de la Ascensión and Los Bajos de San Martín on the coast of Mexico." This was probably one of the Honduras galleons, which disappeared in 1627.

50. **Year 1628.** As the Flota de Nueva España, commanded by Captain-General Juan de Benavides y Bazan, was leaving Veracruz for Havana and Spain near the end of July, the frigate *Larga* was wrecked at the entrance of the port. The *flota* then returned to port while the cargo of this ship was salvaged, then set sail again on August 8.

51. **Year 1628.** The Flota de Nueva España, commanded by Captain-General Hierónimo Gómez de Sandoval and consisting of twenty-one ships, sailed from Cadiz on July 15 and reached Veracruz on September 15. In October an advice boat was sent from Veracruz to carry the news of the *flota's* safe arrival back to Spain but sank on the coast of Campeche, crew and mail saved.

52. **Year 1628.** A hurricane struck the coast of Yucatán on September 8 and many ships and frigates were sunk. This was the same day that the Dutch privateer *Peit Heyn,* with a fleet of warships belonging to the Dutch West Indian Company, captured the

entire Flota de Nueva España, commanded by Captain-General Juan de Benavides y Bazan, in Matanzas, Cuba.

53. **Year 1628 or 1629.** A registered *nao*, sailing alone from the Canaries to Veracruz, was wrecked on the coast near Coatzacoalcos, between Veracruz and Campeche. All of her cargo was salvaged and, when brought to Veracruz, the royal officials discovered that over half of her cargo was contraband. Shortly afterward, another *nao* from the Canaries arrived in Veracruz, and when the officials learned that she too was carrying a great deal of contraband, they tried to seize the ship. However, the ship escaped and later wrecked on the coast of Campeche. Slaves, pepper, wine, and clothes were salvaged from the wreck.

54. **Year 1629.** The governor of Yucatán wrote the King stating that during the month of April they had suffered a great deal of terrible weather and many coastal frigates were lost. A great number of items washed ashore from the wrecks, most of which was contraband. One Indian found three small bars of gold worth over 5,000 pesos.

55. **Year 1631.** The Flota de Nueva España, commanded by Admiral Manuel Serrano and consisting of nineteen ships, sailed from Veracruz for Havana and Spain on October 14. The *flota* was carrying 3,644,198 pesos in silver and gold, 5,408 arrobas (25 pounds each) of cochineal, 3,879 arrobas of an inferior grade of cochineal, 15,413 arrobas of indigo, 10,018 pounds of silk from China, 71,788 hides, 6,858 quintales of brazilwood, 7,972 quintales of palo de Campeche, 119 boxes of chocolate, and 91 quintales of molasses. All of the treasure was carried aboard the *Capitana, Almiranta,* and the *naos* of the captains: Baltasar de Espinosa, Baltasar de Amesqueta, and Francisco Niculas. About a week out of port the *flota* was struck by a hurricane and all ships were lost. The *Capitana, Nuestra Señora del Juncal,* sank 8 leagues north of the Bajo de las Arcas and only 35 of the 335 persons on board were saved by escaping in a small boat. The location of the wreck was never rediscovered and nothing was ever salvaged. The *nao San Antonio,* Captain Antonio Lajust, was wrecked 1 league to windward of the port of Tabasco but most of the cochineal aboard was salvaged. The *nao* of Captain Baltasar de Espinosa (some documents give his name as España) was

wrecked very close to the port of Tabasco and 164,954 pesos in specie, 23 silver bars, and 50 marcos in silver objects and 9 marcos in golden objects were recovered from her by divers. Two other merchant *naos* were wrecked on the coast of Campeche but nothing was salvaged. The identities and fate of the other ships of this *flota* were never discovered.

56. *Year 1635.* The *San Juan el Feo*, a *nao* of the Flota de Nueva España, commanded by Captain-General Martín de Vallecilla, was burnt and totally lost in the port of Veracruz.

57. *Year 1647.* A galleon identified only by the name *Santiago* sank in the "Sonda de Campeche," either near the Bahía de la Ascensión or Bahía del Espíritu Santo. Its people, 276 souls, reached a small island and then made boats and rafts from the wrecked galleon and reached the mainland. Salvage vessels were sent out but the wreck site was never located.

58. *Year 1647.* The Flota de Nueva España, commanded by Captain-General Pablo de Paradas and consisting of only thirteen ships, sailed from Cadiz on July 13 and reached Veracruz on September 10. During the winter two ships of this *flota*—a merchant *nao* and a *patache*—and a merchant *nao* that had arrived from Venezuela were sunk in port because of a "norther."

59. *Year 1649.* A French pirate ship was sunk on the coast of Tabasco and twenty-six pirates were captured and sent back to Spain in the Flota de Nueva España, commanded by Captain-General Juan de Pujadas.

60. *Year 1650.* Unidentified ship carrying Fray Antonio Jesús María left Havana on July 6 and was wrecked on Alacrán Reef on July 15 due to an error by the navigator. Survivors—the number was not mentioned, only that eight persons drowned—lived on the keys for fifty-five days until they made a raft from pieces of the wreck. Then they headed toward the mainland, but in passing a nearby key they found survivors from another ship that had wrecked there three years earlier.

61. *Year 1651.* Unidentified merchant *nao* was lost on the "playa de Jalkun" on the coast of Yucatán.

62. *Year 1657.* Unidentified *nao* of an inward-bound Flota de Nueva España was lost on the coast of Campeche, only the men were saved.

63. Year 1659. Sometime before June four merchant *naos* of the Armada de Tierra Firme, under the command of the Marqués de Villarubia enroute from Cartagena to Havana, were lost on the coast of Yucatán. Only one was identified, the *Santiago*, which had wrecked on the east side of Cozumel during a bad storm. Three hundred survivors were rescued two months later and were suffering from thirst, hunger, and exposure. The other three *naos* were mentioned only as being wrecked "on the coast of Yucatán" during the same storm.

64. Year 1672. Brief mention in an English document that earlier in the year four Spanish ships were wrecked on the coast of Campeche during a hurricane.

65. Year 1675. Two unidentified New England ketches that were enroute to Trist ran aground on the backside of Alacrán Reef and were lost.

66. Year 1675 or 1676. Brief mention that a great quantity of silver pieces of eight were discovered from an unidentified shipwreck —which was located in several fathoms of water—on the coast of Tampico.

67. Year 1683. *Navío El Santo Cristobal, San Agustín y La Magdalena,* Captain Ignacio Antonio de Zarantes, owned by Santiago de la Hava Llaquano, built in Holland, 70 tons, enroute from Spain to Tabasco, stopped in Veracruz to be careened, as she was leaking badly. While being careened she caught fire and was totally lost.

68. Sometime before 1689. Brief mention that some years earlier the *navío Santiago* was lost on the coast of Yucatán and that the location of the wreck was about midway between Chinchorro Reef and Bahía del Espíritu Santo, in 18 degrees of latitude. A Captain Arreynaza was reported to have located the wreck a few years after it was lost, but there was no mention if he carried out any salvage operations on the wreck.

69. Year 1700. Unidentified British ship was wrecked on Alacrán Reef; Richard Falconer was either its captain or was a passenger aboard.

70. Year 1702. While the Flota de Nueva España, commanded by Captain-General Fernando Chacón was preparing for its departure for Spain, the *Almiranta* of this *flota, Santa María de Teas-anos,* Captain Martín González de Vergara, sank at San Juan de Ulúa on January 14.

71. **Year 1706.** The main *patache* of the Flota de Nueva España, the *navío Nuestra Señora de Europa y San José y San Francisco de Padua,* captain and owner Don Manuel Alphonso de Nariega, built in England, 193 tons, sank within sight of Veracruz as the *flota* was entering port.

72. **Year 1706.** An advice boat, *navío Nuestra Señora de la Concepción y San Joseph y Las Animas,* Captain Francisco Barcaeztequi, built in England, 68 tons, enroute from Spain to Veracruz, was chased by an English privateer and ran aground at Conil on the coast of Yucatán. The captain and all his men got ashore, along with the mail they were carrying. The English salvaged the entire cargo, rigging, sails, and ship's fittings before setting it on fire.

73. **Year 1715.** While the Flota de Nueva España, commanded by Captain-General Juan Esteban de Ubilla, was in Veracruz, as well as many merchantmen and warships, a "norther" struck on the night of March 28, causing a great deal of damage both to shipping and the town. Twelve ships were lost, of which four belonged to Ubilla's *flota.* The ships lost were the following: *Gobierno,* Captain Miguel de Lima; a *nao* belonging to Pedro de Cordova; a *nao* belonging to Francisco de Chaves; a newly built frigate from Campeche, Captain Ledesma; *nao Santiago,* Captain Aguirre; small *patache* owned by the King; small merchant schooner, Captain Alvarado; privateer vessel *El Talla Piedra;* frigate owned by Captain Barriga; brigantine owned by the King; merchant *nao* owned by a Greek merchant from Havana; and the frigate *Miseria de Maracaibo.*

74. **Year 1719.** A squadron of three large galleons carrying mercury to Veracruz from Spain, commanded by Admiral Francisco de Cornejo, identified as the *Capitana, Almiranta,* and *Santo Cristo de Maracaibo,* were totally lost on the coast of Campeche.

75. **Year 1725.** The *Capitana* of the Flota de Nueva España, commanded by Admiral Antonio Serrano, caught fire and was totally lost in Campeche Sound, in the Gulf of Mexico, and over four hundred lives were lost.

76. Year 1726. The *navío Nuestra Señora de la Concepción* was burnt in the Gulf of Campeche on April 9.

77. Year 1732. A small squadron carrying mercury to Veracruz, under the command of Jefe de Escuadra Gabriel Pérez de Alderete, sailed from Cadiz on August 18, 1731, but had a very difficult voyage and did not reach Veracruz until early in January 1732. The large galleon *Nuestra Señora de la Concepción*, Captain Quiroga, sank soon after the squadron entered Veracruz and five hundred lives were lost.

78. Year 1733. The warship *Nuestra Señora de la Concepción*, one of two ships sent to escort the Flota de Nueva España back to Spain and commanded by Captain-General Rodrigo de Torres, was lost in Veracruz sometime during spring before the *flota* departed. This *flota* was later lost during a hurricane in the Florida Keys.

79. Year 1735. The Flota de Nueva España, commanded by Lt. General Manuel López Pintado, entered Veracruz on February 24 and a *navío, Santa Rosa,* owned by the King and carrying mercury, was lost trying to enter with the *flota* during a "norther." The crew was saved but not the mercury or any other cargo.

80. Year 1737. The *navío Nuestra Señora de Belem y San Antonio y San Francisco de Asis* was lost in Veracruz between the "Bajo de los Cochinos y el Baluarte del Bonete."

81. Year 1737. An unidentified *nao* or frigate sank 9 leagues south of the Alvarado River, near Veracruz.

82. Year 1738. Brief mention of the *navios Incendio* and *Lanfranco* being lost in Veracruz.

83. Year 1741. News reached England early in 1742 that the large galleon *Europa,* commanded by Admiral Spinola, was lost in the Gulf of Mexico when sailing from Havana to Veracruz.

84. Year 1741. The merchant *nao Nuestra Señora de los Milagros* (alias *El Matanzero*), 270 tons, built in Matanzas, Cuba, Captain Cristobal de Montaño, owned by the Marqués de Casa Madrid, was wrecked "on the coast of Campeche," near Acumal, Quintana Roo, Mexico, on February 22. The ship was partially salvaged soon after the disaster and again salvaged in recent years by myself and CEDAM. More information about the history of this wreck and our recent salvage work can be obtained from my recently published book, *Always Another Adventure,* World Publishing Company, 1967.

85. *Year 1743.* In January the British warship H.M.S. *Oxford,* 70 guns, Captain Perry Mayne, was wrecked in the Gulf of Mexico.

86. *Year 1749.* A *navío* that left Cadiz on October 16, 1748, sailing *suelto* to Veracruz, the *San Antonio de Podera y Nuestra Señora del Rosario* (alias *La Bella Sara*), captain and owner Don Joseph Beatura de Rapaldizan, sank in Veracruz soon after it arrived in January 1749.

87. *Year 1751.* *Navío San Gerónimo* (alias *El Retiro*), Captain Manuel Delfín, owned by Alberto Nicholas Diaz Faxardo and Manuel Silvestre de Ziancaro, sailed from Cadiz on August 6 carrying 10,000 quintales of mercury and other cargo. It struck on a reef 12 leagues to the south of Cabo Catoche, between Isla Contoy and Isla Mujeres.

88. *Year 1752.* Five ships of the Flota de Nueva España, commanded by Captain-General Cristobal de Eraso, sank on the coast of Tabasco.

89. *Year 1755.* *Navío San Raymundo Thae,* Captain Juan Franco de Vilnava, sailed from Cadiz on August 6 and was lost on the coast of Campeche. All of the crew was saved and most of the cargo (of general merchandise) was salvaged.

90. *Year 1758.* Brief mention that a merchant *nao, El Retiro,* was lost on the coast of Campeche.

91. *Year 1760.* Merchant *nao La Fetis,* Captain José Antonio Rivero, sank on its return voyage to Spain after leaving Cartagena, on the east side of Cozumel Island.

92. *Year 1761.* British merchant ship *Tates,* sailing from Cartagena to England, was lost in March on Cozumel Island but its people and money were saved and boats were sent from Campeche to recover her cargo.

93. *Year 1763.* A Spanish frigate, *Mercurio,* which sailed from Cadiz in August with a convoy carrying mercury to Veracruz, was lost near Cabo Catoche.

94. *Year 1765.* The merchant *nao Nuestra Señora de la Luz y San Maura,* Captain Lorenzo de Villas, sailed from Cadiz on March 9 and five days after entering Veracruz it caught fire and sank and lost most of its cargo.

95. *Year 1772.* A *navío* of many guns, *Castilla,* captain the Marqués de Casina, was lost during a violent "norther" in Veracruz on "el bajo de los Hornos." All of her people were saved, but 700 large chests of fine cochineal, which were all the cargo aboard, were lost.

96. *Year 1772.* Spanish frigate *Nuestra Señora de Guadalupe* (alias *La Tetis*), Captain Juan Gil del Barrios, sailed from Cadiz for Honduras on April 15. It then sailed from Omoa, Honduras, for Spain with a cargo of silver and land products. On December 5 it wrecked on Chinchorro Reef. Of the 29 chests of silver aboard her, all but three were salvaged. In *Lloyd's List* it mentions that the ship was carrying 1,580 serons of indigo, which was totally lost.

97. *Year 1780.* Frigate *Santa María* (or *Santa Marta*), 38 cannon, Captain Andrés Valderrama, part of the squadron commanded by Don Juan Bautista Bonet, was lost near the coast of Yucatán on "Bajo de las Mesas de Contreras," which is 2 miles from land, and sank in 3 fathoms of water on a sandy bottom. Her entire cargo consisted of war materials.

98. *Year 1781.* A large ship named *Santa Ana,* coming from Callao, Peru, to Mexico, was lost on a shoal in Acapulco Harbor. This same shoal, which is only 40 meters wide, was named Santa Ana after the ship.

99. *Year 1783.* A large Spanish warship, *Dragon,* 60 cannon, captain the brigadier Miguel de Sousa, was lost on "Bajo Nuevo," in the Gulf of Campeche, and sixty of the crew were drowned.

100. *Year 1786.* Spanish ship *San Rafael* was lost in the Gulf of Mexico.

101. *Year 1794.* Spanish ship *Nuestra Señora del Carmen* (alias *Las Animas*) was lost on Cayo Culebra, one of the Cayos de la Cadena, located 5 leagues from the port of Az——— (rest of word faded on the document) on the coast of Yucatán.

102. *Year 1797.* Spanish advice boat *San Carlos,* sent from San Blas by the Marqués de Banceforte and commanded by Teniente de

Fragata Ramón de Saavedra, sailed to San Francisco, California, with news of war with Great Britain. On March 23 it sank near the port of Yerba Buena and only its people were saved.

103. *Year 1799.* On September 28 the British warship H.M.S. *Fox,* 32 guns, commanded by Lt. William Wooldridge, was wrecked in the Gulf of Mexico but the crew was saved.

104. *Year 1801.* British warship H.M.S. *Meleager,* 32 guns, Captain Honorable T. Bladen Capel, 215 men on board, was lost on June 9 on the westernmost triangle key in the Gulf of Mexico but all its men were saved.

105. *Year 1803.* Spanish merchant ship *María,* Captain Uxaboxa, sailing from Bilbao to Veracruz, was lost in the Gulf of Mexico.

106. *Year 1803.* Spanish merchant ship *Nuestra Señora del Carmen* (alias *La Princesa*), Captain Remachn, sailing from Cadiz to Veracruz with a valuable cargo, was totally lost in the Gulf of Mexico.

107. *Year 1804.* British merchantman *Catherine,* Captain Hayward, sailing from New Orleans to Liverpool, was lost in the Gulf of Mexico.

108. *Year 1805.* Spanish frigate *Nuestra Señora de la O* [*sic*], 64 guns, Captain Miguel de Palacios, was lost in Veracruz during a norther but completely salvaged.

109. *Year 1808.* Spanish frigate *Muros* was lost in the Gulf of Mexico but all her crew was saved.

110. *Year 1808.* Spanish schooner *Felicidad,* Captain José del Castillo, was struck by lightning and blew up while anchored in Veracruz.

111. *Year 1809.* Spanish brigantine *Volador,* 18 cannon, commanded by Teniente de Navío Pedro María de Piedrola, was lost on August 17 in the port of Veracruz "*sobre la zapata del Castillo de San Juan,*" and everyone aboard, 143,000 pesos in specie, and most of the ship's equipment were saved.

112. *Year 1811.* American ship *Sally,* Captain Perkins, coming from New York, was lost in January near Campeche.

113. *Year 1816.* British ship *Rhine,* Captain Gordon, sailing from New Orleans to Campeche, was lost off the coast of Campeche.

114. *Year 1816.* Spanish schooner *Cantabria*, commanded by Teniente de Fragata Antonio Valera, was lost on the Alvarado River on June 9 and eight men were drowned.

115. *Year 1816.* British sloop-of-war H.M.S. *Tay*, 20 guns, Captain Samuel Roberts, was sailing from Campache to Jamaica with about 2 million pesos in treasure when it was lost on Alacrán Reef on November 11. None of the 135 men in her crew were lost. This wreck was recently located by CEDAM members and partially salvaged.

116. *Year 1816.* British sloop-of-war, H.M.S. *Bermuda*, 10 guns, Captain John Pakenham, was wrecked on November 25 near the bar of Tampico and, of seventy-six men in her crew, only one was lost.

117. *Year 1818.* Spanish frigate *Ifigenia*, 38 cannon, commanded by Capitán de Fragata Alejo Gutiérrez de Ribalcava, sank in the harbor of Campeche.

118. *Year 1819.* British ship *Frances Ann*, Captain Mossup, coming from St. Thomas, Virgin Islands, to Campeche, was lost on October 28 off Cabo Catoche.

119. *Year 1819.* Spanish brigantine *Consulado*, 14 cannon, commanded by Teniente de Navío Cipriano Mauleon, and the schooner *Guía* were sunk during a storm at Veracruz on December 30, over 120 men were lost.

120. *Year 1822.* British merchantman *Holliday*, Captain Stewart, sailing from Liverpool to Campeche, was wrecked on May 6 on the Alacrán Reef but the crew was saved.

121. *Year 1822.* American merchantman *Dido*, Captain Dario, coming from Philadelphia, was lost near Alvarado on December 21.

122. *Year 1822.* American merchantman *Catherine Jane*, Captain Storer, sailing from New York to Veracruz, was lost to the eastward of Veracruz.

123. *Year 1823.* British merchantman *Nancy*, Captain Butterfield, sailing from Cuba to Montego Bay, Jamaica, was wrecked on Cabo Catoche to prevent it from sinking, as it had a bad leak, but most of its cargo was saved.

124. *Year 1824.* American ship *Harriet,* Captain Davidson, sailing from New Orleans to Tampico with a valuable cargo aboard, was lost between Soto la Marina and Tampico.

125. *Year 1824.* French ship *Cacique,* Captain Roy, sailing from Bordeaux to Veracruz, was totally lost in the Gulf of Mexico on May 9 but her crew was saved and arrived at the port of Sisal, Yucatán.

126. *Year 1824.* A ship of unknown nationality, *Sancho Panza,* Captain Harris, sailing from New York to Tampico, was lost on Alacrán Reef, crew and passengers saved.

127. *Year 1824.* American ship *Alabama,* Captain Kirk, sailing from Philadelphia to Alvarado, after crossing the bar at the entrance to this port ran aground but all of her cargo was recovered.

CHAPTER FIVE

The Lesser Antilles

THE YEAR-AROUND working conditions in the Lesser Antilles are even better than that of the other, larger islands of the Caribbean, as they are subject to fewer hurricanes and other storms. However, due to the prevailing northeasterly winds, the windward, or eastern, side of these islands is constantly battered by large ocean swells rolling in off the Atlantic, which makes diving generally difficult and hazardous. Off the eastern side of Barbados, for example, the average size of the swells is over 20 feet. Furthermore, there are very few safe harbors or anchorages on the eastern side of most of these islands and a large vessel is needed to do any serious work on shipwreck sites. There are occasional days—generally during the hurricane season—when diving conditions are less unfavorable, but strong ocean swells still roll in and caution must be exercised. With the exception of a few harbors—such as Port of Spain, Trinidad and Bridgetown,

Barbados—the underwater visibility is excellent around all of these islands.

The Dutch government is preparing a law regarding the salvaging of any ancient shipwrecks around their islands, and until the law is put into effect no one can work on a wreck in their waters. The French government has a law requiring that an archaeologist must supervise any work undertaken on shipwrecks in their waters and that the salvor keeps only 40 percent of what he recovers, with the French government having the right to purchase all or any part of the 40 percent belonging to the salvor at a price determined by the government. The British government requires a potential salvor to obtain a permit from the Admiralty Office in London before anyone can work on a site, but no ruling has been passed yet as to what percentage a salvor will receive. Furthermore, in a recent letter to me the Admiralty Office stated that although it has received numerous requests for permission to salvage various wrecks around the British West Indian Islands, it has not granted any permits, as the law governing the salvaging of ancient shipwrecks is not too clear and will have to be modified and rewritten. The islands that have recently won independence from England have no laws concerning the salvaging of shipwrecks and no permission is required unless the shipwreck site is in a harbor or port. None of the islands of the Lesser Antilles requires a permit or permission to search for shipwrecks.

Shipwrecks in the Leeward Islands

ANGUILLA:

1. *Year 1628.* Two unidentified Spanish merchant *naos* sailed from Puerto Rico for Spain but one of them was wrecked on December 12 on the north side of this island and Frenchmen from St. Kitts salvaged some of its cargo.

2. *Year 1733.* English merchantman *Castle Shallop*, owned by Sir William Stapleton, sailing from St. Kitts to England with a cargo of sugar, was wrecked on the south side and only the rigging was salvaged.

3. *Year 1755.* Two ships were lost on the north side: English merchantman *Brown Gally*, Captain Belson, sailing from Rhode

Island to the Leeward Islands, and an unidentified large French merchantman sailing from Martinique to France.

4. **Year 1763.** English merchantman *Temple*, Captain Campbell, sailing from Liverpool to Jamaica, struck on a reef and quickly went to pieces but most of the crew were saved.

5. **Year 1772.** Two large Spanish warships, escorting eighteen merchant *naos* of the Flota de Nueva España, were wrecked off the east end of the island: galleon *El Buen Consejo*, 70 guns, Captain Julio de Urcullo, and the galleon *Jesús, María y Joseph* (alias *El Prusiano*), 40 guns, Captain Juan Baptista de Echeverria. Most of their cargoes were salvaged by the English from surrounding islands.

6. **Year 1773.** English merchantman *William*, Captain Stoodley, sailing from London to the West Indies, was wrecked.

7. **Year 1811.** During a hurricane on October 8, several unidentified American merchantmen were wrecked on the north side of the island.

ST. MARTIN:

8. **Year 1631.** An unidentified Dutch merchantman was wrecked off the south side of this island when it was chased by several ships of the Windward Armada, commanded by Admiral Azevelo. While the Spanish admiral's ship was cruising to pick up survivors from the Dutch wreck, a sudden storm caused it to sink. There were only eight survivors from both wrecks.

9. **Year 1780.** Dutch merchantman *Wynhandelet*, Captain Froon, sailing from this island to Ireland, was totally lost while at anchor during a hurricane on the south side of the island.

10. **Year 1781.** A richly laden Portuguese merchantman, *Santissimo Trinidade*, Captain Dos Santos, sailing from Brazil to Amsterdam, was wrecked and only a small part of its valuable cargo was salvaged.

11. **Year 1792.** During a hurricane on August 1 two unidentified ships foundered in the oyster pond.

12. **Year 1801.** English warship H.M.S. *Proselyte*, 32 guns, Captain

George Fowke (some accounts have a Henry Whitly as captain), was wrecked on a reef on the south side of the island (which is now named Proselyte Reef after this wreck). None of the crew of 215 were lost. In 1960 I spent several days exploring this wreck, which lies in depths of from 15 to 50 feet. I located six anchors, at least twenty cannon, and there were several hundred tons of pig-iron ingots, which were used for ballast during the period this ship was lost. A great section of the wreck was covered over by thick coral growth but some parts were off the reef on a sandy bottom.

13. *Year 1811.* During a hurricane on October 7, several unidentified ships were wrecked.

ST. BARTHELEMY:

14. *Year 1707.* During a hurricane on August 29 a large unidentified ship was sunk in the harbor of this island.

15. *Year 1791.* During a severe gale in September, three unidentified ships were wrecked on this island.

16. *Year 1792.* American merchantman *Nelly,* Captain Shelly, sailing from Antigua to America, was wrecked.

17. *Year 1792.* During a hurricane on August 1, ten unidentified ships were totally destroyed in the main harbor and there was a great loss of life.

18. *Year 1811.* French ship *Guernsey,* Captain Collinette, was totally lost in June and most of her crew perished.

19. *Year 1811.* During a hurricane on October 7 a total of forty ships, most of them American vessels that had come into the harbor for shelter from the hurricane, were wrecked or sunk.

20. *Year 1813.* English warship H.M.S. *Subtle,* 10 guns, Captain Charles Brown, foundered near the island and the crew of fifty perished.

21. *Year 1815.* During a hurricane on September 18, sixty ships, most of them American vessels that had entered the harbor for shelter from the hurricane, were wrecked or sunk. A Swedish sloop-of-war was also lost here.

22. Year 1819. During a hurricane in September, half the town was totally destroyed and washed into the sea and all of the shipping was rendered a mass of ruins at the head of the bay.

23. Year 1821. During a hurricane on September 10, many unidentified sloops and schooners were totally lost in the port.

SABA:

24. Year 1567. Spanish advice boat *La Regla,* 4 guns, Captain Julio Rodriquez Espinosa, was wrecked on the east side of the island while sailing from Spain to Puerto Rico with mail and passengers.

25. Year 1733. English slave ship *Bristol,* Captain Payne, sailing from Africa to Jamaica with a cargo of slaves, was wrecked on this island during a hurricane in June.

ST. EUSTATIUS:

26. Year 1690. During an earthquake on April 6, more than half of the main town of this island—which was located on its west side —was cast into the sea and several hundred lives were lost. At this time the town was used mainly as a base for privateers and contraband traders of various nationalities, so that many of the buidings that fell into the sea were warehouses full of plunder and contraband, the overall value of which exceeded a million pounds sterling. The ruins of these sunken buildings are still visible and are located off the bluff of Orange Town, the island's only settlement. I visited this site in 1960 and, with only fins and mask, recovered a large number of bottles, intact pieces of ceramicware, clay smoking pipes, bricks, and two muskets.

27. Year 1733. During a hurricane in June, two unidentified English merchantmen were wrecked.

28. Year 1737. During a hurricane in October a large fleet of homeward-bound English merchantmen sought shelter off Orange Town but twenty of them were sunk.

29. Year 1758. Italian merchantman *Duke Compagni,* Captain Lambaldi, sailing from this island for Amsterdam after loading a valuable cargo of merchandise for which it received many chests of silver specie, was wrecked as it attempted to round the north side but all of the crew and most of the specie were saved.

30. **Year 1766.** During a violent hurricane on September 21, several unidentified merchant ships were totally lost off Orange Town.

31. **Year 1772.** During a hurricane in August, all four hundred houses in Orange Town were blown down and the Dutch church was thrown into the sea.

32. **Year 1780.** During a hurricane on October 9, seven Dutch ships were totally lost on the coast at North Point and not a soul survived. Orange Town was leveled to the ground and betwen four and five thousand persons perished.

33. **Year 1786.** During a hurricane in August a large number of ships of different nationalities were lost around the island.

34. **Year 1791.** During a hurricane around the end of October, two large Dutch merchantmen were lost off Orange Town.

35. **Year 1792.** During a hurricane on August 1, one large Dutch ship and several of other nationalities were totally lost off the west side. A Spanish brig, sailing between St. Kitts and the island, sank and there were only two survivors.

ST. KITTS:

36. **Year 1629.** During a Spanish attack led by Captain-General Fadrique de Toledo to dislodge the French and English who had recently settled on this island, four small ships were sunk by Spanish cannon fire in the port of Basseterre, off the west side of the island.

37. **Year 1630.** Unidentified merchant *nao* of the New Spain Flota, Captain-General Miguel de Echazarreta, was wrecked on the east side of the island and among the many drowned was the new governor of Santiago, Cuba.

38. **Year 1642.** During a hurricane, twenty-three English ships of various sizes were wrecked at Basseterre, but there was little loss of life, as most of the crews were ashore.

39. **Year 1650.** During two different hurricanes a total of twenty-eight merchantmen of different nationalities, a great number of lives,

and over a half-million pounds sterling in cargoes were lost in and near Basseterre.

40. **Year 1651.** During a hurricane, nine English and twelve Dutch ships were wrecked in Basseterre.

41. **Year 1652.** During a huricane, four or five fully loaded English merchantmen were totally lost off Sandy Point, on the west side of the island.

42. **Year 1667.** While an English squadron of warships was attempting to recapture the island from the French, it burnt one French and one Dutch ship, both of which were anchored at Basseterre.

43. **Year 1680.** During a hurricane on August 3, two shallops were wrecked at Basseterre.

44. **Year 1690.** English merchantman *Thornhills Hill* was wrecked on June 1 against rocks off the west side of the island.

45. **Year 1707.** During a hurricane on August 30, two English warships were wrecked: H.M.S. *Child's Play*, 24 guns, Captain George Doyley, at Palmetto Point, and the H.M.S. *Winchester*, off Sandy Point. The cannon from both wrecks were salvaged

46. **Year 1733.** During a hurricane in June, twelve ships were sunk at Basseterre, three of them identified as English ships: the *Nassau*, *Stapleton*, and *Ancient Britain*. A ship that had just arrived at Sandy Point from Philadelphia suffered a total loss of lives and cargo.

47. **Year 1737.** During an October hurricane an English merchantman, Captain Sutton, main cargo rum and sugar, was sunk at Basseterre and only one of the crew survived.

48. **Year 1741.** Irish merchantman *Rebbec & Martha*, Captain Copythorn, coming from Cork, was wrecked on the east side of the island.

49. **Year 1747.** During hurricanes on September 21 and October 24 a total of twenty-four ships were totally lost at Basseterre, most of them fully loaded with cargoes of sugar for England. All were English merchantmen: *Owen Gally*, Captain Wood; *Rising Sun*, Captain Parker; *Pretty Patsey*, Captain Hays; *Duke of Marlborough*, Captain Denn; *Cornwally*, Captain Sword; *Rowland-*

son, Captain Watson; *Emma,* Captain Faulker; *Mary,* Captain Watson; *Swallow,* Captain Watts; *Plante,* Captain Cains; *Parkham Pink,* Captain Aberdam; *Nisbitt,* Captain Hall; the others were not identified.

50. Year 1751. During a violent gale on July 24, several ships were wrecked at Basseterre but only one was identified: the Irish merchantman *Friendship,* Captain Bodkin, sailing to Cork, none of the crew was saved.

51. Year 1754. During a hurricane on September 13, five unidentified ships were wrecked at Basseterre.

52. Year 1758. During a hurricane an English privateer vessel with two hundred persons aboard sank at Sandy Point with a total loss of life.

53. Year 1765. During a hurricane in August, nine unidentified English merchantmen and one French mail boat were lost around the island.

54. Year 1766. During a gale on September 18 the English merchantman *Betsey,* Captain Mathews, ready to sail for England, was wrecked at Sandy Point and only some rigging was salvaged from it.

55. Year 1766. During a hurricane in October, thirteen English merchantmen and two Dutch sloops were wrecked off the west side of the island and at Basseterre.

56. Year 1772. During a hurricane two ships were totally lost: the English merchantman *Apollo,* Captain Manning, and Scottish merchantman *Thistle,* Captain Hunter.

57. Year 1773. English merchantman *Charlotte,* Captain Williamson, arriving from London, was wrecked off the east side of the island.

58. Year 1775. During a hurricane in October a large number of unidentified ships were lost.

59. Year 1776. During a hurricane on September 6, two unidentified ships were wrecked and three others sank at Basseterre.

60. Year 1779. English storeship H.M.S. *Supply,* 20 guns, Captain John Lockhart Nasmyth, was accidentally burnt at Basseterre.

61. **Year 1780.** During a hurricane on October 11 and 12—described as the worst in over a century—more than one hundred ships of different nationalities and sizes were totally lost all around the island and the loss of lives was in the thousands.

62. **Year 1781.** American privateer *Earl of Cornwallis*, 18 guns and one hundred men, sank at Basseterre and a large number of the crew perished.

63. **Year 1782.** During an attack by several French warships, the English merchantman *Douglas*, Captain Webster, recently arrived from London, was burnt near Basseterre.

64. **Year 1785.** During an August 26 hurricane five English merchantmen were wrecked in Deep Bay, only three of them identified: *Thomas*, Captain Furber; *Spooner*, Captain Lorban; and the *Betsey*, Captain Basdon.

65. **Year 1791.** During a severe gale several ships were wrecked in and near Basseterre but only one was identified: the English merchantman *Yucatán*, Captain Barton, sailing from Cork to Jamaica.

66. **Year 1792.** Before August 1, three English merchantmen were lost on the island: *George & Margaret*, Captain Ashington, sailing to London; *Isabella*, Captain Carnage, sailing to Glasgow; and the *Britannia*, Captain Woodyear, sailing to London.

67. **Year 1792.** During a hurricane on August 1 and 2, more than twenty ships of different nationalities were lost around the island.

68. **Year 1793.** During a hurricane on August 12, thirty merchantmen (English and American) were lost around the island and only a few of the English ships were identified by name: *Hoppitt, Letitia, Flying Delight, Indian Castle, Polly,* and *Nancy*.

69. **Year 1807.** During a gale on July 26, two schooners, two sloops, and the English merchantman *Maria*, Captain Williams, bound for London, were wrecked on the island.

70. **Year 1811.** Three English merchantmen were lost around the island: *Sussex*, only partially loaded; *Venus*, Captain Moore, sailing to Quebec; and the *Dart*, just arrived from England. All three crews were saved.

71. *Year 1813.* During a hurricane that occurred on July 23, seventeen ships were wrecked: ten were American ships seized as war prizes, three were American coastal schooners, and four were English merchantmen: *John & William,* just arrived from France; *Britannia,* Captain Paulson, sailing to England; *Colonest,* Captain Oliver; and the *Bottle,* Captain Ford.

NEVIS:

72. *Year 1629.* During an attack by the Spanish, one unidentified small English merchantman was wrecked on the west side of the island.

73. *Year 1667.* During a battle between thirty French and ten English warships on April 10 in Nevis Roads, one of the English ships was accidentally blown up by her own crew and most of the men aboard her perished.

74. *Year 1669.* During a hurricane on August 16 a large British privateer was totally lost off Charlestown, the island's main port and town.

75. *Year 1690.* An earthquake struck the whole island at seven on the morning of April 6 and most of the town of Charlestown, including the main fort, was cast into the sea. Records concerning this disaster are very brief and vague, and there is no mention of the number of buildings lost, value of property lost, nor of the total loss of lives. During an exploratory dive on the site in 1961, I located at least fifty different brick buildings that were protruding above the sandy sea floor. No doubt many more are buried. Most of the site is in depths of 20 to 30 feet of water, but the walls of the main fort are near shore in only 8 to 10 feet of water, where I sighted over twenty huge iron cannon.

76. *Year 1728.* English merchantman *Campbell,* Captain Goodwin, coming from Bristol, was captured by a French pirate, but on September 10 she was wrecked in a gale at Nevis Point.

77. *Year 1747.* During a hurricane on September 21, eight vessels were wrecked around the island: five sloops, one schooner, a large prize snow, and the English merchantman *Mary,* Captain Herbert, preparing to sail for London.

78. **Year 1761.** English merchantman *Princess Ann,* Captain Tampert, sailing from Barbados to Ireland, was wrecked at Green Point but her cargo of rum was saved.

79. **Year 1772.** During a hurricane a large unidentified English merchantman carrying five hundred hogsheads of sugar was totally lost.

80. **Year 1779.** During a hurricane on September 4, several large French warships of the fleet of the Count d'Estaing, then anchored off Charlestown, were totally lost.

81. **Year 1782.** On January 25, the English warship H.M.S. *Solebay,* 28 guns, Captain Charles Holmes Everritt, while trying to elude three French ships that were chasing it, was wrecked at Nevis Point and burnt by its crew before they escaped ashore.

82. **Year 1790.** During a hurricane in August, twenty unidentified English merchantmen were wrecked in the vicinity of Charlestown and Nevis Point.

83. **Year 1792.** During a hurricane on August 1 the English merchantman *Sarah & Ann,* sailing to London, was totally lost and nothing of her cargo was salvaged.

84. **Year 1804.** Two English ships wrecked on the island: merchantman *Friends,* Captain Donald, coming from London, and the warship H.M.S. *Drake,* 14 guns, Captain William Ferriss, on a reef near the island but none of the crew of eighty-six were lost.

85. **Year 1808.** English merchantman *Grace,* Captain Taylor, coming from London, was totally lost January 30 on a reef at the northeast end of the island, crew and part of cargo saved.

86. **Year 1811.** During a hurricane on October 7 a ship of unknown registry, *Rachael,* was totally lost.

87. **Year 1819.** During a hurricane on September 21 and 22, the Venezuelan cruiser *Brutus* was wrecked.

88. **Year 1823.** A mailboat of unknown registry, *Mackey,* was totally lost on January 16, only the mail was saved.

MONTSERRAT:

89. *Year 1666.* During a hurricane in September a large number of unidentified French warships were wrecked on the island.

90. *Year 1681.* During a hurricane on October 14 an unidentified merchantman coming from New England was wrecked.

91. *Year 1744.* Irish merchantman *Two Brothers,* Captain Brown, coming from Cork, was wrecked but her cargo was saved.

92. *Year 1747.* During a hurricane on September 21 a sloop, several shallops, and two English merchantmen were lost: *Imperial Anne,* Captain Butler, and *Friends Goodwill,* Captain Lesley. And during a hurricane that struck on October 24 the English ship *London Packet,* Captain Tirnam, was totally lost.

93. *Year 1754.* During a September 13 hurricane, eight unidentified English merchantmen were wrecked in Plymouth Harbor, the island's main port and town.

94. *Year 1766.* During a hurricane in October a large number of homeward-bound English merchantmen were totally lost on the west side of the island.

95. *Year 1775.* English merchantman *Gill,* Captain Craig, sailing from St. Eustatius to St. Vincent Island, sank during a hurricane on July 31.

96. *Year 1807.* Two English merchantmen were wrecked during a gale on July 26: *Lady Parker,* bound for London, and *Eliza,* Captain Summers, bound for Bristol.

BARBUDA:

97. *Year 1695.* Unidentified Spanish merchant *nao,* Captain Francisco Morales, carrying 13,000 pesos to pay the garrisons at Maracaibo, was wrecked off the east side of the island. All of the specie and a great deal of merchandise were recovered by divers.

98. *Year 1749.* English slave ship *Pearl,* Captain Dighton, coming from Africa with a cargo of slaves, was wrecked here and seventy slaves and eleven of the crew were drowned.

99. *Year 1749.* English merchantman *Nancy,* Captain Dlam, sailing from Bristol to Jamaica, was wrecked on November 2, only a small part of her cargo was saved.

100. *Year 1752.* Scottish merchantman *Prince Charles,* Captain Walsh, sailing from Dublin to Jamaica, was wrecked on the south end of the island.

101. *Year 1755.* French slave ship *Hazard,* sailing from Africa to Hispaniola, was wrecked and more than eighty slaves were drowned.

102. *Year 1760.* English warship H.M.S. *Griffin,* 20 guns, Captain Thomas Taylor, was wrecked during October.

103. *Year 1761.* A ship of unknown registry, *Boscawen,* Captain Hawkins, sailing from Virginia to Barbados, was wrecked and nothing of her cargo was saved.

104. *Year 1763.* Two English merchantmen were wrecked: *Royal Duke,* Captain Tory, sailing from Guadeloupe to London; and the *John,* Captain Simpson, sailing from England for the West Indies.

105. *Year 1780.* Two English ships wrecked: merchantman *Ceres,* Captain Howes, sailing from London to Antigua, part of her cargo was saved; and privateer *Fortune Teller,* Captain Kay, the crew was saved.

106. *Year 1782.* English merchantman *Telemacko,* sailing from London to Nevis, wrecked on November 9, crew and small part of cargo saved.

107. *Year 1785.* American ship *Betsey,* Captain Woodman, coming from South Carolina, was totally lost near the island.

108. *Year 1790.* American merchantman *Nelly & Nancy,* Captain Dennison, sailing from North Carolina to Guadeloupe, was lost on July 2 but the crew was saved.

109. *Year 1792.* Spanish warship *Lanzerota,* 24 guns, Captain Ignacio Perez, was wrecked on July 23 and very little was saved except for the crew.

110. *Year 1793.* American ship *Grand Sachem,* Captain Cairnes, sailing from St. Helena to Massachusetts, was wrecked on a reef.

111. *Year 1795.* American merchantman *Jeanette,* Captain Anderson, sailing from New England to St. Thomas, was wrecked on the north side of the island, crew and some cargo saved.

112. *Year 1797.* Scottish ship *Castle Semple,* sailing from Glasgow to the West Indies, was totally lost near the island.

113. *Year 1799.* American merchantman *Seaforth,* Captain Phelan, sailing from New York to Barbados, was captured by a French privateer and shortly after wrecked on a reef, most of her cargo was lost.

114. *Year 1801.* Three ships of unknown registry were wrecked near the island: *Argo,* Captain Pindar, sailing from Nassau to Surinam; unidentified sloop sailing from Nassau to Surinam; and an unidentified brig sailing from New England to Antigua.

115. *Year 1807.* English merchantman *Triton,* Captain Newhall, sailing to Antigua, wrecked on April 29, the crew was saved.

116. *Year 1809.* Three English merchantmen were wrecked: *Julia,* Captain Snow, coming from Cadiz, most of her cargo was saved; *Farmer,* Captain Young, sailing from Newcastle to Honduras, only the crew was saved; and the *Kingston,* Captain Bruton, sailing from Liverpool to St. Croix.

117. *Year 1810.* English ship *Adventure,* Captain MacMillon, sailing from Lancaster to St. Thomas, was wrecked during August but her crew was saved.

118. *Year 1813.* English warship H.M.S. *Woolwich,* 40 guns, Captain Thomas Ball Sullivan, wrecked on November 6.

119. *Year 1817.* French ship *Jeune Adolphe,* sailing from Guadeloupe to France, wrecked on August 2 but her crew was saved.

120. *Year 1819.* A ship of unknown registry, *Speculation,* Captain Colburn, coming from Bermuda, was totally lost off the north part of the island on August 25.

121. *Year 1821.* Three ships were lost near the island: French merchantman *Martiniquin,* Captain Garcin, sailing from Martinique to France, lost off the west end of the island on July 24; English merchantman *Hound,* Captain Stronnack, sailing from St. Vincent to London, was totally lost off the southwest end, her

crew was saved; and the Spanish brig *San Josef,* 150 tons, coming from Spain with a cargo of olive oil, brandy, paper, and almonds, wrecked on April 7.

122. *Year 1822.* American merchantman *Monitor,* Captain Whitter, sailing from Philadelphia to St. Eustatius, wrecked on September 25.

ANTIGUA:

123. *Year 1666.* During a hurricane two unidentified English warships were lost in English Harbor with a great loss of life.

124. *Year 1681.* During a hurricane on September 6, an unidentified English ship, Captain Gadbury, was totally lost in the main harbor.

125. *Year 1740.* English merchantman *Eagle,* Captain Long, sailing from London to South Carolina, was wrecked on a reef.

126. *Year 1744.* Two ships were lost: English merchantman *Cape Fear Merchant,* Captain Allen, coming from Bristol, wrecked on the bar while entering the main harbor but most of her cargo was saved; and an unidentified Spanish privateer was destroyed by an English warship after it was forced ashore near the south shore.

127. *Year 1745.* English warship H.M.S. *Weymouth,* Captain Calmady, wrecked on February 16 on a reef near Sandy Island off St. John's Road.

128. *Year 1747.* Two English ships were lost: the *Shirley,* Captain Sherbourn, coming from Boston, driven onshore by some French privateers; and an unidentified sloop lost during a hurricane on September 21.

129. *Year 1748.* Two unidentified English vessels, a brig and a schooner, wrecked off Pope's Head and were totally lost.

130. *Year 1754.* During a hurricane on September 13, more than ten unidentified ships were wrecked off St. John's Harbor.

131. *Year 1762.* English slave ship *Nancy,* Captain Bare, coming from Africa, was lost near Sandy Island but the slaves and crew were saved.

132. *Year 1768*. English slave ship *Dorsetshire*, Captain Traud, coming from Africa, was wrecked on a reef but the slaves and crew were saved.

133. *Year 1770*. An unidentified Spanish ship was wrecked on the island, only her crew was saved.

134. *Year 1772*. During a hurricane on August 30, several English merchantmen sank in St. John's Harbor and four or five English warships were lost in English Harbor.

135. *Year 1773*. American ship *Nester*, Captain Rowland, sailing from New England to Trinidad, was wrecked on the island.

136. *Year 1774*. An unidentified French ship, sailing from Guadeloupe to France, was wrecked on a shoal located 3 miles from the island; only a small part of her cargo of sugar was saved.

137. *Year 1779*. Dutch merchantman *Sarah & Rachel*, Captain Almers, sailing from Amsterdam to St. Eustatius, was lost near the island, only her crew was saved.

138. *Year 1782*. Unidentified merchantman, bound for Belfast, sank shortly after leaving St. John's Harbor.

139. *Year 1786*. English merchantman *Friendship*, Captain Bowen, sailing from Bristol to Honduras, wrecked on a reef but her crew was saved.

140. *Year 1791*. French merchantman *Alliance*, Captain Gamare, sailing from France to Hispaniola, was wrecked on Long Island, off Antigua.

141. *Year 1797*. English slave ship *Lively*, Captain Bell, coming from Africa, was wrecked on the east end of the island.

142. *Year 1802*. Four English merchantmen were wrecked: *Britannia*, Captain Brown, coming from Demarara; *Phaeton*, Captain Billings, coming from Baltimore with a cargo of salt, off Boon Point; *Echo*, Captain Johnson, sailing from London to Jamaica, on Diamond Rock, most of her cargo was saved; and the *Parras*, Captain Sleigh, coming from Bristol, on Guana Island.

143. *Year 1803*. American ship *Alice Bridger*, coming from New York, wrecked on a reef near St. John's Harbor.

144. *Year 1804*. During a hurricane on September 4 the English warship H.M.S. *De Ruyter*, 32 guns, Captain Joseph Becket, was sunk in Deep Bay and none of her crew of 250 men were lost.

145. *Year 1805*. English merchantman *Successful Noney*, sailing to Liverpool, was wrecked on August 16 near Sandy Island.

146. *Year 1809*. English ship *Friends*, Captain Gourley, sailing from Clyde to St. Thomas, wrecked on a reef, most of her cargo was saved.

147. *Year 1811*. During a hurricane on July 7 the English warship H.M.S. *Guachapin*, 10 guns, Captain Michael Jenkins, was wrecked on Rat Island; and during the same hurricane the H.M.S. *Gloire* was forced to cast all of her guns overboard in English Harbor.

148. *Year 1816*. English merchantman *Europe*, Captain Huddlestone, arriving from Liverpool, burnt on August 7 off St. John's Harbor, one man lost.

149. *Year 1817*. Canadian ship *New Providence*, Captain Butler, arriving from Halifax, wrecked on the south side of the island on October 17.

150. *Year 1821*. German merchantman, *Philip & Emelie*, Captain Rentz, sailing from Hamburg to St. Thomas, was wrecked on Belfast Reef on the north side of the island on June 27 and only a small part of her cargo was saved.

151. *Year 1823*. Two ships were lost: American schooner, *Hope*, arriving from Norfolk, wrecked on Little Bird Island on the north side of Antigua; and English merchantman, *Sisters*, Captain Douthwarte, sailing from Demarara to London, wrecked on a reef on the south side of the island.

AVES, OR BIRD ISLAND (*located 130 miles southwest of Guadeloupe*):

152. *Year 1689*. Spanish merchant *nao Santa Ana María*, sailing from Cadiz to Veracruz, was wrecked while carrying a valuable cargo of mercury and general merchandise.

153. *Year 1705*. Unidentified English merchantman, 24 guns, with a main cargo of iron bars and barrels of nails, was wrecked. Eleven days later a French ship rescued the survivors and recovered most of her cargo.

154. **Year 1774.** American slave ship *Rising Sun*, Captain Allanson, sailing from Africa to America with a cargo of slaves, was wrecked on the island.

GUADELOUPE:

155. **Year 1595.** During an English privateering voyage to the West Indies led by Francis Drake and John Hawkins, the ship *Richard* was stripped and then scuttled on the west side of the island because she sailed too slowly.

156. **Year 1603.** The New Spain Flota, commanded by Captain-General Fulgencio de Meneses, made the customary stop to water on the southwest side of the island. While anchored there an onshore breeze caused three of the ships to be wrecked; *Capitana San Juan Bautista*, 700 tons, 45 bronze guns, Captain Domingo de Licona; *nao La Rosa*, Captain Juan Diaz Canpillo; the third was not identified. The value of the cargoes lost on these ships was over a million pesos, and 250 men were left behind to salvage the wrecks. Soon after the *flota* sailed, however, they were attacked by Carib Indians and fled the island before they could recover anything. A few months later the Spaniards captured a French pirate vessel near Puerto Rico that had on board ten of the bronze cannon lost on the *Capitana*.

157. **Year 1609.** Spanish merchant *nao San Juan Bautista*, Captain José de Ybarra, sailing from Cadiz to Veracruz, sank after anchoring in the same area in which the above three ships had wrecked. Carib Indians prevented the Spaniards from salvaging her valuable cargo.

158. **Year 1618.** An unidentified French privateer was wrecked on the east side of the island. Two years later six of the survivors were rescued by an English merchantman bound for Virginia.

159. **Year 1630.** Shortly after the New Spain Flota, commanded by Captain-General Roque Centeno, anchored for water off the south end of the island, the galleon *Nuestra Señora del Pilar*, 1,100 tons, Captain Alonso García del Castillo, sank for no apparent reason quite close to shore but was completely salvaged.

160. Year 1656. During a hurricane a large number of French ships were totally lost at the port of Basseterre and around Maria Galante Island.

161. Year 1666. On August 12 there was a major sea battle between a French fleet and an English fleet commanded by Lord Willoughby. The French lost over twelve major warships and the English lost two near the Isle de Saints. Two days later a hurricane struck and over fifty ships were lost, including all fifteen of Lord Willoughby's fleet. The walls of the fort at Basseterre were washed into the sea, carrying many 14-pound cannon with them.

162. Year 1691. Several English warships forced a French frigate of Admiral De Casse's fleet ashore on the Isle de Saints.

163. Year 1713. During a hurricane in September, over forty ships of different nationalities were lost at Basseterre and other nearby anchorages.

164. Year 1759. English bomb vessel H.M.S. *Falcon*, 8 guns, Captain Mark Robinson, was wrecked on the Isle de Saints.

165. Year 1760. Four English merchantmen were wrecked: *Prosperity*, Captain Wilson, arriving from Cork, was chased onshore by a French privateer; *Armstrong*, Captain Muntford, arriving from Belfast, was chased ashore by the French near Chatron Point and totally lost; *Deliverance*, Captain Whyte, sailing from London to Virginia, was wrecked on the Isle de Saints but her crew was saved; and an unidentified ship of 200 tons arriving from Virginia was also wrecked on the Isle de Saints and some of her crew perished.

166. Year 1762. During a hurricane in July, six unidentified English merchantmen were sunk at Basseterre and several others near Maria Galante Island.

167. Year 1765. During a hurricane on July 31, seventeen English merchantmen were lost at Basseterre but only one was identified: the *Friendship*, Captain Rivoira.

168. Year 1766. During a hurricane on October 6, over fifty large English ships were lost at different ports around the island; and near the Isle de Saints twelve inbound slave ships from Africa were also totally lost.

169. *Year 1774.* A small English trading vessel, *Rose*, Captain Carline, arriving from Dominica, was wrecked at Grand Terre.

170. *Year 1776.* During a hurricane on September 6, over forty ships of various nationalities were wrecked around the island.

171. *Year 1786.* During a hurricane on September 10, three unidentified English ships were sunk at Basseterre.

172. *Year 1792.* French warship *Didon*, 44 guns, was wrecked and totally lost at Pointe-à-Pitre.

173. *Year 1794.* English troop-transport H.M.S. *Britannia* was accidentally burnt at Basse Terre.

174. *Year 1797.* English merchantman *Cornwallis*, sailing from Antigua to Liverpool, was captured by the French and then wrecked off Pointe-à-Pitre.

175. *Year 1800.* English ship *Catherine & Francis*, Captain Smith, sailing from Bermuda to Martinique, was wrecked on Maria Galante Island.

176. *Year 1801.* French merchantman *Syren*, Captain Rohde, sailing from France to St. Thomas, was wrecked on the east side of the island.

177. *Year 1809.* Four warships were lost: the British destroyed two French warships of 40 guns each, *Loire* and *Seine*, on December 18 at Anse la Barque; English sloop H.M.S. *Carieux*, 18 guns, Captain Henry George Moysey, wrecked on September 25 at Petit Terre on Maria Galante Island; and the English warship H.M.S. *Unique*, 12 guns, Captain Thomas Fellowes, burnt at Basseterre on May 31.

178. *Year 1810.* English merchantman *Point-a-Petre*, sailing for London, was lost during a gale on July 29 off Pointe-à-Pitre.

179. *Year 1811.* English warship H.M.S. *Grouper*, 4 guns, Captain James Atkins, wrecked on October 21 on the main island.

180. *Year 1814.* English warship H.M.S. *Rapide*, 6 guns, wrecked on the Isle de Saints.

181. *Year 1821.* A ship of unknown registry, *Kate*, Captain Purdy, sailing to Halifax with a large amount of specie aboard, was captured by pirates and scuttled near Deseada Island.

182. Year 1822. English ship *Virginia*, Captain Burt, sailing from Dominica to Antigua with a large number of soldiers, wrecked on July 20 on the Isle de Saints, but crew and passengers were saved.

183. Year 1823. American ship *Superior*, Captain Shaw, was wrecked on December 20 on Maria Galante Island, crew and cargo saved.

184. Year 1824. Two French merchantmen were wrecked on the main island: *Petit Louis*, Captain Videau, arriving from France, and the *France*, Captain Gerard, leaving for France.

DOMINICA:

185. Year 1565. Unidentified Spanish ship wrecked on the island and the Carib Indians captured and ate most of the survivors. When John Hawkins stopped there for water a few months later he rescued the few remaining survivors.

186. Year 1567. Before the New Spain Flota of Captain-General Juan Velasco de Barrio sailed from Veracruz for Spain it received word that there were two English fleets waiting to intercept the *flota*—one near Havana and the other near the mouth of the Bahama Channel. To protect the treasure they decided to sail back to Spain by a very unusual route. Hugging the coast of Yucatán they turned south, passing south of Jamaica. They planned to sail toward the Virgin Islands, then head directly for Spain. However, when nearing Puerto Rico they were struck by a bad storm and forced to run before it. Six of the major ships of the *flota*—carrying over 3 million pesos in treasure—were wrecked near the northwest tip of Dominica. The lost ships were: the *Capitana, San Juan*, 150 tons, Captain Benito de Santana; the *Almiranta, Santa Barbola*, 150 tons, Captain Vicencio Garullo; galleon *San Felipe*, 120 tons, Captain Juan López de Sosa; nao *El Espíritu Santo*, 120 tons, Captain Juan de Rosales; and two unidentified *naos* of 120 tons each. Due to the storm, none of the other ships in the *flota* could stop to pick up the treasure or the survivors, most of whom reached shore, where they were all cruelly massacred by the Carib Indians. According to several Indians captured the following year by salvors who came to the island, the Indians hid all of the treasure in caves. But even under torture they would not reveal the location of the treasure, and there is no record of it being recovered.

187. *Year 1605.* As the New Spain Flota approached Guadeloupe to stop for water, an unidentified *nao* became separated during the night and anchored at Dominica. While there a large Dutch warship appeared and, after a brief battle, sank the nao. There were only a few survivors, whom the Dutch rescued and placed ashore on Puerto Rico.

188. *Year 1766.* During a hurricane in the month of October, five English merchantmen were totally lost at Roseau: *Phoenix*, Captain Knight, just arriving from Bristol; *Three Friends*, Captain Reef, recently arrived from Newfoundland; and three unidentified vessels.

189. *Year 1769.* During a hurricane on July 26, thirteen ships were totally destroyed at Roseau but only one was identified: the English merchantman *Edward & Ann*, Captain Adnet. Two unidentified sloops were also sunk at Prince Ruperts Bay.

190. *Year 1772.* During a hurricane on August 30, eighteen unidentified English merchantmen were sunk or wrecked at Roseau; several cannon from the fort were also washed into the sea.

191. *Year 1776.* During a hurricane on September 6, two ships were wrecked on the west side of the island: English merchantman *Mary & Jane*, Captain Gerdner, arrived from Lancaster; and the Scottish merchantman *Hunter*, Captain Robinson, some of her cargo was recovered.

192. *Year 1780.* During a hurricane on October 9 the newly built French frigate *Juno*, 40 guns, was wrecked on the east side of the island and over three hundred men perished.

193. *Year 1787.* The island suffered from three different hurricanes this year. The first, on August 3, caused an English slave ship and several schooners to be totally lost. Another, on August 23, sank another English slave ship, three brigs, and many smaller ships. The third hurricane, on August 29, caused another English slave ship and two brigs loaded with rum to be sunk at Roseau.

194. *Year 1792.* During a hurricane on August 1, fourteen English ships were lost in various ports on the west side of the island. Only one was identified: merchantman *Olive*, which was ready to sail for England.

195. *Year 1796.* English warship H.M.S. *Berbice,* 20 guns, Captain John Tresakar, was wrecked during November on a reef near the island.

196. *Year 1804.* English merchantman *Nufus,* Captain Sandland, coming from London, was wrecked with a valuable cargo.

197. *Year 1808.* English merchant schooner *Stag,* Captain Derbyshire, was wrecked at Roseau during a gale on July 14, crew and most of cargo saved.

198. *Year 1809.* During a gale on August 1 or 3, three ships were wrecked: an unidentified American schooner at Roseau; an unidentified British ship on the northern tip of the island; and the English warship H.M.S. *Lark,* 18 guns, Captain Robert Nicholas, off Point Palenqua, with three of her crew of 121 perishing.

199. *Year 1813.* During a hurricane in August, sixteen ships were totally lost near and in the port of Roseau.

MARTINIQUE:

200. *Year 1636.* Spanish warship *San Salvador,* Captain Sancho de Urdanibia, carrying a cargo of war materials to Venezuela for an attack against the Dutch on Curaçao, was wrecked in 2 fathoms on the south side of the island. Due to the fact that the island was settled by the French at this time, the Spaniards threw the twenty-six bronze cannon it carried overboard, then set the ship afire before escaping in small boats. The French tried to reach the wreck, but it blew up before they could get any of its cargo off.

201. *Year 1666.* When the governor of Barbados heard that there were six richly laden French ships in the Bay of All Saints on the island, he sent the H.M.S. *Coventry* and four other large English ships to capture them. When the French saw the English approaching the bay they set fire to all six of their ships, but the English managed to save all but one, which sank. Then, on the following day, while the English were transferring the plunder to their own ships, a storm struck and all five English ships sank. The French recovered over eighty large cannon from these wrecks as well as other items.

202. *Year 1667.* Two accounts differ as to what happened on the island this year. One has it that a large English fleet commanded by Admiral Sir John Harman entered the main port—which was Fort of France—and burnt twenty French warships and merchantmen at anchor. The other account has the event at Governor's Bay and states that nineteen French warships, three fireships, and some Dutch merchantmen were burnt and sunk.

203. *Year 1680.* During a violent hurricane on August 3, over twenty large French ships and two English ships were totally lost in Cul-de-Sac Bay and the loss of lives was great.

204. *Year 1687.* French merchantman *Our Lady of Hope*, Captain Serres, coming from Marseilles, was wrecked on a reef 6 miles off the east side of the island.

205. *Year 1691.* An English warship commanded by Captain Arther forced an unidentified French warship to run aground near Fort of France.

206. *Year 1695.* During a hurricane in October, six or seven large French ships and several smaller ones were totally lost on the west side of the island and over six hundred men perished aboard them.

207. *Year 1740.* During a hurricane in October, two large French warships and many merchantmen were sunk or wrecked in different ports of the island.

208. *Year 1744.* A large unidentified Spanish merchantman, sailing from Cadiz to Cartagena, was forced ashore and destroyed on the south side of the island by several ships of the English fleet commanded by Commodore Knowles.

209. *Year 1745.* As a fleet of forty large French merchantmen escorted by two warships was going around the south side of the island, it was attacked by the English fleet of Admiral Townsend and thirty of the merchantmen and the two warships were forced ashore and destroyed by the English. The cargoes on the merchantmen were valued at over 15 million livres.

210. *Year 1761.* During an attack on the island by an English fleet commanded by Sir James Douglas, one of the ships wrecked near a battery several miles north of Fort of France. She was the

H.M.S. *Raisonable*, 64 guns, Captain Molyneux Shuldham, crew and most of stores saved. The French later recovered her cannon.

211. Year 1762. English merchantman *Brilliant*, Captain Boyd, sailing from London to the West Indies, foundered off the south part of the island but all of her crew was saved.

212. Year 1763. American ship *New Hampshire*, Captain Knight, coming from New England, was lost while entering the port of Fort of France, crew and cargo saved.

213. Year 1765. During a hurricane in July, thirty-three large French merchantmen and many small vessels were lost in different ports on the west side of the island.

214. Year 1766. During a hurricane in October, twenty-eight French and eight English ships were lost at Fort of France; nine other English ships were lost at Flemish Bay; and at La Trinite Bay, eighteen unidentified ships were totally lost.

215. Year 1774. French slave ship *Geraundeau*, Captain Duckerson, arriving from Africa with 450 slaves, was wrecked on the south side of the island, slaves and crew saved.

216. Year 1776. During a hurricane on September 6, over one hundred French and Dutch merchantmen, all in a convoy preparing to sail for Europe, were totally lost at Point Petre Bay and over six thousand persons were drowned.

217. Year 1779. Barely had the island recovered from a previous hurricane when an even worse one struck again on August 28. This time over seventy ships were lost all over the west side of the island, and among the many lives lost were some of the survivors from the last hurricane.

218. Year 1780. The English merchantman *Diligence*, Captain Orr, coming from England, was captured by a French privateer near the island and taken into Fort Royal Bay, where she was burnt along with the ship that had captured her, as ten English warships were coming to her rescue.

219. Year 1780. The hurricane that struck the island on October 12 was the worst one ever to hit the island and no two accounts agree as to the number of ships lost. A French convoy of forty large troop transports that had just reached the island was totally destroyed in some port on the west side. Four large French warships were sunk with a total loss of men in Fort Royal Bay. Three English warships of the fleet of Admiral Rodney were wrecked on the west side of the island: H.M.S. *Andromeda*, 28 guns; H.M.S. *Laurel*, 28 guns; and the H.M.S. *Deal Castle*, 24 guns. An English ship, probably a supply ship of Rodney's fleet, the *Endymion*, was lost on the island. Some accounts place the total number of ships of different nationalities lost on the island at over 150.

220. Year 1788. During a hurricane in September over fifty large French ships were totally destroyed in various ports of the island. Most of the town of Caravel, along with the majority of its inhabitants, was swept into the sea.

221. Year 1794. Two ships were wrecked on the island: American sloop *John*, Captain Richardson, coming from Virginia, and the English troop-transport *Generous Friends*, Captain Harrison, arriving from London.

222. Year 1796. A ship of unknown nationality, *Diana*, Captain Deare, sailing from India to America, was forced to enter a port on the west side of the island and burnt to prevent it from falling into the hands of some English warships.

223. Year 1801. Four English merchantmen were wrecked on the east side of the island: *Edward*, Captain Nash, sailing from London to Honduras; *Hope*, Captain Thompson, sailing from London to Tortola; *Madona*, Captain Vollum, arriving from London; and the *Pacific*, Captain Wilson, also arriving from London.

224. Year 1802. Three English ships were wrecked on the island: merchantman *Dispatch*, Captain McIntire, sailing for Quebec, part of her cargo was saved; merchantman *Susannah*, Captain Stanton, sailing for Dublin; and the slave ship *Kennion*, Captain Robinson, sailing from Africa to Jamaica.

225. Year 1807. English warship, H.M.S. *Thames*, Captain Willoughby, was captured by the French off Barbados but later wrecked near Diamond Rock on the south side of the island.

226. Year 1809. On January 9 the English warship H.M.S. *Morne Fortunee*, 12 guns, Captain John Brown, was wrecked on the island, and forty-one of her crew of sixty-five perished. During an English attack against the French on the island, the English sank the French warship *Amphitrite*, 40 guns, on February 4, at Fort of France. On February 24 the French burnt two of their other warships in the same port to prevent their capture: *Rossollis* and *Carnation*, both of 18 guns.

227. *Year 1811.* Early in the year the American merchantman *Spring Bird*, Captain Lambert, coming from New England, was wrecked on the island. During a hurricane on July 8, four or five unidentified ships were lost at Cul-de-Sac Bay.

228. *Year 1814.* Two Canadian ships were wrecked on the island: sloop *Margaret*, coming from New Brunswick, was lost at Grand Passage Bay but her crew was saved; and the brig *General Hunter*, Captain Perkins, arriving from Halifax, was lost at Fort of France.

229. *Year 1813.* During a hurricane in August a total of forty-two ships of different nationalities were lost in various ports of the island and over three thousand persons perished.

230. *Year 1815.* French merchantman *Madame Royale*, arriving from France, was totally lost on the east side of the island on June 7, no survivors.

231. *Year 1816.* Two French merchantmen were wrecked on the island: *Caroline*, Captain Monnier, sailing from France to Louisiana, in May, crew was saved; and the *Stanislaus*, Captain Berthelet, arriving from France, on September 15.

232. *Year 1823.* French ship *Alfred*, Captain Mony, arriving from France, wrecked on Diamond Rock.

ST. LUCIA:

233. *Year 1780.* During a hurricane on October 10 the following ships were sunk: American merchantman *Champion*, Captain Hall, arriving from New York; English merchantman *Dolphin*, Captain Morrison; and three English warships: H.M.S. *Cornwall*, 74 guns, Captain Timothy Edwards; H.M.S. *Vengeance*, 32 guns; and the *Beaver's Prize*, 18 guns.

234. *Year 1781.* English warship H.M.S. *Thetis*, 32 guns, Captain Robert Linzee, was wrecked on the west side of the island.

235. *Year 1783.* English merchantman *Barbara,* Captain Perry, arriving from Liverpool, wrecked on the northern part of the island, crew and part of cargo saved.

236. *Year 1800.* English slave ship *Prince John,* Captain Hestor, arriving from Africa, lost on the east side of the island, crew and slaves saved.

237. *Year 1805.* English schooner *Dolphin,* coming from Barbados with rum, was wrecked on the east side of the island.

238. *Year 1809.* English merchantman *Lancashire Witch,* sailing from Liverpool to Barbados, was totally lost on the east side of the island but her crew was saved.

239. *Year 1817.* During a hurricane on October 21, seven large English merchantmen were sunk on the west side of the island, over two hundred men perished.

240. *Year 1823.* American merchantman *Suffolk,* sailing from Demarara to New York, was wrecked on the east side of the island on September 15 but her crew was saved.

ST. VINCENT:

241. *Year 1635.* Two unidentified Spanish merchant *naos* were wrecked on the east side of the island while sailing from Spain to Cartagena. Survivors were found on this island in 1667 by the first English settlers.

242. *Year 1780.* During the famous hurricane on October 10 the English warship H.M.S. *Experiment,* 50 guns, and the French warship *Juno,* 40 guns, were totally destroyed on the east coast of this island with almost a total loss of lives.

243. *Year 1784.* English slave ship *Africa,* Captain Brown, arriving from Africa with a cargo of slaves, wrecked while entering the port of Kingstown, crew and slaves saved.

244. *Year 1792.* English packet boat *Willoughby Bay,* was wrecked on the east side of the island on September 21, mail and crew saved.

245. *Year 1793.* A large unidentified ship, apparently English-built, drifted ashore on the east side of the island and quickly went to pieces. No one was on board at the time it wrecked.

246. *Year 1817.* During a hurricane on October 21, ten large unidentified English merchantmen wrecked or sank at Kingstown.

247. *Year 1818.* English merchantman *William,* Captain Landells, sailing from Tobago to London, wrecked on the east side of the island on May 27, crew and some cargo of rum saved.

BARBADOS:

248. *Year 1666.* During a hurricane in July a large unidentified English warship was wrecked on the east side of the island.

249. *Year 1669.* During a hurricane on November 1, many ships were wrecked on the island and over 1,500 coffins from the island's main cemetery were swept into the sea.

250. *Year 1675.* During a hurricane on September 1, twelve large unidentified English merchantmen, some of them loaded with sugar and rum, were sunk at Bridgetown.

251. *Year 1693.* During a hurricane in October, seventeen unidentified English merchantmen were sunk in the vicinity of Bridgetown.

252. *Year 1694.* During a hurricane on September 27, twenty-six English merchantmen were sunk in Carlisle Bay and over a thousand men perished.

253. *Year 1700.* During a hurricane two large and two small unidentified ships were lost.

254. *Year 1716.* A pirate ship of Captain Martel sank a sloop that was guarding the entrance to Carlisle Bay. The following day an English warship chased the pirate ship of 24 guns around the island and sank it by cannon fire on the east side of the island.

255. *Year 1748.* An unidentified richly laden French merchantman, sailing from France to Martinique, was wrecked on the east side of the island. An English sloop-of-war, *Serpent,* was wrecked on the island and seven of her crew perished.

256. *Year 1749.* During a hurricane in October, six ships were sunk near Bridgetown but only the English merchantman *Nancy,* sailing from Bristol to Jamaica, was identified.

257. *Year 1751.* English merchantman *Argo,* Captain Alleyne, sailing for London, wrecked shortly after leaving Carlisle Bay but her crew was saved.

258. *Year 1757.* During a hurricane in July, eight unidentified ships were lost at Carlisle Bay and Bridgetown. In November an American ship, *George,* Captain Hardy, coming from Philadelphia, wrecked on the island.

259. *Year 1758.* During a hurricane on August 23 the following ships were wrecked or sunk in Carlisle Bay: an English privateer brigantine, Captain Franklin; American merchantman *Aurora,* Captain Campbell, coming from North Carolina; American ship *Jenny & Sally,* Captain Boulton, arriving from South Carolina; English merchantman *Rose,* Captain Elmore, arriving from Bristol; and two ships of unknown registry: *Good Intent,* Captain Tucker, and *David & Susanna,* Captain Bartlett. At Bridgetown, six unidentified ships were also lost.

260. *Year 1761.* Scottish merchantman *Blakeney,* Captain Murford, coming from Belfast, was forced ashore on the east side of the island by a French privateer and quickly went to pieces, crew and some cargo saved.

261. *Year 1762.* Two merchantmen were wrecked on the island: English ship *Greyhound,* Captain Walsh, driven ashore by a French privateer on January 8, her cargo was saved; and Irish ship *Cato,* Captain Houseman, sailing from Cork to Guadeloupe, near the entrance to Carlisle Bay, only her crew was saved.

262. *Year 1765.* During a gale or hurricane in August, seven large English merchantmen were lost in Carlisle Bay; at Bridgetown the Scottish ship *Joseph,* Captain McNabb, ready to sail for Dublin, was sunk but her cargo was recovered.

263. *Year 1767.* English slave ship *Rebecca,* Captain Brodie, arriving from Africa, wrecked on a reef near Long Bay on November 17, crew, slaves, and cargo of ivory and wax saved.

264. *Year 1772.* Two English ships were wrecked on the east side of the island: packet boat *Barbadoes,* Captain Twine, arriving from Bristol, burnt after running up on a reef; and the merchantman *Cunriff,* Captain Clapp, arriving from London and Cork, only a small part of her cargo was saved.

265. *Year 1773.* A ship of unknown registry, *Hill,* Captain Coffin, was struck by lightning and blew up off Bridgetown, most of her crew perished.

266. **Year 1775.** During a gale on August 25 the Scottish packet boat *Duncannon*, Captain Goddard, arriving from England, wrecked near Carlisle Bay, crew and mail saved. During a hurricane on September 2 the English ship *Ostall*, Captain Temple, coming from Newfoundland, was wrecked on the island.

267. **Year 1776.** Two ships were wrecked on the east side of the island: English slave ship *Patty*, Captain Johnson, arriving from Africa, crew and slaves saved; and the French ship *Industry*, Captain Carcaud, sailing from Marseilles to Barbados, her crew was saved.

268. **Year 1779.** Privateer ship *Pickering*, 20 guns, forced on shore by the H.M.S. *Aurora* and then burnt.

269. **Year 1780.** During the famous hurricane of October 10, over twenty ships were wrecked around the island. A large number of other ships were blown out to sea, most of them never again heard from. Two English ships, *Happy Return* and the *Edward*, Captain Peoples, which had been blown away during the hurricane, made it back to the island but sank upon returning. One of the main buildings of the Naval Hospital at Bridgetown was carried into the sea by large waves.

270. **Year 1782.** English slave ship *Lark*, Captain Blackhouse, arriving from Africa, wrecked on the east side of the island, crew and all of its 320 slaves saved.

271. **Year 1784.** English merchantman *Euphrates*, Captain Smith, coming from London, was totally lost on a reef on the eastern side of the island but the crew was saved.

272. **Year 1785.** American ship *Rose*, Captain Savage, coming from Philadelphia, was wrecked at Round Rock but part of her cargo was saved.

273. **Year 1786.** During a hurricane on September 2, various accounts state "that every ship in Carlisle Bay was lost." Only two were identified: Scottish ship *Hibernia*, Captain McConnel, and the English merchantman *Generous Planter*, Captain Sands.

274. **Year 1790.** American ship *Betsey*, Captain Brown, sailing from Georgia to Grenada, was totally lost on the east side of the island but her crew was saved.

275. *Year 1791.* English slave ship *King George,* Captain Howard, arriving from Africa, wrecked on the east side of the island and only 80 of its 360 slaves were saved.

276. *Year 1792.* English slave ship *Garland,* Captain Sherwood, arriving from Africa, wrecked on Cobler's Rock, crew and slaves saved.

277. *Year 1794.* Scottish merchantman *Kingston,* coming from Glasgow, wrecked on Cabbin Rock Reef, on the east side of the island.

278. *Year 1798.* English schooner *Star,* shortly after sailing for Trinidad on June 30, was wrecked in a gale on the southern part of the island.

279. *Year 1799.* Two English merchantmen were wrecked on Cobler's Rock: *Edwards,* Captain Wilson, arriving from England, and the *Mary,* Captain Leigh, arriving from Liverpool.

280. *Year 1801.* Two English ships wrecked on the east side of the island: packet boat *Grantham,* Captain Ball, sailing from England to Jamaica, crew and passengers saved; and the merchantman *Chance,* Captain Peters, the crew was saved.

281. *Year 1804.* Large richly laden Portuguese merchantman *Francizhena,* Captain Carros, sailing from Brazil to Lisbon, wrecked on the east side of the island and many men perished.

282. *Year 1806.* English merchantman *Maryann,* Captain Mack, sailing from Newcastle to Grenada, wrecked on the island.

283. *Year 1807.* Four ships were wrecked on the island: English ship *Nelly,* Captain Adamson, arriving from Trinidad, near Bridgetown; American brig *Lark,* Captain Worrel, arriving from Surinam, on the south part of the island; English ship *Cicero,* Captain Turner, sailing from London to Jamaica, on Cobler's Rock; and the English merchantman *Bridgetown,* sailing from London to Jamaica, also on Cobler's Rock.

284. *Year 1808.* English troop transport *Majestic,* burnt and sank in Carlisle Bay, no lives were lost.

285. *Year 1809.* English sloop-of-war H.M.S. *Glommen,* 18 guns, Captain Charles Pickford, wrecked in Carlisle Bay in November, no lives were lost.

286. **Year 1810.** Canadian schooner *Laura,* wrecked during a gale on August 12 at Pier Head, the crew was saved.

287. **Year 1812.** Canadian merchantman *Cruden,* sailing from Newfoundland to Grenada, wrecked on Cobler's Rock on March 7.

288. **Year 1813.** Two English mail packet boats *Sprightly* and *Lady Spencer,* were wrecked on the east side of the island on July 23.

289. **Year 1814.** Two English merchantmen were lost on the island: *Jane,* Captain Ranof, sailing from London and Madeira to Dominica, on the east side of the island, crew and cargo saved; and the schooner *Jonathan,* forced on Marida Reef by an American ship and then destroyed by cannon fire, most of her cargo of dry goods and rum was lost.

290. **Year 1815.** Three merchantmen were lost on the island: Scottish ship *Elizabeth,* Captain Duncan, sailing from England to St. Vincent, on the east side of the island; English ship *Sylph,* Captain Davidson, sailing from Gibraltar to the West Indies, totally lost on August 10 on a reef near the northern end of the island; and a ship of unknown registry, *M'Dowall,* coming from Dominica, on Kettlebottom Rock.

291. **Year 1816.** During a hurricane on September 15, two English ships were totally lost on the island: brig *Commerce,* arriving from England, and the sloop *Economy,* arriving from St. Lucia.

292. **Year 1821.** English packet boat *Lady Georgiana,* Captain Spencer, totally lost in Carlisle Bay on September 1.

GRENADINES:

293. **Year 1611.** An unidentified French slave ship carrying over four hundred slaves was wrecked on one of the islands of the Grenadines. Spaniards later rescued most of the slaves and killed all of the Frenchmen.

294. **Year 1653.** During the month of July a large unidentified French ship was totally lost near one of the smaller cays in this chain of islands.

295. **Year 1675.** During a hurricane in August an unidentified Portuguese slave ship was wrecked on Bequia Island and a large amount of ivory went down.

296. *Year 1768.* English merchantman *Nancy,* Captain Hamilton, sailing from Bristol to Nevis, was lost on one of the islands but her crew was saved.

297. *Year 1769.* English merchantman *Rose,* Captain Farr, sailing from London and Madeira to Jamaica, was wrecked on the east side of Carriacou Island.

298. *Year 1782.* English merchantman *Rebecca,* Captain Sim, sailing from Demarara to Barbados, was totally lost on the east side of Bequia Island.

299. *Year 1794.* A ship of unknown registry, *Adventure Baptista,* Captain Blanckley, was wrecked on a reef near Carriacou Island.

300. *Year 1818.* American schooner *Lily* was wrecked on one of the Grenadines and only the captain was saved.

301. *Year 1821.* English merchantman *March,* sailing from London to Grenada, was wrecked at Carriacou Island in April and was totally lost.

GRENADA:

302. *Year 1768.* During a hurricane on August 9 the following ships were sunk at St. George's Harbor: English ship *Industry,* Captain Wilkinson, arriving from Barbados; Dutch ship, Captain Simpson, arriving from St. Eustatius; and three unidentified brigs. At Grand Once, the English slave ship *Molly,* Captain Woodburn, coming from Africa, was wrecked.

303. *Year 1769.* English slave ship *Sally,* Captain Tonkey, arriving from Africa, wrecked in Grand Roy Bay on June 19, crew and slaves saved.

304. *Year 1772.* English merchantman *Champion,* Captain Glover, arriving from Bristol, was lost at St. George's Harbor.

305. *Year 1773.* English sloop *Ann,* Captain Knotsford, wrecked on a reef near Bacolet, three men were lost.

306. *Year 1774.* Two merchantmen were lost: Scottish ship *Morris & Molly,* Captain Weatherhead, while sailing out of Mergain for Dublin; and the English ship *Rochard,* Captain Bartlet, while leaving Grenville Bay on August 3 for London; some of their cargo was saved.

307. Year 1780. During the famous hurricane of October 10 the following ships were lost: nineteen unidentified Dutch merchantmen sank in Grenville Bay; Swedish merchantman *Prince Frederick Adolph*, Captain Lonstroom, in St. George's Harbor; French ship *Two Sisters*, Captain Townseau, on the east side of the island; French privateer *Comte de Durant*, Captain Lamster, on the south side of the island; and three other French and seven English merchantmen were lost in other ports of the island.

308. Year 1787. English merchantman *Lady Hughes*, Captain Dommet, was totally lost on the island but her crew was saved.

309. Year 1788. American ship *Mary Ann*, Captain Dale, arriving from Virginia, wrecked on the north side of the island on December 2.

310. Year 1790. Two English merchantmen wrecked on the island: *Hope*, Captain Blackman, and the *Amelia*, Captain Burgess, the latter on the north end of the island.

311. Year 1791. American merchantman *Ann & Bridget*, Captain Shaftoe, arriving from Boston, wrecked on the island.

312. Year 1793. Two ships were lost on the east side of the island: English slave ship *Fanny*, Captain Moore, arriving from Africa, only two of the crew were saved; and a ship of unknown registry, *Charlotte*, Captain Cummings.

313. Year 1794. English merchantman *Mary*, Captain Johnson, was totally lost leaving Grenville Bay while sailing for London.

314. Year 1798. American ship *Elizabeth*, arriving from New York, wrecked on a reef near St. George's Harbor but most of her cargo was saved.

315. Year 1800. English merchantman *Charlotte*, Captain Buttery, arriving from London, was wrecked on the south side of the island but most of her cargo was saved.

316. Year 1801. English ship *Love*, Captain Death, arriving from England, wrecked while entering St. George's Harbor but all of her cargo was saved.

317. *Year 1804.* English brig *Surprise,* while leaving for Trinidad, was wrecked at the entrance to Grenville Bay but all of her cargo of rum was saved.

318. *Year 1805.* Large Portuguese merchantman *Armida,* Captain Silva, sailing from Brazil to Venezuela, was wrecked at Point Saline on December 20, most of her cargo was lost.

319. *Year 1807.* English sloop *Neptune,* Captain Hunt, arriving from London, wrecked on the island.

320. *Year 1813.* English merchantman *Four Brothers,* sailing for London, was wrecked on the east side of the island.

321. *Year 1816.* Richly laden Spanish merchant *nao Virgen del Rosario,* Captain Gale, coming from Spain, wrecked on January 22 at Point Saline, only a small part of her cargo was saved.

322. *Year 1822.* Two English merchantmen, *Sophia* and the *Columbine,* Captain Bannatyne, sailing from Tobago, were wrecked on the east side of the island, both crews and cargoes were saved.

323. *Year 1824.* English sloop *Arrow,* Captain Williams, wrecked on La Bays Rock but her crew was saved. The ship was in ballast at the time.

TOBAGO:

324. *Year 1572.* Five unidentified Spanish merchant *naos,* sailing from Spain to Veracruz, were wrecked on the island but most of their cargoes were later salvaged by divers from Margarita Island.

325. *Year 1677.* A big battle took place between a French fleet under Admiral Estres and a Dutch fleet under Vice-Admiral Herr Binkes in Palmit Bay. The French fleet was burnt and sunk; the number of ships or their identities are not known. The Dutch also lost several ships.

326. *Year 1787.* English sloop *Tabago* was totally lost on August 16 on a reef east of Englishman's Bay, on the north side of the island.

327. *Year 1792.* Unidentified French ship of Captain Steur, sailing from Demarara to Amsterdam, was wrecked on the island.

328. *Year 1800.* Two English merchantmen were wrecked on the island: *Recovery,* Captain Abercromby, sailing to London, and the

Mary Ann, Captain Craig, arriving from London. Some cargo from both ships was saved.

329. *Year 1801.* English ship *Rebecca*, Captain Reed, arriving from London, wrecked on the east end of the island but the crew was saved.

330. *Year 1803.* English merchantman *Catherine*, Captain Bodkin, arriving from London, wrecked on the north side of the island.

331. *Year 1805.* English merchantman *Rosalia*, Captain Ferguson, arriving from London, wrecked on a reef while attempting to enter Tyrrel Bay.

332. *Year 1807.* English merchantman *Eclipse*, Captain Vaughan, was totally lost in Courland Bay but her crew was saved.

333. *Year 1812.* English ship *Fame*, Captain Mumford, sailing from Madeira to Tobago, wrecked on August 21 on the island.

334. *Year 1813.* English merchantman *Trafalgar*, Captain Pines, sailing for Bristol, wrecked off the east end of the island in June, some of her cargo was saved.

TRINIDAD:

335. *Year 1731.* Spanish merchant *nao Nuestra Señora de la Concepción*, Captain Gotibo, wrecked on Maracas Bar, only her crew was saved.

336. *Year 1780.* English merchantman *Friends*, Captain Wood, arriving from Africa, wrecked on the east side of the island, only a few of the crew were saved.

337. *Year 1782.* English warship H.M.S. *Rattlesnake* was wrecked on the island, one of the crew perished.

338. *Year 1797.* As an English fleet of warships commanded by Sir Henry Harvey approached to capture the island from the Spaniards on February 17, the Spaniards burnt five large warships off Chaguaramas to prevent them from falling into the hands of the English: *Capitana San Vicente*, 80 guns, Brigadier Jerónimo Mendoza; *Almiranta Arrogante*, 74 guns, Captain Rafael Bennazar; galleon *Gallardo*, 74 guns, Captain Gabriel Sorondo; galleon *San Damasco*, 74 guns, Captain José Jordan; and the frigate *Concha*,

34 guns, Captain Manuel Urtizabel. In recent years amateur divers have located and recovered a few artifacts from these wrecks.

339. *Year 1800.* Two English ships were wrecked on the island: merchantman *Charlotte*, Captain Crow, arriving from Africa, the crew was saved; and the warship H.M.S. *Dromedary*, 20 guns, Captain Bridges W. Taylor, on August 10, at Parasol Rock, but the crew was saved.

340. *Year 1802.* Scottish merchantman *Swan*, arriving from Glasgow, wrecked in the Bocas on September 20.

341. *Year 1803.* English slave ship *Kate*, Captain Good, arriving from Africa, wrecked on the east side of the island, ten people were lost.

342. *Year 1806.* Scottish ship *Governor Picton*, arriving from Clyde, wrecked on the south side of the island on April 19, only her crew was saved.

343. *Year 1810.* Canadian ship *Polly*, Captain Bell, arriving from Newfoundland, sank at Port of Spain but her crew was saved.

344. *Year 1816.* English merchantman *Lion*, Captain Grove, sailing to Demarara, wrecked on the east side of the island but her crew was saved.

345. *Year 1821.* Spanish ship *Tamar*, arriving from Puerto Rico, was wrecked in the Bocas, crew and some cargo saved.

CHAPTER SIX

Bermuda

BERMUDA, in relation to its size, has more shipwrecks than any other area in the Western Hemisphere, with the possible exceptions of the Florida Keys and Cape Hatteras, North Carolina. Although on charts it is nothing more than a dot located 800 miles from the United States, Bermuda played an important role in early navigation. All the Spanish ships, as well as those of all other European nations sailing in the waters of the New World, attempted to pass within sight of Bermuda on their homeward-bound voyages, using it as a checkpoint in their haphazard methods of navigation. Most of the ships bringing colonists to North America either made stops there or passed within sight of it. Due to the fact that these islands are very low in elevation and generally concealed by mist or haze, sighting the islands was not an easy task and many ships ran up on the reefs, some of which are as far as 10 miles out.

From the earliest days of its settlement, many Bermudans were engaged in salvaging the old wrecks around their island. When William Phips first reached the treasure galleon on Silver Shoals, he discovered that Bermudan wreckers had already beat him to it. During World War II a great deal of salvaging for scrap iron went on around the island and many cannon and anchors were raised. The first major treasure recovery in the twentieth century was made in 1955 by Teddy Tucker, a Bermudan and descendant of the first governor of Bermuda (who, ironically, got into trouble over salvaging a Spanish galleon, the *San Antonio,* wrecked in Bermuda in 1621 when he was accused of pocketing a large amount of the recovered cargo). Teddy himself located this same wreck about ten years ago and recovered a large number of artifacts from it. In 1950, while combing the reefs with a glass-bottom bucket to locate several of his fish traps after a storm, he discovered six coral-encrusted cannon in a small sand pocket on a shallow reef. He did not return to the site until the summer of 1955, when, after recovering the cannon for a local museum, he began excavating by hand (using a table-tennis paddle to fan the sand away). His first find was a beautiful gold bar weighing 32 ounces. In less than a week he discovered two small cakes of gold, two smaller gold bars, several gold-studded pearl buttons, and a gold, emerald-studded cross that sold for $100,000. This wreck has not as yet been identified, but is believed to date from the late sixteenth century.

Every summer since 1952, Teddy has been working hard salvaging a wide assortment of different wrecks, usually under the sponsorship of the Smithsonian Institution. The waters are so clear around Bermuda that he has located over one hundred wrecks by light plane, a helium-filled balloon, and by just standing on the bow of his boat and sighting them in the near-transparent water. Of all the divers I have salvaged with around the world, Teddy is the hardest worker, thinking nothing of spending eight or ten hours below each day, wearing a Desco mask, and using an airlift to uncover his wrecks. His many important discoveries were not a matter of luck but of hard work. Of the many wrecks he has worked, the most notable are the following: an unidentified Spanish merchant *nao* dating to 1560; the *San Antonio;* two Virginia Company merchantmen, *Eagle* and *Virginia Merchant,* 1659 and 1660, respectively; an unidentified Spanish *nao* dating around 1700; the *Sir George Arthur,* an English merchantman, 1778; an unidentified French merchantman, around 1780; the *Caesar,* an English merchantman, 1818; and the French warship *L'Herminie,* 1839.

TOP: Surveying a shipwreck in Bermuda that was not buried. The diver on the right is holding a wine bottle and is sitting on round grinding stones. BOTTOM: Mendel Peterson adjusting a measuring device over timbers of an unidentified Spanish ship of ca. 1560–1580 on the southwest reefs of Bermuda (Smithsonian Institution).

LEFT: Gold and emerald cross found on a sixteenth-century Spanish wreck in Bermuda. BELOW: Portuguese gold cruzados, dating from 1578 to 1580, found on a shipwreck in Bermuda (Bermuda News Bureau).

In June 1958 an amateur skin-diver, Robert Downing, discovered the wreck of the *Sea Venture,* which brought the first colonists to Bermuda in 1609. With Teddy Tucker's assistance, they jointly salvaged this wreck, which is of great importance to early Bermudan history. Another native Bermudan, Harry Cox, a wealthy businessman, has been prowling the reefs for as long as Tucker and has located a large number of shipwrecks. His biggest discovery occurred during the summer of 1968, when he excavated the remains of a Portuguese ship sunk around 1580. Among the many items he recovered from this wreck are several gold bars, gold circlets, an assortment of rare mint-condition gold Portuguese cruzado coins, a 15-foot-long solid gold, double-linked chain, a gold manicure set backed by two golden caryatids, an assortment of Spanish silver coins, a pearl cross mounted on a gold frame, several gold rings, and a brass astrolabe, one of the few ever found on shipwrecks anywhere. And there are others who spend most of their spare time working old wrecks. Brian Malpus, who earns his living as a policeman, worked with Tucker for many years but for the past few summers has been working sixteenth- and seventeenth-century Spanish shipwrecks on his own. Although he has not discovered much treasure, his wrecks are yielding a vast array of interesting artifacts—such as a silver bosun's whistle, many types of intact ceramicware, pewterware, and a few Spanish silver coins.

Although Tucker and most of the others work wrecks only during the summer, salvage work on most of the sites can be done most of the year, except when passing hurricanes cause huge swells to break on the reefs. No permits are necessary to explore the reefs and locate wreck sites, but salvage leases are required and may be obtained from the Receiver of Wrecks. The salvor may keep all that he recovers, but the Bermudan government has the right to purchase any part or everything recovered from a wreck at a fair price.

List of Shipwrecks in Bermuda

1. **Year 1500–10.** According to noted British historian Defroy of the nineteenth century, Bermuda is named after a Spanish ship, *La Bermuda,* that wrecked there not long after Columbus' rediscovery of the New World. Other historians claim that the island is named after its discoverer, a Spaniard named Juan Bermúdez.

2. **Year 1533.** An unidentified Spanish merchant *nao* owned by a merchant named Johan de León and carrying an undisclosed amount of gold and pearls, was lost on the reefs. Three years later, two ships sailing from Santo Domingo for Spain passed close to Bermuda and sighted fires on the island but wind and current prevented them from investigating. They recommended to the King that a small ship be sent to pick up the survivors and treasure, but no documents reveal if this was done.

3. **Year 1543.** A Portuguese slave ship, sailing from Santo Domingo with seven Spanish merchantmen, was wrecked on a reef located 4 leagues from the nearest land, at the north end of Bermuda. The thirty survivors got ashore in the ship's boat and made many return trips to the wreck, bringing ashore supplies and part of its cargo. After they spent sixty days on the island they sailed for Santo Domingo in a vessel they had constructed from timbers of the shipwreck. They reported sighting the remains of several other shipwrecks on the reefs.

4. **Year 1550.** Unidentified merchant *nao*, owned by Rodrigo Vago and sailing in the Nueva España Flota, was badly damaged in a storm about 70 leagues west of Bermuda and drifted until it struck a reef at Bermuda. It carried a large amount of gold and silver, none of which was reported recovered.

5. **Year 1551.** A hurricane that lasted for ten days struck the Tierra Firme Armada of Captain-General Sancho de Viedma after it cleared the Bahama Channel. His *Capitana* sprung a bad leak and was deliberately run up on a reef, where her cannon and 150,000 ducats in treasure were saved. Another ship of this fleet, the *Santa Barbola*, 400 tons, Captain Alvarez de los Rios, owned by Cosme Rodríguez Farfan, was also wrecked on a reef but all her treasure was saved.

6. **Year 1560.** When the Tierra Firme Flota of Captain-General Pedro de la Roelas was in sight of Bermuda a storm struck and the *Capitana* disappeared without a trace, either sinking in deep water or on the reefs of Bermuda.

7. **Year 1563.** When the Nueva España Flota of Captain-General Juan Menéndez was in the vicinity of Bermuda, his *Capitana* and several merchant *naos* disappeared without a trace. One of these

is believed to be the unidentified Spanish wreck (dated 1560) that Tucker located.

8. **Year 1588.** Unidentified merchant *nao* of Pedro Menéndez, carrying a cargo of indigo, cochineal, logwood, and a small amount of silver specie, was wrecked on a reef.

9. **Year 1593.** A French ship owned by Monsieur Charles de la Barbotiere sailed from Laguna, Hispaniola, and was wrecked on December 17 against a reef in the northwestern part of Bermuda that the captain reported was 7 leagues from the nearest shore. In a makeshift raft, twenty-six of the fifty persons on board reached shore. They later made a small vessel from the wreck and reached France.

10. **Year 1596.** Merchant *nao San Pedro*, 350 tons, Captain Hierónimo de Porras, of the Nueva España Flota of Captain-General Pedro Menéndez Márquez, was wrecked near the island. It could be this wreck on which Tucker made his big find in 1955.

11. **Year 1603.** Unidentified galleon in the Tierra Firme Armada, Captain-General Luis Fernández de Cordova, separated from the convoy during a storm and was wrecked at Bermuda. Most of the treasure aboard was recovered and, together with the survivors, was rescued twenty-two days later. Crew reported seeing many earlier shipwrecks on the island.

12. **Year 1605.** Merchant *nao Santa Ana*, 200 tons, sailing from Honduras to Spain with a general cargo, sank near Bermuda, only the people on her were saved.

13. **Year 1609.** A squadron of nine English vessels sailed from Plymouth, England, with colonists and supplies for Jamestown, Virginia. The flagship *Sea Venture*, Admiral Sir George Somers, was wrecked at Bermuda and the survivors founded the first settlement on the island.

14. **Year 1619.** An unidentified pinnace, manned mostly by Dutchmen but with a few Englishmen aboard, wrecked on the northwest shoals of Bermuda and went quickly to pieces before anything could be saved. It was returning from a privateering voyage in the West Indies.

15. **Year 1619.** English merchantman *Warwick*, owned by the Virginia

Company, was wrecked in Castle Harbor during a storm in November after it had discharged its cargo and passengers from England. In 1967 this wreck was discovered—with the help of a magnetometer—by Tucker and several persons from the Smithsonian Institution.

16. Year 1621. Merchant *nao San Antonio,* 12 cannon, owned by Simón de Vidacar, was wrecked in Bermuda while the rest of the convoy it was sailing with rode out a storm within sight of the island. Its cargo consisted of 5,000 hides, 1,200 quintals of brazilwood, 6,000 pounds of indigo, 30,000 pounds of tobacco, 5,000 pounds of sarsaparilla, and gold and silver worth 5,000 pounds sterling in English currency. Bermudans, under the direction of the governor, recovered most of its cargo, and the survivors were shipped to England several months later.

17. Year 1622. During a storm that struck the Nueva España Flota of Captain-General Fernando de Sousa, two ships were lost off Bermuda: *nao San Ignacio,* 150 tons, Captain Domingo Hernández, and the *nao Nuestra Señora de la Limpia Concepción,* 116 tons, Captain Juan Calzado.

18. Year 1639. Two small vessels, sailing in the convoy of the Tierra Firme Armada, Captain-General Gerónimo Gómez de Sandoval—*urca La Viga,* Captain Mathew Lorenzo, and the *pattachuelo El Galgo,* a prize vessel captured by the Spaniards—were wrecked on October 22 at Bermuda. The wreck site of *La Viga* was given as 3 leagues from the main village in Bermuda, and survivors from both wrecks reached shore carrying some silver with them.

19. Year 1644. An English chart of Bermuda dated 1740 had the following information marked on it:

> Among these rocks which extend above 3 leagues to the northeast of the island are a great number of wrecks and amongst others, that of a rich Spanish ship lost about the year 1644. It was once discovered, but it is now fished for in vain. Off the southwest and westnorthwest section of the island are great numbers of rocks at 3 to 4 leagues distance from land, whereby an abundance of ships have been lost.

20. Year 1659. English merchantman *Eagle,* Captain Whitby, owned by the Virginia Company, sailing from Plymouth, England, to

Jamestown, Virginia, with trade goods and passengers was wrecked on January 12 on a reef. This wreck has been discovered and partially salvaged by Tucker.

21. *Year 1660.* English merchantman *Virginia Merchant*, Captain Robert Burk, owned by the Virginia Company, sailing from Plymouth to Jamestown, was wrecked on March 26. Of the 189 persons aboard only ten were saved. This wreck has also been discovered and partially salvaged by Tucker.

22. *Year 1669.* During a hurricane a large unidentified ship was sunk at Castle Harbor in Bermuda.

23. *Year 1684.* Spanish *navío San Salvador*, Captain Pedro de Aruide, 567 tons, owned by Admiral Manuel Casadeite, sprung a bad leak and wrecked at Bermuda. After the survivors reached shore in small boats the Spaniards set the ship afire to prevent the Bermudans from salvaging her cargo.

24. *Year 1744.* English merchantman *Friendship*, Captain Hooper, sailing from St. Kitts for Barbados, was driven off course by a storm and lost near Bermuda.

25. *Year 1744.* English ship *Mary and Hannah*, Captain Savage, sailing from Genoa, Italy, for Carolina (both North and South Carolina were called just Carolina at this time) was lost at Bermuda.

26. *Year 1747.* English merchantman *Tryton*, Captain Gibbons, sailing from Carolina to London, was lost near Bermuda.

27. *Year 1747.* A ship of either American or British registry, *Dorothy and Elizabeth*, Captain Simpson, sailing from Boston for the Leeward Islands, was lost on the reefs of Bermuda.

28. *Year 1749.* English ship *Leoftoffe*, Captain Fielding, coming from Jamaica, was lost off Bermuda.

29. *Year 1750.* English ship *Margaret*, Captain Gallagar, sailing from London to Antigua, was lost near Bermuda.

30. *Year 1753.* A large unidentified Danish ship, carrying 700 hogsheads of sugar, was lost on the reefs of Bermuda.

31. *Year 1757.* English ship *Mary*, Captain Daniel, sailing from Philadelphia to Antigua, was lost near Bermuda.

32. *Year 1757.* American sloop *Hunters Galley,* Captain Clement Conyers, sailing from St. Eustatius Island to South Carolina with a general cargo, lost at Bermuda on January 11.

33. *Year 1758.* English ship *Britannia,* Captain Sorogham, sailing for London, struck on a bar leaving Bermuda and sank in 8 fathoms of water.

34. *Year 1760.* English ship *Mancheoneal,* Captain Morgan, sailing from London to Bermuda, was wrecked on the west side of the island but part of its cargo was saved.

35. *Year 1761.* English man-of-war *Griffin,* 20 guns, was lost off Bermuda on October 25, fifty of her crew were drowned.

36. *Year 1762.* English merchantman *Judith Maria,* Captain Ball, sailing from Jamaica to Bristol, England, was wrecked at Bermuda in August, crew, some cargo, and ship's stores saved.

37. *Year 1763.* English brigantine *Katherine,* Captain Simondson, sailing from Philadelphia to Jamaica, was wrecked on a reef on April 4, four of the crew drowned.

38. *Year 1764.* English ship *Peggy,* Captain M'Carthy, sailing from South Carolina to Lisbon, wrecked on a reef on March 18 and her hull slid off into 7 fathoms of water but all the people on board were saved.

39. *Year 1765.* A snow of unknown registry, *Duke,* Captain French, sailing from South Carolina to Oporto, Portugal, was wrecked on a reef.

40. *Year 1766.* English merchantman *Fairfax,* Captain Copithorn, sailing from Virginia to Bristol, was wrecked at Bermuda but part of her cargo was saved.

41. *Year 1766.* English ship *Elizabeth,* Captain Trattle, sailing from New England to Antigua, was wrecked at Bermuda.

42. *Year 1768.* American ship *Penn,* sailing from North Carolina to Bristol, was wrecked on the reefs.

43. *Year 1769.* Two ships, sailing from Jamaica to London, were wrecked in December on a reef 5 or 6 miles northwest of the island: the *Martin,* Captain Mitchell, and an unidentified vessel.

A few days later the English ship *Allitude*, Captain Rains, sailing from Carolina to Tortuga, was wrecked near the two other ships.

44. *Year 1774.* English merchantman *Industry*, Captain Lowes, sailing from Limerick to Virginia, was wrecked at Bermuda on April 13, part of her cargo was saved.

45. *Year 1777.* English warship H.M.S. *Repulse*, 32 guns, Captain Henry Davies, foundered off Bermuda.

46. *Year 1777.* Spanish privateering vessel *Mark Antonio*, Captain Jean-Bautist Hugonne, sailing from St. Eustatius to Cape Henlopen, was wrecked on the island on July 18.

47. *Year 1779.* English ship *Nancy*, Captain Manley, sailing from Jamaica to Bristol, was lost entering a port in Bermuda.

48. *Year 1780.* During a terrible hurricane on October 18, over fifty ships were wrecked or driven aground on the island.

49. *Year 1781.* English merchantman *Lord Frederick*, sailing from Clyde, Scotland, to Charleston, South Carolina, was wrecked at Bermuda.

50. *Year 1783.* Three English warships were lost on the island: H.M.S. *Cerberus*, a 32-gun frigate, Captain Sir Jacob Wheate, was wrecked shortly after leaving Castle Harbor; H.M.S. *Pallas*, 36 guns, Captain Christopher Parker, ran ashore on St. George's Isle; and the H.M.S. *Mentor*, 16 guns, Captain R. Tullidge, was wrecked on a reef.

51. *Year 1783.* A Dutch merchantman, *Stadt Cortrycht*, Captain Harmong, sailing from Dominica Island to Ostend, Holland, carrying a cargo of sugar, was wrecked on a reef while attempting to enter a harbor on June 24.

52. *Year 1784.* Two merchantmen were wrecked on the reefs of Bermuda: Scottish brig *Betsey*, Captain Camarn, sailing from St. Kitts to Cork, Ireland, lost in March, crew and most of cargo saved; and an Irish ship, *Lord Donegal*, Captain Campbell, sailing from Belfast to Virginia, lost on Feburary 9, crew and small part of cargo saved.

53. *Year 1786.* American ship *Kingston*, Captain Farrer, sailing from North Carolina to Grenada Island, was lost off Bermuda but her people were saved.

54. *Year 1787.* A ship of unknown registry, *Swift,* Captain M'Donald, sailing from Grenada Island to Newfoundland, was lost off Bermuda but her crew was saved.

55. *Year 1788.* During a hurricane on July 26 a large number of ships were wrecked on the southwestern side of Bermuda.

56. *Year 1700.* French ship *Marie Thérèse,* Captain Guathier, sailing from Santo Domingo to Bordeaux, France, was lost near Bermuda, only a few bales of cotton were saved.

57. *Year 1792.* French ship *Grand Annibal,* Captain Caisergues, sailing from Santo Domingo to Marseilles, was lost off Bermuda.

58. *Year 1792.* French brig *Le Grand Aanictl,* 350 tons, sailing from Hispaniola to Marseilles with a rich cargo, struck a reef on July 4 off the west side of Bermuda. at a great distance from shore, then slid off into deep water. The captain and several passengers drowned but other survivors reached the island in a boat with only the clothes on their backs. (Note that this may be the same ship mentioned in #57.)

59. *Year 1794.* English warship, the brig *Actif,* 10 guns, Captain John Harvey, foundered off Bermuda on November 26.

60. *Year 1794.* Two merchantmen of unknown registry were lost about the same time near the island: *George Douglas,* sailing from Havana to Newfoundland, was wrecked on a reef on the north side of the island, then slid off into deeper water; and the brig *Harriet,* Captain Monteath, was wrecked on the south side of the island.

61. *Year 1795.* Three merchantmen of unknown registry were lost around the island prior to June: *Minerva,* Captain Arnet, sailing from Norfolk, Virginia, to Tobago Island, was wrecked on a reef, crew and part of cargo saved; an unnamed brig of Captain Clark, sailing from Newhaven, England, to St. Vincent's Island, was wrecked on the north side of the island; and an unidentified ship sailing from Madeira Island to Baltimore.

62. *Year 1796.* Two American vessels were lost: the schooner *Polly,* coming from Norfolk, and the ship *Nancy,* Captain Mitchell, sailing from Philadelphia to' Jamaica. The latter's crew was saved.

63. *Year 1800.* American brig *Humber,* Captain Clough, sailing from New York to Havana, was wrecked on a reef prior to April.

64. *Year 1801.* Three merchantmen were lost: American ship *Dispatch,* Captain Ramsey, sailing from Nevis Island to New England, wrecked on a reef, crew and part of cargo saved; a ship of unknown registry, *Ebenezer,* Captain Sharman, sailing to Santo Domingo; and another ship of unknown registry, the *Mary Ann,* Captain Greave, sailing from New York to Montserrat Island, only the crew was saved.

65. *Year 1802.* Two American merchantmen were lost on January 1 because of fog: brig *Commerce,* Captain English, sailing from New England to St. Croix Island; and the schooner *Roebuck,* Captain Forester, sailing from Boston to the West Indies—both wrecked on reefs, crews and part of cargoes saved.

66. *Year 1803.* American merchantman *Margaret,* Captain Muir, sailing from Virginia to Barbados, was lost near the island on January 19.

67. *Year 1804.* Two merchantmen were lost: English ship *Providence,* Captain Burnet (or Barnick), sailing from Havana to Spain, on October 20, only the crew was saved; and a ship of unknown registry, *Surprise,* Captain Renshaw, sailing from the Cape of Good Hope to Philadelphia, prior to July.

68. *Year 1805.* American ship *Hunter,* Captain Slout, sailing from New York to Martinique Island, was wrecked on November 30, crew and part of cargo saved.

69. *Year 1806.* French ship *Pamela,* Captain Demeul, sailing from Quebec to Jamaica, was lost prior to March. Two merchantmen of English registry were wrecked in December: *Loyal Sam,* coming from London with a valuable cargo, and the *Three Friends,* Captain Pullinge, coming from Philadelphia. Both were lost because of gales.

70. *Year 1807.* Three ships were wrecked on the reefs: the English warship H.M.S. *Subtle,* 8 guns, Captain William Dowers, lost on October 26 near Somerset Island; American ship *Rosannah,* Captain Mull, sailing from Baltimore to Venezuela, lost on February 23; and a ship of unknown registry, the *Merchant,* Captain Day, coming from New London, Connecticut, to Bermuda, on March 21.

71. *Year 1808.* A ship of unknown registry, *Batavia*, Captain Houghton, sailing from Trinidad to Liverpool, was lost on the Bermuda bar, only the crew was saved.

72. *Year 1809.* English ship *William Grey*, Captain King, sailing to Jamaica, was wrecked on a reef on August 29 on the west side of the island, crew and most of cargo saved.

73. *Year 1810.* English merchantman *William & Mary*, Captain Clifton, with a cargo of sherry wine, was wrecked in February, crew and part of wine saved.

74. *Year 1811.* Three merchantmen of unknown registry were wrecked on reefs: small vessel *Montgomery*, Captain Bignell, coming from Bristol, four of the crew were saved and three drowned; ship *Frederick*, Captain White, sailing from New York to the West Indies, on Feburary 1; and the ship *Eliza*, Captain Lord, sailing from New York to Guadeloupe, on April 30, but her cargo was saved.

75. *Year 1812.* Three ships were wrecked on the reefs: English warship H.M.S. *Barbados*, 28 guns, Captain Thomas Huskisson, lost on September 29 at Sable Island, only one of the crew of 195 was lost; Spanish ship *Pensacola del Sol*, sailing from Pensacola, Florida, to London, struck a reef on the west side of the island on March 29 but her cargo was saved; and another Spanish ship, *Antonia*, sailing from Havana to Tenerife in the Canary Islands, was wrecked on a reef to the north of the island on October 24, crew and small part of cargo saved.

76. *Year 1813.* During a hurricane that struck the island on August 1, a large number of ships were driven ashore or sunk in the harbor. Two English ships were wrecked on reefs: *Lady Emily*, a packet boat, was lost in June but the crew and passengers were saved; the merchantman *Pacific*, sailing from Halifax to Barbados, was lost on December 27, only the crew was saved.

77. *Year 1815.* During a hurricane on August 7, many vessels were driven ashore or sunk. On August 15 the English warship H.M.S. *Dominica*, 14 guns, Captain Richard Crawford, was wrecked on a reef.

78. *Year 1816.* English ship *Duke of Wellington*, Captain Williams, sailing from London for Bermuda and Jamaica, was wrecked on a reef in March off the west side of the island, only a small part of her stores was saved.

79. *Year 1817.* Three ships of unknown registry were lost: *Peter*, Captain Chadwick, coming from East Florida, wrecked on a reef in February; *Elizabeth*, Captain Largie, sailing from Barbados to America, on February 19; and the *Emma*, Captain Morgan, sailing from New York to St. Vincent's Island, wrecked on a reef on October 5, crew and part of cargo saved.

80. *Year 1818.* Six merchantmen were lost: English ship *Caesar*, Captain James Richardson, sailing from Newcastle, England, to Baltimore with a cargo of bricks, bottles, and grindstones, was wrecked on a reef on May 17 but part of her cargo and rigging were saved (this wreck has been partially salvaged by Tucker); American ship *Hope*, coming from New York, was wrecked at the island on August 30 during a gale; English ship *Alfred the Great*, sailing from Jamaica to London, was wrecked on a reef on the west side of the island on September 8, part of her cargo was saved; English ship *Admiral Durham*, sailing from Demerara to Bermuda, was wrecked during a gale on a reef off the west side of the island on December 23, one of the crew drowned and some of her cargo of rum was saved; the American ship *Mary*, sailing from New York to St. Thomas, and an unidentified English brig, coming from Barbados to Bermuda, wrecked on reefs off the southwestern point of the island on December 25.

81. *Year 1819.* Three merchant ships were lost: French ship *Lydia*, sailing from Bordeaux to New York, was lost near the island, crew, passengers, and part of cargo saved; a ship of unknown registry, *St. Helena*, sailing from Jamaica to Quebec, wrecked on a reef on May 18, only a small part of her cargo was saved; and English ship *Hamilton*, Captain Adams, coming from Antigua, was wrecked on the east side of the island.

82. *Year 1821.* American ship *Pallas*, coming from Savannah, was lost on June 17.

83. *Year 1822.* American brig *Indian Chief*, Captain M'Vicar, sailing from Jamaica to New Brunswick, was wrecked on a reef on the north end of the island on January 12.

84. **Year 1823.** Three merchantmen were wrecked on the reefs: Dutch ship *Vriendscaap*, Captain de Jong, sailing from Surinam to Amsterdam, off the west end of the island on May 2; American schooner *Collector*, Captain Hall, sailing from St. John's, New Brunswick, to Bermuda and South America with a general cargo, on May 26; and the American ship *Mary*, Captain Campbell, sailing from Philadelphia to St. Thomas, off the northern part of the island on August 15, crew and part of cargo saved.

85. **Year 1824.** American ship *Cyno*, Captain Dessey, sailing from New York to St. Croix, was totally lost on a reef off the northwestern part of the island on August 5.

CHAPTER SEVEN

The Bahamas

THE BAHAMA archipelago is one of the most interesting areas for working on shipwrecks in the Western Hemisphere because of its gin-clear water, ideal year-around weather conditions, and vast number of ancient shipwrecks. Its close proximity to the United States is another advantage to American divers, as there is less expense involved in working a wreck site close to home than one a greater distance away. For this reason, next to Florida, most of the search and salvage work on shipwrecks undertaken by Americans has been done in the Bahamas.

As early as a century before Nassau was first settled by the English in the early 1700s, Bermudan wreckers had bases in different areas of the Bahamas and carried out salvage work. After Nassau was settled, wreck-salvage work—or "wracking," as they called it—was the principal occupation until as late as the end of the American Civil

War. Many of today's wealthy Bahamian families got their start through the "wracking" business. Even now most Bahamian fishermen still use their glass-bottom buckets not only to locate conch and turtles but in the hope of stumbling across a good treasure wreck. Tales of these fishermen occasionally making good discoveries are as numerous as the number of keys and islands in the Bahamas, but rarely can any of the tales be verified. I know of one exception: About ten years ago a fisherman from Grand Cay showed me several gold and silver bars and several hundred gold coins he had discovered somewhere nearby, but he refused to reveal the location of the wreck. About 1933, several fishermen recovered a metal safe containing approximately $100,000 in American gold coins, dating from the American Civil War, on a reef off the north side of Green Turtle Key. Several years later, another fisherman recovered "a boatload" of silver and gold bars off a reef in the Exuma Chain, and all of this treasure was sold for only its metal value. In 1947, after a storm, three Bahamian fishermen living on Gorda Cay discovered five large silver bars and a substantial number of silver coins on a beach on the south side of Gorda Cay. News of their discovery spread quickly and the following year an American diver from Florida, Art McKee, appeared on the scene. One of the fishermen who had discovered the five silver bars showed McKee the location of two small ballast piles offshore from the area where they had discovered the treasure. They were the site of the two Spanish salvage boats that had been wrecked in 1657 while trying to carry some of the treasure salvaged off the galleon *Nuestra Señora de las Maravillas,* sunk north of Memory Rock in 1656. McKee—in helmet-diving equipment—spent several days laboriously moving all the ballast rock. It was well worth the effort, as he discovered three silver bars, a number of iron cannon bars, and some ceramic sherds. Then, in 1950, two Nassau businessmen, Roscoe Thompson and Howard Lightbourn, claimed to have discovered another silver bar from one of the same ballast piles. However, rumor has it that their silver bar was actually one of the five the fishermen had found on the beach and that they had bought it from them for only fifty dollars. During the past twenty years there have been at least two dozen expeditions around Gorda Key, but no one has reported making any other important discoveries.

The major treasure discovery reported in recent years occurred in January 1965, when four American divers—Gary Simmons, Dick Tindale, Jack Slack, and Bissel Shaefer—reported that they had ac-

TOP: A 72-pound silver bar recovered from the Spanish galleon *Nuestra Señora de las Maravillas*, lost in 1656 on the Little Bahama Bank. BOTTOM: Two gold lockets from the same wreck.

TOP: Large sunken building located off the north side of Andros Island, to the east of Bimini from the air. BOTTOM: Two divers inspecting an anchor found on a wreck near *Nuestra Señora de las Maravillas*.

cidentally stumbled on a treasure wreck near Lucava Beach and recovered an immense treasure. At first their find was reported to
be worth over $20 million, but this amount gradually dwindled.
Recently several numismatists were hired by the Bahamian government and they placed the total value of the find at only $40,000,
which is a far cry from $20 million. Actually, the find might someday
reach $20 million if this group or another group eventually discovers
the main section of the wreck from which their silver coins came
or the other Spanish galleon that sank nearby at the time. Both galleons
were carrying a great deal of treasure and were captured in 1628 by
a Dutch fleet in Matanzas Bay, Cuba, and were lost while returning
to Holland with the Dutch fleet.

The most recent discovery in the Bahamas was neither of a shipwreck nor a treasure. Dr. Manson Valentine and Dimitri Rebikoff,
both competent archaeologists, have discovered several submerged
buildings off the northern tip of Andros Island and also what appears
to be an ancient seaport off the west end of Bimini. Although the
press stated that they had found the sunken continent of Atlantis,
they do not believe so. Although they are convinced that it is of
pre-Columbian origin, until excavations are carried out they refuse
to make wild statements. I dived with them on the Bimini site and
believe it may be the remains of a Phoenician or some early-European
seaport. As to the buildings off Andros, my guess is that they may
have been built by the Mayan or some other advanced Mexican-
Indian culture, as none of the Indians of the Caribbean or Florida built
stone structures.

No permission is required for divers to explore for shipwrecks in
the Bahamas. To salvage a wreck, however, a permit must be obtained
from the Ministry of Transportation. Permits are granted on each
wreck site for periods of five years. Salvors keep 75 percent of what
is recovered and the Bahamian government receives 25 percent.
Several years ago an American diver who salvaged a shipwreck
without a permit was arrested and sentenced to a year in prison.

In my files I have over three thousand Bahamian shipwrecks, but I
have selected only those of which I have a fairly accurate location
or those of special importance.

List of Shipwrecks in Bahamian Waters

1. **Year 1500.** In July or August, two unidentified caravels of the four sailing in the squadron of Vicente Yanez Pinzón, from Brazil to Spain, were wrecked near Crooked Island.

2. **Year 1551.** Unidentified galleon, owned by the viceroy of Mexico, Don Luis de Velasco, sailing in the Nueva España Flota, commanded by Captain-General Sancho de Viedma, separated from the convoy during a storm, was wrecked on Silver Shoals, then sank in deeper water. Divers were able to recover only 150,000 pesos of the treasure it carried.

3. **Year 1554.** Two unidentified ships carrying a great amount of silver suffered from a storm in the Bahama Channel and soon after were wrecked on one of the Bahama islands near Hispaniola, but all the persons and treasure were taken ashore. A small frigate was made from the remains of both wrecks and sent to Cuba, but it sank on the way and only two were saved from it. Salvors were sent from Cuba but they were not able to locate the island where the survivors and silver were marooned.

4. **Year 1564.** Galleon *Santa Clara,* 300 tons, Captain Juan Diaz Bozino, sailing in the Tierra Firme Armada of Captain-General Estevan de las Alas, ran aground on October 6 on the El Mime Shoal but all of its people, gold, and silver were saved by other ships of the convoy. On sixteenth-century charts, this shoal was situated several miles north of Memory Rock on the Little Bahama Bank. Later on the shoal was called Mimbres by the Spaniards.

5. **Year 1567.** Unidentified *urca* of Captain Gonzalo de Peñalosa was wrecked on Cayo Romano in the Little Bahama Channel.

6. **Year 1599.** A Spanish merchant ship owned by Hernando del Castillo was sailing to Havana when it was captured by some pirates. The Spaniards and their cargo were taken aboard the pirate vessel, which soon after anchored on Great Inagua Island. The Spaniards escaped in a small boat and headed for Cuba, but enroute they stopped at a large cay for water and accidentally discovered an enormous treasure of gold and silver

bars and pieces of artillery from ships that must have wrecked there. They took some of the treasure with them, then other vessels were sent from Cuba and picked up the remainder.

7. **Year 1628.** Two unidentified Spanish galleons carrying treasures were wrecked during the night near Golden Rock, on the south side of Grand Bahama Island. They were in the Dutch fleet commanded by Piet Heyn and had been captured in Matanzas Bay, Cuba. A section of one of these two ships was discovered several years ago off Lucaya Beach and a considerable amount of silver coins were recovered, but a great amount of treasure remains undiscovered.

8. **Year 1641.** Galleon *Nuestra Señora de la Concepción*, 680 tons, Captain Hernando Rodriquez, sailing in the Nueva España Flota of Captain-General Juan de Campos, was separated from the convoy during a storm in the Bahama Channel and drifted without masts or rudder until wrecking on the north side of Silver Shoals. Most of the six hundred persons aboard managed to swim to a nearby sandbar. Makeshift rafts and boats were constructed from the wreck, and they carried about two hundred of the survivors toward Santo Domingo, but only a few ever reached safety. By the time a rescue vessel reached the area, all of the persons had perished on the sandbar. Bad weather prevented salvage operations for several months, and when the weather finally moderated, the sandbar had been washed away and the rescuers could not locate the wreck site. The story of Sir William Phips's recovery of the treasure from this galleon in 1687 is well-known, but for some unknown reason a myth has persisted stating that he did not recover all of the treasure from this wreck. The fact is that he recovered almost twice the amount that the ship's registers stated she carried, and other salvors worked on the wreck both before and after Phips arrived on the scene, so there is little likelihood that there is much more left. Still, almost every year during the past two decades, there have been major expeditions after this wreck, the last during the summer of 1968, when Jacques Cousteau failed to locate the wreck.

9. **Year 1644.** Three unidentified English privateers in the squadron of General Jacob Jackson were wrecked on Arcas Reef in the Old Bahama Channel.

10. **Year 1656.** Galleon *Nuestra Señora de la Maravillas*, 650 tons, Admiral Mathias de Orelanas, which was the *Almiranta* in the Tierra Firme Armada of Captain General Margues de Montenegro, sank in 5 or 6 fathoms of water on the Little Bahama Bank, about 20 miles north of Memory Rock, after first colliding with another galleon during the night when the whole convoy found itself in shallow water and veered seaward. Of the more than seven hundred persons on this ship, only fifty-six were saved. Spaniards began salvage operations soon afterward and, during the next three years, recovered over 1,500,000 pesos of the 5 million pesos of treasure on this wreck. Shifting sands, however, soon covered the wreck over completely, so they had to abandon future salvage operations. In 1681, Phips stopped at the site of this wreck and recovered only a small amount of silver specie due to the sand over it. In modern times, many treasure-hunters have searched for this wreck, but most of them in the Florida Keys—where other authors have placed the site of the wreck—until I discovered documents in Spain and learned its true location. I passed this information on to a group from Miami in 1960 and they spent several years searching for the wreck, but to no avail. They in turn gave it to others, but so far no one has located it.

In 1657, two small salvage vessels, carrying some of the treasure from this wreck to Puerto Rico, were wrecked on the south side of Gorda Cay. The survivors buried some of the treasure on the cay and most of it—as well as most of what was still on the wrecks—was recovered the following year. The three silver bars discovered by Art McKee, and the one by Roscoe Thompson and Howard Lightbourn, came from these two wrecks.

11. **Year about 1660.** An unidentified English ship, Captain Sayle, was wrecked on Eleuthera Island. Sayle went to Virginia in a small boat, returning later in a larger vessel to rescue the survivors.

12. **Year 1669.** English ship *Port Royal*, Captain John Russel, was wrecked in latitude 26 degrees and 14 minutes at Munsake Island, near Abaco, on January 12. Modern charts do not show an island by this name.

13. **Year before 1687.** On a chart drawn in 1687 by a Captain Salman of the Little Bahama Bank, three shipwreck locations are shown.

Copper Wreck, bearing 10 degrees from Memory Rock, in latitude 27°02'11" North, about 1½ miles from the edge of the bank; *Genovees Wreck,* bearing northwest by about 3½ English leagues from the *Copper Wreck,* in latitude 27°10'11" North, about half a mile from the edge of the bank; *Plate Wreck,* bearing 15 degrees and 10 nautical miles from the *Genovees Wreck,* in about 6 fathoms of water, in latitude 27°20'11" North, and about 3 nautical miles from the edge of the bank.

14. **Year 1694.** Dutch merchantman *Jufron Gertrud,* Captain Derrick Loffrey, carrying 74,000 pieces of eight and a great quantity of merchandise, was wrecked near Great Isaac Cay. Survivors reached Nassau in a small boat and salvors returned to the wreck, recovering all of the treasure and most of her cargo. They sighted another wreck nearby and again recovered things of value.

15. **Year 1702.** Unidentified American brigantine was chased by pirates and forced to run aground on Eleuthera Island, where they plundered her. They also forced another unidentified ship to wreck at Mayaguana Island, where they burnt her to the waterline after plundering her.

16. **Year 1704.** A Bermudan privateer commanded by Captain Peniston captured an unidentified French merchantman sailing from Martinique to France with a cargo of sugar, indigo, cocoa, and drugs. After transferring some of the cargo to the privateer's vessel the French ship was wrecked on Great Abaco Island.

17. **Year 1705.** English packet boat *Barbadoes* was wrecked December 28 on Great Inagua Island, mail and money saved.

18. **Year 1713.** Large French merchantman, *Count de Paix,* Captain Lewis Doyer, sailing from Hispaniola to France with a cargo of gold dust, ambergris, sugar, indigo, and other products, was wrecked on Great Inagua and only the gold dust and ambergris was saved.

19. **Year 1714.** Galleon *San Juan Evangelista,* part of the Armada de Barlovento, sailing from Veracruz to Puerto Rico and Santo Domingo with 300,000 pesos in treasure to pay the royal officials and military at both islands, was struck by a storm in the Bahama Channel and wrecked in 27 degrees of latitude in 4 fathoms of water near Grand Bahama Island. Salvors recovered all of the treasure and the ship's cannon.

20. *Year 1715.* An unidentified Spanish warship with two hundred men aboard, sailing from Havana to St. Augustine, Florida, with chests of silver specie to pay the garrison there, was wrecked on the Little Bahama Bank. Salvors from Havana recovered all of the treasure and then burnt the wreck.

21. *Year 1723.* Ship identified only by the name *Petatch*—which may be the English spelling for a *patache*—was wrecked near Bimini.

22. *Year 1724.* Unidentified French frigate was wrecked at Caye de Argent (or Silver Cay), on the Caicos Bank.

23. *Year 1731.* English merchantman *Bridget & Kitty*, Captain Minshall, sailing from Jamaica to Liverpool, was wrecked on Little Inagua Island but her crew were saved.

24. *Year 1741.* Unidentified Spanish *nao* was wrecked on Lobos Cay, near the Old Bahama Channel.

25. *Year 1744.* An unidentified Spanish merchantman of 300 tons and two hundred men, sailing from Cadiz for Mexico with a cargo valued at over 300,000 pounds sterling, was forced ashore on Sugar Cay by the famous American privateer Captain Lamprier, whose ship was also wrecked nearby.

26. *Year 1750.* English merchantman *Duke of Cumberland*, Captain Prenton, sailing from Jamaica to London, was lost March 27 on the Acklin Keys, crew and part of cargo saved.

27. *Year 1751.* English merchantman *Katherine*, Captain Richards, sailing from Jamaica to Bristol, was lost on Great Inagua Island but the crew was saved.

28. *Year 1751.* English merchantman *Duncanon*, Captain Elphinston, sailing from Jamaica to London, was lost on the Hogsties in the Windward Passage but the crew were saved.

29. *Year 1751.* English merchantman *Jane*, Captain Caton, sailing from Jamaica to London, was wrecked off Acklin's Key but the crew was saved by a French vessel.

30. *Year 1751.* English ship *Warwick*, Captain Manepenny, sailing from Philadelphia to Hispaniola, was lost August 8 at Atwood Key but the crew was saved.

31. *Year 1752.* English merchantman *Lord Duplin,* Captain Thompson, sailing from Jamaica to Liverpool, was wrecked on the Hogsties but the crew were saved.

32. *Year 1753.* American merchantman *Polly,* Captain Walker, sailing from Rhode Island to Jamaica, was lost on Silver Shoals near the Spanish galleon that wrecked there in 1641.

33. *Year 1754.* French merchantman *Anna Maria,* sailing from Hispaniola to France with a cargo of indigo and sugar, was wrecked at Crooked Island.

34. *Year 1755.* A ship of unknown registry, *John and Rebecca,* Captain Rice, sailing from Jamaica to Philadelphia, was lost June 8 on Great Inagua Island.

35. *Year 1758.* Spanish ship *Caesar,* sailing from Havana to Spain, was lost on Annagabes Island but her crew was saved. This island has a different name today, as no island by this name is shown on any charts of the Bahamas.

36. *Year 1758.* A ship of unknown registry, *St. Francis,* sailing from Philadelphia to Antigua was forced ashore on Sandy Cay by a French privateer.

37. *Year 1760.* A ship of unknown registry, *Prince Ferdinand,* Captain Caznean, sailing from Boston to Jamaica, lost January 17 on Great Inagua Island but the crew was saved.

38. *Year 1761.* English merchantman *Eagle Gally,* Captain Nash, sailing from Jamaica to Bristol, was wrecked on the Hogsties but her crew was saved.

39. *Year 1762.* English merchantman *Gambia,* Captain Whiting, sailing from Jamaica to Bristol, was lost on West Caicos Island but the crew was saved.

40. *Year 1763.* English ship *Peter Beckford,* Captain Lovelace, sailing from Jamaica to London, was lost on a reef at San Salvador Island.

41. *Year 1763.* English merchantman *Patty,* Captain Clark, sailing from Bristol, was lost near Nassau.

42. *Year 1764.* Large French ship *Le Bernard,* sailing from Hispaniola to France, was totally lost July 4 on Turks Island.

43. *Year 1765.* English merchantman *Medway Planter,* Captain Leslie, sailing from Jamaica to London, was lost April 25 on a reef near Cat Island but her crew was saved.

44. *Year 1765.* According to an English historian writing in 1775, a very rich unidentified Spanish galleon was wrecked in 1765 on a shoal of sand located 7 miles southwest from Beak Cay, the southernmost cay in the Riding Rock Chain, in 17 feet of water. Some treasure was recovered at the time of the disaster but the wreck sanded over before the majority of it could be recovered.

45. *Year 1768.* English merchantman *Defiance,* Captain Carock, sailing from Honduras to London, was lost March 21 on the Little Bahama Bank, but her crew was saved.

46. *Year 1768.* Two American ships were lost on the Caicos Bank: *Beggars Benizon,* Captain Rogers, lost May 31 while sailing from Charleston, South Carolina, to Jamaica; and *The Charm,* Captain Peggy Stinton, sailing from North Carolina to Jamaica.

47. *Year 1769.* English merchantman *Meylor,* Captain Tyler, sailing from Bristol and Boston to Jamaica, was lost at Caicos but her crew was saved.

48. *Year 1769.* American ship *Nancy Gaer,* sailing from Hispaniola to Georgia, lost May 17 on Great Inagua Island but her crew was saved.

49. *Year 1770.* A large unidentified merchant sloop was wrecked on a reef at Long Key and salvors recovered several chests of Spanish silver species from it.

50. *Year 1772.* English merchantman *Merredith,* Captain Peacock, sailing from Jamaica to London, was lost on San Salvador Island and her cargo totally lost, but crew saved.

51. *Year 1772.* An unidentified three-decked merchantman was lost on the southwest cay of the Caicos Bank.

52. *Year 1773.* English merchantman *John,* Captain Madge, sailing from Jamaica to Bristol, was lost off Gun Cay, to the south of Bimini, but her crew was saved.

53. *Year 1774.* A ship of unknown registry, *Palliser,* was lost on New Providence Island.

54. **Year 1774.** Three unidentified ships were wrecked on the Little Bahama Bank, north of Memory Rock, but the current was too strong for several passing ships to send rescue boats.

55. **Year 1774.** Two English ships were lost on Great Inagua Island: *Hanover Planter*, Captain M'Cullock, sailing from Jamaica to Philadelphia, crew and cargo saved; and the *Martha*, Captain M'Intosh, sailing from Jamaica to London, most of her cargo of rum and sugar saved.

56. **Year 1775.** During a hurricane on November 2, at least eleven merchantmen and several English warships were lost in the Windward Passage near the Caicos Islands.

57. **Year 1775.** A ship of unknown registry, *Expectation*, Captain Wake, was lost August 10 on the windward side of Long Island, crew and part of cargo saved.

58. **Year 1775.** Two ships were lost on the Hogsties: unidentified French ship coming from Port au Prince, and English merchant-man *Port Morant*, Captain Raffles, from Jamaica to London, carrying a cargo of rum and sugar, crew clung to rocks for ten days until rescued.

59. **Year 1780.** English warship H.M.S. *Sterling Castle*, lost October 6 on Silver Shoals and went to pieces in a few minutes, only a small number were saved after floating on wreckage for days.

60. **Year 1781.** American ship *Pink*, Captain Hasrwen, sailing from New York to Jamaica, was lost in January on Silver Shoals but her crew was saved.

61. **Year 1784.** A ship of unknown registry, *David*, Captain Boyd, was lost April 30 at New Providence Island.

62. **Year 1785.** French ship *Marquis de Castries*, sailing from Cape François, Hispaniola, to France, was totally lost on the Caicos.

63. **Year 1785.** Three ships were lost at New Providence Island: English transport *Hope Sherrer*, during a hurricane in September, totally lost; a ship of unknown registry, *Sally*, Captain Croskill, wrecked at Nassau on October 24; and American ship *Rodney*, Captain Jenkins, sailing from Florida to Jamaica, sprung a leak and sank on the Samphire reefs near Nassau.

64. *Year 1786.* Bahamian ship *Bahama,* sailing from Honduras to Nassau, was totally lost during a gale at Bimini on March 4.

65. *Year 1786.* Two American merchantmen were lost at Turks Island: *Sally,* Captain Alexander, sailing from Jamaica to Maryland; and the *Porgey,* Captain Dickson, sailing from New York to Jamaica.

66. *Year 1787.* English merchantman *Charlotte,* Captain Potter, sailing to London, and several unidentified ships were lost at Nassau.

67. *Year 1787.* Large three-decked English merchantman was wrecked on the south end of Acklins Key but her crew was saved.

68. *Year 1787.* Three ships were lost on Great Inagua Island: American ship *Mercury,* Captain Hemsley, sailing from Charleston, South Carolina, to Jamaica; English ship *Jane,* coming from Jamaica; and an unidentified French brig, most of crew and part of cargo saved.

69. *Year 1788.* English merchantman *Lord North,* Captain Maver, sailing from Liverpool for Nassau, was lost on San Salvador Island but part of her cargo was salvaged.

70. *Year 1788.* Spanish brigantine of war, *Infanta,* 18 cannon, Captain Casmiro de Madrid, was wrecked on the reefs of Little Inagua Island, only the crew was saved.

71. *Year 1789.* French ship *Bonne Mère,* 350 tons, Captain David, sailing from Hispaniola to France, was totally lost on San Salvador.

72. *Year 1790.* English merchantman *Triton,* sailing from Jamaica to England, lost June 19 on the Hogsties, crew and part of cargo saved.

73. *Year 1790.* French ship *Le Belisaire,* Captain Kelly, sailing from Hispaniola to Philadelphia, was lost on Salt Pond Reef, crew and part of cargo saved.

74. *Year 1790.* English warship H.M.S. *Endymion,* Captain Woodriff, wrecked on a shoal 4 miles southwest of Sand Key, near Turks Island, in 9 feet of water, but her crew was saved.

75. *Year 1791.* Four ships were wrecked on Great Inagua Island: American ship *St. George,* Captain Vincent, sailing from Jamaica to North Carolina, part of her cargo was saved; English merchantman *Simon Taylor*, carrying cargo of rum and cotton, on May 25, passengers and crew were saved; an unidentified French frigate, sailing from Hispaniola to France, on May 10, troops and crew were all saved; and the French warship *La Fouvette*, 20 guns, sailing from Hispaniola to France, on November 26. After jettisoning all of her guns, provisions, water casks, and part of her ballast, she got off the reef and went to Jamaica for repairs.

76. *Year 1791.* Irish merchantman *Two Sisters*, Captain Sedley, sailing from Cork to Nassau, lost at Royal Island, near New Providence Island.

77. *Year 1791.* Two ships were lost near the northeastern end of Turks Island: American brig *Mary*, Captain Telfair, sailing from New York to Jamaica, on October 25; and the English brig *Dartmouth*, Captain Kimm, on October 26.

78. *Year 1791.* Two ships were lost near Great Abaco Island: American ship *Robert & Mary*, Captain Cameron, sailing from Wilmington to Barbados, on the North Cay near the island; and the English merchantman *Concord*, Captain Forresdale, sailing from London to Nassau, close to the island, part of her cargo was saved.

79. *Year 1792.* French slave ship *L'Armitie*, Captain Jabalet, sailing from Africa to Havana with a cargo of slaves and ivory, lost near Cay Santo Domingo in the Old Bahama Channel.

80. *Year 1792.* American ship *Three Sisters*, Captain Spears, sailing from South Carolina to Nassau, lost on Guana Cay but her crew was saved.

81. *Year 1792.* English merchantman *Cohen*, Captain Davis, sailing from Jamaica to Liverpool, lost near Fish Key.

82. *Year 1792.* Canadian ship *Felicity*, Captain Doty, coming from New Brunswick, Canada, lost near Turks Island.

83. *Year 1792.* French ship *Neckar*, Captain Voltearo, sailing from Santo Domingo to France, was wrecked on the Hogsties.

84. *Year 1792.* Two ships wrecked on Great Inagua Island: French merchantman *Patrice*, Captain Largement, from Hispaniola to

France; and the American ship *Lark*, Captain Barry, from Santo Domingo to New England.

85. *Year 1792*. Two ships were lost on the Caicos Bank: English ship *Friendship*, Captain Riche, sailing from Philadelphia to Jamaica, on the Great Caicos Reef; and an unidentified merchantman on the southwestern part of the bank.

86. *Year 1793*. American ship *Hannah*, Captain Bright, from Hispaniola to Wilmington, lost on Long Island. her crew was lost.

87. *Year 1794*. English merchantman *Active*, Captain Howard, sailing from Jamaica to London, wrecked at Cat Cay, south of Bimini, part of her cargo was saved.

88. *Year 1794*. American ship *Calcutta*, Captain Orange, sailing from New York to Havana, was lost on the Atwood Keys.

89. *Year 1794*. A ship of unknown registry, *Eliza*, Captain Huggins, sailing from Nassau to Santo Domingo, lost on the Crooked Island Reef.

90. *Year 1796*. English warship H.M.S. *Narcissus*, 24 guns, Captain Percy Fraser, wrecked on Sandy Key, near Nassau, her crew was saved.

91. *Year 1796*. Two ships were lost on the Great Inagua Island reef: English merchantman *Hestor*, Captain Pearson, sailing from Santo Domingo to London, in July, crew was saved; and the American ship *Eagle*, Captain Byrnes, sailing from Santo Domingo to Baltimore, a small part of her cargo was saved.

92. *Year 1797*. Two ships lost on Great Inagua Island: Jamaican privateer *Nelly*, sailing from Jamaica to Nassau, and the American schooner *William*, sailing from Baltimore, most of her cargo was saved.

93. *Year 1798*. American ship *Jenny*, Captain Knox, sailing from Havana to Philadelphia, wrecked on Mantanilla Reef, on the Little Bahama Bank, but her crew was saved.

94. *Year 1798*. A ship of unknown registry, *Eliza*, Captain Grant, sailing from the Azores to Santo Domingo, lost September 21 on Gran Caicos Island but her crew was saved.

95. *Year 1799.* English merchantman *Cecilia,* Captain Roach, sailing from Jamaica to Liverpool, lost on the Hogsties, her crew was saved.

96. *Year 1799.* American ship *Hamilton,* Captain Noval, sailing from Savannah to Jamaica, lost on the Caicos Bank.

97. *Year 1800.* English merchantman *Doudswell,* Captain M'Lean, coming from London, was lost at New Providence Island but her crew was saved.

98. *Year 1800.* During August the English warship H.M.S. *Lowestoffe* and eight merchantmen carrying cargoes of colonial produce valued at over 600,000 pounds sterling were totally wrecked on Great Inagua Island.

99. *Year 1801.* During a hurricane in July over 120 ships of various descriptions and sizes were wrecked, sunk, or thrown on the beach near and at Nassau. Only a slave ship named *George* was identified.

100. *Year 1801.* English merchantman *Supply,* Captain Wallace, sailing from Honduras to London, was wrecked at Mohairs Key, near New Providence Island.

101. *Year 1801.* In December a large English merchantman coming from Jamaica was wrecked on the Hogsties but slipped off the reef and sank in deeper water before she could be identified.

102. *Year 1801.* American ship *Endeavour,* Captain Russel, sailing from North Carolina to the Bahamas, was lost on Long Island.

103. *Year 1801.* Three American ships were lost near Little Caicos Island: *Acress,* Captain Lynch, sailing from New York to Jamaica, on July 25; *Hope,* Captain Edmoundson, and the *Hannah,* Captain Larson, both sailing from Philadelphia to Jamaica.

104. *Year 1801.* Six English merchantmen were wrecked at the same time, August 10, on the reefs of Great Inagua Island: *Auspicicus,* Captain Procton, *Milton,* Captain Robley, *Jason,* Captain Watt, *Bushy Park,* Captain Brown, *Fanny,* Captain Warden, and an unidentified ship.

105. *Year 1802.* Spanish merchantman *Argonauta,* carrying a very rich cargo, totally lost at Mantanilla Reef, on the Little Bahama Bank.

106. *Year 1802.* English merchantman *Mars,* Captain Patterson, sailing from Jamaica to London, wrecked on the Hogsties, part of her cargo was saved.

107. *Year 1802.* Three ships were lost near New Providence Island: American ship *Fancy,* Captain Wilson, coming from Philadelphia; English slave ship *Agnes,* Captain Kitts, coming from Africa, slaves and crew saved; and the English merchantman *Ranger,* Captain Lea, arriving from London.

108. *Year 1802.* Two ships were lost at Turks Island: Canadian ship *Minerva,* Captain Potter, coming from New Brunswick, in January; and the American ship *Nancy,* Captain Nevesin, sailing from Virginia to Jamaica, on October 28.

109. *Year 1802.* American ship *General Oglethorp,* sailing from Charleston, South Carolina, to Havana, wrecked on a reef 6 miles north of Whale Key and quickly went to pieces, ten crewmen and thirteen slaves drowned. In the same area, five or six other ships were also lost, one of which was an African slave ship.

110. *Year 1803.* Two American merchantmen were wrecked on Great Abaco Island: *Lilly,* Captain M'Camen, sailing from Georgia to Nassau, on December 5; and the *Adventure,* Captain Bashford, sailing from Charleston to Havana.

111. *Year 1804.* English ship *Morne Fortunee,* Captain Dale, lost December 5 at Crooked Island.

112. *Year 1804.* Two American ships were wrecked on Great Inagua Island: *Lark,* Captain Swan, on February 16, and the *Thomas,* Captain Cobb, on February 5—both sailing from Virginia to Jamaica.

113. *Year 1805.* Two Jamaican ships were lost at Fortune Island: *Ruby,* Captain M'Intosh, and the *John,* Captain Williams—both bound for the United States.

114. *Year 1805.* American ship *Zephyr,* Captain Pace, sailing from Virginia to Jamaica, was lost on Grand Caicos Island.

115. *Year 1806.* American merchantman, *Pyomingo,* Captain Latimer, sailing from London to New Orleans, was wrecked in the Berry Islands.

116. Year 1806. American ship *Jefferson,* sailing from New York to Jamaica, was totally lost February 14 on the Mayaguana Reef.

117. Year 1806. Three ships wrecked on Turks Island: American ship *Heron,* Captain Cullum, sailing from Wilmington to Jamaica; English merchantman *Harnet,* Captain Curry, sailing from Jamaica to Halifax; and the Canadian ship *Ann,* Captain Mackie, sailing from Quebec to Jamaica, but part of her cargo was saved.

118. Year 1806. Seven ships were lost on the Caicos Bank: American merchantman *Eagle,* Captain Toby, sailing from Boston to Jamaica, on July 27; Canadian ship *Jane,* Captain Boyd, sailing from Halifax to Jamaica, on February 19, crew saved; English ship *Martha,* Captain Yates, coming from Liverpool; and four unidentified ships.

119. Year 1806. American merchantman *Polly,* Captain Bigby, sailing from Jamaica to Wilmington, on September 13; English ship *Speedwell,* Captain Fairbotham, sailing from Jamaica to Liverpool, during a hurricane on September 13; and the English ship *Mentor,* Captain Bellowly, carrying the cotton and stores salvaged from the wreck of the *Speedwell.*

120. Year 1806. Four ships were wrecked on Great Inagua Island: American merchantman *Isaac,* Captain Pearson, sailing from Philadelphia to Jamaica, on September 15; American ship *Rattlesnake,* Captain Bessel, sailing from Jamaica to North Carolina, in September; American ship *Brandy Wine,* Captain Miller, sailing from New York to Jamaica; and the English warship H.M.S. *Wolfe,* a sloop of 18 guns, Captain G. C. Mackenzie, 121 in the crew—none of which was lost—on September 4.

121. Year 1807. American ship *Franklin,* sailing from New York to Jamaica, lost February 26 on Great Inagua Island, the crew was saved.

122. Year 1807. English merchantman *Harmony,* sailing from Bristol to the West Indies, was totally lost in the Berry Islands, the crew was saved.

123. Year 1807. Four ships lost on the Caicos Bank: American packet *John,* Captain Sabe, sailing from Washington to Jamaica, lost April 14; a ship of unknown registry, *Martha,* Captain Jackson, coming from St. Vincent Island, the crew was saved; American ship *Four Friends,* Captain Jouffet, sailing from South Carolina to Jamaica, crew and cargo saved; and the English merchantman *Lady Warren,* Captain Kingsbury, sailing from Santo Domingo to London, on November 28, crew and passengers saved.

124. **Year 1807.** English merchantman *Sir Charles Hamilton,* sailing from Liverpool to Santo Domingo, was totally lost on Turks Island.

125. **Year 1808.** English warship H.M.S. *Bermuda,* 18-gun schooner, Captain William Henry Byam, wrecked April 22 at Memory Rock, on the Little Bahama Bank, the crew was saved. (Note: Within a 300-yard radius of Memory Rock there are seven old shipwrecks but all appear to have been thoroughly salvaged.)

126. **Year 1808.** American ship *Hiram,* Captain Anner, sailing from New York to Havana, lost July 21 on Great Abaco Island, crew and part of cargo saved.

127. **Year 1808.** English ship *Elizabeth and Mary,* Captain Graff, sailing from Haiti and Jamaica to London, wrecked April 23 on Grand Caicos Island.

128. **Year 1809.** English merchantman *Victorina,* sailing from Liverpool to New Providence Island, wrecked on the west end of this island, December 9.

129. **Year 1809.** American merchantman *Mary,* Captain Smith, sailing from Cape François, Hispaniola, to Philadelphia, was totally lost on the Caicos Bank, the crew was saved.

130. **Year 1809.** Two ships wrecked on Turks Island: English merchantman *John,* Captain Yates, sailing from Liverpool to Nassau, on August 13, crew and part of cargo saved; and the American ship *Ann,* Captain Nixon, sailing from Amelia Island, Florida, to Jamaica, on May 15, crew and cargo saved.

131. **Year 1810.** A ship of unknown registry, *Orion,* Captain Brown, sailing from Philadelphia to Havana, was wrecked October 28 on Pelican Key, four of the crew drowned.

132. **Year 1810.** English merchantman *Ann,* Captain Robins, sailing from Santo Domingo to Bristol, wrecked October 27 in the Berry Islands, crew and part of cargo saved.

133. *Year 1810.* Two ships wrecked at New Providence Island: a ship of unknown registry, *Olympus,* sailing from New Orleans to England, wrecked in November; and the English ship *Three Brothers.*

134. *Year 1810.* English ship *Good Hope,* Captain Folger, sailing from London to Baltimore, totally lost near San Salvador Island, October 30, the crew was saved.

135. *Year 1810.* French ship *Transit,* Captain Vaux, coming from Haiti, totally lost on a reef off the southwestern end of Great Inagua Island.

136. *Year 1810.* English merchantman *Clarendon,* sailing from Jamaica to London, lost December 11 at Atwood Key, the crew was saved.

137. *Year 1810.* Two ships lost at Turks Island: American ship *Orient,* Captain Hunter, sailing from New York to Jamaica, the crew was saved; and the English ship *Schomer,* Captain Howe, sailing from Haiti to London, September 20, the crew was saved.

138. *Year 1810.* Two American merchantmen wrecked near Great Abaco Island: schooner *Elizabeth Ann,* Captain Blake, coming from Haiti, November 1; and the *Convention,* Captain Allen, sailing from New York to Havana, October 24.

139. *Year 1811.* American merchantman *Union,* Captain M'Known, sailing from Virginia to Jamaica, wrecked January 21 on Great Caicos Reef, the crew was saved.

140. *Year 1811.* English packet boat *Prince of Wales,* Captain Paquet, coming from Jamaica, wrecked on the Great Inagua Island Reef on July 19, crew, passengers, mail, and specie saved.

141. *Year 1811.* Two ships lost near Turks Island: American ship *Fox,* Captain Lippcatt, sailing from New York to Jamaica, December 23, the crew was saved; and the Canadian ship *Harmony,* Captain Penniston, sailing from Newfoundland to Jamaica.

142. *Year 1812.* English warship H.M.S. *Southampton,* 32-gun frigate, Captain Sir James Lucas Yeo, wrecked on a reef 3 leagues from Conception Island in 24 degrees and 3 minutes of north latitude and 69 degrees and 57 minutes of west longitude.

143. *Year 1812.* American ship *Neutrality,* Captain Kimball, sailing from Jamaica to Georgia was totally lost January 13 at Cats Key, south of Bimini, the crew was saved.

144. *Year 1812.* English merchantman *Brown*, Captain Brough, sailing from Santo Domingo to London, wrecked October 5 on the Little Caicos Bank, the crew was saved.

145. *Year 1812.* Four ships were lost near Great Abaco Island: American ship *Twin Sisters*, Captain Owen, sailing from Baltimore to Havana, February 18, crew and most of cargo saved; American ship *Carlton*, Captain Davis, sailing from Virginia to Havana, April 16, crew and part of cargo saved; and the Scottish ship *Irmelinda*, Captain Graham, sailing from Clyde to Nassau, November 9.

146. *Year 1813.* English packet boat *Hinchinbrook*, sailing from Jamaica to England, wrecked at San Salvador Island July 19, only one person drowned.

147. *Year 1813.* English warship H.M.S. *Algerine*, a cutter, Captain Carpenter, wrecked May 20 near Great Abaco Island, the crew was saved.

148. *Year 1813.* English merchantman *Hotspur*, Captain Marshall, sailing from Santo Domingo to London, wrecked July 25 on Atwood Key, the crew was saved.

149. *Year 1813.* Bahamian ship *Fair Bahamian*, Captain Graham, sailing from Nassau to Havana, totally lost August 26 at Cat Cay, south of Bimini.

150. *Year 1813.* English ship *Forester*, Captain Jackson, sailing from Bermuda to Jamaica, lost September 26 on Turks Island, the crew was saved.

151. *Year 1813.* Two English warships wrecked on Silver Shoals: H.M.S. *Laurestinus*, 22 guns, Captain Alexander Gordon, October 22, the crew was saved; and the H.M.S. *Persian*, 18-gun sloop, Captain Charles Bertram, in 7 fathoms of water, none of her crew of 121 men was lost.

152. *Year 1813.* During a violent gale at Nassau on July 26, over forty ships were wrecked, sunk, or cast ashore. Only one was identified: English ship *Dart*, Captain Sweeting, sailing from Jamaica to Nassau, most of her cargo was saved.

153. *Year 1813.* During the same gale the English ship *Conck*, sailing from Nassau to Jamaica, was wrecked on Eleuthera Island.

154. *Year 1814.* Portuguese mail boat *Corriero Lisbonere,* sailing from Liverpool to Havana, was totally lost January 27 on the Little Bahama Bank.

155. *Year 1814.* A ship of unknown registry, *Moreau,* Captain Crosby, sailing from Amelia Island, Florida, to Nassau, was lost on the Nassau Bar.

156. *Year 1814.* Spanish merchantman *María Antonia,* sailing from Florida to Havana, was lost in February on a reef near Great Abaco Island, the crew was saved.

157. *Year 1814.* English ship *Sir James Yeo,* Captain Humble, sailing from Jamaica to Halifax, wrecked on Bird Rock near Crooked Island but most of her cargo was salvaged.

158. *Year 1814.* A ship of unknown registry, *Rose,* Captain Morris, sailing from Haiti to Hamburg, Germany, totally lost in August at Atwood Key.

159. *Year 1815.* American ship *Warrior,* Captain Dickenson, sailing from New York to Havana, lost June 30 on the Great Bahama Bank to the west of Andros Island, the crew was saved.

160. *Year 1815.* American merchantman *William & Mary,* Captain Ross, sailing from Haiti to Baltimore, wrecked August 23 on the Hogsties, the crew was saved.

161. *Year 1815.* Two Spanish merchantmen lost on the Little Bahama Bank: *Barcelones,* sailing from Cadiz to Havana, on January 6, part of her cargo was salvaged; and the *Juncta,* Captain Capillo, sailing from Havana to Cadiz, on December 26, the crew was saved.

162. *Year 1815.* A ship of unknown registry, *Camelcon,* sailing from Norfolk to Havana, was lost on Great Abaco Island.

163. *Year 1815.* American ship *Sceptre,* Captain Simpson, sailing from Philadelphia to New Orleans, was lost on New Providence Island.

164. *Year 1815.* Three ships were lost near Great Inagua Island: a ship of unknown registry, *Port Royal,* sailing from New York to Jamaica; American ship *Intrepid,* Captain Martin, sailing from Jamaica to Baltimore, crew and part of cargo saved; and the American frigate *Statira,* on February 27, the crew was saved.

165. *Year 1815.* American merchantman *Farmer,* Captain Thompson, sailing from Nassau to South Carolina, was lost during a severe gale on June 19 on Wood Key, the crew was saved.

166. *Year 1815.* A ship of unknown registry, *Urbana,* Captain Brittain, sailing from New York to Jamaica, lost on Turks Island, the crew was saved.

167. *Year 1815.* English merchantman *Eliza Ann,* Captain Little, sailing from Honduras to London, wrecked at Memory Rock.

168. *Year 1815.* English ship *Incle,* Captain Thatcher, sailing from Bermuda to Jamaica, wrecked on the Caicos Bank.

169. *Year 1815.* Irish ship *Forest,* Captain Lascell, coming from Norfolk, totally lost December 2 on Great Exuma Island, the crew was saved.

170. *Year 1816.* American ship *Savannah,* Captain Bowers, sailing from Liverpool to New Orleans, was totally lost on the Macories Reef in the Old Bahama Channel, the crew was saved.

171. *Year 1816.* American merchantman *Cooler,* sailing from Philadelphia to Jamaica, wrecked on Mouchoir Bank, near Turks Island, the crew was saved.

172. *Year 1816.* A ship of unknown registry, *Swallow,* Captain Mossop, sailing from Savannah, Georgia, to Jamaica, wrecked December 10 on a reef at the north end of Eleuthera Island, the crew was saved.

173. *Year 1816.* Bahamian ship *Antelope,* Captain Teder, sailing from Nassau to St. Vincent Island, wrecked in October at Atwood Key.

174. *Year 1816.* A ship of unknown registry, *Mary,* Captain Jerault, coming from the Virgin Islands, was wrecked on the Berry Island, crew and part of cargo saved.

175. *Year 1816.* English ship *Phoenix,* sailing from Havana to Nassau, wrecked in March on the Mantanilla Reef, the crew was saved.

176. *Year 1816.* English merchantman *Aldbro,* Captain Suthoff, sailing from Honduras to London, totally lost September 28 near Memory Rock, the crew was saved.

177. *Year 1816.* American ship *Benjamin,* Captain Cushman, sailing from Boston to Havana, wrecked September 21 near Grand Bahama Island, crew and part of cargo saved.

178. *Year 1816.* English ship *Robert,* Captain Wilkes, sailing from Nassau to Liverpool, wrecked on a reef off Egg Island.

179. *Year 1816.* English ship *Britannia,* Captain Middlemas, sailing from Jamaica to New York, wrecked December 24 on Ackland Key, part of her cargo was saved.

180. *Year 1816.* Three American merchantmen were lost near Bimini: *Expedition,* Captain Clare, and the *Charter,* both sailing from Baltimore to Havana, wrecked near Great Isaac Key, the crews were saved; and the *Lardegable,* Captain Leon, sailing from Charleston, South Carolina, to Havana, was totally lost on the Little Isaac Key but the crew was saved.

181. *Year 1816.* Five ships were lost near Great Abaco Island: Spanish ship *Rosa,* sailing from Africa to Havana with three hundred slaves, all people were saved; American ship *Minerva,* Captain Robinson, sailing from New York to Havana, totally lost March 8; American ship *William & Mary,* Captain Cooper, sailing from Philadelphia to Havana, October 17; American ship *New Orleans,* Captain Booth, crew and cargo saved; and the American ship *Alompre,* Captain Prior, sailing from New York to New Orleans, the crew was saved.

182. *Year 1816.* Three ships wrecked on the Caicos Bank: English ship *Amwell,* Captain Hawkins, sailing from London to Jamaica, December 19, at Great Caicos, crew and part of cargo saved; a ship of unknown registry, *Fair Trader,* Captain Haze, sailing from Philadelphia to Cuba, September 23, on the North Caicos Reef; and the American ship *Ann,* Captain Grant, sailing from South Carolina to Jamaica, December 25, the crew was saved.

183. *Year 1816.* Six ships were lost near Great Inagua Island: American ship *Nile,* Captain Turnley, sailing from New York to Jamaica, March 26, crew and cargo saved; American merchantman *Milford,* Captain Dukehard, coming from Baltimore, December 23, crew and part of cargo saved; a ship of unknown registry, *Mary,* sailing from Haiti to Baltimore, August 30; and three unidentified ships during June, one of which was carrying a considerable amount of money.

184. *Year 1817.* German merchantman *Christiansand,* Captain Berge, sailing from Hamburg to Havana, wrecked near Guinches Key, in the Old Bahama Channel, June 28, crew and some of specie saved.

185. *Year 1817.* American merchantman *Fame,* Captain Salisbury, sailing from Boston to Havana, lost January 12 near Harbour Island, the crew was saved.

186. *Year 1817.* American ship *Mohawk,* Captain Harding, sailing from New York to Haiti, wrecked in August on Crooked Island, crew and part of cargo saved.

187. *Year 1817.* Spanish merchantman *Rosa,* wrecked near Little Isaac Island (called *Las Profetas* by the Spanish) in October, on a reef 13 nautical miles and bearing 73 degrees from above island.

188. *Year 1817.* American ship *Miriam,* sailing from Baltimore to Jamaica, wrecked March 27 on Great Inagua Island, her cargo was saved.

189. *Year 1817.* American merchantman *Workenston,* Captain Wilkens, sailing from New England to Veracruz, wrecked on North Caicos Key, crew and part of cargo saved.

190. *Year 1817.* Two ships wrecked on the Great Bahama Bank: American ship *Morning Star,* Captain Bishop, sailing from South Carolina to Havana, January 20; and an unidentified Dutch ship, sailing from Amsterdam to Havana, on the south edge of the bank in July.

191. *Year 1817.* Seven ships were lost near Great Abaco Island: American merchantman *Louisa,* Captain Hayes, sailing from Philadelphia to Havana, in April, part of her cargo was saved; Bahamian ship *Do,* Captain Miller, sailing from Philadelphia to Nassau, November 7, crew and part of cargo saved; a ship of unknown registry, *Adeline,* Captain Marre, sailing from Savannah to Havana, crew and part of cargo saved; American ship *Industry,* Captain Sweet, coming from Boston, March 22; American merchantman *Robert Potter,* sailing from Norfolk to Havana, April 17; American ship *Natchez Belle,* sailing from New York to New Orleans, March 23, crew and cargo saved; and the American merchantman *Frances Mary,* Captain Jennings, sailing from New York to New Orleans, February 12.

192. *Year 1818.* During a bad gale at Nassau on December 14, many ships were wrecked and sunk.

193. *Year 1818.* American ship *Margaret,* Captain Hughes, sailing from Haiti to New York, wrecked March 1 near Little Inagua Island, crew and cargo saved.

194. *Year 1818.* English merchantman *Keddington,* Captain Bacon, sailing from Jamaica to London, lost April 1 at Atwood Key, crew and part of cargo saved.

195. *Year 1818.* English ship *Neptune,* Captain Foller, coming from Antigua, lost September 29 at Turks Island.

196. *Year 1818.* English ship *King George,* Captain Cook, sailing from Jamaica to London, lost on a cay near Bimini, most of her cargo was saved.

197. *Year 1818.* Ship of unknown registry, *Neptune,* Captain Hallowell, sailing from France to New Orleans, was totally wrecked February 5 near James Point on Eleuthera Island, the crew was saved.

198. *Year 1818.* French merchantman *Alexander,* sailing from France to Havana, wrecked in March near New Providence Island, crew and part of cargo saved.

199. *Year 1818.* Two ships of unknown registry wrecked on Silver Shoals: schooner *Alexander,* Captain Stewart, totally lost August 7, coming from Jamaica; and the *John,* bound for Jamaica, on October 10 or 12, the crew was saved.

200. *Year 1818.* American ship *Jane,* Captain Woodward, sailing from Savannah to Jamaica, wrecked on August 16 near Crooked Island, some of her cargo was saved.

201. *Year 1818.* Four ships were wrecked near Memory Rock: Spanish merchantman *Echo,* Captain Rodriquez, sailing from Veracruz to Venezuela, crew and over $100,000 in specie saved; English ship *Elizabeth,* sailing from Jamaica to Liverpool, on March 22; English merchantman *Two Brothers,* Captain Holmes, sailing from New Orleans to Liverpool, the crew was saved; English brig *British Trader,* Captain Gemmell, coming from Jamaica, March 22, but got afloat again after throwing part of her cargo overboard.

202. *Year 1818.* American ship *Horizon,* Captain Johnson, sailing from Philadelphia to New Orleans, wrecked on Fish Key, near Great Abaco Island.

203. *Year 1818.* Five ships were wrecked on Great Abaco Island: a ship of unknown registry, *Shakespeare,* sailing from Le Havre to America, in March; American ship *Caroline,* Captain Seymour, sailing from Norfolk to New Orleans, March 4; English merchantman *Sir John Doyle,* Captain Watts, sailing from Havana to Santiago de Cuba, on September 13, part of her cargo was saved; American packet boat *Savannah,* Captain Fowler, sailing from New York to Mobile, October 14, crew, passengers, and cargo saved; and the American ship *Rival,* sailing from Boston to Mobile, November 18, crew, passengers, and cargo saved.

204. *Year 1818.* American schooner *Lily,* sailing from Port au Prince, Haiti, to Great Exuma Island, wrecked on Andros Island, the crew was saved.

205. *Year 1818.* Scottish merchantman *Pomona,* Captain M'Naught, sailing from Jamaica to Glasgow, lost April 10 on the Caicos Bank, crew, rum, and sails saved.

206. *Year 1819.* A ship of unknown registry, *Sero,* Captain Murdock, sailing from Philadelphia to Cuba, totally lost July 27 at Turks Island.

207. *Year 1819.* English ship *Golden Fleece,* sailing from Jamaica to Liverpool, wrecked in January on Long Key, crew and cargo saved.

208. *Year 1819.* A ship of unknown registry, *Constantia,* Captain Johnson, sailing from Haiti to France, wrecked April 22 on Ginger Key, her cargo was saved.

209. *Year 1819.* American schooner *Walton Grey,* sailing from Baltimore to Havana, wrecked in the Berry Islands, most of her cargo was saved.

210. *Year 1819.* American ship *Hazard,* Captain Crocker, sailing from Boston to Mobile, wrecked January 3 near Nassau, crew and part of cargo saved.

211. *Year 1819.* A large unidentified brig was wrecked on the Crooked Island Reef before April 25.

212. *Year 1819.* English packet boat *Princess Charlotte,* sailing from Jamaica to England, wrecked in early April on the Hogstie Reef, crew, passengers, mail, and specie (with the exception of about $30,000) saved.

213. *Year 1819.* Portuguese ship *Bom Successo,* coming from Brazil with a cargo of sugar, cotton, rice, and hides, was wrecked at Little Island, near Rum Key, most of her cargo was salvaged.

214. *Year 1819.* English merchantman *Fairfield,* Captain Elias, sailing from Haiti to Liverpool, wrecked on a reef at Atwood Key on March 28, crew and some of cargo saved.

215. *Year 1819.* American brig *George Washington,* Captain Baker, sailing from New York to New Orleans, was totally wrecked at Green Turtle Cay, near Great Abaco Island.

216. *Year 1819.* Two American ships wrecked on Great Abaco Island: merchantman *George Washington,* Captain Brethoff, sailing from New York to Havana, January 1, crew and small part of cargo saved; and the sloop *Altezara,* Captain Glover, totally lost at Hole in the Wall.

217. *Year 1819.* Five ships wrecked on the Caicos Bank: an unidentified Dutch brig, sailing from Hamburg to Havana, with a valuable cargo of silks, April 13; American ship *Jonus,* sailing from New York to Haiti, crew and part of cargo saved; Belgian merchantman *Elizabeth Elenor,* Captain Rose, sailing from Antwerp to Havana, April 2, crew and part of cargo saved; Canadian ship *Herman,* Captain Milne, sailing from New Brunswick to Jamaica, part of her cargo was saved; and an unidentified American schooner.

218. *Year 1820.* American ship *Atlantic,* Captain Homer, sailing from Boston to Hispaniola, totally lost December 30 in the Crooked Island Passage, the crew was saved.

219. *Year 1821.* Two ships lost near Cat Cay, south of Bimini: Canadian ship *Prince Regent,* Captain Wickes, sailing from Jamaica to Halifax, on September 5, the crew was saved; and the German ship *Rapid,* Captain Hinman, sailing from Havana to Hamburg.

220. *Year 1821.* English merchantman *Cuba,* Captain M'Gowan, sailing from Liverpool to Havana, totally lost October 15 on Maya-guana Island, the crew was saved.

221. *Year 1821.* American brig *Leopard* was wrecked during a gale on September 14 near Great Exuma Island.

222. *Year 1821.* Two ships were lost on Great Abaco Island: American brig *Perseverance,* sailing from Charleston, South Carolina, to Havana, June 9, the crew was saved; and a ship of unknown registry, *Hero,* Captain Riebeiro, sailing from New York to Havana, in June, crew and most of cargo saved.

223. *Year 1821.* Spanish ship *Santa Rosa,* Captain Torres, sailing from Philadelphia to Havana, lost in March on Egg Island, the crew was saved.

224. *Year 1821.* English ship *Sovereign,* Captain Pierson, sailing from Jamaica to London, was totally wrecked November 17 on the Hogsties, crew and cargo saved.

225. *Year 1821.* English merchantman *Posthumous,* Captain Fisher, lost at Saynee Island, the crew was saved. (Note: Today there is no Bahamian island by this name.)

226. *Year 1821.* Irish ship *James Munroe,* Captain Harwood, carrying a cargo of salt, wrecked on St. Nicolas Key, the crew was saved.

227. *Year 1821.* English brig *Harriet,* sailing from Savannah, wrecked on Ginger Cay, the crew was saved.

228. *Year 1821.* Two ships wrecked near Great Inagua Island: Canadian merchantman *Hope,* Captain Tucker, sailing from Jamaica to New Brunswick, September 13; and the English ship *Anns,* Captain Hodnett, sailing from Bermuda to Jamaica, May 6, near the northeastern end of the island.

229. *Year 1822.* English merchantman *Loyalty,* Captain Atkinson, sailing from Jamaica to London, wrecked January 27 on the Hogsties, crew and part of cargo saved.

230. *Year 1822.* Two ships were lost on Castle Island: American schooner *Jane,* Captain Miller, sailing from Boston to Havana, part of her cargo was saved; and the English brig *Jemima,* coming from Maracaibo, Venezuela, the crew was saved.

231. *Year 1822.* Four American merchant ships wrecked on the Great Bahama Bank: *Maryland, Savannah Packet, Nancy,* and *Speedy Peace,* the latter sailing from Mobile to New York; the crews of all ships were saved.

232. *Year 1822.* American merchantman *Falmouth,* carrying a cargo of soap, lumber, and candles, wrecked near the Exuma Keys.

233. *Year 1822.* Two ships were lost on the Caicos Bank: a ship of unknown registry, *Westmoreland,* Captain Majoribanks, sailing from Quebec to Jamaica, totally lost December 5, her crew was saved; and the English ship *Draper,* Captain Brown, sailing from Bermuda to Jamaica, on November 28, crew and passengers saved.

234. *Year 1822.* Four ships wrecked on Great Abaco Island: Spanish ship *Jupiter,* Captain de Minchaca, sailing from Malaya to Havana, crew and part of cargo saved; Canadian ship *Ann,* sailing from Jamaica to New Brunswick, prior to February 21; American ship *Ranger,* Captain Eldridge, sailing from South Carolina to Havana, totally lost January 26; and the American ship *Washington,* Captain Taylor, sailing from New York to New Orleans in ballast.

235. *Year 1822.* English merchantman *Britannia,* Captain Preble, sailing from Haiti to Wilmington, totally lost November 19 on Sugar Key, the crew was saved.

236. *Year 1822.* Scottish ship *Jemima,* Captain Doyle, wrecked April 2 on a reef near Crooked Island, part of her cargo was saved.

237. *Year 1822.* Canadian ship *Harriet,* Captain Hitchins, sailing from Jamaica to Halifax, wrecked April 26 on the Mira Por Vos Keys, her crew was saved.

238. *Year 1822.* Scottish merchantman *Favorite,* Captain Davis, sailing from Glasgow to Canada, wrecked May 7 on Ragged Island.

239. *Year 1822.* Unidentified merchant brig wrecked at Ackland Key, the crew was saved.

240. *Year 1822.* Two ships of unknown registry wrecked near Great Inagua Island: brig *Hope,* Captain Tooker, coming from Jamaica, her crew was saved; and an unidentified vessel.

241. *Year 1822.* Three ships were totally wrecked at Turks Island: American ship *Washington,* Captain Berry, sailing from New York to Haiti, October 17, her crew was saved; a ship of unknown registry, *Merrimack,* Captain Miltimore, sailing to Haiti, crew and part of cargo saved; and the Canadian ship *Harriet Newell,* Captain Corfield, sailing from New Brunswick to Jamaica, December 1, crew and part of cargo saved.

242. *Year 1823.* Cuban ship *Rio,* sailing from Philadelphia to Havana, wrecked in the Berry Islands.

243. *Year 1823.* Three ships wrecked on Sugar Key: French ship *Ville de St. Pierre,* Captain Scolan, sailing from France to Havana, the crew was saved; a ship of unknown registry, *Warren,* sailing from France to Havana with 400 tons of wine; and an unidentified Dutch ship, sailing from Hamburg to Havana, with a very valuable cargo—most of their cargoes were saved.

244. *Year 1823.* A ship of unknown registry, *Victoria,* Captain M'Killop, sailing from Jamaica to Halifax, wrecked on the Mayaguana Reef, got off, but then was wrecked off the western end of Crooked Island, November 10, where she went to pieces.

245. *Year 1823.* American ship *Orion,* Captain Smith, sailing from Haiti to Wilmington, wrecked December 8 on the Mayaguana Reef, crew and cargo saved.

246. *Year 1823.* English ship *Wanderer,* totally wrecked on Double Headed Shot Key, June 3, crew and passengers saved.

247. *Year 1823.* A ship of unknown registry, *Delight,* sailing from Jamaica to Philadelphia, wrecked near Nassau, part of her cargo saved.

248. *Year 1823.* American schooner *Richard,* Captain Harvey, sailing from New York to Jamaica, lost September 11 on Turks Island, crew and most of cargo saved.

249. *Year 1823.* Two unidentified Jamaican vessels, a brig and a schooner, were wrecked on the Hogsties.

250. *Year 1823.* Spanish brig *Estrella,* sailing from Puerto Rico to Havana, was lost near Great Isaac Key.

251. *Year 1823.* Bahamian schooner *Sarah Ann,* Captain Bannatyne, coming from Cuba, wrecked March 5 on Green Key.

252. Year 1823. A ship of unknown registry, *Friendship*, Captain Wells, sailing from Jeremie to Portsmouth, New Hampshire, wrecked at Castle Island, crew and most of cargo saved.

253. Year 1823. Two ships lost on the Caicos Bank: Spanish ship *Bella Dolores*, captured by a Colombian privateer and then wrecked June 9; and the American ship *Fabius*, Captain Higgins, sailing from Wilmington to Haiti, totally lost, her crew was saved.

254. Year 1823. Five ships wrecked on Great Abaco Island: American schooner *Jane*, Captain M'Williams, sailing from South Carolina to Havana, crew and cargo saved; American merchantman *Essex*, Captain Ladiew, sailing from Rhode Island to Havana; American ship *Franklin*, Captain Taper, sailing from Philadelphia to Venezuela; a ship of unknown registry, *Remittance*, Captain Heter, sailing from New York to Havana; and the American ship *Catherine Rogers*, Captain Griffiths, sailing from New York to Mobile.

255. Year 1824. During a hurricane on September 11, several unidentified ships were wrecked at Rum Key.

256. Year 1824. American ship *Joseph*, Captain Holdrige, sailing from Mobile to New York, totally lost June 3 on the Little Bahama Bank, near Memory Rock.

257. Year 1824. French ship *Eolus*, Captain Dickinson, sailing from Morlaix, France, to Mobile, wrecked on Eleuthera Island.

258. Year 1824. English brig *Providence*, Captain Dunn, sailing from Gibraltar to Havana, wrecked August 8 near Great Exuma Island.

259. Year 1824. English ship *Cleo*, Captain Heath, sailing from Bath to Havana, lost February 23 on Grand Bahama Island, part of her cargo was saved.

260. Year 1824. American schooner *Three Sisters*, Captain Allen, coming from Jamaica, wrecked on the Hogsties.

261. Year 1824. Three ships wrecked on the Caicos Bank: American schooner *Franklin*, Captain Stevenson, sailing from Boston to South America; a ship of unknown registry, *Europa*, Captain Allen, sailing from Liverpool to Havana, June 14, crew and cargo saved; and the Bahamian sloop *Maria*, Captain Bartlett.

262. *Year 1824.* Three ships wrecked on Great Abaco Island: American schooner *George Washington*, Captain Smith, sailing from Philadelphia to Havana, her cargo was saved; a ship of unknown registry, *Chace*, Captain Anderson, sailing from Charleston, South Carolina, to Havana, her crew was saved; and the English ship *Albert*, Captain Philip, sailing from Gibraltar to Mexico, part of her cargo was saved.

263. *Year 1824.* American ship *Live Oak*, Captain Brill, sailing from Gibraltar to Havana, wrecked December 1 near Harbour Island, crew and cargo saved.

264. *Year 1824.* Two American ships wrecked at Turks Island: *Panopea*, Captain Bogle, sailing from South Carolina to Jamaica, December 25, most of her cargo was saved; and the *Jerome Maximilian*, sailing from New York to Haiti, wrecked December 30 with no one aboard.

265. *Year 1825.* English mail boat *Havana Packet*, Captain Jenkins, sailing from England to Jamaica, wrecked March 13 on the Caicos Bank.

266. *Year 1825.* American ship *North America*, sailing from Nassau to Key West, wrecked near Bimini.

267. *Year 1825.* Three ships wrecked on reefs near Mayaguana Island: American ship *Strong*, Captain McGill, sailing from Haiti to Baltimore, part of her cargo was saved; English merchantman *Woodstock*, Captain Paton, sailing from Jamaica to London, small part of her cargo was saved; and the Spanish ship *San Francisco de Paula* (alias *Orionon*), Captain Pugol, sailing from Barcelona to Havana, the crew was saved.

268. *Year 1825.* English ship *Doris*, Captain White, sailing from Santo Domingo to England, was totally lost near Great Inagua Island, her crew was saved.

269. *Year 1825.* American merchantman *Betsy*, Captain Hilton, sailing from New England to Cuba, was totally lost on Double Headed Key, all of crew except one were murdered by pirates.

CHAPTER EIGHT

Cuba

THE ISLAND OF CUBA was considered the most stra-
tegically located island in the Caribbean, as virtually all shipping
going to Mexico, Central America, or the southern sections of the
present United States from Europe or Africa, and all shipping to
Europe or ports in North America from the Caribbean, Mexico, and
Central and South America had to sail close by the island.

When countries were at war with one another, they generally
cruised in search of enemy ships off the western tip of Cuba, which
all ships using the Bahama Channel on voyages to Europe had to
pass. At times, to prevent capture, the Windward Passage between
Haiti and the eastern tip of Cuba was used by shipping, but because
of the difficult navigation through the Bahamian Archipelago, this
route was used only as a last resort. Due to storms, faulty navigation,
and sea battles, more than seven hundred ships were lost in Cuban
waters between the beginning of the sixteenth century and 1825. I

have listed only those in which accurate locations are given or ships of major importance—such as a ship carrying an important treasure.

Under the present Castro government, no foreigners are permitted to salvage shipwrecks, or even sail, in Cuban territorial waters. Since Castro took over, three different American treasure-hunting expeditions had the misfortune of accidentally shipwrecking themselves in Cuban waters; in two of these cases the divers were kept captive for several months even though their original destinations were not in Cuban waters. Even worse, Cuban patrol vessels extend their cruising grounds well out of their own territorial waters, ostensibly to try to intercept Cuban-exile raiders working out of Florida and the Bahamas. Recently a shrimp-boat captain reported sighting a large number of bronze cannon on a reef in Cay Sal Bank—which is in Bahamian waters—but when a group of Miami divers went there to recover these cannon they were chased away by a Cuban gunboat.

There are several unconfirmed stories of American divers recovering treasure in the vicinity of the Isle of Pines prior to the days of the Castro takeover, but I have been unable to verify these reports. In 1957 I was contacted by an amateur diver from Havana who sent me photographs of several silver bars he had recovered from Matanzas Bay, in Cuba. He requested that I aid him in salvaging more treasure, but I was unable to reach there before Castro took over. I identified the bars (from the markings on them) as belonging to one of the Spanish ships wrecked in this bay in 1628 during the attack of the Dutchman Piet Heyn. No doubt there is a great deal more treasure from this disaster in Matanzas Bay that will someday be recovered. Since Castro is himself an avid diving enthusiast, I am surprised that he has not attempted to locate this treasure to augment his depleted treasury.

List of Shipwrecks in Cuban Waters

1. **Early sixteenth century.** The famous Spanish historian Oviedo mentions, without giving the year, that a ship sailing from Santo Domingo to Cuba was wrecked on the coast of Cuba and that a Juan de Rojas and his wife, María de Lobera, were aboard.

2. **Prior to 1515.** An unidentified small Spanish caravel, carrying a valuable cargo, was lost in the port of Cumanacan, at the mouth of the Bani River.

3. *Prior to 1518.* Merchant *nao Jesús Nazareno y Nuestra Señora de Guadalupe,* 112 tons, Captain Bartolome Antonio Garrote, owned by Tomás José Caro, carrying a cargo of tobacco, developed a bad leak after leaving Havana for Spain and was sunk in the port of Guarico, after most of its cargo was removed.

4. *Year 1519.* An unidentified caravel, sailing from the port of Santa María del Antigua, Colombia, for Santo Domingo, was forced (because of bad weather) to pass on the northern coast of Cuba, where it wrecked. Large waves later tossed the ship over 100 yards ashore.

5. *Year 1521.* Merchant *nao San Anton,* 100 tons, Captain Gonzalo Rodríguez, sailing from Havana to Spain, was lost on a reef on the northwestern coast of the island.

6. *Year 1525.* An unidentified ship commanded by Juan de Avalos, a relative of Cortez, was wrecked during a hurricane west of Havana, enroute to Veracruz with supplies for the conquistadors. Of the eighty persons aboard, only eight survived. This occurred toward the end of October.

7. *Year 1527.* During a hurricane on October 14, two large ships of the fleet of Admiral Pánfilo Narváez were lost in the port of Trinidad after arriving from Santo Domingo.

8. *Year 1537.* During a hurricane, two ships were lost: the *nao San Juan,* arriving from Spain with a valuable cargo of merchandise, was lost 5 leagues east of Havana; and the *nao Santa Catalina,* 200 tons, Captain Francisco López, carrying gold and silver from Mexico, sank in Havana Harbor.

9. *Year 1544. Nao Santa María de la Isla,* 180 tons, Captain Vicente Martín, sailing with treasure from Nombre de Dios to Havana, was wrecked on the coast near Havana.

10. *Year 1552.* Two treasure-laden *naos* were wrecked in Havana Harbor: *Santa María de Finisterra,* 200 tons, Captain Juan Rodríguez Zarco, arriving from Panama; and the *San't Andrés,* of 210 tons, Captain Vicente Hernández, owned by Sebastián González, arriving from Honduras, most of her treasure was salvaged.

11. *Year 1555. Nao Santa María de Villacelan,* 220 tons, Captain Mateo de Vides, carrying treasure from Panama and Cartagena to Spain, was wrecked on the coast near Matanzas Bay.

12. **Year 1556.** Four ships of the Tierra Firme Armada, Captain-General Alvaro Sánchez de Aviles, were wrecked on the coast between Cape San Anton and Havana on May 24 during a storm: *nao La Magdalena,* of 220 tons, Captain Cristobal García, and the *nao La Concepción,* 220 tons, Captain Juan Diaz Bozino—both carrying treasure; and two unidentified caravels of 80 tons each.

13. **Year 1563.** A large convoy of ships sailed from Spain for the New World and, after stopping for water at Guadeloupe, those going to South America and those to Mexico split up in two groups. The Nueva España Flota was commanded by Captain-General Pedro de las Roelas. On July 18, six ships of this *flota* were wrecked on the Jardines Reefs on the southern coast of Cuba, in 21 degrees of north latitude at a distance of 12 leagues from the Isle of Pines: the *Capitana, San Juan Bautista,* 150 tons, Captain Juan de Arenas; *nao San Juan,* 250 tons, Captain Gaspar Luys; *galeza* (ship propelled by oars or sail) *San Salvador,* 350 tons, Captain Pedro Menéndez Márquez; *nao Nuestra Señora de la Consolación,* 300 tons, Captain Juan de Barrios; *nao Santa Margarita,* 300 tons, Captain Gonzalo Monte; and the *nao Nuestra Señora de la Concepción,* 250 tons, Captain Pedro del Corro. All six of these ships were carrying large amounts of mercury as well as cargoes of general merchandise. The *Capitana* was also carrying Archbishop Salcedo, who was reported carrying a great amount of church and personal treasure. The wrecks were reportedly in 1½ to 4 fathoms of water. Ships were sent from Havana to rescue the survivors and undertake salvage operations, but only a small part of the mercury and merchandise were recovered and none of the treasure of Archbishop Salcedo was located.

14. **Year 1563.** *Nao San Andrés,* 300 tons, Captain Marco de Nápoles, sailing from Cartagena and Panama with treasure, was wrecked in Havana Harbor.

15. **Year 1565.** Three unidentified Spanish warships under the command of Admiral Esteban de las Alas, sent to the Caribbean to destroy enemy privateers, were wrecked on the island, only the crews were saved.

16. **Year 1567.** An unidentified *urca,* 300 tons, Captain Gonzales de Peñalosa, sailing from Veracruz to Santo Domingo, carrying sev-

eral chests of silver to pay the officials and soldiers garrisoned in Santo Domingo, was lost near Cayo Romano.

17. *Year 1577.* An unidentified *nao* in the Tierra Firme Armada of Captain-General Cristobal de Eraso was separated from the convoy in a storm and forced to enter Puerto Escondido, where it sank. The gold and silver it carried was recovered.

18. *Year 1586.* Unidentified *nao*, sailing from Spain to Veracruz in the Nueva España Flota of Captain-General Francisco de Novoa, was lost at Cape San Anton around the end of September.

19. *Year 1593.* Two treasure-laden *naos*, sailing from Veracruz to Spain in the Nueva España Flota of Captain-General Martín Pérez Olozabal, were lost near Havana: *Santa María de San Vicente*, 180 tons, Captain Miguel de Alcata; and the *Nuestra Señora del Rosario*, 220 tons, Captain Cristobal Castellanos. The treasure from both ships was taken off before they sank.

20. *Year 1595.* Merchant *navío San Gabriel*, 140 tons, Captain Pedro de Morillo, part of the Nueva España Flota, commanded by Captain-General Marcos de Aramburi, was wrecked in Havana Harbor but its silver was recovered by divers.

21. *Year 1605.* Merchant *nao Trinidad* was wrecked near Havana, only a few persons aboard this ship were saved.

22. *Year 1605.* A small mail boat, Captain Diego Ruiz, sank in Havana Harbor after striking on the mast of another shipwreck.

23. *Year 1606.* Unidentified warship in the Armada de Barlovento, commanded by Admiral Juan Alvarez, sent to the Caribbean to capture foreign shipping, was wrecked on the Los Jardines Reefs, near the Isle of Pines.

24. *Year 1610.* Unidentified English privateering vessel, sailing from Plymouth, England, with 150 men on board, sank near the Isle of Pines, there were only eight survivors. This ship was carrying a large amount of treasure captured from Spanish shipping.

25. *Year 1612.* Small unidentified advice boat, sailing from Cartagena to Spain, was wrecked on the Isle of Pines.

26. *Year 1613.* Treasure-laden galleon *Los Peligros*, while preparing to sail for Spain, caught fire and sank in Havana Harbor.

27. **Year 1616.** During a hurricane near the end of September, more than thirty unidentified ships were sunk in several ports of Oriente Province, many by being dashed to pieces against other ships.

28. **Year 1618.** Frigate *San Francisco*, 80 tons, Captain Juan d'Esquibel, sailing as an advice boat between Veracruz and Spain, was lost during a storm while attempting to enter Matanzas Bay, no lives were lost and divers recovered the mail and cargo.

29. **Year 1618.** An unidentified Portuguese merchantman, sailing in the Nueva España Flota of Captain-General Vallecillas, for some unknown reason set fire to his ship as the convoy was entering the port of Havana.

30. **Year 1621.** Advice boat *La Concepción*, 50 tons, Captain Francisco Rodriquiz, sailing from Veracruz to Spain, was wrecked on Cayo del Visal, near the entrance to Rio de Puercos, most of the crew drowned but the mail was recovered.

31. **Year 1628.** A small squadron of privateers owned by the Dutch West India Company attacked two Honduras galleons near Cabo San Anton, forcing one ashore and capturing the other. The cargo of the wrecked ship consisted mainly of indigo and a small amount of silver specie, but only a small part of the indigo was recovered by divers from Havana.

32. **Year 1628.** Another Dutch West India Fleet, commanded by Admiral Piet Heyn, cornered the Nueva España Flota, commanded by Captain-General Juan de Benevides y Bazan, near Havana and forced it into Matanzas Bay on September 8, where all twenty-four Spanish ships were wrecked on the shoals. Some of the treasure on the *flota* ships was thrown overboard before the Dutch fleet entered the bay and the Spaniards fled ashore without firing a shot to protect the treasure or their ships. The Dutch estimate the value of the treasure they took from the ships at 15 million Dutch guilders, and this amount was greater than all that had been captured from Spanish shipping by privateers and pirates since the discovery of the New World. The treasure was so great that it could not be carried aboard the twenty-eight ships of Piet Heyn, so he refloated four of the largest Spanish ships and used them to carry some of the treasure back to Holland. Two of these Spanish ships were separated from the Dutch fleet

in bad weather and wrecked near present Freeport, Grand Bahama Island. A small part of the treasure that one of these ships was carrying was discovered several years ago.

33. *Year 1629.* A Dutch privateer forced the 400-ton *nao Santiago*, Captain Andrés de la Calde, coming from Honduras, to be run aground near Havana, where it was totally lost.

34. *Year 1629.* An unidentified advice boat, sailing between Spain and Veracruz, was forced ashore near Cabo de Cruz by a Dutch privateer but the crew escaped with the mail.

35. *Year 1633.* A large unidentified Portuguese galleon, sailing in the Tierra Firme Armada of Captain-General Antonio de Oquendo, hit a reef and sank at the entrance to Havana Harbor, the crew was all saved and her artillery was later recovered by divers.

36. *Year 1634.* Unidentified merchant *nao* carrying the Mastre de Campo Francisco Riano y Gamboa to Spain, was sunk in the port of Muriel on October 5.

37. *Year 1634.* The galleon *San Juan Agustin*, Captain Bartolome de Larriba, part of a four-galleon squadron commanded by Captain Sancho de Urdaniba to help escort the Nueva España Flota back to Spain, was wrecked during the night in a storm about 15 leagues from Havana, between Rio de Puercos and Bahía Honda, and forty of the crew were drowned.

38. *Year 1635.* Merchant *urca* owned by Captain Diego de Larrasa, was attacked by a Dutch warship off Cape Corrientes and wrecked on the shore but the crew escaped.

39. *Year 1636.* During a hurricane that struck Havana, many houses and warehouses were carried into the sea by torrential floods, a large number of cannon and some of the ramparts of Morro Castle were also flung into the sea.

40. *Year 1636.* When the Nueva España Flota, Captain-General Juan de Vega Bazan, arrived from Veracruz and entered Havana, its *Capitana, Nuestra Señora de la Limpia Concepción,* 600 tons, Captain Alonso Hidalgo, carrying a large amount of treasure, hit a rock near Morro Castle and sank, but due to the rapid action of many nearby ships, all of the treasure and artillery were saved before she went down.

41. *Year 1636.* On January 20, two Dutch privateers forced an *urca* of Captain Juan de Urrutia, which was coming from Maracaibo to Havana with a cargo of cocoa, to run aground at Cape San Anton. After her crew reached shore the Dutch stripped everything of value off the ship.

42. *Year 1638.* A Dutch privateering fleet commanded by the famous Dutch admiral known by the nickname "Wooden Leg" attacked the Tierra Firme Armada of Captain-General Carlos de Ibarra. The battle ensued for two days while the Armada attempted to reach Havana. One of the Spanish galleons, the *Nuestra Señora de Arancacu,* 600 tons, Captain Sancho de Urdaniva, was so badly damaged by cannon fire that, after all of its treasure was transferred to other galleons, it was taken into the port of Bahía Honda and set afire. Later, divers retrieved fifteen of the twenty large cannon from the burnt hulk, but the other five were not raised, as they were buried under sand. All of the other Spanish ships made port safely.

43. *Year 1639.* Merchant *urca Hercules* sank during a storm near Cayo de Libizas, located 22 leagues west of Havana, because she was overloaded. Four frigates with divers sent from Havana recovered all twenty of her cannon, eight of which were bronze.

44. *Year 1640.* Admiral "Wooden Leg" returned again to the Caribbean in an attempt to duplicate Piet Heyn's feat of capturing a treasure fleet; but while cruising near Havana in wait for the Nueva España Flota, a hurricane wrecked seven of his warships on the coast near Xaimanita, Baru, Mosquitos, and La Herradura, located 3, 7, 9, and 11 leagues, respectively, from Havana. The Spaniards captured many of his men and recovered some cannon from a few of the wrecks.

45. *Year 1641.* After the Nueva España Flota, commanded by Admiral Juan de Campos, set sail from Havana for Spain, it was struck by a hurricane in the Bahama Channel and many ships were lost. Four ships of this *flota* were driven back to Cuba, where two were wrecked near Havana; another wrecked 6 leagues from Santiago de Cuba, and the other entered this port.

46. *Year 1642.* The ship of this *flota* that reached Santiago de Cuba was the *nao Nuestra Señora de Atocha y San Josef,* 400 tons, Captain Gerónimo Beleno, which, after making repairs, left this port for Havana in January. Within sight of Havana a bad storm struck and the *nao* was wrecked only a musket-shot distance from the Fort of La Puntal. During this same storm a galleon, *Peña de Francia*, of the Armada de Barlovento, sank 6 leagues from Havana with a total loss of lives. When salvors located this wreck eight months later they were unable to recover anything, as it was completely buried in sand.

47. *Year 1647.* When the Tierra Firme Armada of Captain-General Pedro de Ursua entered Havana, arriving from Cartagena with large amounts of treasure, its *Capitana, San Josef y San Francisco de Paula*, 400 tons, Captain Jacobo de Oyanguren, and an unidentified *patache* were sunk at the entrance to the harbor.

48. *Year 1648.* A pirate ship was sighted cruising off Havana, so the governor armed two large merchantmen and sent them out to capture or destroy it, but both ran aground at a small port near Havana and were totally lost. The pirate ship entered this port and cut the throats of many of the survivors.

49. *Year 1660.* The frigate *La Gallardino*, Captain Juan Gómez Brito, coming from Puerto Rico, was wrecked on a small reef described as about half the size of the main plaza of Havana, where waves are always breaking, located 12 to 14 leagues north of Rio de Puercos.

50. *Year 1672.* Merchant *navío Nuestra Señora de la Concepción y San Francisco*, Captain Juan Ignacio de Cuellar, was accidentally burnt in Havana Harbor.

51. *Year 1672.* A Jamaican privateer commanded by Captain Robert Hewytt, captured a Spanish bark, which was later wrecked at Boga Pavillion, one of the small cays on the south coast of Cuba.

52. *Year 1681.* Merchant *navío Nuestra Señora de la Concepción y San Ignacio*, one of the ships in the Nueva España Flota of Captain-General Fernando Ponce, was wrecked on the shoals of Los Organos, located 14 leagues from Havana.

53. *Year 1687.* Galleon *Nuestra Señora del Rosario y San Joseph*, built in Havana, 424 tons and owned by Governor Francisco Blanco, sank while entering Havana after her sea trials.

54. *Year 1689.* Galleon *San José y Nuestra Señora del Rosario,* Captain Francisco Blanco, 230 tons, sank at the entrance of Havana Harbor, divers recovered her 42 iron cannon and cargo of tobacco.

55. *Year 1693.* English warship H.M.S. *Mordaunt,* 46 guns, Captain Francis Maynard, was wrecked on the Los Colorado Reefs on November 21 with a total loss of life.

56. *Year 1695.* Two treasure-laden galleons were wrecked near Havana: *Nuestra Señora de la Soledad y San Ignacio de Loyola,* near the entrance of the port, all of her treasure was recovered; and the *Almiranta Nuestra Señora de las Mercedes,* Captain Juan Vélez de Larres, at Simarina, near Havana, most of her treasure was recovered.

57. *Year 1696.* An unidentified *navío* was wrecked at Playa de Sabarimar, 7 leagues east of Havana, in 35 feet of water, during a storm, she was completely salvaged soon afterward.

58. *Year 1699.* Merchant *navío Santiago,* 228 tons, Captain Salvador Vanegas, returning to Spain with a cargo of no great value, was wrecked on the Los Jardines Reefs, near the Isle of Pines.

59. *Year 1702.* A French fleet of warships commanded by Chateaurenault was sent to Havana to escort some Spanish treasure galleons back to Spain, but the vice-admiral's ship was burnt in Havana Harbor.

60. *Year 1703.* Another French fleet, commanded by Admiral Ducase, was sent to Havana to escort Spanish ships back to Spain, and the French man-of-war *El Bueno* was wrecked at Castle de la Punta in Havana.

61. *Year 1705.* American privateer ship *New York,* Captain Tongerlou, chased a Spanish ship of 24 guns and 600 tons coming from the Canary Islands and forced it to run aground about 1 league from Baracoa, its cargo of wine and brandy was saved.

62. *Year 1705.* During a hurricane, four large Spanish warships, along with most of their crews, were lost in Havana Harbor.

63. *Year 1707.* Two French frigates, *Diamante* and the *El Conde Torigin,* were wrecked on the Bajos de Santa Isabel, about 3 leagues from Bahía Honda and half a league from shore. One was carrying a cargo of logwood and the other 30 tons of iron bars as ballast.

64. *Year 1711.* Five ships of the Nueva España Flota were wrecked during a "norther" on December 16 about 5 leagues west of Havana: one was its *Almiranta, Santisima Trinidad,* which carried a large treasure, Captain Diego de Alarcón y Ocaño of the Armada de Barlovento; the other four were *flota naos,* of which only one was identified, the *Nuestra Señora del Rosario, San José y Las Animas.* Divers were quickly employed and by January 4 they had recovered over 1,700,000 pesos in treasure from the wrecks. The total amount of treasure carried on these ships was not stated in the documents.

65. *Year 1715.* An unidentified ship bringing eighty-five chests of silver and fifty silver bars—salvaged in 1970—was wrecked during a storm at Jaimanita, located 5 leagues from Havana, but divers recovered all of its treasure.

66. *Year 1715.* Brief mention that a Spanish ship named *Santisima Trinidad* was lost on Los Pasajes Shoals near Havana.

67. *Year 1721.* Treasure-laden galleon *San Juan,* Captain Francisco Maldonado, was lost entering Havana Harbor.

68. *Year 1726.* An unidentified French merchant brigantine, sailing to the Mississippi River, ran aground at Cabo Francés but the majority of her cargo was salvaged.

69. *Year 1727.* Two unidentified French warships commanded by Admiral du Rochet were wrecked on the reefs of Jardines de la Reina, on the southern coast of the island, a bit to the east of Jaqua, and when salvors were sent there they reported sighting several other wrecks in the same area.

70. *Year 1731.* Merchant *navío San Antonio de Padua* (alias *Hercules*), 174 tons, Captain Pedro Sanz y Sagardia, carrying a cargo of mercury, was wrecked in Bahía Mangle, located between Puerto de Principe and Bayano.

71. *Year 1740.* Large galleon *Invencible,* of the squadron of Admiral Rodrigo de Torres, was struck by lightning after anchoring in Havana Harbor and blew up, causing great damage to the city as well. This ship carried 4 million pesos in treasure, none of which was recovered.

72. *Year 1741.* Small unidentified Spanish frigate was wrecked on Cayo Lobos.

73. **Year 1744.** Two unidentified Spanish privateering vessels were run ashore near Santiago de Cuba by two New England privateering ships.

74. **Year 1745.** Two American privateering ships from Philadelphia drove a Spanish sloop ashore at Matanzas Bay and carried her cargo away.

75. **Year 1748.** An English squadron of warships commanded by Admiral Knowles attempted to capture the Nueva España Flota, Captain-General Spinola. During the battle near Havana, the *Almiranta* of the *flota* lost her masts and was forced to run aground on the coast, where the Spaniards set her afire. Within an hour she blew up, scattering the beach with many of the more than 10 million pesos in treasure she carried. A merchant *nao* of this *flota*, in attempting to escape from the English warships, was lost in Ensenada de Vixiras, 95 leagues east of Havana.

76. **Year 1749.** A large unidentified ship was wrecked on the Jardines Reefs, near Cape San Anton.

77. **Year 1751.** Galleon *San Antonio y San Felix*, Captain Ocana, sailing from Cartagena for Spain, was lost during a storm on the coast between capes San Anton and Corrientes, crew and 400,000 pesos saved.

78. **Year 1752.** During a hurricane on September 26, sixteen unidentified ships were lost near Havana.

79. **Year 1753.** English merchantman *Griffin*, Captain Brown, sailing from Jamaica to London, was lost off Cape San Anton.

80. **Year 1755.** Two American merchantmen, *Salisbury*, Captain Ash, and the *Delight*, Captain Fry, both sailing from Honduras to New York, were wrecked on the Los Colorados Reefs. The *Delight*, after throwing overboard part of her cargo, was able to get off the reef; the *Salisbury* lost all of its crew, except for a boy.

81. **Year 1757.** English merchantman *Hawke*, Captain Caine, sailing from Jamaica to London, wrecked on November 3 on the Los Colorados Reef.

82. **Year 1758.** Two unidentified English merchantmen were lost on the Los Colorados Reef, sailing from Jamaica to England.

83. **Year** *1758.* English ship *Lion,* Captain Brown, sailing from Jamaica to Bristol, was wrecked on Isla Blanca, on the northern coast of Cuba, crew and part of cargo saved.

84. **Year** *1760.* English warship H.M.S. *Harwich,* 50 guns, Captain William March, wrecked October 4 on the Isle of Pines.

85. **Year** *1761.* English merchantman *Scorpion,* Captain Quay, sailing from Jamaica to Liverpool, wrecked on the Jardines Reef, near the Isle of Pines.

86. **Year** *1762.* Shortly before the Spaniards surrendered Havana to the English on June 3, they sank their three largest warships at the entrance to the harbor: galleon *Neptuno,* 70 guns, Captain Pedro Bermudas; galleon *Asia,* 64 guns, Captain Francisco Garganta; and the galleon *Europa,* 60 guns, Captain Joseph Vicente. During the English attack on the city, the frigate *La Victoria,* Captain Carlos Joseph de Sarria, sank in the port on "la Colonia del Sacramento."

87. **Year** *1762.* One English warship, H.M.S. *Chesterfield,* and four transports bringing reinforcements to hold the city of Havana in English hands, wrecked on Cayo Confite, north of Havana, but no lives were lost.

88. **Year** *1762.* After the English captured the city of Havana, three English warships were sunk at the entrance of the port while leaving for England with plunder: *Providence,* Captain Strenham, *General Wolfe,* 440 tons, and the *Lion,* 293 tons.

89. **Year** *1763.* A small advice boat sent from Spain, *Nuestra Señora de las Mercedes,* Captain Ramón Ortís Delgado, was wrecked at Cape San Anton on January 26.

90. **Year** *1763.* A ship of unknown registry, *Havana,* Captain Hale, sailing from New England to Jamaica, was lost off Cape Maize.

91. **Year** *1765.* English merchantman *Hare,* Captain Colly, sailing from Jamaica to Liverpool, was wrecked on the Colorado Reef, but the crew was saved.

92. **Year** *1766.* Unidentified Spanish *nao,* carrying the cargo of the *nao El Nuevo Constante* (which had sunk 75 leagues from the mouth of the Mississippi River), sank between El Morro and La Punta in Havana Harbor.

93. **Year 1768.** During a hurricane that struck Havana on October 15, sixty nine ships were sunk, of which seventeen belonged to the King. Of these, only five were identified: *navío Tridente;* three frigates: *Nancy, Perle,* and the *Dorado;* and the packet boat *San Francisco de Paula.* Over five thousand buildings were also destroyed in the city and the surrounding countryside.

94. **Year 1768.** English merchantman *Black River,* Captain M'Taggart, sailing from Jamaica to London, was wrecked on the Isle of Pines but the crew was saved.

95. **Year 1768.** A ship of unknown registry, *Neptune,* Captain Hodgson, sailing from Honduras to Leghorn, Italy, was lost in Bahía Honda but the crew was saved.

96. **Year 1770.** English hydrographic ship, commanded by Lieutenant John Payne, was wrecked on the Colorado Reef in 22 degrees and 22 minutes of latitude, about 4 leagues from Cape Buena Vista. Spaniards rescued them and took them to Havana where they were embarked on a ship for Jamaica, which was also wrecked at Cape San Antonio on February 19.

97. **Year 1770.** Three other ships were lost on the Colorado Reef this year: English warship H.M.S. *Jamaica,* Captain Talbot, all of the crew was saved; English merchantman *Britannia,* Captain Lawrie, coming from the Bay of Honduras; and the American ship *Nonsuch,* Captain Hall, sailing from Jamaica to South Carolina, the crew was rescued from a raft they constructed from the wreck.

98. **About 1771.** English schooner *Rebecca,* Captain Pedro Anson, was wrecked on the Shoals of Santa Isabel. The crew was rescued by a boat from Havana and carried to its port.

99. **Year 1772.** During a hurricane on July 20, more than 150 ships of various sizes and nationalities were destroyed in the ports and on the coast.

100. **Year 1773.** English merchantman *George,* Captain Stenton, sailing from Jamaica to London, was wrecked on the Colorado Reef.

101. **Year 1773.** English ship *Mary,* Captain Aspinal, sailing from Jamaica to London, was wrecked on the Isle of Pines, eight of the crew reached Grand Cayman Island in the ship's longboat.

102. **Year 1776.** English merchantman *Rebecca,* Captain Stott, sailing from Jamaica to Bristol, was wrecked on the Colorado Reef but the crew was saved.

103. **Year 1777.** American merchantman *Sally,* Captain Thompson, sailing from Jamaica to New York, was totally lost on the Jardines Reef, some of the crew were saved.

104. **Year 1778.** During a hurricane (date not stated), many ships were lost in and around Havana Harbor.

105. **Year 1780.** During a hurricane on October 3, thirteen English warships were lost on the Jardines Reefs, on the south coast of the island. They were in the squadron commanded by Sir Hyde Park, sailing from Jamaica to Pensacola, Florida: *Thunderer,* 74 guns; *Stirling Castle,* 64 guns; *Phoenix,* 44 guns; *La Blanche,* 42 guns; *Laurel,* 28 guns; *Andromeda,* 28 guns; *Deal Castle,* 24 guns; *Scarborough,* 20 guns; *Beaver's Prize,* 16 guns; *Barbadoes,* 14 guns; *Camelon,* 14 guns; *Endeavour,* 14 guns; and the *Victor,* 10 guns. Most of the crews on these ships were lost.

106. **Year 1783.** Scottish merchantman *Blandford,* Captain Troup, sailing from Jamaica to Scotland, was totally lost on the Isle of Pines.

107. **Year 1784.** Spanish brigantine *Carlota,* arriving from Spain, sank at the entrance of Matanzas Bay on December 23.

108. **Year 1784.** English ship *Mercury,* Captain Taylor, sailing from Africa and Jamaica to Bristol, was wrecked on the Jardines Reef on March 13.

109. **Year 1785.** English merchantman *Port Maria,* Captain Potter, sailing from Jamaica to London, was totally lost on the Jardines Reefs on the south side of the island but the crew was saved.

110. **Year 1785.** Scottish merchantman *Friendship,* Captain Curry, sailing from Jamaica to Dublin, was lost in Havana Harbor.

111. **Year 1786.** Spanish frigate of war *Santa Tecla,* Captain Carlos Chacón, burnt completely in Havana Harbor.

112. **Year 1787.** Two merchantmen lost in the Colorado Reef: English ship *Ranger,* Captain Patterson, sailing from Jamaica to Bermuda, five men were drowned; and the Irish ship *Hannah,* Captain Williamson, sailing from Jamaica to Cork, struck on a sunken

rock a few leagues northeast of the reef on August 2 but the crew reached Havana in thirteen days in the ship's boat.

113. Year 1788. Spanish schooner *Carmen*, wrecked at Punta Sabanilla, near Havana.

114. Year 1790. English merchantman *Flora*, Captain Fatheringham, sailing from Jamaica to Leith, was lost on the Jardines Reef, near the Isle of Pines.

115. Year 1791. Ship of unknown registry *Ally*, Captain Sparling, sailing from Africa and Dominica to Havana, was wrecked on Cayo Romano, crew and cargo saved.

116. Year 1791. A hurricane on June 21 caused the house of a count named Barretos, at Puestes Grandes, to be swept into the sea. He had died the same day, so his coffin went into the sea.

117. Year 1792. During a hurricane on October 29 an unidentified brig was carried 100 yards ashore at Alarés Castle in Havana, two ships were wrecked near Batabanó, and four others along the coast.

118. Year 1792. Two unidentified English merchantmen were wrecked near the Isle of Pines.

119. Year 1792. Four merchantmen were lost on the Jardines Reef: English ship *Good Intent*, Captain Kennedy, sailing from Jamaica to London; English ship *Sarah*, sailing from Jamaica to Liverpool, her cargo of sugar was lost but some rum and lumber were saved; Scottish ship *Eliza Partridge*, Captain Trenham, sailing from Jamaica to Dublin, crew and part of cargo saved; and the Scottish ship *Charming Mary*, Captain English, sailing from Jamaica to Dublin, part of her cargo of sugar, rum, coffee, ginger, and castor oil was saved.

120. Year 1793. English merchantman *Albion*, Captain Mentor, sailing from Jamaica to Bristol, sank off Cape San Antonio after colliding with another ship but her crew was saved.

121. Year 1794. During a hurricane at Havana on August 27 and 28, seventy-six ships were totally lost and others damaged. Of those lost, twelve were Spanish warships and the others were merchantmen of different countries. Only two ships were identified: Spanish warship *Flor*, and the English merchantman *Sandown*,

Captain Apsey, sailing from Jamaica to Havana. Most of the cargoes were later salvaged.

122. *Year 1796.* During a hurricane on October 2 and 3, five unidentified ships were totally lost in Havana Harbor.

123. *Year 1797.* Spanish frigate of war *Palas*, 34 guns, Captain Pedro Saenz de la Guardia, part of a Spanish squadron going after an English squadron, wrecked in 2 fathoms of water on "el placer de Cayo Blanco," near the Colorado Reef but the ship was later completely salvaged.

124. *Year 1797.* Spanish warship *Ventura*, Captain Luis Cabaleri, was wrecked at Punta del Palo while chasing a pirate ship, several men were drowned.

125. *Year 1798.* American ship *Mable*, Captain Reynolds, sailing from Jamaica to New York, was lost on the Colorado Reef but the crew was saved.

126. *Year 1799.* Spanish frigate *Guadalupe*, Captain José de la Encina, was wrecked on Cape San Antonio on March 15 and 147 persons perished.

127. *Year 1800.* English warship H.M.S. *Diligence*, 18 guns, Captain Charles Baynton Hodgson, was wrecked in September on a shoal near Havana but the crew was saved.

128. *Year 1801.* English warship H.M.S. *Bonetta*, 18 guns, Captain Thomas New, was wrecked on the Jardines Reef on October 25 but the crew was saved.

129. *Year 1802.* Two English merchantmen, sailing from Jamaica to London, were wrecked on the Isle of Pines: *Diana*, Captain Williams, on July 19; and the *Westmoreland*, Captain Smellie, but her crew was saved.

130. *Year 1803.* An unidentified French ship of Captain Gilbert was wrecked on the Shoals of Los Jardines del Rey.

131. *Year 1805.* English merchantman *Paget*, Captain Straycock, sailing from Jamaica to London, was wrecked at Cape San Antonio.

132. *Year 1805.* English warship H.M.S. *Barracouta*, 10 guns, Captain Joel Orchard, was wrecked on Jordan Key on October 2 but the crew was saved.

133. Year 1806. American merchantman *Albert,* Captain Hall, sailing from Boston to Jamaica, was wrecked at Cape Maize but part of her cargo was saved.

134. Year 1807. Spanish schooner *Piedad,* Captain José Fernández de la Peña, sailing from Cartagena to Havana with mail, ran aground on January 19 in Baní but people, mail, and cannon were saved.

135. Year 1807. Two American ships were wrecked on the Colorado Reef: *Merry Quaker,* Captain Brown, sailing from Jamaica to New York, on January 9; and the *Lewis Williams,* Captain O'Brien, sailing from New Orleans to New York, March 23, but the crew was saved.

136. Year 1808. English warship H.M.S. *Muros,* 24 guns, Captain Archibald Duff, lost at the entrance to Balía Honda but the crew was saved.

137. Year 1809. Canadian ship *Cyrus,* Captain Lovitt, sailing from Jamaica to Halifax, was lost on Cape Comentes.

138. Year 1809. A ship of unknown registry, *Spanish Junta,* Captain Murray, sailing from London to Havana, was lost on Stoney Point Reef, located about 3 miles from Guazava Key on the north side of Cuba, but the crew was saved.

139. Year 1809. Two merchantmen were wrecked near the Isle of Pines: Scottish ship *Ann Phillippa,* sailing from Jamaica to Glasgow, on January 22; and a ship of unknown registry, *Tartaruga,* Captain Smith, sailing from Bahía, Brazil, to Havana, on a reef 12 leagues east-southeast of the Isle of Pines.

140. Year 1810. A ship of unknown registry, *May,* Captain Laughton, was burnt at Havana on July 25 but the crew was saved.

141. Year 1810. During a hurricane at Havana from October 23 to 26, thirty-two ships were sunk or wrecked, and the pier, church, and sixty buildings were carried into the sea.

142. Year 1811. Two English merchantmen were wrecked at the Isle of Pines—*Louisa,* Captain Folger; and the *Hannah,* Captain Ellis, on January 29—both sailing from Jamaica to London.

143. Year 1811. American ship *Alexander,* Captain Hall, sailing from Jamaica to the United States, was totally lost on Cape Cruz at the end of May.

144. *Year 1811.* American schooner *Phoebe*, Captain Murray, was burnt off Santiago de Cuba but the crew was saved.

145. *Year 1811.* English ship *Edward Foote*, Captain Smart, sailing from Jamaica to London, was lost off Havana in February but her crew was saved.

146. *Year 1812.* During a hurricane on October 14 at Trinidad de Cuba a number of unidentified ships were sunk.

147. *Year 1813.* A ship of unknown registry, *Catalena*, Captain Ferrer, sailing from San Andrés Island to Jamaica, was wrecked on White Key, near Trinidad de Cuba, July 24, crew and part of cargo saved.

148. *Year 1813.* Canadian ship *Olive*, Captain Vandirey, sailing from Jamaica to Halifax, was lost on September 17 near the Isle of Pines but the crew was saved.

149. *Year 1813.* Two English ships were wrecked at Havana: *Nancy*, Captain Bowden, sailing from Jamaica to London, October 8, very little of her cargo was saved; and the *Lancaster*, Captain Andrews, bound to Liverpool, July 21.

150. *Year 1814.* Two English ships sailing from London to Havana were totally lost near Havana on February 2: *Navigator*, Captain Preda, and the *Esther*, Captain Newman.

151. *Year 1815.* American ship *Pacific*, Captain Clark, sailing from Santo Domingo to Boston, was lost on July 13 on the Jardines Reef, crew and small part of cargo saved.

152. *Year 1815.* A ship of unknown registry, *Sarah*, Captain Kelly, sailing from Jamaica to Halifax, was lost entering Havana Harbor on January 14.

153. *Year 1816.* English sloop-of-war H.M.S. *Briseis*, 10 guns, Captain George Domett, wrecked on a reef November 5 near Punta Pedras but the crew was saved.

154. *Year 1816.* Spanish frigate-of-war *Atocha*, 40 guns, Captain Lorenzo Noriega, caught on fire and sank in Havana Harbor on July 4.

155. *Year 1816.* During a violent gale on June 14, twelve or fourteen unidentified ships were wrecked in Trinidad de Cuba Harbor.

156. Year 1816. A ship of unknown registry, *Clara*, sailing from Rio de la Hacha, Colombia, to Jamaica, put into Santiago de Cuba in distress and sank soon after.

157. Year 1816. Bahamian ship *Minerva*, Captain Whitehead, sailing from Jamaica to the Bahamas, was lost on Cape Maize.

158. Year 1817. A ship of unknown registry, *Lark*, Captain Knight, sailing to Havana, was wrecked on September 17 on the Nuevitas Reef, crew and part of cargo saved.

159. Year 1817. English ship *Jane*, Captain M'Bride, sailing from Jamaica to Greenock, England, wrecked near Cape Corrientes on June 9, crew and passengers saved.

160. Year 1817. Three ships wrecked near Havana: a ship of unknown registry, *Hercules*, during February; English brig *Prince Regent*, arriving from the Bahamas with a cargo of salt, during a gale on March 3; and the English brig *Liberty*, December 20, but her cargo was completely salvaged.

161. Year 1818. French ship *Clementine*, after arriving from St. Malo, France, during a storm on December 15, wrecked in Havana Harbor, crew and part of cargo saved.

162. Year 1818. Scottish merchantman *Amelia*, Captain Williams, sailing from Jamaica to Clyde, Scotland, wrecked on the Jardines Reef, near the Isle of Pines, on May 2.

163. Year 1818. Three merchant ships were wrecked on the Colorado Reef: English ship *Mariner*, Captain Whillis, sailing from London to Havana, crew, silver and gold specie, and small part of cargo saved; American ship *Berkeley*, Captain Dent, sailing from Jamaica to Virginia, during a gale on November 17—after being plundered by Spaniards she was set afire but her crew was saved; and the American ship *Joan*, sailing from Jamaica to Norfolk, July 4, crew and part of cargo saved.

164. Year 1819. Scottish ship *Sir Thomas Graham*, Captain Thomson, sailing from Jamaica to Havana, was lost in March on the Jardines Reef.

165. Year 1819. English merchantman *Syren*, Captain Clark, sailing from Jamaica to London, was totally wrecked on a rocky point near Cape San Antonio on June 9, only her crew was saved.

166. *Year 1821.* Two English merchantmen wrecked near Cape San Antonio: *Aristides,* sailing from Liverpool to New Orleans, was captured by pirates and then wrecked; and the *Duke of Bedford,* Captain Holliday, sailing from Jamaica to London, went to pieces quickly.

167. *Year 1821.* During a gale on September 13, four unidentified Spanish vessels and the American schooner *Olive Branch,* Captain Smith, were lost in the port of Gibara.

168. *Year 1821.* A ship of unknown registry, *Devon,* Captain Carlisle, sailing from Jamaica to Cork, wrecked on a reef off Cape Corrientes on September 16, only some of her crew were saved.

169. *Year 1821.* A ship of unknown registry, *Villorius,* Captain M'Kernly, sailing from the Plate River, Argentina, to Havana, was wrecked at Baracoa at the end of September, most of her cargo was saved.

170. *Year 1821.* French ship *Amie,* Captain Falvey, sailing from Haiti to Havana, lost on September 13 off the Isle of Pines, only the crew was saved.

171. *Year 1821.* English ship *Hall,* sailing from Jamaica to Liverpool, was wrecked at Havana on April 30 during a gale, small part of her cargo was saved.

172. *Year 1821.* American ship *Two Brothers,* Captain Blackman, sailing from Charleston, South Carolina, to Matanzas Bay, was wrecked on Cayo Blanco, located about 30 miles east of Matanzas.

173. *Year 1821.* American merchantman *Hannah,* Captain Lewis, sailing from Santiago de Cuba to Philadelphia, was wrecked during September on the Colorado Reef.

174. *Year 1822.* French ship *Actif,* Captain Belliard, sailing from Havana to Le Havre, was lost near Nuevitas.

175. *Year 1822.* A ship of unknown registry, *Union,* Captain Munro, sailing from Jamaica to Nova Scotia, was lost on a reef 16 leagues from Matanzas Bay.

176. *Year 1822.* Bermudan ship *Carso,* Captain Peabody, sailing from Jamaica to Bermuda, was wrecked 2 leagues east of Havana on January 5.

177. *Year 1822.* Spanish frigate of war *Ligera*, 40 guns, sank in the port of Santiago de Cuba.

178. *Year 1823.* Large Spanish ship *Churrieca*, Captain Aspurua, sailing from Cadiz, Spain, to Veracruz, was totally destroyed by fire near Morro Castle, in Havana Harbor, in April, with a cargo worth over $100,000.

179. *Year 1823.* A ship of unknown registry, *Eliza & Polly*, Captain Forsyth, after leaving Havana, wrecked a few miles west of it.

180. *Year 1823.* A ship of unknown registry, *Freetown*, arriving from Jamaica in ballast, was lost on June 10 entering Santiago de Cuba.

181. *Year 1823.* A ship of unknown registry, *Caesar*, Captain Jars, sailing from Hamburg, Germany, to Havana, was wrecked on Cayo Romano but her cargo was saved by wreckers and carried to Nassau.

182. *Year 1824.* Two ships were wrecked at Cape Corrientes: a ship of unknown registry, *Fleetwood*, Captain Herring, sailing from Jamaica to London, on June 2; and the French ship *Reparateur*, Captain Freore, sailing from Cuba to Bordeaux, France, on June 1.

183. *Year 1824.* Spanish ship *General Palafox*, Captain Abente, sailing from Cadiz to Havana, was totally lost near the Isle of Pines.

184. *Year 1824.* A ship of unknown registry, *Azores*, Captain Bedford, sailing from Jamaica to Trinidad de Cuba, was lost while entering this port on March 2 but her crew was saved.

185. *Year 1825.* Two ships were lost on the coast near Matanzas Bay: American ship *Arinthea Bell*, Captain Pearson, sailing from Baltimore to Havana, crew and part of cargo saved; and a large Dutch ship—with no crew aboard but the decks running with blood—believed to have been plundered and set adrift by pirates.

186. *Year 1825.* A ship of unknown registry, *Telegraph*, Captain Dixon, coming from Alvarado, Mexico, was wrecked near Havana.

CHAPTER NINE

Hispaniola

ALTHOUGH there are a great number of interesting shipwrecks around this island, very little salvage work has been undertaken on them, due to the fact that the governments of Haiti and the Dominican Republic have not passed laws regarding the salvaging of old shipwrecks by foreigners, and getting permission to do so is almost impossible without going through a great deal of difficulty. In the past two decades, many American treasure-hunting expeditions have attempted to work on wrecks around the island but only two groups were given permission.

In 1955 the millionaire Edwin Link and Mendel Peterson of the Smithsonian Institution attempted to locate Columbus' *Santa Maria,* which was wrecked at Cape Haitian in 1492, and although they did not locate the shipwreck they claimed to have discovered an iron anchor from it. Similar anchors—also claimed to be from this shipwreck—

have been found in the same area by Haitian fishermen. In 1967 a group from New Jersey undertook an expedition after this same shipwreck and claimed to have discovered it, but I have been unable to confirm their claim.

During dredging operations in the port of Santo Domingo over the years, large numbers of artifacts and gold and silver coins have accidentally been found. On a recent trip to Santo Domingo I was told by naval officers that some of their divers had recovered several thousand gold coins off a shipwreck a few miles east of the port of Santo Domingo.

In many articles and books concerning sunken treasure, the authors claim that the port of Puerto Plata (Silver Port), on the north coast of the island, was a staging and departure port for the homeward-bound Spanish treasure ships. This is untrue. The port was named for another reason. When Columbus first sighted it, the large mountain behind the port was covered with a silver-colored cloud, so he named it Silver Port. There is another widely circulated erroneous tale in sunken-treasure literature concerning a large table made of solid gold: It was supposedly lost in 1502 near Mona Island. The truth is that a very large gold nugget was found on the island, and when the governor wrote back to Spain telling of the loss of the ship carrying this nugget, he said "that it was big enough to eat off it," meaning that it was as large as a plate and not a table.

Weather and working conditions on shipwreck sites are about the same as they are throughout the rest of the Caribbean, and the calmest months are during the hurricane season, when there are none in the area. Of the more than 430 ships that have been lost around this island, I have listed only those whose locations are fairly accurately given and those that are of major interest. In many cases the documents stated only that they were lost on or at Hispaniola.

Shipwrecks in Waters Around Hispaniola

1. **Year 1492.** Columbus' flagship, the caravel *Santa Maria*, was wrecked on a reef in Caracol Bay, near Cape Haitian. Columbus had the survivors from this wreck completely strip the ship of all its wood, fittings, and supplies, which they used to build a fort with the intention of waiting until Columbus could return to rescue them on his second voyage. If anything of this wreck

remains on the reef, it would probably be only ballast stones (if the ship carried any).

2. *Year 1494.* On Columbus' second voyage he founded a settlement on the north coast and named it Isabela. Two of his caravels —*Mariagalante* and *Gallega*—are believed to have been lost there during a hurricane.

3. *Year 1495.* During the month of October a hurricane struck the port of Isabela and six or seven caravels were reported lost here. One account states that two of Columbus' ships—*San Juan* and *Cordera*—and four ships of the explorer Juan Aquardo were lost. Another account states that these six plus another of Columbus' ships—named *Gallega*—were lost. This second account may be confusing the loss of the *Gallega* during the hurricane in 1494 with the 1495 hurricane.

4. *Year 1500.* Two unidentified caravels of the explorer Vicente Yañez Pinzon were wrecked during a storm on the Shoals of Babura.

5. *Year 1501.* Two unidentified *naos* of the captains Rodrigo de Bastidas and Juan de la Cosa, with cargoes of gold nuggets and dust as well as brazilwood and other products, were lost in Puerto Principe.

6. *Year 1502.* Columbus was in the port of Santo Domingo while a large fleet of thirty caravels and *naos* was preparing to sail for Spain. He attempted to prevent their departure, claiming there were signs of a hurricane. But Governor Bodadilla, who was his enemy, would not heed his advice, so the fleet sailed, carrying a large amount of gold (including the gold nugget the size of a plate) and other valuables. The fleet, commanded by Admiral Antonio de Torres, left port around the beginning of July, and about thirty or forty hours later the hurricane struck and all but four ships were lost. Most of them were wrecked on the coasts 8 to 10 leagues east of the port; others sank on the high seas near Mona Island. Over five hundred persons perished.

7. *About 1505.* After the fleet of the lawyer Lucas Vázquez de Ayllon reached Santo Domingo from Spain, one ship—*El Breton* —was sent to carry colonists to new lands, but bad weather forced into Puerto Plata, where it sank at anchor.

8. **Year 1508.** During a hurricane on August 3 in which most of the town of Santo Domingo was leveled to the ground, more than twenty unidentified caravels and *naos* were sunk or wrecked in the port or along the nearby coast. When the hurricane first struck, many ships threw their cannon overboard in the port to lighten the ships.

9. **Year 1509.** Another hurricane struck this same port on August 8 and eighteen or twenty ships of various sizes—including several that Columbus' son Diego had just brought from Spain—were sunk. During this same storm a small vessel owned by a religious named Mariscal was wrecked on the small key of Alto Velo, located 50 leagues west of the port of Santo Domingo, with six of the eight persons aboard drowning.

10. **Year 1526.** *Nao Santa María,* 110 tons, Captain Pedro Núñez, sank in Puerto Plata after loading aboard a cargo of sugar. Other accounts place the sinking in 1524 and 1525.

11. **Year 1528.** Unidentified ship of Captain Alonso Durán was wrecked in the port of Puerto Real sometime before April.

12. **Year 1541.** A small French pirate vessel with a crew of only thirty-five men captured and plundered a large Spanish merchant-man, then wrecked it on Mona Island.

13. **Year 1542.** *Nao San Miguel,* a ship in the fleet of Admiral Francisco de Montejo, sailing from Santo Domingo to Spain, was lost near Cape Cabrón, about 15 leagues from Puerto Plata, carrying a large amount of gold and silver.

14. **Year 1545.** Two hurricanes struck the town and port of Santo Domingo. The first occurred on August 20 and many ships in port were lost. The second, which was even worse, occurred on September 18 and destroyed all the ships that had not been lost in the first hurricane. Roughly ten ships were lost in the Ozama River in the port, five near the fort, several others by the house of Columbus, more on the coast near the port, and one ship of Captain Cruzado on Saona Island. The total number of ships lost during this second hurricane was eighteen to twenty.

15. **Year 1547.** During a hurricane the *nao San Juan,* 200 tons, Captain Martín de Zavalo, sailing from Spain to Nombre de Dios, Panama, was wrecked in Puerto Hermoso. Another account gives the date as 1549.

16. **Year 1551.** A French pirate ship with a crew of 150 men was wrecked on the coast of Iaquana and only a few escaped.

17. **Year 1551.** The *flotas* of Nueva España and Tierra Firme joined in Havana with the Armada de Tierra Firme, commanded by Captain-General Sancho de Veidma, and entered the Bahama Channel for the return to Spain. During a storm in the channel, the galleon *San Miguel*, 200 tons, Captain Salvador Garrido, owned by the viceroy of Mexico, Don Luis de Velasco, carrying a very valuable cargo of gold and silver specie and bullion, lost her mainmast and rudder and drifted until wrecking on a reef between Cape Francés and Cape Cabrón, about 30 leagues from Puerto de Plata. All of her people were saved and divers recovered all of her treasure.

18. **Year 1553.** Treasure-laden *nao La Salvadora*, Captain Juan Rodríquez, sailing from Mexico to Spain, was caught in a storm in the Bahama Channel, losing all her masts, and drifted until being wrecked on the coast near Monte Cristi. All of her gold and silver was recovered by divers.

19. **Year 1553.** During a hurricane that struck the port of Santo Domingo, sixteen merchantmen, loaded and ready to set sail for Seville, were totally lost. At the same time, three *naos* and one *patache*, commanded by Cristobal Colón (the nephew of the famous discoverer), were also lost on the coast.

20. **Year 1556.** Nao *San Bartolome*, 120 tons, Captain Blas Alonso, sailing from Santo Domingo to Spain, was wrecked on the coast close to the port of Santo Domingo shortly after sailing but divers recovered her cargo of gold, silver, and hides.

21. **Year 1564.** Nao *Santa María de Guadalupe*, 250 tons, Captain Salvador Gómez, after receiving the cargo of gold and silver from a ship that had sunk in the Bahama Channel during a storm, lost her masts and drifted until it wrecked near Monte Cristi, where divers later recovered all of the treasure she carried.

22. **Year 1584.** An oared galley, *Santiago*, sent from Santo Domingo to search for pirates, was wrecked on the reefs in front of Puerto de Plata, all of the galley slaves perished.

23. **Year 1603.** An unidentified merchant *nao* in the Nueva España Flota of Captain-General Fulgencio de Meneses, sailing from

Spain to Veracruz, was wrecked on the southern coast of the island.

24. **Year 1605.** An unidentified Spanish advice boat was lost on Mona Island enroute from Spain to Santo Domingo.

25. **Year 1609.** Small *navío San Vicente Ferrer,* 84 tons, Captain Gaspar Alvarez, sailing from Puerto Rico to Havana and Spain, was wrecked near Samana Bay, only her crew was saved.

26. **Year 1626.** *Nao La Candelaria,* 300 tons, Captain Juan de Patermina, sailed from Santo Domingo for Spain with three other *naos* all carrying products of the island, but when near La Saona Island, three enemy ships gave chase and forced it to run aground on this small island, where it broke into pieces and sank.

27. **Year 1631.** An unidentified Dutch warship was wrecked during a storm near the port of Santo Domingo.

28. **Year 1635.** The Spaniards launched an attack on the Island of Tortuga, which pirates had been living on for about six years. During the attack the Spaniards burnt two ships and one pinnace after murdering all of the pirates and their families.

29. **Year 1652.** During a hurricane in September the English ship *Honest Seaman* was cast ashore at Porto Pina.

30. **Year 1658.** Portuguese slave ship of Captain Juan Bautista Pluma was sunk in Santo Domingo Harbor, and the divers who recovered twelve iron cannon of 6- to 8-pound shot from this wreck, were paid 158 reals in silver.

31. **Year 1669.** English privateering frigate *Oxford,* 240 tons, caught fire on January 12 while anchored at the Isle of Ash and blew up with the loss of over two hundred lives. This ship had just returned from a successful attack on Porto Bello, Panama, and was carrying a great deal of plunder.

32. **Year 1670.** During a storm in October, when the privateer Henry Morgan was waiting for other ships to join his fleet, ten of his eleven ships were run ashore on the Isle de Vache, all were refloated except three.

33. **Year 1673.** An English privateering ship that operated out of Port Royal, Jamaica, the *Jamaica Merchant,* Captain Knapman—on

which Henry Morgan was aboard—was wrecked on February 25 on the east side of the Isle de Vache (also called Vaca and Vacour), due to the pilot's faulty navigation. Five or six days later they were rescued by another Jamaican privateering vessel and carried back to Jamaica. The governor of Jamaica sent salvage sloops to the wreck site and they recovered twenty large cannon and 212 cannonballs.

34. **Year 1677.** A Dutch fleet attacked all the French ships in the port of Petit-Goâve and, after sacking them, burnt them.

35. **Year 1680.** During a hurricane at the port of Santo Domingo on August 15, twenty-five French warships commanded by the Count de Estre and several Spanish merchantmen carrying a very valuable cargo of treasures from South America, were all totally lost with almost a complete loss of lives.

36. **Year 1702.** An English fleet forced ashore a large French man-of-war at Petit-Goâve. Rather than let it fall into English hands, the French blew it up. Nearby, the English captured and burnt two French merchantmen.

37. **Year 1706.** English warship H.M.S. *Dunkirk Prize*, 24 guns, Captain George Purvis, while in pursuit of a French ship on October 18, ran on a rock off Cape Francés and broke into pieces.

38. **Year 1721.** An unidentified *nao*, sailing from Spain to Veracruz, was wrecked in Sancana Bay.

39. **Year 1724.** The Nueva España Flota, commanded by Captain-General Baltasar de Guevara, sailed from Veracruz on August 25, but after leaving the Bahama Channel and heading toward Bermuda a hurricane forced it to head south and an undisclosed number of ships, carrying a great amount of treasure, were lost in the area of Samana Bay. Its *Capitana, Nuestra Señora de Guadalupe y San Antonio,* sank on September 12 in deep water near this bay; the *Almiranta, La Tolosa,* wrecked at Cape Samana, and other merchant *naos* wrecked on the reefs of the bay. Over 120 lives were lost, but all the ships, with the exception of the *Capitana,* were completely salvaged.

40. **Year 1737.** During a hurricane on October 5 at the port of Santo Domingo, the whole town was leveled to the ground and a large number of ships were wrecked or sunk in the harbor.

41. *Year 1742.* English warship H.M.S. *Tiger,* 50 guns, Captain Edward Herbert, wrecked on January 12 on a small key near Tortuga Island.

42. *Year 1747.* An English privateer forced a large French privateer to run ashore near Monte Cristi but her crew was saved.

43. *Year 1749.* French merchantman *Atlas,* Captain Tegail, was lost leaving the port of Cape Francés while sailing for Bordeaux but the crew was saved.

44. *Year 1754.* During a September hurricane at the port of Santo Domingo, twelve merchantmen were wrecked and more than 1,700 hogsheads of sugar were lost with them.

45. *Year 1757.* English warship H.M.S. *Assistance* chased two French privateering vessels, along with an English vessel they had captured, into Tiberoon Bay, where the French had a fort. The French burnt all three vessels near the shore under the guns of the fort.

46. *Year 1762.* French warship *Dragon,* 64 guns, was wrecked at Cape François.

47. *Year 1770.* French merchantman *Mecca,* Captain Merle, sailing from Hispaniola to Bordeaux, was wrecked near Cape François.

48. *Year 1772.* During a violent gale at the end of August, twenty-eight French ships were lost near the northwestern tip of the island, and 280 bodies were washed ashore the following morning.

49. *Year 1772.* English merchantman *Intelligence,* Captain Hubbert, was lost on January 2 entering Cape François, twenty-one slaves drowned and most of her cargo was lost.

50. *Year 1774.* English slave ship *Ellis,* Captain Rylands, sailing from Africa and Barbados to Jamaica, was lost on the Isle of Ash but her crew and all 450 slaves were saved.

51. *Year 1779.* French warship of the fleet of the Count D'Estaing, *Tounant,* was badly damaged in a storm and sank a few days afterward at Cape François around the beginning of December.

52. *Year 1782.* Two large English warships drove the French warship *Scipion,* 74 guns, ashore near Cape François on October 18.

53. Year 1783. A ship of unknown registry, *Delight*, Captain Anderson, sailing from Grenada Island to Havana, was wrecked on June 3 at Tortuga Island, part of her cargo was saved.

54. Year 1784. A ship of unknown registry, *Friendship*, Captain Reily, sailing from Dublin to Philadelphia, was wrecked at Cape François.

55. Year 1785. English ship *Cornwallis*, Captain M'Gowan, sailing from Antigua to Port Royal, Jamaica, was wrecked during a hurricane on August 25 at Neve Bay and totally lost but the crew was saved.

56. Year 1788. During a hurricane at Port-au-Prince on August 16, more than twenty-five ships were lost. Another twenty-five were wrecked on the coasts nearby.

57. Year 1790. Large Scottish merchantman *Active*, Captain Douglas, sailing from Glasgow to Jamaica, was lost on the Isle de Vache on March 7, crew and part of cargo saved.

58. Year 1792. French merchantman *Clement*, Captain Omalin, sailing for Bordeaux, was lost leaving the port of Santo Domingo.

59. Year 1792. French merchantman *Jume Eiema*, Captain Camden, after arriving from Bordeaux, was lost in the Harbor of Cape François.

60. Year 1796. English warship H.M.S. *Salisbury*, 50 guns, Captain William Mitchell, wrecked on May 13 on Isle de Avanche but none of her crew of 343 men was lost.

61. Year 1796. English sloop-of-war H.M.S. *Cormorant*, 18 guns, Captain Thomas Gott, accidentally blew up at Port-au-Prince and 95 of her crew of 121 men were lost.

62. Year 1797. English warship H.M.S. *Tartar*, 28 guns, Captain Charles Elphinstone, was wrecked on July 1 when leaving the port of Puerto de Plata but none of her crew of 195 men was lost.

63. Year 1798. A ship of unknown registry, *Cornelia*, Captain Gilbert, sailing to Charleston, South Carolina, was lost in the port of Jeremie, on the northwest Tiburon Peninsula of Haiti.

64. Year 1802. English merchantman *Arethusa*, Captain Dods, sailing from London to Jamaica, was wrecked on the Isle of Ash, crew and part of cargo saved.

65. *Year 1803.* English warship H.M.S. *Garland,* 22 guns, Captain Frederick Cottrell, was wrecked at Cape François in November.

66. *Year 1806.* Two French warships, *Imperial,* 120 guns, and the *Diomede,* 74 guns, were sunk during action with an English fleet commanded by Vice-Admiral Sir J. T. Duckworth off the port of Santo Domingo.

67. *Year 1808.* English schooner-of-war H.M.S. *Flying Fish,* 12 guns, Captain J. Glassford Gooding, was wrecked on December 15 on a reef eastward of Point Salines but her crew was saved.

68. *Year 1808.* Ship of unknown registry, *Catherine,* Captain Dohlin, sailing from St. Thomas, Virgin Islands, to Jacmel, Haiti, was lost on December 19 on the reef at Saona Island.

69. *Year 1809.* English merchantman *Queen,* Captain Sherwood, sailing to London, was wrecked near the Aux Cayes.

70. *Year 1810.* English merchantman *Caerwent,* Captain Browner, sailing to London, was lost on May 31 when leaving Jacmel Harbor, Haiti.

71. *Year 1810.* During a gale on September 27, about ten Haitian vessels were driven ashore at Jeremie, and the English ship *Ellen* was wrecked near Aux Cayes.

72. *Year 1812.* American merchantman *Frederick William,* Captain Henchman, sailing from Lisbon to Boston, was wrecked on Isle de Vache on May 17, four of the crew perished.

73. *Year 1816.* During a hurricane on September 19, all of the shipping at Port-au-Prince was wrecked or sunk.

74. *Year 1816.* English ship *Shark,* arriving from London, was accidentally burnt at Port-au-Prince about February 4.

75. *Year 1817.* American schooner *Roxano,* coming from Nantucket, was lost on Isle de Ash, crew and part of cargo saved.

76. *Year 1817.* French ship *Jean Marie,* Captain Bowie, sailing from Marseilles to Hispaniola, wrecked on the coast near Samana Bay around the end of May, crew and part of cargo saved.

77. *Year 1818.* American ship *Latona*, Captain Low, sailing from London to New Orleans, was lost in Samana Bay, but her crew was saved.

78. *Year 1819.* A ship of unknown registry, *Sally*, Captain Brockesby, sailing from Amsterdam to Havana, was totally lost near Puerto Principe.

79. *Year 1819.* An unidentified brig, sailing to England, was lost on July 30 at Port-au-Prince; and a Scottish merchantman, *Lord Belhaven*, sailing from Glasgow to Port-au-Prince, was lost about 20 miles from this latter port.

80. *Year 1821.* English ship *Favorite*, Captain Hayward, coming from Jamaica, was wrecked on April 19 at St. Jago port but her crew was saved.

81. *Year 1821.* American merchantman *Intrepid*, Captain Crofts, arriving from Charleston, South Carolina, was wrecked in Jacmel Harbor, Haiti, during a gale on January 30.

82. *Year 1821.* A ship of unknown registry, *Felix*, Captain Condon, was lost on Cape Engano on July 2.

83. *Year 1821.* During heavy gales from September 2 to 4, four merchantmen were wrecked at the Aux Cayes: a ship of unknown registry, *Peace*, Captain Clarkson, and three American ships—*Rover*, Captain Johnson, *Ann*, Captain Berchier, and an unidentified vessel.

84. *Year 1822.* American ship *Commerce*, Captain M'Knight, sailing from St. Thomas, Virgin Islands, to Hispaniola, was totally lost on Cape St. Nicolas Mole on June 10 but her crew was saved.

85. *Year 1823.* American ship *Jefferson*, Captain Marlore, sailing from Philadelphia to Dominica Island, was totally lost on January 10 on the Isle de Vache but her crew was saved.

86. *Year 1824.* A Jamaican cutter, *Swallow*, Captain Robertson, sailing from Jamaica to Barbados, was wrecked due to strong currents on Isle de Vache on November 12, crew and part of cargo saved.

CHAPTER TEN

Jamaica and
the Cayman Islands

BETWEEN 1504 AND 1825, over nine hundred ships of many nationalities and descriptions were lost in Jamaican waters, but in this chapter I have again listed only those in which the exact location of the shipwreck is given or those of special interest.

The reason there are so few Spanish shipwrecks around Jamaica is that the island was one of the least important Spanish New World colonies and very few ships visited it. There were periods in the sixteenth and seventeenth centuries when no large ship visited the island in as long as ten years, as the inhabitants were very poor and not able to purchase goods from Spain; nor did they have precious metals or other products to ship back to Spain. It was not until the English captured the island that large numbers of ships visited.

In the past decade, there have been several large-scale treasure expeditions to Pedro Shoals by American divers, and although a large number of interesting artifacts have been recovered from several wreck sites no treasure has been found. The Jamaican government has since enforced strict laws concerning old shipwrecks, and in 1967 and 1968 three American diving groups were arrested there for illegally diving. The government now requires a salvage group to apply for a permit and then leave a bond of $10,000 as a guarantee that the shipwreck will be excavated properly and the salvors won't disappear with their recovery before splitting with them. The government offers one of the most unattractive agreements of any country in the Western Hemisphere: It receives 100 percent of all artifacts recovered, as well as 50 percent of any treasure, and it has the right to purchase any or all of the 50 percent of the treasure belonging to the salvor at bullion value.

Fortunately, I worked on the other side of the fence when I lived in Jamaica. Employed as the government marine archaeologist from 1965 to 1968, I had no problems about obtaining a fair shake with what I recovered: The government received every single item my team and I recovered. Most of my time was spent excavating the sunken city of Port Royal, but I also found time to explore several dozen shipwreck sites around the island. Our excavation of Port Royal remains the largest underwater excavation undertaken anywhere in the world. Although limited by insufficient funds, we managed to recover the greatest amount of artifacts. In fact, we recovered more than has been recovered off all the old shipwrecks worked in the Western Hemisphere in the past two decades.

All experts consider the sunken city of Port Royal the most important marine archaeological site in the Western Hemisphere. The sudden cataclysm that caused Port Royal to sink into the sea is quite similar to the volcanic eruption that destroyed the Roman city of Pompeii in A.D. 79. When archaeologists began excavating Pompeii more than fifty years ago, they discovered a fantastic time capsule of history, since the site had been covered over quickly by volcanic ash and remained virtually untouched for almost two thousand years. After a long, arduous excavation and close study of the findings, archaeologists were able to determine what life was like in Pompeii at the time of the disaster. Because of the similarity in the way the two cities met their end, a thorough excavation of Port Royal should reap the same dramatic and spectacular results as Pompeii.

Port Royal was founded very shortly after the British captured Jamaica from the Spaniards in 1655. It first served as a base for the English invasion fleet and soon afterward became the principal army garrison on the island. During the next decade (1660–70), Port Royal served as the most important buccaneering base in the West Indies. Henry Morgan was only the most successful (and is the most infamous) of a long list of privateers who brought immense riches in plunder from their raids on Spanish settlements and shipping. When in 1670 Spain and England signed a peace treaty, the heyday of the privateers ceased and Port Royal became even more famous.

By the time of the earthquake in 1692, Port Royal had been transformed in a few decades from a deserted cay to the most important trading center in the New World. The spacious harbor was always crowded with shipping, and the amount and variety of goods that passed over its wharves was astonishing—the large majority of which entered the very lucrative contraband trade with the Spanish colonies and brought in much greater riches than the plunder obtained by the privateers. From historical documents we know that the town consisted of two thousand buildings, the majority of which were made of bricks, and many were two stories high. The population was about eight thousand and, although most contemporary accounts claim that the vast majority of the inhabitants were "Godless men," there were several Protestant churches (including a Quaker meeting house), a Roman Catholic chapel, and a synagogue. The wharves, warehouses, and houses of the wealthy merchants were located on the harbor, or north side of the town, where the water was deep enough for ships of large tonnage to tie up right against the shore. Three large forts —Charles, James, and Carlisle (the latter two sank during the earthquake)—as well as several smaller batteries protected the town. The most outstanding buildings were the King's house, where the island's council met; the governor's house; St. Paul's Church (Anglican); the Exchange, the center for the town's main business transaction; the Marshallsea, a prison for men; and Bridewell, a prison for women. At twenty minutes before noon on June 7, 1692, disaster struck: an earthquake quickly followed by a tidal wave. Within a matter of minutes, nine-tenths of the town had either sunk or slid into the sea and no more than ten acres of land remained out of the water by the end of the day; and over twenty ships were sunk by the tidal waves. More than two thousand lives were lost that day, and within a month an additional three thousand persons died from epidemics that followed the disaster. Most of the survivors moved across the harbor and founded the town of Kingston. Salvage operations began on the very day of the disaster and continued for many years, but the

RIGHT: Silver pocket watch found at Port Royal, Jamaica. BELOW: Archaeologist Nancy Farriss studying silver pieces of eight found in a treasure chest at Port Royal.

Silver, pewter, brass and glass from one of the sunken buildings of Port Royal.

Silver and pewter from the sunken city of Port Royal.

TOP: One of the few underwater pictures from Port Royal—a diver inspecting the wreck of the H.M.S. *Swan*, lost during the earthquake. BOTTOM: Diver attaching lines to an old treasure chest, ca. 1860, off the coast of Colombia.

bulk of the things lost during the disaster was missed by the salvors; either they sank in water too deep for them to dive in or the walls of the buildings covered them over.

The first six months of our work on the site was utilized in mapping the overall site, locating the walls of the buildings buried under the harbor sediment with long metal rods, locating large metallic deposits with metal detectors, and removing tons of modern debris that covers the overall site.

The actual excavation began on May 1, 1966, and was carried on six days a week, with each diver averaging nine hours under water a day until June 1968, when the excavation was brought to a halt because of the vast amount of artifacts that were awaiting proper preservation. Using a 4-inch-diameter airlift, we systematically excavated a rectangular hole 400 feet by 150 feet to an average depth of 15 feet below the sea floor. We estimated that this area originally contained about thirty to forty buildings at the time of the disaster, and by comparing the owners' initials on pewter and silverware with the old property records we were able to identify the owners of many of these buildings and what they were used for. Although the majority of the buildings had been private homes, we also located two taverns, a carpenter's shop, a silversmith's shop, the fish and meat markets, and two turtle crawls. In this same area we also located two shipwrecks dating from the 1692 disaster and a French warship that sank during a hurricane in 1722.

Working conditions were very bad, as underwater visibility was never more than a few inches and constant landslides of the sediment into the hole the divers were working in resulted in twenty-four serious accidents requiring medical attention. On several occasions divers were trapped under large brick walls that collapsed on top of them. In coral-encrusted iron objects alone, we recovered over 50,000 items —such as tools, weapons, household items, ship's fittings, and thousands of other artifacts still awaiting preservation. Other artifacts included 2,000 glass bottles, 12,000 clay smoking pipes, over 500 pewter and silver items, 2,500 copper and brass items, as well as two large hoards of silver coins and numerous pieces of valuable jewelry.

Yet my team and I have barely scratched the surface of what remains on the site. We actually excavated the least important section of the sunken city—because this section was slated to be dredged for use as a deep-water port—and the total area we uncovered is less than 5 percent of the overall site, so there are still many years of work left to be done there. A preservation laboratory is under construction at Port Royal to cope with the vast amount of material we recovered, and until all of these artifacts are properly preserved—which may take many years—no further excavation is planned on the site. And unless the Jamaican government makes a more attractive division arrangement with potential salvors, I doubt if any serious work will be undertaken on the numerous shipwrecks in these waters.

Due to the excellent diving conditions in the waters of the Cayman Islands, large numbers of divers have been visiting the islands mainly for underwater photography and spearfishing but very little work has been done on old shipwrecks. Ballast piles and many iron cannon have been located around all three of the Cayman Islands but no elaborate excavation equipment has been used and only a small number of artifacts have been recovered. Several professional salvage firms have attempted to work these wrecks but permission was not obtained from the island's authorities, as they state that all these wrecks are Crown property and anything recovered from them must be turned over to the British government.

List of Shipwrecks in Jamaican Waters

1. **Year 1504.** On Columbus' fourth and last voyage of discovery, he lost two of his ships, *Capitana* and *Santiago*, in St. Anne's Bay, on the northern coast of Jamaica. After spending some months exploring along Panama and Central America—where he was forced to abandon two of his caravels—he started for Santo Domingo but ran out of food and water, and the two ships mentioned above were leaking very badly because of sea worms. When he was off the northern coast of Jamaica, contrary winds prevented him from heading toward his destination, and with both ships barely afloat from the great amount of water in them, he was forced to enter St. Anne's Bay, where he ran both ships aground to prevent them from sinking. For a year he and his men lived in the fore-and-aft castles of both ships, which were the only parts above the water, before they were finally rescued.

Using historical data and assisted by Dr. Harold Edgerton of M.I.T.—with his sediment-penetrating sonar equipment—we located both of these shipwrecks in February of 1968 and carried out a small excavation on one of the wrecks to obtain samples of artifacts to positively identify our discovery, which we did. At the time of writing I am trying to obtain a grant from UNESCO to undertake a major archaeological excavation on these ship-wrecks, which are buried under 12 to 14 feet of mud.

2. *Year 1512.* A small caravel under the command of Valdivia, the regidor of Darien, was sailing from Panama to Hispaniola for supplies and reinforcements and carrying a great deal of treasure it had obtained from the Indians when it struck upon Pedro Shoals, located about 130 miles south of the island of Jamaica. The caravel broke up quickly and the crew was unable to escape with anything more than a small boat, in which it drifted for thirteen days until reaching the Yucatán Peninsula.

3. *Year 1579.* The *Capitana La Trinidad,* 350 tons, Captain Manuel de Rodas, on which Captain-General Alvaro Manrique was travel-ing, was lost on the south side of Jamaica. No details on whether it was carrying any treasure at the time.

4. *Year 1602.* A large unidentified merchant *nao,* sailing in the Nueva España Flota of Captain-General Alonso de Chaves Galindo, carrying a great deal of merchandise and missionaries from Spain to Yucatán, was wrecked in bad weather on Pedro Shoals when it was accidentally separated from the convoy. After the ship broke up on the reef, survivors made rafts and reached the southern section of Jamaica in a few days. The governor of Jamaica sent a salvage boat, but it could not locate the shipwreck. The owner of the ship was Tome Cano, one of the leading ship designers in Spain at that time.

5. *Year 1662.* A Spanish merchant ship, sailing from Caracas, Vene-zuela, to Veracruz, was wrecked on Bajo Nuevo Shoals, striking on a reef and quickly breaking up. Forty persons drowned and only a few reached Jamaica. This shoal is located about 150 nautical miles south of the western tip of Jamaica. Colombia claims jurisdiction over it, so permisison must be obtained from the Colombian government before salvaging a wreck there.

6. *Year 1670.* During a hurricane on October 7, about twenty Eng-lish warships and a large number of privateering vessels were wrecked in Kingston Harbor.

7. *Year 1961.* Four galleons, part of the Tierra Firme Flota, the Marqués de Vado, sailing between Cartagena, Colombia, and Havana, were wrecked on Pedro Shoals, 776 persons were saved

from these wrecks by fishing boats from Port Royal. The lost ships were: the *Almiranta*, Admiral Leonardo de Lara; *Nuestra Señora del Carmen*, Captain Salvador Velez de Guevara; *Nuestra Señora de la Concepción*, Captain Pedro Azpil Cueta; and the *Santa Cruz*, Captain Vicente López. As soon as the wrecks were abandoned by the Spaniards, a large number of salvage sloops from Port Royal descended upon them and began salvage operations. England and Spain were then at peace, and the Spaniards demanded all the treasure recovered. The British agreed that the treasure should be seized and turned over to the Spaniards; however, many chests of treasure were concealed by the salvors, so there is no way to know just how much was salvaged. The Spaniards also carried on their own salvage operations, and as late as 1698 salvage boats from Havana were recovering cannon from these wrecks.

8. *Year 1699.* Small Spanish advice boat *Jesús, María y José*, of 80 tons, sent from Veracruz to Santo Domingo, was wrecked on the north coast of Jamaica.

9. *Year 1714.* During a hurricane that struck Kingston Harbor on August 9, several large English men-of-war were sunk as well as several small trading sloops and schooners.

10. *Year 1726.* During a hurricane that struck the island on October 22, over fifty ships of different descriptions were wrecked or sunk at Port Morant, St. Anne's Bay, Port Royal, and Kingston Harbor. At Port Royal, several dozens of wooden houses were also blown into the harbor.

11. *Year 1730.* Spanish galleon *Genovesa*, 54 guns, Captain Francisco Guiral, sailing from Cartagena to Havana, struck on a reef on Pedro Shoals and was lost. She was sailing alone and not in a convoy at the time, carrying over 3 million pesos in gold and silver plus many important passengers, several of whom drowned with the crew. Soon after the ship wrecked, an English frigate, the H.M.S. *Experiment*, arrived on the scene and took off the survivors and a large amount of the treasure. Other salvage vessels arrived from Port Royal and recovered undisclosed amounts of treasure and many of the ship's cannon. The ship broke up within a few weeks, however, and a great deal of the treasure was scattered and buried under sand. Over the years, various treasure-hunters claimed to have located this wreck, but I have examined

all of the artifacts they recovered and have determined that they had located another Spanish shipwreck in the same area, one that dates at least fifty years later.

12. **Year 1741.** English merchantman the *London*, Captain Hayes, was almost fully loaded for her voyage to London when she was accidentally destroyed by fire in Old Harbour.

13. **Year 1741.** An English troop transport, *Vease Pink*, Captain Horn, was lost in July on the Morant Keys, off the south coast of Jamaica, where she hit a reef and broke up quickly, with most of the persons aboard drowning.

14. **Year 1744.** A Spanish privateering vessel was sunk by the H.M.S. *Solebay* under the watch tower at Pedro Point. The present lighthouse is located near the ruins of the watch tower, and there are four different old wrecks in 30 feet of water—one of which might be this one.

15. **Year 1744.** During a hurricane that struck the island in October, 105 ships—nine warships and ninety-six merchantmen—were wrecked or sunk in Kingston Harbor and Port Royal. Many of the wharves and warehouses in Kingston—which were full of merchandise—were also carried into the harbor. Only five of the warships that were lost were identified: H.M.S. *Albans*, 50 guns, Captain William Knight; H.M.S. *Greenwich*, 50 guns, Captain Edward Allen; H.M.S. *Bonetta*, 14 guns, Captain William Lea; bomb ship H.M.S. *Thunder*, 8 guns, Captain Thomas Gregory; and the store ship H.M.S. *Lark*, no guns, captain's name unknown. Many of these ships were reflected and a great amount of their cargoes recovered. In shallow water, on the western side of Kingston Harbor, I have dived on over thirty different wreck sites from this disaster, and although I did not use any excavation equipment I recovered a wide variety of ceramicware, bottles, clay pipes, cannonballs, and other artifacts.

16. **Year 1747.** Two English merchantmen were lost entering Port Morant, on the eastern end of the island: *Culloden*, Captain Harris, coming from London, and the *Pembeston*, Captain Nunns, coming from Liverpool.

17. **Year 1748.** English merchantman *Dragon*, Captain Lawson, with a cargo of sugar and rum, wrecked leaving St. Anne's Bay, on her way to London.

18. **Year 1748.** English merchantman *Greyhound*, Captain Palliser, with a cargo of sugar, molasses, rum, and some silver specie, was chased ashore near Cape Morant by two Spanish privateers.

19. **Year 1748.** English merchantman *Industry*, Captain Graham, sailing from Boston to Kingston, was lost off Port Morant.

20. **Year 1748.** English merchantman *Happy Success*, Captain Paterson, was lost leaving Port Antonio, heading for London, but part of her cargo was recovered.

21. **Year 1749.** English merchantman *Dragon*, Captain Wall, was lost on May 14 at Port Morant, only the crew was saved.

22. **Year 1751.** During a hurricane on September 25, twenty-four merchant ships and one man-of-war were lost in Kingston Harbor and at Port Royal. The warship was the H.M.S. *Fox*, 20 guns. Four of the merchantmen were American, one was Dutch, and the rest were English.

23. **Year 1752.** English merchantman *Phebe*, Captain Lawson, coming from Liverpool, was wrecked on September 17 on the Morant Keys with a rich cargo of trade goods and some pieces of artillery for the island's forts.

24. **Year 1755.** English ship *Montfort*, Captain Clutson, sailing from Kingston to Bristol, carrying several chests of specie, was wrecked on the Morant Keys but the treasure was recovered.

25. **Year 1755.** Large Spanish galleon *La Andalucía*, sailing alone from Cartagena to Spain, was wrecked on Pedro Shoals on June 9, treasure and crew saved.

26. **Year 1757.** English merchantman *Craven*, Captain Stewart, sailing to London with a cargo of sugar products, was lost leaving St. Mary's harbor.

27. **Year 1760.** English merchantman *Sally*, Captain Bland, sailing for London, was lost on the reefs near St. Anne's Bay, crew and most of cargo saved.

28. **Year 1762.** A large unidentified Spanish merchantman, laden with indigo, cocoa, and specie, sailing from Venezuela to Veracruz, was wrecked on the coast near Port Morant, most of her cargo was salvaged.

29. **Year 1762.** English merchantman *Prince George,* Captain Clapperton, coming from London, was lost in a gale while entering the harbor of Martha Brae, only the crew was saved.

30. **Year 1764.** English ship *Marquis of Grandby,* Captain Calvert, coming from London, struck a rock near Portland Bight and went to pieces quickly, only the crew was saved.

31. **Year 1765.** English merchantman *Fanny,* Captain Boyd, coming from London, was sunk at Pidegon Island, in Old Harbour, on March 8.

32. **Year 1766.** English merchantman *Portland,* Captain Kendal, after arriving from London, was lost in Manchaneal Bay.

33. **Year 1766.** English ship, a snow, *Friendship,* Captain Johnson, coming from Tortola, Virgin Islands, was wrecked onshore February 16, 3 miles west of Annoto Bay, crew and part of cargo saved.

34. **Year 1766.** During a hurricane on August 18, seventeen ships were wrecked in Kingston Harbor, and others were lost at Black River, Savanna la Mar, and Port Morant.

35. **Year 1768.** English merchantman *Minerva,* Captain Smith, loading for a voyage to London, was accidentally burnt on April 19, having on board 300 hogsheads of sugar and 17 puncheons of rum, very little of which was saved.

36. **Year 1769.** English merchantman *Lyon,* Captain Irwin, sailing for London, was lost leaving the harbor of Oracabeza.

37. **Year 1770.** English slave ship *Cecelia,* Captain Dunn, coming from Africa with a cargo of slaves, was wrecked in the Morant Keys.

38. **Year 1770.** English merchantman *King David,* Captain Broad, was sunk in Port Royal Harbor, when it struck upon a large anchor sticking up from the sea floor.

39. **Year 1770.** English ship *Industry,* Captain Haste, arriving from Liverpool, was wrecked on the Palisadoes, several miles east of Port Royal, and was a total loss.

40. **Year 1770.** English merchantman *Caesar,* Captain Raffes, sailing to London, was lost on a reef west of Port Morant on July 23.

41. *Year 1774.* Unidentified Dutch slave ship, coming from Africa with over five hundred slaves on board, was wrecked in the Morant Keys.

42. *Year 1774.* American ship *Jamaica Planter,* Captain M'Fadzen, coming from Boston with a cargo of trade goods, and another vessel identified only by the captain's name—Todd—were both lost on Plumb Point, near Port Royal.

43. *Year 1776.* A ship of unknown registry, *Caton,* Captain Glyn, coming from Africa with a cargo of slaves, ivory, and beeswax, was lost due to fire at Kingston.

44. *Year 1779.* Jamaican schooner *Speedwell,* on a sponging and wrecking voyage to the Bahamas, was lost leaving Manchaneal Bay.

45. *Year 1779.* English warship H.M.S. *Glasgow,* 24 guns, Captain Thomas Lloyd, was accidentally lost by fire on June 19 at Kingston.

46. *Year 1780.* A hurricane on February 23 caused six large ships to sink at Montego Bay: *Echo,* Captain Cragie, from London; *Petersfield,* Captain Thomas, from Bristol; *Nancy,* Captain Marshall, from Bristol; *Hero,* Captain Logget, from New York; *Cornelia,* Captain Smith, from New York; *Orangefield,* Captain Farris, from New York; and the *Charles and Martha,* Captain Elston, from Liverpool.

47. *Year 1780.* American ship *Pallas,* arriving from Charleston, South Carolina, with trade goods, was lost entering Port Morant on March 24.

48. *Year 1780.* During a hurricane in October, many ships were lost at various ports. At Lucea Harbor the H.M.S. *Badger* was sunk. At Port Morant, three large ships were thrown over a quarter of a mile onshore and were totally lost.

49. *Year 1781.* A ship of unknown registry, *Duke of Cumberland,* Captain Le Geyt, arriving from St. Eustatius Island, was lost entering Montego Bay.

50. *Year 1781.* During a hurricane that struck Jamaica on August 1 and 2, many ships were destroyed. In Kingston Harbor, ninety ships of various descriptions were wrecked or sunk; another thirty were lost at Port Royal; and seventy-three were lost in other ports of the island. The H.M.S. *Pelican,* 24 guns, Captain Cuthbert Collingwood, was wrecked on the Morant Keys. This wreck was discovered by a group of treasure-hunters from Florida who recovered a small bronze cannon, one gold coin, and other artifacts. But they worked on it for only one day before being driven away by a Jamaican naval launch.

51. *Year 1782.* English warship H.M.S. *Hinchinbrooke,* 20 guns, Captain Nelson, wrecked on a reef off St. Anne's Bay. This wreck was reported being located by a Jamaican diver in 1965.

52. *Year 1782.* English merchantman *Blagrove,* Captain M'Neil, with a cargo of sugar products, was sunk in Buckness Bay due to a leak.

53. *Year 1783.* English merchantman *Ann & Mary,* Captain Graham, sailing to London, was wrecked on rocks while leaving Kingston.

54. *Year 1783.* Spanish merchant *nao Nuestra Señora de la Concepción,* Captain Joaquin Fernández, sailing from Cartagena to Cadiz, Spain, was wrecked on the Morant Keys on November 15, only a small part of her cargo was salvaged.

55. *Year 1784.* Hurricane struck the island on July 30 and over eighty ships were destroyed or sunk in various ports around the island. At Port Royal, many houses were blown into the harbor.

56. *Year 1785.* A hurricane struck the island prior to October and over fifty ships were wrecked or sunk in Kingston Harbor and Port Royal. Several others were lost at Savanna la Mar, Bulls Bay, and Bush Cay in Old Harbour.

57. *Year 1785.* English merchantman *John,* Captain Churnside, sailing to Bristol, was wrecked at John's Point, near the west end of the island, part of her cargo was saved.

58. *Year 1786.* A hurricane struck the island on October 20 and about twenty ships were lost at Kingston Harbor and several others at Montego Bay.

59. *Year 1787.* Two English ships were wrecked on the reefs near Port Royal: slave ship *Enterprize,* Captain Wilson, arriving from Africa with a cargo of slaves; and merchantman *Marianne,* arriving from Santo Domingo.

60. *Year 1790.* English ship *Columbus,* Captain Mason, laden with sugar products for Leith, England, was burnt at Bluefields.

61. *Year 1790.* English merchantman *Two Friends,* Captain Brookbank, sailing to England, was wrecked in Old Harbour, most of the cargo was saved.

62. *Year 1791.* Jamaican sloop *Fly,* Captain Saise, driven onshore by wind on November 18 in St. Anne's Bay.

63. *Year 1791.* Scottish merchantman, a brig, *Exuma,* Captain Aylward, loaded with sugar and rum, bound for Dublin, wrecked onshore at Oracabeza by strong winds and quickly went to pieces.

64. *Year 1792.* American merchantman *Scipio,* Captain Carr, after arriving from Virginia, was wrecked during a storm on April 11 at Annotto Bay, most of her cargo of timber was washed ashore.

65. *Year 1792.* Irish merchantman *Ritson,* Captain Fairclough, was lost due to fire on June 20 at Old Harbour.

66. *Year 1792.* English merchantman *Rosemary,* Captain Woodham, loaded with sugar, struck a reef and sank at Jack's Bay.

67. *Year 1792.* American ship *Griffin,* Captain Vassey, sailing to Savannah, was wrecked on the Port Royal Bank on December 19.

68. *Year 1793.* English merchantman *Emerald,* Captain Kilgour, struck on her own anchor and sank with 400 hogsheads of sugar in Martha Bay.

69. *Year 1793.* Seven ships were wrecked or sunk in a gale at Montego Bay: *Langrest,* Captain Fitzhenry; *Active,* Captain Williams; *Young Eagle,* Captain Jones; *Palliser,* Captain James—all arriving from London; the other three were not identified.

70. *Year 1794.* English warship H.M.S. *Rose,* 28 guns, Captain Mathew Henry Scott, was wrecked on June 28 at Rocky Point.

71. *Year 1794.* Scottish ship *Sampson,* Captain Bowie, sailing to Santo Domingo and London, was lost in Cow Bay.

72. *Year 1795.* English ship *Hankey,* Captain Kirky, sailing to London, sank in Port Antonio, crew and cargo saved.

73. *Year 1796.* English warship H.M.S. *Undaunted*, 38 guns, Captain Robert Winthrop, was wrecked on August 27 in the Morant Keys. She was originally the French warship *Aréthuse* captured by the English.

74. *Year 1796.* English warship H.M.S. *St. Pierre*, Captain Christopher Paule, was wrecked on February 12 on some rocks off Point Negrille.

75. *Year 1796.* English slave ship *Old Dick*, Captain Birdy, arriving from Africa with a cargo of slaves, gold dust, and ivory, wrecked near Morant Bay, slaves and part of cargo saved.

76. *Year 1796.* English merchantman *Maria*, sailing to Exeter, England, was lost on a reef near Port Royal.

77. *Year 1797.* Scottish ship *Hope*, arriving from Glasgow, was lost on the Palisadoes, near Port Royal.

78. *Year 1798.* English ship *Carletch*, Captain Hamilton, arriving from New Brunswick, Canada, was lost near Jack's Bay, part of her cargo was saved.

79. *Year 1798.* English troop ship *Aurora*, Captain Milner, was wrecked at Old Harbour.

80. *Year 1800.* Two English merchantmen were wrecked in a gale at Oracabeza: *St. Andrew*, Captain Howard, from London; and the *Mary Ann*, Captain Bannerman.

81. *Year 1800.* English merchantman *Britannia*, Captain Compton, sailing to London, was lost at Buckner's Bay, none of her cargo was saved.

82. *Year 1800.* English merchantman *King George*, Captain Eilbeck, sailing from Kingston to London, was lost on Pedro Point but the crew was saved.

83. *Year 1801.* English ship *Lady Milford*, Captain Higgs, sailing to London, was lost on a reef near Savanna la Mar, crew and part of cargo saved.

84. *Year 1802.* A violent gale struck the north coast of the island on February 23 and many ships were driven ashore at Montego Bay, Annotto Bay, and Rio Bueno.

85. *Year 1802.* Three merchantmen were lost at Oracabeza during a gale: English ship *Generous Planter,* Captain Beattie; English ship *Fortune,* Captain Saunders; and the American brig *William,* Captain Clark.

86. *Year 1802.* Two English merchantmen were lost at Rio Bueno: *Jupiter,* Captain Plank, was burnt; and the *Grace,* Captain Cook, wrecked—both were total losses.

87. *Year 1802.* During a violent gale on March 16, four unidentified ships were totally lost at Port Antonio and two in Buckner's Bay: English merchantman *Hannah,* Captain Lenox, from Greenock, England; and an unidentified American schooner.

88. *Year 1803.* American schooner *Mary,* Captain White, was totally lost in St. Anne's Bay on December 25.

89. *Year 1804.* American merchantman *Sisters,* Captain Richards, arriving from the Canary Islands with a cargo of wine and brandy, was lost on the reefs at the entrance to Port Royal.

90. *Year 1804.* English merchantman *Triumph,* Captain Johnson, arriving from New Brunswick, Canada, was burnt in January at Kingston and was a total loss.

91. *Year 1804.* English ship *Henry Addington,* Captain Lacey, arriving from London, was wrecked on Barebush Cay in Old Harbour on April 14.

92. *Year 1804.* English merchantman *Margaret,* Captain Goodwin, sailing for London, was lost in Manchaneal Harbour on July 12.

93. *Year 1805.* Two English warships foundered near Jamaica: schooner, H.M.S. *Redbridge,* 10 guns, Captain Francis Blower Gibbs, in May; and H.M.S. *Orquijo,* 18 guns, Captain Charles Balderson, in October.

94. *Year 1805.* English merchantman *Scarbro,* Captain Scott, bound for London, sprung a leak and sank at Port Royal.

95. *Year 1805.* Two merchantmen were lost at Plaintain Garden: American ship *Minerva,* Captain Harding, sailing to Boston; and the English ship *William,* Captain M'Iver.

96. *Year 1805.* English merchantman *Jamaica,* Captain Clarke, bound for London, was totally lost during a gale on John's Point on June 30 but some of her cargo of rum was saved.

97. *Year 1806.* English merchantman *Vulcan,* Captain Gardner, bound for Bristol, was totally lost on Bare Bush Keys on July 26.

98. *Year 1806.* A ship of unknown registry, *Hercules,* Captain Cushing, arriving from Boston and sailing to the Spanish Main, was wrecked at Pedro Point on March 3.

99. *Year 1806.* American ship *Venus,* Captain Dony, arriving from New York, was totally lost at Rio Bueno in December.

100. *Year 1807.* American ship *Jane,* Captain Rust, arriving from Boston, was wrecked in Montego Bay on February 14.

101. *Year 1808.* Two English ships were wrecked at Bare Bush Key in Old Harbour: the frigate *Daedalus,* July 30, three men were drowned; warship H.M.S. *Meleager,* 36 guns, Captain Frederick Warren, July 30. This wreck was located about ten years ago and a large anchor raised, which is now on exhibit in Port Royal.

102. *Year 1808.* Two merchantmen were lost on the reefs at the entrance to Manchaneal Harbour: Jamaican schooner *Robert,* Captain Clarke, fully loaded, June 16; and the English ship *Dryade,* Captain Hoisbro, sailing to London, April 15, crew and small part of cargo saved.

103. *Year 1810.* Large Spanish warship *Nuestra Señora del Amparo,* carrying a valuable cargo of mercury and wine and sailing from Spain to Veracruz, was wrecked in the Morant Keys.

104. *Year 1810.* English troop-transport *Hannah,* Captain Harrison, was lost in Montego Bay on September 1 but the crew was saved.

105. *Year 1810.* English ship *Humphreys,* Captain Hastings, sailing to Honduras, was wrecked on Half Moon Key near Old Harbour on February 28.

106. *Year 1810.* English merchantman *Mary,* Captain Stafford, bound for London, was wrecked at Port Maria, December 18, during a gale, 167 hogsheads of sugar were lost.

107. *Year 1811.* American merchantman *Active,* after arriving from Boston, was wrecked near Port Royal on May 14 but part of her cargo was saved.

108. *Year 1811.* American ship *Ohio,* Captain Sinclair, arriving from Portsmouth, England, was wrecked in Plaintain Garden River on November 14.

109. *Year 1812.* During a hurricane from October 12 to 14 a great number of ships were destroyed in Kingston Harbor.

110. *Year 1812.* English merchantman *Leander,* Captain Keen, arriving from Liverpool, was totally lost at Alligator Pond.

111. *Year 1812.* English merchantman *Mariner,* Captain Allurd, sailing to London, was wrecked at Oracabeza in December.

112. *Year 1813.* Five ships were lost around Port Royal prior to July: English warship H.M.S. *Colibri,* 18 guns, Captain John Thompson wrecked in Port Royal Harbor; English brig-of-war H.M.S. *Rhodion,* arriving from Porto Bello, Panama, wrecked on shore 2 miles from Port Royal on February 20; Jamaican sloop *Chance,* arriving from Cuba with a cargo of cotton, sank in Port Royal Harbor during a gale on July 18; Scottish merchantman *Mercater,* sailing to Glasgow, wrecked on the Port Royal Keys; and an unidentified American ship sank in Port Royal Harbor.

113. *Year 1813.* On July 13, both a hurricane and an earthquake struck, causing twelve large ships to be lost at Kingston; forty to fifty small vessels were lost at Port Royal; and eight ships at Morant Bay.

114. *Year 1814.* English ship *Hibernia,* Captain Vaas, arriving from Halifax, was lost on the Morant Keys on November 17.

115. *Year 1814.* English merchantman *Metcalf,* bound for London, was lost in April, sailing out of Port Maria.

116. *Year 1814.* English warship H.M.S. *Halcyon,* was wrecked off Annotto Bay in May but the crew was saved.

117. *Year 1815.* American merchantman *Planet* (or *Patent*), arriving from New York, was wrecked near Frankfork Bay during a gale on October 18–19.

118. *Year 1815.* Jamaican schooner *Mary,* Captain Brackenbridge, sailing from Kingston, was wrecked in Orange Bay.

119. *Year 1815.* American ship *Watson,* arriving from New York, was driven ashore at Blue Hole and went to pieces on October 18, all of the cargo was lost and thirteen men drowned.

120. *Year 1815.* Two ships were lost on the reefs at Port Antonio: Spanish brig *Solo,* Captain Dick, arriving from Cuba, eight men drowned; and the Jamaican schooner *Two Friends.*

121. *Year 1815.* During a bad gale in October, two ships were lost at Port Maria, one in Orange Bay, one in Annotto Bay, and another at Goat Island.

122. *Year 1816.* A warship of unknown nationality, *Briseis,* sailing to Nassau, was lost on November 5 at Pedro Point, crew and greater part of stores saved.

123. *Year 1816.* A ship of unknown registry, *Anaconda,* Captain Pinel, sailing to Philadelphia, wrecked near Montego Bay but part of its cargo was saved.

124. *Year 1816.* English ship *Eliza,* Captain Johnston, arriving from Canada, was wrecked on the Grand Reef at Negril on March 8.

125. *Year 1816.* American ship *Agnes,* Captain Livingston, arriving from Charleston, South Carolina, wrecked entering Annotto Bay on December 23.

126. *Year 1817.* American ship *Isabella,* Captain Roach, sailing to Philadelphia, was wrecked in February on the Morant Keys.

127. *Year 1817.* Jamaican sloop *Happy Return,* with a cargo of sugar, was lost on June 11 coming out of Port Maria Harbor but the crew was saved.

128. *Year 1817.* Two ships wrecked in Morant Bay: English brig *Johanna,* Captain Caldwell, and the American schooner *Mary,* Captain Eswell.

129. *Year 1817.* Canadian ship *Five Sisters,* arriving from Nova Scotia, wrecked in St. Anne's Bay on December 20 but some of her cargo was saved.

130. *Year 1818.* Bahamian ship *Duke of Wellington,* Captain Chancellor, arriving from Norfolk, Virginia, wrecked in Montego Bay on November 11.

131. *Year 1818.* Two ships were lost near Kingston Harbor: English ship *Triton,* Captain Carzia, arriving from Liverpool, totally lost on December 5 off Plumb Point, passengers, crew, and part of cargo saved; and the Jamaican sloop *Young March,* Captain Brown, wrecked at Healthshire Point on February 11 but part of her cargo was saved.

132. *Year 1819.* Bermudan ship *Julian,* Captain Brown, sailing to Bermuda, wrecked at Orange Bay, crew and cargo saved.

133. *Year 1819.* English merchantman *Ann,* Captain Fortune, sailing to Cuba, capsized on August 1 and sank near Oracabeza but the crew was saved.

134. *Year 1819.* Jamaican cutter *John Shand,* Captain Tucker, was totally lost in Port Morant on January 1.

135. *Year 1820.* English ship *Martins,* Captain Ramsey, sailing from Coro, Venezuela, to Kingston was wrecked on the Morant Keys on December 14, crew and most of cargo of mules saved.

136. *Year 1821.* Bahamian ship *Three Brothers,* Captain Hanson, was lost off Port Antonio on February 14.

137. *Year 1821.* English ship *Mackerel,* Captain Thompson, sailing to the Spanish Main, wrecked on September 20 near Port Morant.

138. *Year 1821.* American sloop *Brutus,* Captain Brakenbridge, was lost at Downers Bluff on September 19.

139. *Year 1821.* Scottish ship *Countess of Bute,* sailing between Kingston and Montego Bay, was lost on Sandy Reef Key on February 8 but the crew was saved.

140. *Year 1821.* Canadian ship *Lowland Lass,* Captain Kyle, arriving from New Brunswick, was totally lost in St. Mary's Bay but the crew was saved.

141. *Year 1822.* Two ships of unknown registry were lost at Montego Bay: *Mary Charlotte,* Captain Richards, but the crew was saved; and an unidentified ship.

142. *Year 1822.* Dutch ship *Johanna,* Captain Benoist, sailing to Curaçao, wrecked off Rocky Point on a reef, crew and cargo saved.

143. *Year 1823.* Spanish ship *Graciosa,* sailing from Cadiz to Honduras, wrecked on Bajo Nuevo Shoals in April but the crew was rescued by a Dutch schooner.

144. *Year 1824.* English cutter H.M.S. *Dwarf,* 10 guns, Captain Nicholas Gould, wrecked on a pier at Kingston on March 3, one man was lost.

145. *Year 1824.* American merchantman *Thomas & Edward,* Captain Chevenick, arriving from Wilmington, North Carolina, sank near Kingston.

List of Shipwrecks in the Cayman Islands

146. Year 1631. Unidentified Dutch ship, carrying 30 iron cannon, owned by the Dutch West India Company, was wrecked on Grand Cayman Island.

147. Year 1715. English sloop H.M.S. *Jamaica* lost her mast in a storm and drifted on the rocks on Grand Cayman Island, where it was lost but the crew was saved.

148. Year 1722. During a hurricane about the beginning of September, the pirate ship *Morning Star*, Captain George Bradley, was totally lost on the reefs of Grand Cayman Island but the crew was saved.

149. Year 1730. Spanish *patache Señor San Miguel*, Captain Juan Bautista de la Hondel y Zevallos, was wrecked on Little Cayman Island. She was sailing in the Nueva España Flota, Admiral Rodrigo de Torres, en route to Veracruz from Spain, and none of her cargo of mercury was salvaged.

150. Year 1764. English merchantman *Augustus Caesar*, Captain Duffell, sailing from Jamaica to London, was lost on Grand Cayman Island but her crew was saved.

151. Year 1766. English merchantman *Mary*, Captain Sullivan, sailing from Jamaica to London, was wrecked on Grand Cayman Island.

152. Year 1774. Spanish merchantman *Infante*, Captain Aspillage, sailing from Bilbao, Spain, to Havana, was lost at Little Cayman Island but her crew was saved.

153. Year 1783. English merchantman *Catherine*, Captain Miller, sailing from Jamaica to Bristol, was lost in the Cayman Islands, a small part of her cargo was salvaged and sold in Jamaica.

154. Year 1783. Two English merchantmen were lost on Grand Cayman Island: *Fidelity*, Captain Hewson, sailing from Jamaica to London, crew and part of cargo saved; and the snow *Rodney*, sailing from Jamaica to London.

155. Year 1794. English warship *Convert*, 32 guns, Captain John Lawford, was wrecked on Grand Cayman Island on February 8 but her crew was saved. Originally she was the French warship *Inconstant* until captured by the English.

156. *Year 1794.* English merchantman *Fortune,* Captain Merryman, sailing from Jamaica to Bristol, was lost on Grand Cayman Island but the crew was saved.

157. *Year 1795.* English merchantman *Maria,* Captain Allison, sailing from Jamaica to Liverpool, was lost in the Cayman Islands but part of her cargo was saved.

158. *Year 1806.* A ship of unknown registry, *Allegator,* Captain Rust, sailing from France to New Orleans, was lost on Grand Cayman Island but the crew was saved.

159. *Year 1807.* American merchantman *Three Brothers,* Captain Jeffries, sailing from Jamaica to New York, was totally lost on December 17 off the Cayman Islands.

160. *Year 1808.* English merchantman *Cygnet,* Captain Bale, sailing from Jamaica to London, was lost in the Cayman Islands.

161. *Year 1810.* Scottish merchantman *Duncan,* sailing from Jamaica to Dublin, was lost in the Cayman Islands.

162. *Year 1810.* English merchantman *Cambria,* Captain Robertson, sailing from Jamaica to London, was lost on Grand Cayman Island.

163. *Year 1812.* English merchantman *Lion,* Captain Wilmot, sailing from London to Honduras, was lost on Grand Cayman Island on June 4 but the crew was saved.

164. *Year 1817.* English merchantman *Sisters,* Captain Swiney, sailing from Jamaica to London, was lost on August 3 on Grand Cayman Island but the crew was saved.

165. *Year 1819.* English merchantman *Constantine,* Captain Allen, sailing from Jamaica to London, wrecked on Grand Cayman Island at the end of July but most of her cargo of coffee was saved.

166. *Year 1822.* Canadian schooner *Dorchester,* coming from St. John's, New Brunswick, was wrecked on Grand Cayman Island.

167. *Year 1823.* A ship of unknown registry, *Grove,* Captain Reid, sailing from Cadiz to Veracruz, was lost on June 1 at Grand Cayman Island but her crew was saved.

168. *Year 1823.* Large American schooner, sailing from the Mediterranean to New Orleans, was wrecked on Grand Cayman Island in September but part of her cargo of wine and silks was saved.

169. *Year 1824.* Spanish merchantman *Zamore*, sailing from France to Mexico, was wrecked on Grand Cayman Island but her crew was saved.

CHAPTER ELEVEN

Puerto Rico and
the Virgin Islands

PUERTO RICO:

Compared with the majority of the other islands of the Caribbean, Puerto Rico has relatively few shipwrecks in her waters predating 1825. Jamaica, for example, although only slightly larger than Puerto Rico, has over nine hundred recorded ship disasters predating 1825, and even the small Island of Anegada, in the British Virgin Islands, has at least four times the number of shipwrecks that Puerto Rico has.

There are various explanations for the scarcity of shipwrecks around Puerto Rico. Firstly, the island is high in elevation and can be sighted at quite a distance from sea, which decreases the possibility of a ship running upon its shores. Unlike many of the other Caribbean islands, there are very few dangerous offshore reefs—as at Barbuda or most of the Bahamas—thus eliminating the danger of ships running aground.

The waters surrounding virtually the whole coastline of Puerto Rico are quite deep and there are very few, if any, shoals or sandbanks. Then, the question of how much maritime traffic there was around Puerto Rico must be taken into consideration. The island, mainly because it lacks precious metals and other important export commodities, was never considered an important settlement by the Spaniards, so there was very little shipping to it during the sixteenth, seventeenth, and eighteenth centuries. In fact, there were occasional periods of as long as five years when no ships reached the island from Spain or left the island sailing for Spain. Most of the maritime commerce carried on in the island during this period was with small coastal sailing vessels that traded between Hispaniola and Puerto Rico.

Each year, after the Nueva España Flota made its Caribbean landfall at either Martinique, Guadeloupe, or Dominica islands, where it usually stopped to obtain fresh water and fruits, it would pass within sight of the southern coast of Puerto Rico on its way to Veracruz, but this generally occurred in early summer, before the hurricanes were a threat. Around the middle of the seventeenth century, when the above three islands were settled by foreigners, the *flota* changed its pattern and began making its Caribbean landfall near the islands of St. Barthélémy or Anguilla, and it would pass within sight of the northern coast of Puerto Rico while heading west to Veracruz. Throughout the three centuries of the *flota* system, only a few of these ships were lost at Puerto Rico.

No permits of any type are needed to salvage shipwrecks on this island, except cases where a shipwreck might be located at the mouth of a harbor or in an area where there is a great amount of marine traffic. In this case, permission must be granted by the Harbor Master of the nearest port. Puerto Rico enjoys relatively good weather the year around, except during the hurricane season. The United States National Park Service has several archaeologists and historians working in San Juan and they, along with several historians at the University of Puerto Rico, can be helpful in identifying and dating artifacts recovered from shipwrecks in this area.

List of Shipwrecks in Puerto Rico

1. **Year 1515.** Caravel, *San Nicolas*, 80 tons, Captain Domingo de Guedin Bermeo, owned by Antonio de Norcia of Seville, sailing from Spain for Puerto Rico and Santo Domingo, sank in the

harbor of San Juan *"en una isleta llamada Berberia"* sometime before October 25.

2. **Prior to 1550.** Unidentified caravel lost "on the coasts of Puerto Rico" and only the people saved off it.

3. **Year 1550.** Merchant *nao Santa María de Jesús,* Captain Diego Bernal, enroute from Spain to Mexico, was lost 1 league from the port of San Juan. The governor of the island wrote stating that this ship was one of the richest galleons ever to come to the Indies. Some salvage work was undertaken on the wreck but the majority of the cargo was not recovered. The accident occurred shortly before August 27.

4. **Year 1554.** Three *naos, San Salvador, Doña Juana,* and *Regina Caelis,* of the Nueva España Flota of Don C. Rodríguez Farfan, were lost in the port of San Juan but the majority of their cargoes were salvaged.

5. **Year 1562.** *Nao San Estevan,* 120 tons, Captain Lazaro Morel, was lost "at San Juan de Puerto Rico."

6. **Year 1606.** Two ships entered Saulúcar de Barrameda in Spain on January 10 and reported that on October 26, 1605, while sailing from Santo Domingo to Spain, the *Capitana* of their fleet sank because of a leak when they were north and south of Punta de la Aguada and only the men were saved.

7. **Year 1623.** Sometime before September 22, eight merchant ships left Santo Domingo for Spain but one of them was run aground by bad navigation and was lost on the northern coast of Puerto Rico.

8. **Year 1623.** Galleon *N.S. de Begoña,* of a squadron of the Armada de Mar Oceano, commanded by Captain-General Thomas de Larraspuru, was lost on a shallows inside the port of San Juan. As the squadron was entering the port, a rain squall struck and caused this ship to run aground and then sink in deeper water. It was carrying only war munitions as its cargo, part of which was later salvaged along with some of the ship's cannon. No lives were lost in the disaster.

9. **Year 1625.** During the Dutch attack on San Juan, the Dutch totally destroyed by fire a merchant *nao* of 300 tons.

10. **Year 1625.** After the attack upon San Juan by the Dutch, one of the Dutch *urcas* sank in the harbor as the enemy fleet was sailing from that port. The Spaniards later salvaged six iron cannon from this wreck.

11. **Year 1649.** A Swedish ship of 200 tons was wrecked on a small island near Puerto Rico named Isla Palominos. This ship carried sixteen cannon, two of which were brass, and the Spaniards recovered all of them from the wreck and imprisoned the Swedes.

12. **Year 1659 or 1660.** An advice boat, or *aviso*, owned by Captain Francisco de Liende, on its way from Spain to Veracruz, was forced to enter San Juan because of a bad leak, but it sank soon after. Only a part of the mail, papal bulls, and a little money was recovered.

13. **Year 1673.** Unidentified French ship reported to have hit a reef and sunk off Puerto Rico during February. Its location was not given in this letter, but in another one in the same *legajo* there was a brief mention that a ship was wrecked this same year at El Arecibo, and it was probably the same ship.

14. **Year 1673.** The French governor of the Island of Tortuga, located off the northern coast of Haiti, had a large warship built, which he named *Ogeron*. It was manned by five hundred pirates of various nationalities and sent by this governor to aid in the capture of Curaçao. But when the ship was off the west side of Puerto Rico a violent storm wrecked the ship on the rocks near some islands called Guadanillas, where the ship quickly broke up. Most of the pirates made it ashore to Puerto Rico but were massacred the next day by the Spaniards.

15. **Prior to 1720.** The pirate Captain George Lowther captured two ships near Puerto Rico: a small ship from Bristol of Captain Smith and a Spanish privateer that had just captured the ship of Captain Smith. After stripping both prizes he burnt them near the island.

16. **Year 1720.** Warship *Carlos V*, 50 cannon, was lost during a hurricane at Puerto Rico and over five hundred men drowned.

17. **Year 1720.** Spanish ship *La Victoria* was lost in Bahía Anegada, at Puerto Rico.

18. Year 1739. Spanish galleon *N.S. del Pilar y San Antonio*, Captain Domingo Casares Goicochea, bound from Maracaibo for Cadiz, was lost near Puerto Rico but the people and goods were saved.

19. Year 1742. A Spanish sloop privateer was chased onshore and dashed to pieces and another of 24 cannon and full of men was sunk off Puerto Rico in an engagement with the H.M.S. *Scarsborough*, Captain Liste.

20. Year 1743. The H.M.S. *Litchfield* arrived at Kingston, Jamaica, on November 8, reporting that she had sunk a Spanish privateer on the west end of Puerto Rico and burnt a Spanish sloop in Bahía La Aguada.

21. Year 1745. Unidentified French ship of 36 guns was accidentally lost while entering the port of San Juan.

22. Year 1764. British merchantman *Elizabeth*, Captain Alexander, going from Antigua to London, foundered off Puerto Rico but crew and captain saved.

23. Year 1780. British merchantman *Revenge*, Captain Kerr, sailing from Newfoundland to Jamaica, was lost at Puerto Rico.

24. Year 1787. A slave ship of British registry, *Sisters*, Captain Alworthy, going from Africa to Havana, was overset by a strong gust of wind while in the Mona Passage on May 17 with five hundred slaves on board. All except two crew members and three slaves perished.

25. Year 1804. A large number of ships were sunk off the western end of Puerto Rico during a severe hurricane on September 3.

26. Year 1818. German ship *Nautilus*, captain either Korff or Miltenburg, was lost off the northern coast of Puerto Rico.

27. Year 1818. Spanish schooner *Eugenia*, 2 cannons, Captain Francisco Gómez, was lost at Puerto Rico on August 13.

28. Year 1821. Spanish brigantine schooner *Proserpina*, 10 cannon, lost on the coast of Aguadilla.

29. Year 1822. British ship *Fountain*. Captain Howard, of St. John's, New Brunswick, going from Trinidad to Boston, was lost on December 23 on the island of Puerto Rico but the crew was saved.

THE VIRGIN ISLANDS:

The waters of both the American and British Virgin Islands offer a good cross-section of shipwrecks of various types and nationalities that cover a wide date range; however, there is only one documented shipwreck throughout the whole sixteenth century, and there were only a few wrecks in the seventeenth century. The explanation for this lies in the fact that there was virtually no shipping of any kind passing through or even near these waters until late in the seventeenth century, when the Nueva España Flota changed its sailing patterns. In the early days this *flota*, after making its Caribbean landfall at Guadeloupe, or one of the other nearby islands, would head for Mexico, passing within sight of the southern coast of St. Croix. When the *flota* later made its landfall at Anguilla or St. Barthélémy islands, it would pass around the northern edge of the Virgin Islands, generally sighting Anegada, on which some of these ships were lost. With the exception of Anegada—on which several historians claim that over one hundred ships were wrecked prior to 1850—all of the other islands in this group are of considerable elevation, which results in fewer ships wrecking on them because of faulty navigation, since they could be spotted even in the dark. Most of the wrecks occurred in bad weather, when the ships were driven by stress of wind and seas upon the reefs and islands.

No permits are required to work on shipwrecks in the American Virgin Islands; however, to work a shipwreck in the British Virgin Islands a permit must be obtained from the Keeper of Wrecks in Roadtown, on the Island of Tortola. The weather pattern is about the same as for Puerto Rico.

The Virgin Islands have long been a major center for diving, and although many wrecks were accidentally discovered by amateurs, no serious attempts have been made to salvage any wrecks. The only major wreck discovery in these waters occurred in February 1969, when the harbor was being dredged at Roadtown. The dredge buckets brought up over four hundred artifacts, which included silver and pewter plates, cutlery, a silver sword handle, a cutlass, carpenter's tools, various types of shot, clasp knives, a flintlock rifle, ship fittings, caulking tools, clay pipes, and many different types of rigging.

Dr. Edward Towle, director of the Caribbean Research Institute, which is affiliated with the College of the Virgin Islands, created a department of Marine Archaeology in his Institute during the spring of 1968 and is the area's leading authority on shipwrecks. His intention is to hire a full-time archaeologist to work on different shipwrecks in both the British and American Virgin Islands as well as assisting any-one else working on shipwrecks in this same area. Provided he can raise the funds, he also intends to set up a preservation laboratory at his Institute that would handle artifacts recovered not just in the Virgin Islands but from all over the Caribbean. UNESCO has shown great interest in his projected plans and subsequent funds are ex-pected from this source.

List of Shipwrecks in the Virgin Islands

1. **Year 1523.** Two merchant *naos,* sailing from Spain for Santo Domingo, one under command of Captain Francisco Vara and the other under Captain Diego Sánchez Colchero, were lost in the Virgin Islands. The location of Vara's ship was given only as on some "shallows," but Colchero's was reported wrecked on the Island of Anegada. After several days, Colchero was able to re-float his ship by having most of its cargo and anchors thrown overboard. Then, going 2 leagues away, they located Vara's wrecked ship but could save the men only.

2. **Year 1625.** The governor of Puerto Rico wrote the King of Spain stating that an English-built ship of 70 tons with eighteen men on it sank at Anegada Island. They had sailed from Virginia for Bermuda to salvage a shipwreck, but the ship was damaged in bad weather and driven onto the reefs of Anegada.

3. **Year 1647.** The *Bark,* commanded by Jean Pinart, carried French settlers from St. Christophers and was burnt by Spaniards, most likely in one of St. John's harbors.

4. **Year 1652.** Prince Maurice, in the British ship *Defiance,* while privateering in the Caribbean with a convoy commanded by his brother, Prince Rupert, admiral of Charles I of England, wrecked off Anegada.

5. **Year 1678.** Unidentified French frigate, part of the war fleet of the Count D'Estrees, was wrecked on Crab Island.

6. Year 1683. British naval officer Captain Carlile of the H.M.S. *Francis* wrote: "31 July 1683, attacked a pirate ship at anchor in the harbour of Charlotte Amalie, of 32 guns and six *patararoes*, by the name of *La Trompeuse*, commanded by the Frenchman John Hamlin . . . setting her afire and she blew up. . . ."

7. Sometime between 1692 and 1705. In a description of Anegada, Pere Labat wrote:

> It is said that a year ago a great Spanish galleon laden with treasure was wrecked on Anegada, and that the treasure was buried on the island. There it still remains, or so they say, because most of the men who buried it were lost at sea, and the few survivors did not know where the treasure was hidden and were never able to find it. This treasure has caused many men including several filibusters to waste their time. I knew a man who stayed four or five months on the island, digging and sounding. He said that he had found something, but no one has yet found the real treasure . . . [Speaking of another shipwreck he wrote] . . . one of our priests was wrecked on L'Isle Noyee or Anegada and had been captured with the rest of his crew by the people of Panestown, also known as Virgin Gorda. He told me that he had remained a prisoner for two months with these Englishmen on Panestown . . .

8. Year 1713. Captain Lewis Doyer, of French ship *Le Count de Poix*, sailing from Santo Domingo to Havre de Grace, France, wrecked on Anegada.

9. Year 1730. An English-built ship converted to a Spanish treasure galleon, *N.S. de Lorento y San Francisco Xavier*, 212 tons, commanded by Captain Juan de Arizon, coming from Spain and sailing in convoy with a fleet of treasure galleons commanded by General Manuel López Pintado for Cartagena and Porto Bello, sank on Anegada Island.

10. Year 1731. Unidentified Spanish galleon, carrying a very valuable cargo of mercury or quicksilver and destined for the silver and gold of Mexico, was wrecked on the reefs of Anegada.

11. Year 1734. "While I was in England, they [inhabitants of Anguilla, Spanish Town (Virgin Gorda), and Tortola] pyrated upon a Spanish ship wrecked on the Anegadas. . . ."

12. **Year *1738*.** Spanish warship *Victory*, commanded by Captain Don Carlos Casamara, was cast away on the Anegada Shoals.

13. **Year *1742*.** Spanish merchant ship *San Ignacio*, belonging to the newly formed Caracas Company, was lost on Anegada Island.

14. **Year *1742*.** Spanish warship *St. Auguasies* (English spelling of its name, possibly the same ship as in #13), from 30 to 60 guns, was wrecked on Anegada on March 20, 1742, and four hundred of its six hundred persons were drowned. It was sailing with two other warships from San Sebastián, Spain, for Havana, carrying two thousand troops and supplies.

15. **Year *1749*.** British merchantman *Purcell*, Captain Fuller, from Bristol for Tortola, was lost on the rocks near Tortola.

16. **Year *1750*.** Sloop returning from the wreck of the *Nuestra Señora de Soledad* (lost on Cape Hatteras, North Carolina), and supposedly carrying the valuables from that ship, wrecked off Anegada.

17. **Year *1751*.** *Katherine*, commanded by Captain Richards, sailing from Jamaica to Bristol, was lost on Anegada but the crew was saved.

18. **Year *1757*.** Spanish merchantman *El Cesar*, Captain Josef Bernabe Madero, owned by the Marqués de Casa Madrid, was lost on Anegada Island.

19. **Year *1758*.** Spanish merchantman *Santa Rosa* wrecked on the reefs of Anegada.

20. **Year *1760*.** *Prince Ferdinand*, Captain Caynoon, sailing from Boston to Jamaica, was lost on Anegada Reef but her crew was saved.

21. **Year *1769*.** British merchantman *Graham*, Captain M'Intosh, was cast away off the back reef of St. Croix, both ship and cargo were a total loss but the crew was saved. The *Graham* had been sailing from Grenada to London.

22. **Year *1769*.** British ship *Brothers*, Captain Briggs, from Virginia for Lisbon, sprung a leak at sea and, bearing away for the West Indies, ran ashore upon a reef off St. Croix, both ship and cargo were lost but the crew was saved.

23. *Year 1769. Nancy Gaer* was lost off Anegada but her crew was saved.

24. *Year 1773.* British ship *Lord Mount Cathell*, Captain Fisher, previously commanded by the late Captain Taylor, was lost on the island of St. Croix in July, only part of the cargo was saved.

25. *Year 1774. Martha*, Captain McIntosh, sailing from Jamaica to London, was lost May 25 on Anegada.

26. *Before 1775.* Written on a chart of the Virgin Islands in a book was the following note: "On Anegada is Ye Treasure Point, so called by ye freebooters from the gold and silver supposed to have been buried there abouts after the wreck of a Spanish galleon."

27. *Year 1775.* A Spanish snow called *Spirito Santo* (Spanish spelling would be *Espíritu Santo*), bound from La Coruña, Spain, to Havana, wrecked night of March 19 on the rocks of Anegada (at the point called the Horseshoe), the people and a great part of the cargo were saved but the vessel was lost.

28. *Year 1776.* British slave ship *Fox*, Captain Jones, from Africa for America, was lost at St. Thomas.

29. *Year 1778.* Dutch ship *Neptune*, Captain Spranges, lost at Tortola.

30. *Year 1781.* British merchantman *Swallow*, Captain Heblethwaith, of Liverpool, was lost coming out of Tortola but the crew was saved.

31. *Year 1782.* Originally a Spanish ship taken by the British on September 14, 1779, the *Santa Monica*, Captain John Linzee, was lost near Tortola. All of her crew but one were saved, as well as many of her guns, stores, and cargo.

32. *Year 1783. Ortello*, Captain Johnson, sailing from Africa to Tortola, was cast away in Tortola, 213 slaves were saved.

33. *Year 1784.* British ship *Ranger*, Captain Stewart, from Tortola to London, was lost on a reef of rocks near Tortola.

34. *Year 1785. Constantine*, Captain Langdon, sailing from Dominica to Bristol, was lost in hurricane August 26 on Thatch Island, near St. Thomas but the crew was saved.

35. **Year 1786.** American ship *Cruger,* Captain Williams, from Philadelphia to St. Croix, was wrecked on September 3 on the Horseshoe Reef of Anegada.

36. **Year 1789.** British ship *Neptune,* Captain Casey, of London, was lost at the Island of St. John, Virgin Islands.

37. **Year 1790.** Spanish ship *El Rayo,* sailing from Bilbao to Puerto Rico, ran ashore on Anegada but the crew abandoned her safely.

38. **Year 1792.** Spanish ship *Nevarro* (probably correctly spelled *Navarro*), Captain Belandia, from St. Andero (Santander), Spain, to Havana, was lost at Anegada Island.

39. **Year 1792.** During a hurricane on August 1, two vessels were wrecked on the Island of St. Thomas, and a packet boat was run aground at Tortola Island.

40. **Year 1793.** British slave ship *Recovery,* Captain Walker, from Africa, was blown out of Nevis Roads (on Nevis Island) and driven by winds and wrecked on Tortola Island.

41. **Year 1793.** A ship of unknown nationality, but probably French, named *Christopher,* Captain Mollyneaux, from Africa, struck on a submerged anchor in the harbor of St. Croix and sank.

42. **Year 1795.** British ship *Hebe,* Captain Gray, from Cork to Jamaica, was lost on the rocks near Tortola.

43. **Year 1795.** British ship *Perseverance,* Captain Oriel, from Dublin to Jamaica, was totally lost on the north side of Anegada near Tortola.

44. **Year 1796.** British merchant ship *Jamaica,* Captain Alexander, from Tobago and Grenada to London, was captured by the French and run ashore at St. Croix.

45. **Year 1797.** British ship *Mary,* Captain Hunter, from Africa, was lost near St. Croix but her cargo was saved.

46. **Year 1801.** British ship *Albion,* Captain Robertson, from Montserrat to London, was lost at Tortola.

47. **Year 1801.** Ship, nationality unknown, named *Lavinia,* Captain Elles, from Tortola to Quebec, was lost near Tortola but a great part of her cargo was saved.

48. *Year 1803.* British ship *General Abercrombie,* Captain Booth, from Africa to West Indies, was lost at St. Croix but most of her cargo was saved.

49. *Year 1805.* British merchant ship *Ocean,* Captain Brown, from St. Vincent's Island to Bristol, was lost near the Island of Tortola.

50. *Year 1806.* British ship *Partridge,* Captain Miller, from Bristol and the Island of Madeira to St. Thomas, was lost near Tortola but part of her cargo was saved.

51. *Year 1807.* British merchant ship *Henry,* Captain Retson, of Liverpool, was lost off Water Island, St. Thomas, on April 26.

52. *Year 1808.* British frigate *Astrea,* 32 guns, Captain Edward Heywood, was lost on May 23 on a reef at the Island of Anegada, only four men were lost.

53. *Year 1808.* Spanish felucca was lost off Anegada, three men were lost.

54. *Year 1809.* British ship *Good Hope,* Captain Watson, from London to the Spanish Main, was lost near Anegada but most of the cargo was saved.

55. *Year 1809.* British war brig *Dominica,* Captain Charles Welsh, 10 guns, foundered near Tortola, sixty-two of her crew of sixty-five perished, including the captain.

56. *Year 1810.* Spanish merchant ship *Aftrivedo,* Captain Laporta, coming from Tarragona, was lost on July 22 on Anegada Island but part of the cargo was saved and carried to Tortola.

57. *Year 1810.* British ship *London,* Captain Cromie (might be Cramie), from London to Haiti, was lost on Anegada Island.

58. *Year 1810.* Unidentified ship lost off Anegada.

59. *Year 1811.* American brig *Lioness* wrecked on Anegada Reef.

60. *Year 1812.* British ship *Ocean,* Captain Stewart, from London to Honduras, totally lost in February on Anegada Reef but the crew was saved.

61. *Year 1812.* Spanish ship *N.S. de la Victoria,* coming from Málaga, was lost on December 5 on Anegada Reef.

62. *Year 1813.* A brig, name unknown, struck a rock between Buck Island and St. Thomas and stuck there. Incident took place the same day the *Thomas*, of Bristol, coming from St. Vincent, struck the same rock and was run ashore to keep from sinking.

63. *Year 1813.* Spanish ship *Anrora* (correct spelling is probably *Aurora*) Captain Aldayturriaga, from Cadiz to Veracruz, was totally lost on Anegada on November 29 but the crew was saved.

64. *Year 1814.* A ship of unknown nationality, *Caroline*, Captain DaSilva, from Madeira to Jamaica, was lost off Tortola on November 15 but the crew was saved and carried to Puerto Rico.

65. *Year 1815.* British ship *Marina*, Captain Littlewood, from Barbados to St. John and New Brunswick, was wrecked on a small island to the westward of St. Thomas but part of her cargo was saved.

66. *Year 1816.* British cutter *Jane* was lost on the north side of Tortola, her port of origin, at the end of February.

67. *Year 1816.* British ship *Dash*, Captain Falls, of London, from Puerto Rico to Barbados, with 120 head of oxen, was totally lost on May 23 on Anegada Reef, the crew, twenty head of oxen, and some rigging were saved.

68. *Year 1816.* British ship *Warwick*, Captain Simpson, from Liverpool to St. Thomas, struck a rock between Buck Island and St. Thomas and was lost with her cargo but the crew was saved.

69. *Year 1817.* A ship of unknown nationality, *Arabella*, Captain Spiller, from Pará, Brazil, to New York, was totally lost near St. Thomas.

70. *Year 1817.* A ship of unknown nationality, *Mary*, Captain Autman, from Jamaica to Veracruz, was lost on Anegada.

71. *Year 1817.* American ship *Falcon*, Captain Brothoff, wrecked at Anegada on May 26.

72. *Year 1817.* A large unidentified Spanish ship with over three hundred African slaves aboard ran aground on the Horseshoe part of Anegada. After throwing many heavy objects overboard she was light enough to be pulled off and proceeded on her voyage.

73. *Year 1818.* *Paterson* sank at Anegada.

74. **Year 1818.** British ship *Bulwark*, from New Brunswick to Jamaica, wrecked on Anegada on December 13.

75. **Year 1819.** Portuguese ship *Dona Paulo*, Captain Viana, of Pará, totally wrecked on the Anegada Shoals the night of September 3, 235 African slaves and the crew were saved.

76. **Year 1819.** British ship *Agno*, Captain Park, from London to (St.) Petersburg, lost on the south end of Hogland (Hog Island?) in the Virgin Islands.

77. **Year 1819.** During a hurricane in September an unidentified vessel was driven onshore at Tortola.

78. **Year 1819.** English ship *Ajax* wrecked, captain and three men drowned, off Anegada, September 1819.

79. **Year 1819.** American schooner *Maxwell* sank at Anegada.

80. **Year 1819.** American schooner *James Edwards* sank at Anegada.

81. **Year 1819.** Danish brig *Volvent* sank at Anegada.

82. **Year 1819.** British brig *Argus* sank at Anegada.

83. **Year 1819.** Dreadful hurricane struck St. Thomas as well as throughout the Leeward Islands on September 20–22. At St. Thomas alone, 104 vessels were totally lost.

84. **Year 1821.** A ship of unknown nationality, *Mary*, Captain Hellyer, from New York to St. Thomas, was lost on February 22 on Anegada Shoals but the crew and cargo were saved.

85. **Year 1821.** American ship *General Brown*, Captain Godfrey, from New York to the west end of Puerto Rico, was totally wrecked on the Anegada Shoals but most of its cargo was saved and sold at Tortola.

86. **Year 1821.** British ship *Bryon* (or *Byron*), Captain Anderson, of and for Cork from Trinidad, was totally lost on Anegada Shoals on November 23 but the crew and passengers were saved.

87. **Year 1822.** British ship *Sophia Sarah*, Captain Stairs, of and from Halifax to Jamaica, was totally lost in July on the Anegada Shoals but the crew and part of her cargo were saved.

88. **Year 1822.** American brig *Caroline*, from Boston to Puerto Rico, was totally lost on Anegada Shoals about November 25.

89. *Year 1822.* Spanish felucca on Anegada.

90. *Year 1823.* British schooner *Sophia,* of Antigua, bound to Curaçao with cargo of mahogany wood, ran on the Anegada Reef and was totally lost, crew, rigging, and part of cargo saved.

91. *Year 1823.* British ship *Eliza,* Captain Filliul, from Liverpool to St. Thomas, wrecked on Horseshoe Reef near Anegada, cargo and crew saved.

92. *Year 1823.* British ship *Acadia,* Captain Venham, of and for Trinidad from Puerto Rico, lost on the Anegada Shoals on March 4, only about fifty head of cattle were saved.

93. *Year 1823.* British ship *Union,* Captain Purrington, from Barbados to Bath, was lost on December 12 on Anegada.

94. *Year 1824.* American ship *James Barron,* Captain Fisher, from Charleston, South Carolina, to Barbados, was totally lost on January 7 on the Anegada Reef.

95. *Year 1824.* French ship *Aimable Eulalie,* Captain Alleaume, from Guadeloupe to Le Havre, wrecked on Anegada Shoals on May, only a small part of the cargo was saved.

96. *Year 1824.* British ship *Sector,* from Trinidad to St. Thomas, wrecked on Anegada Shoals on May 6, crew and some of cargo of dry goods saved.

97. *Year 1824.* A ship of unknown nationality, *Angelica,* Captain Treby, from New York, was totally wrecked on Buck Island, off St. Croix, crew and small part of cargo saved.

CHAPTER TWELVE

Central America
and Off-Lying Areas

WHEN COMPARED with most other areas of the Western Hemisphere, Central America and the areas adjacent to it do not have a large number of shipwrecks. The main reason for this is because of the relatively small amount of shipping in these waters during the period covered in this book. There were only a few small Spanish settlements along the coastline of Central America, on both the Caribbean and Pacific sides, and these were not very important when compared with many of the other Spanish settlements in South America and Mexico. Only the ports in Panama were considered of major importance, and they only served as transshipment points between Spain and Peru. Throughout most of the sixteenth, seventeenth, and eighteenth centuries, shipping was forbidden in the Pacific Ocean between ports of Mexico, Panama, and all South-American ports. During the same period the only important shipping on the Caribbean side of Central America was carried on by the Honduras galleons, two of which were permitted to sail annually between Spain and Honduras, but there were many years when none sailed for periods as long as ten years, especially in wartime. In the eighteenth century, when the English started settlements in British Honduras and some of the Bay Islands, shipping increased, and so did the number of ship losses, but most of these ships carried insignificant cargoes, such as mahogany and dyewoods.

In this chapter I have to exclude over one hundred shipwrecks, most of them English and dating after 1650, because the documents list them only as being lost at such ambiguous locations as the "Bay of Honduras" or "on the Coast of Honduras," and until as late as the early part of the last century the whole of the Caribbean coastline of Central America from Panama up to Yucatán was simply called "Honduras." And all of the western part of the Caribbean, from the Cayman Islands to the west, was called the "Bay of Honduras"—and not merely the body of water near the coast.

With the exception of the Islands of Old Providence and San Andrés, which belong to Colombia (see Chapter 13), none of the other areas or countries covered in this chapter have any laws concerning the salvaging of old shipwrecks. Except for a few small expeditions undertaken around Panama, and my own work at Old Providence Island and Serrana and Serranilla banks, virtually no work has been done on old shipwrecks.

List of Shipwrecks off Central America and Off-Lying Areas

OFF-LYING AREAS:

1. *Year 1526.* A small unidentified Spanish merchant *nao*, sailing between Santo Domingo and Venezuela, encountered a severe storm and lost its masts and rudder. After drifting for six days it was wrecked on a reef in front of Southwest Key (now Serrana Bank). Only a man identified as Master Pedro Serrano reached the key safely. The others drifted away on pieces of the wreckage and were lost. He lived on the key for eight years before a passing ship sighted his smoke signals and picked him up. The

bank was named after him. I located this shipwreck several years ago and recovered a number of interesting artifacts from it.

2. Year 1531. While Pedro Serrano was living on Southwest Key, another unidentified Spanish ship was wrecked on a reef about 6 miles to the east of Southwest Key. The only survivor from this wreck managed to reach Southwest Key and he lived with Pedro Serrano until both were rescued in 1534.

3. Year 1534. Several months after Pedro Serrano and his companion were rescued, another unidentified Spanish ship, carrying a large amount of treasure on board, was wrecked on the reefs at the eastern end of Serrana Bank. A few survivors from this wreck reached Jamaica in a small boat, but there are no records indicating if the treasure from it was ever recovered.

4. Year 1571. Small Spanish merchant *nao Nuestra Señora de la Limpia Concepción,* sailing from Spain to Panama, was wrecked on a reef off Old Providence Island. Using documentation from the Archives of the Indies, I located this shipwreck in 1964 and partially salvaged it the following year.

5. Year 1605. Seven treasure-laden galleons of the Armada de Tierra Firme, commanded by Captain-General Luis de Cordova, were struck by a hurricane between Serrana and Serranilla banks. One of the ships managed to return to Cartagena and two others reached Jamaica. The other four, carrying over 8 million pesos in treasure, were wrecked on Serranilla Bank. They were the *Capitana, San Roque,* 600 tons, Captain Ruy López; *Almiranta, Santo Domingo,* 747 tons, Captain Diego Ramírez; *Nuestra Señora de Begonia,* 500 tons, Captain Pedro Muñoz de Salto; and the *San Ambrosio,* 450 tons, Captain Martín de Ormachea. Although there were no survivors from these four wrecks, the Spaniards sent out salvage teams all over the western Caribbean trying to locate them, which they failed to do. They were accidentally located in 1667 by Spanish fishermen from Cuba who recovered an undisclosed amount of silver coins from two of the wrecks. During the following six years, Spanish authorities sent many expeditions to salvage these wrecks but all failed because of bad weather. Several modern-day expeditions, including one of my own in 1963, have attempted to salvage these rich wrecks but also failed due to bad weather and the incessant large seas that break over the area of the reef in which these wrecks are located. From the air I have sighted six large ballast piles in the area where these ships were lost, and from artifacts I found on the inside of the reef, which date from the period of the disaster, I am sure that at least one of the six ballast piles I sighted is one of these 1605 wrecks.

6. **Year 1633.** While the Armada de Tierra Firme, commanded by Captain-General Antonio de Oquendo, was sailing between Cartagena and Havana, it encountered a bad storm near Serrana Bank. The galleons *Almiranta* and *San Juan,* both carrying a great amount of treasure, were wrecked on Serrana Bank, and there are no records indicating if they were ever salvaged.

7. **Year 1641.** The Spaniards sent an expedition commanded by Admiral Pimienta from Cartagena to dislodge the English from their newly founded settlement on Old Providence Island. The Spanish attack was successful, but one of the ships of the attacking squadron, a Portuguese *nao, Santa María de la Ayuda,* of 230 tons, struck on a reef off the western end of the island and sank in 10 fathoms of water.

8. **Year 1643.** A small Spanish frigate of 6 bronze cannon was sent from Porto Bello with supplies for the Spanish garrison on Old Providence Island but was wrecked en route on a reef at San Andrés Island, located 55 miles south of Old Providence Island.

9. **Year 1666.** A small Spanish warship was sent from Cartagena to dislodge a band of pirates then living in Old Providence Island but due to faulty navigation was wrecked on the reefs of Quita Sueño Bank, located north of the island.

10. **Year 1675.** An unidentified large Dutch warship was wrecked on Roncador Reef, located to the east of Old Providence Island. Some survivors managed to reach the southern coast of Cuba in a raft, where they were captured by the Spaniards.

11. **Year 1688.** Several Spaniards petitioned the King of Spain for permission to salvage several very rich galleon wrecks located near Swan's Island, but they neither identified the ships nor when they were lost. Records do not indicate if they were granted permission.

12. *Year 1788.* English merchantman *Richard*, Captain Watson, sailing from Jamaica to Honduras, was wrecked at San Andrés Island but the crew was saved.

13. *Year 1794.* English merchantman *June*, Captain Gardner, sailing from Honduras to London, was wrecked at Old Providence Island on August 17..

14. *Year 1796.* Spanish frigate *Palas*, 34 cannon, Captain Pedro Saenz de la Guardia, was wrecked at Old Providence Island on December 29.

15. *Year 1801.* Spanish merchantman *El Paysano*, Captain Chicey, sailing to Jamaica, was wrecked near San Andrés Island, her crew was lost.

16. *Year 1816.* American schooner *Charming Sally*, Captain Vincent, sailing from South Carolina to Cartagena, was wrecked on Serrana Bank.

17. *Year 1817.* American merchantman *Rolla*, Captain Lewis, coming from Philadelphia, was wrecked in April on Serranilla Reef but all of the crew was saved.

18. *Year 1819.* Three English merchantmen were wrecked on some reefs located south of San Andrés Island: *St. Lawrence*, Captain Williamson; *Friends*, Captain Howard; and the *Beckles*, Captain Hall.

BRITISH HONDURAS:

19. *Year 1749.* During a hurricane on September 18, more than twenty English merchantmen were totally lost on the coast and off-lying keys and reefs.

20. *Year 1751.* English merchantman *Monmouth*, Captain Wadham, sailing to London, was wrecked on Glover's Key but the crew was saved.

21. *Year 1751.* Two sloops from Rhode Island and a snow from Jamaica were lost on the "North Keys."

22. Year 1764. English merchantman *Mary Oxford*, coming from Jamaica, was wrecked on Turneffe Island.

23. Year 1769. English merchantman *Liberty*, Captain Beard, coming from Jamaica, was wrecked on the southern end of Chinchorro Reef but her crew was saved.

24. Year 1771. American ship *Andrew*, Captain Passgrove, sailing from Honduras to Philadelphia, was wrecked October 22 on Chinchorro Reef.

25. Year 1773. American merchantman *Industry*, Captain Glen, sailing from Honduras to New York, carrying a cargo of indigo and mahogany, was wrecked on Chinchorro Reef.

26. Year 1774. Two ships wrecked on Glover's Reef: English merchantman *Argyle*, Captain Fisher, about 5 leagues from the southwestern end of the reef; and the American ship *Polly*, Captain Waid, sailing to New York, on the northeastern end of the reef—crews and part of cargoes saved.

27. Year 1776. Irish merchantman *Hercules*, Captain Norwood, sailing from Honduras to Dublin, was wrecked on Chinchorro Reef.

28. Year 1780. English ship *Live Oak*, sailing to Jamaica with a cargo of mahogany, was wrecked on the coast at Black River, the crew was saved.

29. Year 1786. English merchantman *Assistance*, Captain Galt, coming from Jamaica, was lost crossing the bar at Black River.

30. Year 1786. Unidentified Scottish ship, Captain Carr, was wrecked on Glovers Reef but the crew was saved.

31. Year 1787. During a hurricane on September 2, more than thirty English merchantmen were wrecked on the coast and off-lying areas. Of these, fifteen were lost in the port of Belize. The only ship identified by name was the HMS *Triumvirate*, lost at St. Georges Key, which was carrying a large amount of silver specie.

32. Before 1792. An English chart dated 1792 states that some years earlier a Spanish galleon named *Santa Yaga* was lost off the Three Brothers, which are several small keys near the northeastern tip of Ambergris Key.

33. *Year 1793.* English gunship H.M.S. *Advice*, 4 cannon, Captain Edward Tyrell, was lost to the leeward of Key Bokell but her crew was saved.

34. *Year 1793.* English merchantman *Chance*, Captain Reed, coming from Jamaica, was wrecked on Glovers Reef.

35. *Year 1803.* English merchantman *Fishburn*, Captain Leake, sailing to London, was lost on a reef near Belize on February 19.

36. *Year 1804.* A ship of unknown registry, *Mentor*, Captain Simpson, coming from Jamaica, was lost on "the Main Reef" near Belize but part of her cargo was saved.

37. *Year 1807.* English ship *General Don*, Captain Messeroy, coming from France, was lost on Glovers Reef.

38. *Year 1808.* English merchantman *Perseverance*, Captain M'Nutt, coming from Jamaica, lost near Belize on December 20 but the crew was saved.

39. *Year 1814.* A ship of unknown registry, *Pompey*, Captain Cowan, was wrecked on "the Main Reef" on March 31 but her cargo of wine was saved.

40. *Year 1815.* Scottish merchantman *Lord Blandtyre*, Captain M'Lea, coming from Jamaica, was wrecked in August on the "Southern Four Keys."

41. *Year 1818.* American ship *Enterprize*, Captain Wayne, sailing from the Bahamas to New Orleans, was lost on March 9 near Belize but her crew was saved.

42. *Year 1818.* English merchantman *John Winslow*, Captain Hodges, coming from Liverpool, was lost on July 26 on the "Main Reef," cargo and crew saved.

43. *Year 1819.* English merchantman *Vestol*, Captain Hutchinson, sailing to London, was wrecked on Corker Key in August, crew and part of cargo saved.

44. *Year 1821.* English merchantman *Barrosa*, Captain Anderson, coming from London, was totally lost on November 8 on the "Southern Fourth Reef," crew and most of cargo saved.

45. **Year 1821.** French ship *Ceres*, Captain Mourant, coming from France, was wrecked on July 18 on Chinchorro Reef, only the crew was saved.

46. **Year 1822.** American ship *Phoebe Ann*, sailing to New York, was wrecked near Belize about April 11.

47. **Year 1822.** English ship *Comet*, Captain Merrill, sailing to England, was wrecked on Ambergris Key on August 16.

HONDURAS:

48. **Year 1524.** After learning of the revolt of Captain Olid, Cortez sent two ships full of soldiers commanded by Captain Francisco de las Casas to quell the mutiny. After entering the port of Triunfo de la Cruz, a battle ensued between the mutineers and de las Casas' ships in which one of Olid's vessels was sunk by cannonfire. Soon after, a violent gale hit the port and both of de las Casas' ships were sunk.

49. **Year 1530.** Two large ships from Spain arrived in the port of Trujillo, with supplies and the new governor of that province, Don Diego de Albitez. Only minutes after anchoring, both ships were wrecked by a violent gust of wind and only a small part of their cargoes was salvaged.

50. **Year 1545.** A big unidentified galleon commanded by Captain Nicolás Castellón sailed from Puerto Caballos for Spain with a large number of passengers and a great amount of gold. She was wrecked at Cabo de Honduras and the majority of her passengers and gold was lost.

51. **Year 1605.** Two large galleons were sent from Spain to the port of Trujillo and met with misfortune. As the *Almiranta* was entering port it was struck by lightning and sank quickly, with only eleven of the 101 persons aboard being saved. After the *Capitana* had taken on a valuable cargo in that port, including a substantial amount of gold and silver, it sailed for Spain. But the following day a storm drove it ashore on the coast, where it quickly went to pieces. Several months later, pieces of the wreck, including some bodies and a few bars of gold and silver, were found on a beach but the wreck was never located.

52. *Year 1607.* A squadron of twelve Dutch ships entered the port of Puerto Caballos and attempted to capture two Spanish galleons that were then loading for the voyage to Spain. During the battle that ensued and lasted for a period of nine days, one Dutch ship was sunk in the port and the other left without capturing the two Spanish galleons.

53. *Year 1617.* Two galleons sent from Spain to Honduras were lost. The *Capitana La Limpia Concepción de Nuestra Señora* sank on September 28 while entering Trujillo, and several days before the *Almiranta Santiago* had wrecked on Guanaja Island.

54. *Year 1618.* The following year, Spain sent only one galleon to Honduras, and it too met with disaster. She was the 450-ton galleon *San Francisco*, Captain Sebastián Rodríguez de Caranca, and when attempting to enter the port of Santo Tomás de Castilla she was wrecked and totally lost on a reef. Of her thirty bronze cannon only two were salvaged, and of her cargo only a few casks of wine.

55. *Year 1644.* Six English warships were sighted off the port of Santo Tomás de Castilla on May 12, and to prevent the capture of a frigate that had just arrived from Veracruz, the Spaniards quickly took off her cannon and then sank the ship at the mouth of the port.

56. *Year 1647.* Shortly after two large galleons from Spain had arrived at Trujillo, they were quickly unloaded and then sunk by the Spaniards, as they believed that an English fleet was coming to attack that port.

57. *Year 1660.* The Spanish *nao Santiago,* part of the Tierra Firme Flota of Captain-General Juan de Echeverri, sailing from Cartagena to Havana, was wrecked near a deserted island off the coast of Honduras. Most of the persons aboard the ship managed to reach the island and spent fifty-three days there building a small vessel from the timbers of their wreck.

58. *Year 1690.* Due to a shortage of mercury in Mexico, the viceroy sent a small ship with over a million pesos in silver specie aboard for the purpose of buying mercury in Peru. Several days after sailing from Acapulco, it was struck by a storm and soon afterward wrecked near a point of land on the southwest side of the

Gulf of Fonseca. Salvors were able to recover only a small part of the treasure, as most had been buried under shifting sands.

59. *Year 1751*. English merchantman *Lamport*, Captain M'Namara, carrying a cargo of 300 tons of logwood to England, was wrecked on Roatan Island.

60. *Year 1768*. English merchantman *Ward*, Captain Kelly, sailing from Honduras to the Windward Islands, was wrecked on Utila Island.

61. *Year 1769*. English merchantman *Windsor*, Captain Burden, sailing to England, was wrecked on Roatan Island but most of its cargo was saved.

62. *Year 1773*. A ship of unknown registry, *St. Paul*, Captain Maes, sailing from Montserrat Island to Honduras, was lost on Roatan Island but the crew was saved.

63. *Year 1774*. Scottish merchantman *Willingmaid*, Captain Bray, was accidentally burnt while at anchor at Guanaja Island.

64. *Year 1785*. English merchantman *Quebec*, Captain Rattle, sailing from Honduras to Bristol, was wrecked at Guanaja Island.

65. *Year 1803*. English merchantman *Oliver*, Captain Hood, sailing for England with a cargo of logwood, was wrecked on Utila Island.

NICARAGUA:

66. *Year 1577*. Unidentified Spanish *nao*, carrying a large number of religious from Cartagena to Trujillo, Honduras, was wrecked about 20 leagues south of Cabo Gracias a Dios.

67. *Year 1680*. An unidentified English privateer, coming from Jamaica, was wrecked several leagues north of Cabo Gracias a Dios.

68. *Year 1766*. English sloop *Fanny*, Captain Henderson, coming from Jamaica, was lost October 31 off Cabo Gracias a Dios.

69. *Year 1822*. Dutch warship *Fox*, sailing from Puerto Cabello to Havana, was wrecked at Cabo Gracias a Dios.

COSTA RICA:

70. *Year 1567.* Small Spanish advice boat *La Rapidez,* Captain Hernando Martín López, was wrecked near the mouth of the San Juan River, on the Caribbean side of the country.

71. *Year 1675.* Two unidentified merchant *naos,* sailing from Callao, Peru, to Acapulco, each carrying several chests of silver specie as well as several tons of mercury, were wrecked near Cabo Blanco on the Nicoya Peninsula, which is in the Pacific.

PANAMA:

72. *Year 1503.* While Columbus was on his fourth voyage of discovery, two of his caravels were so worm-eaten that he was forced to scuttle them. The *Gallega* was scuttled near Santa María de Belem and the *Vizcaina* off Porto Bello. Both vessels were first stripped of all items of value.

73. *Year 1514.* Two or three small Spanish ships, under the command of Governor Pedrarias Davila, were lost during a storm near Cabo Tiburon, on the Caribbean side of the isthmus.

74. *Year 1544.* At the orders of the conquistador Francisco de Pizarro, an undisclosed number of ships were scuttled in the port of Nombre de Dios after being stripped of their cannon and rigging.

75. *Year 1551.* An unidentified Spanish *nao* of the Tierra Firme Flota of Captain-General Sancho de Viedma, was wrecked on the coast about 25 leagues from the port of Nombre de Dios.

76. *Year 1563.* While the Tierra Firme Flota of Captain-General Antonio de Aquayo was anchored in Nombre de Dios, seven ships were sunk during a storm. None had their cargoes aboard at the time, the cannon from five of them was recovered.

77. *Year 1567.* An unidentified merchant *nao* of the Tierra Firme Flota of Captain-General Diego Flores de Valdes struck upon an anchor in a shallow area while entering Nombre de Dios and sank with all of her cargo still aboard.

78. *Year 1584.* Shortly after the Tierra Firme Flota of Captain-General Francisco de Novoa Feijo entered the port of Nombre de Dios, two merchant *naos* sank with their cargoes from Spain still

aboard: *Espíritu Santo,* 500 tons, Captain Cristobal García de la Vega, and an unidentified *nao* of 300 tons, Captain Nufio Rodriquez.

79. *Year 1609.* An unidentified Portuguese caravel, coming from Angola, Africa, with a cargo of slaves, ivory, and gold dust, sank a bit north of the Bay of Acla but all of her cargo and slaves were saved.

80. *Year 1619.* Several flat-bottomed boats that were transporting treasure from Panama to the galleons anchored in Porto Bello overturned on the Chagres River and a large amount of treasure was lost.

81. *Year 1631.* The *Almiranta* of the South Seas Armada, the galleon *San José,* while carrying a great amount of treasure from Callao, Peru, to Panama, was wrecked on a reef about 40 leagues from Panama City, between the islands of Garachine and La Galera. Divers were quickly sent to the wreck site and recovered twenty-five of the ship's twenty-eight cannon and over a million pesos in treasure. However, a year later the president of Panama reported that there was still over 400,000 pesos in silver specie and forty-four silver bars still on the wreck, but diving operations had to be suspended because of rough seas and fast currents; also because the remainder of the treasure was buried under sand.

82. *Year 1632.* The *patache Margarita,* owned by Miguel de Garnica, was wrecked at Isla del Rey, located 15 leagues from Panama City, but her complete cargo of silver bullion and specie was recovered.

83. *Year 1634.* Two unidentified Spanish merchant *naos* were sunk during a storm in the port of Porto Bello but the cargoes and cannon from both wrecks were salvaged.

84. *Year 1635.* While the Tierra Firme Armada, commanded by Captain-General Carlos de Ibarra, was in Porto Bello loading on the treasure for Spain, one galleon—the *Santa Ana María*—was in such bad condition from multiple leaks that she was stripped and then sunk.

85. *Year 1670.* While approaching the coast of Panama before his attack on Panama City, the flagship of the pirate Henry Morgan

and four other ships in his fleet were wrecked on a reef at the mouth of the Chagres River. After all five were stripped of all valuable items they were burnt to the waterline by the pirates.

86. *Year 1681.* After the Tierra Firme Armada, commanded by the Marqués de Bienes, had taken on treasure and set sail from Porto Bello it was struck by a storm that scattered many of the ships to various places near the coast of Panama. An unidentified rich treasure galleon of Captain Antonio de Lima struck on a reef off Punta de Brujas and quickly broke up with more than 280 persons drowning and her treasure totally lost. The merchant *nao Chaperon* sank at the mouth of the Chagres River with only eleven men lost; and another *nao, La Boticaria,* was wrecked on a reef near Isla de Naranjos, but only two men were lost and some of her cargo was eventually recovered.

87. *Year 1740.* During the English attack led by Admiral Vernon against Porto Bello, a small Spanish sloop was sunk at Porto Bello and two large Spanish vessels were sunk at the mouth of the Chagres River.

88. *Year 1746.* A Spanish privateer, *Golgoa,* was driven ashore near Porto Bello by two English warships after a short battle and quickly went to pieces.

89. *Year 1818.* Two schooners were wrecked near Porto Bello during a storm: the *Lion,* coming from Jamaica, and an unidentified vessel from Havana.

90. *Year 1819.* A large French brig, *Jeune Robert,* was totally lost on Sapelo Island, on the Caribbean side of the isthmus.

CHAPTER THIRTEEN

South America

IN THIS CHAPTER I have excluded 123 shipwrecks—for the reasons previously given. To the Spaniards and the Portuguese, all of the east coast of South America—from Venezuela to the Straits of Magellan—was considered "Brazil" until later in the eighteenth century. Although the majority of the shipping off the East Coast of South America was composed of Portuguese ships during the sixteenth, seventeenth, and eighteenth centuries (and no doubt hundreds of their ships were lost), due to the almost total destruction of old Portuguese documents, relatively few of their wreck locations are known.

None of the countries in South America have any laws regarding salvaging old shipwrecks, with the exception of Colombia, which passed a law in 1968. Their law is very similar to that of Florida, such as the salvor getting 75 percent and the country 25 percent of all treasure and artifacts recovered. In addition, a foreigner must give the government a bond of about $25,000 to protect the Colombian government from someone locating a treasure and then fleeing the country with it. Another problem in Colombia is that although the salvor retains 75 percent of everything he recovers, no gold in any form can leave the country; and if a Colombian museum wishes to obtain anything belonging to a salvor, they can buy it at a price they deem reasonable—which certainly makes working there difficult.

List of Shipwrecks in South America

COLOMBIA:

1. *Year 1504.* During an exploration voyage along the coast of Colombia the flagship of Captain Cristobal García was wrecked on a reef near Punta de Canoas, which is located between Cartagena and Barranquilla. The crew was rescued by the two other vessels in the flotilla, but an undisclosed amount of gold nuggets and emeralds that the explorers had traded from the natives went down with the ship.

2. *Year 1504.* Another flotilla of four larger vessels commanded by Captain Juan de la Cosa was sent later this same year to continue exploring and mapping the Colombian coast, but all four were wrecked during a storm in the Bahía de Uraba and 175 of the two hundred men on board the *naos* were drowned.

3. *Year 1513.* A large *nao* was sent from Santo Domingo to the new Spanish settlement named Darien, located close to the present boundary of Panama and Colombia. The *nao* was carrying a large number of colonists and supplies, but the pilot erred in his navigation and the *nao* wrecked a bit west of Darien, there were only a few survivors.

4. *Year 1542.* Three unidentified ships carrying over a half-million pesos in gold and silver were sunk near Boca Chica, in Cartagena Harbor, while entering the port. At the admiral's orders the main pilot of the convoy was hanged and, later, divers were able to recover only a small part of the treasure, as it was reported to be in a depth too deep for them to work in.

5. *Year 1544.* A large unidentified Spanish *nao*, carrying a bishop to Cartagena from Spain along with a rich cargo of merchandise, was wrecked on the coast near Santa Martha.

6. *Year 1546.* An unidentified Spanish merchant *nao* was wrecked on a reef near Cartagena and thirteen of the 104 persons aboard perished.

7. *Year 1553.* After the Tierra Firme Armada, commanded by Captain-General Bartolome Carreno, sailed from Nombe de Dios with a great amount of treasure, the *nao Santa María de Villacelan,* 120 tons, Captain Martín García, was wrecked on the coast about 10 leagues south of Cartagena but all of her treasure was salvaged by Indian divers brought from the pearl fisheries of Margarita Island.

8. *Year 1556.* Unidentified merchant *nao* of Captain Juan Estevan sank while at anchor in Cartagena Harbor but all of her treasure was recovered by Indian divers.

9. *Year 1559.* A richly laden unidentified galleon sailing from Nombe de Dios with over 900,000 pesos in gold and silver aboard parted from its convoy and attempted to enter Cartagena Harbor at night, but the pilot made a mistake as to where the entrance was and the ship ran aground a bit south of the port and quickly broke up. Only a small amount of the treasure was recovered.

10. *Year 1562.* Treasure-laden *nao Santa María de Begonia,* 250 tons, Captain Cosme Andrés, ran aground when entering Cartagena Harbor and was lost but all of her treasure was saved.

11. *Year 1564.* An unidentified treasure-laden galleon in the Tierra Firme Armada, commanded by Captain-General Esteban de las Alas, was wrecked on a reef near Cartagena and thirteen persons drowned. The wreck fell off the reef into deeper water before her treasure could be saved and divers were unable to recover anything because of the depth in which the wreck sank.

12. *Year 1572.* Treasure-laden galleon *San Felipe,* 550 tons, Captain Galdomez, caught fire while sailing between Nombre de Dios and Cartagena and was run aground near Isla Tesora, where it blew up before the majority of the treasure she carried could be taken off.

13. *Year 1575.* Shortly before the Tierra Firme Armada was to sail for Havana, two unidentified galleons collided while at anchor in Cartagena and one of them, carrying an immense treasure in

silver bullion and specie, sank. Because of the water's depth, divers were only able to recover some of the ship's rigging and a few bronze cannon.

14. **Year 1600.** Unidentified merchant *nao* of Captain Bodes, coming from Margarita Island with a large amount of pearls, was wrecked near the mouth of the Medellín River.

15. **Year 1615.** Soon after arriving from Spain the *nao Nuestra Señora del Rosario*, 250 tons, Captain Baltazar Rodriquez Carreno, sank at anchor in Cartagena Harbor.

16. **Year 1616.** A small unidentified ship, coming from Venezuela with a cargo consisting mainly of tobacco, ran aground while entering the port of Santa Martha.

17. **Year 1626.** Treasure-laden galleon of the Tierra Firme Armada, Captain-General Thomas de Larraspuru, the *Nuestra Señora de la Candelaria*, 600 tons, Captain Juan de Campos, was wrecked on the Salmedina Reef when the Armada was leaving Cartagena enroute to Havana but most of her treasure was recovered by divers.

18. **Year 1629.** Due to bad leaks the galleon. *Nuestra Señora de la Concepción y San Francisco*, 550 tons, sank while at anchor in Cartagena Harbor, but she did not have any treasure or other cargo aboard at the time.

19. **Year 1631.** While the Tierra Firme Armada, Captain-General Thomas de Larraspuru, was sailing between Porto Bello and Cartagena, an unidentified *patache* was wrecked on a reef off Isla Baru.

20. **Year 1632.** An unidentified *patache*, sailing from Margarita Island to Cartagena with a valuable cargo of pearls, was wrecked on Isla Tesoro but most of the pearls were recovered by divers.

21. **Year 1634.** When the Tierra Firme Armada, Captain-General Antonio de Oquendo, was arriving at Cartagena, coming from Porto Bello with a vast amount of treasure, four ships were lost: galleon *San Juan Bautista*, 600 tons, Captain Hernán Martínez de Velasco, was wrecked on Salmedina Reef but her treasure and cannon were recovered; *patache Nuestra Señora del Carmen*, 80 tons, was wrecked at the entrance of Boca Chica but was totally salvaged later; two merchant *naos, Nuestra Señora del Rosario,*

450 tons, and the *Los Tres Reyes,* 600 tons—both sank because of leaks shortly after entering the inner harbor. A week later an unidentified merchant *nao* from Santo Domingo also sank after accidentally striking some part of the sunken *patache* at Boca Chica.

22. **Year 1637.** The *patache* of the Tierra Firme Armada, Captain-General Carlos de Ibarra, was sailing between Venezuela and Cartagena with a cargo consisting of 60 tons of copper ingots when it wrecked on a reef near Cartagena. Salvors were able to recover most of the cargo.

23. **Year 1640.** Due to the outbreak of war between Spain and Portugal this year, the Tierra Firme Armada intercepted the richly laden Portuguese Armada when it was sailing between Brazil and Portugal and forced it to sail with the Spanish Armada to Cartagena. The leader of the Portuguese Armada, Admiral Rodrigo Lobad da Silva, had no idea that there was a war between the two countries but suspected foul play, so as both armadas were entering Cartagena Harbor he deliberately wrecked his three richest galleons on a reef near the entrance of Boca Grande. The treasure on these three galleons—consisting of gold, diamonds, and other precious stones—was estimated at over 5 million pesos, and the records do not state if any of it was ever recovered.

24. **Year 1652.** An unidentified Spanish advice boat was wrecked off Cabo de la Vela. Her crew reached shore but was captured and eaten by the Carib Indians. These same Indians recovered the mail from the wreck and sold it to the Spaniards.

25. **Year 1660.** An unidentified Portuguese slave ship struck on a rock in 1½ fathoms of water near Punta de la Canoa, then sank in deeper water.

26. **Year 1680.** An unidentified advice boat arriving from Spain was totally lost on the Salmedina Reef.

27. **Year 1681.** After the Tierra Firme Armada, Captain-General Marqués de Brenes, sailed from Cartagena for Porto Bello, four ships were lost: galleon *Santa Teresa;* galleon *Nuestra Señora de la Soledad;* merchant *nao Nuestra Señora de la Asunción;* and the *patache Nuestra Señora de la Encarnación.* The cause or

location of these four ship losses was not stated in the documents. After receiving the treasure at Porto Bello, the armada returned to Cartagena, then sailed for Havana, but shortly after leaving Boca Chica, four more ships were wrecked on nearby reefs: galleons *Santa Teresa* (another by the same name as the one above) and *Santiago;* an unidentified small *nao;* and the armada's *patache.* The loss of treasure and lives was great, and only four persons were rescued from all four ships.

28. **Year 1682.** The galleon *Catheresa* sank in sight of Cartagena Harbor but records do not indicate whether she was in a convoy or carried any treasure. The records do indicate that in 1963 several bronze cannon were recovered from this wreck.

29. **Year 1697.** A French fleet under the command of Admiral Pointi attacked Cartagena, and to prevent the French from entering the inner harbor the Spaniards sank two large galleons near Castillo Santa Cruz and then burnt two other large ships, two galleys, and many small vessels in the inner harbor to prevent their capture by the French. The French bomb galliot *Eclatant* was so badly damaged by Spanish cannonfire that the French burnt it in the harbor before leaving.

30. **Year 1705.** The French merchantman *La Armona,* which had permission to trade with the Spaniards, was wrecked on Salmedina Reef while carrying a valuable cargo of merchandise.

31. **Year 1707.** While giving chase to a small French sloop, the English warship H.M.S. *Margaret* was lost at Punta de la Canoa.

32. **Year 1708.** The richest single Spanish galleon ever lost in the Western Hemisphere was the *San José,* carrying over 11 million pesos in treasure. Because of the War of Spanish Succession, no treasure had been sent from South America to Spain in six years, and this year a fleet of seventeen ships arrived at Porto Bello to receive the treasure. Since only four of the ships were heavily armed, all of the 22 million pesos in treasure received at Porto Bello was placed on these four ships: the *Capitana San José,* 64 guns; the *Almiranta San Martín,* 64 guns; the galleon *Gobierno,* 44 guns; and an unidentified *urca* commanded by Captain Francisco Neito. As the fleet was approaching Cartagena, an English squadron commanded by Commodore Wager appeared on the

horizon between the Spanish fleet and Cartagena and closed in on the Spaniards. Soon afterward a battle ensued between the four Spanish ships and the English warships and continued into the night. The *San José* exploded and quickly sank, with only five of her crew of six hundred surviving. The *Gobierno* was captured by the English, the *urca* was run aground and set afire by the Spaniards on the tip of the Baru Peninsula, and the *San Martín* managed to reach the safety of Cartagena, along with the other Spanish merchantmen. The exact location of the *San José* is not given in the records, only that it sank off Baru Island. Most of the treasure on the *urca* was later recovered by the Spaniards.

33. *Year 1740.* An unidentified Spanish merchant *nao* was lost near Isla de los Sombreros.

34. *Year 1741.* Spanish warship *Guipuscoa,* 70 guns, was sent from Cartagena to search for some English privateers operating near Santa Martha, but during a storm she was wrecked near the entrance to Santa Martha.

35. *Year 1741.* During the English attack on Cartagena led by Admiral Vernon, the Spaniards sank six galleons, six large warships, and several merchant *naos* in the harbor. Only the warships and a French merchantman were identified: *Galicia,* 70 guns; *San Carlos,* 70 guns; *Africa,* 60 guns; *San Felipe,* 80 guns; the French ship *El Leon de Nantes,* Captain José Lesvin; all of the other Spanish ships were scuttled across the mouth of the outer harbor near Castillo Grande to prevent the English ships from entering the port. The following day the two remaining Spanish warships—*Conquistador,* 60 guns, and the *Dragon,* 60 guns—were also sunk in the inner channel of the port. Most of the superstructures of the Spanish ships remained above the water, and the Spaniards burnt these parts of the ships to prevent the English from obtaining anything of value from them. While the English were still at Cartagena, a large Spanish ship named *Galicia* unsuspectingly entered the harbor and was captured by the English, who after stripping it, burnt it.

36. *Year 1751.* Spanish merchant *nao Nuestra Señora del Carmen* (alias *Bristol*), Captain Joseph de Artecona, coming from Cadiz, was wrecked on Sunzen Shoals, near San Bernardo Island.

37. **Year 1761.** A terrible storm struck Cartagena on December 12 and two large unidentified Spanish warships were wrecked in the harbor. During the same storm, many cannon from the two forts at Santa Martha were thrown into the sea.

38. **Year 1765.** English merchantman *Friendship*, Captain Morgan, coming from Jamaica, was wrecked off Punta Gallinas.

39. **Year 1773.** Spanish *nao San Joseph*, Captain Arestiqui, arriving from Cadiz, was lost while entering Cartagena Harbor.

40. **Year 1790.** Spanish warship *San Miguel*, Captain Juan Elizalde, struck a submerged rock between Punta de la Canoa and El Palmarita and then sank in 14 fathoms of water on January 3 with only one of her crew drowning.

41. **Year 1793.** Spanish merchant *nao Nuestra Señora de Cortijo* (alias *La Serrana*) wrecked on the north side of the point of Isla de Galera Zamba.

42. **Year 1795.** Spanish warship *Victoria*, 10 guns, Captain Francisco de Raula Escudero, was wrecked on March 28 on the shallows of Bajo de Negrillo, located near Cartagena. She was originally a French ship captured by the Spaniards.

43. **Year 1801.** English warship H.M.S. *Legere*, 18 guns, Captain Cornelius Quinton, was wrecked in Jamba Bay, east of Cartagena, on February 2, one of her crew of 121 men was lost.

44. **Year 1808.** A ship of unknown registry, *Chalmers*, Captain Tyack, bringing slaves from Africa to the West Indies, was wrecked on February 24 near Cabo de la Vela, its crew and slaves were all saved.

45. **Year 1808.** Two English warships were wrecked within sight of Cartagena: the brig H.M.S. *Bassora*, 12 guns, Captain James Violett, on February 13, none of her crew of fifty was lost; and the frigate H.M.S. *Raposa*, 10 guns, on February 15, the crew was saved.

46. **Year 1813.** English merchantman *Confeance*, Captain Molloy, coming from Jamaica, was lost at the end of March near Cartagena.

47. *Year 1814.* English merchantman *Clara,* Captain Roberts, coming from Jamaica, sank on September 23 off St. Blas, in the Gulf of Darien, the crew was saved.

48. *Year 1817.* A ship of unknown registry, *Martin,* Captain Bull, sailing from Barcelona to Santa Martha was lost on December 10 near Rio de la Hacha, crew and part of cargo saved.

49. *Year 1818.* Spanish schooner *Amistad,* Captain Manuel de Zaragosa, was wrecked on the bar of the Magdalena River, the captain and several of the crew perished.

50. *Year 1822.* English merchant brig *Martins,* Captain Ramsey, coming from Jamaica, was wrecked off Cartagena.

VENEZUELA:

51. *Year 1531.* Three Spanish merchant *naos* commanded by Captain Diego de Ondas were lost in the Gulf of Venezuela, near the entrance of Lake Maracaibo.

52. *Year 1561.* An unidentified caravel carrying the Count of Nieva, the new viceroy of Peru, and other important persons, was lost on the coast of the Paraguana Peninsula and there were no survivors.

53. *Year 1586.* Two Spanish galleys were sent after a French pirate vessel anchored at Puerto Santo on Margarita Island, and during the battle the French ship exploded and forty-six of the fifty Frenchmen aboard her were lost.

54. *Year 1605.* The Dutch had established a thriving salt industry at Punta de Araya several years earlier, and this year a large armada of Spanish warships was sent after the Dutch. They surprised twenty-two Dutch ships there, burnt and sank all of them, then massacred all of the Dutchmen.

55. *Year 1610.* As the Tierra Firme Armada, Captain-General Hierónimo, was sailing between Spain and Cartagena, its *Capitana, San Felipe,* 850 tons, 42 bronze cannon, Captain Gaspar de Vargas, and the *patache* of the armada were wrecked off the east side on Bon Aire Island. Over a period of five years divers were able to recover all the cannon from both wrecks as well as a great amount of the cargo of the *Capitana.*

56. **Year 1613.** An unidentified *patache* carrying a large amount of pearls was wrecked on Aves Island. Two years later the owner of the vessel stated that it had not yet been salvaged.

57. **Year 1622.** Unidentified *patache* was wrecked on Isla Beata in Lake Maracaibo.

58. **Year 1622.** An unidentified frigate owned by the King of Spain, carrying 30,000 pesos' worth of tobacco, sank near the port of Coro.

59. **Year 1630.** Merchant *nao Nuestra Señora de Lantigua*, Captain Benito Sánchez, sank on June 1 on the north side of Tortuga Island (not to be confused with the island of the same name located off Hispaniola) and was later salvaged by the Dutch.

60. **Year 1660.** Three large unidentified Spanish *naos* commanded by Captain Antonio Campos were lost in Lake Maracaibo.

61. **Year 1669.** While the pirate Henry Morgan was attacking and sacking various settlements on Lake Maracaibo, three large frigates of the Windward Armada, commanded by Admiral Alonso de Espinosa, were sent to fight the pirates. The three Spanish ships were anchored under the guns of the fort at the entrance to Lake Maracaibo, and the pirates had to pass there when leaving the lake. The pirates sank one with the use of a fire ship, the Spaniards burnt another to prevent its capture, and the third was captured by the pirates.

62. **Year 1678.** A French fleet consisting of eighteen warships and two privateers, commanded by Count D'Estre, was sent to capture Curaçao from the Dutch. During the night of May 3 all but one of the warships and one of the privateers were totally lost on a reef on Aves Island. Over 1,200 men perished and 250 brass and 300 iron cannon were lost. The Dutch were able to salvage most of the cannon, and later the French recovered most of those not recovered by the Dutch.

63. **Year 1733.** Spanish *navío San Miguel* was wrecked near the port of Cumana and was later salvaged by the English.

64. **Year 1734.** Unidentified Spanish schooner was wrecked on the reefs in front of Puerto de la Guayra on the mouth of the Orinoco River.

65. *Year 1763.* English merchantman *Edward,* Captain Darby, sailing from Hispaniola to Curaçao, was wrecked on Aruba Island.

66. *Year 1766.* Irish merchantman *John & Stephen,* Captain Kent, sailing from Cork to Curaçao, was wrecked on August 10 during a storm on Bon Aire Island but most of her cargo was saved.

67. *Year 1779.* Spanish advice boat *San Antonio,* sailing from Caracas to Spain, was wrecked on June 4 on Bon Aire Island.

68. *Year 1780.* A ship of unknown registry, *Good Hope,* Captain Dirks, coming from France, was totally lost near Curaçao Island.

69. *Year 1784.* During a hurricane that struck at Curaçao Island, several large ships were wrecked in the main harbor and others forced to sea, where they were lost without a trace.

70. *Year 1791.* Spanish ship *San Francisco de Paula* was totally lost on the bar at the entrance to Lake Maracaibo.

71. *Year 1802.* A ship of unknown registry, *Escape,* coming from Martinique Island was lost near Curaçao Island.

72. *Year 1803.* Spanish schooner of war *San Carlos,* Captain Juan Casteñeda, lost in May on Aves Island during a voyage from Puerto Rico, crew and some cannon saved.

73. *Year 1807.* English warship H.M.S. *Pert,* 14 guns, Captain Donald Campbell, wrecked on October 16 on Margarita Island.

74. *Year 1807.* English warship H.M.S. *Firefly,* 12 guns, Captain Thomas Price, foundered on November 11 near Curaçao Island, most of the crew perished.

75. *Year 1808.* English slave ship *Chalmers,* coming from Africa, was wrecked on Margarita Island.

76. *Year 1808.* English warship H.M.S. *Volador,* 16 guns, Captain Francis George Dickins, wrecked on October 24 in the Gulf of Coro.

77. *Year 1808.* During a hurricane on October 16 that struck the Island of Curaçao, many of the buildings in the main town were carried into the sea, as well as many graves in the churchyard and cannon from the forts.

78. *Year 1809.* Scottish merchantman *Jason*, Captain Stewart, sailing to Curaçao Island, was wrecked on August 17 on Orchella Island, crew and small part of cargo saved.

79. *Year 1809.* English merchantman *Penelope*, Captain Boon, sailing from London to Curaçao, was lost near Curaçao, crew and part of cargo saved.

80. *Year 1813.* Spanish brigantine-of-war *Manuel*, Captain Martín María Espinó, sank in Puerto Cabello on April 27, crew and some equipment saved.

81. *Year 1815.* A large fleet of Spanish warships and troop transports was sent from Spain to suppress the revolution in Venezuela, and after reaching the Caribbean the fleet anchored off Coche Island, located near Margarita Island. One of the largest warships in the fleet was the *San Pedro Alcantara*, 64 guns, Captain Jávier de Salazar. During the afternoon of April 24 this ship caught fire and blew up, costing over fifty men their lives. There was over 800,000 pesos in silver specie aboard, as well as tons of weapons and munitions, all of which scattered over a wide area because of the explosion. Salvage operations were started the following day, and as late as 1871 salvors were still recovering treasure from this wreck. Due to incomplete records, however, it is not known just how much was recovered nor if anything remains. In recent years, amateur divers from Caracas have dived on the wreck and recovered a few cannon and artifacts.

82. *Year 1817.* Dutch merchantman *Ceres*, Captain Jucometti, sailing from Rotterdam to Curaçao, was wrecked on December 27 on Bonaire Island, only a small part of her cargo was saved.

83. *Year 1819.* Spanish merchantman *Mariposa*, sailing to Spain, was totally lost on Aves Island but her crew was saved.

84. *Year 1822.* English merchantman *Mary*, Captain Richardson, coming from London, was wrecked on September 17 on the bar in front of the port of Maracaibo but the crew was all saved.

85. *Year 1822.* English merchantman *Robert*, Captain Neilson, coming from Liverpool, was wrecked on a reef near the port of Maracaibo on May 20 but most of her cargo was saved.

86. *Year 1822.* Scottish ship *Thetis,* coming from Clyde, was lost near the port of La Guaira, part of her cargo was saved.

87. *Year 1822.* American ship *Eliza,* Captain Bicker, sailing from New York to Curaçao, was lost on November 30 off Bonaire Island.

88. *Year 1822.* American schooner *Cecila,* Captain Hampton, sailed from Curaçao with a valuable cargo of dry goods, cocoa, indigo, etc., then sank off the west end of Curaçao.

89. *Year 1822.* During a bad gale that struck the port of La Guaira on December 22, over twenty large ships of different nationalities were lost.

90. *Year 1824.* A ship of unknown registry, *Caledonia,* sailing from Philadelphia to La Guaira, wrecked on Los Roques Reefs, part of her cargo of soap and flour was saved.

91. *Year 1824.* American merchantman *Morning Star,* Captain Waring, sailing from New York to Curaçao, was totally lost on November 14 on Aves Island, only the crew was saved.

WEST COAST:

92. *Year 1586.* During a violent earthquake in Peru, two or three large unidentified merchant *naos* that had just arrived from Mexico were sunk in the port of Callao.

93. *Year 1600.* During a storm the Spanish merchant *nao San Juan Bautista* sank in the port of Valparaiso, Chile, but her cargo was salvaged.

94. *Year 1600.* Spanish caravel *Buen Jesús,* 60 tons, Captain Francisco de Ibarra, was approaching the port of Valparaiso when it sighted Dutch warships commanded by Admiral Oliver von Noort. Because the caravel carried no cannon and the Dutch were certain to capture it, the captain ordered her cargo (which consisted of over 125,000 pesos in gold and silver bullion and specie) thrown overboard.

95. *Year 1610.* A large Spanish *nao,* carrying over 1 million pesos in gold and silver, was wrecked on its voyage to Panama, several leagues south of the port of Chiclayo, and divers were able to recover only about 150,000 pesos from it.

96. *Year 1623.* A large fleet of Dutch warships attacked the port of Callao and burnt eleven large Spanish ships anchored there at the time.

97. *Year 1632.* A large merchant *nao* owned by Martín López Caballón was sailing from Panama to Callao with a cargo of merchandise valued at 1 million pesos and 125 slaves. On February 27 it was lost on some rocks at Las Hormigas, located 7 leagues from Callao, and everyone aboard perished except two men—one of them was the pilot and was later hanged for losing the ship.

98. *Year 1647.* During an earthquake that struck Peru and Chile on May 13, large numbers of ships were lost in ports and on the coasts of both countries. At the port of Arica, Chile, the *navío San Nicholás*, which had over a million pesos of treasure on board, was lost. Divers were able to recover only a small part of this treasure.

99. *Year 1650.* Spanish warship *San José* sailed from Concepción, Chile, with soldiers, supplies, and over 125,000 pesos in silver specie for several garrisons located to the south. On March 26 it wrecked at Punta Dotolauquen, near the port of Valdivia, and although most of the crew and soldiers made it ashore they were massacred by hostile Indians.

100. *Year 1654.* In May, four large galleons sailed from Callao, heading for Panama with several years' accumulation of treasure from the mines of South America. During a dark rainy night, the *Capitana*, commanded by Admiral Francisco de Sosa, was wrecked on Chanduy Reef, near the mouth of the Guayaquil River, in Ecuador, and went to pieces quickly with almost everyone aboard perishing. Of the more than 3 million pesos in treasure aboard, salvors were able to recover only a small amount, as the rest was buried under shifting sands within days after the disaster.

101. *Year 1680.* An unidentified Spanish merchantman sailing from Callao to Guayaquil, Ecuador, carrying over 100,000 pesos in specie, was wrecked in August near Santa Clara, Ecuador.

102. *Year 1684.* Spanish *nao San Juan de Dios*, sailing from Callao to Concepción, Chile, and carrying the new bishop of Concepción and other important persons, was totally lost on Playa de Panque, Chile.

103. *Year 1685.* An unidentified Spanish merchant *nao* caught fire and sank at Callao. A diving bell was used to recover her cannon and cargo.

104. *Year 1688.* An unidentified merchant *nao* owned by Nicolás de Zarza, not carrying any cargo at the time, wrecked near Esmeraldas, close to the port of Amapola.

105. *Year 1721.* English pirate ship *Speedwell,* Captain George Shevelocke, carrying a large amount of plunder it had obtained by attacking Spanish settlements and shipping, was wrecked on rocks while entering a cove of one of the islands in the Juan Fernández islands group. The pirates managed to recover the greater part of their treasure, then built a schooner from the wreckage and escaped.

106. *Year 1721.* Treasure-laden galleon *Jesús María y Limpia Concepción* was wrecked on Chanduy Reef, Ecuador. Records do not indicate if she was ever salvaged.

107. *Year 1746.* On October 28, Peru suffered the worst earthquake since it was colonized by the Spaniards. Both Lima and the port of Callao were leveled to the ground and thousands of persons perished. At Callao, twenty-three ships were wrecked or sunk, of which only two were identified: galleon *San Fermin,* 30 guns, and the merchant *nao Santo Cristo de León.* In the port of Guacacho, another merchant *nao, San Cristobal,* was sunk.

108. *Year 1760.* A large galleon, *San Martín,* Captain Caconba, sank during a voyage between Valparaiso and Callao but her crew was saved.

109. *Year 1762.* Three Spanish trading frigates, *Encarnación, San Juan Evangelista,* and *San Judas Tadeo,* were wrecked among the islands of the Chiloe archipelago, Chile.

110. *Year 1765.* After arriving from Spain to Valparaiso, and with most of her cargo taken off, the galleon *San Lorenzo del Arco,* Captain Juan Lacomba, sank in port.

111. *Year 1770.* The largest ship to sail directly from Spain to Chile was the 1,200-ton galleon *L'Orriflamme,* which originally was a French warship. Her cargo was valued at over 4 million pesos and she carried a crew and passengers numbering over seven hundred.

During a storm she was totally lost on the coast near Valparaiso and there were only a few survivors. Salvage attempts were made but very little was recovered.

112. **Year 1788.** Spanish galleon *Nuestra Señora de la Balvanera,* 470 tons, Captain Antonio Ordóñez, was wrecked on the Guapacho Reefs near the port of San Carlos, Chile. All of her crew perished and several chests of gold and silver specie were never recovered from her.

113. **Year 1800.** Spanish frigate-of-war *Leocadia,* 34 guns, Captain Antonio Barreda, was wrecked on November 7 near Punta Santa Elena, Ecuador, carrying over 2 million pesos in treasure. Of her crew, passengers, and English prisoners, 140 perished and forty-eight were badly injured. Within three weeks, salvors had recovered the greatest part of her treasure.

114. **Year 1822.** English merchantman *Maria,* Captain Quincey, sailing from Rio de Janeiro to Valparaiso, was totally lost off Conceicas, located near Valparaiso.

115. **Year 1823.** Italian merchantman *Diana,* sailing from Italy to Lima, while attempting to enter the port of Pisco, Peru, and in passing between the islands of Gallon and Maise, struck a rock in 9 feet of water and immediately sank but her crew was saved.

EAST COAST:

116. **Year 1582.** Three Spanish merchant *naos, Capitana, Almiranta,* and *Santiago,* commanded by Captain Juan Ortiz de Zarate, were sunk in the Plate River, close to Buenos Aires.

117. **Year 1625.** The Spanish *urca Puerto Cristiana* was sent to search the seas for Dutch ships and while doing so was wrecked on a reef at Pernambuco (today called Recife), Brazil, the men and cannon were saved.

118. **Year 1625.** In 1624 a large Dutch fleet captured Salvador, the most important town in Brazil, and during its attack sank several small Portuguese merchantmen. The following year a massive armada of Portuguese and Spanish warships commanded by Captain-General Fadrique de Toledo was sent to recapture the town from the Dutch. During the attack three unidentified Dutch warships were

sunk by cannonfire and a Portuguese warship was wrecked on the reefs near the entrance to this port.

119. **Year 1673.** Spanish merchant *nao San Joseph*, Captain Sebastián de la Menarala, sank shortly after sailing for Spain from Buenos Aires.

120. **Year 1679.** Spanish galleon *Jesús, María y Joseph*, 350 tons, Captain José López de Villavicencio, sank while anchored at the mouth of the Plate River during a violent storm, all of its crew of 174 men perished.

121. **Year 1681.** Spanish *nao Nuestra Señora del Milagro*, 129 tons, Captain Cristoval de Aquenni, sank on October 19 while at anchor off Buenos Aires but was not carrying anything of value.

122. **Year 1687.** A fleet of nineteen Dutch merchantmen were wrecked during a storm off Cayenne, French Guiana, and over seven hundred men perished.

123. **Year 1688.** Two unidentified French warships were wrecked on a reef near Paramaribo, Surinam, due to faulty navigation.

124. **Year 1698.** A large richly laden Portuguese carrack was wrecked on the coast near present-day Georgetown, British Guiana, over four hundred persons perished and only three were saved. Nothing of the 1½ million of cruzadoes in treasure the ship carried was ever recovered.

125. **Year 1722.** A small unidentified French merchantman was wrecked on Devil's Island, located off French Guiana.

126. **Year 1744.** A ship of unknown registry, *The Duke of Chartres*, sailing from Cadiz to Buenos Aires, was lost at the mouth of the Amazon River and Indians massacred the majority of the survivors who reached shore.

127. **Year 1750.** Spanish merchant frigate *La Purisima Concepción y San Francisco de Asis*, owned by the Marqués de Casa Madrid, sank during a bad storm at the mouth of the Plate River, which is the boundary between the present-day countries of Uruguay and Argentina.

128. **Year 1752.** Large French East Indiaman, *Prince*, Captain Morin, with a cargo valued at over 5 million livres aboard, caught fire off the coast of Brazil and was run aground near Natal, where she

was totally lost. Of her crew of over four hundred, only nine survived.

129. *Year 1752.* Spanish merchant frigate *Esperanza*, coming from Cadiz, was wrecked near Rio de Janeiro and all except the captain perished. She was carrying 624,232 pesos in treasure from Peru.

130. *Year 1752.* Spanish galleon *Nuestra Señora de Luz*, sailing for Cadiz with 2 million pesos of treasure, sank near Buenos Aires, all but 62,000 pesos was recovered by divers.

131. *Year 1753.* Spanish galleon *Nuestra Señora del Rosario*, 460 tons, Captain Poloni, carrying 819,752 pesos in treasure from Peru, sank at the mouth of the Plate River but her crew was saved.

132. *Year 1762.* An unidentified English ship was lost on the Plate River. In 1793, parts of the river went dry because of some strange phenomenon caused by a freak wind and many wrecks, including this one, were left high and dry and many things were salvaged from them.

133. *Year 1776.* Spanish frigate-of-war *Clara*, 30 guns, was wrecked on Banco Inglés, located off Montevideo, and 120 persons of her crew were lost.

134. *Year 1776.* A ship of unknown registry, *M of Marbourn*, coming from Africa with a cargo of slaves, was wrecked near Cayenne, French Guiana.

135. *Year 1779.* English merchantman *Prince Edward*, Captain Clerk, sailing from Australia to London, was lost near Cape Frio, Brazil.

136. *Year 1801.* Two English slave ships, *Enterprize* and *Earl*, of Liverpool, Captain Hume, both coming from Africa, were lost on the coast of Surinam.

137. *Year 1805.* English merchantman *Duke of Clarence*, Captain Killiner, arriving from Liverpool, was sunk at the mouth of the Plate River.

138. *Year 1805.* Spanish warship *Asunción*, 36 guns, Captain Juan Domingo Deslobbes, was wrecked on the Plate River during May.

139. *Year 1807.* English merchantman *Mary*, Captain Athol, sailing from Montevideo to Virginia, was lost near Aracaju, Brazil, and only two of her crew were drowned.

140. *Year 1807.* Three ships were lost on the Plate River: French privateer *Dart*, Captain Le Pelley, all hands perished; a privateer of unknown nationality, *Venus*, the crew was saved; and the English troop-transport *Royal Charlotte* during a gale on March 10.

141. *Year 1809.* Two English ships were lost on the Plate River: merchantman *Fanny*, Captain Bonsfield, shortly after sailing for London, the crew was saved; and the warship H.M.S. *Agamemnon*, 64 guns, Captain Jonas Rose.

142. *Year 1809.* Spanish merchantman *Galzo*, Captain Echeverriara, sailing from Cadiz to the Plate River, was wrecked near Montevideo but part of her cargo was saved.

143. *Year 1809.* Portuguese merchantman *Fama de Lisboa*, Captain Ramos, coming from London, was lost on August 18 while entering Recife, Brazil, but the crew was saved.

144. *Year 1809.* Portuguese ship *San Juan Rey de Mar*, sailing from Maraham to Cayenne, was wrecked at Para, Brazil.

145. *Year 1810.* Two English merchantmen were lost on the Plate River: brig *Adventure*, after arriving from Rio de Janeiro; and the ship *Little Venus*, Captain Bamber, heading for Liverpool.

146. *Year 1813.* Spanish ship *Fernando Séptimo*, was burnt at anchor in La Enseñada, near Buenos Aires, by the revolutionaries from Montevideo.

147. *Year 1815.* English warship H.M.S. *Cygnet*, 16 guns, Captain Robert Russell, was wrecked off the Courantyne River, which is the boundary between Surinam and British Guiana.

Selected Bibliography

THE SHIPS AND THEIR HISTORY:

Artinano y de Galdacano, Gervasio de
La arquitectura naval española. 1920, Madrid.
Historia del comercio de las Indias. 1917, Barcelona.

Baker, William A.
Colonial vessels. 1962, Barre, Mass.
Sloops & shallops. 1966, Barre, Mass.

Boxer, Charles R.
The Dutch seaborne empire: 1600–1800. 1965, New York.
The Portuguese seaborne empire: 1415–1825. 1969, New York.

Chaunu, Huguette & Pierre
Seville et L'Atlantique (1504–1650). Nine vols., 1955, Paris.

Clowes, William L.
The Royal Navy. Three vols., 1898, Boston.

Cowburn, Philip
  The warship in history. 1965, New York.
Duhamel Du Monceau, Henri L.
  Elemens de l'architecture navale. 1758, Paris.
Duro, Fernández Cesareo de
  La armada española. Nine vols., 1895–1903, Madrid.
  Disquisiciones nauticas. Six vols., 1876–81, Madrid.
Fincham, John
  A history of naval architecture . . . 1851, London.
Hamilton, Earl J.
  American treasure and the price revolution in Spain, 1501–1650. 1934,
    Cambridge, Mass.
Haring, Clarence H.
  Trade and navigation between Spain and the Indies in the time of the
    Hapsburgs. 1918, Cambridge, Mass.
  The buccaneers in the West Indies . . . 1910, Cambridge, Mass.
Landström, Björn
  The ship. 1961, New York.
Martínez-Hidalgo, José María
  Columbus' Ships. 1966, Barre, Mass.
Marx, Robert F.
  The treasure fleets of the Spanish main. 1968, Cleveland.
  The battle of the Spanish Armada: 1588. 1965, Cleveland.
Morison, Samuel Eliot
  Admiral of the ocean sea. 1942, Boston.
Pares, Richard
  War and trade in the West Indies. 1936, New York.
Parry, J. H.
  The age of reconnaissance. 1963, London.
  The Spanish seaborne empire. 1966, New York.
Schurz, William L.
  The manila galleon. 1939, New York.
Veitia Linage, Joseph de
  Norte de la contratación de las indias occidentales. 1672, Seville.

EARLY SALVAGE AND MARINE ARCHAEOLOGY:
Bass, George F.
  Underwater archaeology. 1966, New York.
Blair, Clay, Jr.
  Diving for pleasure and treasure. 1960, Cleveland.

Bush Romero, Pablo
 Under the waters of Mexico. 1964, Mexico City.

Davis, Robert H.
 Deep diving and submarine operations. 1951, London.

Diolé, Philippe
 4,000 years under the sea. 1954, New York.

Dugan, James
 Man under the sea. 1956, New York.
 Men under water. 1965, New York.

Dumas, Frédéric
 Deep-water archaeology. 1962, London.

Franzen, Anders
 The warship Vasa. 1960, New York.

Frost, Honor
 Under the Mediterranean. 1963, London.

Karraker, Cyrus H.
 The Hispaniola treasure. 1934, Philadelphia.

Latil, Pierre de and Rivoire, Jean
 Man and the underwater world. 1954, London.

Marx, Robert F.
 They dared the deep. 1967, New York and Cleveland.
 Pirate port: the story of the sunken city of Port Royal. 1967, New York and Cleveland.

McKee, Alexander
 History under the sea. 1968, London.

Peterson, Mendel
 History under the sea. 1969, Washington.

Rackl, Hanns-Wolf
 Diving into the past: archaeology underwater. 1968, New York.

Taylor, Joan du Plat, editor
 Marine archaeology. 1965, London.

Throckmorton, Peter
 The lost ships. 1964, Boston.
 Shipwrecks and Archaeology. 1969, Boston.

DIVING AND MODERN-DAY SALVAGE:

Borhegyi, Suzanne de
 Ships, shoals and amphoras. 1961, New York.

Carrier, Rick and Barbara
 Dive: the complete book of skin diving. 1955, New York.

Ciampi, Elgin
> Skin diver. 1960, New York.

Cousteau, Capt. Jacques Yves
> The silent world. 1953, New York.
> The living sea. 1963, New York.

Ellsberg, Edward
> On the bottom. 1929, New York.
> Men under the sea. 1939, New York.

Falcon-Barker, Capt. Ted
> Roman galley beneath the sea. 1964, New York and London.

Hass, Hans
> Diving to adventure. 1951, New York.

Jefferis, Roger and McDonald, Kendall
> The wreck hunters. 1966, London.

Le Prieur, Yves
> Premier de plongee. 1956, Paris.

Link, Marion C.
> Sea diver, a quest for history under the sea. 1959, New York.

Marx, Robert F.
> Always another adventure. 1967, Cleveland.

Masters, David
> The wonders of salvage. 1924, New York.
> Epics of salvage. 1952, Boston.

Morris, Roland
> Island treasure. 1969, London.

Nesmith, Robert I.
> Dig for pirate treasure. 1958, New York.

Owen, David M.
> A manual for free divers. 1955, New York.

Rebikoff, Dimitri
> Free diving. 1956, New York.

Slack, Jack
> Finders losers. 1967, New York.

Stenuit, Robert
> The deepest days. 1966, New York.

Tucker, Teddy
> Treasure diving with Teddy Tucker. 1966, Bermuda.

Wagner, Kip (as told to Taylor, L. B., Jr.)
> Pieces of Eight. 1967, New York.

SHIPWRECK LOCATIONS:

Anonymous
    Shipwrecks and disasters at sea. 1851, London.

Barrington, George W.
    Remarkable voyages and shipwrecks. 1883, London.

Bowen, Dana Thomas
    Shipwrecks of the lakes. 1952, Daytona Beach, Florida.

Deperthes, Jean L.
    Histoire des naufrages. Three vols., 1828, Paris.

Duffy, James
    Shipwreck and empire. 1955, Cambridge, Mass.

Duro, Fernández Cesareo de
    Armada española. 1878, Madrid.

Gibbs, James A., Jr.
    Shipwrecks of the Pacific coast. 1957, Portland, Oregon.

Layton, J. F.
    Memorable shipwrecks and seafaring adventures. No date, Glasgow
    and Sydney.

Lonsdale, Adrian L., and Kaplan, H. R.
    A guide to sunken treasure in American waters. 1964, Arlington, Va.

Marx, Robert F.
    Shipwrecks in Florida waters. 1969, Eau Gallie, Florida.

Neider, Charles
    Great shipwrecks and castaways. 1952, New York.

Nesmith, Robert I., and Potter, John S., Jr.
    Treasure: how and where to find it. 1968, New York.

Paine, Ralph D.
    Lost ships and lonely seas. 1942, Garden City, N.Y.

Potter, John S., Jr.
    The treasure diver's guide. 1960, New York.

Shepard, Birse
    Lore of the wreckers. 1961, Boston.

Snow, Edward R.
    Great storms and famous shipwrecks of the New England coast. 1943,
    Boston.
    The vengeful sea. 1956, New York.

Stick, David
    Graveyard of the Atlantic. 1952, Chapel Hill, N.C.

Stirling, Nord B.
    Treasure under the sea. 1957, Garden City, N.Y.
Villiers, Alan J.
    Wild ocean: the story of the North Atlantic and the men who sailed
        it. 1957, New York, Toronto, and London.
Wilkins, Harold T.
    Hunting hidden treasures. 1929, New York.
Wood, Walter
    Survivors' tales of famous shipwrecks. 1932, London.

PRESERVATION:

Albright, Alan
    The preservation of small water-logged wood specimens with poly-
        ethylene glycol. Curator 1966, vol. IX, no. 3, pp. 228–34.
Barkman, Lars
    The preservation of the Vasa. No date, Stockholm.
Caley, Earle R.
    Coatings and incrustations on lead objects from the Agora and the
        method used for their removal. Studies in Conservation, 1955, vol. 2,
        no. 2, pp. 49–54.
Erickson, Egon, and Tregel, Svend
    Conservation of iron recovered from the sea. 1966, Copenhagen.
Graham, John Meredith
    American pewter. 1949, Brooklyn.
Katsev, Michael, and Doornick, Fredrick van
    Replicas of iron tools from a Byzantine shipwreck. Studies in Con-
        servation, August 1966, vol. 11, no. 3, pp. 133–42.
Organ, R. M.
    The conservation of fragile metallic objects. Studies in Conservation,
        November 1961, vol. 6, no. 4, pp. 135–36.
Pittsburgh Plate Glass Company
    Embedding objects in selectron 5000 resins. 1946, Pittsburgh.
Plenderleith, H. J.
    The conservation of antiquities and works of art. (The most com-
        prehensive work on the subject.) 1956, London.
Smith, James B., Jr., and Ellis, John P.
    The preservation of under-water archaeological specimens in plastic.
        Curator, 1963, vol. VI, no. 1, pp. 32–36.
Thomas M. W., and Dunton, John V. N.
    Treatment for cleaning and preserving excavated iron objects. 1954,
        Williamsburg, Va.

Townsend, Samuel P.
Heat methods of preserving cast iron artifacts recovered from salt water. Report presented at the Third Conference on Underwater Archaeology, Miami, Florida, March 23–25, 1967.

Werner, A. E.
Consolidation of fragile objects. Studies in Conservation, November, 1961, vol. 6, no. 4, pp. 133–35.

IDENTIFICATION OF ARTIFACTS:

Artillery:

Foulkes, Charles
The gun founders of England. 1937, Cambridge, England.

Gibbon, John
The artillerists manual. 1863, New York.

Grant, Michael
Armada guns. 1961, London.

Hime, Henry W. L.
The origin of artillery. 1915, London.

Hogg, Oliver F. G.
English artillery 1326–1716. 1963, London.

Manucy, Albert
Artillery through the ages. 1949, Washington, D.C.

Mountaine, William
The practical sea-gunners' companion or an introduction to the art of gunnery. 1747, 3rd edition, London.

Muller, John
A treatise of artillery. 1780, 3rd edition, London.

Museo del Ejército
Catálogo del Museo del Ejército. Four vols., 1956, Madrid.

Robins, Benjamin
New principles of gunnery. 1742, London.

Saint-Remy, Pierre Surirey de
Memoires d'artillerie . . . Two vols., 1741, The Hague, Holland.

Smith, George
An universal military dictionary. 1779, London.

Streete, Thomas
The use and effects of the gunne [*sic*]. 1674, London.

Thomas, Capt.
A treatise on gunpowder. 1789, London.

Vigon, Jorge
> Historia de la artillería española. Three vols., 1947, Madrid.

Weapons:

Greener, W. W.
> The gun and its development. Ninth edition, 1967, New York.

Jackson, H. J.
> European hand firearms of the 16th, 17th & 18th centuries.

Peterson, Harold L.
> The treasury of the gun. 1962, New York.
> Arms and armor in colonial America, 1526–1783
> Daggers and fighting knives of the western world.

Stone, George Cameron
> A glossary of the construction, decoration and use of arms and armor in all countries and in all times. (The most comprehensive work on the subject.) 1934, New York.

Tunis, Edwin
> Weapons: a pictorial history. 1954, Cleveland and New York.

Wilkinson, Frederick
> Swords and daggers. 1968, New York.

Navigation Instruments:

Brewington, M. V.
> Navigating instruments. 1963, Salem, Mass.

García France, Salvador
> Instrumentos nauticos en el Museo Naval. 1959, Madrid.

Mountaine, William, and Wakely, Andrew
> The mariner's compass rectified. 1754, London.

Waters, David W.
> The art of navigation in England in Elizabethan and early Stuart times. 1958, London.

Zinner, Ernst
> Astronomische instrumente. 1967, Munich, Germany.

Clay Smoking Pipes:

Brongars, G. A.
> Nicotiana Tabacum. 1964, Amsterdam.

Dunhill, Alfred
> The pipe book. 1924, New York.

Harrington, J. C.
> Dating stem fragments of 17th and 18th century tobacco pipes. Bull. Arch. Soc., 1954, vol. 4.

Marx, Robert F.
  Clay smoking pipes recovered from the sunken city of Port Royal: May 1, 1966–September 3, 1967. March 1968.
  Clay smoking pipes recovered from the sunken city of Port Royal: October 1, 1967–March 31, 1968. August 1968.
  (Both reports were published by the Jamaica National Trust Commission, Kingston, Jamaica.)

Oswald, Adrian
  English clay tobacco pipes. 1967, London.

Glassware and Bottles:

Buckley, Francis
  The glass trade in England in the 17th century. 1914, London.

Corning Glass Museum
  Glass from the Corning Glass Museum. 1965, Corning, N.Y.

Frothingham, Alice Wilson
  Hispanic Glass. 1941, New York.

Harrington, J. C.
  Glassmaking at Jamestown. 1953, Richmond, Va.

Hayes, E. Barrington
  Glass through the ages. 1966, Baltimore.

Honey, W. B.
  Glass. 1946, London.

Hume, Ivor Noel
  Dating English glass wine bottles. Wine and Spirit Trade Record, February 1955.
  Here lies Virginia. 1963, New York.

Lee, Ruth Webb
  Victorian glass. 1939, Framington, Mass.

Marx, Robert F.
  Wine glasses recovered from the sunken city of Port Royal: May 1, 1966–March 31, 1968. Jamaica National Trust Commission, Kingston, Jamaica, May, 1968.
  Glass bottles recovered from the sunken city of Port Royal, Jamaica: May 1, 1966–March 31, 1968. Caribbean Research Institute, St. Thomas, Virgin Islands, January, 1969.

McKearin, Helen and George
  Two hundred years of American blown glass. 1956, New York.

Rider, Dennis
  A history of glass bottles. 1956, London.

Ruggles-Brise, Sheelah
    Sealed bottles. 1949, London.

Gold Plate:

Castro, J. P. de
    The law and practice of marking gold and silver ware. 1935, London.
Heal, A.
    The London goldsmiths, 1200–1800. 1935, Cambridge, England.
Hill, H. D.
    Antique gold boxes, their lore and their lure. 1953, New York.
Jackson, C. J.
    English goldsmiths and their marks. 1949, London.
Jones, E. A.
    Old English gold plate. 1907, London.
Prideaux, W. S.
    Memorials of the goldsmiths' company, 1335–1815. Two vols., 1896–97, London.

Silverware:

Cripps, W. J.
    Old English plate, ecclesiastical, decorative and domestic: its makers and marks. 1926, London.
Jackson, C. J.
    An illustrated history of English plate, ecclesiastical and secular. Two vols., 1911, London.
Jones, E. A.
    Old silver of Europe and America. 1928, London and New York.
Wyler, S. B.
    The book of old silver: English, American, and foreign. 1947, New York.

Pewterware:

Bell, Malcolm
    Old pewter. 1905, New York.
Cotterell, Howard H.
    Old pewter: its makers and marks. (The most comprehensive work on the subject.) 1929, London.
Markham, C. A.
    Pewter marks and old pewterware. 1909, London.
Welch, C.
    History of the worshipful company of pewterers of London. 1902, London.

Pottery and Porcelain:

Chaffers, William
 The new collector's handbook of marks and monograms on pottery and porcelain. 1914, London.

Cushion, J. P., and Honey, W. B.
 Handbook of pottery and porcelain marks. 1956, London.

Frothingham, Alice Wilson
 Talavera pottery. 1944, New York.
 Lustreware of Spain. 1951, New York.

Garner, Frederic H.
 English delftware. 1948, New York.

Godden, Geoffrey A.
 British pottery and porcelain. 1966, New York.

Goggin, John M.
 The Spanish olive jar, an introductory study. Yale University publications in Anthropology, no. 62, 1960, New Haven.
 Spanish majolica in the new world: types of the sixteenth to eighteenth centuries. 1968, New Haven.

Savage, George
 Porcelain through the ages. 1963, Baltimore.

Shepard, Anna O.
 Ceramics for the archaeologist. 1965, Washington, D.C.

Thorn, C. Jordan
 Handbook of old pottery and porcelain marks. 1965, New York.

Towner, Donald C.
 English cream-colored earthenware. 1957, London.

Watkins, Lura W.
 Early New England potters and their wares. 1950, Cambridge, Mass.

Wills, Geoffrey
 The book of English china. 1964, New York.

Spanish Coinage:

Beals, Gary
 Numismatic terms of Spain and Spanish America. 1966, San Diego.

Dasi, Tomás
 Estudio de los reales de a ocho. Five vols., 1950, Valencia, Spain.

Harris, Robert P.
 Pillars and portraits. 1968, San Jose, California.

López-Chaves y Sánchez, Leopoldo
 Catálogo de la onza española. 1961, Madrid.

Catálogo de la media onza o doblón de a cuatro. 1961, Madrid.
Catálogo de las onzas de la America independiente. 1961, Madrid.
Nesmith, Robert I.
   The coinage of the first mint of the Americas at Mexico City. 1955, New York.
Pradeau, Alberto F.
   Numismatic history of Mexico from the pre-columbian epoch to 1823. 1938, Los Angeles.
Yriarte, José de
   Catálogo de los reales de a ocho españoles. 1955, Madrid.

Coinage of other nations:

Brooke, George C.
   English coins from the seventh century to the present day. 1932, London.
Ciani, Louis
   Catalogue de monnaies françaises . . . Three vols., 1926–31. Paris.
Dieudonne, A.
   Monnaies royales françaises. 1916, Paris.
Lindheim, Leon
   Facts and fiction about coins. 1967, Cleveland and New York.
Peck, C. Wilson
   English copper, tin and bronze coins: 1558–1958. 1960, London.
Santos, Leitao & Cie.
   Catálogo de monedas brasileiras de 1643 a 1944. No date, Rio de Janeiro.
Wood, Howland
   The coinage of the West Indies, and the sou marque. 1915, New York.
Yeoman, R. S.
   A catalog of modern world coins. 1965, Chicago.
   A guide book of United States coins. 1965, Chicago.

Brass and Copper objects:

Marx, Robert F.
   Brass and copper items recovered from the sunken city of Port Royal: May 1, 1966–March 31, 1968. Jamaica National Trust Commission, Kingston, Jamaica, May 1968.
Wills, G.
   Collecting copper and brass. 1954, Glasgow. Privately published.

Miscellaneous Reference Books:

Bradford, Ernle
> Four centuries of European jewelry. 1953, Feltham, England.

Bruton, E.
> Clocks and watches. 1965, London.

Hume, Ivor Noel
> A guide to artifacts of Colonial America. (This comprehensive book is useful in the identification of hundreds of different types of artifacts, such as bells, buckles, buttons, cooking vessels, cutlery, locks and padlocks, and tools.) 1970, New York.

Mercer, Henry C.
> Ancient carpenters' tools. 1960, Doylestown, Pa.

Raising an old anchor.

Raising a bronze cannon.

Diver searching for small items beneath the ballast on the lower deck of a wreck.

Diver sending a 70-pound bar to the surface.

Archaeologist sawing the timbers of an early seventeenth-century Dutch merchant ship.

Index

ABOUT THE AUTHOR

ROBERT F. MARX is one of the most successful and well-known specialists in the field of marine archaeology and has an equally strong reputation for his work in naval and maritime history. His particular area of interest is Spanish naval activity in the Caribbean during the colonial period. He has written fifteen books covering his wide range of interests and has published more than one hundred scientific and popular articles and reports. He studied at UCLA and at the University of Maryland and served in the United States Marine Corps, where he worked in diving and salvage operations.

He is perhaps best known to the general public for such feats as the voyage from Spain to San Salvador of the *Niña II*, a replica of Columbus's ship, on which he served as co-organizer and navigator. For this voyage he was made a Knight Commander in the Order of Isabella the Catholic by the Spanish government, the highest honorific order given to any foreigner. He also participated in the location of the Civil War ironclad USS *Monitor*, the discovery of several Mayan temple sites in Central America, the discovery of many famous Spanish, French, and English wrecks from the colonial period and, more recently, the mapping and excavation of the sunken city of Port Royal. He has also been an editor for *Argosy* and *The Saturday Evening Post*.

A CATALOG OF SELECTED
DOVER BOOKS
IN ALL FIELDS OF INTEREST

A CATALOG OF SELECTED DOVER
BOOKS IN ALL FIELDS OF INTEREST

DRAWINGS OF REMBRANDT, edited by Seymour Slive. Updated Lippmann, Hofstede de Groot edition, with definitive scholarly apparatus. All portraits, biblical sketches, landscapes, nudes. Oriental figures, classical studies, together with selection of work by followers. 550 illustrations. Total of 630pp. 9⅛ × 12¼.
21485-0, 21486-9 Pa., Two-vol. set $29.90

GHOST AND HORROR STORIES OF AMBROSE BIERCE, Ambrose Bierce. 24 tales vividly imagined, strangely prophetic, and decades ahead of their time in technical skill: "The Damned Thing," "An Inhabitant of Carcosa," "The Eyes of the Panther," "Moxon's Master," and 20 more. 199pp. 5⅜ × 8½. 20767-6 Pa. $4.95

ETHICAL WRITINGS OF MAIMONIDES, Maimonides. Most significant ethical works of great medieval sage, newly translated for utmost precision, readability. Laws Concerning Character Traits, Eight Chapters, more. 192pp. 5⅜ × 8½.
24522-5 Pa. $4.50

THE EXPLORATION OF THE COLORADO RIVER AND ITS CANYONS, J. W. Powell. Full text of Powell's 1,000-mile expedition down the fabled Colorado in 1869. Superb account of terrain, geology, vegetation, Indians, famine, mutiny, treacherous rapids, mighty canyons, during exploration of last unknown part of continental U.S. 400pp. 5⅜ × 8½. 20094-9 Pa. $7.95

HISTORY OF PHILOSOPHY, Julián Marías. Clearest one-volume history on the market. Every major philosopher and dozens of others, to Existentialism and later. 505pp. 5⅜ × 8½. 21739-6 Pa. $9.95

ALL ABOUT LIGHTNING, Martin A. Uman. Highly readable non-technical survey of nature and causes of lightning, thunderstorms, ball lightning, St. Elmo's Fire, much more. Illustrated. 192pp. 5⅜ × 8½. 25237-X Pa. $5.95

SAILING ALONE AROUND THE WORLD, Captain Joshua Slocum. First man to sail around the world, alone, in small boat. One of great feats of seamanship told in delightful manner. 67 illustrations. 294pp. 5⅜ × 8½. 20326-3 Pa. $4.95

LETTERS AND NOTES ON THE MANNERS, CUSTOMS AND CONDITIONS OF THE NORTH AMERICAN INDIANS, George Catlin. Classic account of life among Plains Indians: ceremonies, hunt, warfare, etc. 312 plates. 572pp. of text. 6⅛ × 9¼. 22118-0, 22119-9, Pa. Two-vol. set $17.90

ALASKA: The Harriman Expedition, 1899, John Burroughs, John Muir, et al. Informative, engrossing accounts of two-month, 9,000-mile expedition. Native peoples, wildlife, forests, geography, salmon industry, glaciers, more. Profusely illustrated. 240 black-and-white line drawings. 124 black-and-white photographs. 3 maps. Index. 576pp. 5⅜ × 8½. 25109-8 Pa. $11.95

THE BOOK OF BEASTS: Being a Translation from a Latin Bestiary of the Twelfth Century, T. H. White. Wonderful catalog real and fanciful beasts: manticore, griffin, phoenix, amphivius, jaculus, many more. White's witty erudite commentary on scientific, historical aspects. Fascinating glimpse of medieval mind. Illustrated. 296pp. 5⅜ × 8¼. (Available in U.S. only)   24609-4 Pa. $6.95

FRANK LLOYD WRIGHT: ARCHITECTURE AND NATURE With 160 Illustrations, Donald Hoffmann. Profusely illustrated study of influence of nature—especially prairie—on Wright's designs for Fallingwater, Robie House, Guggenheim Museum, other masterpieces. 96pp. 9¼ × 10¾.   25098-9 Pa. $8.95

FRANK LLOYD WRIGHT'S FALLINGWATER, Donald Hoffmann. Wright's famous waterfall house: planning and construction of organic idea. History of site, owners, Wright's personal involvement. Photographs of various stages of building. Preface by Edgar Kaufmann, Jr. 100 illustrations. 112pp. 9¼ × 10.

23671-4 Pa. $8.95

YEARS WITH FRANK LLOYD WRIGHT: Apprentice to Genius, Edgar Tafel. Insightful memoir by a former apprentice presents a revealing portrait of Wright the man, the inspired teacher, the greatest American architect. 372 black-and-white illustrations. Preface. Index. vi + 228pp. 8¼ × 11.   24801-1 Pa. $10.95

THE STORY OF KING ARTHUR AND HIS KNIGHTS, Howard Pyle. Enchanting version of King Arthur fable has delighted generations with imaginative narratives of exciting adventures and unforgettable illustrations by the author. 41 illustrations. xviii + 313pp. 6⅛ × 9¼.   21445-1 Pa. $6.95

THE GODS OF THE EGYPTIANS, E. A. Wallis Budge. Thorough coverage of numerous gods of ancient Egypt by foremost Egyptologist. Information on evolution of cults, rites and gods; the cult of Osiris; the Book of the Dead and its rites; the sacred animals and birds; Heaven and Hell; and more. 956pp. 6⅛ × 9¼.

22055-9, 22056-7 Pa., Two-vol. set $21.90

A THEOLOGICO-POLITICAL TREATISE, Benedict Spinoza. Also contains unfinished *Political Treatise*. Great classic on religious liberty, theory of government on common consent. R. Elwes translation. Total of 421pp. 5⅜ × 8½.

20249-6 Pa. $7.95

INCIDENTS OF TRAVEL IN CENTRAL AMERICA, CHIAPAS, AND YUCATAN, John L. Stephens. Almost single-handed discovery of Maya culture; exploration of ruined cities, monuments, temples; customs of Indians. 115 drawings. 892pp. 5⅜ × 8½.   22404-X, 22405-8 Pa., Two-vol. set $15.90

LOS CAPRICHOS, Francisco Goya. 80 plates of wild, grotesque monsters and caricatures. Prado manuscript included. 183pp. 6⅛ × 9⅜.   22384-1 Pa. $5.95

AUTOBIOGRAPHY: The Story of My Experiments with Truth, Mohandas K. Gandhi. Not hagiography, but Gandhi in his own words. Boyhood, legal studies, purification, the growth of the Satyagraha (nonviolent protest) movement. Critical, inspiring work of the man who freed India. 480pp. 5⅜ × 8½. (Available in U.S. only)

24593-4 Pa. $6.95

ILLUSTRATED DICTIONARY OF HISTORIC ARCHITECTURE, edited by Cyril M. Harris. Extraordinary compendium of clear, concise definitions for over 5,000 important architectural terms complemented by over 2,000 line drawings. Covers full spectrum of architecture from ancient ruins to 20th-century Modernism. Preface. 592pp. 7½ × 9⅝. 24444-X Pa. $15.95

THE NIGHT BEFORE CHRISTMAS, Clement Moore. Full text, and woodcuts from original 1848 book. Also critical, historical material. 19 illustrations. 40pp. 4⅝ × 6. 22797-9 Pa. $2.50

THE LESSON OF JAPANESE ARCHITECTURE: 165 Photographs, Jiro Harada. Memorable gallery of 165 photographs taken in the 1930's of exquisite Japanese homes of the well-to-do and historic buildings. 13 line diagrams. 192pp. 8⅜ × 11¼. 24778-3 Pa. $10.95

THE AUTOBIOGRAPHY OF CHARLES DARWIN AND SELECTED LETTERS, edited by Francis Darwin. The fascinating life of eccentric genius composed of an intimate memoir by Darwin (intended for his children); commentary by his son, Francis; hundreds of fragments from notebooks, journals, papers; and letters to and from Lyell, Hooker, Huxley, Wallace and Henslow. xi + 365pp. 5⅜ × 8. 20479-0 Pa. $6.95

WONDERS OF THE SKY: Observing Rainbows, Comets, Eclipses, the Stars and Other Phenomena, Fred Schaaf. Charming, easy-to-read poetic guide to all manner of celestial events visible to the naked eye. Mock suns, glories, Belt of Venus, more. Illustrated. 299pp. 5¼ × 8¼. 24402-4 Pa. $7.95

BURNHAM'S CELESTIAL HANDBOOK, Robert Burnham, Jr. Thorough guide to the stars beyond our solar system. Exhaustive treatment. Alphabetical by constellation: Andromeda to Cetus in Vol. 1; Chamaeleon to Orion in Vol. 2; and Pavo to Vulpecula in Vol. 3. Hundreds of illustrations. Index in Vol. 3. 2,000pp. 6⅛ × 9¼. 23567-X, 23568-8, 23673-0 Pa., Three-vol. set $41.85

STAR NAMES: Their Lore and Meaning, Richard Hinckley Allen. Fascinating history of names various cultures have given to constellations and literary and folkloristic uses that have been made of stars. Indexes to subjects. Arabic and Greek names. Biblical references. Bibliography. 563pp. 5⅜ × 8½. 21079-0 Pa. $8.95

THIRTY YEARS THAT SHOOK PHYSICS: The Story of Quantum Theory, George Gamow. Lucid, accessible introduction to influential theory of energy and matter. Careful explanations of Dirac's anti-particles, Bohr's model of the atom, much more. 12 plates. Numerous drawings. 240pp. 5⅜ × 8½. 24895-X Pa. $5.95

CHINESE DOMESTIC FURNITURE IN PHOTOGRAPHS AND MEASURED DRAWINGS, Gustav Ecke. A rare volume, now affordably priced for antique collectors, furniture buffs and art historians. Detailed review of styles ranging from early Shang to late Ming. Unabridged republication. 161 black-and-white drawings, photos. Total of 224pp. 8⅜ × 11¼. (Available in U.S. only) 25171-3 Pa. $13.95

VINCENT VAN GOGH: A Biography, Julius Meier-Graefe. Dynamic, penetrating study of artist's life, relationship with brother, Theo, painting techniques, travels, more. Readable, engrossing. 160pp. 5⅜ × 8½. (Available in U.S. only) 25253-1 Pa. $4.95

HOW TO WRITE, Gertrude Stein. Gertrude Stein claimed anyone could understand her unconventional writing—here are clues to help. Fascinating improvisations, language experiments, explanations illuminate Stein's craft and the art of writing. Total of 414pp. 4⅜ × 6⅜. 23144-5 Pa. $6.95

ADVENTURES AT SEA IN THE GREAT AGE OF SAIL: Five Firsthand Narratives, edited by Elliot Snow. Rare true accounts of exploration, whaling, shipwreck, fierce natives, trade, shipboard life, more. 33 illustrations. Introduction. 353pp. 5⅜ × 8½. 25177-2 Pa. $8.95

THE HERBAL OR GENERAL HISTORY OF PLANTS, John Gerard. Classic descriptions of about 2,850 plants—with over 2,700 illustrations—includes Latin and English names, physical descriptions, varieties, time and place of growth, more. 2,706 illustrations. xlv + 1,678pp. 8½ × 12¼. 23147-X Cloth. $75.00

DOROTHY AND THE WIZARD IN OZ, L. Frank Baum. Dorothy and the Wizard visit the center of the Earth, where people are vegetables, glass houses grow and Oz characters reappear. Classic sequel to *Wizard of Oz*. 256pp. 5⅜ × 8. 24714-7 Pa. $5.95

SONGS OF EXPERIENCE: Facsimile Reproduction with 26 Plates in Full Color, William Blake. This facsimile of Blake's original "Illuminated Book" reproduces 26 full-color plates from a rare 1826 edition. Includes "The Tyger," "London," "Holy Thursday," and other immortal poems. 26 color plates. Printed text of poems. 48pp. 5¼ × 7. 24636-1 Pa. $3.95

SONGS OF INNOCENCE, William Blake. The first and most popular of Blake's famous "Illuminated Books," in a facsimile edition reproducing all 31 brightly colored plates. Additional printed text of each poem. 64pp. 5¼ × 7. 22764-2 Pa. $3.95

PRECIOUS STONES, Max Bauer. Classic, thorough study of diamonds, rubies, emeralds, garnets, etc.: physical character, occurrence, properties, use, similar topics. 20 plates, 8 in color. 94 figures. 659pp. 6⅛ × 9¼. 21910-0, 21911-9 Pa., Two-vol. set $15.90

ENCYCLOPEDIA OF VICTORIAN NEEDLEWORK, S. F. A. Caulfeild and Blanche Saward. Full, precise descriptions of stitches, techniques for dozens of needlecrafts—most exhaustive reference of its kind. Over 800 figures. Total of 679pp. 8⅛ × 11. Two volumes. Vol. 1 22800-2 Pa. $11.95
Vol. 2 22801-0 Pa. $11.95

THE MARVELOUS LAND OF OZ, L. Frank Baum. Second Oz book, the Scarecrow and Tin Woodman are back with hero named Tip, Oz magic. 136 illustrations. 287pp. 5⅜ × 8½. 20692-0 Pa. $5.95

WILD FOWL DECOYS, Joel Barber. Basic book on the subject, by foremost authority and collector. Reveals history of decoy making and rigging, place in American culture, different kinds of decoys, how to make them, and how to use them. 140 plates. 156pp. 7⅞ × 10¾. 20011-6 Pa. $8.95

HISTORY OF LACE, Mrs. Bury Palliser. Definitive, profusely illustrated chronicle of lace from earliest times to late 19th century. Laces of Italy, Greece, England, France, Belgium, etc. Landmark of needlework scholarship. 266 illustrations. 672pp. 6⅛ × 9¼. 24742-2 Pa. $14.95

ILLUSTRATED GUIDE TO SHAKER FURNITURE, Robert Meader. All furniture and appurtenances, with much on unknown local styles. 235 photos. 146pp. 9 × 12. 22819-3 Pa. $8.95

WHALE SHIPS AND WHALING: A Pictorial Survey, George Francis Dow. Over 200 vintage engravings, drawings, photographs of barks, brigs, cutters, other vessels. Also harpoons, lances, whaling guns, many other artifacts. Comprehensive text by foremost authority. 207 black-and-white illustrations. 288pp. 6 × 9. 24808-9 Pa. $9.95

THE BERTRAMS, Anthony Trollope. Powerful portrayal of blind self-will and thwarted ambition includes one of Trollope's most heartrending love stories. 497pp. 5⅜ × 8½. 25119-5 Pa. $9.95

ADVENTURES WITH A HAND LENS, Richard Headstrom. Clearly written guide to observing and studying flowers and grasses, fish scales, moth and insect wings, egg cases, buds, feathers, seeds, leaf scars, moss, molds, ferns, common crystals, etc.—all with an ordinary, inexpensive magnifying glass. 209 exact line drawings aid in your discoveries. 220pp. 5⅜ × 8½. 23330-8 Pa. $4.95

RODIN ON ART AND ARTISTS, Auguste Rodin. Great sculptor's candid, wide-ranging comments on meaning of art; great artists; relation of sculpture to poetry, painting, music; philosophy of life, more. 76 superb black-and-white illustrations of Rodin's sculpture, drawings and prints. 119pp. 8⅜ × 11¼. 24487-3 Pa. $7.95

FIFTY CLASSIC FRENCH FILMS, 1912–1982: A Pictorial Record, Anthony Slide. Memorable stills from Grand Illusion, Beauty and the Beast, Hiroshima, Mon Amour, many more. Credits, plot synopses, reviews, etc. 160pp. 8¼ × 11. 25256-6 Pa. $11.95

THE PRINCIPLES OF PSYCHOLOGY, William James. Famous long course complete, unabridged. Stream of thought, time perception, memory, experimental methods; great work decades ahead of its time. 94 figures. 1,391pp. 5⅜ × 8½. 20381-6, 20382-4 Pa., Two-vol. set $23.90

BODIES IN A BOOKSHOP, R. T. Campbell. Challenging mystery of blackmail and murder with ingenious plot and superbly drawn characters. In the best tradition of British suspense fiction. 192pp. 5⅜ × 8½. 24720-1 Pa. $4.95

CALLAS: PORTRAIT OF A PRIMA DONNA, George Jellinek. Renowned commentator on the musical scene chronicles incredible career and life of the most controversial, fascinating, influential operatic personality of our time. 64 black-and-white photographs. 416pp. 5⅜ × 8¼. 25047-4 Pa. $8.95

GEOMETRY, RELATIVITY AND THE FOURTH DIMENSION, Rudolph Rucker. Exposition of fourth dimension, concepts of relativity as Flatland characters continue adventures. Popular, easily followed yet accurate, profound. 141 illustrations. 133pp. 5⅜ × 8½. 23400-2 Pa. $4.95

HOUSEHOLD STORIES BY THE BROTHERS GRIMM, with pictures by Walter Crane. 53 classic stories—Rumpelstiltskin, Rapunzel, Hansel and Gretel, the Fisherman and his Wife, Snow White, Tom Thumb, Sleeping Beauty, Cinderella, and so much more—lavishly illustrated with original 19th century drawings. 114 illustrations. x + 269pp. 5⅜ × 8½. 21080-4 Pa. $4.95

SUNDIALS, Albert Waugh. Far and away the best, most thorough coverage of ideas, mathematics concerned, types, construction, adjusting anywhere. Over 100 illustrations. 230pp. 5⅜ × 8½. 22947-5 Pa. $5.95

PICTURE HISTORY OF THE NORMANDIE: With 190 Illustrations, Frank O. Braynard. Full story of legendary French ocean liner: Art Deco interiors, design innovations, furnishings, celebrities, maiden voyage, tragic fire, much more. Extensive text. 144pp. 8⅞ × 11¾. 25257-4 Pa. $10.95

THE FIRST AMERICAN COOKBOOK: A Facsimile of "American Cookery," 1796, Amelia Simmons. Facsimile of the first American-written cookbook published in the United States contains authentic recipes for colonial favorites—pumpkin pudding, winter squash pudding, spruce beer, Indian slapjacks, and more. Introductory Essay and Glossary of colonial cooking terms. 80pp. 5⅜ × 8½. 24710-4 Pa. $3.50

101 PUZZLES IN THOUGHT AND LOGIC, C. R. Wylie, Jr. Solve murders and robberies, find out which fishermen are liars, how a blind man could possibly identify a color—purely by your own reasoning! 107pp. 5⅜ × 8½. 20367-0 Pa. $2.50

ANCIENT EGYPTIAN MYTHS AND LEGENDS, Lewis Spence. Examines animism, totemism, fetishism, creation myths, deities, alchemy, art and magic, other topics. Over 50 illustrations. 432pp. 5⅜ × 8½. 26525-0 Pa. $8.95

ANTHROPOLOGY AND MODERN LIFE, Franz Boas. Great anthropologist's classic treatise on race and culture. Introduction by Ruth Bunzel. Only inexpensive paperback edition. 255pp. 5⅜ × 8½. 25245-0 Pa. $6.95

THE TALE OF PETER RABBIT, Beatrix Potter. The inimitable Peter's terrifying adventure in Mr. McGregor's garden, with all 27 wonderful, full-color Potter illustrations. 55pp. 4¼ × 5½. (Available in U.S. only) 22827-4 Pa. $1.75

THREE PROPHETIC SCIENCE FICTION NOVELS, H. G. Wells. *When the Sleeper Wakes, A Story of the Days to Come* and *The Time Machine* (full version). 335pp. 5⅜ × 8½. (Available in U.S. only) 20605-X Pa. $6.95

APICIUS COOKERY AND DINING IN IMPERIAL ROME, edited and translated by Joseph Dommers Vehling. Oldest known cookbook in existence offers readers a clear picture of what foods Romans ate, how they prepared them, etc. 49 illustrations. 301pp. 6⅛ × 9¼. 23563-7 Pa. $7.95

SHAKESPEARE LEXICON AND QUOTATION DICTIONARY, Alexander Schmidt. Full definitions, locations, shades of meaning of every word in plays and poems. More than 50,000 exact quotations. 1,485pp. 6½ × 9¼. 22726-X, 22727-8 Pa., Two-vol. set $31.90

THE WORLD'S GREAT SPEECHES, edited by Lewis Copeland and Lawrence W. Lamm. Vast collection of 278 speeches from Greeks to 1970. Powerful and effective models; unique look at history. 842pp. 5⅜ × 8½. 20468-5 Pa. $12.95

THE BLUE FAIRY BOOK, Andrew Lang. The first, most famous collection, with many familiar tales: Little Red Riding Hood, Aladdin and the Wonderful Lamp, Puss in Boots, Sleeping Beauty, Hansel and Gretel, Rumpelstiltskin; 37 in all. 138 illustrations. 390pp. 5⅜ × 8½. 21437-0 Pa. $6.95

THE STORY OF THE CHAMPIONS OF THE ROUND TABLE, Howard Pyle. Sir Launcelot, Sir Tristram and Sir Percival in spirited adventures of love and triumph retold in Pyle's inimitable style. 50 drawings, 31 full-page. xviii + 329pp. 6½ × 9¼. 21883-X Pa. $7.95

THE MYTHS OF THE NORTH AMERICAN INDIANS, Lewis Spence. Myths and legends of the Algonquins, Iroquois, Pawnees and Sioux with comprehensive historical and ethnological commentary. 36 illustrations. 5⅜ × 8½.
25967-6 Pa. $8.95

GREAT DINOSAUR HUNTERS AND THEIR DISCOVERIES, Edwin H. Colbert. Fascinating, lavishly illustrated chronicle of dinosaur research, 1820's to 1960. Achievements of Cope, Marsh, Brown, Buckland, Mantell, Huxley, many others. 384pp. 5¼ × 8¼. 24701-5 Pa. $7.95

THE TASTEMAKERS, Russell Lynes. Informal, illustrated social history of American taste 1850's–1950's. First popularized categories Highbrow, Lowbrow, Middlebrow. 129 illustrations. New (1979) afterword. 384pp. 6 × 9.
23993-4 Pa. $8.95

DOUBLE CROSS PURPOSES, Ronald A. Knox. A treasure hunt in the Scottish Highlands, an old map, unidentified corpse, surprise discoveries keep reader guessing in this cleverly intricate tale of financial skullduggery. 2 black-and-white maps. 320pp. 5⅜ × 8½. (Available in U.S. only) 25032-6 Pa. $6.95

AUTHENTIC VICTORIAN DECORATION AND ORNAMENTATION IN FULL COLOR: 46 Plates from "Studies in Design," Christopher Dresser. Superb full-color lithographs reproduced from rare original portfolio of a major Victorian designer. 48pp. 9¼ × 12¼. 25083-0 Pa. $7.95

PRIMITIVE ART, Franz Boas. Remains the best text ever prepared on subject, thoroughly discussing Indian, African, Asian, Australian, and, especially, Northern American primitive art. Over 950 illustrations show ceramics, masks, totem poles, weapons, textiles, paintings, much more. 376pp. 5⅜ × 8. 20025-6 Pa. $7.95

SIDELIGHTS ON RELATIVITY, Albert Einstein. Unabridged republication of two lectures delivered by the great physicist in 1920–21. *Ether and Relativity* and *Geometry and Experience*. Elegant ideas in non-mathematical form, accessible to intelligent layman. vi + 56pp. 5⅜ × 8½. 24511-X Pa. $2.95

THE WIT AND HUMOR OF OSCAR WILDE, edited by Alvin Redman. More than 1,000 ripostes, paradoxes, wisecracks: Work is the curse of the drinking classes, I can resist everything except temptation, etc. 258pp. 5⅜ × 8½. 20602-5 Pa. $4.95

ADVENTURES WITH A MICROSCOPE, Richard Headstrom. 59 adventures with clothing fibers, protozoa, ferns and lichens, roots and leaves, much more. 142 illustrations. 232pp. 5⅜ × 8½. 23471-1 Pa. $3.95

PLANTS OF THE BIBLE, Harold N. Moldenke and Alma L. Moldenke. Standard reference to all 230 plants mentioned in Scriptures. Latin name, biblical reference, uses, modern identity, much more. Unsurpassed encyclopedic resource for scholars, botanists, nature lovers, students of Bible. Bibliography. Indexes. 123 black-and-white illustrations. 384pp. 6 × 9.   25069-5 Pa. $8.95

FAMOUS AMERICAN WOMEN: A Biographical Dictionary from Colonial Times to the Present, Robert McHenry, ed. From Pocahontas to Rosa Parks, 1,035 distinguished American women documented in separate biographical entries. Accurate, up-to-date data, numerous categories, spans 400 years. Indices. 493pp. 6½ × 9¼.   24523-3 Pa. $10.95

THE FABULOUS INTERIORS OF THE GREAT OCEAN LINERS IN HIS-TORIC PHOTOGRAPHS, William H. Miller, Jr. Some 200 superb photographs capture exquisite interiors of world's great "floating palaces"—1890's to 1980's: *Titanic, Ile de France, Queen Elizabeth, United States, Europa*, more. Approx. 200 black-and-white photographs. Captions. Text. Introduction. 160pp. 8⅜ × 11¼.
                                                                                24756-2 Pa. $9.95

THE GREAT LUXURY LINERS, 1927-1954: A Photographic Record, William H. Miller, Jr. Nostalgic tribute to heyday of ocean liners. 186 photos of Ile de France, Normandie, Leviathan, Queen Elizabeth, United States, many others. Interior and exterior views. Introduction. Captions. 160pp. 9 × 12.
                                                                                24056-8 Pa. $10.95

A NATURAL HISTORY OF THE DUCKS, John Charles Phillips. Great landmark of ornithology offers complete detailed coverage of nearly 200 species and subspecies of ducks: gadwall, sheldrake, merganser, pintail, many more. 74 full-color plates, 102 black-and-white. Bibliography. Total of 1,920pp. 8⅜ × 11¼.
                                                       25141-1, 25142-X Cloth. Two-vol. set $100.00

THE SEAWEED HANDBOOK: An Illustrated Guide to Seaweeds from North Carolina to Canada, Thomas F. Lee. Concise reference covers 78 species. Scientific and common names, habitat, distribution, more. Finding keys for easy identification. 224pp. 5⅜ × 8½.   25215-9 Pa. $6.95

THE TEN BOOKS OF ARCHITECTURE: The 1755 Leoni Edition, Leon Battista Alberti. Rare classic helped introduce the glories of ancient architecture to the Renaissance. 68 black-and-white plates. 336pp. 8⅜ × 11¼.   25239-6 Pa. $14.95

MISS MACKENZIE, Anthony Trollope. Minor masterpieces by Victorian master unmasks many truths about life in 19th-century England. First inexpensive edition in years. 392pp. 5⅜ × 8½.   25201-9 Pa. $8.95

THE RIME OF THE ANCIENT MARINER, Gustave Doré, Samuel Taylor Coleridge. Dramatic engravings considered by many to be his greatest work. The terrifying space of the open sea, the storms and whirlpools of an unknown ocean, the ice of Antarctica, more—all rendered in a powerful, chilling manner. Full text. 38 plates. 77pp. 9¼ × 12.   22305-1 Pa. $4.95

THE EXPEDITIONS OF ZEBULON MONTGOMERY PIKE, Zebulon Montgomery Pike. Fascinating first-hand accounts (1805-6) of exploration of Mississippi River, Indian wars, capture by Spanish dragoons, much more. 1,088pp. 5⅜ × 8½.   25254-X, 25255-8 Pa. Two-vol. set $25.90

A CONCISE HISTORY OF PHOTOGRAPHY: Third Revised Edition, Helmut Gernsheim. Best one-volume history—camera obscura, photochemistry, daguerreotypes, evolution of cameras, film, more. Also artistic aspects—landscape, portraits, fine art, etc. 281 black-and-white photographs. 26 in color. 176pp. 8⅜ × 11¼. 25128-4 Pa. $13.95

THE DORÉ BIBLE ILLUSTRATIONS, Gustave Doré. 241 detailed plates from the Bible: the Creation scenes, Adam and Eve, Flood, Babylon, battle sequences, life of Jesus, etc. Each plate is accompanied by the verses from the King James version of the Bible. 241pp. 9 × 12. 23004-X Pa. $9.95

WANDERINGS IN WEST AFRICA, Richard F. Burton. Great Victorian scholar/adventurer's invaluable descriptions of African tribal rituals, fetishism, culture, art, much more. Fascinating 19th-century account. 624pp. 5⅜ × 8½. 26890-X Pa. $12.95

FLATLAND, E. A. Abbott. Intriguing and enormously popular science-fiction classic explores the complexities of trying to survive as a two-dimensional being in a three-dimensional world. Amusingly illustrated by the author. 16 illustrations. 103pp. 5⅜ × 8½. 20001-9 Pa. $2.50

THE HISTORY OF THE LEWIS AND CLARK EXPEDITION, Meriwether Lewis and William Clark, edited by Elliott Coues. Classic edition of Lewis and Clark's day-by-day journals that later became the basis for U.S. claims to Oregon and the West. Accurate and invaluable geographical, botanical, biological, meteorological and anthropological material. Total of 1,508pp. 5⅜ × 8½.
21268-8, 21269-6, 21270-X Pa. Three-vol. set $26.85

LANGUAGE, TRUTH AND LOGIC, Alfred J. Ayer. Famous, clear introduction to Vienna, Cambridge schools of Logical Positivism. Role of philosophy, elimination of metaphysics, nature of analysis, etc. 160pp. 5⅜ × 8½. (Available in U.S. and Canada only) 20010-8 Pa. $3.95

MATHEMATICS FOR THE NONMATHEMATICIAN, Morris Kline. Detailed, college-level treatment of mathematics in cultural and historical context, with numerous exercises. For liberal arts students. Preface. Recommended Reading Lists. Tables. Index. Numerous black-and-white figures. xvi + 641pp. 5⅜ × 8½.
24823-2 Pa. $11.95

HANDBOOK OF PICTORIAL SYMBOLS, Rudolph Modley. 3,250 signs and symbols, many systems in full; official or heavy commercial use. Arranged by subject. Most in Pictorial Archive series. 143pp. 8⅛ × 11. 23357-X Pa. $6.95

INCIDENTS OF TRAVEL IN YUCATAN, John L. Stephens. Classic (1843) exploration of jungles of Yucatan, looking for evidences of Maya civilization. Travel adventures, Mexican and Indian culture, etc. Total of 669pp. 5⅜ × 8½.
20926-1, 20927-X Pa., Two-vol. set $11.90

DEGAS: An Intimate Portrait, Ambroise Vollard. Charming, anecdotal memoir by famous art dealer of one of the greatest 19th-century French painters. 14 black-and-white illustrations. Introduction by Harold L. Van Doren. 96pp. 5⅜ × 8½.
25131-4 Pa. $4.95

PERSONAL NARRATIVE OF A PILGRIMAGE TO ALMANDINAH AND MECCAH, Richard Burton. Great travel classic by remarkably colorful personality. Burton, disguised as a Moroccan, visited sacred shrines of Islam, narrowly escaping death. 47 illustrations. 959pp. 5⅜ × 8½.　21217-3, 21218-1 Pa., Two-vol. set $19.90

PHRASE AND WORD ORIGINS, A. H. Holt. Entertaining, reliable, modern study of more than 1,200 colorful words, phrases, origins and histories. Much unexpected information. 254pp. 5⅜ × 8½.　20758-7 Pa. $5.95

THE RED THUMB MARK, R. Austin Freeman. In this first Dr. Thorndyke case, the great scientific detective draws fascinating conclusions from the nature of a single fingerprint. Exciting story, authentic science. 320pp. 5⅜ × 8½. (Available in U.S. only)　25210-8 Pa. $6.95

AN EGYPTIAN HIEROGLYPHIC DICTIONARY, E. A. Wallis Budge. Monumental work containing about 25,000 words or terms that occur in texts ranging from 3000 B.C. to 600 A.D. Each entry consists of a transliteration of the word, the word in hieroglyphs, and the meaning in English. 1,314pp. 6⅝ × 10.
23615-3, 23616-1 Pa., Two-vol. set $35.90

THE COMPLEAT STRATEGYST: Being a Primer on the Theory of Games of Strategy, J. D. Williams. Highly entertaining classic describes, with many illustrated examples, how to select best strategies in conflict situations. Prefaces. Appendices. xvi + 268pp. 5⅜ × 8½.　25101-2 Pa. $6.95

THE ROAD TO OZ, L. Frank Baum. Dorothy meets the Shaggy Man, little Button-Bright and the Rainbow's beautiful daughter in this delightful trip to the magical Land of Oz. 272pp. 5⅜ × 8.　25208-6 Pa. $5.95

POINT AND LINE TO PLANE, Wassily Kandinsky. Seminal exposition of role of point, line, other elements in non-objective painting. Essential to understanding 20th-century art. 127 illustrations. 192pp. 6½ × 9¼.　23808-3 Pa. $5.95

LADY ANNA, Anthony Trollope. Moving chronicle of Countess Lovel's bitter struggle to win for herself and daughter Anna their rightful rank and fortune—perhaps at cost of sanity itself. 384pp. 5⅜ × 8½.　24669-8 Pa. $8.95

EGYPTIAN MAGIC, E. A. Wallis Budge. Sums up all that is known about magic in Ancient Egypt: the role of magic in controlling the gods, powerful amulets that warded off evil spirits, scarabs of immortality, use of wax images, formulas and spells, the secret name, much more. 253pp. 5⅜ × 8½.　22681-6 Pa. $4.50

THE DANCE OF SIVA, Ananda Coomaraswamy. Preeminent authority unfolds the vast metaphysic of India: the revelation of her art, conception of the universe, social organization, etc. 27 reproductions of art masterpieces. 192pp. 5⅜ × 8½.
24817-8 Pa. $5.95

CHRISTMAS CUSTOMS AND TRADITIONS, Clement A. Miles. Origin, evolution, significance of religious, secular practices. Caroling, gifts, yule logs, much more. Full, scholarly yet fascinating; non-sectarian. 400pp. 5⅜ × 8½.
23354-5 Pa. $6.95

THE HUMAN FIGURE IN MOTION, Eadweard Muybridge. More than 4,500 stopped-action photos, in action series, showing undraped men, women, children jumping, lying down, throwing, sitting, wrestling, carrying, etc. 390pp. 7⅞ × 10⅝.
20204-6 Cloth. $24.95

THE MAN WHO WAS THURSDAY, Gilbert Keith Chesterton. Witty, fast-paced novel about a club of anarchists in turn-of-the-century London. Brilliant social, religious, philosophical speculations. 128pp. 5⅜ × 8½.
25121-7 Pa. $3.95

A CEZANNE SKETCHBOOK: Figures, Portraits, Landscapes and Still Lifes, Paul Cezanne. Great artist experiments with tonal effects, light, mass, other qualities in over 100 drawings. A revealing view of developing master painter, precursor of Cubism. 102 black-and-white illustrations. 144pp. 8¾ × 6⅜.
24790-2 Pa. $6.95

AN ENCYCLOPEDIA OF BATTLES: Accounts of Over 1,560 Battles from 1479 B.C. to the Present, David Eggenberger. Presents essential details of every major battle in recorded history, from the first battle of Megiddo in 1479 B.C. to Grenada in 1984. List of Battle Maps. New Appendix covering the years 1967–1984. Index. 99 illustrations. 544pp. 6½ × 9¼.
24913-1 Pa. $14.95

AN ETYMOLOGICAL DICTIONARY OF MODERN ENGLISH, Ernest Weekley. Richest, fullest work, by foremost British lexicographer. Detailed word histories. Inexhaustible. Total of 856pp. 6½ × 9¼.
21873-2, 21874-0 Pa., Two-vol. set $19.90

WEBSTER'S AMERICAN MILITARY BIOGRAPHIES, edited by Robert McHenry. Over 1,000 figures who shaped 3 centuries of American military history. Detailed biographies of Nathan Hale, Douglas MacArthur, Mary Hallaren, others. Chronologies of engagements, more. Introduction. Addenda. 1,033 entries in alphabetical order. xi + 548pp. 6½ × 9¼. (Available in U.S. only)
24758-9 Pa. $13.95

LIFE IN ANCIENT EGYPT, Adolf Erman. Detailed older account, with much not in more recent books: domestic life, religion, magic, medicine, commerce, and whatever else needed for complete picture. Many illustrations. 597pp. 5⅜ × 8½.
22632-8 Pa. $8.95

HISTORIC COSTUME IN PICTURES, Braun & Schneider. Over 1,450 costumed figures shown, covering a wide variety of peoples: kings, emperors, nobles, priests, servants, soldiers, scholars, townsfolk, peasants, merchants, courtiers, cavaliers, and more. 256pp. 8⅜ × 11¼.
23150-X Pa. $9.95

THE NOTEBOOKS OF LEONARDO DA VINCI, edited by J. P. Richter. Extracts from manuscripts reveal great genius; on painting, sculpture, anatomy, sciences, geography, etc. Both Italian and English. 186 ms. pages reproduced, plus 500 additional drawings, including studies for *Last Supper, Sforza* monument, etc. 860pp. 7⅞ × 10¾. (Available in U.S. only) 22572-0, 22573-9 Pa., Two-vol. set $31.90

THE ART NOUVEAU STYLE BOOK OF ALPHONSE MUCHA: All 72 Plates from "Documents Decoratifs" in Original Color, Alphonse Mucha. Rare copyright-free design portfolio by high priest of Art Nouveau. Jewelry, wallpaper, stained glass, furniture, figure studies, plant and animal motifs, etc. Only complete one-volume edition. 80pp. 9⅜ × 12¼. 24044-4 Pa. $9.95

ANIMALS: 1,419 COPYRIGHT-FREE ILLUSTRATIONS OF MAMMALS, BIRDS, FISH, INSECTS, ETC., edited by Jim Harter. Clear wood engravings present, in extremely lifelike poses, over 1,000 species of animals. One of the most extensive pictorial sourcebooks of its kind. Captions. Index. 284pp. 9 × 12.
23766-4 Pa. $9.95

OBELISTS FLY HIGH, C. Daly King. Masterpiece of American detective fiction, long out of print, involves murder on a 1935 transcontinental flight—"a very thrilling story"—NY Times. Unabridged and unaltered republication of the edition published by William Collins Sons & Co. Ltd., London, 1935. 288pp. 5⅜ × 8½. (Available in U.S. only) 25036-9 Pa. $5.95

VICTORIAN AND EDWARDIAN FASHION: A Photographic Survey, Alison Gernsheim. First fashion history completely illustrated by contemporary photographs. Full text plus 235 photos, 1840–1914, in which many celebrities appear. 240pp. 6½ × 9¼. 24205-6 Pa. $8.95

THE ART OF THE FRENCH ILLUSTRATED BOOK, 1700–1914, Gordon N. Ray. Over 630 superb book illustrations by Fragonard, Delacroix, Daumier, Doré, Grandville, Manet, Mucha, Steinlen, Toulouse-Lautrec and many others. Preface. Introduction. 633 halftones. Indices of artists, authors & titles, binders and provenances. Appendices. Bibliography. 608pp. 8⅜ × 11¼. 25086-5 Pa. $24.95

THE WONDERFUL WIZARD OF OZ, L. Frank Baum. Facsimile in full color of America's finest children's classic. 143 illustrations by W. W. Denslow. 267pp. 5⅜ × 8½. 20691-2 Pa. $7.95

FOLLOWING THE EQUATOR: A Journey Around the World, Mark Twain. Great writer's 1897 account of circumnavigating the globe by steamship. Ironic humor, keen observations, vivid and fascinating descriptions of exotic places. 197 illustrations. 720pp. 5⅜ × 8½. 26113-1 Pa. $15.95

THE FRIENDLY STARS, Martha Evans Martin & Donald Howard Menzel. Classic text marshalls the stars together in an engaging, non-technical survey, presenting them as sources of beauty in night sky. 23 illustrations. Foreword. 2 star charts. Index. 147pp. 5⅜ × 8½. 21099-5 Pa. $3.95

FADS AND FALLACIES IN THE NAME OF SCIENCE, Martin Gardner. Fair, witty appraisal of cranks, quacks, and quackeries of science and pseudoscience: hollow earth, Velikovsky, orgone energy, Dianetics, flying saucers, Bridey Murphy, food and medical fads, etc. Revised, expanded In the Name of Science. "A very able and even-tempered presentation."—The New Yorker. 363pp. 5⅜ × 8.
20394-8 Pa. $6.95

ANCIENT EGYPT: ITS CULTURE AND HISTORY, J. E Manchip White. From pre-dynastics through Ptolemies: society, history, political structure, religion, daily life, literature, cultural heritage. 48 plates. 217pp. 5⅜ × 8½. 22548-8 Pa. $5.95

SIR HARRY HOTSPUR OF HUMBLETHWAITE, Anthony Trollope. Incisive, unconventional psychological study of a conflict between a wealthy baronet, his idealistic daughter, and their scapegrace cousin. The 1870 novel in its first inexpensive edition in years. 250pp. 5⅜ × 8½. 24953-0 Pa. $6.95

LASERS AND HOLOGRAPHY, Winston E. Kock. Sound introduction to burgeoning field, expanded (1981) for second edition. Wave patterns, coherence, lasers, diffraction, zone plates, properties of holograms, recent advances. 84 illustrations. 160pp. 5⅜ × 8¼. (Except in United Kingdom) 24041-X Pa. $3.95

INTRODUCTION TO ARTIFICIAL INTELLIGENCE: SECOND, EN-LARGED EDITION, Philip C. Jackson, Jr. Comprehensive survey of artificial intelligence—the study of how machines (computers) can be made to act intelligently. Includes introductory and advanced material. Extensive notes updating the main text. 132 black-and-white illustrations. 512pp. 5⅜ × 8½. 24864-X Pa. $8.95

HISTORY OF INDIAN AND INDONESIAN ART, Ananda K. Coomaraswamy. Over 400 illustrations illuminate classic study of Indian art from earliest Harappa finds to early 20th century. Provides philosophical, religious and social insights. 304pp. 6⅜ × 9⅜. 25005-9 Pa. $11.95

THE GOLEM, Gustav Meyrink. Most famous supernatural novel in modern European literature, set in Ghetto of Old Prague around 1890. Compelling story of mystical experiences, strange transformations, profound terror. 13 black-and-white illustrations. 224pp. 5⅜ × 8½. (Available in U.S. only) 25025-3 Pa. $6.95

PICTORIAL ENCYCLOPEDIA OF HISTORIC ARCHITECTURAL PLANS, DETAILS AND ELEMENTS: With 1,880 Line Drawings of Arches, Domes, Doorways, Facades, Gables, Windows, etc., John Theodore Haneman. Sourcebook of inspiration for architects, designers, others. Bibliography. Captions. 141pp. 9 × 12. 24605-1 Pa. $7.95

BENCHLEY LOST AND FOUND, Robert Benchley. Finest humor from early 30's, about pet peeves, child psychologists, post office and others. Mostly unavailable elsewhere. 73 illustrations by Peter Arno and others. 183pp. 5⅜ × 8½. 22410-4 Pa. $4.95

ERTÉ GRAPHICS, Erté. Collection of striking color graphics: Seasons, Alphabet, Numerals, Aces and Precious Stones. 50 plates, including 4 on covers. 48pp. 9⅜ × 12¼. 23580-7 Pa. $7.95

THE JOURNAL OF HENRY D. THOREAU, edited by Bradford Torrey, F. H. Allen. Complete reprinting of 14 volumes, 1837–61, over two million words; the sourcebooks for Walden, etc. Definitive. All original sketches, plus 75 photographs. 1,804pp. 8½ × 12¼. 20312-3, 20313-1 Cloth., Two-vol. set $125.00

CASTLES: THEIR CONSTRUCTION AND HISTORY, Sidney Toy. Traces castle development from ancient roots. Nearly 200 photographs and drawings illustrate moats, keeps, baileys, many other features. Caernarvon, Dover Castles, Hadrian's Wall, Tower of London, dozens more. 256pp. 5⅜ × 8¼. 24898-4 Pa. $6.95

CATALOG OF DOVER BOOKS

AMERICAN CLIPPER SHIPS: 1833–1858, Octavius T. Howe & Frederick C. Matthews. Fully-illustrated, encyclopedic review of 352 clipper ships from the period of America's greatest maritime supremacy. Introduction. 109 halftones. 5 black-and-white line illustrations. Index. Total of 928pp. 5⅜ × 8½.
25115-2, 25116-0 Pa., Two-vol. set $17.90

TOWARDS A NEW ARCHITECTURE, Le Corbusier. Pioneering manifesto by great architect, near legendary founder of "International School." Technical and aesthetic theories, views on industry, economics, relation of form to function, "mass-production spirit," much more. Profusely illustrated. Unabridged translation of 13th French edition. Introduction by Frederick Etchells. 320pp. 6⅛ × 9¼. (Available in U.S. only)
25023-7 Pa. $8.95

THE BOOK OF KELLS, edited by Blanche Cirker. Inexpensive collection of 32 full-color, full-page plates from the greatest illuminated manuscript of the Middle Ages, painstakingly reproduced from rare facsimile edition. Publisher's Note. Captions. 32pp. 9⅜ × 12¼.
24345-1 Pa. $4.95

BEST SCIENCE FICTION STORIES OF H. G. WELLS, H. G. Wells. Full novel *The Invisible Man*, plus 17 short stories: "The Crystal Egg," "Aepyornis Island," "The Strange Orchid," etc. 303pp. 5⅜ × 8½. (Available in U.S. only)
21531-8 Pa. $6.95

AMERICAN SAILING SHIPS: Their Plans and History, Charles G. Davis. Photos, construction details of schooners, frigates, clippers, other sailcraft of 18th to early 20th centuries—plus entertaining discourse on design, rigging, nautical lore, much more. 137 black-and-white illustrations. 240pp. 6⅛ × 9¼.
24658-2 Pa. $6.95

ENTERTAINING MATHEMATICAL PUZZLES, Martin Gardner. Selection of author's favorite conundrums involving arithmetic, money, speed, etc., with lively commentary. Complete solutions. 112pp. 5⅜ × 8½.
25211-6 Pa. $2.95

THE WILL TO BELIEVE, HUMAN IMMORTALITY, William James. Two books bound together. Effect of irrational on logical, and arguments for human immortality. 402pp. 5⅜ × 8½.
20291-7 Pa. $7.95

THE HAUNTED MONASTERY and THE CHINESE MAZE MURDERS, Robert Van Gulik. 2 full novels by Van Gulik continue adventures of Judge Dee and his companions. An evil Taoist monastery, seemingly supernatural events; overgrown topiary maze that hides strange crimes. Set in 7th-century China. 27 illustrations. 328pp. 5⅜ × 8½.
23502-5 Pa. $6.95

CELEBRATED CASES OF JUDGE DEE (DEE GOONG AN), translated by Robert Van Gulik. Authentic 18th-century Chinese detective novel; Dee and associates solve three interlocked cases. Led to Van Gulik's own stories with same characters. Extensive introduction. 9 illustrations. 237pp. 5⅜ × 8½.
23337-5 Pa. $5.95

Prices subject to change without notice.
Available at your book dealer or write for free catalog to Dept. GI, Dover Publications, Inc., 31 East 2nd St., Mineola, N.Y. 11501. Dover publishes more than 175 books each year on science, elementary and advanced mathematics, biology, music, art, literary history, social sciences and other areas.